THE ALMANAC OF RURAL LIVING

THE ALMANAC OF RURAL LIVING

by HARVEY C. NEESE

WILLIAM MORROW AND COMPANY, INC.

NEW YORK   1979

ACKNOWLEDGEMENTS

Appreciation is extended for information in THE ALMANAC to the following people and organizations; Mel Ott, Mervina Milton and Stan Hilliard for some of the photographs; Paul Dammarell and Duffie Miller for general information and sketches on gold panning techniques; especially the Cooperative Extension Services of the University of Idaho, Washington State University and other extension services for the use of their bulletins; VITA (Volunteers in Technical Assistance) for some of the illustrations; Dee and Winnie for their help and all the pioneers of yesterday who helped develop and demonstrate the innovations and skills found in THE ALMANAC OF RURAL LIVING.

———

First Morrow Quill Paperback Edition

Library of Congress Cataloging in Publication Data

Neese, Harvey C.
    The almanac of rural living.

    1. Agriculture—Handbooks, manuals, etc.   2. Home
economics, Rural—Handbooks, manuals, etc.   I. Title.
[S501.2.N44   1979]   630   78-23295
ISBN 0-688-03411-X
ISBN 0-688-08411-7 pbk.

Printed in the United States of America.

1   2   3   4   5   6   7   8   9   10

BETWEEN THE COVERS

FOREWORD

THE ALMANAC OF RURAL LIVING was written to aid those who are searching for helpful innovations, skills and plans on how to do things for themselves. There is useful information in THE ALMANAC for farmers as well as rural dwellers and just plain city folks. There is an education for those who want to learn different ways of doing things and monetary savings for those who want to become self-sufficient, wherever they might live.

Community development and rural village workers abroad will find a multitude of ideas that could ease the burdens of life for rural dwellers in these developing countries.

Since the book was put together mainly for small farmers, rural dwellers and city folks, most of the recommendations are slanted to these groups of people. In animal husbandry techniques and facilities for instance, THE ALMANAC is geared for small production. Recommendations for large scale production would be much different. Suggestions for use of pesticides are limited to the least toxic to humans and the chemicals least likely to be banned because of their toxicity. These are for the most part derivatives of plant sources. Other types of pesticides are listed in Part III in the order of their toxicity so that users of these chemicals will understand the dangers in these toxic compounds.

Even though smallness is emphasized in the pages of THE ALMANAC mastering the messages on each and every page will reward you with big dividends. It is intended to help you do things for yourself, and this it will do, if you will give it half a chance.

The Author

PART I AGRONOMY

CLIMATE

Temperature Distribution

The distribution of temperature over the world and its variations through the year depend primarily on the amount and distribution of the radiant energy received from the sun in different regions This in turn depends mainly on latitude but is greatly modified by the distribution of continents and oceans, prevailing winds, oceanic circulation, topography, and other factors.

In the winter of the Northern Hemisphere the poleward temperature gradient (that is, the rate of fall in temperature) north of latitude 15° is very steep over the interior of North America. The temperature gradient is also steep toward the cold pole over Asia. In western Europe, to the east of the Atlantic Ocean and the North Atlantic Drift, and in the region of prevailing westerly winds, the temperature gradient is much more gradual. In the winter of the Southern Hemisphere the temperature gradient toward the South Pole is very gradual because continental effects are largely absent.

In the summers of the two hemispheres—July in the north and January in the south—the temperature gradients poleward are very much diminished as compared with those during the winter. This is especially marked over middle and higher northern latitudes because of the greater warming of the extensive interiors of North America and Eurasia than of the smaller land areas in middle and higher southern latitudes.

Effects of Climatic Factors on Growing Plants

Climate largely determines the type of vegetation that grows naturally in any part of the world and the kinds of agricultural production that are possible. The three most important factors in climate from the standpoint of plant response are temperature, water supply, and light. Temperature is the main factor that determines where native species or crop plants can be grown in great belts north and south of the Equator. Precipitation or water supply is the most important factor in determining the distribution of plants and crops within these great belts of somewhat similar temperature conditions. Light varies greatly in intensity in different areas, and the length of daily illumination varies in different regions and at different seasons of the year. Both light intensity and the length of the daily illumination period profoundly affect plant behavior.

Other elements of climate are less important from the standpoint of crop production. Wind increases the water requirement of plants. Hailstorms, tornadoes, or hurricanes may destroy crops locally. Near salt water, the salt spray may be destructive to many forms of vegetation.

All of these elements of climate are interrelated in their effect on the plant organism. Temperature and light affect the water requirement. The available moisture supply greatly influences the effects of high temperatures and light intensities. Although these elements of climate are discussed separately, the reader should keep in mind that the plant is a complicated organism, affected by all factors in its environment, nutritional as well as climatic, and that these effects are usually interrelated in plant response. The following values for latitude, longitude, and elevation are generally suggested for determining the time at which plants of the same species will flower:

1. For each degree of latitude north or south of the Equator, flowering is retarded 4 calendar days.
2. For each 5 degrees of longitude, from east to west on land areas, flowering is advanced 4 calendar days.
3. For each 400-foot increase in altitude, flowering is retarded 4 calendar days.

1

Temperature and Plant Growth

Temperature influences every chemical and physical process connected with plants—solubility of minerals; absorption of water, gases, and mineral nutrients; diffusion; synthesis, growth and reproduction. Thus temperatures delimit the areas of successful production of most agricultural crops. Such well-defined areas in America as the Cotton Belt, the Corn Belt, the winter and spring wheat areas, and the Michigan fruit belt are determined essentially by temperatures. This limiting influence on crop distribution results primarily from (1) too short a period of favorable temperature for crop maturity; (2) unfavorably high or unfavorably low growing season temperatures for proper development of the crop; (3) occurrence of temperatures, either high or low, that cause injury or death to growing plants; (4) winter temperature conditions that injure or kill dormant plants; and (5) temperature conditions particularly favorable to the development of injurious diseases or insect pests.

In its evolution the plant kingdom has become adapted to a wide range of temperatures. There are few places on earth too hot or too cold to sustain some form of plant life. Certain blue-green algae thrive in hot springs where the water is constantly near the boiling point. Plants of arctic regions survive where winter temperatures reach —90° F. Many plants can adapt themselves to great extremes of temperature by entering resting stages. Dormant trees that withstand —65° F. in winter are killed when they are in summer growing condition by temperatures a few degrees below freezing. Dried seeds and spores withstand temperatures of liquid air and liquid oxygen. Spore stages of certain fungi can survive temperatures up to 266° F. (130° C.)

The temperature range within which growth takes place is much more limited than that within which plants in inactive stages can survive. Mention has already been made of the hot-springs algae that grow at temperatures of about 90° C. (199.4° F.). At the other extreme are fungi that develop in cold storage at about —6° C. (21.2° F.) and certain marine algae that complete their life cycle in sea water below 0° C. (32° F.). These, however, are exceptional cases, interesting because they show the enormous adaptability of plant protoplasm. By far the greater number of both higher and lower plants are capable of carrying on growth only within a comparatively narrow range, from about 32° F. (0° C.) to about 122° F. (50° C.).

For each species and variety there is a minimum and maximum growth temperature. Between these limits there is an optimum temperature at which growth proceeds with greatest rapidity. These three points are called the cardinal growth temperatures. At the minimum point growth proceeds very slowly. From somewhat above the minimum to the optimum, the rate of growth follows Van Hoff's law; that is to say, for every 10° C. (18° F.) rise in temperature the rate of growth approximately doubles. Above the optimum, the growth rate falls off rapidly until it stops. Thus the optimum and maximum points are closer together than are the optimum and minimum.

These cardinal growth temperatures vary considerably among the different kinds of plants. With typical cool-season crops, such as oats, rye, wheat, and barley, these points are all comparatively low—minimum 0°-50° C. (32°-41° F.), optimum 25°-32° C. (77°-87° F.), and maximum 31°-37° C. (87.8°-98.6° F.). For hot-season crops, such as melons and sorghums, the temperatures are much higher—minimum 15° 18° C. (59°-64.4° F.), optimum 31°-37° C. (87.8°-98.6° F.), and maximum 44°-50° C. (111.2°-122° F.). However, there are other crops such as hemp that embrace the whole range of growth temperatures, having the minimum of the cool-season crops and the maximum of the hot-season crops. The cardinal temperatures for growth may vary considerably with the stages of plant development, such as germination, seedling stage, and maturity. Thus seedlings

2

often have lower temperature requirements than plants in later stages.

The optimum temperature that produces the highest growth rate is not necessarily the most favorable for the general welfare of the plant and is often undesirable from an agricultural standpoint. Too rapid growth may delay or entirely prevent fruiting; it may produce plants that are structurally weak, susceptible to disease or insect attacks, and subject to damage by wind, hail, or other climatic influences. However, wide departures from the optimum will so reduce growth as to make production unprofitable.

Temperature requirements for the same variety of plant vary greatly under different growing conditions. The greater light duration during the summer in more northern latitudes may partly compensate for less heat. Thus, while plants may be classed as requiring much, moderate, or little total heat, a definite number of degree-hours or degree-days does not result in similar development under widely varying conditions.

Unlike warm-blooded animals, plants have no mechanism for controlling temperature independent of environment or for maintaining a uniform temperature throughout the organism. Plant parts have approximately the same temperature as their surroundings.

Effects of Low Temperatures

Wherever freezing temperatures occur, plants are in danger of frost injury. There are, however, many habits and modifications by which they are able to survive in regions having temperatures at or below the freezing point. Tender annuals escape freezing by completing their life cycle, from seed to seed, during the period between frosts. Herbaceous perennials die back to the ground but maintain life in underground organs—roots, bulbs, tubers, or rhizomes—which produce new tops when temperatures are favorable. Beneath the soil these organs are either entirely protected from freezing or subjected to much less cold than aerial parts. Coverings of snow or leaves also afford protection from low temperatures, and many low-growing half-hardy plants are able to survive in cold regions because of such covering during periods of extreme cold. Natural protection is frequently supplemented in farming by such practices as mulching.

Cold-hardy plants have the ability to develop cold resistance within their tissues. The degree of resistance varies with different species and varieties. Some herbaceous types, such as cabbage, withstand ice formation in their leaves but are killed by winter temperatures in the colder parts of the country. Hardy wood plants-trees, shrubs, and vines—that endure cold winters without protection develop the greatest degree of cold resistance among higher plants. The exact nature of this remarkable physiological adaptation to cold is still a partial mystery. Within limits, it is possible to secure increased resistance to many species by breeding.

Many correlations have been noted between cold resistance and certain plant characteristics, such as structure and the chemical and physical properties of the cells. None of these factors, however, seems to be common to all cold-hardy plants and none can therefore be regarded as the causal mechanism of cold resistance. The exact nature of cold resistance, as well as the mechanism of injury from freezing, must await a better knowledge of the structure and the physiology of plant protoplasm.

Bark, bud scales, and hairy coatings, often regarded by enthusiastic amateur naturalists as a means of keeping the plant warm, actually have little value in protecting it from cold. At best such coverings only slightly retard the rate of temperature fall, and the plant soon comes to equilibrium with the temperature surrounding it.

In their efforts to extend production into colder regions, farmers and gardeners have persistently carried plants beyond the temperature range to which they are

naturally adapted. Consequently, cold injury is common in cultivated plants. Since frost occurs in practically every part of the continental United States, low-temperature injury is an agricultural problem of the entire country, and none of our agricultural areas are entirely free from this hazard.

The nature of freezing damage to crops varies in different regions and with the different kinds of crop plants. In winter-garden sections frosts may kill outright fields of tender crops, such as beans, melons, and tomatoes. Subtropical-fruit districts may experience winter frosts that freeze and ruin green or ripening fruit on the trees. With more severe freezing, the leaves and even the trees are killed.

Over much of the United States late-spring frosts constitute a major hazard of plant production. They may damage or kill young plants of corn, flax, potatoes, cotton, tender garden vegetables, and even seedlings of such comparatively hardy crops as wheat and alfalfa. Plants such as tomatoes, which are normally transplanted into the fields, are usually started in the South under glass to escape the frost hazard. Deciduous fruits and nuts suffer damage to opening buds, flowers, or young fruit, often to the extent of completely destroying the crop. Flowers, shoots, and leaves of ornamental trees, shrubs, and perennials may be killed or damaged so that their aesthetic value is largely lost for the season. Forest trees suffer damage from late spring frosts through destruction of the seed crop, killing back or injury of new growth, and development of frost rings in the wood, which later yields lumber of inferior quality.

Plants overwintering in cold regions are subject to various types and degrees of cold injury. Since not all parts, organs, or tissues are equally cold-resistant, one part may be killed or badly injured while another is undamaged. For this reason, plants apparently hopelessly injured by cold often make a surprising recovery. On the other hand, the effects of winter injury are not always immediately evident. Injured trees or branches may suddenly wither and die after opening their buds, or they may flourish until summer and even flower and fruit before dying. Injury to roots or interference with the conducting system by excretions or outgrowths from cold-injured tissue in the wood may be the cause of such surprising behavior.

Winter injury to herbaceous plants may consist in complete killing, as frequently happens with winter wheat, grasses, alfalfa, clover, strawberries, and many ornamental perennials. Less severe cold may kill buds or injure crowns or roots, as is common with alfalfa and strawberries.

Woody plants may have terminals killed back, and with lower temperatures killing may extend to the snow cover or the ground. Injury to certain tissues or internal structures of woody stems is common and is generally recognizable by discoloration of the affected part. "Black heart" is an extreme case of such injury prevalent in cold regions, in which pith and often one or more annual rings of wood will be dark-colored. The cambium—the region between the wood and bark where new wood and bark cells are formed—is usually one of the most cold-resistant parts of a dormant stem and often remains uninjured, later laying down new rings of sound wood outside the discolored layers.

Roots are sometimes killed or injured even though the top is unharmed. Hardy fruit or nut varieties budded or grafted on tender rootstocks are likely to suffer from root killing. Winter killing of flower buds is common in many parts of this country, particularly on such crops as peach, cherry, and almond. It also occurs on apple, pear, and many ornamental plants. Local killing of the bark occurs on trees at crotches, at the base of the trunk, and in patches variously located on branches and trunk. Frost cracks and splitting and loosening of bark are mechanical injuries to trees resulting from freezing.

Sunscald is a cold injury occuring on the south and west sides of tree trunks and branches. In cold weather, sunlight falling directly on the bark may warm it several degrees above shaded parts. At sunset the temperature drops suddenly, and killing of the bark results either from the rapid fall in temperature or from

4

freezing of tissues temporarily started into growth by the heating effect of the sun. Such practices as shading or wrapping the trunk or whitewashing to reduce absorption of heat from the winter sun reduce the sunscald types of injury.

Indirect effects of low temperatures on overwintering plants are heaving of soil, resulting in breakage or exposure of roots; the smothering effect of ice sheets; and breaking of trees and shrubs by snow and sleet.

Deleterious effects may result when plants are subjected to low temperatures above freezing. Growth is slowed down, elongation is reduced, and plants become dwarfed and more compact in habit. Definite injuries result from chilling many typically warm-climate plants. Exposure of a day or two at temperatures from slightly above 0° C. (32° F.) to 10° C. (50° F.) may result in yellowing of foliage, dead areas in the leaves, the dropping of leaves, and even the death of the plant.

Not all low-temperature effects are harmful. Many plants, including all of our deciduous fruit trees, have a "rest period," during which no growth takes place, even when all external conditions are favorable for growth. Shoots of woody plants, seeds, bulbs, tubers, and crown buds may exhibit this phenomenon. Some rather drastic treatments, by cold, chemical vapors, or heat, are necessary to break this rest. Cold is the natural means of accomplishing this result. Seed stratification, cold storage of bulbs, and chilling of rhubarb roots and flowering stems of lilac and other woody plants before forcing are commercially applied to break the rest period.

Certain plants seem to require a period of low temperature during germination and early seedling stages in order that later stages of development may be normal. Winter wheat sown in spring does not head; but if the seed is partly germinated and held from 1 to 2 months at temperatures around freezing and then spring-sown, a crop will be produced. This method of shortening the vegetative period and hastening seed production is called vernalization. Many cool-climate plants respond to this treatment.

Effects of High Temperatures

The effects of high temperatures on plants are difficult to separate from the usually accompanying factors of high light intensity and rapid transpiration. Above the optimum growth temperature the rate of growth drops rapidly, and plants become dwarfed. Temperate Zone plants under tropical conditions tend to make only vegetative growth and fruit sparingly or not at all. Fruits grown where summer temperatures are excessive for the variety ripen their crop prematurely, and the fruit is poor in flavor, color, and keeping quality. High temperatures cause in certain varieties and strains pollen abnormalities that result in sterility and failure to produce seed or fruit. Heat treatment of floral parts is used as a means of inducing polyploidy (multiplication of the number of chromosomes) in plants. Tissue injuries resulting from high temperatures may kill local areas on leaves, as in tipburn of lettuce and potatoes; scald fruits—such as strawberries and gooseberries; discolor and cause malformation of flowers, as in early blooming crysanthemums and dahlias; and produce heat cankers on tender plants such as flax, and on the bark of fruit trees. General effects of excessive heat are defoliation, premature dropping of fruits, and, in extreme cases, death of the plant.

Water Supply and Plant Development

Water supply, from rainfall or irrigation, ranks with temperature as the great determiner of where plant species grow naturally or can be grown agriculturally. Within the great belts of similar temperature conditions, it is more important than any other factor in determining the distribution of plant species and agricultural crops.

5

Plants may be divided into three great groups on the basis of the moisture condition to which they are adapted: (1) Hydrophytes—water plants or water-loving plants; (2) mesophytes—plants adapted to medium moisture conditions; and (3) xerophytes—plants able to survive under conditions of extreme moisture shortage.

Hydrophytes may grow entirely under water, or, more frequently, with part of the plant structure above water or floating on water. Plants in this group are usually large-celled and have thin cell walls and thin epidermal covering. They often have a relatively poorly developed root system that can survive in the absence of oxygen. They have relatively little protection against water loss. Among important agricultural crops, rice most nearly approaches the typical hydrophyte. Such crops can be grown only where water, from either rainfall or irrigation, is extremely abundant.

The mesophytes, requiring a medium amount of water, include the greater proportion of our agricultural crops. Such plants need moderate soil moisture and also good aeration around their roots, as the root system must have oxygen for development. They have moderately large root systems in proportion to the tops. Their structures are composed of medium-sized cells with surface covering well developed to prevent excessive water loss. Stomata, or pores, in the leaves usually close under conditions of incipient leaf wilting. Thus the plants are moderately well protected against water loss.

The third class, xerophytes, includes plants highly resistant to drought conditions. Usually their structure is such that water loss is reduced to a minimum—leaves are small, all epidermal coverings are thick and heavily covered with waxy material (cutinized), stomata are small and are frequently set in pits instead of on the surface of the leaves, and cells are small and thick-walled. Much of the true xerophytic vegetation has large root systems. Such plants usually grow slowly when moisture is available but are highly resistant to water loss and can survive long period of drying. Since they are generally slow growing. they are not of great importance agriculturally. However, the native xerophytic vegetation of arid sections provides some feed for livestock and is important in reducing soil erosion.

In arid regions, in addition to xerophytic plants, there is usually an additional flora of quickly maturing plants that grow from seed and produce flowers and fruits during short seasons when rainfall occurs. The seed then remain in the ground until moisture and temperature conditions are again favorable for growth. Such plants are mesophytic in type and develop only when moisture is ample.

A plant properly classed as a mesophyte tends to assume some of the characteristics of xerophytes when grown with a shortage of moisture and some of those of hydrophytes under conditions of abundant moisture. Thus the individual plant grown with abundant moisture will generally have larger leaves, larger cells, thinner cell walls, and less highly developed surface coverings than plants of the same variety or species grown under conditions of deficient water.

The Role of Water in Plants

Most growing plants contain much more water than all other materials combined. C. R. Barnes has suggested that it is as proper to term the plant a water structure as to call a house composed mainly of brick a brick building. Certain it is that all essential processes of plant growth and development occur in water. The mineral elements from the soil that are usable by the plant must be dissolved in the soil solution before they can be taken into the root. They are carried to all parts of the growing plant and are built into essential plant materials while in a dissolved state. The carbon dioxide from the air may enter the leaf as a gas but is dissolved in water in the leaf before it is combined with a part of the

6

water to form simple sugars—the base material from which the plant body is mainly built. Actively growing plant parts are generally 75 to 90 percent water. Structural parts of plants, such as woody stems no longer actively growing, may have much less water than growing tissues.

The actual amount of water in the plant at any one time, however, is only an infinitesimal part of what passes through it during its development. The processes of photosynthesis, by which carbon dioxide and water are combined—in the presence of chlorophyll and with energy derived from light—to form sugars, require that carbon dioxide from the air enter the plant. This occurs mainly in the leaves. The leaf surface is not solid but contains great numbers of stomata, or pores, through which the carbon dioxide enters. The same structure that permits the one gas to enter the leaf, however, permits another gas—water vapor—to be lost from it. Since carbon dioxide is present in the air only in trace quantities (3 to 4 parts in 10,000 parts of air) and water vapor is near saturation in the air spaces within the leaf (at 80° F. saturated air would contain about 186 parts of water vapor in 10,000 parts of air), the total amount of water vapor lost is many times the carbon dioxide intake. Actually, because of wind and other factors, the loss of water in proportion to carbon dioxide intake may be even greater than the relative concentrations of the two gases. Also, not all of the carbon dioxide that enters the leaf is synthesized into carbohydrates.

While the air spaces inside the leaf are normally at or near saturation in plants or in a wilted condition, the moisture in the air surrounding the leaf may vary from full saturation to as low as 10-percent saturation. The drier and hotter the air surrounding the plant in general the more rapid the water loss in proportion to carbon dioxide intake. Thus in the drier, hotter areas the total water required to grow a plant to a given size will be greater than in areas where the air contains greater average quantities of moisture. Also water loss is more rapid when there is much wind than on a still day with the same temperature and humidity.

Water enters the plant primarily through the root system, which in most plants, at least those growing in a medium to dry environment, is usually more extensive than is generally realized. Some sources state that corn in open soil will root almost as deeply as the height of the stalk; that the roots of a single lima bean or cabbage plant may ramify through 200 cubic feet of soil, and that many grasses and legumes have roots 16 feet deep in the soil. In open soils planted to such crops it may be impossible to find even a cubic inch of soil in the upper 2 or 3 feet that is not penetrated by roots.

The amount of moisture that the soil will hold against the downward force of gravity is termed the "field capacity" and varies in general with the fineness of the particles making up the soil. The moisture is held in the soil as films of water around the soil particles, and the total amount held is roughly proportional to the total amount of these surfaces. As the young roots penetrate the soil they are in contact with these moisture films, and the water enters them largely as a result of the physical process called osmosis.

Not all the water in the soil, however, can be absorbed by the plant. If the films of water surrounding each soil particle become thin, the rate of capillary flow becomes less until the root is no longer able to absorb water. If this condition is reached in much of the root zone the plant wilts, because water is lost more rapidly from the top than it is supplied by the roots. The point at which the roots are no longer able to absorb appreciable moisture from the soil is termed the "wilting percentage," the moisture below that point being unavailable for plant use. The available moisture capacity of the soil is the amount of water available for plant use that it will store, or the amount between field capacity and wilting percentage is a little less than half that of field capacity, though this varies in different soils.

7

The amount of available water that the soil will hold varies greatly with the soil texture and structure. Thus coarse, sandy soils may not hold more than half an inch of available water per foot of depth. Moderate-textured loam soils will usually hold 1½ to 2 inches of available water per foot of depth, while some clay soils will hold as much as 3 inches. Thus the light, coarse textured soils that hold little available water are known as droughty and are of value agriculturally only under conditions of very frequent and regular rainfall or where abundant irrigation water is available. On the other hand, soils of high available water-holding capacity frequently will store enough water to mature satisfactory crops even though no rainfall occurs during the period of crop growth.

The most critical period of water shortage in a plant is when it is making its most rapid growth, or when cell division is occuring most rapidly. In crops grown for their seed, the most critical period is likely to be the time of fertilization of the flowers, since lack of water then is likely to result in failure to form seed. In plants grown primarily for their leaves and stems, such as the forage crops, water shortage is likely to reduce production more during the earlier stages of development than during the later stages before harvest. With tree fruits such as cherries and peaches, the period of rapid growth just before maturity is the most serious in reducing production.

In perennial plants, which form their flower buds during the season preceding that in which the buds flower and fruit, moderate water shortage tends to result in increased fruit-bud formation. Thus seasons of moderate water shortage usually are followed by abundant bloom the following spring in many fruit and forest trees.

Many of the basic farm practices, particularly in regions of limited rainfall, are based on conservation of water. Summer fallowing is primarily to secure 2 years' rainfall for one crop. Contouring and mulching are based in part on securing penetration into the soil of all water that falls. Clean tillage of cultivated crops during the growing season removes the competition of weeds for water. It can also cause severe erosion on steep areas and light soil structures. Irrigation is supplying water to plants that could not develop properly without it. Finally, much has been accomplished and more is possible in breeding varieties of agricultural plants that will thrive under conditions of limited water supply.

SOILS, THEIR FLORA AND FAUNA

There are many different sorts of soils and many different conditions of soils. The first cannot be altered, the second can, and it is the farmers' object to maintain it as the most acceptable medium for plant growth.

In order that a plant's roots may thrive they need moisture, food, air, warmth and anchorage. An ideal soil, then, will hold and conduct moisture, contain an abundance of available food, permeated with an extensive network of cracks and channels, yet compact to aid water movement and anchorage. We have already studied the plant's food, but the remaining items are mainly bound up with soil structure.

Natural undisturbed soils consist of a friable surface layer filled with a mat of roots perhaps 2 or 3 in. thick and containing a quantity of decaying plant remains. Underneath there is another layer of crumbly earth of a dark color about 6 in. thick, but in which the crumbs are all fitted compactly together like a jig-saw, being separated merely by fine cracks. Fine roots penetrate between these cracks and expand, squeezing the plastic soil crumbs into different shapes and, at the same time, closing up some cracks and opening others so that a constant supply of fresh feeding surfaces is available to the plant.

8

In addition to these cracks there are the larger perforations made chiefly by earth-worms, more especially on well-drained but moisture-retentive soils. These form the main conduits for the access of air and for the drainage of surplus moisture. Worms are constantly feeding on soil in one place and dumping it, in a more finely divided and mixed condition, in another.

In some parts of the world there are no earth-worms to provide drainage. Such places have long dry periods so that waterlogging is remote in any case. The need for these burrows, therefore, is not great, unless long wet periods intervene, as in the Tropics, where ants often serve the same purpose. In rather dry temperate climates, where microbial activity is low, a fibrous type of organic matter accumulates at the surface and its slow decay gives a finely granulated but fairly well aerated soil—the prairie soil.

Going deeper, the cracks become fewer but larger, so that the individual soil crumbs become soil blocks with more or less vertical divisions formed by the alternate drying and shrinking, and wetting and expansion, of the body of the soil. Down these cracks the plant tap roots go in their search for moisture and often for minerals also. The worm-holes, too, become fewer but larger, only the large worms are found below 9 in., the great majority of worms living mainly in the top 6 in. Disused worm-holes again become easy passages for roots.

These larger channels, in well-drained loamy soils, often go down 6 ft., and many of our crops go to this depth, especially root crops and others possessing tap roots. Roots of lucerne in some dry American soils have been found at 30 ft. There is seldom any need for roots to travel such distances for moisture in this country except on shallow soils overlying fissured rocks.

Plants use a lot of water while building up their substance, though only about $1/2$ to 1 per cent of the water taken up is actually built into the sugars and other materials that make up the plant body or used in plant processes. The remainder is evaporated by the plant through its leaves and stems during transportation, drawing up a good deal of nutrients from the root at the same time.

It has been found that a plant needs at least 20 gallons of water to form 1 lb. of dry weight, and up to 80 gallons in dry climates—in the latter case simply to keep the plant tissues from wilting under the intense evaporation.

The water content of average soils on a rough basis is the equivalent of about 1 in. of rain for every foot of sandy soil and 2 in. for every foot of clay soil, with loam soils taking an intermediate position.

There are a variety of soils, more or less extreme cases, with high proportions of sand, clay or silt. A loamy soil containing about 40 per cent of sand, 40 per cent of silt and 20 per cent of clay may be taken as the standard, in which the sand and silt particles are bound together by clay to form the small soil crumbs. Only clay, of the mineral constituents, has this binding property—a sort of gelatinous stickiness which is only too obvious to those afflicted with clay soil. Silt, which is a grade of soil particles intermediate between clay and sand does not possess this stickiness. For that reason, it does not hold itself together in crumbs but easily breaks down to dust or mud with cultivation, and in wet weather effectively seals off soil pores with the possibility of suffocation of plant roots.

Sand particles, being coarser still, though having no binding properties again, will nevertheless allow air to penetrate into the soil. There is sometimes a danger, however, that if it contains a proportion of silt this will wash down and accumulate at a lower layer, forming a kind of pan.

All these extreme types have one thing in common. They are all improved, cumulatively, by decaying organic matter. They are improved in two ways. By an improvement in structure and an improvement in water-holding capacity. This is brought about by the presence of large numbers of bacteria and fungi and their remains, which are of a mucilaginous or gummy nature. This helps the silt and sand particles to combine into crumbs. Fungal hyphae have a similar effect. It also

9

permits the cracks in clay soils to remain open; this mucilage being of a much less sticky material than the clay itself. It creates lines of weakness between the clay crumbs and blocks. Unfortunately, these effects only hold as long as the micro-organisms are supplied with organic matter. A good soil with a good structure is one that will work to a tilth over a wide range of moisture conditions without the individual crumbs losing their entity under rain.

Water-holding capacity is improved in two ways: by the presence of these mucilaginous materials and, in the case of clay and silt soils, by the formation of fine cracks which hold thin films of moisture. Though the relative quantity of these colloidal materials is not great they can hold up to ten times their bulk of water. An annual dressing of 14 tons of manure per acre, over many years, has been shown to increase the water content of the top 9 in. of the soil by about a third, that is, from 2 in. to about 2¾ in. And consequently reducing the loss by drainage, as the following figures from Rothamsted show.

Average number of days on which the field drains were running:
Manured land   0.7 days ⎫
Non-manured land   19.5 days ⎬ during the same period

Note: 1 hectare = 2.4 acres

ORGANIC MATTER AND HOW TO MAINTAIN IT

Soil organic matter is dynamic material. It changes continually through further decomposition, but it maintains a degree of stability in quantity and in quality through the additions of new raw materials.

Organic matter is a temporary product—a stage in a natural cycle of elements. Each increment remains in the soil while it passes through the several slow biological oxidation changes that eventually reduce it to carbon dioxide, water, and mineral elements. As it passes through the cycle, it is replaced by organic matter formed from fresh residues.

Organic matter is formed in the biological decomposition of plant and animal residues. In the decomposition process, some of the plant substances are converted rapidly to carbon dioxide, water, and mineral elements (mineralization), and other substances may be only chemically altered at first.

The microbiological activity is high when fresh plant residues begin to decay. As the micro-organisms consume the more easily decomposable materials, the level of activity gets less and less. When only the more resistant plant substances remain along with the series of new organic materials synthesized by the micro-organisms, the microbial activity becomes slow—akin to a smoldering fire—and is the cause of constant loss of organic matter from soil.

The amount of organic matter in soil at any time hinges on the speed of the microbiological activity and the amount of fresh residue material that is added each year. The principles that regulate microbiological decomposition—which affect mechanical losses of soil and determine the amount and kind of residues returned to the soil—therefore are the principles that govern the level of organic matter in soil.

A number of things affect the speed of activity of soil microbes. We can control some of them. Others depend on the weather. Some are determined by early geological processes and the kind of plant cover that prevailed before men became interested in soil organic matter. Among the factors are temperature, moisture, aeration, acidity, supply of plant nutrients, tillage, and the kind and the amount of crop residues and manures returned to the soil. Cropping systems and soil management exert strong influences on most of these factors.

10

Microbes are most active in a moist soil. Microbial activity is depressed when a soil is extremely wet or dry. Air is excluded from the soil pore spaces in a wet soil, and the lack of air slows decomposition.

Composting

The purpose of composting plant and animal residues is to provide the plant with food in a more easily available form than that contained in the original residues. There are, in addition, a number of other benefits to be gained from this preparation of the food.

(a) The food is presented to the plant in a steadily available form, being broken down by soil organisms during the course of the season as and when the plant requires it.

(b) The organic matter provides a useful soil conditioner in a form less readily destroyed than animal manure, as it contains a better balance of carbon and nitrogen compounds.

(c) Weed seeds and pathogenic organisms are destroyed by the heat and microbial activity of the composting process.

(d) The bulk of the materials used is reduced to about a third, and is in a friable condition, thus considerably reducing handling costs over the original bulk of materials.

(e) The highly concentrated and sometimes harmful compounds in some animal manures are converted to more suitable and better balanced materials for plant use.

(f) The conservation of nitrogen and other easily lost nutrients.

In order that the decomposition of residues shall come about rapidly and efficiently, three factors must be present—namely, air, moisture and sufficient nitrogenous matter, phosphates and trace elements, for the micro-organisms to build up their bodies.

Air, naturally, is required for the micro-organisms' respiration, during which they burn up the carbohydrates in the plant residues with the evolution of considerable heat. If we are to obtain this heat (140-160°F.), the air supply must be adequate. On the other hand, too much air will cool and dry the heap—the supply must be controlled. This is best achieved by wrapping small heaps with some porous material—sacking or slatted boards—or, in the case of large heaps, by situating them out of winds, or, better still, in pits with a network of air channels on the bottom to provide a steady percolation of air from the bottom upwards. It is for the reason of excessive air supply that heaps of less than half a cubic yard are difficult to heat properly except in warm weather, or unless extremely well insulated.

The actual rate of passage of air can vary within quite wide limits: an increase in flow, though carrying away the heat, also gives the organisms the opportunity to work faster and produce more heat, so that the process is to some extent compensatory. Care must be taken to avoid extremes.

In practice, a mixture of soft leafy or grassy material, and plant stems in equal proportions, or straw, with the addition of the commonly recommended one-quarter by bulk of farmyard manure, will give good results. Sawdust, coffee grounds and similar close-textured materials are almost impossible to decompose quickly, mainly because of poor aeration. The addition of sufficient nitrogenous matter and moisture for complete decomposition would effectively stop air from entering these materials. It is better, therefore, if quick results are required, to mix these materials with more fibrous matter.

11

The loss of nitrogen through composting close-textured materials, particularly if high in nitrogen, is well borne out in the following table:

Table 1: Changes of Nitrogen Content In Compost Heaps

Material	Nitrogen at Start lb.[2]	Nitrogen at End lb.	Gain or Loss lb.	Percentage Gain or Loss
Weeds	44.2	25.7	—18.5	—41.8
½ Weeds and ½ Crotalaria[1]	42.8	28.4	—14.5	—33.8
Ditto	49.7	29.2	—20.5	—41.3
Mixed Crop Residues	28.3	29.5	+1.3	+4.4

1. Crotalaria is a leguminous plant. Heaps of approximately 2 tons at start.
2. 1 kilogram = 2.2 lbs.

It will be noted that the higher the proportion of nitrogen the greater the loss. While a well-aerated heap low in nitrogen finally contained the most. It has been found also that mixed wastes decompose more quickly than single materials partly, no doubt, owing to the improved texture of the heap. But it seems that many micro-organisms thrive better on a mixed diet, and these will be better catered for.

Fig. 1. Two bins permit turning compost by moving it from one bin to the other.

Fig. 2 - Composting autumn leaves (top) in a circular bin of woven wire fence. City gardeners collect the leaves that gave them summer shade (bottom) and compost them for mulching the soil in next year's garden.

Moisture is necessary and needs to be present within comparatively narrow limits—sufficient to provide a film of moisture for the micro-organisms to travel in, but not so much as to impede aeration or even to run through the heap and cool it. While water passing through will probably not carry away much nutrient, providing the heap is warm and well aerated, should the heap become cold and the micro-organisms inactivated, there is a decided risk of this occuring. In practice, a water content of 50-70 per cent is found to be satisfactory; in effect, the materials will be holding just as much water as they can without any surplus to drain away. Too much water will also impede the activity of fungi which is necessary to decompose the ligneous fractions.

Nitrogen is the chief food element, apart from carbohydrate, required by the micro-organisms. In order to provide a balanced diet for micro-organisms the nitrogen must be between 1.2-3 and 2.8 per cent of the carbohydrate on a dry-weight basis, which represents a carbon-nitrogen ratio of about 33:1. On this basis, a ton of fresh animal manure containing 10 lb. of nitrogen would suffice for 1,000 lb. of straw already containing about 0.5 per cent of nitrogen. A smaller quantity will result in a somewhat slower decomposition, while a greater quantity will not be utilized by the microbes and will be destroyed by denitrifying organisms or lost to the atmosphere as ammonia or evil-smelling compounds. From the point of view of economy, therefore, it is probably wiser to err on the lower side.

It is interesting to note in this connection that a compost heap is to a large extent self-compensatory in its nitrogen requirements, as micro-organisms feeding on the material can fix considerable amounts from the atmosphere, as shown by the following table:

Table 2: Fixation of Nitrogen by Organisms

Amount of Manure Used	Total N. at Start lb. [1]	Total N. at End lb.	Percentage Gain of N.	Gain N. in lb.
Full quantity	32.70	34.87	6.6	2.17
¼ quantity	29.12	32.36	11.1	3.24

1. Kilogram = 2.2 lbs.

It will be noted that the low-nitrogen heap has gained 1.7 lb. more of nitrogen over the full-nitrogen heap. This effect is also dependent on the aeration of the heap, as shown below.

Table 3: Aeration and Nitrogen Fixation

	Pit 4 ft. Deep [1]	Pit 2 ft. Deep
Total at start (lb)	31.25	29.12
Total N. at end (lb.)	29.49	32.36
Loss or gain N. (lb.)	− 1.76	+ 3.24
as percentage	− 6.1	+11.1

Both these tables refer to pits containing about 2 short tons of wastes.
1. 1 ft. = 30.36 cm.

For those farmers having abundant supplies of manure, providing the proportion of this material does not exceed a quarter by bulk to strawy or other low-nitrogen wastes, there will be little loss or gain. For the market gardener, however, who has to buy his manure, only one-sixteenth part of farmyard manure is needed, provided it is fresh, or less if the wastes contain a fair proportion of discarded vegetables, tomato vines, etc., which are generally a good deal higher in nitrogen than straw. In practice, all that is required is sufficient to ensure satisfactory heating of the heap, permitting a large degree of latitude in proportions of materials used. On this basis, very much less of other nitrogenous materials used for composting than has hitherto been recommended seems necessary.

Temperature has some influence on the nitrogen and organic matter content. Less organic matter and nitrogen is lost as the temperature rises from 113° F, (45° C.) to 167° F. (75° C.), and the same applies to temperatures below 86° F. (30° C.). In the intermediate range organic matter decomposes more quickly, while the nitrogen content may increase.

The energy food of the organisms, almost entirely carbohydrates, with a little protein, can take many forms varying in digestibility. The most easily decomposed are the sugars which provide food for some nitrogen fixing organisms, notably azotobacter. There are further small quantities of starch and pectins, but the great bulk, as a rule, consists of celluloses and hemi-celluloses which provide food for a great variety of bacteria and fungi. The last group of energy-providing materials are the lignins which, so far as we know, can only be broken down by fungi. Curiously enough, the heat-loving bacteria that live in the heap in its early stages seem to prefer proteins. This possibly accounts for the fact that material low in nitrogenous compounds and activated with sulphate of ammonia or other artificial nitrogen may fail to heat up satisfactorily.

The course of events taking place in a compost heap are roughly as follows. The hemi-celluloses surrounding the cellulose fibres are strongly attacked by fungi and bacteria with the evolution of much heat. This releases the celluloses for attack, mainly by bacteria. This stage is needed after about a week, when the temperature reaches its highest peak. With a gradual fall in temperature the fungi reinvade the heap and its celluloses, and also attack the ligneous fractions, but their action is slow and lasts over several months, according to temperature and aeration. If the material contains as much as 20-30 per cent of lignins, as in wood, decomposition is very slow as the lignin encloses much of the cellulose material, thus protecting it from decomposition. Sawdust, from its finely divided nature, is a good deal more accessible, though this is counterbalanced to some extent by its close texture impeding aeration. The processes are exemplified in the table:

Table 4: Rate of Decomposition Of Rye Straw At 350° C.[1]

Duration of Decomposition	0 days	4 days	8 days	24 days	84 days
Total Organic Matter	100	97	78	62	49
Celluloses	57	56.1	41.9	30.4	24.2
Hemi-celluloses	21.85	18.35	10.81	8.42	6.85

As percentage of original organic matter

1 Degrees farenheit $= 1.8 \text{x} C + 32°$

Composts, Peat, Sewage Sludge and Their Availability

Organic materials once were the only fertilizers used by farmers. They were mainly plant and animal products high in protein and were used for their nitrogen-supplying value. The demand for many of them in making feed and the lower cost and greater availability of plant nutrients in mineral fertilizer have led to the replacement of most of them as fertilizer.

Other organic materials, such as composts, peat, and sewage sludge, continue to be used to improve soil. They are called soil amendments rather than fertilizers because of their low content of plant nutrients.

They may be incorporated into the soil or used as mulches. Heavy rates of application are the rule. Thus they have the double effect of contributing some plant nutrients and improving the physical condition of the soil.

Sometimes the amendments represent utilization of materials that otherwise would be wasted. Some have an unusual composition, and special practices are needed to use them successfully.

In composting, a microbiological process, organic materials are partially decomposed by the activity of microbes. Hemicelluloses (the gumlike substances), cellulose (the plant fiber), and lignin, (the woody material) make up 50 to 85 percent of mature plant materials. The lower percentages occur in the leguminous plants, the intermediate ones in nonleguminous crops, and the higher amounts in wood. The rest of the plant is largely water-soluble substances and protein and small amounts of fat and ash.

Microbes readily attack the water-soluble substances, hemicelluloses, and cellulose, which rot quickly.

Lignin is quite resistant to attack. Its nature changes somewhat, but it disappears only slowly.

From the readily decomposable substances, microbes get energy to carry on their activities and the carbon they need for building their cells.

About 20 percent of the carbon in the decomposed part may be synthesized into microbial cells. The remainder enters the air as carbon dioxide and becomes available for photosynthesis by new generations of plants.

About one-half of the total dry matter originally present is decomposed by the time the compost is ready for use. Three-fourths of this loss is represented by a decrease in hemicelluloses and cellulose.

Microbial cells contain 5 to 10 percent of nitrogen. So, if large amounts of energy substances are present, considerable nitrogen is needed for synthesis of cells. The amount of energy available and consequently the amount of nitrogen needed depend on the amount of material susceptible to decomposition by the microbes.

Materials like sphagnum plants and highly lignified wood tissues, which resist decomposition, have low nitrogen requirements. For the usual farm crop residues, a nitrogen content of 1.5 percent is enough for a maximum rate of decomposition. Microbes do not assimilate all the nitrogen in materials that have higher nitrogen values, and the excess is subject to loss by volatilization, leaching, or denitrification. Actually, values of 1 to 1.25 percent of nitrogen are adequate.

Mature nonleguminous plant residues are low in nitrogen and high in substances that supply energy for microbial growth. When they are incorporated into soil, microbes assimilate available nitrogen from the soil and cause a shortage of nitrogen for crop growth.

This nitrogen-depleting effect can be overcome by adding enough available nitrogen to supply the needs of the microbes. The nitrogen may be supplied by commercial fertilizer added with the organic matter if it is turned under directly. If used as bedding for livestock, the feces and urine of animals supply the

16

nitrogen. The third (but more expensive) way to overcome the nitrogen-depleting effect is to compost the material.

Two main objectives are accomplished by composting.

First, readily decomposable substances are removed, and the percentage of nitrogen content is increased. Thus there is no danger that a nitrogen shortage will be induced when composts are added to soils.

Second, the physical nature of the material is changed. The decomposition of cellulose causes the plant material to lose its strength and to break easily. It becomes friable, crumbly, and easier to handle and incorporate into the soil. That is important when hand tools or small tillage implements are used.

With some materials, such as manure or municipal garbage, a third result of composting is the removal of obnoxious odors.

The composition of composts is variable. The moisture content is usually in the neighborhood of 75 percent, but it may be as low as 40 percent. A high moisture content makes the finished compost weigh more than the dry weight of the material originally placed in the heap. That is the basis of statements that 1 ton of plant residues will produce 2 tons or more of compost. Its value, of course, is in the dry matter.

Composts commonly contain 2 percent of nitrogen, but the content may be 1.5 to 3.5 percent in the dry matter.

The phosphorus content of dry composts is about 0.5 to 1.0 percent. Potassium values probably are twice as high. These values will be correspondingly higher if phosphate and potash are added to the compost.

The nitrogen of composts is only slowly available and never approaches that of inorganic sources of nitrogen. Its slow availability lowers the possibility of leaching and extends availability over the entire growing season. Presumably the availability of phosphorus and potassium in composts approaches that of inorganic sources.

Composts are essentially low-analysis fertilizers, and large amounts must be used to obtain adequate additions of plant nutrients to soils.

The maximum effects of composts on soil structure—increased aggregation, pore space, and water-holding ability—and on crop yield usually occur only after several years.

Uses of Compost

Composts increase crop yields as much as do equal additions of manure from the bedding of horses and cattle. Composts should be used in much the same way as manure with regard to amount and method of application and reinforcement. Because compost is like farmyard manure in physical nature, composition, and value, we sometimes call it synthetic manure.

Composts are good to use as mulches in gardens or around shrubbery. Applied 2 or 3 inches deep, they conserve soil moisture, lower soil temperatures in hot weather, help control weeds, and contribute nutrients.

Applications on small areas of large amounts of compost may supply the entire nutrient needs for the successful production of crops. If the composted materials come from a large area, the land from which they come loses its share of organic matter. One can overcome some of that loss by using rotations of sod crops whose roots restore the physical condition of the soil. The amount of organic matter that can be returned to the soil over any large area of land can be no larger than the amount produced on it. Because, furthermore, some is used by animals and man, only moderate rates of compost applications can be attained over any large area.

Before you decide whether to practice composting in practical farming operations, you should compare the soil-improving value of compost and that of the fresh residues from which it is made.

In 12 years of comparisons at the Rothamsted Experimental Station in England, turning under fresh straw to which nitrogen was added gave 10 to 20 percent greater yields of potatoes, barley, and sugar beets than composts prepared from the same amount of straw and nitrogen.

At the New Jersey Agricultural Experiment Station, fresh residues, applied on an equal organic-matter basis, produced double or triple the aggregation of silt and clay particles produced by composts prepared from the same materials.

One must also realize that (since one half the organic matter is lost in composting) fresh residues applied at the same rate will cover twice the area that can be covered by composts. When it is feasible to do so, one should return plant residues directly to the soil in preference to composting; doing so leads to greater soil improvement and saving of labor. Sufficient nitrogen and other nutrients in the form of commercial fertilizers should be added to meet the needs of the crop.

In some situations, however, composting meets a need and is a highly desirable practice.

The first is when commercial fertilizers are expensive, labor is cheap, and implements are simple. Composts prepared from plant, animal, and human wastes have been used extensively for many centuries in India, Japan, and China. More than one-half the nitrogen and a higher proportion of the phosphorus and potassium returned to the soil in Japan in 1946 were supplied by composts. Composting practices in some countries include the use of town garbage and night soil; a supplementary benefit thus is improved sanitation.

Composts are also used when soil is used intensively as in market gardening, in which frequent tillage and almost complete removal of crops (sometimes even the roots) may lead to soil deterioration. Composts are used to overcome this effect.

Special composts are needed for growing mushrooms. They used to be prepared from horse manure, but more and more they are made from definite mixtures of plant products and commercial fertilizers, which supply nitrogen and potash.

Compost Production

The most prevalent composting in the United States is by gardeners who save garden residues, weeds, tree leaves, lawn clippings, and kitchen wastes.

Compost is produced commercially in many places.

A plant at Wyster, Holland, produces 120,000 tons of compost a year from municipal refuse. The annual production of compost is sold at a low price to farmers, and the demand for it is great.

In general, it may be said that commercial production of compost is limited to situations where the cost of assembling the material is not charged to the composting operation itself.

Two sources of compostable material may get greater—wood residues (from lumbering, woodworking plants, and improvement cuttings in forests) and organic wastes in cities.

The total annual quantity of unutilized wood residues was estimated in 1956 by the Forest Service to be 1.4 billion cubic feet at sawmills and woodworking plants. An almost equal quantity was left as logging residues in the forests. About 700 million cubic feet of the residues at sawmills and plants was fine material, such as sawdust, which requires no further reduction in size for use in soil improvement. A large part of the wood residues accumulate, at points remote from possible agricultural use, but in some sections as in the North Central States, nearly all lumbering operations are on farms. Wood residues are also quite accessible for agricultural use in the Northeast and the South.

The use of these residues has been confined mainly to sawdust and shavings because of their favorable physical form and accumulation in large amounts.

18

All available supplies of sawdust and shavings in parts of New England are used as bedding for dairy cows. The manure is used on crops. Waste wood is also converted to chips for use as bedding. The cost may be so high, however, that the use of chips may be restricted to localities where supplies of sawdust and other forms of bedding are inadequate and transportation costs make wood chips competitive with other bedding materials.

Wood residues can be incorporated directly into the soil. They also can be composted. Both sawdust and woodchips make excellent mulches for blueberries, strawberries, fruit trees, ornamentals, and garden crops. Because woody plant materials are low in plant nutrients, they need extra nitrogen and phosphate when they are composted or added to soil.

Municipal organic wastes of garbage and street refuse are composted for agricultural use in many European cities and in the Far East. In this country they have been disposed of mostly by land filling, soil burial, or incineration, but there is an increasing interest in the possibility of disposing of them by composting because of the growing scarcity of areas to be filled in, objections to air pollution produced by incineration, and the possibility of reducing costs of waste disposal from the sale of the compost.

The staff of the Sanitary Engineering Research Project of the University of California in 1953 completed a series of experiments on composting municipal wastes. They found that a wide variety of wastes could be composted successfully. Shredding the material (after cans and bottles have been removed) to permit uniform mixing was found desirable. No further modification was found necessary. Turning the heaps every 3 or 4 days meant that finished compost could be produced in 2 or 3 weeks. The composts contained as much plant nutrient as did composts from crop residues. Its value for soil improvement should equal those of manure or composted farm residues.

Making Compost

Almost any natural organic product can be composted with proper care—cornstalks, straw, hay, tree leaves, wood residues, coconut husks, animal and human excreta, garbage, wastes from wineries and breweries, and many more. The microbes are not choosy.

For making composts, you must provide proper aeration, moisture, nutrients, and temperature for microbial decomposition. Those factors and the nature of the material affect the time required for preparation and the final composition. Composting is usually carried out by piling organic materials into heaps where reasonable control of these factors can be maintained.

Air should penetrate the entire compost heap to allow microbes to act and finish the compost in a minimum of time. Aeration depends on size of air spaces within the heap, the height of the pile, and the moisture content.

The coarse materials, like cornstalks, cause large air spaces, excessive aeration, and rapid loss of moisture and heat from the heap. They should be cut to 6-inch lengths or mixed with finer materials before composting. Excessive aeration can be reduced by compacting the pile and by increasing its height. Fine materials, such as sawdust, are hard to aerate and may be mixed with coarser materials or turned oftener. Cereal straws and tree leaves have good properties for composting.

Compost heaps should be built no more than 6 feet high so air can penetrate to the bottom of the pile. Width and length may be adjusted for convenient handling.

Excessive moisture cuts aeration by filling air spaces in the material and by increasing compaction.

Only a slow partial decomposition takes place when aeration is insufficient. Intermediate products of anaerobic microbes, such as organic acids and reduced nitrogenous and sulfur compounds, are formed. Many have offensive odors.

The physical nature of the composting material frequently is altered little under anaerobic conditions, and it remains hard to handle. Poor aeration is overcome by turning the heap.

The composting material should be kept damp but not wet enough to cause liquids to trickle down and collect at the bottom of the heap. The weight of the moisture should be 1 to 2.5 times that of the dry organic material. Decomposition is slowed down when the heap is drier than that: anaerobic conditions set in, particularly at the bottom of the heap, when it is wetter. Water is best applied to the layers as the pile is built up.

Many fresh dry plant residues are somewhat hard to wet. They can be wetted best by applying the water in a fine spray. If necessary, water should be added on 2 or 3 successive days at the start of the composting period.

Letting water run out at the bottom of the pile should be avoided because nutrients are lost. Fresh green materials, such as grass clippings, contain too much moisture for proper composting. They should be left to wilt before piling or should be mixed with about one-third their weight of dry material. Rainfall may increase moisture in the heap. If the moisture becomes excessive, it can be reduced by turning and loosening the pile. Small heaps that have a high proportion of exposed surface may become unduly dry. Water should be added to them as needed.

Most plant residues will form composts in time if they simply are put in a heap and kept moist.

Adding Nutrients

Sometimes nutrients are added. Mature residues of nonleguminous plants require the addition of about 15 pounds of actual nitrogen per ton of dry material—equal to the nitrogen in 70 pounds of ammonium sulfate or calcium cyanamide, 45 pounds of ammonium nitrate, or 30 pounds of urea. Any of them are satisfactory. Calcium cyanamide and urea give a slightly basic reaction, which promotes rapid decay. If ammonium sulfate is used, an equal amount of finely ground limestone should be added to neutralize the acidity arising from the sulfate anion.

Residues of leguminous plants and young nonleguminous plants may contain 1.5 to 3.5 percent of nitrogen and need no additional nitrogen. Substantial losses of nitrogen occur if such residues are composted directly, because the amount of nitrogen present is in excess of that assimilated by the microbes. Such materials should be mixed with residues of low nitrogen content. Two or three parts of mature, nonleguminous residues mixed with young plants or with leguminous plants give a satisfactory mixture.

Other organic nitrogenous substances, such as cottonseed and soybean meals and dried blood, may be added to composts to give the proper nitrogen content. The cost of nitrogen in these forms is greater than in the inorganic form. Liquid and solid excreta of animals and sewage sludge also may be used to supply nitrogen to composts.

The microbes need so little phosphate and potash that ordinary plant residues supply enough for composting. To sawdust or plant residues that become leached before composting, it may be wise to add phosphate and potash—about 20 pounds (or 3 gallons) of superphosphate and 5 or 10 pounds of potassium sulfate or potassium chloride to a ton of residue.

The phosphate and potash increase the fertilizing value of the resulting compost. A complete fertilizer with an analysis such as 10-6-4 may be used to supply nitrogen, phosphate, and potash. The fertilizer should be added to give the proper amount of nitrogen in the beginning compost. Extra care should be taken to prevent leaching. If that cannot be done, it is preferable to reinforce the compost when it is applied to the soil instead of in the pile.

20

Temperature on Compost

Rotting proceeds slowly at temperatures near freezing. Microbial processes increase at higher temperatures. The rate nearly doubles for every rise of 18° F. in temperature.

Microbes themselves produce heat as a byproduct of the decomposition. They release large amounts of heat in the pile; since it is nearly self-insulating, the temperature of the pile rises. Microbes that grow best at ordinary temperatures initiate the decomposition and carry it on until a temperature of about 115° F. to 120° F. is reached. That temperature kills them, and another group of microbes takes over. They are called thermophiles, or thermophilic organisms, because they can carry on at high temperatures. They raise the temperature inside the heap to 140° F. to 170° F. This rise in temperature, which usually persists 2 or 3 weeks, indicates that the composting is proceeding normally. It greatly shortens the time required for the decay of the plant material. The rapid dissipation of heat in small or open heaps may keep temperatures down too low.

The high temperature also kills disease-causing organisms, insects, and weed seeds, except in the outer parts and the bottom of the heap. When the heap is turned, those parts should be turned to the center of the pile so that they also will be subjected to the high temperatures.

Residues of diseased plants should be composted only if they can be completely subjected to the high temperatures in the interior of the heap. That is seldom possible with small piles; if so, they should be turned to avoid spreading disease.

Turning the compost heap hastens the decomposition by increasing the supply of air for the microbes. Heaps may be turned every 3 or 4 days in commercial operations. In some mechanized processes, air is blown continuously through the composting mixture. In farm and garden practices, the compost should be turned at least once about every 3 weeks after its preparation. More frequent turning is desirable to assure mixing and more uniform decomposition of the heap. The number of turnings may be adjusted to facilities available and the desired time for completing the compost.

Occasionally some practices are advocated that are not essential. Inoculation with prepared cultures of microbes is sometimes said to hasten the process and lead to a better product.

Experiments at the University of California tested soil, horse manure, partially composted material, and a commercial preparation of selected cultures as inoculants. None had any significant effect on the course of composting. It appears that the materials used in composting have enough of the microbes on their surfaces to start and continue decomposition.

Mixing small amounts of soil into composts is unnecessary, but the soil may help conserve nitrogen and other nutrients. A thin layer of soil on the outside surfaces of a heap will aid in retaining moisture. A shallow pit does the same, but the pit should be in a well-drained place, because accumulation of water in a poorly drained pit will produce anaerobic conditions.

Compost Completion and Bin Construction

When is the composting process completed? In large, well-prepared heaps, a drop in the interior temperature to values near air temperature and easy crumbling of the materials in the hand indicate completion.

Full composting in small heaps usually requires 3 months under favorable conditions of moisture and temperature. Composts prepared late in the fall in regions of cold winters may not be ready for use until early the next summer. Under commercial conditions, with large heaps and frequent turning, composting time may be shortened to 2 or 3 weeks. With some mechanized processes, only 10 days are required for fresh material, and that may be shortened to 3 days if the beginning material is already partly decomposed.

Bins of simple construction are desirable for home or garden-scale composting. A bin will help to maintain moisture at the edgesof the heap and prevent blowing. It should be about 4 feet wide, 5 feet high, and as long as needed to hold the material available for composting. No floor is needed.(See Figures 1 & 2)

It is well to have two bins side by side with one common wall. The compost may be forked then from one bin to the other for turning and mixing. The compost that is ready for use may be kept in one bin while fresh compost is started in the other.

Snow fencing with posts at the corners makes a satisfactory bin. A variety of timbers, arranged in log-cabin fashion, or boards nailed to corner posts provide satisfactory enclosures. Only narrow cracks should be left between the timbers or boards. More permanent structures may be built of concrete blocks or bricks. Small openings should be left near the bottom of such walls to permit penetration of air. One end of the bin should be closed with removable boards to permit access for mixing and removal of the compost.

Peat is a widely used organic soil amendment. It is made up of plant remains that have accumulated over the centuries under relatively airless conditions in bogs.

Other Soil Improvements

Peats improve the water-holding ability of most soils and give better physical structure to fine soils. Heavy applications equal to 25 to 50 percent of the volume of the soil often are made with that in mind. They are used mostly on specialty crops and home grounds.

Undecomposed or slightly decomposed forms of sphagnum, if incorporated into the soil, require small amounts of nitrogen. Acid peats are used for acid-loving plants as a direct growth medium or by mixing into the soil or as a mulch on the place where they are grown. The acidity of such peats may need to be neutralized with ground limestone if they are to be used for ordinary plants.

Peats, especially the coarser grades of sphagnum, are good livestock bedding and poultry litter. In 1950 in the United States an estimated 161,000 tons of peat were used for soil improvement and 31,000 tons for stable bedding and poultry litter.

Sewage sludge is the solids remaining from the treatment of sewage in disposal plants. Various methods of digestion and removal of the solids reduce the organic matter in the plant effluent to a safe point. The resulting sludge is filtered off and may be burned or sold or given away for use as a fertilizer.

The value of the sludge for soil improvement depends on the method used for treating the sewage.

Activated sludge comes from disposal plants in which aerobic treatment is obtained by bubbling large quantities of air through the digesting sewage. The sludge is then allowed to settle in large settling tanks, drawn off, and filtered. The filtered material still contains 80 to 85 percent of water. If it is to be sold as fertilizer, it is dried by heat to a moisture content of 5 to 10 percent. Activated sludge contains 30 to 40 percent of ash, 5 to 6 percent of nitrogen, and 1 to 3.5 percent of phosphorus.

Digested sludges come from disposal systems in which solids are allowed to settle out and are then digested anaerobically. On a dry-matter basis, they contain 35 to 60 percent of ash, 1 to 3 percent of nitrogen, and 0.5 to 1.5 percent of phosphorus. They are allowed to air-dry on sand filter beds outside or in greenhouses where they are protected from rain. Because of their low content of plant nutrients, they are seldom sold for fertilizer.

Activated sludge has a higher nutrient content, lower moisture, better physical condition, and no odor. Available nitrogen in activated sludge is almost equal to that in cottonseed meal and costs about the same. When it is added to soil, about one-half the nitrogen is nitrified in 4 weeks.

All sewage sludges are low in potassium because compounds of potassium dissolve readily in water. they must then be supplemented with a potash fertilizer when used on soils that have too little potassium. Additional phosphate also is needed on some soils, depending on the amount of sludge used.

Sludges contain appreciable quantities of the minor elements, copper, boron, manganese, molybdenum, and zinc. A few experiments indicate that they are available for plant growth.

Sanitary aspects must be considered when digested sludges are applied. Pathogenic organisms may escape the treatment process. It is not advisable to use digested sludge on root crops or low-growing vegetables that are to be eaten raw. Incorporation into the soil 3 months ahead of planting leads to destruction of the disease organisms. Digested sludges give rise to bad odors, which can be overcome by immediate incorporation into the soil. Activated sludges have no bad odor and microbes are killed in the heat treatment.

PROVIDING THE FOOD BY ORGANIC MATTER

It remains now to discuss the mechanisms by which these crops are produced.

In order to produce good crops, plants need a steady and liberal release of nitrogenous compounds, potash, and phosphates, and all other necessary adjuncts to the plant's health.

All this is provided, under natural conditions, by one means, through the activity of soil organisms. These in turn require food, mainly as a source of energy. There is a great distinction here—the plant provides its own energy from light and often some to spare for symbiotic organisms. The micro-organism has to find its energy requirements direct from the soil particles.

The need of soil organisms for nitrogenous materials in the shape of manure, and so forth, has been stressed to the point of imbalance. Certainly they need nitrogen (and minerals), but they need fifty times as much energy-providing food. We give them ample roast beef but forget their bread and butter.

This energy supply consists of carbohydrates which are in turn plant remains, plant skeletons. It may be divided into various fractions varying slightly in their chemical constitution and considerably in their rate of availability as food to the micro-organisms. The most easily used fractions are sugar and starch; next come the hemi-celluloses and celluloses used for plant skeletons in herbaceous plants; and finally the lignins, found in trees and other hard, woody stems, sometimes to the extent of 30-40 per cent of the total carbohydrate. Lignin, it seems can only be decomposed by fungi, whereas the first two groups can be utilized by bacteria as well. These materials are converted to carbon dioxide with the evolution of energy; indeed, the quantity of carbon dioxide liberated is a direct indication of the biological activity of the soil and consequently of its current fertility. (But not necessarily of its total or potential fertility, except under natural conditions, as biological activity can be stimulated by cultivations, addition of nitrogen and other nutrients, etc.)

A notable point of the natural cycle of plant growth and decay is its economy of nutrients. This is obvious enough in tropical climates where fallen leaves and branches decay rapidly and the plant foods they contain are equally rapidly assimilated by the surrounding growth. In most temperate climates, where most of the rain falls in autumn, the mildness and warmth of the soil at this time—coupled with the fact that plants can no longer grow very much on account of the shortage of light—decay and nitrification—release a good deal of nitrogen into the soil which is in danger of being washed away. In fact, it is at this time of year that the fungi come into their own feeding on the freshly-fallen leaves and stems, or dead grasses, and incorporating this free nitrogen into their protoplasm

23

where it is held until the following year. Then, with a diminution in food supply and alternate droughts and rains of spring and summer, much of this fungal material dies and the nutrient is absorbed by the plants again. Worms also are active in autumn and assist by dragging plant remains into the soil or feeding on them, thus rendering them more suitable for fungal use. It would seem wise, then, to imitate Nature by applying undecomposed residues to the soil in autumn.

Bacteria, of course, are active more or less throughout the year, but their activities, which are greatest in autumn, would be rather in a secondary capacity after the plant remains had been incorporated with the soil by worms and fungi.

A soil well supplied with organic matter and in its natural uncultivated condition does not lose nitrogen readily by leaching with heavy rain for another reason. It appears that the water percolates rapidly down cracks and worm-holes to the subsoil, leaving the bulk of the plant food in the body of the soil granules or crumbs.

The ideal situation for this organic matter, it seems, is as near the surface as possible. Here again evolution can provide us with a clue. Plant and animal remains, with the exception of plant roots and soil animals, are deposited on the surface and dragged under bit by bit by worms and to a limited extent by other animals. Here it is either mixed up with finely-divided soil particles by the worm and excreted in an ideal form for further breakdown by bacteria and fungi, or it is acted on by these agents directly at the soil surface where the lower layers of litter are moist and shaded. It will be noted that the decay is invariably aerobic, encouraging nitrogen-fixing and nitrifying bacteria, and it is also adjusted to the plants' needs, giving an increased supply of plant foods in warm and damp weather when plants are growing quickly, and decreasing during cold or dry weather when plant foods cannot be used. A very different set of events takes place when organic matter is ploughed under, especially under modern conditions of deep ploughing and artificial manuring.

The plant and animal residues are put into a permanently damp atmosphere at the bottom of the furrow with a varying degree of aeration according to the depth of ploughing and type of soil. Providing the soil is not cold, e.g. winter time, decomposition is immediate and rapid, resulting in a large microbial and fungal population. Providing the residues contain 1½ per cent or more of nitrogen, there will be sufficient of this element to support the plant as well as the micro-organisms. But also, if plenty of nitrogen is present, the carbohydrates in the organic matter will be used up quickly, giving a further and rapid release of nitrogen on the death of micro-organisms by starvation. The crop may be able to take up quickly all this nitrogen, but generally excess nitrogen in the soil is liable to severe losses. This rapid evolution of nitrogen is followed subsequently by a comparative shortage and the plant may starve if not already mature, even though large amounts were added in the first place. When quickly available nitrogenous fertilizers or manure are used these effects occur even more rapidly.

There is another reason why the organic matter should be left near the surface. The carbohydrate of plant remains is converted to humus chiefly by fungi and to a comparatively small extent by bacteria. When these remains are turned under by the plough much carbon dioxide is evolved by bacterial action, which in turn suppresses the fungi, so that carbon dioxide rather than humus is formed.

It is obvious that a superabundance of a particular kind of food will result in a rapid increase in the particular kind of organism that enjoys that food: take, for example, the growth of yeast in a sugary solution or the prolificacy of rabbits where there is plenty of winter food. So it is when we add nitrogenous manures to the soil. These are added as, or are soon converted into nitrates. Certain organisms can obtain both body-building materials and oxygen for their energy by breaking down nitrates—the denitrifying organisms. These can work without or with air, but more commonly without—so the process is more rapid when the manures are turned under by the plough. They destroy the nitrates and convert

24

them to atmospheric nitrogen—they are then lost to the plant. Indeed, the fact that these organisms can work under any conditions seems to indicate that nitrates have a short life in the soil. In warm weather this destruction of nitrogenous fertilizer takes two to three weeks under suitably moist conditions, that is why in market gardening top dressings have to be applied at about this interval.

The best we can manage, when using concentrated nitrogenous nourishment for the plant, is to provide a rapidly fluctuating food supply, very dependent on rain for its solution and consequent assimilation, and with a risk of scorching the roots or depriving them of water in dry weather. It is for this reason that these crop yields vary so widely from year to year.

The other wasteful effect of nitrogenous manures not generally known is that it stimulates bacteria, including the nitrifying and denitrifying types, to search around for any possible source of carbonaceous matter for energy, and they will decompose the forms of humus (peaty material) which are normally fairly resistant to breakdown and have a great influence on soil structure. It is this effect that has, above all others, given artificial manures a bad name in many quarters—but it is not confined to artificial manures. We have the curious anomaly whereby the ploughing-in of a succulent green crop leaves the soil with rather less organic matter than before, owing to the fact that it contains much nitrogen. Even manure almost entirely decomposes itself, as can be seen in the case of a heap of manure left for twelve months on a paved yard. An annual application of 14 tons per acre is just sufficient to keep the organic matter at an economic level and, as already shown, the losses of nitrogen are enormous. If only for this reason, it is much more economical to compost manure either with fibrous plant residues or by spreading on grassland (sheet composting) so as to bring the proportion of nitrogen to about 1½ per cent of the carbohydrate. Again, this effect is aggravated by our agricultural customs.

When ploughing under a young green crop a rapid decomposition and release of plant foods takes place which unfortunately is completed in 1-2 months and may be followed by starvation of the subsequent crop. So the crop has to be kept going with top dressings, hoping for rain to render them effective. Or it is given a heavy dressing of artificials, in the first place, in the hope that it will see the crop through—with a further loss of organic matter.

The above wastages takes place when the manure or green crop is ploughed under immediately before spring sowing. It seems more usual, however, to plough in these materials in autumn. The losses of humus and nitrogenous plant foods are much more severe—the period of maximum nitrification coincides with the autumn rains and much of the soluble nutrient is washed away. We are faced again with the necessity of a spring top dressing.

Supposing the crop of green manure is allowed to become mature and woody, and ploughed under. The proportion of nitrogen is much less than 1½ per cent, probably more like ½ per cent. All the available nitrogen in the soil is seized by the microbes to build up their bodies for the attack on the celluloses and their conversion to humus. The crop goes short. Another top dressing of fertilizers or basal application is ploughed in, to compensate. There is, as before, a gradual decay and consequent release of plant food from this woody material. Unfortunately, the crop may not get the benefit from it until late in the season, or perhaps not at all. The decomposition may be completed by the onset of autumn and the wet weather will soon get rid of the hoped-for benefit.

If, however, this woody material had been left on or near the surface, micro-organisms would not have been able to attack it in entirety, and absorb all the soil nitrogen, as it would not have been in a permanently moist condition. It would also have provided to surface living nitrogen-fixing organisms with food to fix some nitrogen for the crop. Thus by ploughing in organic matter, not only do

25

we not gain any nitrogen but we also lose some of what we had.

It can be said that the more nitrogen used the faster the organic matter is used up. The less organic matter, the poorer the soil aeration; the poorer the aeration, the deeper one must plough and cultivate. The deeper one ploughs, the more nitrogen must be used in an attempt to balance the activity of the denitrifying organisms.

SOIL CLASSIFICATION, NUTRIENTS AND ACIDITY

Soil maps are a basic tool for selecting a system of soil management. The maps show the kinds of soil in a field and farm—essential knowledge for selecting from the various available soil-management practices the combination of practices that is best suited to the soil and to the resources, skills, and desires of the farmer and rancher.

If they know the effect of a given practice on a field, whose kind of soil also is known, they can foresee the effect of that practice on other fields with the same kind of soil. Just as they can predict the behavior of a particular variety of hybrid corn, so they can predict the response to management of a particular soil.

Soils are classified and named, just as plants and animals are. Plants are identified by such characteristics as the structure of the flower and the form of the leaf. Soils are identified by such characteristics as the kinds and numbers of horizons, or layers, that have developed in them. The texture (the relative amounts of stones, gravel, sand, silt, and clay), the kinds of minerals present and their amounts, and the presence of salts and alkali help distinguish the horizons.

Most of the characteristics that identify soils can be determined in the field. A few can be determined only in the laboratory, but even without laboratory tests you often can get an accurate knowledge of them from standard works on soils and geology. For example, you can estimate the amount of sand in a soil from its feel when you rub it between your fingers, but for an accurate knowledge you would have to depend on laboratory analyses.

The "type" is the smallest unit in the natural classification of soils. One or a few types constitute a "soil series." These are the common classification units seen on soil maps and survey reports.

A soil series is a group of soils that have horizons that are essentially the same in the properties used to identify soils, with the exception of the texture of the surface soil and the kinds of layers that lie below what is considered the true soil.

The names of soil series are taken from the towns or localities near the place where the soils were first defined.

The soil type, subdivision of the soil series, is based on the texture of the surface soil. Stones, gravel, sand, silt, and clay have been defined as having the following diameters: Gravel, between 0.08 inch and 3 inches; sand, between 0.08 and 0.002 inch; silt, between 0.002 and 0.00008 inch; and clay, less than 0.00008 inch.

The full name of soil type includes the name of the soil series and the textural class of the surface soil equivalent to the plow layer—that is, the upper 6 to 7 inches. Thus, if the surface of an area of the Fayette series is a silt loam, the name of the soil type of "Fayette silt loam."

The "soil phase" is not a part of the natural classification. It can be a sub-division of the soil type, series, or one of the higher units in the classification.

Phases shown on soil maps commonly are subdivisions of soil types and are based on characteristics of the soil significant to its use for agriculture.

Phases shown on large-scale soil maps generally have reflected differences in slope, degree of erosion, and stoniness, but other bases for defining phases include drainage and flood protection, climate, and the presence of contrasting layers below the soil. (A comparable subdivision in the classification of animals

might be classes according to their age, such as old animals, old cows, or old Holstein cows.)

The legends that accompany soil maps generally include such names for the units on the map, as "Sharpsburg silty clay loam, eroded rolling phase," or "Fayette silt loam, 8-14 percent slopes, eroded." Those names identify the soil series, the soil type, and the phase. They represent names of the most specific kinds of soil, comparable to the name of a practical subdivision of a variety of a plant, such as old Jonathan apple trees.

The world "Fayette" in the second soil name we mentioned is the name of the soil series. This name, plus the words "silt loam," identify the soil type, and the phase is identified by the words, "8-14 percent slopes, eroded." In this name, the word "phase" is not used but is understood.

Higher units in the classification system include families, great soil groups, suborders, and orders. They are seldom used on any but small-scale soil maps.

Soil series, types, and phases do not occur at random in the landscape. They have an orderly pattern of occurrence that is related to the land form; the parent material from which the soil was formed; and the influence of the plants that grew on the soils, the animals that lived on them, and the way men have used them.

On a given farm, the different kinds of soil commonly have a repeating pattern, which is associated with the slope.

The relationships between the soils and landscapes vary in details in different parts of the country, but the relationships generally exist. Anyone who is familiar with the soils can visualize the landscape from a soil map; or, if he sees the landscape, he can predict where the boundaries are.

A soil survey includes finding out which properties of soils are important, organizing the knowledge about the relations of soil properties and soil use, classifying soils into defined and described units, locating and plotting the boundaries of the units on maps, and preparing and publishing the maps and reports.

The soil survey report consists of a map that shows the distribution of soils in the area, descriptions of the soils, some suggestions as to their use and management, and general information about the area.

Reports usually are prepared on the soils of one country, although a single report may cover several small countries or only parts of countries.

Soil surveys in America are made cooperatively by the Soil Conservation Service (SCS) of the Department of Agriculture, (USDA) the agricultural experiment stations, and other state and federal agencies. Plans for the work in any area are developed jointly, and the reports are reviewed jointly before publication.

Soil maps have many uses, but generally they are made for one main purpose—to identify the soil as a basis for applying the results of research and experience to individual fields or parts of fields. Results from an experiment on a given soil can be applied directly to other areas of the same kind of soil with confidence. Two areas of the same kind of soil are no more identical than two oak trees, but they are so similar that (with comparable past management) they should respond to the same practices in a similar manner.

But many thousands of kinds of soil exist in the United States. Research can be conducted on only a few of them. The application of the research results must usually be based on the relationships of the properties of the soil on which the experiment was conducted to the properties of the soils shown on the maps. This can be done best by the soil classification system.

The significant properties that can be known from the soil maps include physical properties, such as the amount of moisture that the soil will hold for plants, the rate at which air and water move through the soil, and the kinds and amounts of clays, all of which are important in drainage, irrigation, erosion con-

trol, maintenance of good tilth, and the choice of crops.

Some important chemical properties can be known from the soil maps. The ability of a soil to convert phosphate fertilizer to forms unavailable to plants is an example. Generally speaking, however, the ability of a soil to supply nutrients needed by plants cannot be known with precision from the soil map alone, for the supplies of the nutrients are changed when a farmer applies fertilizers.

Soil tests on individual fields are becoming more and more important. Considered in relation to the kind of soil, they form the most reliable background for recommending the application of fertilizers.

The soil map shows the distribution of specific kinds of soil and identifies them through the "map legend." The legend is a list of the symbols used to identify the kinds of soil on the map.

The most common soil units shown on maps are the phases of soil types, but other kinds of units may be shown.

The "soil bodies," areas occupied by the individual soil units, generally range from a few acres to a few hundred acres. Often within one soil body are small areas of other soils—series, types, or phases. If the included soils are similar in nature, they are generally not identified unless they represent more than 10 or 15 percent of the soil body in which they are included. If the properties of the included soils differ markedly from those of the rest of the soil body, they usually are indicated by special symbols.

But occasionally the individual parts of a unit are so small and so mixed with other units that they cannot be shown. Then the legend will indicate the area occupied by the intricate mixture as a "soil complex" if all of the included units are present in nearly every area.

A complex may consist of two or more phases of a soil type, but commonly it consists of two or more series. The names of complexes may carry a hyphen between the names of two soil types or phases, as "Barnes-Buse loams." If several series or types are included in the complex, the names of one or two of the most important series or types will be followed by the word "complex," for example, "Clarinda-Lagonda complex."

The other kinds of units are common on soil maps—"the undifferentiated group" and the "miscellaneous land type."

Two or more recognized kinds of soil that are not regularly associated in the landscape may be combined if their separation is costly and the differences between them are not significant for the objective of the soil survey. This kind of undifferentiated group is shown in the legend with the names of the individual units connected by a conjunction—for example, "downs or Fayette silt loams."

The miscellaneous land types are used for land that has little or no natural soil. The map units then are given descriptive names, such as "steep, stoney land," "gullied land," and "mixed alluvial land."

The relationships between the units that appear on the maps and legends and the use and management alternatives are explained in the text that accompanies the soil survey report.

HOW TO DETERMINE NUTRIENT NEEDS

You can tell whether soil needs fertilizers by the health and productiveness of the plants that grow on it.

Plants in poor health may be stunted or—when nutrients are critically low—show signs of sickness on leaves, stems, or fruits. In some plants, however, the need for more or different nutrients is less easily seen. Often they may not appear stunted or show deficiency symptoms, but they will respond to the addition of nutrients to the soil. This hidden hunger will become more common as farmers increase their yields.

Three steps are necessary to determine the nutrient needs of soil:

The problem must be diagnosed.

The degree of deficiency must be determined.

The amount of fertilizer needed for the desired yield must be found.

Plants and soil conditions must be examined in detail in the field. There is no way of getting around that. This diagnosis can then be checked by simple fertilizer tests in the field or greenhouse, by quick tests of plant tissues, and by analysis of soils and plants.

Often you can easily see that a crop is not making proper growth. Sometimes plants exhibit general or specific symptoms of poor nutrition. Two little sulfur and nitrogen, for example, produce a general chlorosis—a yellow or pale-green color over the entire plant. Some deficiencies, like that of iron, show up mostly in the younger tissues; the young leaf blades are white or pale yellow but the veins may be normal.

Although symptoms are a useful guide to the need for nutrients, one has to be careful in interpreting them, particularly when two or more deficiencies exist at the same time. Climate also may affect the expression of symptoms. Therefore the diagnosis should be confirmed by chemical tests of the plant tissues or by applying the nutrient to the soil or the foliage and seeing how the plant responds.

Of particular importance in diagnosis is the influence of the soil profile. Poor drainage may induce symptoms of deficiency. An example is so-called lime-induced chlorosis, or iron deficiency, which is common on susceptible crops or poorly drained sites in the West. Plants in fields where surface soil has been removed by erosion or in preparation for irrigation often are deficient in nitrogen, phosphorus, iron, potassium, or zinc, especially if the sub-soil contains lime. Overliming can induce some deficiencies on acid soils. Deficiencies of one or more elements frequently occur where sand or gravel underlies shallow soil.

It is important but not always easy to exclude other possible causes of poor growth or symptoms that look like mineral deficiencies. Some insects suck juices from plants and so reduce growth. The toxins of some insects deform plants and produce symptoms like those of mineral deficiency. Nematodes may retard development of roots.

Some plant diseases, particularly the virus diseases, produce leaf patterns that can be confused with symptoms of mineral deficiency. So do various organisms that produce dead areas in leaves. Root rot can reduce the ability of a plant to forage for nutrients.

Excess salts in the soil reduce the entry of water into plants and restrict their growth without producing specific symptoms of deficiency. This problem is common in western irrigated areas and may become so in the Eastern States. Accumulation of sodium on the clay of soils leads to an alkali condition that often is linked with poor growth or no growth of crops and the presence of deficiency symptoms of iron and sometimes zinc.

The damage done by drought may be mistaken for nitrogen deficiency in grains, corn, sorghum, and grasses.

Frost damage may also produce symptoms that may appear to be deficiencies of nutrients.

Applying fertilizers too close to the seed at planting or side-dressing fertilizers at too high rates or too close to the plants may produce injuries that reduce growth or kill plant tissues.

Improper cultivation may result in deficiency symptoms. Lightning may sear small areas in a field.

After you have made a field diagnosis, you can confirm it by pot experiments in a greenhouse or strip tests in the field. These tests are made by adding (singly or in various combinations) the fertilizer elements suspected of being deficient and observing the plant growth that results.

29

The next step is to determine the extent of the deficiency.

One way to do that is to make an experiment in the field itself. The deficiency is estimated by adding nutrients and determining what effect the additions have on the plants. The fertilizer containing the nutrient is added to the soil or sprayed on the plants at various rates of application—more than one nutrient may be deficient, and several rates of each nutrient may be added in combination with different rates of the others.

Several kinds of information may be had from these experiments. The simplest is the response curve of yield in relation to the amount of nutrient supplied. It gives information about the supplying power of the unfertilized soil in terms of bushels or tons of produce. If the increase in yield is great, the experiment shows that the soil has too little of the nutrient in question. The shape of the response curve also shows how much nutrient is needed to produce the desired yield level under the existing set of conditions.

pH, SOIL ACIDITY, AND PLANT GROWTH

When crop plants do not grow well, one of the first questions the soil scientist usually asks is, "What is the pH of the soil?" or, "Is the soil acid, neutral, or alkaline?"

The reason for these questions lies in the fact that the pH, or degree of acidity of the soil, often is a symptom of some disorder in the chemical condition of the soil as it relates to plant nutrition.

A measurement of soil acidity or alkalinity is like a doctor's measurement of a patient's temperature. It reveals that something may be wrong but it does not tell the exact nature of the trouble.

The acidity or alkalinity of every water solution or mixture of soil and water is determined by its content of hydrogen ions and hydroxyl ions. Water molecules break up, or in chemical language, ionize, into two parts—hydrogen ions and hydroxyl ions. When there are more hydrogen ions than hydroxyl ions, the solution is said to be acid. If there are more hydroxyl ions than hydrogen ions, the solution is alkaline (or basic). Solutions with equal numbers of hydrogen and hydroxyl ions are called neutral.

Only a very small percentage of the water molecules present are broken up into hydrogen and hydroxyl ions at any one time. If one attempts to express the concentration of these ions in conventional chemical ways, some cumbersome decimal fractions result. In order to avoid these cumbersome numbers, the Danish biochemist S.P.L. Sorenson devised a system called Ph for expressing the acidity or alkalinity of solutions.

The pH scale goes from 0 to 14. At pH 7, the midpoint of the scale, there are equal numbers of hydrogen and hydroxyl ions, and the solution is neutral.

pH values below 7 indicate an acid solution, where there are more hydrogen ions than hydroxyl ions, with the acidity (or hydrogen ion concentration) increasing as the pH values get smaller. (See Table 2, Part II, Horticulture)

pH values above 7 denote alkaline solutions, with the concentration of hydroxyl ions increasing as the pH values get larger.

The pH scale is based on logarithms of the concentration of the hydrogen and hydroxyl ions. This means that a solution of pH 5 has 10 times the hydrogen ion concentration of a solution of pH 6. A solution of pH 4 has 10 times more hydrogen ions than one of pH 5 and 10 times 10, or 100 times, the hydrogen ion concentration of a solution of pH 6.

IRRIGATION AND RURAL WATER SUPPLY

The following tables and illustrations are given to acquaint the reader with some basic facts and figures on irrigation and water sources for the farm. There is sufficient information provided for the reader to calculate some of the more usable data that might be needed in setting up an irrigation system or establishing a farm water supply.

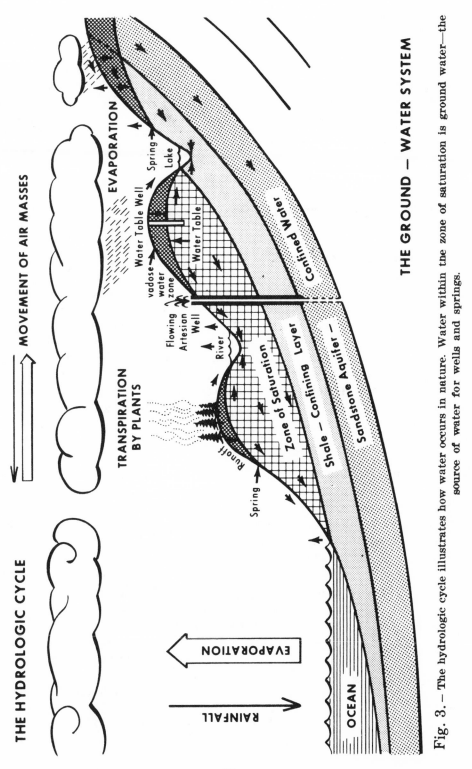

Fig. 3. — The hydrologic cycle illustrates how water occurs in nature. Water within the zone of saturation is ground water—the source of water for wells and springs.

WEIRS

A weir is a regularly shaped overpour notch in a vertical well bulkhead placed across the stream. It is the simplest form of water-measuring device for open channels and is easily constructed on the farm. Under standard conditions it will give reliable results. Discharge tables are given for triangular, rectangular, Cipolletti, and rectangular suppressed weirs.

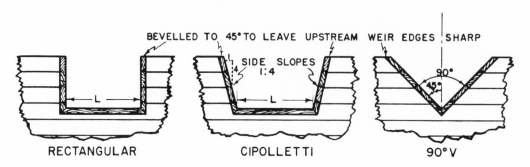

Figure 4. Downstream side of wooden contracted weir notches.

Standard Conditions for Weirs

The weir wall or bulkhead must be vertical (not leaning upstream or downstream), set at right angles to the direction of flow of the stream, and must extend far enough into the bank to be secure. The weir box, or weir pond, must be large enough to reduce the velocity of the water approaching the weir to less than ½ foot per second (practically still water), and to bring it to the weir in a straight even flow without eddies or swirls. Baffles may be put in the weir pond to reduce velocity and equalize the flow. The weir box or pond must be kept clean of silt accumulations or the velocity of approach will be increased due to the reduction in section, and more water will pass over the weir than the gauge indicates.

The height of the crest above the bottom of the ditch upstream from the weir should be at least twice the maximum head to be measured. The crest being above the ditch bottom is referred to as "bottom contraction." To meet standard conditions, then, the bottom contractions must be 2H or greater.

The side of the weir extending into the stream past the side of the ditch is referred to as "end contraction." Each end contraction must be equal to or greater than twice the head being measured.

The weir notch must be regular in shape and its edges must be rigid, straight, and sharp on the upstream face. The edges need not be knife edges but they must not be rounded nor more than 1/8 inch thick except for large discharges. When cut directly from a wooden bulkhead, the weir notch should be beveled on the downstream side to an angle of 45 degrees so that the water flowing over the weir will not touch the bulkhead or weir notch except at the upstream edge and will have an air pocket under the sheet of falling water. When the edges of the weir notch are made of metal strips nailed to the wall, the wooden notch is beveled or is cut enough larger to obtain the same effect as wooden weir notches are likely to crack and warp, metal strips are always desirable.

The weir crest must be level and accurate as to length (1/8 inch error in the length of a 12-inch weir will change the discharge approximately 1 percent.)

Weir Scales or Gauges

The weir scale consists of a strip of wood or metal graduated in inches and fractions, feet and decimals, or directly in units of flow or discharge per minute. A scale graduated directly in units of flow will fit all weirs of the same design and size when operated under standard conditions but will not fit another weir of a different design, or of a different crest length.

The scale or gauge may be set in the weir pond as stated under "standard conditions" or may be set in a stilling well or box at the side of the pond. The stilling well is connected to the weir pond by a small pipe set below the water level. The function of the stilling well is to present a water surface at the same elevation as the water surface of the weir pond completely without turbulence or surges. The connecting pipe must be small in comparison to the area of the well or it will transmit surges. The pipe must be kept freely open or the well will not give a reliable reading.

The practice of reading the head by holding a rule on the crest and allowing the velocity of the water to "pile up" on the rule is not recommended although, with a rule of the right proportion and operated by an expert, it gives very close results. If the rule is not of the proper width or leans from the vertical, the reading will not be correct. Gauges are not read directly on the crest of the weir for the reason that the surface of the water has a decided curve downward as it approaches the weir.

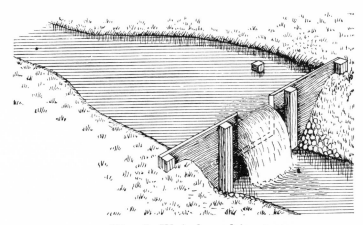

Fig. 5. Weir board in stream.

Equivalents

1 cubic foot = 7.48 gallons or approximately 7.5 gallons.

1 cubic foot of water weighs about 62.4 pounds.

1 cubic foot per second (c.f.s.) = 448.8 gallons per minute or approximately 450 gallons per minute = 50 miner's inches (Idaho).

1 cubic foot per second flowing 24 hours = 1.9835 acre-feet or approximately 2 acre-feet.

1 cubic foot per second flowing 12 hours = .9917 acre-feet or approximately 1 acre-foot.

1 cubic foot per second flowing 1 hour = .9917 acre-inches or approximately 1 acre-inch.

The table of equivalents may be used to determine the depth of water applied to a field when the time and flow are known.

Definition of Terms

Gallon: The gallon is 231 cubic inches.

Cubic foot: A volume equal to that of a cube 12 inches in length, 12 inches in breadth, and 12 inches in thickness. (1,728 cubic inches)

Acre foot: The volume necessary to cover 1 acre to a depth of 1 foot. (43,560 cubic feet).

Acre inch: The volume necessary to cover 1 acre to a depth of 1 inch. (3,630 cubic feet)

Gallon per minute: A continuous flow amounting to 1 gallon passing a point each minute.

Cubic foot per second: (c.f.s., or second foot) A continuous flow amounting to 1 cubic foot passing a point each second.

Head: The depth of the water above the weir crest measured at a distance from the weir notch so as to be unaffected by the curve of the water surface as the water flows over the weir.

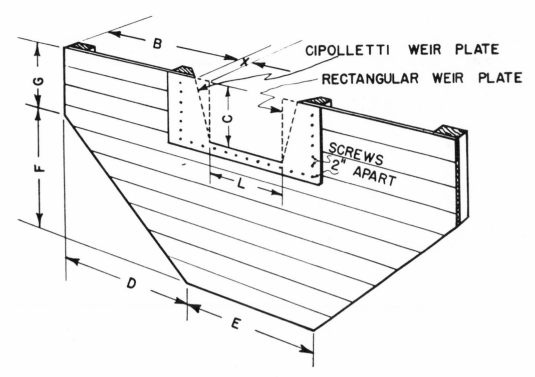

Fig. 6. Bulkhead for rectangular or Cipolletti weirs. . . suitable for medium and heavy soils.

Table 5 — Symbol dimensions and capacities for weir bulkhead shown in Figure 6.

Crest length L ft.	Recommended range of measurement in C.f.s.		Symbol dimensions						
	Rectangular	Cipolletti	B ft. in.	C ft. in.	D ft. in.	E ft. in.	F ft. in.	G ft. in.	X in.
1.0	.2 to .6	.2 to .6	1 10	8	1 6	2	1 6	10	2
1.5	.3 to 1.7	.3 to 1.8	2 7	1	2 3	2 8	2 3	1 1	3
2.0	.4 to 3.5	.4 to 3.7	3 2½	1 2	2 11	3 2	2 11	1 1	3½
3.0*	.6 to 9.5	.6 to 10.0	4 7½	1 6	4 2	4 8	4 2	1 4	4½
4.0*	.8 to 19.5	.9 to 20.7	6 2	2	5 6	6 4	5 6	1 10	6

*Requires heavier construction than shown in drawing.

35

Table 6 — Discharge table for rectangular weirs having complete contractions.

Head H Ft. or In.		Discharge, Q, in cubic feet per second — Crest length					Head H Ft. or In.		Discharge, Q, in cubic feet per second — Crest length				
Ft.	In.	1.0 ft.	1.5 ft.	2.0 ft	3.0 ft.	4.0 ft.	Ft.	In.	1.0 ft.	1.5 ft.	2.0 ft	3.0 ft.	4.0 ft.
0.10	1 3/16	0.105	0.158	0.212	0.319	0.427	0.81	9¾	2.25*	3.41*	4.59*	6.95	9.33
0.11	1 5/16	0.121	0.182	0.244	0.367	0.491	0.82	9 13/16	2.29*	3.47*	4.67*	7.08	9.50
0.12	1 7/16	0.137	0.207	0.277	0.418	0.559	0.83	9 15/16	2.33*	3.54*	4.75*	7.21	9.67
0.13	1 9/16	0.155	0.233	0.312	0.470	0.629	0.84	10 1/16	2.37*	3.60*	4.84*	7.33	9.84
0.14	1 11/16	0.172	0.260	0.348	0.524	0.701	0.85	10 3/16	2.41*	3.66*	4.92*	7.46	10.01
0.15	1 13/16	0.191	0.288	0.385	0.581	0.776	0.86	10 5/16	2.46*	3.72*	5.01*	7.59	10.19
0.16	1 15/16	0.210	0.316	0.423	0.638	0.854	0.87	10 7/16	2.50*	3.79*	5.10*	7.72	10.36
0.17	2 1/16	0.229	0.346	0.463	0.698	0.934	0.88	10 9/16	2.54*	3.85*	5.18*	7.85	10.54
0.18	2 3/16	0.249	0.376	0.504	0.760	1.02	0.89	10 11/16	2.58*	3.92*	5.27*	7.99	10.71
0.19	2¼	0.270	0.407	0.546	0.823	1.10	0.90	10 13/16	2.62*	3.98*	5.35*	8.12	10.89
0.20	2⅜	0.291	0.439	0.588	0.887	1.19	0.91	10 15/16	2.67*	4.05*	5.44*	8.25	11.07
0.21	2½	0.312	0.472	0.632	0.954	1.28	0.92	11 1/16	2.71*	4.11*	5.53*	8.38	11.25
0.22	2⅝	0.335	0.505	0.677	1.02	1.37	0.93	11 3/16	2.75*	4.18*	5.62*	8.52	11.43
0.23	2¾	0.358	0.539	0.723	1.09	1.46	0.94	11¼	2.79*	4.24*	5.71*	8.65	11.61
0.24	2⅞	0.380	0.574	0.769	1.16	1.55	0.95	11⅜	2.84*	4.31*	5.80*	8.79	11.79
0.25	3	0.404	0.609	0.817	1.23	1.65	0.96	11½	2.88*	4.37*	5.89*	8.93	11.98
0.26	3⅛	0.428	0.646	0.865	1.31	1.75	0.98	11⅝	2.93*	4.44*	5.98*	9.06	12.16
0.27	3¼	0.452	0.682	0.914	1.38	1.85	0.98	11¾	2.97*	4.51*	6.07*	9.20	12.34
0.28	3⅜	0.477	0.720	0.965	1.46	1.95	0.99	11⅞	3.01*	4.57*	6.15*	9.34	12.53
0.29	3½	0.502	0.758	1.02	1.53	2.05	1.00	12	3.06*	4.64*	6.25*	9.48	12.72
0.30	3⅝	0.527	0.796	1.07	1.61	2.16	1.01	12⅛		4.71*	6.34*	9.62*	12.91
0.31	3¾	0.553	0.836	1.12	1.69	2.26	1.02	12¼		4.78*	6.43*	9.76*	13.10
0.32	3 13/16	0.580	0.876	1.18	1.77	2.37	1.03	12⅜		4.85*	6.52*	9.90*	13.28
0.33	3 15/16	0.606	0.916	1.23	1.86	2.48	1.04	12½		4.92*	6.62*	10.04*	13.47
0.34	4 1/16	0.634*	0.957	1.28	1.94	2.60	1.05	12⅝		4.98*	6.71*	10.18*	13.66
0.35	4 3/16	0.661*	0.999	1.34	2.02	2.71	1.06	12¾		5.05*	6.80*	10.32*	13.85
0.36	4 5/16	0.688*	1.04	1.40	2.11	2.82	1.07	12 13/16		5.12*	6.90*	10.46*	14.04
0.37	4 7/16	0.717*	1.08	1.45	2.20	2.94	1.08	12 15/16		5.20*	6.99*	10.61*	14.24
0.38	4 9/16	0.745*	1.13	1.51	2.28	3.06	1.09	13 1/16		5.26*	7.09*	10.75*	14.43
0.39	4 11/16	0.774*	1.17	1.57	2.37	3.18	1.10	13 3/16		5.34*	7.19*	10.90*	14.64
0.40	4 13/16	0.804*	1.21	1.63	2.46	3.30	1.11	13 5/16		5.41*	7.28*	11.04*	14.83
0.41	4 15/16	0.833*	1.26	1.69	2.55	3.42	1.12	13 7/16		5.48*	7.38*	11.19*	15.03
0.42	5 1/16	0.863*	1.30	1.75	2.65	3.54	1.13	13 9/16		5.55*	7.47*	11.34*	15.22
0.43	5 3/16	0.893*	1.35	1.81	2.74	3.67	1.14	13 11/16		5.62*	7.57*	11.48*	15.42
0.44	5¼	0.924*	1.40	1.88	2.83	3.80	1.15	13 13/16		5.69*	7.66*	11.64*	15.62
0.45	5⅜	0.955*	1.44	1.94	2.93	3.93	1.16	13 15/16		5.77*	7.76*	11.79*	15.82
0.46	5½	0.986*	1.49	2.00	3.03	4.05	1.17	14 1/16		5.84*	7.86*	11.94*	16.02
0.47	5⅝	1.02*	1.54	2.07	3.12	4.18	1.18	14 3/16		5.91*	7.96*	12.09*	16.23
0.48	5¾	1.05*	1.59	2.13	3.22	4.32	1.19	14¼		5.98*	8.06*	12.24*	16.43
0.49	5⅞	1.08*	1.64	2.20	3.32	4.45	1.20	14⅜		6.06*	8.16*	12.39*	16.63
0.50	6	1.11*	1.68	2.26	3.42	4.58	1.21	14½		6.13*	8.26*	12.54*	16.83
0.51	6⅛	1.15*	1.73*	2.33	3.52	4.72	1.22	14⅝		6.20*	8.35*	12.69*	17.03
0.52	6¼	1.18*	1.78*	2.40	3.62	4.86	1.23	14¾		6.28*	8.46*	12.85*	17.25
0.53	6⅜	1.21°	1.84°	2.46	3.73	4.99	1.24	14⅞		6.35*	8.56*	12.99*	17.45
0.54	6½	1.25*	1.89*	2.53	3.83	5.13	1.25	15		6.43*	8.66*	13.14*	17.65
0.55	6⅝	1.28*	1.94*	2.60	3.94	5.27	1.26	15⅛				13.30*	17.87
0.56	6¾	1.31*	1.99*	2.67	4.04	5.42	1.27	15¼				13.45*	18.07
0.57	6 13/16	1.35*	2.04*	2.74	4.15	5.56	1.28	15⅜				13.61*	18.28
0.58	6 15/16	1.38*	2.09*	2.81	4.26	5.70	1.29	15½				13.77*	18.50
0.59	7 1/16	1.42*	2.15*	2.88	4.36	5.85	1.30	15⅝				13.93*	18.71
0.60	7 3/16	1.45*	2.20*	2.96	4.47	6.00	1.31	15¾				14.09*	18.92
0.61	7 5/16	1.49*	2.25*	3.03	4.59	6.14	1.32	15 13/16				14.24*	19.12
0.62	7 7/16	1.52*	2.31*	3.10	4.69	6.29	1.33	15 15/16				14.40*	19.34
0.63	7 9/16	1.56*	2.36*	3.17	4.81	6.44	1.34	16 1/16				14.56*	19.55*
0.64	7 11/16	1.60*	2.42*	3.25	4.92	6.59	1.35	16 3/16				14.72*	19.77*
0.65	7 13/16	1.63*	2.47*	3.32	5.03	6.75	1.36	16 5/16				14.88*	19.98*
0.66	7 15/16	1.67*	2.53*	3.40	5.15	6.90	1.37	16 7/16				15.04*	20.20*
0.67	8 1/16	1.71*	2.59*	3.47*	5.26	7.05	1.38	16 9/16				15.20*	20.42*
0.68	8 3/16	1.74*	2.64*	3.56*	5.38	7.21	1.39	16 11/16				15.36*	20.64*
0.69	8¼	1.78*	2.70*	3.63*	5.49	7.36	1.40	16 13/16				15.53*	20.86*
0.70	8⅜	1.82*	2.76*	3.71*	5.61	7.52	1.41	16 15/16				15.69*	21.08*
0.71	8½	1.86*	2.81*	3.78*	5.73	7.68	1.42	17⅛				15.85*	21.29*
0.72	8⅝	1.90*	2.87*	3.86*	5.85	7.84	1.43	17 3/16				16.02*	21.52*
0.73	8¾	1.93*	2.93*	3.94*	5.97	8.00	1.44	17¼				16.19*	21.74*
0.74	8⅞	1.97*	2.99*	4.02*	6.09	8.17	1.45	17⅜				16.34*	21.96*
0.75	9	2.01*	3.05*	4.10*	6.21	8.33	1.46	17½				16.51*	22.18*
0.76	9⅛	2.05*	3.11*	4.18*	6.33	8.49	1.47	17⅝				16.68*	22.41*
0.77	9¼	2.09*	3.17*	4.26*	6.45	8.66	1.48	17¾				16.85*	22.64*
0.78	9⅜	2.13*	3.23*	4.34*	6.58	8.82	1.49	17⅞				17.01*	22.85*
0.79	9½	2.17*	3.29*	4.42*	6.70	8.99	1.50	18				17.17*	23.08*
0.80	9⅝	2.21*	3.35*	4.51*	6.83	9.16							

USABLE IRRIGATION TABLES

Table 7—Number of gallons of water per minute required per acre for covering tract in specified periods.

| | Water to be applied in— | | | | Water applied to a depth of— | | | | | |
Hours	10-hour days	12-hour days	20-hour days	24-hour days	1 inch [1]	1½ inches [2]	2 inches [3]	3 inches [4]	4 inches [5]	6 inches [6]
Number	*Number*	*Number*	*Number*	*Number*	*Gallons*	*Gallons*	*Gallons*	*Gallons*	*Gallons*	*Gallons*
30	3				15.08	22.62	30.16	45.24	60.32	90.48
40	4				11.31	16.97	22.62	33.93	52.64	78.96
50	5				9.06	13.59	18.12	27.18	36.24	54.36
55	5½				8.23	12.35	16.46	24.69	32.92	49.38
60	6	5			7.54	11.31	15.08	22.62	30.16	45.24
66		5½			6.86	10.29	13.72	20.58	27.44	41.16
70	7		3½		6.47	9.71	12.94	19.41	25.88	38.82
80	8		4		5.66	8.49	11.32	16.98	22.64	33.96
90	9		4½		5.03	7.55	10.06	15.09	20.12	30.18
100	10		5		4.52	6.78	9.04	13.56	18.08	27.12
110			5½		4.11	6.17	8.22	12.33	16.44	24.66
120		10	6	5	3.77	5.66	7.54	11.31	15.08	22.62
140			7		3.23	4.85	6.46	9.69	12.92	19.38
160			8		2.83	4.25	5.66	8.49	11.32	16.98
180			9		2.51	3.77	5.02	7.53	10.04	15.06
200			10		2.06	3.09	4.12	6.18	8.24	12.36
240				10	1.89	2.84	3.78	5.67	7.56	11.34

[1] Suitable for sprinkling irrigation, eyelet or porous hose.
[2] Suitable for surface irrigation, heavy soil, little waste.
[3] Suitable for surface irrigation, average soil, short runs, careful handling, limited waste.
[4] Suitable for surface irrigation, average soil, average waste, some subirrigation.
[5] Suitable for surface irrigation, sandy soil, large waste, some subirrigation.
[6] Suitable for much subirrigation.

Table 7 has been prepared to indicate the quantity of water necessary to irrigate an acre of land in a specified length of time. It is applicable to any field and any type of irrigation. From this table the number of gallons of water required per minute of continuous flow to irrigate an acre of ground to different depths may be read directly. Multiplying this number of the number of acres in the tract to be watered will determine the needed capacity of the water supply, in gallons per minute. For instance, to irrigate 1 acre to a depth of 2 inches in 60 hours—either in six 10-hour days or in five 12-hour days—requires 15.08 gallons per minute; to irrigate 10 acres to the same depth in the same time required a rate of flow 10 times as great, or 150.8 gallons per minute.

Table 8—Carrying capacities of ditches

Size of ditch	Fall per 100 feet	Carrying capacity per minute
	Inches	*Gallons*
Top width 2 feet, bottom width 1 foot, depth 6 inches, cross-sectional area 0.7 square foot.	4	340
	6	410
	8	480
	12	590
	18	720
Top width 3 feet, bottom width 1½ feet, depth 9 inches, cross-sectional area 1.7 square feet.	2	760
	3	930
	4	1,070
	5	1,200
	6	1,320
Top width 3 feet 8 inches, bottom width 2 feet, depth 10 inches, cross-sectional area 2.3 square feet.	2	1,190
	3	1,460
	4	1,690

Size of ditch	Fall per 100 feet	Carrying capacity per minute
	Inches	*Gallons*
Top width 4½ feet, bottom width 2½ feet, depth 1 foot, cross sectional area 3.5 square feet.	1	1,460
	1½	1,790
	2	2,070
	3	2,550
Top width 5½ feet, bottom width 3 feet, depth 1 foot 3 inches, cross-sectional area 5.3 square feet.	1	2,620
	1½	3,220
	2	3,730
Top width 7 feet, bottom width 4 feet, depth 1½ feet, cross-sectional area 8.2 square feet.	¾	4,150
	1	4,800
	1½	5,900
	1¾	6,380
Top width 9 feet, bottom width 5 feet, depth 2 feet, cross-sectional area 14 square feet.	⅜	6,080
	½	7,070
	¾	8,700
	1	10,070

Table 9—Approximate horsepower required for irrigation

Horsepower required for an elevation of—

Quantity per minute (gallons)	10 feet Hp.	15 feet Hp.	20 feet Hp.	30 feet Hp.	40 feet Hp.	50 feet Hp.	60 feet Hp.	70 feet Hp.	80 feet Hp.	90 feet Hp.	100 feet Hp.	125 feet Hp.	150 feet Hp.	175 feet Hp.	200 feet Hp.	250 feet Hp.	300 feet Hp.
5	0.025	0.038	0.05	0.07	0.10	0.12	0.14	0.16	0.20	0.22	0.25	0.31	0.37	0.43	0.50	0.62	0.75
10	.050	.075	.10	.15	.20	.25	.30	.35	.40	.44	.50	.62	.75	.87	1.00	1.24	1.50
15	.075	.113	.15	.22	.30	.37	.45	.52	.60	.68	.75	.94	1.12	1.31	1.50	1.88	2.25
20	.100	.150	.20	.30	.40	.50	.60	.70	.80	.90	1.00	1.25	1.50	1.75	2.00	2.50	3.00
25	.125	.188	.25	.37	.50	.62	.75	.88	1.00	1.12	1.25	1.56	1.87	2.18	2.50	3.12	3.75
30	.150	.225	.30	.45	.60	.75	.90	1.04	1.20	1.35	1.50	1.87	2.25	2.62	3.00	3.74	4.50
35	.175	.263	.35	.52	.70	.87	1.05	1.22	1.40	1.58	1.75	2.19	2.62	3.15	3.50	4.38	5.25
40	.200	.300	.40	.60	.80	1.00	1.20	1.40	1.60	1.80	2.00	2.50	3.00	3.50	4.00	5.00	6.00
45	.225	.338	.45	.67	.90	1.12	1.35	1.56	1.80	2.02	2.25	2.81	3.37	3.94	4.50	5.62	6.75
50	.250	.376	.50	.75	1.00	1.25	1.50	1.74	2.00	2.24	2.50	3.12	3.75	4.37	5.00	6.24	7.50
60	.300	.450	.60	.90	1.20	1.50	1.80	2.10	2.40	2.70	3.00	3.75	4.50	5.25	6.00	7.50	9.00
70	.350	.525	.70	1.05	1.40	1.75	2.10	2.44	2.80	3.14	3.50	4.38	5.25	6.12	7.00	8.76	10.50
80	.400	.600	.80	1.20	1.60	2.00	2.40	2.80	3.20	3.60	4.00	5.00	6.00	7.00	8.00	10.00	12.00
90	.450	.675	.90	1.35	1.80	2.25	2.70	3.14	3.60	4.04	4.50	5.62	6.75	7.87	9.00	11.24	13.50
100	.500	.750	1.00	1.50	2.00	2.50	3.00	3.50	4.00	4.50	5.00	6.25	7.50	8.75	10.00	12.50	15.00
125	.625	.938	1.25	1.87	2.50	3.12	3.75	4.36	5.00	5.62	6.25	7.81	9.37	10.94	12.50	15.62	18.75
150	.750	1.125	1.50	2.25	3.00	3.75	4.50	5.24	6.00	6.75	7.50	9.37	11.25	13.12	15.00	18.74	22.50
175	.875	1.313	1.75	2.62	3.50	4.37	5.25	6.12	7.00	7.88	8.75	10.94	13.12	15.31	17.50	21.88	26.25
200	1.00	1.500	2.00	3.00	4.00	5.00	6.00	7.00	8.00	9.00	10.00	12.50	15.00	17.50	20.00	25.00	30.00
250	1.25	1.875	2.50	3.75	5.00	6.25	7.50	8.75	10.00	11.25	12.50	15.62	18.75	21.87	25.00	31.24	37.50
300	1.50	2.25	3.00	4.50	6.00	7.50	9.00	10.50	12.00	13.50	15.00	18.75	22.50	26.25	30.00	37.50	45.00
350	1.75	2.625	3.50	5.25	7.00	8.75	10.50	12.25	14.00	15.75	17.50	21.87	26.25	30.62	35.00	43.74	52.50
400	2.00	3.000	4.00	6.10	8.00	10.00	12.00	14.00	16.00	18.00	20.00	25.00	30.00	35.00	40.00	50.00	60.00
450	2.25	3.375	4.50	6.75	9.00	11.25	13.50	15.75	18.00	20.25	22.50	28.13	33.75	39.37	45.00	56.26	67.50
500	2.50	3.750	5.00	7.50	10.00	12.50	15.00	17.50	20.00	22.50	25.00	31.25	37.50	43.75	50.00	62.50	75.00
600	3.00	4.50	6.00	9.00	12.00	15.00	18.00	21.00	24.00	27.00	30.00	37.50	45.00	52.50	60.00	75.00	90.00
700	3.50	5.25	7.00	10.50	14.00	17.50	21.00	24.50	28.00	31.50	35.00	43.75	52.50	61.25	70.00	87.50	105.00
800	4.00	6.00	8.00	12.00	16.00	20.00	24.00	28.00	32.00	36.00	40.00	50.00	60.00	70.00	80.00	100.00	120.00
900	4.50	6.75	9.00	13.50	18.00	22.50	27.00	31.50	36.00	40.50	45.00	56.25	67.50	78.75	90.00	112.50	135.00
1,000	5.00	7.50	10.00	15.00	20.00	25.00	30.00	35.00	40.00	45.00	50.00	62.50	75.00	87.50	100.00	125.00	150.00
2,000	10.00	15.00	20.00														
3,000	15.00	22.50	30.00														

38

FRICTION LOSS AND PUMPING HEAD

Movement of water in a pipe produces friction, a form of resistance that increases with the length and roughness of the pipe and the rapidity with which the water moves. Wherever much water is to be delivered through a long pipe, the power or head necessary to overcome friction should be determined. This is called friction loss or friction head. Its effect is to increase the vertical height against which a pump operates. Bends, especially sharp turns, in a pipe line also increase the friction, but ordinarily the farmer may neglect this loss in discharge pipes. Excessive loss due to friction may be avoided by increasing the size of the pipe. Table 10 shows the friction head (number of feet to be added to the vertical height) for each 100 feet of iron pipe (not new) to overcome friction when discharging given quantities of water. The comparative discharging power of pipes of the several sizes also is shown.

Table 10—Friction head or loss and comparative discharging power of pipes.

Discharge in gallons per minute	Diameter of pipe in inches												
	¼	⅜	½	¾	1	1¼	1½	2	2½	3	4	5	6
	Friction loss in feet for each 100 feet length of pipe												
0.5	7.8												
1	28.0	6.4	2.1										
2	103.0	23.3	7.4	1.9									
3		49.0	15.8	4.1	1.26								
4			27.0	7.0	2.14	0.57	0.26						
5			41.0	10.5	3.25	.84	.40						
6				14.7	4.55	1.20	.56	0.20					
8				25.0	7.8	2.03	.95	.33	0.11				
10				38.0	11.7	3.05	1.43	.50	.17				
12					16.4	4.3	2.01	.70	.24				
14					22.0	5.7	2.68	.94	.32				
16					28.0	7.3	3.41	1.20	.41				
18						9.1	4.24	1.49	.50				
20						11.1	5.2	1.82	.61	0.25			
25						16.6	7.8	2.73	.92	.38	0.09		
30						23.5	11.0	3.84	1.29	.54	.13		
35							14.7	5.1	1.72	.71	.17		
40							18.8	6.6	2.20	.91	.22		
45							23.2	8.2	2.76	1.15	.28		
50								9.9	3.32	1.38	.34	0.11	
60								13.9	4.65	1.92	.47	.16	
70								18.4	6.2	2.57	.63	.21	
80								23.7	7.9	3.28	.81	.27	
90									9.8	4.08	1.00	.34	
100									12.0	4.96	1.22	.41	
120									16.8	7.0	1.71	.58	0.24
140									22.3	9.2	2.28	.76	.32
160										11.8	2.91	.98	.40
180										14.8	3.61	1.22	.50
200										17.8	4.4	1.48	.61
240										25.1	6.2	2.08	.86

WELLS

WELLS

Dug Wells

Dug wells may be constructed with either hand tools or powered tools. They are usually 3 to 4 feet in diameter but may be much larger. While usually less than 50 feet deep, they must sufficiently penetrate the water table. Dug wells may fail during dry periods.

Bored Wells

Bored wells are much like dug wells, but they may be deeper and are usually smaller in diameter.

They are constructed with either hand augers or powered augers.

Hand-bored wells are usually 8 inches or less in diameter; power-bored wells may be as large as 3 feet in diameter.

Driven Wells

A driven well consists of coupled pipe sections with a well point and screen on the end. The point is driven down into the ground until the screen is below the water table level. Water enters the well through the screen.

In areas with relatively coarse sand, driven wells can be an excellent and very cheap means of obtaining water. Local dealers can advise on installation in these areas.

Drilled Wells

Drilled wells are constructed with special well-drilling equipment. Some of the equipment can drill to great depths through rock formations.

Two types of drilling equipment or methods are used—percussion (cable tool) and rotary (conventional and reverse-rotary methods). Geology of the site; desired well diameter, quantity, and depth; and other factors determine which to use.

Drilled wells for household water supply are usually about 6 inches in diameter.

Jetted Wells

Jetting or hydraulic well drilling is most successful in sandy soils. It is difficult in clay and hardpan formations and may be impossible in rock formations.

Jetting techniques and equipment used may vary depending on the soil formation, but the basic principle is the same. The hole is made by the force of a high velocity stream of water. The water loosens the material.

Table 11—Practical depths, usual diameters, and suitable geologic formations for the different types of wells.

Type of well	Depth	Diameter	Geologic formation
Dug_____	0 to 50 feet_	3 to 20 feet_	*Suitable:* Clay, silt, sand, gravel, cemented gravel, boulders, soft sandstone, and soft, fractured limestone. *Unsuitable:* Dense igneous rock.
Bored_____	0 to 100___ feet.	2 to 30 inches.	*Suitable:* Clay, silt, sand, gravel, boulders less than well diameter, soft sandstone, and soft, fractured limestone. *Unsuitable:* Dense igneous rock.
Driven_____	0 to 50 feet_	1¼ to 2 inches.	*Suitable:* Clay, silt, sand, fine gravel, and sandstone in thin layers. *Unsuitable:* Cemented gravel, boulders, limestone, and dense igneous rock.
Drilled: Cable tool__	0 to 1,000 feet.	4 to 18 inches.	*Suitable:* Clay, silt, sand, gravel, cemented gravel, boulders (in firm bedding), sandstone, limestone, and dense igneous rock.
Rotary_____	0 to 1,000 feet.	4 to 24 inches.	*Suitable:* Clay, silt, sand, gravel, cemented gravel, boulders (difficult), sandstone, limestone, and dense igneous rock.
Jetted_____	0 to 100 feet.	4 to 12 inches.	*Suitable:* Clay, silt, sand, ¼-inch pea gravel. *Unsuitable:* Cemented gravel, boulders, sandstone, limestone and dense igneous rock.

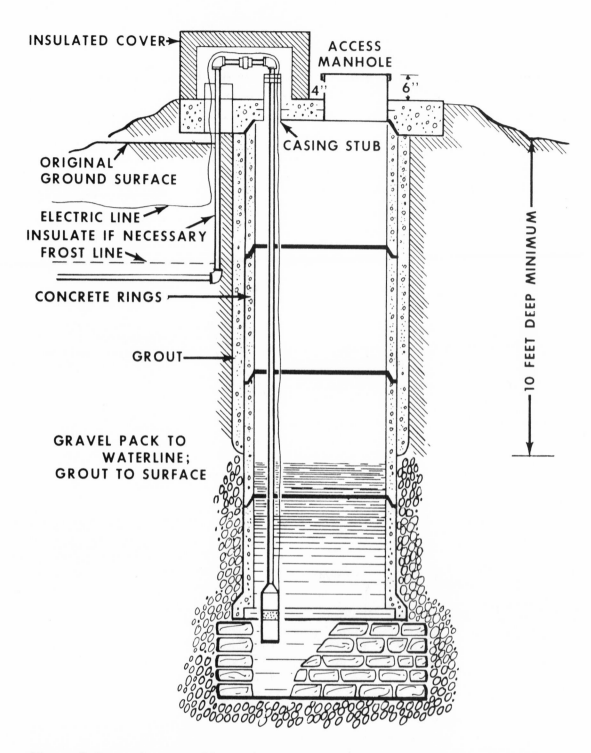

Figure 7: In good, permeable sand or gravel formations, dug wells can yield an ample supply of water. This well is lined with concrete rings. The protective layer of concrete extends down 10 feet to insure waterrightness of the upper walls.

SPRINGS

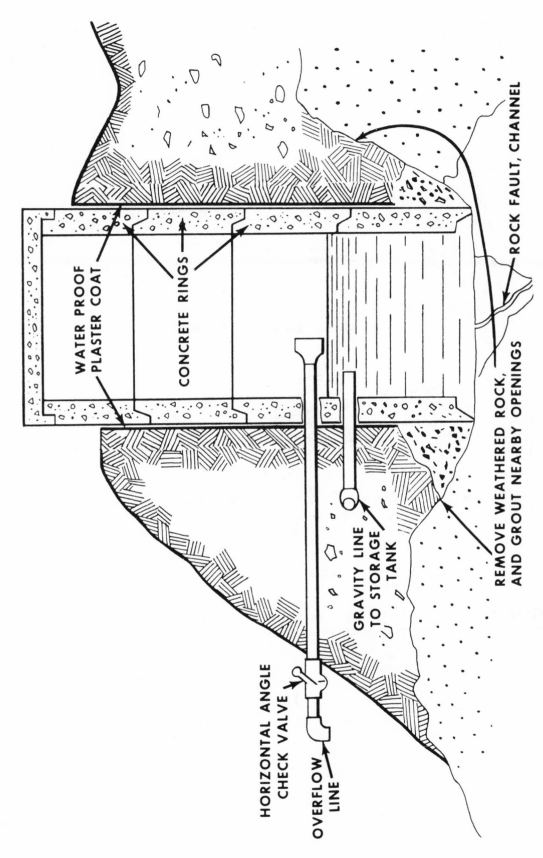

WATER PROOF
PLASTER COAT

CONCRETE RINGS

ROCK FAULT, CHANNEL

REMOVE WEATHERED ROCK,
AND GROUT NEARBY OPENINGS

GRAVITY LINE
TO STORAGE
TANK

HORIZONTAL ANGLE
CHECK VALVE

OVERFLOW
LINE

Figure 8. Development of spring in rock formation. Proper protection to avoid pollution of the water is essential.

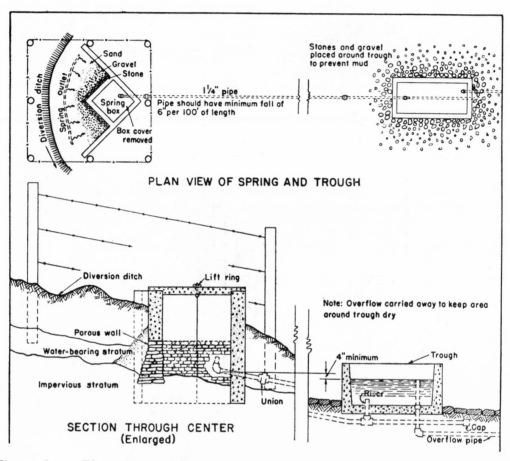

Figure 9. Plan view and cross section of an installation for a contact spring.
The spring box is provided with a removable cover.

44

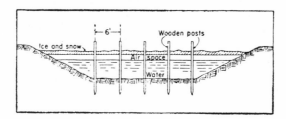

Figure 10. Cold-weather protection for a dugout.

To minimize the freezing hazard a unique method has been suggested by the agricultural engineering department of the Manitoba Agricultural College. This method is shown in figure 10. It consists of cutting holes in the ice after it has frozen to about an 8-inch thickness. The holes should be spaced about 6 feet apart. Posts are then driven through the holes and into the mud bottom far enough to find some support. The water will freeze around the posts, and as water is withdrawn they will act as columns to support the ice sheet, leaving an air space between the water surface and the ice. The air space acts as an insulator and thus reduces further freezing considerably.

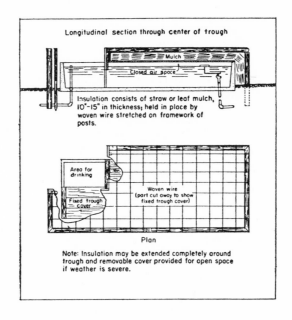

Fig. 11. A simple but effective way to insulate a watering trough against freezing.

HYDRAULIC RAMS, CISTERNS AND WINDMILLS

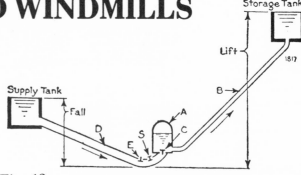

Fig. 12. General layout of a hydraulic ram installation. *D*, Drive or supply pipe; *E*, escape valve; *C*, check valve; *A*, air chamber; *B*, delivery or discharge pipe; *S*, sniff or air valve

HYDRAULIC RAMS

Hydraulic rams are not mechanical toys. They are the most economical pumps known and have been used to raise large quantities of water. Hydraulic rams utilize the principle of water hammer. Their operation will be understood from Figure 12 and the following description: Water flows from the source of supply through a straight iron pipe **D**, wasting through escape valve **E** until the velocity is sufficient to force the valve outward to its seat. This creates a "kick" or water hammer in pipe **D** and opens check valve **C**, through which some of the flow is forced into air chamber **A** and delivery pipe **B**. The greater pressure in pipe **B** quickly overcomes the movement and causes a reaction or backward pulsation closing valve **C** and unseating valve **E**, whereupon the water in pipe **D** flows again and the whole operation is repeated. On the recoil, a little air is sucked through the sniff valve **S** to maintain the supply in chamber **A**.

The approximate quantity of water raised by a good ram, properly installed, may be estimated from Table 12.

Table 12 — Quantity of water raised by a hydraulic ram

Lift (feet) divided by fall (feet)	2	3	4	5	6	7	8	9	10	11	12	13	14	15	18	20
Gallons raised in 24 hours for each gallon per minute to the ram	605	370	260	195	150	120	100	85	70	60	50	45	40	35	22	16

Table 13 — Capacity of round cisterns and tanks

Depth in feet	Diameter in feet								
	4	5	6	7	8	9	10	11	12
	Capacity in gallons								
4	376	588	846	1,152	1,504	1,904	2,350	2,844	3,384
5	470	735	1,058	1,439	1,880	2,380	2,938	3,555	4,230
6	564	881	1,269	1,727	2,256	2,855	3,525	4,265	5,076
7	658	1,028	1,481	2,015	2,632	3,331	4,113	4,976	5,922
8	752	1,175	1,692	2,303	3,008	3,807	4,700	5,687	6,768
9	846	1,322	1,904	2,591	3,384	4,283	5,288	6,398	7,614
10	940	1,469	2,115	2,879	3,760	4,759	5,875	7,109	8,460
11	1,034	1,616	2,327	3,167	4,123	5,235	6,463	7,820	9,306
12	1,128	1,763	2,537	3,455	4,512	5,711	7,050	8,531	10,152

46

Table 14— **Approximate capacity of windmills**

Lift	Velocity of wind per hour	Diameter of wheel							
		6 feet		8 feet		10 feet		12 feet	
		Diameter of cylinder	Capacity per hour	Diameter of cylinder	Capacity per hour	Diameter of cylinder	Capacity per hour	Diameter of cylinder	Capacity per hour
Feet	*Miles*	*Inches*	*Gallons*	*Inches*	*Gallons*	*Inches*	*Gallons*	*Inches*	*Gallons*
25	10	2½	140	3½	320	4¼	420	5½	1,010
35	10	2	120	3	270	4	360	5	675
50	10	1¾	110	2¾	180	3½	305	4	520
75	10	------	------	2½	135	3	235	3	365
100	10	------	------	2	105	2½	160	2¾	265
125	10	------	------	1¾	90	2	125	2½	200
25	15	3½	250	5	560	7	1,190	9	2,190
35	15	3	175	4	400	6	880	7	1,595
50	15	2½	125	3½	280	5	610	6	1,165
75	15	2	85	2¾	190	4	375	5	766
100	15	1⅞	60	2½	140	3½	305	4½	565
125	15	------	------	2¼	115	3¼	250	3¾	450

PART II HORTICULTURE

Local conditions will determine the feasibility of attempting to improve existing systems of fruit or vegetable production. Disease and insect problems make the introduction of new plants extremely difficult. Cross breeding and/or grafting may help to solve disease problems but these should be considered only at the advanced stages of development. Mechanical control or hand killing of insects may prove adequate where labor is plentiful and spraying impractical.

The Almanac makes no attempt to discuss varieties of vegetables, fruits or crops, because of extreme variations of species and growth factors in different locales. Study and observe the existing situation before making recommendations. Expand and improve the growing and uses of local fruits and vegetables as the most feasible means to improve horticulture. Methods of curing and storage often provide a means to a yearly supply of vegetables and some fruits. An underground potato cellar may provide storage, natural cooling and drying might suffice. (For drying, see Sun Drying of Fruits and Vegetables under Home Industries.)

1. **Fruits.** Principal fresh fruits of world commerce are the grapes, apple, orange, pear, plum and banana; principal nuts are the almond, Brazil nut, chestnut, coconut, filbert, pecan and walnut. Large quantities of fruits are dried, canned, frozen and otherwise processed. The grape, including grapes grown for wine, for drying and for table use, is the leading fruit of the world.

The apple is the most important tree fruit of the temperate zone. The orange is the most important commercial tree fruit of tropical and subtropical regions. The date is an important crop in the drier areas of the world. There are more species of fruit in the tropics than in any other region, but most of them are only of local importance because of their highly perishable nature. The four of greatest commercial value are the banana, pineapple, coconut and Brazil nut. Others include mango, avocado, papaya, guava, durian, rambutan and prickly pear. The mango is as important to the people of India as is the apple to the inhabitants of the temperate regions. The banana is the great starch food of the tropics.

In the growing of fruits, the first factor to consider is the kind of fruit to be grown. The variety selected should be well adapted to the particular section of the country in which the enterprise is to be located. Successful fruit growing requires careful attention to all production practices, particularly pest control.

Having selected the location and the kinds of fruits to be grown, the particular area of the farm on which the fruits are to be grown should receive consideration next. Soil is the most important factor in selection of the site. Fruits will grow on a fairly wide range of soil types but, in general, fruit plants grow and produce most satisfactorily in a soil that is at least moderately fertile, well drained, well

48

aerated (so that the roots may penetrate deeply) and adequately supplied with moisture. The presence of an abundance of organic matter in the soil is a great aid in retaining moisture. Fruits usually do best on slightly acid soils.

2. **Vegetables.** Because of their bulk and their perishable nature, fresh vegetables do not figure prominently in world commerce as do fruits and nuts. In domestic commerce, however, vegetables surpass fruits in value. The sweet potato is a universal food crop in the tropics and offers much promise for development.

The vegetable garden is primarily to provide food for the family, yet it may reach considerable economic importance in the aggregate. The size of the garden will be dictated by the size of the family, the interest in gardening, the labor available and the geographical location. Following is a suggested plan for a garden 30 to 60 ft. for temperate zone conditions and arranged in numbered rows according to season of planting : (1) asparagus; (2) lettuce and radishes; (3) spinach, followed by cucumbers and bush squash; (4) onion sets; (5) early turnips, mustard, cress; (6) early beets, followed by late cabbage; (7) onions; (8) parsley, carrots; (9) parsnips; (10) early peas, followed by string beans; (11) cabbage, cauliflower; (12) lettuce, followed by celery; radishes, followed by celery; (13) late peas; (14) string beans; (15) early sweet corn, followed by turnips; (16) late sweet corn; (17) dwarf lima beans, peppers; and (18) tomatoes and eggplant.

3. **Propagation of Plants.** Horticultural plants are propagated (i.e., increased in numbers) by two methods, namely by seeding (sexual propagation), and by vegetative means (asexual propagation) involving the use of a portion of the plant other than the seed. Propagation by seed is employed for plants which provide an abundance of seed and which can be bred readily to uniform and pure lines, as most annual flowers and many vegetables. Hybrid seed, such as that used for sweet corn, is produced by developing two pure lines and then combining them by cross-fertilization. Such seed may produce superior yields, but seed taken from plants raised from hybrid seed should not be used for reseeding.

Seed of herbaceous plants, such as tomato, onion and zinnia, will germinate as soon as it is mature. On the other hand, seed of many wood plants must lay dormant before it will germinate. Thus, peach seed requires 12 weeks at about 41° F. for the period of time required for the particular seed under treatment.

Plants are propagated vegetatively from portions of leaves, stems or roots. Although in propagation by seed each plant varies somewhat from every other plant in the lot, in vegetative propagation all daughter plants are identical in genetic make-up and are also identical to the parent plant from which they are secured. This is of great importance in horticulture, since it means that a single plant with desirable characteristics can be retained and perpetuated, identical in all respects to the original. None of the common tree fruits, such as the apple, pear, cherry, plum and peach will produce true from seed; distinctive horticultural varieties, such as the Northern Spy apple and the Washington Navel orange, are propagated by vegetative means.

A combination of both seeding and vegetative propagation is common with many woody plants, such as fruit trees and roses, in which an inexpensive seedling root is raised from seed and upon which the desired variety is then budded or grafted. The portion of a plant which serves for the root or underportion is called the rootstock or stock, and the portion of a plant which is placed upon the stock is called the scion. The resulting plant is thus composed of a seedling root and a known-varietal top and may be termed a stion (combination of stock and scion). In combining a stock and a scion, various techniques are employed, all of which are a form of grafting. A common form is called budding in which a single bud is grafted onto the stock during the active growing season, as contrasted with grafting with dormant scions in midwinter or early spring. Strains of plants which are propagated by vegetative means are called clones. (See next section for de-

tailed explanation of budding and grafting.)

Humidity, light, temperature, soil, rooting medium and the nature of the material itself play important parts in the method of propagation selected and the results secured. Continuous artificial mist has aided in the rooting of softwood cuttings; synthetic growth substances, such as indolebutyric acid, have increased the speed and degree of rooting; and synthetic plastic films, such as polyethylene, having proved of great value in air layerage and in propagation of cuttings.

4. **Pest Control.** Pests of horticultural plants are controlled by both natural and artificial means. The development of varieties which are resistant to certain pests has become one of the important functions of plant breeding. For example, resistance to mosaic virus has been bred into red raspberries, wilt resistance into tomatoes, powdery mildew resistance into canteloupe and nematode resistance into peach understocks. Artificial controls include crop rotation, purification and grading of seeds, soil cultivation, sanitation, soil fumigation, placing of mechanical guards as protection against rodents and spraying, dusting and dipping with various fumigants, fungicides and insecticides.

Common insecticides include arsenate of lead, pyrethrum, rotenone, malathion and oils. Common fungicides include various sulfur compounds, bordeaux mixture and copper and mercury compounds.

5. **Harvesting and Storing.** The time of harvest is dependent upon the nature of the crop itself, the use which is to be made of it and the facilities of storage. Beans are harvested in the green, immature stage when used as snap beans, but are left until full maturity when used as hard-shell beans. Among the indexes of maturity are changes in color, changes in the pressure required to puncture the flesh as measured by a mechanical pressure tester, and the predetermined time interval between full bloom and the usual harvest season.

Both common storage and artificial cold storage are used for horticultural products. Common storage depends upon natural outdoor temperatures and is provided by basement storage rooms in residences, by boxes or barrels sunk into the ground and by specially designed pits, caves and ventilated buildings. Cold storage is provided by refrigeration in specially constructed and insulated buildings. (See Home Industries and Self Help Engineering—Part VIII).

GRAFTING AND BUDDING FRUIT TREES

What you can graft

You can usually graft most varieties of one particular kind of fruit interchange-ably. But, because some varieties grow faster than others, placing a strong variety on a weak variety often results in considerable overgrowth. Delicious apple on Jonathan and sweet cherries on Montmorency sour cherry are examples (Fig. 1). Such combinations can stimulate earlier production, as with sweet cherries on Montmorency, but may cause structural weaknesses.

With apples, certain combinations appear to be better than others. Delicious grafted onto several varieties, such as Ben Davis, Arkansas Black, or Red Astrachan, grows almost as though no top-working had been done. But certain other combinations, growth is sub-normal and unsatisfactory. Delicious on Winesap is an example, and in some locations, Van cherry on Mahaleb.

In general, only those combinations known to be satisfactory are commonly used. For practical use, it is usually safe to combine varieties of about the same growth rates.

In some cases you can graft one kind of fruit onto a different kind as long as stone fruits are grafted onto stone fruits and apple onto apple. Occasionally, there is an advantage in grafting one stone fruit onto another. Plum on peach stock sprouts less than plum on plum. Standard pear varieties grafted onto quince stock produce trees that start bearing early.

FIG. 1—Graft in which scion (upper left) has overgrown stock. The scion is Delicious apple and the stock is Jonathan. It is usually better to combine varieties that grow at about the same rate. Generally only combinations known to be satisfactory are used.

FIG. 2—Top: Fine-toothed saw for sawing off stub to be grafted. Bottom (left to right): Leather strap glued to 1—inch board, budding knife with curved cutting edge, budding knife with straight cutting edge, grafting tool, and hand clippers.

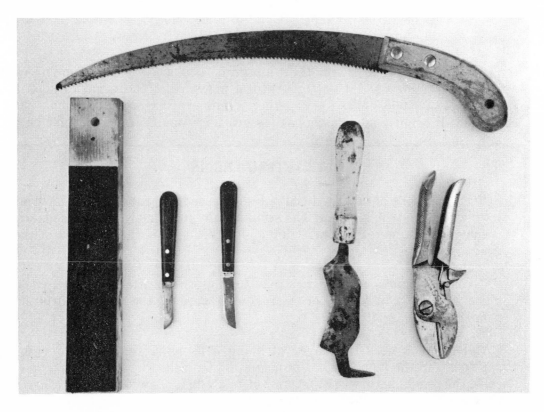

There are several reasons why grafting is advantageous to even the small fruit grower:

1. Fence rows and old fields often have wild fruit trees, sprouted probably from seeds dropped by men or animals. Apple seed, for example, doesn't reproduce the variety of apple it came from. Trees from seed usually bear fruit that is small or generally unsatisfactory. But the young wild tree can supply the trunk and branches on which to graft a variety to your liking.

2. An apple tree will take scions or branch grafts from any other apple tree. You can graft several different varieties from the same tree. Yellow plum, red plum, Italian prune plum, apricot, almond and peach are interchangeable on the same tree. In other words, any of these fruit varieties can be grafted onto the other's stock.

3. It takes two or three years for grafted scions to reach production, while saplings from the nursery can take as many as four to six years.

4. It is cheaper to graft than purchase trees from nurseries.

Tools and materials

A *sharp knife* has no substitute. Almost any pocket knife that takes and holds a sharp edge will do, but regular grafting and budding knives have worthwhile advantages.

The grafting tool is designed especially for making the cleft graft. It has a curved blade that is used to split the stub and a non-cutting wedge that is used to hold the two sides of the cleft apart as you insert the scion (Fig. 2). If you do not have a grafting tool, a heavy knife and some type of wedge will do. The wedge should be at least 2 inches long and fairly wide. If the wedge is too short, it will slip out of the cleft. If it is too narrow, it will bury itself in the wood without opening the cleft enough.

A *mallet or hammer* is needed to pound the grafting tool when splitting the stub.

Nails are required for veneer, bridge, and inarch grafts. You need long, thin nails, preferably 19 or 20 gauge, with flat heads. The nails should be long enough to go well into the sapwood of the stock. For bridge grafting you need nails about ¾ inch long. For inarch grafting, unless the bark is very thick, ½ inch nails are long enough and are easy to drive without bending.

Grafting tape is necessary for the whip graft. It is also good for binding cleft grafts in which there is not enough natural pressure of the wood to keep the cambiums of the stock and scion together. Some grafters use it to bind veneer grafts, too. If regular non-elastic canvas grafting tape is used, it must be slit

---

GRAFTING TERMS

SCION—A piece of detached twig or shoot used in propagating the plant from which the twig is taken. The scion usually contains two or three buds. It may contain more. For most kinds of grafting it is the top part of the graft.

STOCK—The portion of the graft to which the scion is attached. It may be a piece of root, a seedling, or a tree with part of the top removed in preparation for grafting.

CAMBIUM—A very thin layer of living cells lying between the outer sapwood and the inner bark. Because cambium cells divide and make new cells, the cambiums of two different but related plants will grow together if they are fixed and held firmly in contact.

before it starts to girdle the branch. There also is a non-canvas grafting tape which does not require slitting. Electrician's tape and masking tape can also be used without being slit. Masking tape is excellent for whip grafts that do not require a lot of pressure for binding.

Budding strips are important for holding the bud shield, and the stock bark covering it, firmly in place. Raffia was used at one time, but now rubber budding strips are most common. Rubber maintains continual pressure and doesn't girdle the stock. The most commonly-used size of budding strip is ¼ inch wide, 5 inches long, and 16/000 inch thick. There are 1,200 of these in 1 pound.

Grafting wax is necessary to protect cut surfaces from drying and from rot organisms. It must stick without peeling or sloughing off. Either hand or brush wax may be used. Some brush waxes can be applied cold. Others need to be heated to brushing consistency. They should be heated just enough to brush well — about like thick paint. Wax that runs freely like water or milk is too hot. It will burn the tissue of the graft. Commercial grafting compounds are available at your local garden store, feed store, or fruit supply store. Do not use unproved materials; they may injure the cambial tissue and cause considerable loss.

A *brush* is needed to apply the grafting wax. An inexpensive paintbrush, about 1½ inches wide, is satisfactory. Between jobs, the brush should be thoroughly cleaned and wrapped tightly in a piece of plastic. It can be cleaned by rubbing the bristles energetically in loose soil and then washing it out. One brush can easily last a season.

FIG. 3—Bundle of scion wood. One-year-old wood is preferable for most grafting. It should be free from disease or winter injury and well hardened.

When to Graft

The sooner you graft after conditions are ready, the better. Grafts set in March or April or even earlier usually become established before hot weather sets in. (Pertains to Northwest U.S.A.)

For some fruits certain periods are definitely better than others. For example, while you can cleft graft any time you can get dormant scion wood, the ideal time with apples is just as the buds start to swell. For peaches and cherries, earlier is better.

53

Collecting and storing scion wood

A graft can be no better than the scion wood, so the scion wood must be disease-free wood that will grow.

For most grafting, one-year-old wood is preferable to older wood although there are cases in which older wood has been used satisfactorily. The wood should be of average vigor and well hardened. Wood grown in sunlight is better than wood grown in shade.

It is usually best to use wood about lead pencil size, or ¼ inch in diameter (Fig. 3). Wood of this size is usually firm enough to be cut into a well-shaped, solid wedge. Smaller wood is hard to handle and the pressure of the cleft graft stock may crush it. For long bridge grafts it may be necessary to use wood ½ inch or more in diameter.

Wood that has been injured by low winter temperatures, particularly in early fall, is not satisfactory. Injured wood turns brown in the cambial area soon after the freeze. Discoloration at the base of the bud is common. Slightly discolored buds seem to grow all right, but if the inner bark is seriously discolored, scion wood probably will not grow.

Most scion wood is collected while the wood is dormant, in the late fall immediately after leaves drop. This safeguards against winter damage. Some good bridge grafting has been done with wood collected after growth had started. These grafts were put on right after being collected.

As you collect scion wood, tie it in convenient bundles. Store the bundles in a cold, moist place. About 34° F. is a good temperature. Protection from mice may be necessary.

A convenient way to store scion wood is to bury the bundles in soil or sawdust on the north side of a building. Bury them deep enough so they will stay cold even in late spring. If you have just a few sticks, you can put them in a plastic bag and store them in the refrigerator. Scion wood can also be stored in a warehouse if it is kept moist and cool. If properly stored, scion wood can be kept well into the following growing season.

The Cleft Graft

The cleft graft is commonly used to top-work a tree, changing it from one variety to another. To cleft graft, choose small branches—1 to 2 inches in diameter. Large branches do not heal as fast as small ones. Using small branches shocks the tree less and reduces the danger of rot.

Branches that are fully exposed to sunlight and in the stream of sap flow are better than those in shaded or inactive areas of the tree. Grafts on upright branches grow better than those on horizontal branches.

Any number of cleft grafts may be made on a tree as long as the grafts do not crowd each other out. The more there are on a tree the sooner it comes into bearing.

Preparing the stock

Branches have to be sawed off to provide a stock for the scion. Before sawing, select a smooth, knot-free, straight-grained section of the branch.

To avoid tearing the bark where you want to put the graft, first saw the branch off several inches above the straight-grained section. Then, saw the branch off again in the upper part of the smooth section at right angles to the grain. Avoid tearing or splitting the bark.

54

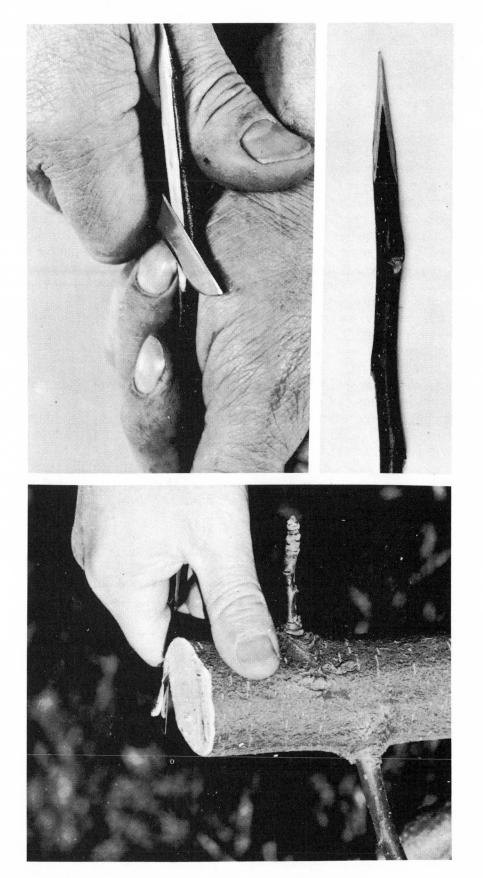

FIG. 4—If the saw cut is not smooth, use a knife to trim off the rough edge on the stub to be grafted. Trimming helps make sure the bark is tight and helps insure a good seal in waxing so the graft will heal rapidly.

Fig. 5—Cleft graft scion with one side of wedge cut, showing position of knife to make cut. Make cut toward you, with single, straight stroke, leaving smooth, level surface.

FIG. 6—Scion after both sides of wedge have been cut. One edge is thicker than the other. Wedge is usually cut so bottom bud is on the thick side.

If you do not make a smooth cut all the way across, trim off the rough edge with a knife (Fig. 4). This trimming helps make sure the bark is tight where you put the graft. It also helps exclude air as you cover the graft with wax.

Using the grafting tool, split the stock so a crack extends through the center of the branch. You will usually not have to drive the grafting tool more than 2 inches into the branch. Driving the tool too far splits the branch more than needed. If there are slivers in the crack, cut them with a knife. Otherwise, slivers interfere with inserting the scion.

Preparing the scion

The cleft graft scion should be healthy, one-year-old wood that is about ¼ inch in diameter. Smaller wood is hard to handle and to cut into a well-shaped, solid wedge. Also, the pressure of the stock may crush it.

To prepare the scion for grafting, cut a wedge on the butt end of the scion stick. Start about 2 inches from the end and make a long, smooth cut toward you that has a surface about 1 to 1½ inches long (Fig. 5). Cut with a single straight stroke that leaves a smooth level surface such as you would make with a carpenter's plane. Just whittling will help you develop skill for making well-fitting wedges.

Some grafters like to start cutting the wedge just below a bud. This leaves the bottom bud of the scion near the top of the wedge.

Turn the scion over and make a similar cut on the opposite side. These two cuts make a two-sided wedge (Fig. 6). When making the second cut, hold the knife so that you make one side of the wedge slightly thicker than the other. Be sure the wedge is about 1½ inches long.

The wedge is usually cut so that the bottom bud is on the thick side. This bud sometimes grows when others fail.

The wedge does not need to come to a sharp point. A blunt point is preferable, particularly when grafting large branches. The cut surfaces of a blunt-pointed wedge more nearly parallel the split surfaces in the stock.

After cutting the wedge, shorten the scion to the desired length, usually three buds. You may get fewer takes if you leave more than three buds. If wood is scarce or expensive, you can leave just one or two buds.

Inserting the scion

The cambiums of the scion and stock must be in contact for the graft to grow. To insure contact, slant the scion slightly. Although maximum contact is obtained when you set the scion straight, there is also a chance that the cambiums will not touch at all if you do not slant it. It is better to be sure of getting some contact by slanting the scion than to try to get more and miss completely.

Where the cambiums touch is important. They must touch where the stock is tight against the scion (Fig. 7). It is better for this contact point to be about ¼ inch below the shoulder of the stock.

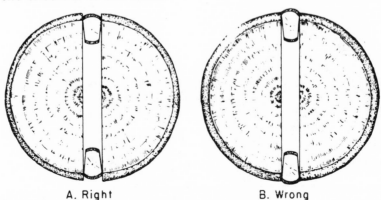

A. Right   B. Wrong

Fig. 7. Cambiums must touch where stock is tight against scion. Point of contact should be ¼ inch below shoulder.   56

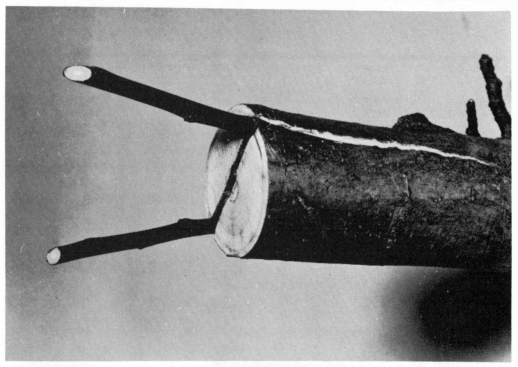

Fig. 10

Fig. 9

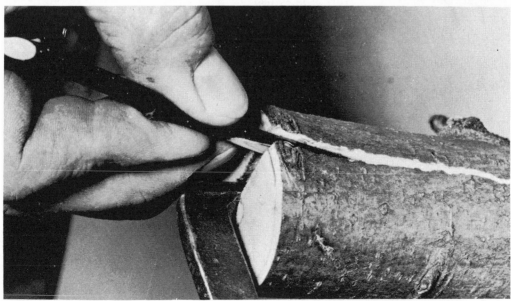

Fig. 8

57

With the non-cutting edge of the grafting tool, open the crack in the stock wide enough to insert the scion without much force. Insert the scion so the thick side of the wedge is toward the outside and its cambium is in contact with the cambium of the stock. (Fig. 8). Then the pressure of the stock against the scion will be greatest at the point where the cambiums touch. Be sure to push the scion wedge down into the crack far enough to hide nearly all its cut surface.

Two scions are usually inserted in each cleft (Fig. 9). This gives you two chances of getting the graft to grow. Two growing scions cover the stock faster than one. When using only one, insert it on the top side of the stub.

Waxing the graft

Wax the graft so that all cut surfaces are well covered. Pay special attention to the cracks on the top and sides of the stock. Coat the side of the stock to about ½ inch below the shoulder to be sure the top surface is well covered (Fig. 10).

As you finish, coat the cut end of the scion and recheck to see that all cut surfaces are covered. Cracks sometimes develop as the wax sets. It is well to check a few days later and then several weeks later to be sure all cut surfaces are kept covered.

Care of the graft

Making the graft properly doesn't finish the job. You must give it attention as it grows.

The graft usually produces one to several branches each growing season. Allow all branches to grow without pruning during the first season. You can, however, pinch back very vigorous shoots that would otherwise grow several feet without producing lateral branches. When these shoots reach the point where you want a lateral branch, pinch out the end. This pinching will give some protection from wind. Grafts that are growing more slowly and do not appear likely to grow more than 2 or 3 feet during the first season do not need to be pinched.

For most cleft grafts, light pruning is definitely preferable to heavy pruning. Heavy pruning stimulates the graft. As a rule, cleft grafts are vigorous and need to be slowed down rather than stimulated. Light pruning can shape them and at the same time permit them to bear early. Light pruning also helps to speed the growth of new tissue over the wound and reduce the danger of infection.

After the first growing season you will need to do some training and branch selection (Fig. 11). Do it in late winter or early spring. Even if both grafts on a stub grow, and they usually do, one is usually better than the other. If one is on the top side of the stub and the other on the bottom, generally the top one is preferable. It is less apt to pull out. Remove weak crotches from it and do any other structural pruning that may be necessary. If the branch is long and whippy, head it.

Shorten the other graft enough so that it will permit free branching of the selected one, but do not take it off. Keeping both grafts helps to cover the wound faster. Follow this same practice when there are several scions on any particular stub.

When pruning top-worked trees, leave stock branches of the variety you are replacing as long as they do not interfere with the grafts. When grafting only small wood, you can remove nearly all the stock branches during the first dormant pruning after grafting (Fig. 12). When grafting larger wood, removing all of the stock wood during the first or second year usually shocks the tree unnecessarily, complicates training and delays bearing. You should take two or three years to get rid of larger wood.

It is a good idea to check the wax as you prune, even during the second year, to be sure that the wound is completely covered. It may be necessary to recover some areas, particularly in the cracks.

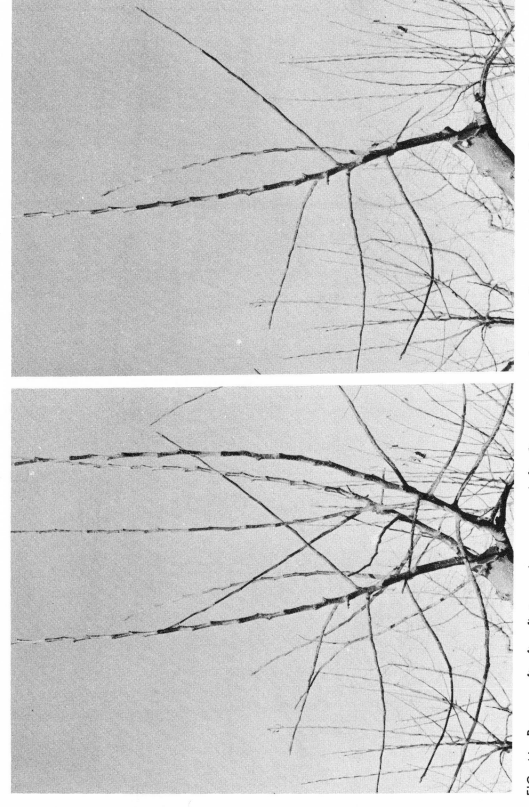

FIG. 11—Prune graft after first growing season. Left: One-year-old graft without any summer pinching or dormant pruning. Both scions have grown vigorously. Right: The same graft after pruning. Lower graft was pruned to keep from crowding upper one. Remaining main stem of upper graft was not headed; if there had been no side branches, it would have been headed at 18-24 inches.

FIG. 12—Nearly all the stock branches can be removed during the first dormant pruning if you are grafting only small wood.   Left: A top-worked apple tree before pruning.   Right: The same branch after pruning.

60

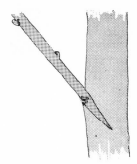

The Side Graft

The side graft is simple and easy to do. It is considerably faster than the cleft graft. More side grafts are usually put on a tree than cleft grafts because side grafts are put on smaller branches.

When choosing the stock branch, select one that is from ½ to 1 inch in diameter. The scion should be about ¼ inch in diameter.

Shape the butt end of the scion into a two-sided wedge like that used for the cleft graft, but make the wedge shorter.

Making the graft

Select a smooth area near the base of the stock. Using a strong sharp knife, make a slanting cut about halfway through the branch.

To insert the scion, spring open the crack by bending the branch away from the crack. Insert the scion with the thick side of the wedge out (Fig. 13). Only the top surface of the wedge should be exposed above the crack. Then let the branch spring back to its natural position. The spring holds the scion in place, so no tacking or binding is necessary.

Care of the graft

Stub the stock branch at 5 or 6 inches beyond the graft. As soon as the graft is made, remove any lateral branches on the stub that will crowd the graft. Over a period of two or three years remove any lateral branches that may be on the stub. Wax the graft carefully so that all cut surfaces of both scion and stock are covered. Cover the tip of the scion and the wounds made by removing lateral branches from the stub.

Fig. 13. Insert scion of side graft with thick side of wedge toward outside of cut. Stock should be stubbed off 5 or 6 inches above graft and all cut surfaces should be covered with wax.

61

The Whip, Tongue, or Bench Graft

The whip graft is easy to do and heals over rapidly. It is generally used on small trees, particularly in propagating nursery stock. It is also used for top-working trees and is especially useful on young trees.

The bench graft is a variation of the whip graft in which a piece of root is used for the stock. To make this graft, remove a piece of root from a healthy tree and whip graft the variety you are propagating onto it. You can then plant the graft with the graft union at the soil line or a little lower.

For all whip grafts the stock should be smooth and straight grained. It is important to avoid side branches in the area where the graft is to be made. In the

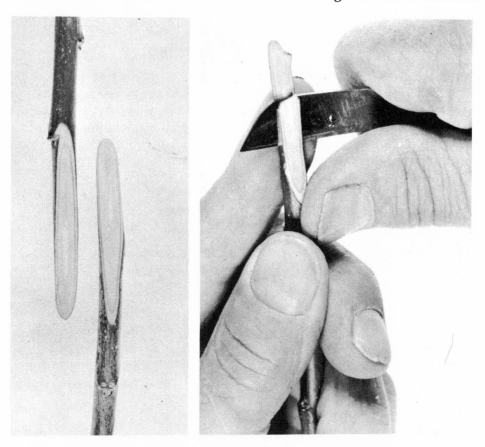

Fig. 14 Scion and stock of whip graft cut into one-sided wedges and ready for next cut. Note that scion and stock are of same diameter. Cut surfaces are about 1½ inches long.

Fig. 15. To make final cut, hold the one-sided wedge up with cut surface facing toward you. Start about one-third of distance down from tip of cut surface and cut straight down for about ½ inch. Cut should extend to ½ inch from lower end of cut surface.

case of root grafts you may have to trim off side roots.

When selecting the scion, choose one-year-old wood, preferably the same size as the stock. When the stock is larger than the scion, you can get contact on only one side.

Preparing the stock and scion

How you cut the stock is important. Starting about 2 inches from the butt of the whip, make a smooth, straight cut about 1½ inches long (Fig. 14). With practice and a sharp knife you can make this cut with one good sweeping movement. It should not be necessary to do any extra whittling to make it straight and even.

You are now ready to make the final cut. Hold the one-sided wedge up with the cut surface facing you and support the wedge with your pointing finger. Starting about one-third of the way down from the tip of the cut you have already made, make a downward cut about ½ inch long (Fig. 15.) Make the cut approximately parallel with the grain of the wood. Prepare the scion in the same way and leave it two or three buds long.

With scion and stock cut, fit them together (Fig. 16). Push them together far enough so the cut surfaces match. The toe of the scion then just comes to the heel of the stock. If the scion and stock are not the same size, be sure to match the cambiums on one side only.

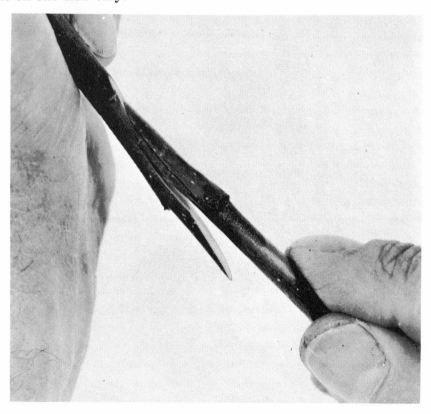

Fig. 16. Fitting scion and stock of whip graft together. Push them far enough together so cut surfaces match.

Wrapping the graft

Whip grafts must be wrapped to maintain contact (Fig. 17). When wrapping see that the scion does not move out of position. The tips of both wedges should be bound tightly against matching cut surfaces.

When using non-elastic binding material that may girdle the graft, or material that will not disintegrate as the graft grows, you can either slit the material as

you complete the wrapping or do it several weeks later.

Although it is not considered necessary to wax whip grafts, doing so often increases the percentage of takes. This is especially true of grafts that are not covered with soil. Waxing may not be needed when you use highly elastic material, such as electrician's tape, because you can make a fairly tight wrap. But with masking tape, waxing is certainly an improvement.

Care of the graft

Because the whip graft heals rapidly and grows straight, it needs only a minimum amount of care. When whip grafting seedlings, be sure that sprouts from the stock do not develop and interfere with the graft.

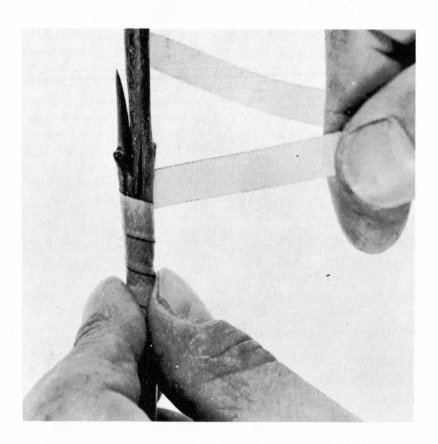

Fig. 17. Wrapping Whip Graft. Tips of both wedges should be bound tightly against matching cut surfaces.

Budding

Budding is the most common method of propagating new trees. On seedlings it is easier than whip grafting. It is also often used on young trees that are from one to three years old.

The time of year when you will be propagating can determine whether you whip graft or bud. Whip grafting is done from January to March using dormant wood, while most budding is done during July and August.

Some people prefer the whip graft because the resulting branch grows straight out from the stock. A branch grown from a bud usually has a slight crook in it. This is simply a matter of personal preference. Both make good unions and reasonably straight trees.

When to bud

Budding can be done almost any time if buds are fully developed and the bark of the stock slips. But most budding is done in July or August. Buds set at this time ordinarily remain dormant until the following spring.

Growth in the fall is undesirable because new shoots are susceptible to winter injury. Because some fruits start growing immediately if budded early, it is better to bud these late. Apple varieties in Malling IX rootstock are good examples.

Bud peach or apricot trees first. Cherry trees are budded last because the "take" of cherry buds set during hot weather is usually poor. Budding is usually done in this sequence—peaches, apricots, prunes, pears, apples, cherries.

Preparing the stock

Nursery stock which is to be budded must first be prepared. In early summer, strip off the lateral shoots on the lower 6 inches of the trunk. When you get ready to bud, you will then have a smooth surface on which to work.

You need to develop some good, new growth on which to bud. You can force it by heavy pruning or dehorning, but young trees will usually produce plenty of good wood without heavy pruning.

On nursery trees you usually place the bud 2 or 3 inches above the ground. Apple trees budded onto certain dwarfing stocks are exceptions. They are budded 6 to 18 inches above the ground.

The budstick

The budstick is a twig usually of the current season's growth, taken from the plant you want to propagate. It should be from a healthy tree. Mature wood of average vigor, with plump, well-developed buds is preferable to weak or succulent wood. Buds from the top or base of the stick are not as good as those from near the middle. As soon as budsticks are removed from the tree, the leaves should be clipped off. (Fig. 18). This reduces transpiration and keeps the buds fresh.

Although it is best to use budsticks as you take them from the tree, you can hold them for several weeks. Keep them cool and moist while they are being stored (Fig. 19).

Removing buds from the budstick

Each budder has his own technique for cutting buds off the budstick. Most commercial fruit tree budders remove both the wood and the bud from the budstick in one smooth stroke.

When following this practice, you should be sure your knife is sharp. Start ½ to ¾ inch below the base of the bud. Make a smooth slicing cut upward that extends ½ to ¾ inch above the bud (Fig. 20). As you complete the cut, use the thumb to pinch the bud shield against the knife blade. You will then have the detached bud in position for inserting it into the stock. There will be no chance of its becoming dry or dirty before it is inserted.

The cut surface of the bud shield should always be straight from one end to the other. With a straight cut you will get good contact all the way between the bud

65

Fig. 18. Clip leaves from budstick to reduce transpiration and keep buds fresh. Leave short stubs of leaf petioles.

Fig. 19. Apple budsticks after leaves have been clipped off. Buds should be plump and well developed.

Fig. 20. —To remove bud, start cut about ¾ inch below bud. Make smooth, slicing upward cut to ½ to ¾ inch above bud. Then pinch bud shield against knife with thumb.

Fig. 21.—Surface of left bud is straight. It will have good contact with stock for its entire length. Right bud has bulge which makes good contact unlikely.

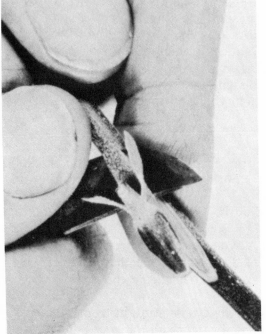 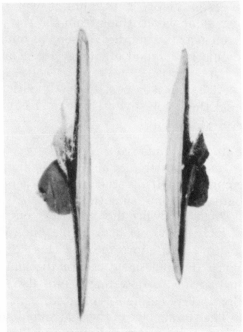

and the stock. If there is a big bulge in the middle of the shield, good contact is unlikely (Fig. 21). Avoid "rocking chair buds."

Or, if you prefer to remove the wood from the bud, start ½ to ¾ inch below the base of the bud and cut into the wood about twice the thickness of the bark. Hold this depth until you reach the end of the cut, ¾ inch above the bud. Then remove the knife and make a crosscut about ¾ inch above the bud. Cut only through the bark, not into the wood. As you complete the crosscut, grip the top of the bud shield between your forefinger and the knife blade (Fig. 22). As you remove the bud from the stick, you will have it in position for inserting. To remove the bud, peel it free so that the sliver of wood is left attached to the stock.

Fig. 22. —To remove wood from bud shield, cut upward to ¾ inch above bud. Remove knife and make crosscut in bark. Peel bud free, leaving sliver of wood attached to stock.

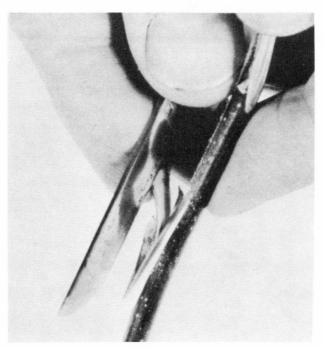

Inserting the bud

To make the opening where you insert the bud, select a smooth, branch-free place on the stock. In this smooth area make a vertical cut parallel with the grain of the wood. Start it about ¾ inch below the place where you want to set the bud. Draw the knife upward for about 1½ inches. If the stock is in good condition for budding this cut is free and easy. But when the bark is tight, more pressure is needed. Extend the cut only through the bark.

Next, make a crosscut which forms a T with the vertical cut. By holding the knife blade at a slightly acute angle with the trunk, you can open the bark as the cutting edge passes the vertical cut (Fig. 23). This opening will make it easy to start the bud. When making the crosscut, just cut through the bark and not into the wood. If you chafe the wood the bud will not slide down freely.

To insert the bud, place the tip of the bud shield in the opening at the top of the T cut. If the opening is property made, you should have no difficulty in starting the bud. Slide the bud down so the top of the shield is even with or below the crosscut (Fig. 24.)

It is important that the bark slips easily. If the bark is in good condition, the bud will go in readily. If the bark is too tight, you can't force the bud in.

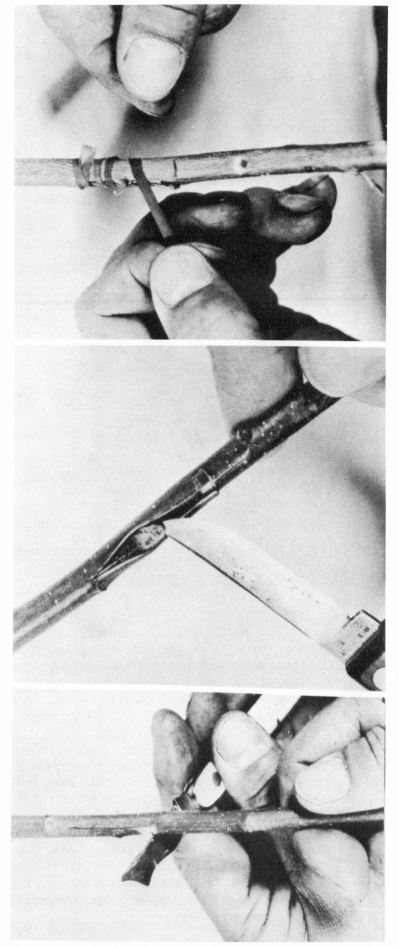

Fig. 23.—Make vertical cut on stock, then make a crosscut to form a T. Cut just through bark, not into wood.

Fig. 24.—Slide bud shield into place on stock. Top of shield should be even with crosscut or below it.

Fig. 25.—Start wrap with self-binding loop. Make three or four wraps below bud and several above it.

Wrapping the bud

When the bud is in place, you are ready to wrap it. Rubber budding strips are commonly used, although you can use raffia or string of almost any sort. To make the wrap, start with a self-binding loop slightly beyond the tip of the bud shield (Fig. 25).

Ordinarily, you can start either above or below the bud. If the bark is very loose, you should start above the bud and wrap downward to keep it from pushing the bud out. Make three or four wraps above the bud and several below it. When completing the wrap, make a self-binding loop as you did when starting. It is probably worthwhile to cover the top of the T cut when you wrap.

Care of the bud

A bud starts getting nourishment from the stock soon after you set it. In about a week you can tell if it is going to grow. Examine it then. If both the bud and the surrounding bark of the bud shield are shriveled and dry, you may still have time to set another bud. If you used a non-elastic binding material such as raffia, cut it when examining the bud at this time. Adhesive bands can be cut almost any time after budding.

In the spring, as soon as the buds start swelling, cut off the stock just at the cross of the T cut or 4 or 5 inches beyond the bud. Sometimes buds developing from stocks cut off just at the T are broken by birds lighting on them. Cutting the stock off beyond the bud avoids such breakage.

The bud shoot will soon grow over the stub. While the bud is starting, numerous other buds usually develop below it. Remove these as they appear or before they are more than 2 or 3 inches long.

It is not advisable to prune the new branch during the summer unless it is very vigorous or there is danger of the wind blowing it out. Even so, a support to which the whip can be tied is usually preferable to pruning.

HOME GARDENS

The management of our garden soils follows the same principles as the management of field soils, but we use different practices. In our gardens we aim for variety, and we have a wide range of plants—grasses, annuals, perennials, shrubs, vines, and trees.

We try to have flowers and fruits through the seasons and ornamentals for sun and shade. Yet the total number of plants is small, and we can treat them individually. Even with simple handtools, we have a chance to apply the principles of soil management over a wide range of combinations more precisely than the farmer can do for a few crops in big fields.

We have little choice in selecting our garden soils. Rarely can we choose level, stone-free, sunny, "rich loam" soils, which are recommended so blithely in the garden books and on the backs of seed packets. Once the location of the house is fixed, we must take the soils we find and make the best of them. Oftener than not, the soils around the house are not well suited, as they are, to the plants we want to grow, especially if builders have destroyed the natural surface soil and left thin topsoil over fills of trash and raw earth.

Thus many new home gardeners may begin with soils that are too hilly, too sandy, too clayey, too dry, too wet, or too infertile for good gardens. But good garden soils can be made from them.

By "garden," I refer to all the cared-for soils and plants around the home—the kitchen garden, flowerbeds, lawns, and plantings of trees and shrubs. Included is a variety of plants that have unlike soil requirements. Some need shade. Others

want full sun. Some prefer a slightly acid or neutral soil. Others do best in strongly acid ones. Some should have high soil fertility, others do well in poor soil.

The central problem of soil management in gardens is to develop and maintain a proper relationship between each plant and the immediate soil in which it grows.

Aside from pure luck, the gardener's success depends upon knowing two sets of factors: The requirements of the different plants he can grow and the characteristics of the soils in his garden.

Some plant can be found for almost any kind of soil as it is. And almost any kind of soil can be modified by management to grow any climatically adapted plant if one is willing to go to the trouble. Most successful gardeners try to find satisfying combinations of plants that require a minimum of soil change for good growth. Yet others go to a lot of trouble to change their soils to make them suitable for particular plants they want to have in their gardens. Some may even make drastic changes in a soil already about ideal for azaleas to have one suitable for roses, or the other way around.

One could hardly overemphasize the critical relationship between a plant and the soil in which it grows. Admiration of a plant in the catalog, at the flower show, or in a friend's garden is not enough of a basis for deciding to put it in our own garden, unless we know that its requirements can be satisfied by our garden soil as it is or as we can change it.

Gardening is an art, and many home gardens are outdoor living rooms. No one can say what is practical for home gardeners in general. Some are satisfied with almost any kind of green and growing things as long as the soil is nearly covered and the plants look healthy—a sensible goal for persons with only a mild interest in gardening.

A large money budget is not necessary for a good garden, even on poor soil. Far more important is the work budget—the care and attention the garden will be given throughout the season, not simply during a short spring bustle that is followed by neglect in summer and autumn.

The place for the garden is normally near the house. Even the kitchen garden is best there unless the soil in some distant place is a great deal better for vegetables and fruits. Near the house there is time to do the little things, before a pest, a drought, or a nutrient deficiency becomes serious. The watchful eye of the gardener is the best fertilizer for his garden.

What We Need To Know About The Soil

To begin a garden, we need to know several things about our own place:

The basic soil conditions; the air drainage and frostiness; the water supply we can count on, both natural and artificial; the light that falls on the plants during the seasons; and the protection required against hazards of wind, tree roots, and animals.

To learn about the soils we must dig—not simply into the surface, but down to about 3 feet or even more, if deep hardpans or other barriers to roots and water are suspected. The lower layers of soil control the supplies of nutrients, air, and water for deep roots. The movement of water out of the surface soil itself depends upon permeable layers beneath.

Most soils consist of a series of definite layers, or horizons, one above the other, with different colors and other properties. The horizons have been produced by the longtime effects of the climate and vegetation acting on the mineral matter. The horizons collectively are called the soil profile. Very young soils may not have horizons. Examples include those in the flood plains along streams, recent sand dunes, or new soil made by earthfills. If the gardener digs into an ordinary upland soil and finds no regular horizons, he can be reasonably certain that the soil has been moved about and mixed up not long before.

70

The main things to look for are depth, texture, structure, color, drainage, the slope and exposure, acidity, nutrients, and contamination.

Depth. Three kinds of soil depth are important. The dark-colored surface soil is normally the most mellow and most fertile. This is deepest in the black soils developed under grass, like those in Iowa and the Dakotas. It is normally very thin in the desert and only moderately thick under the forest of humid regions. On steep slopes it is commonly very thin. Builders often destroy this dark-colored surface soil completely or may cover it with raw, earthy material from excavations.

Then we need to know the depth of the whole soil, both surface soil and subsoil (or A and B horizons), over the raw substratum of weathered rock or other earthy material that has not been changed to true soil.

Finally, we should know how deep the whole soil and other loose, earthy material is over solid rock. The material under many soils is loose and porous to great depths. Other soils are thin over hard rocks with only a small space for roots and water storage. Such soils generally can support only drought-resistant plants that normally have shallow roots.

Texture. The relative proportion of sand, silt, and clay, or soil texture, of each horizon is important because it affects many other properties and because many recommendations are keyed to it. The texture in most soils changes from horizon to horizon. Commonly the subsoil, or B horizon, contains more clay than the surface soil above it or the substratum beneath it.

Classes of soil texture start with sand, which has only a little silt and clay. Then with increasing amounts of clay, the principal classes are loamy sand, sandy loam, loam, silt loam, clay loam, and clay.

With a little practice, you can easily distinguish them by squeezing a moist sample of the soil between your fingers. The sands are harsh and gritty, and the particles scarcely hold together at all. Loamy sands are gritty, too, but the particles cling together when moist. At the other extreme, clay can be squeezed into a smooth smear. The silt loam makes a rough and broken smear. Clay loams are intermediate. Loams give only a very rough smear; sandy loams give scarcely any.

Garden soils of intermediate texture—the sandy loams, loams, and silt loams—are easiest to handle. Sands and loamy sands are permeable, but they hold rather small quantities of water and are said to be droughty soils. Clays tend to become hard and massive unless they are handled carefully.

Structure. The individual soil particles in the ideal garden soil are grouped into stable granules or crumbs. Next best are blocky, nutlike aggregates, between which roots and water can move. Worst of all are the structureless soils.

At the one extreme are sands, in which each grain is by itself. Such soils hold little water between rains and are easily blown about by the wind.

At the other extreme are massive soils with no regular structural forms. Commonly clayey soils deficient in organic matter become massive if plowed, stirred, or walked on when they are wet. But massive hardpans can form from loams and even from sands with some cementing material to hold the particles together. Wherever they occur within the depth of normal rooting for garden plants, such massive soil must be reworked to make it granular or blocky. It is not enough simply to break up massive clods of clay. Organic matter must be added, or the fragments flow back together into masses when they are wet again.

Color. Soil color by itself is not important, but it suggests other conditions that are. Color, along with other evidence, can tell the gardener a great deal about drainage, the amount of organic matter in the soil, and the general level of productivity.

Brownish-black and dark-brown colors generally suggest a good supply of organic matter. In wooded areas where the normal upland soils are brown, black colors in the surface of soils in low ground suggest a good supply of organic

matter. In wooded areas where the normal upland soils are brown, black colors in the surface of soils in low ground suggest muck and poor drainage. Well-drained soils developed under tall grasses, like many in the Middle West, have black or nearly black surface soils. But a few black soils are poor in organic matter and easily lose their structure and become massive.

Solid red or yellow colors generally (but not always) suggest fairly good to free drainage. Yellow suggests leaching and a low supply of plant nutrients. So do the grays or whites in upland areas of good drainage. But in low ground, especially if the surface soil is nearly black, gray horizons (called gley) indicate poor drainage—too poor for ordinary garden plants. White colors in dry regions suggest too salty or too limy for most plants.

Some horizons beneath the surface are mottled. Imperfectly weathered rock just above the solid rock may look like this. But the commonest cause of mottling in soils is imperfect drainage, now or in the recent past: The soil is saturated with water, or waterlogged, part of the time and pervious to air, or aerated, part of the time.

Drainage. Imperfectly drained soils that are well drained during the summer and wet only in winter and early spring can support annual garden plants, but the roots of perennials cannot live over the winter in them. Even annuals do poorly if periods of waterlogging occur during their growing seasons. Often there is little evidence in the surface soil alone of poor drainage beneath. Thus it is important that you identify such conditions in advance so you can take appropriate steps for drainage or for plant selection.

If you have any doubt about drainage, you can dig some holes to the depth that roots normally grow—say to 2 or 3 feet, depending on the plants—and fill them with water. For all garden plants that require well-drained soils, the water should disappear within 30 minutes or an hour. If it does not disappear within 24 hours, only shallow-rooted plants could be expected to survive.

Slope and exposure. The slope of the surface soil has a lot to do with drainage, runoff, and erosion. Highly permeable soils that admit water rapidly can be used for cultivated plants on fairly steep slopes. On soils of slow to moderate permeability, small terraces are needed to slow down the runoff water, partly to give it more time to soak into the soil and partly to prevent washing.

You need to look at the whole slope, since it may begin above your garden and carry water from higher ground over your garden. If so, you should plan a diversion terrace on the upper side of the garden to intercept the excess runoff water and to guide it harmlessly to a prepared outlet.

Water tends to accumulate on nearly flat soils that are only slowly permeable unless ditches or special drains are made.

The direction of the slope is often critical. South-facing slopes in warm areas may be too hot for plants that do well on north-facing slopes. Many gardeners in warm areas find it easier to maintain good blue grass lawns on north-facing slopes than on south-facing ones. The south-facing slopes in cool sections may be much better than north-facing ones for vegetables and flowers that require a warm surface soil.

Acidity and nutrients cannot be seen, of course. They can be guessed at from the vigor of growing plants. The soil in which blueberries and the like grow wild is strongly acid. If roses and bluegrass are doing well, blueberries are probably not.

Acidity and nutrients can be measured accurately only on samples in the laboratory. I suggest that field tests be made for acidity only, but if you have some flair for chemistry you can try the tests for nutrients.

Most upland soils in humid forested regions are likely to be too acid for vegetables, a bit too acid for most flowers, and too low in plant nutrients for best growth. A generous application of fertilizers rich in phosphorus and potassium usually should be given at the start. But many shrubs and flowers and a few fruits

72

demand an acid soil. Most of the flowers need medium rather than high fertility, and some of the herbs want even low fertility.

Until you get a representative sample of each kind of your soil tested for acidity and plant nutrients, you are working a great deal in the dark. Samples should be taken carefully to represent an even slice or core of the surface soil that is normally spaded, down to 5 to 8 inches, say, and of the soil beneath to about 20 inches. If the layers above 20 inches are strongly contrasting, it is better to have a separate sample of each. Samples of unlike soils, or of unlike horizons from the same soil, should not be mixed. Generally it is best to write to a laboratory before you collect the samples to meet any special requirements of the laboratory.

Contamination. In areas of disturbed soil, you need to be on the lookout for buried trash. Fragments of tar paper, concrete, and other rubbish should be removed. Any buried pieces of plaster or concrete are bad for acid-loving plants like azaleas and may cause chlorosis, or yellowing, of the leaves.

Commonly the worst places for buried materials are near the house, where shrubs and flowerbeds are needed. The excavations for basements usually are made somewhat larger than necessary so that after the walls are finished a V-shaped space is left just outside the wall. Careless builders allow rubbish to accumulate in this space and at the end simply cover it with a layer of topsoil. It should have been filled with soil and packed to protect the basement wall from accumulations of water. For plantings near the house it often is necessary therefore to remove a large amount of miscellaneous rubbish.

Other bad spots that your examination may uncover include old buried roadways or sidewalks and spots of oil-soaked soil. They must be dug up and removed.

The air drainage of the garden affects its frostiness. If the garden is relatively high on a slope, the cold air moves or drains away from it into the low ground, so that plants escape the late-spring and early-autumn frosts that kill plants in the low ground. The gardener in low ground thus cannot count on so long a growing season as his neighbors on high ground with good air drainage. Plants growing on muck soils on low ground are even more subject to frost damage than plants growing on mineral soils on low ground. When you receive the frost-free days from the reports of the County Agent's office or agricultural services, you should take these local ground conditions into account.

Water should be available for all of the garden except the parts that have only naturalized wild plants entirely adapted to the natural soil. A dependable source of irrigation water is essential in dry regions; short periods of drought cause damage that nullifies much of the benefit from other good practices.

You can conserve soil water so that you need only a little if you prepare the soil properly, build terraces where they are helpful, and use mulches to protect the surface. But this little is often critical for carrying through fine plants in the kitchen garden and among the ornamentals.

Evergreens need watering during severe winter droughts as well as summer droughts.

In cities where the use of water for gardens may be regulated during dry spells, the resourceful home gardener may find a way to store some of the rainwater in a pond or cistern.

The light requirements of plants vary greatly. You need to study the place to determine the hours of sunshine for the various parts of it, remembering that under deciduous trees there is little shade in winter and early spring and heavy shade in summer.

Nearly all vegetables and fruits do best in full sun, although the salad crops need shade in warm sections. Tomatoes, one of the most important vegetables in a small garden, grow fairly well in half the normal sunshine. The moving shade of a tree is less harmful to sun-loving plants than the dead shade of a building.

Other plants prefer shade. A few fine ornamentals flourish in the continuous

shade of the north side of a building. Several of the ornamentals do well with winter and spring sun and summer shade, as under an oak tree.

Some lawn grasses prefer full sun and others partial shade. Ivy or other ground cover is more satisfactory than grass in heavy shade.

Many ornamental plants that seem to wither in full sun are really injured by high soil temperatures. If good mulches keep their roots cool, they do all right in full sun. Ordinarily clematis is one of these. Azaleas prefer partial shade, but they may do well in the sun if kept well mulched with something like sawdust.

Some of the trouble with plants growing near trees and big shrubs that is commonly put down to shade is due to root competition.

Plants need protection from competing roots, wind, and animals.

Roots from a competing tree may be pruned by digging a trench along one side—or even more if the tree is growing normally. A steel barrier may be placed in the trench to whatever depth the roots penetrate, say 2 to 4 feet, as a permanent protection for flowerbeds, vegetables, and shrubs.

Plants vary in their reaction to the roots of other plants. Azaleas, for example, grow well among oak trees, but roses do not. Yet azaleas grow poorly in competition with elm or maple roots. In fact, lawns, flowerbeds, and fine shrubs do badly near elms, maples, cottonwoods, poplars, and willows, which are not for small gardens.

In very large gardens near a woods, some gardeners dig deep, open trenches as a protection against roots, but they are unsightly and dangerous.

Many failures due to competing roots are incorrectly laid to the soil or its shade. Even small plants can rob the others. Forsythia roots, for example, are very bad robbers, and so are those of American bittersweet. Some iris are bad. Unless the roots of strong growers are kept pruned, they take over in a mixed garden. Flowerbeds may be protected from grass roots with 4-inch steel barriers and from most shrub roots with 12-inch barriers.

Wind is a serious hazard in many parts of the country—hot winds in summer, cold winds in winter, or both. Usually windbreaks of ornamental trees, especially evergreens, can be planted if the soil is suitable and if water is available. Winds may be very destructive in a few places around the garden during the winter. Those spots can be identified by their barrenness of snow when the rest of the garden is covered with it. Mature shrubs often thrive in such places if moved into them, but little shrubs of the same kind perish.

Animals are not useful in the garden. Home gardens can be destroyed by rabbits. Dogs are probably the most commonly destructive animals in most home gardens. It is not worth while trying to grow fine flowering shrubs in some communities without fences.

Tilling The Soil

Tillage is commonly the first step in preparing the garden soil. Organic matter, fertilizers, and other soil amendments are commonly mixed into the soil at the same time.

Large gardens can be plowed with machines, but small plots and small areas for flowerbeds and individual shrubs or trees should be spaded. Deep, fertile, granular soil, receptive to roots and water, may not have to be plowed or spaded very much, but usually some tillage is necessary.

The objectives of tillage are to produce and to maintain as deep a rooting zone of fertile granular soil as possible, control weeds, and keep the soil receptive to water.

For the development and maintenance of good structure is the main reason for plowing and spading. Considering the soil most gardeners have, this means

working a great deal of organic matter into the soil—not just once, but often.

For spading or stirring, a sample of the soil should just crumble in the hand after it has been formed into a ball and squeezed. Tillage of wet and sticky soils causes them to lose their granular structure and become massive, especially if they contain much clay and little organic matter. Once a clayey soil is badly puddled, it often takes years of careful handling to produce good structure.

It often is convenient to apply fertilizer and lime, besides organic matter, to the lower layers when spading. Most plant nutrients in time are carried down into the soil by rain and irrigation water if applied to the surface, but the movement is slow in clayey soils. Phosphorus especially moves down very slowly, although deeply rooted plants move it from their surface roots into their deep roots, where it becomes available to new plants after the old roots decompose.

Deep spading of the surface soil is rarely good practice in the garden except in the few soils that have little or no contrast between the horizons. The surface soil should be spaded to a depth of about 5 inches in dry sites and 7 or 8 inches in normally moist ones, without mixing in more than a very little of any lighter colored subsoil at any time.

Subsoil spading usually is necessary in most garden soils for good, deep rooting. That is, very many garden soils should be spaded to a considerable depth, but each major layer should be spaded separately and not mixed with the others. That is called double or triple spading if two or three layers are spaded separately.

Let us take as a common example a soil that has a dark-colored surface horizon of intermediate texture about 7 inches thick overlying a clayey subsoil that goes to 20 inches with a fairly pervious substratum below that.

Double spading is called for. You start spading at one end of the garden or flowerbed by removing entirely a 2- or 3-foot strip of surface soil to 7 inches and piling it to one side. Then you spade the subsoil for 13 inches—making a total depth from the surface of 20 inches—and mix in the necessary sawdust, compost, or manure (as organic matter to improve structure), any needed lime (to correct acidity), and the basic fertilizers. When you have spaded and prepared the subsoil in this first strip, you spade the surface soil from the next similar strip over it and at the same time mix the necessary organic matter and fertilizers into it. Then the newly uncovered subsoil is spaded as before—and so on across the entire bed or plot. The surface soil you remove from the first strip you carry over to cover the spaded subsoil in the last strip.

If the substratum below the subsoil is also massive and needs improvement for proper rooting and for proper movement of water, you carry out surface soil from the first two strips at the end of the plot and the subsoil from the first strip to one side.

Then the substratum is spaded and treated. The subsoil from the second strip is treated with organic matter and other materials, and you spade it over the freshly spaded substratum of the first strip. The surface soil from the third strip you place over the freshly spaded subsoil of the first strip. This triple spading is carried across the whole plot. The subsoil from the first strip is used in the last one and the surface soil from the first two strips covers the last two.

If the soil is massive, mere spading does little good: When it is wet again, the soil particles settle back together—deeper layers are heavily pressed by the weight of the ones above them.

Organic Matter: Mulch, Compost, Manure

Besides spading, you need to add abundant organic matter and the basic fertilizers for good structure and adequate nutrition of deep roots.

The organic matter has a direct effect in bringing about lines of weakness and

preventing the settling of the soil particles into solid masses. But more important, in well-drained soils the organisms decompose the organic matter and produce compounds that lead to natural soil granulation.

These organisms need nutrients, especially nitrogen and phosphorus, which are deficient in sawdust, peat, and most organic materials (except high quality compost and manure) that a gardener can add. The relation of nitrogen to organic matter is explained later in the text.

Once the lower horizons are loosened thoroughly and supplied with organic matter and plant nutrients and if they are kept free of excess water by natural and artificial drainage, the roots of many kinds of plants extend down into them. The roots supply further organic matter to the lower layers.

If organic matter is not available, triple spading with good fertilization can be successful if the soil is planted immediately to a deep-rooted legume like sweet-clover or kudzu. After a year or two of vigorous growth, these plants produce a large amount of organic matter above and below the surface. The aboveground part can be cut and spaded into the surface soil or mixed with other materials for the compost. Such treatments may delay the garden for a year or so, but they are often worthwhile.

The soil for small beds and little places for individual shrubs and trees can be improved in the same way. Each soil layer is removed and piled to one side separately. It is replaced after organic matter and fertilizers are added to it. If the soil has hardpans or very heavy claypans, it is best to discard those layers and replace them with good garden soil, with surface soil from a fertile field, or (for acid-loving plants) with soil from a woods.

Cultivation after the soil is spaded and during the growing season follows the same general rule about soil moisture. If the clayey soils are stirred or tramped when wet, they lose their granulation. If the garden must be walked on, broad boards should be laid down yet garden soils should be kept free of weeds and porous to water. Since so many of our rains in the United States come as sharp showers, a hard crust on the surface allows much of the water to run off and be lost before the soil becomes permeable. Then, too, after plants have fair size, surface tillage needs to be shallow and gentle so as not to harm surface roots. A good mulch can go a long way in substituting for tillage—it helps prevent crusting, promotes the entry of water, and suppresses weeds.

Organic matter is a vital material of which most gardeners rarely have enough.

Organic matter has several functions in the garden soils—as food for microorganisms and tiny animals within the soil, as a source of plant nutrients, and as a mulch. It also improves soil structure.

Its promotion of granular structure aids root growth and the entrance of water and air into the soil, reduces crusting and losses of surface soil by blowing or washing, and increases the ability of the soil to hold both water and nutrients for use by plants. Mulches help to control temperature, to reduce evaporation losses, and to suppress weeds. (Mulches of coarse sand and small stones have some of the same effects, too.) Organic matter, especially manure or compost derived from a wide range of normally growing plants, furnishes the growing plants a balanced supply of slowly available nutrients, including the trace elements.

The living roots, micro-organisms, and small creatures, such as earthworms, are a part of the total organic matter in the soil. Besides them, the garden soil contains three general classes of organic matter—the fresh remains of plants, partly decomposed materials, and the more or less stable, dark-colored humus, which is slowly decomposed to water, carbon dioxide, and ash. During the decomposition of fresh materials, a vast number of intermediate organic compounds appear before the formation of humus. Some of them are toxic in large amounts, but in normally well-drained soils they are transitory, and are themselves decomposed so soon that large amounts are never present. This decomposition is carried

76

out by the tiny animals and the micro-organisms. The organic matter furnishes them food for growth and the nutrients in it are thereby released for use by plants.

The fresh materials vary widely in their rates of decomposition and in the amounts of plant nutrients they release, especially the amounts of nitrogen.

Cottonseed meal and meat scraps, for example, decompose rapidly and furnish so much nitrogen that they are regarded primarily as fertilizers. Next come freshly cut clover and grass. Wheat straw decomposes moderately fast but is low in protein and so furnishes little nitrogen. Oak leaves and pine needles are even more resistant. Finally, sawdust and wood chips decompose very slowly and furnish negligible amounts of plant nutrients to the soil. Because they decompose slowly they are good mulches, especially in warm, moist regions. As we shall see in a moment, dry straw, tree leaves, and sawdust actually reduce the nitrogen available to plants when first added to the soil.

Among the partly decomposed materials, animal manure is important. Nearly pure manure is also a kind of fertilizer; often it is dried and sold in bags. It decomposes rapidly and gives the soil a balanced supply of plant nutrients. Manure that has much dry straw and wood chips with it decomposes more slowly.

Leaf mold, the partially decomposed leaves just above the mineral soil in the woods, is an excellent material, especially for mulching acid-loving plants. It decomposes slowly and furnishes some nutrients. Most peats decompose slowly and furnish minor supplies of nutrients.

Compost is a major source of organic matter to the gardener who has trees. It can be used as a slowly available source of nutrients and as a mulch and to improve the structure of soils.

The chief aim in composting is to produce an organic matter approximately like that in a fertile soil, in which the organic matter has about 10 parts of carbon for each part of nitrogen, or, as we say, a C/N ratio of 10.

The plant materials most commonly available to the gardener—autumn leaves and straw or other plant stems—are dry, coarse, and much higher in carbon, with a C/N ratio of 30 or higher. If they are added directly, it is hard to mix them evenly with the soil, considerable moisture is needed to moisten them in advance of decomposition, and the excess carbon as carbohydrate furnishes the bacteria a great deal of energy food. With this food, which acts like sugar, they increase enormously in numbers, taking out of the soil phosphorus and nitrogen, which otherwise would be available to plants.

For a field or a very large garden, it is most practical to add these materials directly to the surface soil, together with enough nitrogen and phosphorus to balance the carbohydrate, and plow all of it into the soil. But for small gardens and flower beds it is best to arrange for partial decomposition in advance in a compost pile. The product can be added as needed in preparing beds or as a mulch.

You should have a rick or open bin in which to make the compost. You can use ordinary wire fence or boards attached to solid posts, or open brickwork, to make such a rick some 3 to 8 feet high and 3 to 5 feet wide and of any convenient length. One end should be made with removable sides for convenience in building up the compost and for taking out the material. (See Compost Bins, Part I)

Materials like autumn leaves can be laid down in layers some 6 to 12 inches thick. To each layer is added some nitrogen and phosphorous (and magnesium sulfate—or epsom salt—in the humid East, or dolomitic limestone, if none of the compost is to be used for acid-loving plants) and a half-inch layer of soil.

As it is built up, the material should be packed with the feet around the margins but only lightly in the middle—so that the center will settle more than the margins and water added to the surface will gradually moisten the whole.

77

Some gardeners use pits, but it is better to build from the surface of level ground. The material needs to be moist but not soggy. Decomposition without air leads to loss of nitrogen.

If lime is needed in compost intended for the kitchen garden, wood ashes can be used instead. If nitrogen and phosphorus are not available separately, a mixed fertilizer can be used. If considerable manure or fresh clover hay is used, the amounts of nitrogen and phosphorus can be reduced proportionately.

The following table suggests some alternative mixtures in making compost with leaves or straw as the main material.

Table 1. Material To Add in Making Compost

Material	Rate in cups per tightly packed bushel of compost material

For General Purposes, Including Acid-loving Shrubs:

Combination A:
Ammonium sulfate 1
Superphosphate (20 percent) 1/2
Epsom salt 1/16

Combination B:
Mixed fertilizer 10-6-4 . . . . .1-1/2
   or
Mixed fertilizer 5-10-5 . . . . .2-1/2

For Kitchen Garden or Flowers Not Requiring Acid Soil:

Combination C:
Ammonium sulfate 1
Superphosphate (20 percent) 1/2
Ground dolomitic limestone or wood ashes. 2/3

Combination D:
Like B, above, plus ground colomitic limestone or wood ashes 2/3

[1] 1 U.S. bushel = 2150 cu. in. = 35.24 liters

After 2 or 3 months of moderate to warm weather, the pile should be turned for best results, although that is not entirely necessary. In turning into another rick, you can cut down vertical sections in the old one and put them horizontally in the new one, being careful to keep any dry materials to the inside.

In regions having cool, frosty winters, compost made from autumn leaves in November and December may be turned the following May or June.

A pile that is made too large may overheat, with a loss of nitrogen.

If the material is kept reasonably moist and has a cap of garden soil (besides the soil between the layers), it should have no odor.

Applications of good compost or stable manure to the garden are about 4 to 40 bushels to 1,000 square feet.

Other organic materials may be used as mulches. Straw free of weed seeds is good, especially for small fruits, although it is a fire hazard and does not look neat in a garden.

Sawdust and wood chips are useful to mix into clayey soils to improve their structure and as mulches. Since they contain some slowly soluble carbohydrates, nitrogen must be added with them over and above that recommended for the soil

otherwise. Nitrogen can be added by placing 3 to 4 inch layers of pure animal manure to each 18 inches of compost. Perhaps well-rotted sawdust is somewhat better, but fresh sawdust is used successfully. When moistened, it gives nearly ideal acidity for azaleas and other acid-loving plants. For the kitchen garden and the rose garden it is well to use about one-fourth to one-half cupful of finely ground dolomitic limestone with each bushel.

A 3- to 5-inch mulch of sawdust is recommended around shrubs and other tall plants. Gardeners particular about the appearance of their intimate gardens can put a light covering of well-rotted compost over the sawdust or wood chips.

Cover crops are helpful on garden soils used for annual plants, both flowers and vegetables. Winter wheat, rye ryegrass, or other winter-hardy crops may be planted in autumn. They protect the soil and absorb nutrients that would otherwise be lost. In the spring you have a supply of succulent, nutrient-rich organic matter to spade into the surface. This is very fresh organic matter and makes little contribution to the basic supply of humus.

Water For The Garden

The control of water is essential for the garden except in spots naturalized to wild plants that can endure wet, dry, or alternately wet and dry conditions.

Most soils lose a part of the water that falls on them through runoff from the surface, percolation through the soil, evaporation from the surface, and transpiration through plants.

Much of a gardener's success depends upon keeping these losses to a minimum, except the transpiration from his wanted plant, and on being sure that excess water does not accumulate in the pore spaces of the soil at the expense of air. Actually, it is not the excess water that injures plants in poorly drained soils, but the lack of air.

The ideal garden soil admits nearly all the water that falls on it, holds a large quantity within the fine capillaries between rains, allows any excess to drain away is protected by surface mulches from excessive evaporation, and has no weeds. It should be added that a sandy garden soil subject to heavy leaching during the cool, rainy periods should have a cover of growing plants that take in nutrients that would otherwise be leached away. These are returned to the surface soil again when the plants are spaded under in the spring or the material can be taken to the compost pile.

Terraces are needed on sloping soils. To make full use of the water that falls during sharp showers, we need to have the soil granular. But in addition, on sloping soils, little, winding terraces, usually at a slight angle to the contour, to slow down the water are necessary. You can make several individual level terraces out of small stones the size of quart cans or gallon jugs with low walls on the downslope side of each large plant or small group of plants. These stones guide the water into the soil. With terraces, most of the plants can thus be planted or set out on level ground.

Drainage of wet soils can be accomplished in several ways. The simplest method is to throw up beds of soil above the original ground level, with places between for the excess water to collect and to flow away.

Irrigation is needed to some degree in most gardens. In fact, the more we do to improve our soils and to protect our plants, the more important it becomes to provide water for the critical periods so that we do not lose the benefit from all our other work.

A soil in good tilth, properly fertilized and well mulched, requires much less irrigation than a poorly managed one. Yet critical periods are fairly common when even the best garden soil needs water for fine plants.

Most of us irrigate when we see that our plants have started to wilt. That is too

late for best results. When plants wilt, at least some damage has already been done. For a few dollars you can buy an instrument (called a tensiometer) to keep in your garden soil during the summer. Such an instrument indicates the moisture content and tells you when to irrigate before plants begin to wilt.

Depending on convenience, you may irrigate in small ditches, with a porous hose, or by sprays. The important thing is to irrigate well when it is done.

pH and Acidity

Excess salts can do a lot of harm. They are commonly associated with poor drainage in arid and semiarid regions, or with the use of salty irrigation water, or both.

Controlling the reaction of the garden soil is one of the important adjustments the gardener can make for his plants. Many plants grow quite well over a wide range of soil reaction (acid-neutral-alkaline), especially when other growing conditions are good, but most plants do best within a rather narrow range.

The garden vegetables, most of the common annual flowers, most lawn grasses, and many herbaceous perennials and shrubs do best in slightly to very slightly acid soil—about pH 6.1 to 6.9. The term "pH" is a quantitative measure of the degree of acidity:

Table 2. pH Measurements

	pH
Extremely acid	Below 4.5.
Very strongly acid	4.5-5.0.
Strongly acid	5.1-5.5.
Medium acid	5.6-6.0.
Slightly acid	6.1-6.5.
Neutral	6.6-7.3.
Mildly alkaline	7.4-7.8.
Moderately alkaline	7.9-8.4.
Strongly alkaline	8.5-9.0.
very strongly alkaline	9.1 and higher.

A more acid soil than pH 6.5 is better for many plants, especially those that grow naturally under a forest with acid leaf litter.

Any plants like these having an ideal soil pH range so far on the acid side usually do better in soil that has no free lime within the rooting zone. Such free lime occurs naturally in some soils, especially in subhumid and semiarid regions. It may have been added accidentally as ashes or in rubbish. Or it may have been added when garden soils were treated to make them best for vegetables, lawns, or other plants intolerant of strong acidity.

Other things being equal, such as structure, moisture, or organic matter, the micro-organisms that decompose organic matter, that transform organic nitrogen into forms most suitable to plant roots, and that fix nitrogen from the air grow best about pH 6.5. Near this same soil pH, 6.5, conditions are best for the availability to plants, without toxic amounts, of most plant nutrients.

Table 3. Suitable pH Ranges for Various Crops and Ornamental Plants

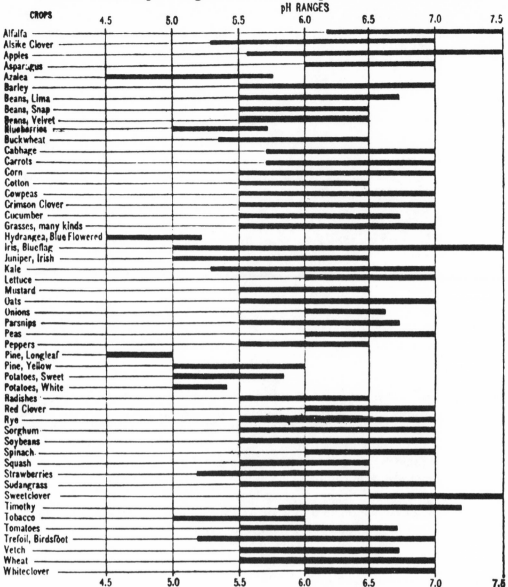

Among the trace elements, iron, manganese, copper, and zinc become less available as the pH rises. Iron chlorosis, a yellowing disease of plant leaves due to iron deficiency, is a common symptom of acid-loving plants growing on soils containing free lime.

On the other hand, availability of nearly all important plant nutrients except iron diminishes with increasing acidity, phosphorus especially.

Most upland soils developed under forests in the humid sections are too acid for the best growth of lawns, vegetables, and many other plants. They require liming. Most soils developed under grass and shrubs in the subhumid or dry sections do not need lime.

Since pH measures only the intensity of soil acidity, and not the total amount, applications of lime for soils of the same pH increase with increasing total amounts of clay, with increasing activity of the clay, and with increasing amounts of organic matter.

Table 4 gives some general guidelines for the application of finely ground limestone, all of which passes through a 100-mesh screen. Only one-half as much burned lime should be used. If the organic matter in the soil is very high, the amounts should be increased about one-fourth over those given in the table. If the organic matter is very low, the amounts of lime should be reduced by about one-fourth.

81

Table 4. Suggested Applications of Finely Ground Limestone to Raise the pH of a 7-inch Layer of Several Textural Classes of Acid Soils, in Pounds per 1,000 Square Feet

Textural class	pH 4.5 to 5.5		pH 5.5 to 6.5	
	Northern and Central States	Southern Coastal States	Northern and Central States	Southern Coastal States
Sands and loamy sands ..	25	15	30	20
Sandy loams	45	25	55	35
Loams	60	40	85	50
Silt loams	80	60	105	75
Clay loams	100	80	120	100
Muck	200	175	225	200

You should bear in mind that the individual horizons of your soil may have quite different pH values and lime requirements. For example, many soils are medium acid in the surface, strongly acid in the subsoil, and only slightly acid or even slightly alkaline in the substratum.

Overliming must be avoided. It is easy to overlime very fertile soils in which only small amounts are required to make a big change. Overliming causes problems of nutrient deficiency, especially with the trace elements. Partly for this reason it is better to use burned lime or hydrated lime, both of which are strong. Any unevenness in spreading may lead to overliming.

The best material of all is finely ground dolomitic limestone. It contains magnesium carbonate and calcium carbonate. Most soils needing lime are likely to be deficient to some degree in both magnesium and calcium as plant nutrients. Furthermore, because dolomitic limestone becomes nearly insoluble at pH 7 or higher, the danger of overliming with uneven spreading is greatly reduced. Finally, if a very strongly acid soil is to be used for vegetables or lawns, it is better to raise the pH in two applications a year or so apart than in one big application.

For the acid-loving plants, you may have the problem of increasing the acidity of the soil. If the soil contains free lime, the most practical thing to do is to remove it, say to about 20 inches for blueberries and azaleas, and replace it with naturally acid surface soil from the woods. But for soils containing little or no free lime, sulfur can be added according to the amount shown in the table below.

Amounts for sandy loams are intermediate between those for sand and loam. It is not commonly practical to use soils more clayey than loam for acid-loving plants. The gardener can grow acid-loving plants by removing the clayey soil and replacing all or a part of it with sandy soil mixed with acid organic matter.

Although aluminum sulfate often is recommended to gardeners for increasing the acidity of the soil, it has a toxic salt effect on plants if it is used in large amounts. Small amounts are not very effective. About 7 pounds of aluminum sulfate is required to accomplish the same effect as 1 pound of sulfur.

Table 5. Suggested Application of Ordinary Powdered Sulfur to Reduce the pH of an 8-inch Layer of Soil, as Indicated in Pints per 100 Square Feet.

Pints of sulfur for 100 square feet to reach pH of --

Original pH of soil	4.5		5.0		5.5		6.0		6.5	
	Sand	Loam	Sand	Loam	Sand	Loam	Sand	Loam	Sand	Loam
5.0	2/3	2	....	....	....	....	....	....	....	....
5.5	1 1/3	4	2/3	2	....	....	....	....	....	....
6.0	2	5 1/2	1 1/3	4	2/3	2	....	....	....	....
6.5	2 1/2	8	2	5 1/2	1 1/3	4	2/3	2	....	....
7.0	3	10	2 1/2	8	2	5 1/2	1 1/3	4	2/3	2

The soil to be treated must be well drained. A mixture of sulfur and organic matter in wet soils produces hydrogen sulfide, an ill-smelling substance that is toxic to plants.

Whenever possible, it is best to prepare the soil at the proper pH for acid-loving plants in advance. The soil can be kept moist while the reactions take place, followed by a thorough moistening to leach out any soluble materials before planting. If the plants are already established before you discover that the soil is not acid enough, you can mix one-half to 1 tablespoonful of sulfur into the surface soil just above the roots for an area of about 1 square foot.

Besides sulfur, the use of acid mulches (such as pine needles, sawdust, and acid peat) and the continued use of ammonium sulfate as a nitrogen fertilizer tend to increase soil acidity.

Nutrients in the Soil

A balance of plant nutrients in the soil is essential for good growth. Most gardeners realize this and may tend to oversimplify the problem of soil productivity by getting a big bag of fertilizer from the store, spreading it on the soil, and then feel they have done the job. That can be helpful, but the plant nutrients are no more important than proper structure, adequate supplies of water, and the control of soil temperature with mulches.

Besides the carbon, oxygen, and hydrogen from air and water, plants take at least 12 essential elements from the soil. Deficiencies in nitrogen, phosphorus, and potassium are most widespread; those elements are most commonly contained in mixed fertilizers. Calcium and magnesium ordinarily are included in liming materials, and at least small amounts are in most mixed fertilizers. Sulfur is abundant in most arid soils; it is contained in some fertilizers; and enough falls in the rain near cities. Six trace elements are needed by plants in tiny amounts: Iron, boron, manganese, copper, zinc, and molybdenum. Each of the 12 elements is important as a fertilizer somewhere in the world.

Vanadium and chlorine also are essential to plants, but we would not expect them to limit plant growth in garden soils. Occasionally, however, a soil may be found that contains toxic amounts of some of these trace elements or of others.

Each of the 12 elements is contained in manure and in compost made from normally growing plants, although usually not in the best proportions to make a good garden soil from a naturally infertile one. It would take a long time to build up the phosphorus content of a highly phosphorus deficient soil with compost and manure alone. It is more practical to use chemical fertilizer in addition to organic matter.

When there is a scarcity of good manure and good compost and a general use of mixed fertilizers rich in nitrogen, phosphorus, and potassium, gardeners must pay increasing attention to the trace elements in order to have a proper balance among the nutrients at a high level of fertility.

The balance among the nutrients—not only the total amounts of them—is important. In many of the naturally infertile, leached soils of the eastern part of the country, for example, a lack of boron may be the factor that limits plant growth. Unless it is added, the gardener does not get the advantage of other fertilizers and good practices. Boron is especially important for tomatoes and other plants in the kitchen garden. Zinc also is rather commonly deficient; white streaks on the leaves of sweet corn indicate its lack.

The common basic elements, especially calcium, magnesium, and potassium, must be in proper relationship to one another for good nutrition.

Thus the use of a large amount of pure calcium liming material can bring on magnesium deficiency, often exhibited by a chlorosis, or yellowing, of the older leaves, which spreads to the younger leaves. An excess of either magnesium or potassium can depress the intake of the other by plants.

Phosphorus, potassium, and nitrogen need to be in reasonable balance. An excess of nitrogen causes spindly, flabby plants susceptible to disease. Where gardeners use a lot of manure or compost and fertilizers rich in nitrogen, they are inclined to have big plants with lots of leaves and relatively few flowers and fruits. The addition of potassium to such a soil strengthens the plant. The addition of phosphorus encourages more fruiting, earliness, and root growth.

An excess of both phosphorus and nitrogen together, and especially where potassium is low, may stimulate iron deficiency, which causes chlorosis. This, of course, is especially bad for acid-loving plants if the soil pH is too high anyway.

Chlorosis can also be caused by manganese deficiency and by zinc deficiency, but it is most commonly due to either iron deficiency or magnesium deficiency. In the latter, the old leaves turn yellow early, and the yellowing spreads to the new leaves. With iron deficiency, the yellowing starts with the young leaves and progresses to the old ones. A nitrogen deficiency also can cause grayish or yellowish leaves, which tend to mature abnormally yearly.

The serious gardener finds it well worth his time to become familiar with the functions of the individual nutrients in plants and their common reactions in the soil, as explained in other chapters.

Estimating the amounts of fertilizer to apply depends upon three separate sets of more basic estimates: The nutrients already in the soil, plus those normally added in any compost or manure; the general requirements of the specific plants to be grown; and the amounts of the nutrients contained in the various fertilizer materials available for use.

None of the fertilizers consists 100 percent of plant nutrients. The actual plant nutrients are parts of other compounds, and some other materials may have been added to keep the fertilizer in good physical condition. Thus, if you use ordinary superphosphate as a source of phosphorus and 20 pounds of phosphoric oxide are called for, you would apply 100 pounds of the material, because ordinary superphosphate has only 20 percent of phosphoric oxide.

Our calculations are further complicated by the old trade practice of expressing the amounts of phosphorus in terms of phosphoric oxide(P_2O_5)rather than as elemental phosphorus (P). Similarly, the plant nutrient content of a potassium fertilizer is expressed as potash (K_2O), rather than as potassium (K). It is hoped that these practices will be changed, so that all nutrients are shown as the elements. That is now done with nitrogen (N).

A laboratory soil test is the best means for estimating the existing supplies of available plant nutrients, along with the appearance and abundance of previous plant growth. But these results cannot be followed blindly since the same test result indicates somewhat different fertilizer recommendations for different soils in the various parts of the country. A qualified soil-testing laboratory takes these factors into account in the interpretation of their tests. Thus when you send samples to the laboratory for testing, the more precise the information about

previous plant growth and about the soil that you furnish the laboratory, the better the recommendations you receive from the laboratory.

The following suggestions about groups of garden plants are given as rough general guides. Readers should be aware that individual plants within these groups vary considerably. After each group of plants, it is indicated roughly their fertility requirements for nitrogen, phosphorus, and potassium as high, low, or medium.

Vegetables . . . . High
Herbs . . . . Medium to low
Lawn grasses . . . . Medium to high
Fruits . . . . Medium
Annual flowers . . . . Medium
Perennial flowers . . . . Medium to low
Shrubs, deciduous . . . . Medium to low
Shrubs, evergreen . . . . Low
Shade trees, deciduous . . . . Medium to low
Shade trees, evergreen . . . . Low

Table 6 is designed as a rough guide to the amounts of nitrogen, phosphorus, and potassium to use on garden soils of various textures and of low or high fertility, as indicated by present plant growth or soil tests. The figures given are not for the fertilizers themselves; they refer to the net plant nutrients in fertilizers as nitrogen, phosphoric oxide, and potash. The high part of the range is for plants responding to high levels of fertility for the element, and the low range is for plants needing only low amounts of the element.

Table 6. The Amount of NPK to Use on Soil

GENERAL SOIL CLASS		NUTRIENTS (Pounds per 1,000 square feet)		
TEXTURE	FERTILITY LEVEL	NITROGEN (N)	PHOSPHORIC OXIDE (P_2O_5)	POTASH (K_2O)
Sandy soils . . . Low		1 to 4	2 to 5	1 to 4
	High	0 to 2	0 to 3	$\frac{1}{2}$ to 3
Loamy soils . . . Low		1 to 4	2 to 5	1 to 4
	High	0 to 2	0 to 3	0 to 2
Clayey soils. . . Low		1 to 4	3 to 6	2 to 5
	High	0 to 2	0 to 3	0 to 3
Muck soils . . . Low		$\frac{1}{2}$ to 3	3 to 6	1 to 7
	High	0 to 2	1 to 4	0 to 3

Suppose that our garden soil is a loam of low fertility and we want to prepare it for vegetables. As a general guide, we should need about 2 pounds of nitrogen, 3 of phosphoric oxide, and 2 of potash. That would amount to 20 pounds per 1,000 square feet of a 10-15-10 mixed fertilizer, containing 10 percent of nitrogen, 15 percent of phosphoric oxide, and 10 percent of potash. Instead of a 10-15-10, we could use 40 pounds of the more common 5-10-5, which would give us just what we need of nitrogen and potassium with a little extra phosphorus.

When preparing a garden soil for vegetables, flowers, and lawns, the necessary limestone and basic fertilizer, as suggested above, can be spread on the surface

and tilled in along with about 10 to 20 bushels of manure or good compost for each 1,000 square feet. If the lower layers also need improvement, they may be given similar treatments with variations in the lime according to the degree of acidity.

Many gardens also need one or more of the trace elements, especially where little manure or compost is used.

Magnesium can be had with dolomitic limestone where it is used. Most mixed fertilizers contain some. If limestone is not used, as for acid-loving plants, ordinary epsom salt can be used at a rate of one-half cupful per 100 square feet for sandy soils and twice that for clayey soils.

For iron, gardeners have usually depended upon sprays having around 1 to 2 percent of iron as ferrous sulfate. One wants to be sure to use high-quality materials containing no residual acids. With woody plants, such spraying may need to be done every year to prevent chlorosis if the soil pH is too high or if it contains free lime. More effective iron fertilizers have appeared on the market under various trade names. They are some kind of iron chelates. Commonly they are added to the soil in water solutions, in accordance with the suggestions for the specific materials, although some spray them on the plants. But such spraying is not necessary except for curing an immediate situation. Some rather serious cases of iron chlorosis in azaleas have been cured within 10 days after treatment of the soil directly under the plant with an iron chelate dissolved in water.

Ordinary borax may be used to supply boron, which often is important in the kitchen garden on soils that were originally acid. You must be careful to spread it evenly at low rates of about 5 ounces, or 1 tablespoonful, to 100 square feet for sandy soils, or up to 3 times that amount for clayey soils. Such small amounts can be spread more easily if they are mixed with the bulkier fertilizers or with sand. For safety, a whole garden and lawn can be given a light application every 2 or 3 years. Although celery, cauliflower, apples, beets, and tomatoes are especially sensitive to a deficiency of boron, beans are easily harmed by a slight excess of boron.

To treat soils deficient in manganese you may use about a tablespoonful of manganese sulfate per 100 square feet. If plants are already suffering chlorosis from manganese deficiency, a 1- or 2-percent solution of manganese sulfate may be sprayed on the plants, as with iron.

Zinc deficiency is rather uncommon except with citrus, pecans, and sweet corn. All plants need at least a little. Where deficiencies are suspected, zinc sulfate may be sprayed or applied to the soil in the same amounts as recommended for manganese sulfate.

Copper deficiencies are most likely in newly developed peat soils or in old, highly leached sandy soils. Applications of copper sulfate should not exceed 1.5 teaspoonfuls on peat soil for 100 square feet.

Very old, leached soils may have too little molybdenum for growing clover in the lawn mixture. If you suspect such a deficiency you may use approximately one-half teaspoonful of sodium molybdate for each 100 square feet. Excessive amounts are toxic.

Sulphur is a limiting factor in parts of the Pacific Northwest, the Northern Lake States, and some of the highlands of the Middle Atlantic States far from cities or industrial establishments. If ordinary superphosphate is used, either directly or in low-analysis mixed fertilizers, sufficient sulfur is obtained that way. If a deficiency is known or suspected, it may be overcome by the use of ordinary powdered sulfur at the rate of about 1 cupful for 100 square feet. Certainly it is not needed on many gardens.

Fertilizer companies offer to gardeners a few special mixed fertilizers to supply the minor nutrients. Those from dependable companies are good to use if you are sure that none of the nutrients is already present in excessive amounts.

The amounts of fertilizer materials discussed so far are based upon broadcast applications over an area. Once the soil for the kitchen garden is well built up in fertility—especially in calcium, magnesium, phosphorus, potassium, and the trace elements—it is usual to place the fertilizer in bands about 1.5 inches beneath and to one side of the seeds. You may dig a V-shaped trench on each side of the guide line for the row and add the fertilizer. These little trenches may be filled, and a shallow one made for the seeds themselves directly on the line for the row. Similar local placement can be made in bands around individual tomato plants, cabbages, and others. For such local placement, the recommended amounts of fertilizers are reduced by about half.

With high applications of compost or manure, the broadcast treatments may also be reduced by about half.

With sweet corn, tomatoes, and long-season salad crops, especially in gardens below the 42d parallel, it is helpful to give the plants additional nitrogen after they are well started. With tomatoes, this is after the first set of fruit. The application on sweet corn should be made when the plants are about 24 inches high. Nitrogen fertilizer is added in a small band by the side of the plants within the surface inch or so of soil. One may use about three-fourths cupful of ammonium sulfate, or its equivalent in some other nitrogen fertilizer, for each 100 feet of row, with the rows about 2 feet apart. Slightly lower amounts are used for plants in narrower rows and slightly higher if they are in wider rows. For an individual tomato plant about 2 teaspoonfuls of ammonium sulfate can be mixed into the surface inch of soil in a circular band beginning 4 inches from the plant and extending to about 12 inches from it.

These recommendations are very generalized, but they may still seem a bit complicated to a few readers. Those in a hurry can treat the "average" kitchen garden or flowerbed (if there is an "average") with 1,000 pounds of manure and 20 pounds of 10-10-10 fertilizer per 1,000 square feet and hope for fair success. This will not fit all plants.

Recommendations as to fertilizers in bulletins and those based on the results of soil tests from a reliable laboratory are usually given in terms of pounds per acre or pounds per 1,000 square feet. Since most gardeners do not have proper scales for weighing these materials, tables are given to show how such recommendations may be converted into ordinary household measures—pints, cups, tablespoons, and teaspoons. The values are not precise but are near enough for applications in the ordinary garden. One pint is equivalent to 2 cups, or 32 tablespoons, or 96 teaspoons.

A pint of water weighs 1.0427 pounds. So for materials having that same weight, one may convert directly from pounds to pints, although most of them are lighter than water. (See Part XI for measurements)

PART III
PESTICIDES

PROPERTIES OF SYNTHETIC PESTICIDES

The more extensively used of the modern synthetic pesticides are either *chlorinated hydrocarbons* (ch) or *organic phosphorus* (op) compounds. Although there is a considerable overlapping in toxicity between these groups, the acute toxicity of the organic phosphorous, is, on the average, somewhat greater than that of the chlorinated hydrocarbon compounds. However, the *chlorinated hydrocarbons*, due to their greater stability, are considered more of a residue problem than are the phosphorous materials.

The exact physiologic mechanism by which chlorinated hydrocarbons exert their toxic action is not known; however, their primary effect is on the nervous system. The chlorinated hydrocarbons are fat soluble and tend to accumulate in body fat in animals (including humans) exposed to them. Lactating animals that have been exposed also excrete the chlorinated hydrocarbon materials or their derivatives in milk. *It is important that dairy animals not be exposed to chlorinated hydrocarbon materials.* The drift of these pesticides onto forage crops which are intended for use as cattle feed should be avoided.

Among the more hazardous of the chlorinated hydrocarbons are aldrin, dieldrin and endrin. Exposure to the chlorinated hydrocarbons can be established by analysis of blood and body fat and for certain of these materials, such as DDT, by urine tests.

The organic phosphorous compounds are chemically related to the so-called "nerve gases". Their effect on the human body is also through the nervous system. However, the specific mechanism of action is known more exactly than is the case with the chlorinated hydrocarbons. The organic phosphorous materials inhibits the enzyme cholineasterase, which functions in the transmission of nerve impulses.

The following tables are shown to give users of pesticides known data which will hemp them to choose the least dangerous of these chemicals when synthetic pesticides are deemed necessary.

Table 1. Toxicity Data On Pesticides

In the following table are shown the chemical class, the toxicity classification, and the LD50 values to rats for many of the commonly used pesticides. The chemical classes are designated as follows: C, carbamate; CH, chlorinated hydrocarbons; M, miscellaneous; N, nitro; and OP, organic phosphorus. It should be noted that the classification into toxicity groups is both approximate and relative. The classifications are as follows: (1) most dangerous; (2) dangerous; (3) less dangerous; and (4) least dangerous. The LD50 values refer to the amount of the chemical which is required to kill 50 percent of the test animals: thus, the lower figures are associated with the more toxic compounds. The LD50 values listed are for male white rats and were, unless otherwise designated, carried out under standardized conditions at the FDA, Division of Pesticides, Toxicology Branch Laboratory, Atlanta, Georgia. Estimates of comparative toxcity based on these figures should be meaningful. The values shown in parenthesis were determined by other laboratories. It should be kept in mind that there may be differences in susceptibility to these chemicals between the rat and man and thus estimates of toxic hazard based on these figures may not be exact.

Insect Groups

GRASSHOPPERS, ROACHES, AND THEIR KIN (Orthoptera)   Medium to large insects. Live on land. Forewings leathery. Hindwings folded fan-like (some have no wings). Development gradual. Chewing mouth-parts.

EARWIGS (Dermaptera)   Small insects with typical pincer-like tail. Usually four small wings. Segmented antennae. Development gradual.

TERMITES (Isoptera)   Ant-like insects, small and soft-bodied. Some have four long wings. Live in colonies. Specialized "castes" for working, fighting. Chewing mouth-parts. Development gradual.

LICE (Anoplura)   Small, wingless insects with piercing and sucking mouth-parts. Body flattened. Legs with claws for clinging to warm-blooded animals.

LEAFHOPPERS, APHIDS, AND SCALE INSECTS (Homoptera)   Small to medium insects, most with two pairs of similar wings held sloping at sides of body. Jointed beak for sucking attached to base of head. Land insects. Some scale-like.

TRUE BUGS (Hemiptera)   Range from small to large in size. Two pairs of wings, with forewings partly thickened. Jointed beak for sucking arises from front of head. Development is gradual.

DRAGONFLIES AND THEIR KIN (Odonata),   Fairly large insects with two pairs of long, equal-sized wings. Body long and slender. Antennae short. Immature insects are aquatic. Development in three stages.

MAYFLIES (Ephemerida) **AND STONEFLIES** (Plecoptera)   Both with two pairs of transparent, veined wings. In mayflies, hind wings are smaller; in stoneflies they are larger. Mayflies have long, 2- or 3-pronged tails.

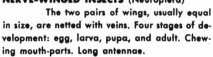

NERVE-WINGED INSECTS (Neuroptera)   The two pairs of wings, usually equal in size, are netted with veins. Four stages of development: egg, larva, pupa, and adult. Chewing mouth-parts. Long antennae.

SCORPIONFLIES (Mecoptera)   Small insects with two pairs of slender, generally spotted wings. Legs long. Antennae long also. Beak-like, chewing mouth-parts. Larvae live in soil.

CADDISFLIES (Trichoptera)   Most larvae live in fresh water. Some build ornamented case. Adults with two pairs of wings with long, silky hairs and with long antennae. Mouth-parts reduced.

MOTHS AND BUTTERFLIES (Lepidoptera)   Medium to large insects with two pairs of scaly wings. Sucking mouth-parts. Antennae knob-like or feathery. Development in four stages.

FLIES AND THEIR KIN (Diptera),   Two-winged, small to medium insects, with sucking mouth-parts. Antennae small, eyes large. Second pair of wings reduced to balancing organs. Development in four stages.

BEETLES (Coleoptera)   Forewings modified to thickened covers. Hind wings thin, folded. Size from small to large. Chewing mouth-parts. Antennae usually short. All have four life stages. Some aquatic.

BEES, WASPS, AND ANTS (Hymenoptera)   Small to medium-size insects; many social or colonial. Two pairs of thin, transparent wings. Hindwings smaller. Mouth-parts for chewing or sucking. Only insects with "stingers." Development in four stages.

TOXICITY DATA ON PESTICIDES

Compound	Chemical Class	Estimated Toxicity Hazard to Spraymen	LD$_{50}$ (mg/kg)	
			Oral	Dermal
Abate	OP	4	4700	--
Akton	OP	3	146	177
Alar	M	4	8400	--
Aldrin	CH	2	39	98
Aramite	M	4	(6300)	--
Azodrin	OP	1	17	120
Baygon	OP	2	83	>2400
Baytex (Entex)	OP	3	215	330
BHC	CH	3	600	--
Bidrin	OP	1	21	43
Binapacryl (Morocide)	N	3	63	810
Bromophos	OP	4	1600	4700
Bux	C	2	(95)	(242)
Captan	M	4	(15,000)	--
Carbaryl (Sevin)	C	4	850	>4000
Carbofuran (Furadan)	C	1	8.7	>1000
Carbophenothion (Trithion)	OP	2	30	54
Chlordane	CH	3	335	840
Chlorobenzilate	CH	4	1040	--
Co-Ral	OP	3	41	860
2, 4-D	M	4	(500)	--
Dasanit	OP	1	4.1	19
DDD (TDE) (Rhothane)	CH	4	>4000	--
DDT	CH	4	113	2510
Delnav	OP	2	43	235

> more than the amount shown

Compound	Chemical Class	Toxicity Classi-fication	LD50 (mg/kg) Oral	LD50 (mg/kg) Dermal
Dessin	N	2	59	--
Demeton (Systox)	OP	1	6	14
Diazinon	OP	3	108	900
Dicapthon	OP	3	400	790
Dichloroethyl ether	M	3	(105)	--
Dichlorovos (DDVP)	OP	2	90	107
Dieldrin	CH	2	46	90
Dilan	CH	4	600	6900
Dimethoate	OP	3	215	--
Dinitrocresol (DNOC)	N	2	(26)	--
Dinitrobutylphenol (DNOSBP)	N	2	(37)	--
Dipterex (Dylox)	OP	3	630	> 2000
Di-Syston	OP	1	7	15
Dyfonate	OP	1	(7.9)	(147)
Endosulfan (Thiodan)	CH	3	43	130
Endrin	CH	2	18	18
EPN	OP	2	36	230
Ethion	OP	3	65	245
Fundal	M	3	300	325
Galecron	M	3	300	325
Gardona	OP	4	1125	4000
Guthion	OP	3	13	220
Heptachlor	CH	3	100	195
Imidan	OP	3	113	2000
Kelthane	CH	4	1100	1230
Kepone	CH	3	125	> 2000
Lead Arsenate	M	3	1050	2400
Lindane	CH	3	88	1000
Malathion	OP	4	1375	> 4444
Methomyl (Lannate)	C	1	(17)	> (1500)
Methoxychlor	CH	4	--	> 6000
Methyl parathion	OP	2	14	67
Mevinphos (Phosdrin)	OP	1	6	5
Mirex	CH	4	740	> 2000
Monitor	OP	1	(18.9)	(118)
Morestan	M	4	1800	> 2000
NAA	M	4	(1000)	--

> more than the amount shown

Compound	Chemical Class	Toxicity Classification	LD$_{50}$(mg/kg)	
			Oral	Dermal
Naled (Dibrom)	OP	3	250	800
Nicotine	M	2	83	285
Omite	M	4	1480	--
Oxydemetonmethyl (Meta-Systox-R)	OP	2	47	173
Parathion	OP	1	13	21
Perthane	CH	4	>4000	--
Phorate (Thimet)	OP	1	2	6
Phosphamidon	OP	2	24	143
Phostex	OP	4	350	480
Piperonyl butoxide	M	4	(11,500)	--
Ronnel (Korlan)	OP	4	1250	--
Rotenone	M	4	(132)	--
Ruelene	OP	3	635	--
Schradan (OMPA)	OP	1	9	15
Sulphenone	M	4	(1400)	--
Temik	C	1	0.79	3
TEPP	OP	1	1	2
Tetradifon (Tedion)	M	4	>(14,700)	--
Toxaphene	CH	3	90	1075
Tranid	C	2	30	>2000
Vapam	M	3	(800)	--
VC-13	OP	3	(270)	--
Zectran	C	2	37	1500-2500
Zinophos	OP	1	6	17
Zolone	OP	2	(96)	>(2000)

> more than the amount shown

Table 2. Different Formulations Of Pesticides

The common type of insecticide formulations are wettable powders, emulsifiable concentrates, dusts, solutions, aerosols, baits, granules, and flowables.

Wettable powders (WP) are dry forms of insecticides in which the toxicant is adsorbed or absorbed on powders that can be readily mixed with water because a wetting agent has been added. These form a suspension-type spray which must be kept agitated in a sprayer tank.

Emulsifiable concentrates (EC) contain an insecticide and an emulsifying agent in a suitable solvent. These are diluted with water to form an emulsion and applied as sprays.

Dusts (D) are usually made by diluting the toxicant with finely ground, dried plant materials or minerals. These include wheat, soybean, walnut shells, talc, clay or sulfur.

Solutions are liquid forms of insecticides which are dissolved in suitable solvents such as petroleum distillates, or liquid gas. Oil-base cattle sprays, household sprays, and gas-propelled aerosols are examples of insecticide solutions.

Aerosols are air suspensions of solid or liquid particles of ultramicroscopic size which remain suspended for long periods.

Baits consist of a poison or poisons plus some substances which will attract the insect.

Granules (G) are formed by impregnating the insecticide upon an inert carrier of 30 to 60 mesh particle size.

Soluble powder (SP) - a power formulation that dissolves in water.

Flowable (FI) - a liquid or viscous concentrate of suspendible pesticide in water.

Fumigant - a substance or mixture of substances which produce gas, vapor, fume or smoke intended to destroy insects, bacteria, rodents, or other organisms.

Table 3. Equivalents For Teaspoonful, Tablespoonful and Cup

The weight of solid insecticides varies so greatly that it is not possible to give accurate measures in terms of teaspoons, tablespoons, or cups.

A measuring cup and measuring spoons, the latter obtainable in several sizes, are useful in making dilutions under practical conditions where great accuracy is not required. The values given below are also useful in transposing the precise measurements of the laboratory into commonly used and understood units when an insecticide is recommneded to home gardeners.

1 teaspoon	= 1/3 tablespoon	= 0.17 ounce
1 tablespoon	= 3 teaspoons	= 1/2 ounce
1 ounce	= 2 tablespoons	= 1/8 cup
2 cups	= 16 ounces	= 1 pint
1 cup	= 8 ounces	= 1/2 pint

16 tablespoons {
¼ Quart
½ Pint (1 cup)
8 Fluid ounces
237 Milliters

1 pint	= 2 cups	= 1/2 quart	= 1/8 gal.	= 16 fl. ounces
1 quart	= 2 pints	= 1/4 gallon	= 32 fl. ounces	
1 gallon	= 4 quarts			

93

TABLE 4 - DILUTION FOR WETTABLE POWDER AND EMULSIFIABLE CONCENTRATES

Type of Material	Quantities of Material for Indicated Quantities of Water			
	100 Gallons	5 Gallons	3 Gallons	1 Gallon
Wettable powder	5 lbs.	15 T.	10 T.	3 T.
	4 lbs.	13 T.	8 T.	8 t.
	3 lbs.	10 T.	6 T.	2 T.
	2 lbs.	8 T.	4 T.	4 t.
	1 lb.	3 T.	2 T.	2 t.
	1/2 lb.	5 t	1 T.	1 t.
Emulsifiable concentrate	5 gals.	1 qt.	1 1/4 pts.	13 T.
	4 gals.	1 1/2 pts.	1 pt.	10 T.
	3 gals.	1 1/4 pts.	3/4 pt.	1/4 pt.
	2 gals.	3/4 pt.	1/2 pt.	5 T.
	1 gal.	1/2 pt.	8 T.	3 T.
	1 qt.	3 T.	2 T.	2 t.
	1 pt.	5 t.	1 T.	1 t.

TABLE 5 - EQUIVALENT QUANTITIES FOR LIQUID INSECTICIDE DILUTIONS IN WATER

Dilution	100 gals.	50 gals.	25 gals.	12 1/2 gals.	10 gals.	6 1/4 gals.	5 gals.	3 1/8 gals.	2 1/2 gals.
1:50 (2%)	2 gals.	1 gal.	2 qts.	1 qt.	1.6 pts.	1 pt.	12.8 oz.	1/2 pt.	6.4 oz.
1:100 (1%)	1 gal.	2 qts.	1 qt.	1 pt.	12.8 oz.	1/2 pt.	6.4 oz.	4 oz.	3.2 oz.
1:200	2 qts.	1 qt.	1 pt.	1/2 pt.	6.4 oz.	4 oz.	3.2 oz.	2 oz.	1.6 oz.
1:400	1 qt.	1 pt.	1/2 pt.	4 oz.	3.2 oz.	2 oz.	1.6 oz.	1 oz.	0.8 oz.
1:600	1 1/2 pts.	3/4 pt.	6 oz.	3 oz.	2.4 oz.	1 1/2 oz.	1.2 oz.	3/4 oz.	0.6 oz.
1:300	1 pt.	1/2 pt.	4 oz.	2 oz.	1.6 oz.	1 oz.	0.8 oz.	1/2 pt.	0.4 oz.
1:1600	1/2 pt.	4 oz.	2 oz.	1 oz.	0.8 oz.	1/2 oz.	0.4 oz.	1/4 oz.	0.2 oz.
1:3200	4 oz.	2 oz.	1 oz.	1/2 oz.	0.4 oz.	1/4 oz.	0.2 oz.	1/8 oz.	0.1 oz.

TABLE 6 EQUIVALENT QUANTITIES FOR SOLID INSECTICIDE DILUTIONS IN WATER

100 gals.	50 gals.	25 gals.	12 1/2 gals.	10 gals.	6 1/4 gals.	5 gals.	3 1/8 gals.	2 1/2 gals.
4 oz.	2 oz.	1 oz.	1/2 oz.	0.4 oz.	1/4 oz.	0.2 oz.	1/8 oz.	0.1 oz.
1/2 lb.	4 oz.	2 oz.	1 oz.	0.8 oz.	1/2 oz.	0.4 oz.	1/4 oz.	0.2 oz.
1 lb.	1/2 lb.	4 oz.	2 oz.	1.6 oz.	1 oz.	0.8 oz.	1/2 oz.	0.4 oz.
2 lbs.	1 lb.	1/2 lb.	4 oz.	3.2 oz.	2 oz.	1.6 oz.	1 oz.	0.8 oz.
3 lbs.	1 1/2 lbs.	3/4 lb.	6 oz.	4.8 oz.	3 oz.	2.4 oz.	1 1/2 oz.	1.2 oz.
4 lbs.	2 lbs.	1 lb.	1/2 lb.	6.4 oz.	4 oz.	3.2 oz.	2 oz.	1.6 oz.
5 lbs.	2 1/2 lbs.	1 1/4 lbs.	3/4 lb.	8 oz.	5 oz.	4 oz.	2 1/2 oz.	2 oz.

NON-SYNTHETIC PESTICIDES AND THEIR PROPERTIES.

Publications are available through your county agent on control of garden and animal pests relying chiefly on short residual, low hazard, synthetic insecticides such as malathion, diazinon, carbaryl, dicofol, naled, korlan (ronnel) and others.

The following recommendations are not based entirely on nonpesticide approaches. The few suggested pesticides are not synthetics but are now hazard materials derived from plants, dormant and summer petroleum oils, and lime-sulfur and elemental sulfur.

Pyrethrins.

These insecticides are derived from the dried flowers of a species of *Chrysanthemum* and have been used for controlling insects since ancient times. They have the property of "Quick knockdown" and very short residual effects. Therefore, they must be used often. They are sold most frequently with an activator or synergist (piperonyl butoxide, piperonyl cyclonene, or some other synergist). The use of pyrethrins without these low hazard and safe activators would be much less effective, difficult to obtain, and almost prohibitive in cost. An insecticide chemically similar to pyrethrins has been developed. Called allethrin, it has similar properties to pyrethrins. The pyrethrins kill insects only by contact. They are effective against a wide range of garden pests especially the soft-bodied forms, but will not control mites. Do not spray around fish ponds. Consult the labes for specific usages. Sprayed edible portions of fruits and vegetables can be safely eaten soon after application, but read and follow the label carefully.

Rotenone.

For centuries natives of tropical Africa and South America used this plant derivative as a fish poison. Fortunately, although this chemical is highly toxic to most cold-blooded animals, it is safe for most warm-blooded types, including man. Natives make powder of the root of the *Derris* plant or related plants containing rotenone and place the material in a lake or stream to kill fish. The fish die quickly and can then be eaten. This chemical is still used to rid lakes from unwanted "trash" fish. In the mid-19th century, its properties as an insecticide were discovered and it became widely used until the mid-forties, when DDT and other synthetics largely replaced it. It has longer residual action than the pyrethrins, but also requires repeated applications. *Rotenone is probably the best general-purpose, nonsynthetic garden insecticide available.* It can be used either as a dust or spray and kills a wide range of garden insects such as caterpillars, aphids, and certain beetles, but is ineffective against spider mites and soil insects. Read the label carefully for specific usages.

Nicotine

This old-timer unfortunately controls only aphids, related soft-bodied sucking insects, thrips, and a few species of caterpillars. It does not control most chewing insects. It is derived from the tobacco plant and is usually sold as a 40 per cent liquid concentrate of nicotine sulfate (Black Leaf 40) which is then diluted with water and applied as a spray. Nicotine dusts are not normally sold for garden use because of the irritation to the operator. Nicotine is much less effective when applied during cool weather. It has short residual effects and can be used on vegetables very close to harvest. *Nicotine concentrate is extremely poisonous.*

There are several other plant-derived insecticides, such as sabadilla, Ryania, and hellebore, but unfortunately, with the exception of Ryania, which is used primarily for codling moth on apples and pears in southeast Canada, these are rarely available in parts of the U.S.

Dormant and Summer Oils

Petroleum oils have been used for insect control as early as 1787 and are still popular, although not used as extensively as they might. *Apply them only on woody plants.* There are two principal types: the dormant oils which should only be applied on trees or shrubs which are in a dormant or delayed-dormant condition, and summer oils which can be used during the growing season but are also restricted to *woody plants.* To apply a strictly dormant oil during the growing season will severly burn foilage. For summer use, be certain to purchase oil especially prescribed for this purpose and apply only on those plants for which the material is recommended. There are some special oils which can be applied either summer or winter; however, the concentration used in summer is far less.

Oils control many insects and their eggs, such as overwintering leafrollers, and aphid and mite eggs, as well as nymphs and adults of aphids, scale insects, and mites. These oils must be first diluted with water. They contain emulsifying agents which facilitate their mixing when added to water. The oils cause little or no harm to most beneficial insects and resistance of pests to these sprays does not occur. They are particularly nonhazardous to human health.

Lime-Sulfur [Liquid]

This old-timer is still in commercial use. You use it much the same as for the dormant oils diluted with water. Do not apply to apricot trees at any time; you may injure the foilage. *Use only on woody plants and only during the dormant season,* or up to prebloom on some plants. The only exception is on caneberries where it can be used for dryberry mite and redberry mite in the spring when vegetative buds are ½ inch long. This material is particularly effective against pearleaf blister mites, rust mites and their close relatives, as well as for many insect eggs. These sprays also have fungicidal value. On fruit trees, lime-sulfur is often mixed with dormant oil to increase its efficiency. Use lime-sulfur with caution when you treat ornamentals near your house. The spray drift when dried is most difficult to remove from buildings and may cause stains on all types of painted surfaces.

Elemental Sulfur.

This finely ground powder can be applied either as a dust or spray. In addition to controlling fungus diseases, it will also control spider mites, especially during hot weather. Warning: do not use sulfur on most vegetables just prior to harvest if you plan to can the produce. *Small amounts of sulfur in the can will produce sulfur dioxide which will cause the container to explode. It may also cause off-flavor.* Sulfur can be used safely on berries and other fruits without these hazards and on vegetables eaten fresh, dried, or processed for freezing. Sulfur is very safe—in fact it is an element essential for good health.

Soaps as Insecticides

Soap diluted with water has been recommended for certain soft-bodied insects, such as aphids, since 1787. Most often these soaps were derived from either plants (coconuts, olive, palm, cotton seed) or from animal fat, such as whale oil, fish oil, or lard. Vegetable or plant-derived soaps are more effective than those derived from petroleum. Unfortunately, commercial soaps vary tremendously in composition and purity, therefore vary widely in effectiveness.

A gardener might try true soap suds from a known brand of inexpensive laundry soap against aphids on a limited scale first. Should this prove successful, the practice could be extended. Or some old-fashioned homemade soap may be prepared using inexpensive waste lard or tallow, lye, water, and borax (optional). Six pounds of fat and a can of lye will make 6 pounds of soap. (See part VII)

96

NONINSECTICIDE APPROACHES TO INSECT CONTROL

Many cultural practices reduce the susceptibility of garden plants to insect attack just as they do against disease attack.

1. Rotate your garden plot if you possibly can. This is often possible on the farm since land suitable for gardens is more readily available. If an alternative crop cannot be grown on land suitable for gardens, you can at least change the sequence of plants grown in the garden plot. Should you develop a soil insect problem, such as wireworms or white grubs, avoid growing tuber or root crops, such as potatoes or carrots. Do not grow the same kinds of garden produce in the same place each year. Avoid planting your garden on recently plowed sod.

Avoid or restrict the growing of insect-susceptible crops. Unfortunately, we have no nonsynthetic insecticides suitable for soil insects. Therefore, white grubs, wireworms, cabbage maggots, onion maggots, carrot rust fly, and other soil insects may continue to bother you. The cole crops (radishes, cauliflower, cabbage, broccoli, turnips, etc.,) are highly susceptible to attack by both foilage insects, particularly the cabbage worm, and by cabbage maggots in the soil. Minimize or discontinue planting these crops and grow instead more insect-tolerant vegetables, such as beans, peas, chard, spinach.

2. Fertilize, cultivate, and water well to induce good, healthy growth. Insect injury is less damaging on a healthy plant.

3. Use interplantings (as opposed to solid plantings of a given species) to isolate the infestation and reduce damage.

4. Handpick and destroy pests when feasible by knocking pests from foliage into a bucket containing a mixture of water and kerosene or oil.

5. Use transplants. The longer a plant is growing in a garden, the greater is its exposure to potential insect attack. For this reason, plants of the cabbage family will avoid early and often devastating attacks of cabbage maggot if you purchase healthy, mature transplants or else grow them under glass for transplanting later. A healthy transplant will more likely overcome subsequent insect attack than a small plant developing from seed in the field.

6. Cold frames. Cold frames are recommended during the early growing season, not only for preserving heat, preventing wind and hail damage, but also for preventing early insect attack.

7. Sanitation. Since many garden insects overwinter in plant debris, spade under old plants; such as spinach, lettuce, etc., during the summer or add these plant residues to your compost. The cabbage aphid, for example, may overwinter as an egg on the cabbage plant; the adult asparagus beetle overwinters in the hollow stems of asparagus; and several species of leafhopper overwinter in or on plant debris. Immediately dispose of your cull onions as the onion maggot will continue to breed in them. Whenever a garden plant is no longer producing, spade it in or relegate it to the compost pile. Keep your garden free of weeds and volunteer plants: these can be harborages of pests—particularly certain aphids which may transmit disease organisms.

8. Cultivation. Cultivating a garden exposes those stages of pests which live near the surface of the soil to birds and injures or kills some insects. Fall cultivation is preferred since it also exposes pests to the rigors of winter.

9. Other methods. There is much publicity on the use of light traps, reflective materials such as aluminum foil, irradiation, electric shock, repellents, and the use of sex hormones. None of these methods can be recommended for the gardener at present, although eventually they may be of considerable value.

BIOLOGICAL CONTROL OF INSECT PESTS

Biological control is the use of any form of life to control a pest. A controlling

agent may be a disease organism, a predacious or parasitic insect, predacious spiders and mites, insect-feeding birds, rodents, toads, or other vertebrates. A number of companies now supply insect and mite predators and parasites to gardeners and farmers. For a current and complete listing, refer to any magazine on organic gardening. Many of these beneficial organisms occur naturally, but often effective numbers develop too late to control the pest before severe damage occurs. One must keep in mind also that when one introduces an insect to prey upon or parasitize a pest animal, its numbers can only be increased in nature if it has sufficient prey to feed upon. If you are experiencing little insect damage or the pest species are in low numbers or absent, the beneficial insects or other animals must move elsewhere, where food is available to survive. To allow prey insects or other animals that feed on pests to increase in number sufficiently to control pest insect, you must accept a certain amount of insect damage. You can't have insect-free garden produce and encourage beneficial insects at the same time. Releasing predators or parasites can be very beneficial in establishing them in new areas.

The insecticides mentioned in this section are definitely less hazardous to beneficial insects than many of the synthetic pesticides, *but*, they should be used only when absolutely necessary in order to preserve as many beneficial forms as possible.

Birds are far more important in preventing insect outbreaks than in controlling them. All bird species feed upon insects to some degree. The flycatchers, swallows, warblers, vireos, creepers, nuthatches, and woodpeckers are almost entirely insectivorous, while blackbirds, robins, crows, gulls, magpies and even the birds of prey, the hawks and owls, commonly feed on insects. To develop bird numbers near gardens one must encourage those species which feed largely upon insects. If you encourage all species of birds, including those which damage gardens, such as starlings, robins, blackbirds, etc., you may be asking for trouble. Insect-feeding birds can best be encouraged by providing cover, supplementary feed, and prevention of predation from cats and other predators.

Many insectivorous birds can be attracted to your home by planting those ornamentals which provide suitable bird cover and food. Some especially valuable plants are:

	Hawthorn
	Highbush Cranberry
Dogwood	Cherry
Mountain Ash	Wild Plum
Russian Olive	Coteneaster
Firethorn	Red Cedar
Crabapple	Bittersweet
Elderberry	Holly
Sumac (Aromatic and Staghorn)	Sunflowers

PART IV ANIMAL HUSBANDRY

BEEF CATTLE

You can convert feeds produced on your farm into beef under a number of systems:

1. Beef breeding herd, with all calves except necessary replacements sold as feeders at weaning or at yearling ages. A variation of this system, more important in the South than elsewhere, is to sell fat calves for slaughter at weaning.

2. Beef breeding herd combined with feeding operation. All surplus young cattle fattened on the farm where produced.

3. Feedlot operations with purchased feeder cattle.

4. Combination grazing and feeding operations with purchased feeder cattle.

5. Dual-purpose breeding herd, with calves either fattened on farm where produced or sold to feeders.

The particular system of beef production that will suit your farm depends on—
• Size of your farm.
• What markets are available in your area.
• Your financial situation.
• How much help is available and what you pay for it.

You can vary your feeding plan—the ratio of concentrates to roughage—to use your available feed to the best advantage. Table 1 gives realistic estimates of the amounts of feed required per head for various production programs. Cost of feed \will dictate, in the end result, how much can be economically used. Beef production has been swinging back to more grasses, roughages and less grains because of recent record high prices of grains.

Cow herds are particularly adapted to farms that produce large amounts of pasture and harvested roughage and limited amounts of grains. Drylot full feeding of weaned calves, either steers or heifers, requires no pasture—only moderate amounts of harvested roughage and relatively large amounts of grain.

Other feeding operations with older cattle and deferred feeding systems with calves effectively use larger proportions of roughage than calf feeding systems. These operations, however, also require grain production on the farm or a local source of grain at reasonable prices if they are to be successful.

Your farm may be best adapted to a system in which cattle are both raised and fattened. For example, part of your farm may be rough, broken, non-tillable land that is best suited for grazing cow herds. If your farm also has tillable land from which you can harvest grain and roughage, a system of fattening the animals raised as calves or yearlings may be your choice.

Dual-purpose cattle systems were an important part of the Nation's cattle economy in earlier years. They have become less important with the trend toward larger farms, more specialization, more expensive labor, and more rigid sanitary requirements for the production of dairy products for human use.

Today, the dual-purpose cattle system probably is suitable only to small or medium-sized farms in areas where there is not a ready market for fluid milk and where unpaid family labor is available.

This section discusses the management of beef-cow herds. Suggestions are included on raising the calves produced to market ages.

99

TABLE 1.—*Approximate amount of feed required per head under various beef-production programs* [1]

Program	Pas-ture	Average per day			Average per year or per animal		
		Har-vested roughage (hay equiva-lent)	Grain	Protein supple-ment	Har-vested roughage (hay equiva-lent)	Grain	Protein supple-ment
1. 1,000-pound beef cow and calf to weaning (no creep):	*Days*	*Pounds*	*Pounds*	*Pounds*	*Pounds*	*Pounds*	*Pounds*
Pasture	215						
Winter lot, 150 days		20		1	3,000		150
2. Additional to creep-feed calf for 100 days			5			500	
3. Feeding steer calves from 450 to 950 pounds:							
Dry lot, 250 days (average daily gain, 2 pounds)		5	12	1.5	1,250	3,000	375
4. Feeding steer calves from 450 to 1,050 pounds: [2] Winter, 150 days (average daily gain, 1.5 pounds)		8	5	1			
Pasture, 120 days (average daily gain, 1.5 pounds)	120				1,900	2,150	250
Dry lot, 100 days (average daily gain, 2.0 pounds)		7	14	1			
5. Feeding heifer calves from 400 to 750 pounds:							
Dry lot, 200 days (average daily gain, 1.75 pounds)		4	11	1	800	2,200	200
6. Feeding yearling steers from 700 to 1,050 pounds:							
Dry lot, 150 days (average daily gain, 2.30 pounds)		7	13	1	1,050	1,950	150
7. Feeding 2-year-old steers from 950 to 1,200 pounds:							
Dry lot, about 100 days (average daily gain, 2.5 pounds)		10	15.8	1.1	1,000	1,580	110
8. 1,200-pound dual-purpose cow milked 250 days and her calf to weaning [3]	215				4,000	1,300	650

[1] This table is based largely on published data. Amounts are approximate and will differ in various sections of the Nation, particularly because of differences in the length of the grazing seasons.

[2] Deferred Kansas System.

[3] Assuming that the cow is milked 250 days and produces 6,500 pounds of milk. She is fed a 16-percent concentrate mixture at the rate of 1 pound for each 4 pounds of milk produced, and is fed a protein supplement during her dry period (winter).

NOTE: This data was published prior to historically high grain prices of the early 1970's.

100

Size of Herd and Expected Production

The herd should include 20 to 25 cows. One bull can service a herd of 25 or somewhat larger. Small herds cost more per cow for bull service. Often, inferior bulls are used in small herds—and calf quality is lower.

Partnership or community ownership of bulls or use of artificial insemination may make smaller herds feasible. Artificial insemination is successful with beef cattle if the cows are observed carefully so that heat can be detected accurately, but it may not be available in some areas.

The profit you can expect from your beef herd depends to a large extent on the percentage of cows that produce calves each year. A survey in 1955 indicated that less than 80 percent of the Nation's beef cows produced calves each year. Properly managed farm herds should exceed this figure, but herds with average calf crops of above 95 percent over a period of years are exceptional. A calf crop of 90 percent is about the attainable average under good management.

Weaning weights vary with the type of cattle and feed supplies, but your calves should weigh an average of 450 to 500 pounds at 7½ to 8 months of age if you are to make money.

Selecting Breeding Stock

Crossbred calves of British types (Shorthorn, Hereford and Angus) have conflicting results in limited experiments, but they probably are more vigorous and grow faster on the average than purebreds or grades with parents of similar quality. However, their superiority is not great, and it is difficult for a small-herd owner to follow a systematic crossbreeding program.

Unless you have a herd large enough to use two or more sires, you probably should use a bull of the same breed as your cows. This will involve a period of "grading up" if you start with a mixed or nondescript group of cows. In some areas, it is difficult to market crossbreds to advantage.

In the Deep South, experiments have shown that crosses between Brahman and British breeds exhibit vigor and growth rates superior to either parental type. They produce carcasses equal to or only slightly inferior to those from British-type cattle at least when marketed at young ages. The value of Brahman blood is particularly apparent in the cow's calf-raising ability. If you live in an area where some Brahman blood is desirable, you can use a continued crossbreeding program or grades or purebreds of one of the new breeds based on Brahman-British crossbred foundations.

More important than selecting the breed or the crossbreeding plan is selecting breeding stock from within the breed or breeds chosen.

Selecting Herd Bulls

If you can find one, an older bull that has been proved on the basis of his progeny to be a superior breeding animal probably would be your "best buy," provided he is free of reproductive disease. Such bulls seldom are available, however, so you probably will be forced to purchase young, untried bulls.

A bull 12 to 14 months of age can be handbred to 20 to 25 cows in a season or can be allowed to pasturebreed smaller herds. Using bulls this age is risky, however, since their fertility and breeding behavior tend to be uncertain. It is preferable to use a bull at least 18 months old. Under pasture breeding conditions, bulls of this age and older usually will breed 25 to 30 cows satisfactorily in a 70- to 120-day breeding period.

Consider the following factors in selecting a young bull:

• He should be from a sire and dam with good fertility records. If possible, choose a bull from a sire and dam whose other offspring have above-average performance records.

• He should have been raised by his own mother and have had a satisfactory weaning weight. Such a bull will have a good chance of transmitting satisfactory calf-raising ability to his daughters and thus contribute to the longtime improvement of the herd's performance.

• He should have exhibited good gaining ability after weaning and should have a high weight-for-age at 12 to 14 months of age.

• He should be a thick-fleshed animal of desirable conformation, of acceptable breed character, and of an inherent skeletal size that is compatible with producing finished progeny at popular market weights.

• He should be disease free and from a herd with a good health history.

Selecting Females

As far as possible, use the same standards when buying females for your herd as when buying bulls. Ordinarily, you cannot be so selective.

Cull the cow herd on the basis of regularity of calving and weight and quality of calves produced. If a cow's first calf is poor, her later calves are likely also to be below average. You can safely cull cows in the lower 10 to 25 percent of a herd on the basis of performance records of 1 or 2 of their calves.

For replacements in an established herd, 20 to 40 percent of the heifers raised must be saved if herd numbers are to be kept up (depending on percentage of calf crop, culling intensity among cows, and the age at which cows are replaced). Select heifers with heavy weaning weights, good rate of gain and fattening qualities, and acceptable beef-type conformation.

Keep performance records to help you cull older animals and select replacement animals intelligently. These records need not be elaborate but should include the following:

• Identification of each animal by means of ear tattoos, ear notches, brands, or neck straps.

• A record of the parentage of each calf.

• A record of the birth date of each calf.

• A weight and grade taken at or near weaning to evaluate the dam's maternal ability.

If you keep your calves past weaning age, you should feed and manage all those of each sex alike so that you can evaluate rate of gain from weights taken 6 months to a year after weaning. Grade animals at this time.

When buying herd sires or females from other herds, look for animals from herds where performance records are available. Because management practices and feed supplies have a great influence on records, do not rely solely on the absolute size of the records. Instead, select animals from among the tops in a herd.

Raising Replacement Breeding Animals

Good pasture is the best and, usually, the cheapest feed for developing replacement heifers following weaning. However, heifers usually are weaned in the fall and must be fed through the winter in dry lot. The level of feeding to be used the first winter following weaning should depend largely on whether you plan to breed the heifers at 14 to 16 months of age to calve at about 2 years of age or whether you plan to breed them to calve first at about 3 years of age.

If you plan to breed them for early calving, feed them during the first winter so that they gain 1 to 1½ pounds per day and weigh 600 pounds or more at breeding.

Table 2. Rations to Gain 1 to 1½ Pounds Per Day

	Pounds
1. Corn or sorghum silage	25 to 30
Grain	3 to 5
Protein supplement	1
2. Legume or mixed hay	12 to 15
Grain	3 to 5
3. Corn or sorghum silage	20 to 25
Legume hay	3 to 4
Grain	3 to 5
4. High-quality grass hay	12 to 15
Grain	3 to 5
Protein supplement	1

These heifers will require similar rations during their second winter just before calving.

If you postpone breeding so that heifers drop their first calves as 3-year-olds, you can feed them more limited and economical winter rations and depend on summer pasture to produce most of the growth.

Table 3. Rations That Can Be Expected To Produce Gains of ¼ to ¾ Pound Daily During the First Winter

	Pounds
1. Legume hay	4 to 6
Low-quality nonlegume roughage, such as straw, low-quality grass hay, or cottonseed hulls	6 to 8
2. Corn or sorghum silage	20 to 25
Cottonseed, soybean, or linseed meal, or other high-protein supplement	1
3. High-quality grass hay	12 to 15
4. Low-quality grass or legume hay	10 to 15
Protein supplement	1
5. Legume hay	3 to 5
Corn or sorghum silage	6 to 10
Grain	2 to 3

In many parts of the U.S. you can winter heifers more cheaply on permanent pasture than in dry lot on harvested feed even if pastures are low in quality. Feed protein supplements at the rate of 1 to 2 pounds daily if you do this.

Usually, bulls should be fed rather liberally from weaning to 12 to 14 months of age. This promotes rapid development and makes breeding use possible at minimum ages. Also, liberal rations during this period give a bull an opportunity to show his inherent ability to gain, fatten, and develop satisfactory conformation. His ability in these respects is related to the potential performing ability of his progeny. Thus, selecting and using bulls with above-average performance during this period should lead to improved herd performance.

Feeding and Caring for Breeding Bulls

As a general rule, a bull requires more feed than a cow. How much more depends on his size and age and how heavily you use him.

Fertility is likely to be best if bulls are kept in medium flesh and can exercise at will. Too much fat wastes feed and money and may result in poor fertility. Bulls that are too thin also may have breeding difficulties.

During the grazing season, good pasture will provide most of the bull's nutritional needs. Usually, however, young growing bulls need some supplementary grain to keep in satisfactory flesh. If used on a seasonal basis, most bulls are likely to lose 200 to 300 pounds during breeding season. They must gain 1 to 1½ pounds a day during the rest of the year to regain this loss.

Older bulls usually will maintain desirable condition on good pasture in summer and roughage in winter. To provide enough carotene, which the animal can convert to vitamin A, at least half of the roughage fed (dry basis) should be good legume hay or corn, sorghum, or grass silage. If none of the roughage is legume, 1 to 2 pounds daily of a high-protein supplement should be fed.

Although there is no scientific evidence to confirm their idea, many breeders think it is desirable to stop feeding silage about 30 days before the breeding season, and during the breeding season when this is possible, to improve breeding performance. One pound of protein supplement and 5 pounds of grain daily should be ample for most bulls. The condition of the bull should govern the amount of feed offered.

Do not allow the herd bull to run with the cows the whole year. If possible, keep him in a separate enclosure during the nonbreeding season. If you cannot keep him in a pasture by himself after the breeding season, pasture him with steers or pregnant cows. A bull in good breeding condition is likely to be temperamental. Always handle him with care.

The fence around the lot or corral where you keep the bull should not stop him from seeing other cattle but should be securely constructed. For an added safety factor, install a battery-operated "charged-wire" device on the inside of the fence enclosing the lot or corral. Find the best location for the wire by trial; a height of about 2 feet is suggested.

Feeding and Caring for the Cow Herd

Cows produce fewer pounds of meat per hundred pounds of live weight than any other class of farm animal. Because feed required for maintenance is roughly proportional to live weight, beef cows must be fed as much as possible on low-cost roughage and waste and byproduct feeds if they are to compete successfully with

other classes of livestock.

In all beef-cow herd operations a middle level of nutrition is the most profitable. Feeding above this level will increase expense without commensurate increase in production. Keeping cows too fat may decrease fertility and milk flow. Undue limitations on feed quality and quantity will reduce productivity—particularly the percentage of calf crop—and thus reduce net income.

Pastures are the natural feed for beef cattle, and cows on good pasture ordinarily will not need supplemental feed. Some cattlemen think that beef cows on extremely succulent pasture early in the spring benefit if they are fed some hay or other dry roughage.

If you wean your calves in the fall, you may be able to maintain your beef cow herd until well into the winter on meadow or small grain aftermath, on stalk fields after corn has been harvested, or on permanent pasture where grass has been allowed to accumulate during the late summer. They can get most of their roughage from such material—feed that might otherwise be wasted. Usually this roughage is low quality, because it is mature and low in protein. If this is so, feed about 1 pound of protein concentrate per head daily.

Start winter feeding when pasture conditions demand it and before the cows lose much weight. Supply feed in small amounts at first and increase as necessary. Usually, feed the poorest hay or silage first and save the best roughage for late winter and the calving season. In many climates you can feed your herd on permanent pasture sod. This saves cleaning and manure hauling during the busy spring season.

Feed cows, yearlings, and calves separately. Separate cows into small groups for winter feeding so that the "bossy" cows can be separated from timid ones.

Rations for dry beef cows can vary widely, because they depend on the feed available. Include a source of vitamin A in the ration. You can meet a cow's daily requirements for vitamin A by feeding about 5 pounds of green-colored hay or 15 or more pounds of silage preserved so that its green color is well maintained.

A succulent feed is desirable but not essential in the ration of a dry beef cow. Silage is the most widely used feed of this type. Corn, sorghum, and various types of grass silage are excellent. Stock carrots or other root crops also are excellent, but they are not used much because of the labor needed to grow and harvest them.

To maintain weight, a beef cow needs about 2 pounds of dry matter daily per 100 pounds of live weight. Much of this can be straw, low-quality grass hay, corn stover, ground corncobs, cottonseed hulls, and similar materials. Feed good-quality hay or silage in limited amounts or a cow will eat more than she needs and increase feed costs unduly.

Table 4. Some Examples of Suitable Rations for Dry, Pregnant Cows Weighing About 1000 Pounds

	Pounds
1. Legume or mixed grass-legume hay	16 to 25
2. Legume hay	5 to 10
Straw or low-quality grass hay	10 to 15
3. Corn or sorghum silage	30
Legume hay	5
Straw, low-quality grass hay, cottonseed hulls, ground corncobs, or other low quality roughage	Unlimited
4. Cereal straw	Unlimited
Protein supplement	1
5. Corn or sorghum silage	50 to 60
Protein supplement	1
6. Prairie or grass hay	Unlimited
Protein supplement	0.5 to 1.0
7. Grass silage	30 to 40
Straw or low-quality grass hay	Unlimited

There has been some interest in wintering cows or heifers entirely on low-quality roughage such as ground corncobs or cottonseed hulls plus 2 to 3½ pounds daily of a highly fortified protein supplement like Purdue Supplement A.

Table 5. Formula of 32-percent Crude Protein Purdue Supplement A

	Pounds per ton of mix
Soybean meal (44 percent)	1,286.2
Molasses feed (45 percent molasses)	571.6
Bonemeal	102.8
Salt	34.4
Vitamin A and D concentrate[1]	5.0

1 Concentrated cod-liver oil with potency of 2,250 International Units of vitamin A and 300 International Units of vitamin D per gram.

A ration of 14.5 pounds of ground cobs, 3.5 pounds of supplement A, and 1 pound of ground alfalfa has proved satisfactory for wintering pregnant cows. Feed prices and availability determine whether you should use rations of this general type. Cost easily can be greater for rations of this type than for more conventional rations and no evidence indicates better results.

Unless your hay or silage is of very good quality, to stimulate milk flow you must feed concentrates to cows that drop fall calves and nurse them during the winter. Add 3 to 5 pounds of a 16-percent protein concentrate mixture to any of the rations listed. Silage is especially valuable for cows nursing calves.

When cows calve in early spring before pasture is available, feed them more liberally after their calves are large enough to benefit from an increased milk flow.

Except in the Deep South most of the perennial summer pasture grasses used for permanent pastures are dormant and have low nutritional value during the winter. If you use them for grazing during winter, feed a protein supplement. Usually it is more economical to feed harvested forage for a time each winter except in the most extreme southern areas.

In much of the South, well-fertilized temporary winter crops such as rye, oats, ryegrass, or mixtures of these with crimson clover will furnish grazing during the winter months. Productivity varies greatly, depending on the severity of the winter and moisture conditions, and these crops furnish better grazing than is needed. Even cows nursing calves fatten excessively on such pastures. Grazing cows on such pastures for limited periods of 2 to 4 hours daily and feeding harvested roughage for the remainder of the daily ration can be economical and highly satisfactory.

Caring for Cow at Parturition (Calving)

The average gestation period of the cow is about 283 days, or about 9½ months. A variation of as much as 10 days either way from the average gestation length is not unusual.

As parturition approaches, the udder becomes distended with milk and there is a marked "loosening" or falling away in the region of the tailhead and pinbones. The vulva swells and enlarges considerably.

When cows calve during the grazing season, a clean pasture is the best place for calving. Chance of infection and injury is less than in a barn. Often, you can segregate cows expected to calve in a small pasture near the farmhouse where they can be frequently observed. If this is not possible, check the pasture at least twice daily during the calving season.

If you expect a cow to calve during severe weather, put her in a clean, well-ventilated box stall that has been disinfected or in a small pasture with underbrush or protected shelter. Cows in large herds normally calve without any change in ration. If you can provide individual care, reduce the daily ration as calving approaches and incorporate into the diet some mildly laxative feeds such as linseed meal or bran mash. This is helpful if the cows are on dry feed. Silage or other succulent feed is valuable at this time. However, cows getting only high-quality dry roughage usually get along well at calving time.

Most cows will calve normally without assistance. Be alert for signs of trouble and assist or call trained help if needed. If the cow has severe labor for more than 1 to 2 hours without result, assistance usually is needed.

If the calf does not immediately begin breathing when it is born, wipe out any mucus in its mouth or nostrils. Induce natural breathing either by forcing air into the lungs with a bellows or by alternate compression and relaxation of the walls of the chest.

In cold weather, protect the calf and keep it warm until it is dry and on its feet. Disinfect the navel of the newborn calf with iodine, as a precaution against navel ill.

After the cow has calved, give her all the water (preferably lukewarm) she desires. Return ration to normal in a few days. If the cow is an exceptional milk producer, she may have more milk than the calf can take the first few days. Milking out the surplus milk for a few days may make the cow more comfortable. However, many cattlemen in recent years have adopted the practice of milking only when the calf fails to nurse one or more teats. The milk output quickly adjusts to what the calf can take. Failing to remove excess milk does not increase the frequency of spoiled udders.

Age at Which to Breed Heifers

If calves are to be dropped in a herd at only one season of the year, the owner must decide whether to breed heifers to calve first as 2-year-olds or 3-year-olds. At present no general recommendation can be made.

Several experiments have been carried out on this problem. It has been found that heifers bred to calve first as 2-year-olds will raise an average of approximately 0.7 more calves during their lives than heifers bred to calve first as 3-year-olds. Mature size is affected little if at all and length of productive life apparently is not reduced.

Disadvantages of calving first at 2 years of age are:

1. Heifers raise a smaller calf crop in their first calving season than if bred to calve first at 3.

2. A higher than average number of heifers calving at 2 often fail to rebreed to calve the next year.

3. A high number (about 50 percent in one survey) of heifers require help at calving.

4. Death losses may be higher than average.

5. Calf losses usually are higher than average.

The importance of these disadvantages has varied from experiment to experiment—in some cases, results have been so bad as to discourage the practice.

It would appear that breeding to calve first at 2 is profitable and is to be encouraged if (1) heifers can be grown rapidly and weigh 600 pounds or more at breeding, and (2) experienced help will be available at calving time and will have the necessary time to give special attention to the heifers. Breeding heifers to small, fine-boned bulls will minimize calving troubles but if this is done all the resulting calves should be marketed. This usually is not feasible in small farm herds where only one bull is used annually.

Seasonal Calving

In many farm beef herds, the bull is allowed to run with the cow herd the year around with the result that calves of all ages are on hand.

Although this system may result in more calves being raised over a period of years, if your herd is small it usually is preferable to limit breeding to a season of 2 to 4 months. If you limit breeding to a short period, you can choose the most favorable season for calving for your area. This system facilitates uniform and systematic management of the calves. If your herd is large, systematic calving at two seasons a year may be desirable and may increase calving percentages slightly since cows failing to settle in one season can be bred in the next. You can breed heifers to calve first at about 2½ years of age, which may be preferable to either 2 or 3 years.

Most beef calves are dropped in the spring. If weather is suitable, have calves born 6 weeks to 3 months before pasture season begins so that the calf is large enough to use the increased milk flow when the dam goes to pasture. Because it usually is necessary to wean calves at the end of the pasture season in the fall, having them born fairly early in the spring will result in older, heavier, and more valuable calves at weaning.

Fall calving requires more harvested feed for the cow herd. In the North, fall calves seldom do as well as calves born in the spring; fall calving, therefore, is justified only under special circumstances. In the South late fall or early winter calving often is desirable because of the relative freedom from screwworms at this season. Local circumstances and feed supplies should determine the time of the breeding season.

Creep Feeding Calves

Creep feeding is feeding concentrates to nursing calves in enclosures that their dams cannot enter. (See Part VII for Creep and Feeders.)

Giving 80- to 90-day-old nursing calves access to a concentrate mixture in a creep placed in the pasture where shade and water are available and where cows gather usually increases gains and the amount of finish carried at weaning.

Whether creep feeding will be profitable depends on the system of management and, to some extent, on the milk-producing ability of the dams. Calves from dams with good bred-in milk-producing ability get little benefit from creep feeding. Creep feeding often must be resorted to in drought years when feed supplies for cows are short and their milk production is reduced.

Since milk is high in protein, grain alone is a satisfactory creep feed. Feed grain, whole, cracked, or coarsely ground. Often, adding a small proportion of protein supplement (1 part of supplement to 6 to 9 parts of coarsely ground grain) will improve palatability. Calves eat an average of about 500 pounds of feed if they have free access to creeps after they are about 90 days old. The amount eaten varies greatly from herd to herd, however.

Creep feeding often will pay (1) in purebred herds where the finish that calves exhibit at weaning may have advertising value, (2) in commercial herds when the calves are to be marketed at or soon after weaning as fat baby beeves, and (3) during drought or other emergency.

Creep feeding ordinarily will not pay if calves are to be carried through a winter on limited rations prior to grazing for one or more seasons before marketing.

Calves from Dual-Purpose Cows (Milk and Meat Breeds)

Calves from dual-purpose cows formerly made up a substantial proportion of the Nation's beef supply. Raising calves from dual-purpose cows is not likely to be

profitable unless unpaid family labor is available. They usually are raised by one of two systems. With the double-nursing system, 2 calves of about the same age are suckled by 1 cow. The calves get along nearly as well as when they run with their own mothers in a strictly beef herd, although considerably more labor is involved. With this plan, half of the cows in the herd may be used for the production of milk.

With the other system, calves are taken from their dams on the fourth or fifth day after birth and bucket fed.

To teach a calf to drink milk, first permit the calf to suck your fingers and then immediately immerse your fingers in a bucket of milk. When the calf begins to take the milk in this way, withdraw your hand from the bucket. Buckets with rubber nipples often are used. This eliminates having to teach the calf to drink. After each feeding, clean and disinfect buckets and other utensils. Use a chlorine solution or a similar disinfectant.

Three or four pounds of whole milk are enough for a day or two after weaning. If the calf refuses to drink, do not force it; take the milk away. Twelve hours later, at the next feeding time, the calf probably will take milk. Increase the quantity by about a pound a day until the calf is getting 8 to 10 pounds a day. (1 quart equals 2.15 pounds)

After feeding whole milk for 10 days to 2 weeks, gradually replace it with skim milk. Make the change over a period of 5 to 7 days. Skim milk contains less energy and less vitamin A than whole milk. Feed a small quantity of cod-liver oil or other fish oil rich in vitamin A. If you have enough skim milk, increase the amount gradually each week until you are feeding 15 to 20 pounds per calf per day. If you want to conserve the milk supply, 12 to 14 pounds will be enough, provided you feed the calves enough suitable grain mixture, a protein supplement, and good hay.

Stop feeding cod-liver oil or other source of vitamin A after calves begin to eat hay, silage, or grass, provided the hay is green and leafy or the silage or grass has some green color. Be sure the calves have access to clean, fresh water and salt at all times. Calves readily learn to eat grain and should receive a limited amount each day from the time they are about 3 weeks old. Equal parts, by weight, of wheat bran, ground oats, and coarsely ground corn or barley is a suitable grain mixture.

As soon as possible, put the calves on pasture. If pasture is not available when calves are about a month old, cut and feed some growing crop or give them a small quantity of silage or carrots. Feed calves running on green pasture or confined in a lot or corral a little clean, bright hay from a rack.

Weaning Calves

Wean calves that have been running with their dams on pasture by taking them away from the cows and confining them in a pen or barn out of sight of their dams and other cattle. Preferably, they should be far enough away from their dams to be out of hearing distance, but this is difficult on most small farms. Offer the calves some good hay and a small amount of grain during this period. Unless they were creep fed, they will eat little for a few days.

It formerly was recommended that calves being weaned be put back with their dams to nurse at increasingly less frequent intervals over a period of about 2 weeks. It was felt that this was necessary to prevent spoiled udders in cows and that it was less disturbing to the calf.

It now is known, however, that the safest and most effective method of drying off even high-producing dairy cows is to quit withdrawing the milk. The pressure built up stops further secretion. It is believed that both the dams and the calves will be better off if the calves are taken away and not put back with the cows.

109

Weaning bucket-fed calves is comparatively simple. Milk usually is withdrawn from the ration by the time they are 6 to 7 months old. If they have learned to eat hay and grain, the quantity of milk fed may be greatly reduced or eliminated several weeks earlier without stunting the calves.

Dehorning and Castrating

In commercial herds, and often in purebred herds, it is advisable to dehorn calves of horned breeds. This can be done most easily before the calves are 3 weeks old. At that age, the tender horn "buttons" first appear. Scrape them with a knife to irritate the surface. Prevent horn growth by carefully applying the slightly moist tip of a caustic pencil (stick of potassium hydroxide). The caustic causes a scab to form on the irritated area. After a few days, the scab shrivels and falls off, leaving a hornless or "polled" head.

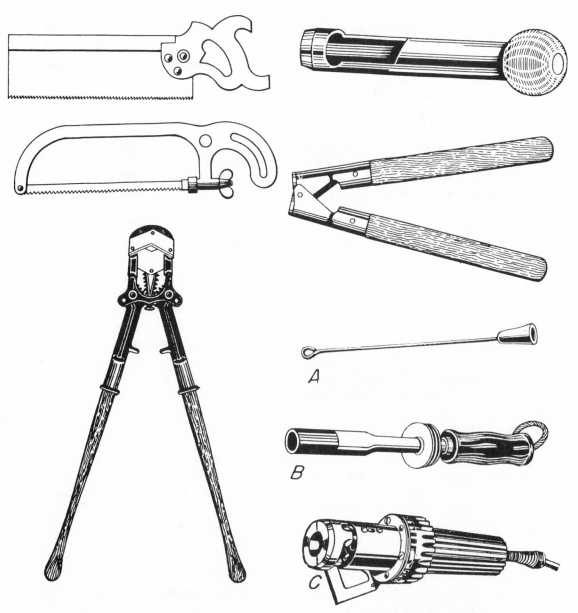

Fig. 1. Types of Dehorners for Cattle. Top Left; Hand Saws commonly used in dehorning. Top Right; Mechanical Dehorners for calves. Bottom left; Dehorner for large horns. Bottom Right; Dehorning Irons. B and C are electrically heated.

Commercial liquid and paste preparations may be easier for many people to use than the caustic sticks. Young calves also can be dehorned by applying a heated iron to the base of the horn button. Electrically heated irons are convenient and satisfactory for use on many farms. (See Fig. 1)

Male calves must be castrated to produce beef meeting American market requirements. Perform the operation preferably at a time of year when flies are not prevalent and before the calves are 3 to 4 months old. Some cattlemen castrate calves when taking birth weights.

Spaying of heifers seldom is practiced in farm herds. Contrary to the former belief, spayed heifers actually make slower gains and have no carcass superiority. Heifers should be spayed only on farms where they are being fattened and it is impossible to keep them separated from bulls.

Salt and Other Mineral Requirements

At all times, supply stock with clean, fresh water and loose or block salt. On the average, cattle will consume about 2 pounds of salt a month—less for calves and more for steers on full feed and mature cows.

Requirements of cattle for other minerals vary from area to area and with the type of ration. Consult your county agricultural agent about probable needs in your area.

In some parts of the country, iodine is deficient. This deficiency leads to goiter or "big neck" in newborn calves. In these areas iodized salt should be fed. In other areas cobalt, copper, iron, and possibly other trace minerals are known to be deficient. These should be supplied.

Calcium often will be needed if beef cattle are not fed legumes or if the pasture is low in calcium. Phosphorus is deficient in the soil in many areas. Plants grown on these soils also are low in this element. Low-quality roughage, and mature, weather hay and grasses that are low in protein and carotene also are likely to be low in phosphorus.

Ground limestone usually is the cheapest calcium supplement. Phosphorus may be supplied in the form of steamed bonemeal, dicalcium phosphate, or defluorinated phosphates. Supplements should be fed as required in specific localities. Both calcium and phosphorus supplements usually are fed in mixtures with salt.

Feeding Cattle for Market

Many farmers with beef herds find it practicable to fatten the calves raised. The system used may be immediate full-feeding on heavy concentrate rations. An increasingly popular system of handling farm-raised steers, however, is to winter them at moderate nutritional levels the first winter, graze them a season, and then full feed them for 60 to 100 days just prior to marketing. This system permits marketing 18- to 20-month-old steers at approximately 1,000 pounds that grade in the high-good to low-choice range. Heifers can be handled under either system but ordinarily should be marketed at lighter weights than steers since they fatten more rapidly.

111

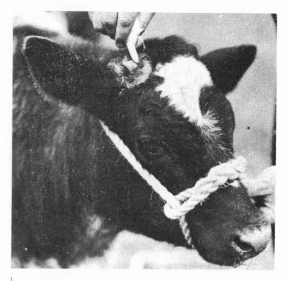

Fig. 2 — *Left*, Hair has been clipped and petrolatum applied around the undeveloped horn. *Right*, Applying caustic to the undeveloped horn.

Fig. 3 — Using a mechanical dehorner and branding in one operation.

Fig. 4 —Cattle squeeze chute.

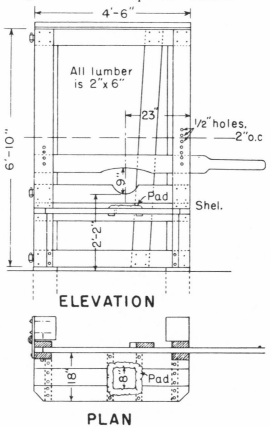

ELEVATION

PLAN

Fig. 5. —A practical type of stanchion gate. In this type the nose is placed in a hole and held there by a bar pressing downward against the top of the neck.

113

FORAGE FROM IMPROVED PASTURES

Livestock are wasteful in their grazing habits. Instinctively, they search out the most palatable plants and plant parts—literally the cream of the pasture crop – and are inclined to avoid a less palatable forage.

Recognizing this, farmers and scientists have searched for ways to encourage livestock to eat more of the forage that is available to them from pastures, thus cutting down on waste and increasing the efficiency of forage use. One way this has been done is through use of various systems that help control the availability of forage to livestock.

Three forage utilization systems that have evolved in recent years are rotation grazing, strip grazing, and green feeding. These systems can be used not only to encourage forage consumption by livestock, but also to protect plants from over-grazing and other damage.

The systems provide patterns for grazing and harvesting forage that are designed for efficient and practical management of improved grasslands. Their successful operation depends on skillful judgment that is based in turn, on an intimate knowledge of both plants and livestock.

Highly important to the success of the systems is the ability of farmers to recognize signs of inefficient forage use and to correct conditions that bring them about. These signs show up in either plants or livestock, or both. They can be avoided if grazing or harvesting is started and ended at the correct time and stage of plant growth, if the proper numbers and kinds of livestock are grazed on an area, and if plants are provided sufficient opportunity to recover before grazing or harvesting is repeated.

Skill in making these management decisions is actually the key to efficient use of pastures. With good management, it is possible to use forage efficiently with any of the utilization systems. Rotation grazing, strip grazing, and green feeding provide ways for reinforcing managerial skill with such features as planned plant rest periods and a high degree of control over grazing and harvest.

No single system of forage utilization fits all farming situations. Each farm has its own set of requirements and such factors as animal and seasonal needs for forage should be carefully considered before selecting a system.

Increasing Livestock Production with Forage

There may be a number of ways that livestock production can be increased with forage on a particular farm. These include: (1) Increasing the forage potential of a pasture through use of more productive plants and better cultural methods and by intelligent use of different plant species that mature at different times during the season; (2) decreasing waste of forage during grazing, harvesting, and feeding; (3) decreasing damage to plants from trampling or overuse; and (4) by combining two or more of these possible changes.

Pasture with a high forage yield potential is the starting point for high animal production per acre. Efforts to improve production through grazing management may be fruitless if pastures are poor. Skillful management becomes increasingly important as pastures are made more productive, because the possibilities of wasteful use and damage to plants are also increased. Dense, fast-growing plants are particularly vulnerable to damage from trampling and overgrazing.

Development of Modern Forage Utilization Systems

Modern systems for utilizing forage resulted from research and practical experience. Dating from 1930, scientists and farmers made some of the most significant contributions toward improving pastures and their use. Refinements were made

in pasture fertilization, irrigation, and other cultural practices. Plant breeders developed better pasture plants. As these were released to growers, more and more land was seeded to adapted, highly productive grasses and legumes. Annual, biennial, and semi-permanent pastures gained places of prominence alongside permanent pastures.

Interest also centered on improving methods of grazing and harvesting pasture forage. Dairy farmers, in particular, attempted to find better ways to utilize forage, extend grazing periods, and obtain more uniform levels of milk production. Some of them experimented with a grazing method developed in Germany called the "Hohenheim System." Designed especially for dairy cattle, it involved heavy fertilization. Pastures were divided into smaller grazing areas and cattle were permitted to graze the areas in rotation.

The Hohenheim system was the forerunner of modern rotation grazing. The rotation system was first used with bluegrass and other low-growing plants in permanent pastures. Later, it was found to fill an important requirement in grazing improved pastures containing erect, highly productive new species of grasses and legumes. Unlike low-growing plants, these new species proved to be especially sensitive to overgrazing and continuous grazing. The rotation system provided a way to control grazing so that the highly productive plants could be protected.

Strip grazing is a variation of rotation grazing that has been used in New Zealand and Australia for over three decades and for a shorter period in the United States. With this system, livestock are moved onto a new strip of pasture each day.

Green feeding is a modern version of a system of cutting and hand feeding fresh forage that was first used in this country more than 150 years ago. With the present system, livestock never enter the pasture, but forage is harvested by machine and brought to them.

Rotation Grazing

The rotation grazing system provides a way to utilize forage by confining livestock to an area so small that they will eat all pasture plants to a desired height in a given period of time. When grazing is completed on an area, plants are allowed to establish new growth before being grazed again. These rest periods help prevent destruction of highly productive grasses and legumes.

Maintenance of desirable pasture plants as well as more efficient utilization of forage are the two major factors that contribute to the efficiency of rotation grazing. The individual contribution of these two factors is usually difficult to determine.

Rotation grazing helps to reduce damage to forage from trampling, which can cause great waste in dense, tall crops if grazing is poorly managed. Cattle in rotationally grazed pastures usually obtain the forage they require in less time than cattle on pastures grazed continuously and therefore conserve energy for meat and milk production.

Because pastures are alternately grazed and left idle during rotation grazing, such jobs as fertilization, clipping for weed control, and irrigation can be done on areas not in use without the interference of grazing livestock. For the same reason, excess forage can easily be harvested for hay or silage, thereby, in effect, temporarily reducing the area required for grazing. This permits considerable flexibility in the number of animals that can be grazed on an area during the season.

From the standpoint of management rotation grazing is relatively simple to use. A pasture is divided into several grazing areas with electric fences. The number of grazing areas, size of the areas, and livestock numbers are adjusted so that each area is grazed to a height that best maintains the seeded species, and

the time for plant rest periods is geared to the growth rate of the pasture.

Plant growth rate varies during the season, a factor that will regulate both the number of grazing livestock and the size of the grazing areas. During the period of flush plant growth in the spring, for example, it may be impossible to move animals through all pasture areas and adequately graze each area. Surplus forage may be harvested for hay or silage. Later, as the rate of plant growth slows down, animals may graze through all areas at a relatively rapid pace.

Livestock are usually turned onto the first area as soon as they can get a "good bite", or at the earliest time compatible with the animals' obtaining a reasonable amount of forage, yet not damaging desirable plant species.

During the first round of grazing in the spring, livestock are permitted to progress through the pasture areas, grazing forage down to the recommended height, until the area on which grazing was first begun has recovered sufficiently to be grazed again. The animals are then moved back to this area and the areas untouched during the first round of grazing are cut for hay or silage.

Milk production may fluctuate during the period dairy cows are grazing an area of pasture under the rotation system. Production may be at a high level for a few days after the animals are turned onto an area, then slacken after the more nutritious plants are eaten, usually reaching its lowest point just before the cows are moved to a new area. This cyclic pattern of production usually does not lower total seasonal milk production.

A variation on conventional rotation grazing, called the split-herd system, is sometimes used with dairy cattle. The herd is divided into low and high producers, and cattle are rotated through grazing areas so that high producers are first to be turned onto a new area. They remain on the area for a short period of time, usually a week or less, then are moved to another new area. The low producers then are moved onto the pasture area partially grazed by the high producers.

The split-herd system gives high-producing cattle the advantage of being first to graze nutritious new pasture growth. Theoretically, the quality of forage they consume is consistently high. Studies indicate that some increases in milk production may be expected from this system, compared with conventional rotation grazing, provided that sufficiently large differences in milk-producing capabilities exist between the high-and low-producing groups of cows.

Strip Grazing

Strip grazing is a method of intensified rotation grazing that provides smaller grazing areas and shorter grazing periods. Livestock are moved onto new forage each day, helping to lessen the chance of fluctuations in animal production such as those sometimes experienced with conventional rotation grazing.

There appears to be no convincing evidence that strip grazing will result in appreciably greater animal production or more cow-days of grazing per acre than a well-managed rotation grazing system. In comparisons of strip and rotation grazing in which the number of animal units permitted to graze an area were kept equal, total seasonal animal production from pastures under the two system was identical.

Strip grazing is more complicated than rotation grazing because of the chore of moving livestock to a fresh strip of pasture each day. Most farmers use a single strand of electric fence that can be readily shifted from strip to strip.

Bloat is less likely to occur during strip grazing than during continuous rotation grazing because the more limited grazing area encourages cattle to eat coarse, more mature forage along with the bloat-causing immature, leafy portions of legumes.

When dairy cattle are strip grazed on pastures at the Agricultural Research Center, Beltsville, Md., the width of pasture strips is adjusted each day so that

forage is well utilized. This involves daily observation of both livestock and pasture to determine if the animals are receiving adequate forage and if there is damage to the pasture stand. As the cattle progress through the pasture, forage on ungrazed areas that obviously will not be needed for grazing is harvested for hay or silage.

Clipping of pasture areas is recommended. This practice helps control weeds, removes clumps of uneaten forage, and promotes young and nutritious forage growth. Hay and silage may be made from any pasture area if excellent growing conditions cause a surplus of plant growth for grazing.

Green Feeding

The green feeding system is also called soiling, green chop, mechanical grazing, zero pasture, and zero grazing. As some of these terms indicate, pasture forage is harvested with machinery, rather than livestock. This way, energy normally used by livestock for grazing is used in meat and milk production.

Green feeding is an adaptation of a method of cutting and feeding forage crops first used in this country in the early 1900's to supplement pastures. The early system never became generally popular because it was complex, involved much hand labor, and the growing of a succession of crops throughout the season.

Interest in feeding fresh cut forage revived with the development of high-yielding forage crops and much labor-saving machinery as field forage choppers and self-unloading wagons.

Equipment and labor requirements are still relatively high with the modern system of green feeding because forage is cut, chopped, and fed once or twice daily. On the other hand, the need for fencing, watering facilities, shade, and other requirements associated with grazing is reduced or eliminated.

A dairy herd of at least 35 to 40 cows is required to make green feeding economical.

The principal advantage of green feeding is the possibility of meeting forage needs with fewer acres than would be required with grazing. The system helps avoid waste caused by selective grazing, trampling, or fouling with droppings for two reasons: (1) livestock never enter the fields, and (2) both leaves and stems of plants are harvested and fed.

The prospect of reducing acreage requirements for forage is especially attractive on farms where operating costs are high, labor is plentiful, and where land for pasture is scarce. However, green feeding of improved pasture forage has seldom resulted in more animal products per acre than well-managed rotation grazing when animals have been allowed equal time to utilize the crop. Production per animal has also been about equal in such comparisons.

In some cases, the success reported with green feeding has resulted from not only changing the forage utilization system, but also from changing from low-yielding to high-yielding forage crops. Studies in which ladino clover—orchardgrass forage was utilized either by rotation grazing, strip grazing, or green feeding, showed no advantage in animal production that favored green feeding over the other systems.

A high degree of crop management skill is necessary for successful operation of green feeding. Excellent management is required to produce a continuous succession of crops and to harvest them and feed them during their most nutritious stage of growth.

Generally, green feeding involves more risks than a grazing system. Machinery breakdowns and rainy weather can slow down or prevent daily harvest. Some risks can be offset by providing emergency pasture near feedlots or by having an emergency supply of hay or silage. Other factors related to green feeding, but not

117

to grazing systems, include hauling of manure from feedlots, the need for surfaced feedlots, and sanitation and disease problems that may occur as a result of confining livestock to drylot. A current handicap in green-feeding is the increased cost of fuel. This is a major determining factor on whether green-feeding is feasible.

The Role of Mangement in Forage Utilization

Determination of the best way to improve livestock production through better use of forage is a complicated process because two biological systems are involved; livestock and the pasture plants. Every decision about one in some way affects the other. Understanding certain basic interrelationships that exist between plants and livestock is important in making forage management decisions. The better these interrelationships are understood, the greater are the possibilities of making effective decisions.

The forage utilization system selected for a farm should result in maximum net dollar returns from pasture and livestock. To accomplish this, it would appear that the ideal system should provide the highest possible animal production by the use of all forage that grows in a pasture. In practice, however, top animal production is possible when livestock consume only the most nutritious plants in the pasture and avoid coarse, more mature plants. This is the pattern of wasteful selective grazing cattle instinctively follow if not controlled. When livestock are compelled to eat all plants in the pasture, the overall nutritive value of the forage they consume is lowered by the mature forage plants and weeds it contains. The result is less-than-maximum animal production.

In the interest of efficiency, it is good management to compromise between obtaining maximum animal production and the using of all forage in a pasture. This compromise is accomplished through management decisions that avoid excessive waste of forage and damage to the pasture from overuse without sacrificing animal production unnecessarily to favor pasture growth. They result in a pasture utilization plan that takes into account the fact that various ages and classes of livestock have different forage requirements and the fact that ample forage should be available throughout the season, including critical production periods.

Decisions About Intensity of Pasture Use

Successful forage management decisions affect a satisfactory balance between the capacity of a pasture to produce quality forage and the capacity of livestock to produce meat or milk. This balance is mutually beneficial to the plants and livestock. In the final analysis, such management decisions involve the determination of a correct stocking rate for grazing (animal days of grazing per acre) or a correct rate of harvest for green feeding.

Accurate rates for stocking or for harvesting take into account individual animal differences. This requires an intimate knowledge of the productive capacities of the animals.

Livestock differ in their inherited capacities to produce meat and milk. Some animals may eat more forage than they can possibly convert into animal products. Others may make efficient use of a relatively high intake of forage, supplemented with concentrates, because of their inherited high capacity for production.

There also are seasonal variations in the productive capacities of pastures. A special problem occurs during the period of flush plant growth in the spring, when livestock usually cannot eat all of the forage that is available. This problem may be solved by reducing the size of the pasture area grazed and by harvesting excess forage for silage or hay, or by increasing the number of livestock grazing the pasture.

118

Signs of inefficient pasture use are most likely to develop when livestock are permitted to graze a pasture continuously with a minimum of control. The animals are free to follow their natural tendencies to select only palatable, tender leaves and plants and to avoid more mature and less palatable plants.

The signs are characterized by areas of over-mature forage, areas of extremely short forage that has been frequently and closely grazed, and changes in the pasture stand from more productive to less productive species and weeds.

Close observation of both pasture and livestock can result in early detection of the signs of inefficient pasture use. Rotational and strip grazing generally result in closer management than continuous grazing. Condition of both pasture and livestock may be observed regularly as animals are moved from area to area. Danger signs may be noted and adjustments made in the size of grazing area or the length of grazing period.

Green feeding provides an opportunity for close regulation of the use of pasture forage, since it makes possible strict control over the entire operation. Harvest may be done in a manner that prevents plant damage and waste. In addition, daily contact with livestock permits adjustments in the amount of forage fed to achieve a desired level of animal production.

Rest Periods for Plant Recovery

The rest periods for plant recovery that are an integral part of rotation and strip grazing and green feeding help bring about a balance between production and consumption of forage. Used correctly, they protect pastures from overuse and help assure that enough nutritious forage will be available to livestock throughout the pasture season.

Managing forage in such a way as to include adequate rest periods has become an important feature of the three pasture systems because the plants predominant in improved pastures are especially sensitive to close, continuous grazing or frequent harvesting. These plants are more erect and more productive than the low-growing plants in permanent pastures and include such legumes and grasses as Ladino clover, alfalfa, the fescues, coastal bermudagrass, Dallisgrass, orchardgrass, bromegrass, and timothy.

Because of their height, a larger amount of the leaf surface of plants in improved pastures may be easily eaten or trampled by livestock. Loss of leaf surface is a setback to plants. Leaves that are removed ordinarily would be used to manufacture carbohydrates for continued growth and reserves stores in roots. When defoliated, plants rely on root reserves, and continuous defoliation results in depletion of these reserves and death of the plants. If grazed too frequently and too close, the improved plants may be forced out of the pasture stand, often to be replaced by weeds.

During rest periods, forage plants produce new foliage from shoots near the ground. This foliage is highly digestible and high in protein content. When regular rest periods are provided, the plants will continually produce new shoots and the foliage remains young and nutritious. New foliage has a very high vitamin A value because it is rich in carotene. It is also rich in B-complex vitamins, vitamin E, ascorbic acid, and certain other essential vitamins. Calcium and phosphorus contents also are higher than in mature forage.

Livestock generally prefer young plants, or the young and actively growing leaves and stems of plants. In their search for these, they will pass by more mature plants. This selective grazing may be a special problem when grazing is continuous and poorly controlled. On the other hand, the greater degree of control of forage use provided by rotation grazing, strip grazing, and green feeding minimizes the problem by compelling livestock to eat all plants and plant

119

parts. Production of high-producing animals may suffer, however, if they are compelled to eat low quality forage.

The Importance of Timing

Management involves determining when grazing should be started, how long it should be continued on each pasture area, and when and how often forage should be harvested for green feeding.

For maturity, leafiness, and yield of forage at the time it is grazed or harvested are important in determining the feeding value of any pasture crop. Best yields of nutritious forage are obtained when plants are young, vegetative, and actively growing. In this stage, the plants are more palatable, more nutritious, and more digestible than when they are mature.

Grazing should be started in the spring as soon as livestock can obtain an adequate amount of forage, yet not damage the plant stand. Rotation grazing may be continued on each pasture area until such mixtures as bromegrass and alfalfa are grazed to a minimum average height of 3 to 4 inches, and mixtures such as orchardgrass and clover are grazed to an average height of 2 inches. During hot, dry weather, however, these minimum heights should be raised an inch or more. The size of strip-grazed pasture areas should be so adjusted that the forage is grazed to the minimum height desirable for the plants at the end of a 24-hour period.

The sequence for chopping for green feeding should be so timed that forage is cut when nutritious and adequate recovery periods are provided between harvests. Cutting for green feeding generally should be started when plants are in the early hay stage, which occurs a week or more after the plants are ready for grazing.

MILK GOATS

Present Status of the Industry

Goats are especially useful to those who need a small quantity of milk and do not have the room or cannot afford to keep a cow. A goat can be kept where it is impossible to keep a cow, and the goat will consume considerable feed that

Fig. 6 – A mature doe with outstanding body development and good mammary system.

otherwise would be wasted. The raising of goats is not limited to family use, however; many commercial dairies have been established successfully in areas where markets for the milk are favorable. The fact that goats are rarely affected with tuberculosis is another point in their favor. Milk goats are exceptionally clean animals and are more fastidious in eating habits than any other type of domestic animals.

Yield

About the first question that most people ask concerning milk goats is, "How much milk will one produce?" This is important, of course, as the value of a doe is estimated largely by her milk production. Even if a doe is purebred, she is of little value from the utility standpoint unless she is capable of giving a good quantity of milk. Many persons, in purchasing grade or even purebred goats, have been disappointed to find that the milk could be measured in pints and not quarts or gallons, as expected.

A doe that produces 1,000 pounds or about 500 quarts of milk (1 quart equals 2.15 pounds) during a lactation period of 10 months is considered a fair milker. A production of 1,200 pounds of milk is good, and 1,600 pounds and up is excellent provided it is produced in a lactation period of 10 months or less. Good does will produce 8 to 10 months in a year and from 8 to 15 times their weight in milk in a lactation period.

Characteristics

Goat's milk is nearly always pure white in color. The small size of the fat globules and the soft curd are two of its chief characteristics. The cream rises very slowly and never so thoroughly as in cow's milk. This condition makes impracticable the ordinary method of allowing cream to rise. It has been stated that goat's milk will not keep sweet so long as cow's milk, but tests have shown that this is not the case. The keeping quality of any milk depends on the conditions under which it is produced and handled.

In tests made by the Department of Agriculture it was found that goat's milk could be thoroughly separated in a separator. After milk testing 4.4 percent of fat was run through the separator, the milk then tested only 0.03 percent of fat.

Composition and Nutritive Properties

Goat's milk is a healthful and nutritious food. The milk of Saanen and Toggenburg goats resembles that of Holstein cows in percentage of water, lactose, fat, protein, and ash, although subject to greater variation with the advance of lactation than milk of either Holstein or Jersey cows (Table 6). The percentage of total solids in goat's milk ranged from 13.05 in February to 10.78 in August.

The small fat globules and the soft curd of goat's milk contribute to its ease of digestibility. Some persons who are allergic to cow's milk can consume goat's milk readily, due largely perhaps to its easier digestibility. In a great many cases goat's milk has proved especially valuable for infants and invalids.

The U. S. Department of Agriculture in cooperation with Johns Hopkins University conducted a series of studies on the nutritional properties of goat's milk as compared with those of the milk of Holstein-Friesian and of Jersey cows. Under the supervision of the University, normal infants were fed milk from the three sources. The milk was boiled for 1 minute and supplemented with orange juice and cod liver oil. No essential differences in health, general appearance, and well-

being of the infants were observed, good results being obtained with each milk. The gains in weight were in proportion to the total nutritive content of the milk. In these studies, no attempt was made to use babies with a history of malnutrition.

TABLE 6. Comparison of the composition of goat's milk and that of two common breeds of dairy cows.

Source of milk	Water	Total solids	Fat	Protein	Lactose	Ash
	Percent	Percent	Percent	Percent	Percent	Percent
Goats	88.02	11.98	3.50	3.13	4.55	0.80
Holstein-Friesian	87.50	12.50	3.55	3.42	4.86	.68
Jersey	85.31	14.69	5.18	3.86	4.94	.70

In one of a series of nutrition studies in Pennsylvania and Texas, a preliminary investigation was made of the value of goat's milk in the diet of growing children. This work has been summarized as follows:

"In an institutional nutritional investigation, 38 children ate the same basic dietary, with the children divided into two equal groups, each consisting of 19 children (10 girls and 9 boys). One of the groups drank 1 quart of goat's milk and the other 1 quart of cow's milk daily, in the 5-month study.

"Numerous medical-nutrition observations and tests were made on the children before the study began and at its close.

"(1) The children who drank goat's milk surpassed those who drank cow's milk to an extent which was statistically significant in the following respects: (a) Weight for the sex, age, body size, and body build; (b) skeletal mineralization, or bone density; (c) blood plasma vitamin A; (d) blood serum calcium; (e) urinary excretion of thiamine, or vitamin B_1; (f) urinary excretion of riboflavin, or vitamin B_2 and (g) urinary excretion of F_2, a fluorescent substance related to niacin.

"(2) The group of children who drank cow's milk exceeded the goat's-milk group by an extent which was statistically significant in growth, although both groups made excellent growth progress.

"(3) The goat's-milk group tended to exceed the other group in the following respects, although the differences between the two groups were not statistically significant (a) Skin dryness as observed biomicroscopically; (b) hemoglobin concentration in the blood; (c) total protein in the blood serum; (d) reflex action; (e) overall score by the medical examiner.

"(4) The two groups showed no difference in their progress from the initial to the final test in the following: (a) Skeletal maturity; (b) condition of the conjunctiva, or normally transparent covering of the eyeball; (c) corneal vascularization; (d) condition of the tongue; (e) condition of the gums; (f) condition of the skin except for unusual dryness (see above); (g) red cell count; (h) packed cell volume; (i) leucocyte or white cell count; (j) differential cell count; (k) blood plasma carotene; (l) blood plasma vitamin C; (m) protein fractions in the blood; (n) blood serum phosphorus; (o) functioning of the heart; and (p) resistance to fatigue.

"This 5-month study must be regarded as preliminary. Whereas the results of this study are strongly indicative of the fact that goat's milk has some superior qualities, the work should be extended before final conclusions are drawn."

Goat's Milk Products

Goat's milk can be utilized for the same purposes as cow's milk, although for some it is not nearly so well suited. For general use, such as drinking or cooking, the milk has proved to be very satisfactory. Where a market exists for fluid milk this is by far the most profitable. Goat's milk is less satisfactory than cow's milk for making butter, but large quantities of goat's-milk cheese are manufactured, especially in Europe.

The milk of some of the largest herds in the country is evaporated and sold in that form. Goat's milk frequently may be purchased at drug or health-food stores in evaporated, dehydrated, or powder form.

Butter

Good butter can be made from goat's milk, but ordinarily very little is produced. The cream rises very slowly, and only a portion of it reaches the top. By the use of the separator, however, practically all the butterfat can be obtained. Unless artificially colored the butter is very white and resembles lard in appearance. If colored, it resembles cow's butter, although it does not have the same texture. It can be used for the table or for cooking. A good quality of butter with no objectionable features is produced when the milk and cream are properly handled. However, when a good price is obtained for the milk, it does not pay to make butter, as cow's butter is cheaper.

Cheese

Several varieties of cheese, known under various names, are made from goat's milk. In France, goat's-milk cheese is called Chevret, or Chevrotin; in Italy, Formaggio di Capra; and in Germany, Weichkase aus Ziegenmilk (soft cheese from goat's milk). Goat's-milk cheese has a characteristic and individual flavor all its own depending on the process and cultures used. The products closely resemble cow's milk cheeses made by the same process. The cheese may be made either entirely of goat's milk or, better with from one-fourth to one-third cow's milk; the mixture materially improves the quality of the product.

Hard cheese may be made by the following method: "A junket tablet is dissolved in ½ cupful of cold water and stirred into a gallon of milk which has been heated to 88°F. After 30 minutes the curd is cut into cubes about 1 inch in diameter. For this purpose a large knife is used and after cutting in two directions vertically a horizontal cutting is made to complete the cubes. Sometimes it is convenient to make the horizontal cuttings with a bent wire.

"The container with the curd is placed in a pan of water at 100°F. This temperature is maintained so that the temperature of the curd will be 98°F. after 1 hour. The curd is stirred frequently while being heated. In from 30 minutes to 1 hour after heating, the curd is poured with the whey into a muslin bag. After 2 or 3 hours the curd can be removed and placed in a mold formed by rolling the cheese in a small square piece of muslin. This cheese ball is then placed in the container (a cylinder), using an inverted plate as a false bottom. Another plate is placed on top of the cheese. This is weighed down.

"After 24 hours the cheese is removed from the musin cloth and rubbed with salt. It is rubbed in salt again the following day. These cheeses can then be stored in a cool place and rubbed daily for a week to prevent mold growth and to get a good rind formation. This cheese is ready for eating when 10 days old. If the cheese cracks while it is curing, its surface can be rubbed with a neutral oil or butter."

Cottage cheese may also be made from goat's milk. By one method "Skim milk

is held at a temperature of about 75°F. until it develops a firm curd. When this curd is sufficently firm, it is cut into pieces about 2 inches square with a long knife or large spoon. Then the vessel containing the broken curd is placed on the edge of the stove or in a vessel of water, and heated very slowly to 100°F. The mass is kept at that temperature for about 45 minutes to firm the curd. During the heating and holding period the curd is stirred gently with a spoon or ladle to prevent it from lumping and to secure uniform heating. When it is sufficiently firm so that the pieces yield no milky whey and do not bind together when gently squeezed in the hand, the curd is poured into a porous sack or a colander to drain. The flavor and the keeping quality of the cheese will be improved if the curd is washed in cold water when the draining is practically complete. After this wash has been thoroughly drained from the curd, about 1 teaspoonful of salt is added for each pound of cheese, is mixed in well, and the product is stored in a cool place."

Goat Dairies

Numerous goat dairies are in operation in different parts of the country. These dairies have been established both for the production of milk and the manufacture of milk products. One of the largest goat dairies in the country is devoted to the manufacture of condensed milk. If only a few goats are kept it is not necessary to have much equipment, but if a considerable number of does are milked it is best to have the proper equipment for handling the work advantageously. This does not mean, however, that expensive buildings must be provided. Any clean, dry quarters free from drafts may be used. The building should have proper ventilation and an abundance of light, and be so arranged that each goat can be fed and handled properly.

Breeding and Selection

The development of superior individuals or lines of breeding in milk goats as with other animals is dependent upon the interactions of heredity and environment. Good breeding will develop outstanding individuals only if the right kind of feeding and management practices are followed. Similarly, the best feed and management possible will not produce a desirable type of goat with high milk and butterfat yields unless the individuals carry the breeding for these characteristics.

Improvement in goats is brought about chiefly through hereditary factors transmitted through the germ cells. Effort, therefore, should be concentrated toward improvement by so mating the animals as to recombine these factors in more desirable forms. The various recombinations which may take place are the hope and despair of animal breeders. Without such variations, there is no opportunity for improvement; with them there is no assurance of fixing a type without constantly selecting animals with desirable characters and discarding those with undesirable ones.

Through selection, the goat breeder has the means of controlling the inheritance of his animals. He can decide which of his animals shall have many offspring, which shall have few, and which shall have none. As a guide in estimating whether an animal has the hereditary factors that will enable it to approach the desired ideal, certain procedures are of value and should be used in practical breeding. Individuality, ancestry, and performance must all be taken into account. Each has its value or its limitations, and no single formula for the amount of attention to give to each can be generally prescribed.

125

Fig. 7. Alpine Doe

The Alpine dairy goat is a medium-to-large animal. It is the only breed with upright ears that offers all colors and combinations of colors, giving it distinction and individuality. They are hardy adaptable animals that thrive in any climate. This breed is composed of several varieties, including the British, Rock, and Swiss Alpine. The French Alpine is by far the most popular in the United States.

Fig. 8. La Mancha Buck

La Mancha

The La Mancha was developed in the late 1930's in Oregon. It was developed from a short-eared Spanish breed crossed with the leading purebreds. It has excellent dairy temperament and is an all-around sturdy animal that can withstand a great deal of hardship and yet produce. They may be any color but are distinguished by their external ears which are either absent or very short and are known as "gopher" ears. The hair is short, fine, and glossy.

Nubian

The Nubian is a relatively large, proud, and graceful dairy goat of Oriental origin. It is known for high-quality, high-butterfat milk production.

The head is the distinctive breed characteristic. The ears are long, wide, and pendulous. It is one of the largest breeds. It contains both horned and hornless animals. The colors range from black to white with many reddish shades. They may be solid in color or any combination of colors in a spotted or dappled pattern.

Fig. 9. Nubian Doe

Saanen

The Saanen is the largest of the Swiss breeds. Its predominating color is pure white to creamy white

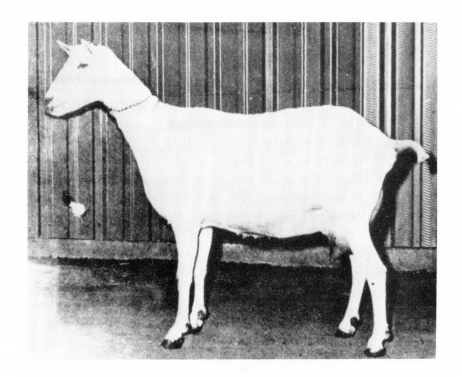

Fig. 10. Saanen Doe

with a flesh-colored muzzle. The hair is short and fine. They are generally considered a hornless breed but many have horns. The hornless animals are preferred when all other factors are equal. Ears should be erect and alertly carried.

Toggenburg

The Toggenburg is a Swiss dairy goat from the Toggenburg Valley of Switzerland. This breed is of medium size, sturdy, vigorous, and alert in appearance. The hair is short or medium in length, soft, and fine. The color is always some shade of brown with a white stripe down each side of the face. The legs are white, as are the inside of the thighs and under the tail. This breed is the most numerous and popular for general purposes in the United States.

Fig. 11. Toggenburg Doe

Selection of the Buck

The buck is usually considered half the herd and, in order to make progress in breeding, care should be exercised in making this selection. As good bucks are scarce, it is not always possible to get the type desired, but the best obtainable should be procured even if the cost is a little greater. Select a buck from a good-producing doe that is a persistent milker. There is nothing more important in the matter of breeding than evidence that the entire family to which the sire belongs is especially good in performance and in conformation. The success of breeding any class of animals depends largely on the selection of the sires. The selection of a single sire has made many herds famous.

A buck should be masculine in appearance, of at least medium size for his age, and of good conformation. As regards the latter, a good depth of body is one of the most important considerations. The masculinity of the buck can be determined by the size and conformation of the head, amount of bone, and the quality and length of the hair on various portions of the body. The legs should be straight and well placed. Always select a vigorous buck. Thinness is no objection if the buck is healthy and a good feeder. A good buck is seldom in good flesh, especially during the breeding season.

Most breeders at the present time prefer bucks that are naturally hornless. The kids of such bucks are usually without horns. The type of doe to which the buck is bred will, of course, have some influence in this respect.

When only a few does are kept, it is cheaper and more convenient to send them away to be bred. A buck is usually a troublesome individual, and must be kept away from the rest of the herd. The charges made for outside breeding are usually reasonable.

Many small breeders are compelled to use crossbred or grade bucks; in such cases selection should be made upon conformation and breeding. Always use purebred bucks when available.

Selection of the Doe

Although it is not always possible, it is much more satisfactory in making selections to see does during their lactation period. This not only gives an opportunity to study their conformation when they are producing, but the udder development, which is so important, can be better observed.

A good doe should have a feminine head, thin neck, sharp withers, well-defined spine and hips, thin thighs, and rather fine bone. The skin should be fine and thin over the ribs. She should have good digestive capacity, as shown by the spring of rib and size of stomach. The so-called wedge shape of the dairy cow is clearly defined in a good milk doe. The constitution, an important item, is indicated by the depth and width of the chest. The udder should be of good size when filled with milk and very much reduced when empty. A large udder does not always indicate a high milk yield unless it is of the so-called "genuine" type. The teats should be large enough to make milking easy.

In selecting a doe, the first questions that are naturally asked are: How much milk will she produce and how long will she milk? While some does milk for only a few months after kidding, others continue producing for 8 to 10 months or even longer.

In selecting does, especially when they are giving milk, avoid those that are fleshy; this is a strong indication that they are not good producers. Select those of the dairy conformation.

Owing to the scarcity of good purebred does and the prices asked for them, it is much more economical to begin a herd by selecting good grade does, such as are found in many sections of the country, and breeding them to superior bucks of the leading breeds. By keeping the best young stock and breeding them back to good

bucks selected for high producing offspring, a grade herd can be developed that will out-produce purebreds of the quality most breeders are willing to sell. Another way is to buy the best purebred doe kids that the buyer can afford from reliable breeders.

Methods of Breeding

Since the ultimate success of the goat breeder in the improvement of his animals depends not only on his skill in their selection but upon the judicious mating of them as well, it is essential that he has at least a general understanding of the systems of breeding used in the improvement of goats and other livestock.

Inbreeding is the mating of animals which have a closer relationship to each other than the average relationship within the species or breed concerned. Only animals of excellent merit and few defects should be used in such a system. Mating of sire to daughter, son to dam, full brother and sister are examples of this system. Animals resulting from such matings are more likely to transmit their good characteristics than animals which are possibly as good individually but which have resulted from outcrossing or random breeding. However, this type of breeding also tends to bring out recessive characteristics not apparent in the parents which may be undesirable. (Inbreeding should be left to experienced breeders who are interested in long-term results.)

Linebreeding is mating animals so that their descendants will be kept closely related to some animal regarded as unusually desirable. It is accomplished by mating animals that are both closely related to the unusually desirable ancestor but little if at all related to each other through any other ancestor. Since both parents are related to the animal toward which the linebreeding is being directed, they are related to each other.

This system is used extensively and is recommended when the ancestor to which all offspring trace is of special merit and free from serious defects. However, the chances of getting inferior offspring are too great to employ it on average stock in order to avoid the purchase of a new buck.

Crossbreeding is the mating of two animals which are both purebred but belong to different breeds. The hybrid vigor often results in superior individuals. These are not usually satisfactory as breeding stock due to their complex genetic inheritance. However, on account of the general dominance of genes favorable to size, vigor, fertility, and production, goat raisers interested primarily in milk production employ this system with good results.

Out crossing is the mating of animals of the same breed but which show no relationship for at least the first 3 or 4 generations. It is a relatively safe system to use, for it is unlikely that two unrelated animals in a breed, selected more or less at random, will be carrying the same undesirable genes and pass them along to the offspring.

Grading up is the practice of using purebred sires of a given pure breed on native or grade females. Its purpose is to develop uniformity and to increase productivity and quality in the progeny. This system of breeding is the most economical way of rapidly lifting the milk production of commercial stock.

Age of Breeding

Goats are in their prime when from 4 to 6 years of age, but choice individuals and good breeders may often be kept to advantage several years longer. The general practice is to breed young does when they are 15 to 18 months of age, at which time they will be practically grown if they have been well cared for. Most breeders have their does kid in the months of February, March, and April, and

breed them but once a year. However, some people who keep only a few goats desire a milk supply during the entire year and breed a part of the does to freshen during the fall or early winter. Well-grown young does can be bred to advantage from 12 to 15 months of age.

Does will sometimes breed at an early age and care should be taken not to allow them to become pregnant too young. Cases are recorded in which does have kidded when less than 9 months of age.

Periods of Heat

Does come in heat regularly between September and January, and somewhat irregularly and with less intensity from January to March. After this only an occasional doe can be bred until late in August, when the entire herd will come in heat again. When they come in heat and desire the attention of the buck they make their condition known by uneasiness and constant shaking of the tail. They usually remain in heat from 1 to 2 days. The period between heats is ordinarily about 21 days. From the record kept of one herd, most does have returned in from 17 to 21 days, but sometimes they will return in from 5 to 7 days after service. This, however, may be an indication that something is wrong with the doe. Bucks are continually of use for service from the fall to the spring season. It is during this time that they have such a strong odor. The number of does to breed to one buck depends on his age and condition. An early spring buck kid, if well grown and properly handled, can be bred to a few does the following fall. A buck from 12 to 18 months of age can be bred to at least 25 does, and a mature buck is sufficient for from 40 to 50 does.

Out-of-season Breeding

Breeders experience much difficulty in getting does to breed during the late spring and summer months. This seasonal restriction in the breeding of does creates a problem of maintaining a fairly uniform level of milk production throughout the year and is of much concern to goat dairymen and others who would prefer a fairly constant supply of milk. Several possible means of spreading the period over which does come in milk have been investigated by research workers and in some instances applied by breeders. Probably the most practical ones are: (1) Delayed breeding of a part of the does in a herd so that some are bred at different times during the breeding season, (2) pen breeding virgin or dry does during the spring and summer months, by permitting a buck to run with them, and (3) selection of does that tend to come in estrus outside the usual breeding season, thereby increasing the spread in possible breeding dates.

Until other methods can be developed, the first and second ones can be considered the most practical. Even these are not so easy of application in small herds as in large ones where there is more opportunity for separation of animals into groups for early and late breeding. Reserving some does for late breeding may also result in a few dry does since goats do not breed with as much certainty during the latter part as in the early months of the breeding season.

To develop a strain of goats which would consistently breed out of season, if possible, would require many generations of vigorous selection for the trait.

The injection of hormones to produce out-of-season breeding has not proved effective and in some cases has proved detrimental in retarding the occurrence of natural estrus and thereby delaying the effective breeding. Therefore, this practice cannot be recommended to the practical breeder.

Gestation Period

The gestation period, which is the time between the effective service of the buck and the birth of the kid or kids, ranges from 146 to 152 days. It is usually spoken of as 5 months. The average gestation period recorded for several years in the Beltsville herd of Toggenburg does was 146 days.

Number of Kids

Milk goats are very prolific. The usual number of kids at one time for mature does is 2, but frequently there are 3, and it is not a rare thing, especially among the common American goats, to have a doe produce 4. Yearling Toggenburg does at Beltsville have produced kids at a rate of 168 per 100 does, while the mature Toggenburg does have produced kids at the rate of 196 per 100 does. Records indicate little difference between Toggenburg and Saanen breeds in this respect.

Feed and Management

Successful goat production, as with other livestock, requires the use of proper feeding methods. The ability to convert feed into milk is inherited. Consequently, one of the most important problems of the goat breeder is to so feed his goats that this inherited ability is utilized to the maximum. Unless feeding permits full development, intelligent selection cannot be made of the animals which can transmit the desired characteristics. Undernourished does that never had an opportunity to demonstrate their capacity to produce milk, and bucks lacking in growth and vigor, are difficult to appraise accurately.

The Buck

In handling goats, the bucks are a considerable problem. Their strong odor and disgusting habits cause many people to take a great dislike to goats. Bucks should be kept away from the does except when desired for service. If they are kept in the same barn or room where the does are milked, some of the strong odor is likely to be absorbed by the milk. Place the bucks in a separate barn or shed, with a lot sufficient for exercise and pasture.

The best results can be expected only when the bucks are kept in a healthy condition. During the winter months the ration should consist of a hay—alfalfa, clover, or mixed hay—and corn stover, with some succulent feed such as silage and turnips, and a sufficient quantity of grain.

Bucks are usually wintered on 3 pounds of alfalfa or clover hay, 1 to 1½ pounds of silage, and 1½ pounds of grain a day, the grain mixture consisting of 100 pounds of corn, 100 pounds of oats, 50 pounds of bran, and 25 pounds of linseed meal. During the breeding season the grain ration for mature bucks is usually increased to 2 pounds per head daily. When the bucks are on good pasture, no grain is necessary.

During the breeding season it is usually necessary to keep the bucks separate, or they will fight and are likely to injure one another. A wood lot with plenty of browse is an excellent place for them during the summer. Goats are browsers by nature and prefer leaves, twigs, and weeds to grass.

It is often necessary to protect the trees in the lots and pastures by putting around them a framework covered with close-woven wire. This is true especially of the young trees. If no lot, or only a small lot, is available for feed and exercise, the buck may be tethered out. Vacant lots can often be utilized to advantage. Fresh feed as well as a variety is thus afforded.

134

Most of the feeds that are valuable for the production of milk for dairy cows are also suitable for does. From 6 to 8 goats can be kept upon the feed required for 1 cow. When does are in milk, they should be allowed all the roughage that they will consume, such as alfalfa, clover, or mixed hay and corn stover. They should receive a liberal quantity of succulant feed, such as silage, mangel-wurzels, carrots, rutabagas, parsnips, or turnips. The grain feeds best suited for their ration are corn, oats, bran, barley, and linseed meal or linseed cake. Other feeds that are often available and that can be utilized are cottonseed meal, brewers' grains, corn bran, gluten feed, and beet pulp.

A ration that has proved to be very satisfactory for does in milk during the winter season consists of 2 pounds of alfalfa or clover hay, 1½ pounds of corn silage or roots, and from 1 to 2 pounds of grain. The grain ration consists of a mixture of 100 pounds of corn, 100 pounds of oats, 50 pounds of bran, and 25 pounds of linseed meal. When the does are on pasture they receive from 1 to 1½ pounds per head daily of the grain mixture.

There is a great difference in individual goats; one goat may readily eat a ration that another may not like so well. As in the case of dairy cows, each doe should be studied if the best results are to be obtained. It is best to feed separately each doe that is giving milk. This not only affords an opportunity to study each individual but also insures that each one receives the quantity intended for her. A good practice is to feed grain on the basis of a doe's milk production; that is, at a ratio of 1 pound of grain for each 3 or 4 pounds of milk produced, with a daily minimum allowance for all does of 1½ pounds of grain per head.

With Toggenburg does, an average of 1.0 pound of grain is required to produce a quart of milk, on the basis of the daily consumption of grain throughout the entire period of lactation. Approximately 500 pounds of hay and 450 pounds of grain a year are required for a mature doe, provided of course, that good pasture is afforded as much as 6 months of the year. If no pasture is available about twice the amount of hay and 20 percent more grain is required. It is estimated that 1 acre of good pasture is sufficient for 2 to 3 mature goats during a grazing season 5 to 6 months in length. If grain and hay are to be grown for the goats, additional acreage must be provided for this purpose. Goats relish browse, but a doe cannot be expected to produce milk at her maximum level without the addition of good legume hay or other pasture plus a grain ration.

Young does should be kept growing. In the spring, summer, and fall, if they have plenty of browse and pasture, no grain is necessary. If no browse is afforded and the pasture is short during certain months, give them a little grain. In winter they should be fed about 1 pound of grain, 1 to 1½ pounds of silage or roots, and all the hay or fodder they will consume. They should have a shed for shelter and protection from the wind. Goats must be kept dry and out of cold winds for best results.

Some goat breeders make it a practice to gather leaves in the fall and store them for winter use. This practice should be resorted to only in cases of shortage of more desirable feed. Leaves may be used for bedding, but even for this purpose they are only fairly satisfactory. If only 1 or 2 goats are kept, refuse from the kitchen, such as potato and turnip peelings, cabbage leaves, and waste bread may be utilized for feeding. If necessary, does may be tethered out, as described in connection with handling the buck.

All feed offered to goats should be clean. Rations should be made up from the best feeds available and those most relished by the goats. Salt should be provided in the form of medium fine stock salt with trace minerals. Phenothiazine can be mixed with this in the proportion of 12 to 17 parts salt to 1 part phenothiazine without coloring the milk. This provides some protection from internal parasites as the does consume their salt requirement. In order to be sure they get enough

phenothiazine to protect them, no other salt should be provided and mixed feed containing salt should not be used. A good supply of fresh water is necessary; goats should not be compelled to drink from pools where the water has been standing.

Lactation period

The lactation period, which is the time that a doe produces milk, varies considerably in the different breeds and types of goats. It ranges all the way from 3 to 10 months, or even longer. A lactation period ranging from 8 to 10 months is considered very satisfactory. There are certain conditions, such as the breed, individuality, health, feed, and regularity and thoroughness of milking, which may influence it. Purebred does of any of the leading breeds, as a general rule, will milk longer than any of the so-called common, or American type. The breed that has been developed the longest should, of course, excel in this respect if the animals have been properly selected. There are always individuals in a breed that excel along certain lines, and this is especially true as regards length of lactation period.

The health of the does while giving milk is of special importance. When does are out of condition frequently their milk yield shrinks, and in many cases, they have to be dried up. Proper feed and regular feeding have a tendency to extend the lactation period not only by stimulating the production but by causing a more uniform flow during this time. The milking must be done regularly and thoroughly if good results are desired. Irregularity and neglecting to draw all the milk from the udder have a tendency to shorten the period.

Milking

As young does usually object at first to being milked, a stanchion arrangement is an excellent method of handling them. For the first few times at least it is best to give the does a little grain feed in the box attached to the stanchion. Does soon become accustomed to being milked and after a few times will jump up on the stand and put their heads through the stanchion without being assisted.

The doe's udder should always be either washed or wiped thoroughly before being milked. Ordinarily a damp cloth is sufficient to remove all foreign material. The first milk drawn should not be saved, as the openings in the teats may be partially filled with foreign matter which will be removed after a little milk has been drawn. It is best to have a room for milking separate from the main goat barn. This prevents the milk from absorbing any odors in the stable.

There are two systems of milking goats: From the side, as cows are milked, and from the rear. This latter method is largely a European style and is used very little in the United States as there is more opportunity for contamination of the milk from dirt and droppings. Commercial dairies usually make milking arrangements to conform to local health regulations.

There are also two systems of drawing milk from the udder: One consists in pressing the teat in the hand, as is usually practiced in milking cows, and the other is "stripping." The first can be adopted when the teats are of sufficient size to be grasped by the hand. The other method is necessary only for goats with small teats or for goats in their first lactation, before the teats are fully developed. In stripping, the teat is grasped between the first finger and the thumb close to the udder and drawn down the entire length, sufficient pressure being exerted to cause the milk to flow freely.

A heavy producer may have to be milked three times a day for a short time, but twice is sufficient for most does. The period between milkings should be divided

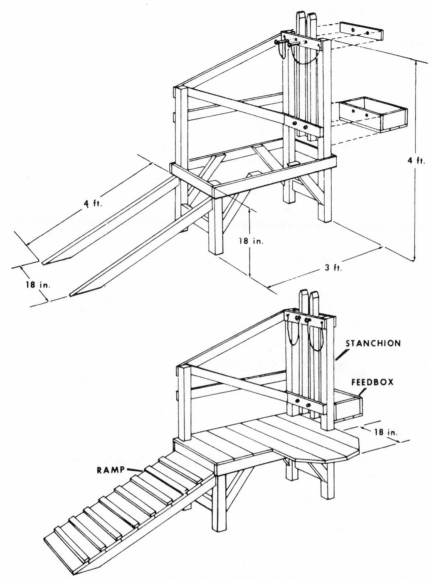

Fig. 12.

Dimensions on these drawings can be used as a guide for building a milking stand. The upper drawing shows construction of framework without flooring boards. Bolts at top of stanchion pull out so that uprights can be spread apart to admit the doe's head. Then bolts are put back, and the uprights hold the doe in place. The lower drawing shows the finished stand. For platform, cross supports, feedbox, ramp, and ramp cleats, use 1-inch-thick boards. Use 2- by 4-inch lumber for leg braces and ramp frame. Use 4- by 4-inch lumber for leg frame.

up as equally as possible. Milk should not be used for human consumption until the fourth or fifth day after the doe gives birth to kids. Some authorities recommend waiting longer, but this is not necessary if everything is normal. Regularity in milking is important, and kindness and gentleness should be regarded as essential. It is advisable that the milking be done by the same person so far as possible. Milking machines especially designed for goats are used in many commercial dairies.

Care of the Milk

Utensils used in handling the milk may be purchased from goat dairy supply houses. All utensils should be kept clean. A sanitary stainless steel milking pail with detachable hood has been satisfactory at Beltsville. These pails are of 4-quart capacity. As soon as the milk is drawn it should be weighed, strained, and cooled. The weighing is necessary if one is to determine accurately how much a doe produces. Milk records are especially valuable to the breeder in selling stock as well as in selecting breeding animals.

The milk should always be thoroughly strained to remove any foreign matter. The best method is to use commercial filters or strainers, but it is possible to use a layer of sterilized absorbent cotton between two cloths, or to pass the milk through several thicknesses of cloth. Cheesecloth is best for this purpose.

To check the growth of bacteria the milk should be cooled to a temperature of 40°F. as soon after milking as possible. This may be done by placing the cans in a tank containing cold water. One of the best systems of cooling the milk rapidly, however, is to run it over a cooler inside of which is cold, running water. Milk should be kept cool until wanted for use.

Sometimes undesirable flavors appear in the milk. These may be due to strong feeds such as wild garlic or strong-flavored weeds or vegetables consumed by does too near to milking time. Good flavored milk results from proper handling, such as keeping bucks separate from the milking does, using perfectly clean utensils, cooling the milk rapidly after it is drawn, and keeping it refrigerated. Occasionally, owing to ill health or some systemic disorder, individual does will give poorly flavored milk. Theories have been advanced that individual does vary in the amount of fatty acids secreted in the milk, and thus does receiving the same feed sometimes produce differently flavored milks. Some breeders believe that off-flavored milk is an inherited characteristic. Still others have observed that does milked for unusually long lactation periods tend to produce milk of poor flavor. Experimental study of this problem is needed.

Because pasteurization of goat's milk distributed for human consumption is required by public-health authorities in many localities, its effects on nutritive values are important. Studies by the U.S.D.A. have shown that the solubility of calcium and phosphorus is slightly increased and the curd tension is reduced by pasteurization. This process improves the keeping quality more than the flavor of fresh goat's milk. Pasteurization by holding the milk at not less than 142°F. for 30 minutes caused a decrease of from 33 to 45 percent in the content of reduced ascorbic acid, or vitamin C.

Care of the Doe during kidding

Ordinarily the doe and kid need no special care during and after kidding. A few days before expected parturition the doe should be given a small stall where she may be alone. Plenty of clean bedding, such as straw, leaves, or shavings should be provided. She should have all she will eat. If she is indifferent about food, adding carrots, beets, or small pieces of apples to her ration may induce her to eat.

138

Assistance at birth is seldom required. Small or young does kidding for the first time may need help. Parturition may require an hour. If it is not completed by the end of 2 hours, assistance should be given. Wash the hands and arms with soap and warm water and a mild disinfectant, such as a 10-percent solution of therapogen. This is made by taking one part of therapogen and diluting with 9 parts of water.

Examine with the hand the position of the kid in the uterus. Normally the two front feet should be felt first with the nose resting on the front legs. Fasten a stout cord which has been disinfected in the solution to the kid's front legs and pull gently as the doe strains. The kid's head should move along with the legs. Once the forelegs and head are passed there will usually be no further trouble. If one leg is doubled back, it should be straightened out so that it lies alongside of the other so that both will come out together. Never pull on the front legs unless the head is coming along with them.

If the kid is in a posterior position, the two hind feet must be expelled together. Attach a cord to them and proceed as in a forward presentation.

In a backward presentation the kid's back is sometimes downward. In this case the kid should be turned in the passage so that its belly will be downward before any pulling is done.

After the kid is out, dry it off with a clean dry cloth and put it near the doe. She will usually lick it clean and otherwise care for it. A second or third kid may be born following removal of the first one. The afterbirth as soon as passed should be burned or buried. If the afterbirth is retained for more than 24 hours, or if there is inflammation of the uterus, 2 to 3 ounces of mineral oil containing one-half dram of iodoform may be introduced into the uterus through a sterile soft rubber tube. This loosens the attachment of the afterbirth to the womb and prevents bacterial infection.

After the kid gets up and starts to nurse, make certain that it is getting milk. Stripping the teats a few times will indicate the presence or absence of milk. If the teat is not open a veterinarian should be called. The kid or kids should receive the first milk, or colostrum. If hand feeding is to be used the kid should not be allowed to nurse the doe at all, but should be fed from a bottle with a nipple for the first few days, then taught to drink from a pan. If the kid nurses the doe, see that both halves of the udder are emptied uniformly. The udder should not be allowed to become hard.

Raising the Kids

The raising of the kids is especially important when it is desired either to sell or use the milk for family purposes. If the kids are not to be raised, they can frequently be sold for pets or for meat when 2 to 3 months old. Kids that are allowed to suckle their dams not only make good growth but require very little attention as compared with those raised by hand. However, hand-raising helps avoid ill-shaped udders which sometimes result from uneven suckling, prevents weaning difficulties, and provides a check on milk production.

The quantity of milk to be fed and the length of time that it should be fed depends on several conditions. Kids dropped in the spring do not require so much milk or need to be fed so long as those dropped in the fall or early winter. The quantity of milk required for a kid can be determined readily from the fact that a doe producing from 3 to 4 pounds of milk a day can easily raise two kids satisfactorily. This means that each kid needs 1½ to 2 pounds of milk a day, or 1½ to 2 pints. An experiment allowed several does with records of a little above 4 pounds of milk a day to suckle 3 kids, feeding the kids also some hay and grain. The kids made a fairly good growth, which shows that the amount of milk can be decreased if other feed is supplied.

139

Studies in the feeding of kids by hand have shown that after they have reached 10 weeks of age the milk may be replaced in a large measure by good alfalfa hay and mixed grain without sacrificing body weight and development. During the period of 10 to 18 weeks of age, the kids in one lot were given 60 pounds less of milk than the check lot, and all were fed all the hay and grain they would clean up. The kids on the restricted milk diet consumed on the average 9 pounds of grain and 2 pounds more of hay during this 8-week period than the kids in check lot. The average weight of the kids in the 2 lots was identical at the close of the feeding test. This substitution of grain and hay for milk in kid feeding is economical, as it takes approximately 1 pound of grain to produce 2.2 pounds of milk.

Kids to be raised by hand should not be allowed to nurse the doe. They should, however, be given the colostrum or first milk which is so valuable to them during the 2 days following birth. This milk should be fed at frequent intervals from a bottle and nipple.

Kids can be raised satisfactorily on whole cow's milk, and some goat breeders have adopted a system whereby skim milk has been used with a fair degree of success. The kids should be changed from whole to skim milk very gradually, the quantity of skim milk being gradually increased until it makes up the entire milk ration. After this has been done the kids will usually consume from 2 to 3 pounds a day. They should be given just as much as they will drink readily, and until they are at least 6 weeks old they should be fed three times a day. During this time the milk should be warmed and fed at a temperature ranging from 90°F. to not more than 98°F. The kids can be weaned from milk when they are from 3 to 4 months old. At about 8 weeks of age the digestive system of kids is usually sufficiently developed so that they can obtain substantial nourishment from solid feeds. At weaning age they will consume sufficient hay, grain, and pasture to make a good growth. Some of the leading goat breeders do not wean the kids until they are about 5 months of age. The age of weaning, however, should depend upon the system of raising the kids. If raised by nursing the does, they can be allowed to remain in the herd until 5 months of age; but if they are raised by hand feeding and the supply of milk is limited, they may be weaned much earlier without serious results.

Kids will eat a little hay and grain at an early age, and they should be provided with them. Alfalfa or clover hay should be given in a rack and the grain mixture in a trough. Arrangements should be made to keep the kids out of both the rack and the trough. A good grain ration for the kids consists of cracked corn, crushed or rolled oats, and bran mixed in the proportion of one part cracked corn, one part crushed or rolled oats, and one-half part bran. They should be allowed as much as they will clean up during the 24-hour period until they are eating one-half pound a day. All grain that is not eaten should be removed from the trough each day and fresh grain provided, as kids are very delicate in their eating habits.

If the kids are fed by hand, they can either be given the milk from a bottle with a nipple or a tank with a number of nipples attached, or they may be fed from pans. Most kids can easily be taught to drink from a pan or trough, and this system is less troublesome. Some kids, however, are very slow in learning to drink and do much better when fed from a bottle. Cleanliness is absolutely essential for the successful raising of kids. The pans, pails, bottles, and nipples should be kept clean. After the kids are a few weeks old and have learned to drink, they can be fed from a galvanized-iron trough. Care should be taken, however, to see that each kid receives its share of the milk.

Kids are very playful creatures and require considerable exercise. If they are kept in a small enclosure, it is a good plan to put a box from 18 to 20 inches in height in the center, so that they may run and jump upon it. This will give them plenty of exercise, and they will have keen appetites. Pasture or browse should be afforded as early as possible.

Castration

All buck kids not to be kept or sold for breeding purposes should be castrated when they are from 10 days to 3 weeks of age. The older they are, the more severe the operation. The operation of castration is very simple and can be performed by the elastration or pincer methods or by cutting the lower third of the scrotum off and grasping above the testicles forcing them out so that they can be grasped and pulled away one at a time with the spermatic cord attached.

The elastration method is accomplished by expanding a rubber band by an instrument, which is released around the scrotum, above the testicles, stopping the flow of blood to the extremity below the band. The pincer method is performed by clamping pincers, the jaws of which do not come entirely together across the scrotum above the testicles. This pincer crushes the cord but does not sever the outside layers of skin. These are known as bloodless methods of castration.

In case the knife is used when the kids are more than 4 months of age, the cords should not be pulled out but scraped off just above the testicles. The wound should be bathed with some good disinfectant after the operation.

Buck kids should be separated from the doe kids when they are about 4 months of age. Doe kids come in heat when young, and the young bucks worry them a great deal if allowed to run with them. Occasionally doe kids become pregnant when they are only 4 to 5 months of age.

Marking

Each goat in the herd should be marked in some manner for identification. This may be done by the use of metal ear labels, by notching the ears, or by tatooing the ears. In some instances all three of these systems are used. When this is done, the kids' ears are notched as soon after birth as possible, and when they are from 3 to 6 months of age and ear label is inserted and the tatooing done. The ear label is only a fairly satisfactory method of marking and never should be used as a sole means of identification as the label is liable to be torn out. Care should always be taken to insert the label rather close to the head and far enough up into the ear to make it fairly tight.

Notching the ears can be done with the punch used for inserting the ear label. Notches on certain parts of the ears indicate certain numbers, the sum of the numbers represented by the notches being the number of the goat. Numbers up into the hundreds involve a rather complicated system, but they are not usually necessary in a small herd. To avoid a complex system, each crop of kids may be numbered from one upward. The notch system is especially valuable, as it not only serves as a means of identification but it is not always necessary to catch the goats to read their numbers. A person can stand at some distance, and if the goat is facing him the notches can be seen readily.

Tatooing on the inside of the ear is the most satisfactory method of marking goats. There are on the market tatooing instruments having adjustable numbers and letters, with which a combination containing 3 or 4 of either or both can be made. Some breeders tatoo their initials in one ear and a number in the other. Tattooing is an excellent method of recording the identity of goats as the numbers are easily read and when properly inserted are practically permanent. Special nonfading tattoo ink can be obtained from all livestock equipment houses. Care should be used to make sure the ink is rubbed well into the indentures made by the needles.

141

Mature goats may be dehorned safely. This is done best by sawing the horns off close to the head with a saw such as veterinarians use. The operation should be performed if possible when the weather is fairly cool and when flies are not troublesome. As soon as the horns are removed, apply a little pine tar to the wounds.

The horns on kids can be prevented from developing by using caustic soda or potash sticks, commercial horn removing preparations, or the disbudding iron. Regardless of the method used it is highly important to make sure that the kid to be disbudded actually requires disbudding; that is, be certain that the kid is not naturally hornless. To determine whether a kid has horn buds, the hair should be clipped closely from the top of the head where the horn buds would be expected. If two shiny hairless spots show up, the size of a pinhead or larger, and if the skin is tightly attached to the skull at these points, it is highly probable that the kid has horn buds. On a naturally hornless kid, the skin can be moved from side to side by pushing with the finger, as the skin is not attached. However, there is an enlargement at the point at which the horn would be attached to the skull. The most favorable time to disbud is the day after the kid is born, provided the kid is of normal vigor, and it has been determined that the kid has horn buds. The sooner the operation is performed the less developed the horn buds will be and the easier it is to stop their growth.

Caustic sticks of soda or potash may be obtained from the drug store. These should be used with care, as they may injure the skin of the person handling them. The stick caustic should be wrapped in a piece of paper to protect the fingers, leaving one end uncovered. Moisten the uncovered end and rub it on the horn buttons. Care should be taken to apply the **caustic to the horn button only**, but it should be blistered well. This is best effected by clipping the hair close to the head for some distance around the horn button and coating the surface with petrolatum, leaving the skin close to the horn button and the button itself free from the coating.

The caustic may then be applied to the uncoated portion without danger of its burning the remainder of the head or running into the eyes. The application should be made when the kids are from 2 to 5 days old.

The disbudding iron probably gives more uniformly successful results and is easier on both the kid and the operator than the other methods. A disbudding iron can be purchased from goat dairy supply firms or made by anyone handy with tools. It resembles a soldering iron with the tip sawed off. Irons, the ends of which are slightly concave, are preferable to irons sawed off with plain end, although these also give good results. For disbudding the iron should be heated so that at least 2 inches are cherry-red. Having two irons so that a fresh one is ready for the second horn bud accelerates the operation. For small doe kids a 7/8-inch (diameter) iron is sufficiently large, but for large does and especially buck kids a 1-inch iron is better. The iron should be centered on the horn buds, and applied with a rotary motion and light pressure, for from 5 to 10 seconds or more depending on the size and development of the horn buds. When the iron has burned enough the clean skull will show. It is important that the iron be a cherry-red heat, because at a lower temperature a longer time is required which is more exhausting to the kid. Unguentine or carbolated vaseline should be applied to each disc immediately after disbudding.

Care of the Hoofs

If goats are more or less confined and not allowed to run upon gravelly or rocky soil their hoofs grow out and should be trimmed. A goat should have its hoofs

trimmed so that it will stand squarely on its feet. A sharp pruning or hoof knife is best for this operation. The horny edge of the hoof should be trimmed level with the soft tissue which comprises the sole, and if this tissue is overgrown or unbalanced it may also require a little trimming.This part of thehoof is sensitive and must be trimmed carefully and not too deeply. Excessive horny portions of the heel should be trimmed so that the entire foot will set squarely on the ground. If the hoof is overgrown and badly out of shape, it will be necessary to restore it gradually to normal shape by drawing it to form a little more at each trimming. The need for hoof trimming will vary with individual goats, but examination of the hoofs should be made at monthly intervals.

Goat Meat and Goatskins

There has always been a rather general prejudice in this country against the use of goat meat as food. However, in some sections a great many goats of the milk type, especially kids, are consumed and are in demand. They are sold for slaughter when from 8 to 12 weeks of age. The flesh of young goats, or kids, is palatable and has a flavor suggesting lamb.

The prices of goats sold on the market for slaughter are always considerably less than those received for sheep. Goats do not fatten and carry flesh as sheep do.

The United States imports in normal times about 40,000,000 goatskins annually, so it would seem that there should be a ready market for all skins that could be produced. Skins from the shorthaired goats, such as the common type of American goat and the milk breeds, are the kind used in the manufacture of shoes, gloves, bookbindings, pocketbooks, and like articles. However, as a rule these skins have only a small commercial value.

Health Problems With Goats

Although considered very healthy, goats are subject to disease and have their troubles as well as any other animal. Goats are less subject to disease than sheep, but the two species are so closely allied that, in general, the treatment in cases of disease is the same for both. Since the diagnosis and treatment of diseases require special knowledge and experience, the services of a veterinarian should be obtained whenever disease problems arise.

A matter of great importance and one on which breeders lay considerable emphasis is the fact that goats are rarely affected with tuberculosis. When confined to close quarters with cows that have tuberculosis, they may, however, contract the disease. Goats that are in good condition are not very liable to contract disease, but some maladies may affect them if they are allowed to get in poor condition.

In the Federal meat inspection the cause of most of the condemnation for goats on both ante mortem and post mortem inspections is emaciation. Emaciation may be due to any one of a combination of factors such as stomach worms, flukes, tapeworms, and abortion. It is necessary, of course, to determine the cause before treatment can be administered.

Brucellosis

This term covers infection due to germs belonging to the genus known as *Brucella.* Organisms of this class are responsible for brucellosis, also known as Bang's disease and infectious abortion, in cattle and other animals, Malta fever in goats, and undulant fever in man who contracts the disease directly or indirectly from infected animals or their products.

143

Brucellosis in goats is most frequently caused by the germ, *Brucella melitensis*. Signs of infection may vary considerably. Abortions are common in herds where the disease has been recently introduced as well as in young does from herds where infection has been present for a considerable time. Other symptoms occasionally observed are lameness, retarded milk secretions, and inflammation of the udder.

Suspicion as to the presence of brucellosis can be verified by tests of the animal's blood. In herds found to be infected, repeated tests are usually desirable. The test, known as the agglutination test, is the same as that commonly used for brucellosis, or Bang's disease, in cattle. Milk and milk products from infected animals are dangerous unless pasteurized or boiled. Persons caring for infected animals are exposed to the infection.

The chief method of prevention is frequent blood testing. Newly acquired animals should always be subjected to test, preferably by an authorized agent of the State, before they are added to healthy goat herds. This is especially desirable in goat dairies, and is mandatory in some States. The reacting animals should either be isolated pending replacement or slaughtered under veterinary supervision.

Abortion

Goats, like all other species of farm animals, sometimes abort. The abortion may be caused by infection, lack of some necessary element in the diet, or other factors about which little or nothing is known.

If several repeated abortions should occur in the herd, infection of some kind may be suspected. In such a case it would be advisable to have the aborting goats, or even the entire herd, blood-tested for Malta fever. Goats affected with this disease are apt to abort. Malta fever is not likely to appear among goats except in those restricted localities where the disease is known to exist. The test for Malta fever is the same as that for Bang's disease.

If a doe aborts she should be placed in a pen by herself, away from the herd, and kept isolated until discharges from the generative organs cease and recovery is complete.

The fetus and after birth, provided the latter has been expelled, should be disposed of in such a manner as to be inaccessible to the rest of the herd. Similar disposition should be made of the discharges from the genital organs and of contaminated bedding.

Pens in which abortive goats have been isolated should be well cleaned and disinfected before being used again.

Little can be done or is necessary in the way of treatment beyond attention to the comfort and nourishment of the animal. If the afterbirth is retained for more than 24 hours, the subcutaneous or intramuscular injection of diethylstilbestrol or estradiol diproprionate is recommended. This treatment produces contraction of the uterus which aids in the expulsion of fluids and eventual detachment of afterbirth.

Constipation

Constipation sometimes occurs, especially in the kids. Simple constipation may be due to digestive disturbances resulting from accumulations of poorly digested dry feed, lack of exercise, or gorging.

A change of diet and adequate exercise may serve to relieve this condition. When medication is required such simple drugs as Epsom salts or oil may usually be safely administered as a drench.

The dosage for mature stock is from 2 to 4 ounces of salts dissolved in 1 pint of

warm water. Weaning kids should receive only half that dosage. Castor oil or raw linseed oil in place of Epsom salts will be effective, and the dosage should consist of the same number of liquid ounces.

Mastitis, or caked udder

When mastitis is present the udder usually feels hard and is hot and swollen, but an occasional case may be found in which there are flakes in the milk and very little swelling of the udder. The condition is caused very frequently by the presence of bacteria which multiply in the milk and tissues of the udder, and set up inflammatory changes. Injuries, excessive accumulation of milk in the udder, rough milking, chilling, and systemic derangements favor the development of the disease-producing germs. The diseased animal should be promptly removed from the herd and treated. Treatment consists in milking the animal thoroughly but gently every hour or two during the day. The application of hot towels or water as hot as the hand will stand for 20 minutes 4 to 5 times a day will also be of benefit.

Antibiotics and sulfonamides are also useful for intramammary injection in cases of chronic mastitis or parenterally in acute cases. If these drugs are injected through the teat canal then frequent stripping of the udder is not necessary. Treatment by use of antibiotics and sulfonamides should be administered by a competent veterinarian.

Sore Teats

This condition may be caused by the teeth of the kids, warty growths on the teats, or an injury. After the teats have been washed and dried, carbolated petrolatum should be applied.

Foot Rot

Unless properly managed, goats may have foot rot. The first evidence of this trouble to attract attention is a slight lameness, which rapidly becomes more marked. The foot will become swollen and warm to the touch. There is no specific treatment for this condition. A treatment may be successful under certain conditions and worthless under others. In a treatment sometimes used, the affected feet are first trimmed thoroughly so as to expose the site of infection, and then soaked in a saturated solution of copper sulphate (2½ pounds to 1 gallon of water) for several minutes. The animal is removed to clean dry quarters and the copper sulphate treatment repeated, when necessary. Pine tar applied to the feet helps to promote healing after the infection has been controlled. Sulfonamides and antibiotics are also used in the treatment of foot rot.

Parasites

Goats and sheep become infested with about the same kinds of internal and external parasites, and are adversely affected in a similar manner.

Goats are known to harbor different kinds of parasites, but those concerned in parasitic gastroenteritis cause the greatest economic loss. The most important of these are stomach worms, intestinal hairworms, and nodular worms. Heavy infestations of the common stomach worm produce a severe anemia; stomach hairworms cause an inflamation of the lining of the fourth or true stomach, resulting in gastritis, diarrhea, and loss of appetite. The effects of intestinal hairworm infestations are similar to those caused by stomach hairworms, except that the inflammation is in the small intestine and is known as parasitic enteritis. Nodular worms may produce somewhat similar effects in the large intestine. Emaciation

145

and death of kids and adult goats may result from heavy infestations of one or more of these parasites, unless measures are promptly taken to expel a significant proportion of the worms. Even if death losses do not result from parasitic infestations, there may be serious effects on growth, interference with milk production, and interruptions in breeding activities. Other internal parasites, such as liver flukes, tapeworms, lungworms, and coccidia, also can be troublesome to goats. Certain external parasites also are injurious but, in general, are considered of lesser importance.

Phenothiazine is the most effective drug that can be used for the removal of internal parasites from goats. This drug should be given in doses of 35 to 40 grams (about 1⅓ ounces) to adult goats, and 20 grams (⅔ ounce) to kids under 6 months of age or 60 pounds or less in weight. Treatment with phenothiazine twice a year is recommended in cases where parasitism tends to be troublesome. More frequent treatments may be given if necessary. If goats are in production, the milk should be discarded, or used for other than human consumption, for a period of 4 days immediately following treatment, as phenothiazine imparts a pink discoloration to the milk for a few days after medication.

Phenothiazine may be given as a drench or in capsule. Animals may be treated individually or in groups by mixing the proper amount of the drug in their feed. This method is not recommended, however, for goats in production. In order to obtain an accurate diagnosis, to assure proper dosage, and to avoid injury to the animals, the treatment should be given by, or under the supervision of, a veterinarian.

Other chemicals, such as copper sulphate, nicotine sulphate, a combination of these, or tetrachloroethylene, are used to treat worm parasitism in goats, but none of these is more generally useful than phenothiazine except perhaps in the case of animals in poduction.

Measures other than specific medication can play an important part in effective control of goat parasites. A wide range and dry, hillside pastures tend to prevent parasitic infestation, whereas small, wet low-lying pastures favor the spread of parasites. Enclosures free from vegetation are not as dangerous as lush pastures. Cleaning out the manure frequently and thoroughly is another aid in keeping enclosures safe. Pasture rotation is an important control measure. The longer the pastures are rested the greater is the destruction of the free-living stages of the parasites. If it is not feasible to use these aids for parasite control one must resort to periodic medication with phenothiazine or other antiparasitic drugs.

Lice

Goats infested with lice may be treated by dipping, spraying, washing, or dusting with suitable insecticides. The method of choice will depend upon the number of animals to be treated, the insecticide used, prevailing weather conditions, and available facilities. Washing and dusting are probably the most practical methods for most dairy herds, the latter being particularly useful in cold weather. Spraying and dipping are very effective but they are generally feasible only when large numbers of animals are to be treated. Whatever method is selected, however, all goats in the herd should be treated regardless of the number of animals infested. It may be noted that clipping long-haired goats discourages lice and is an excellent sanitary measure as well.

A suitable dusting powder may be prepared by thoroughly mixing 3 ounces of derris or cube powder (containing 5 percent of rotenone). The mixture must be well rubbed into the hair over the entire body surface. Ordinarily, 1 or 2 ounces is sufficient for a single application which can usually be relied upon to protect the animals from serious reinfestation for at least 3 or 4 weeks.

Rotenone wash, or dip, may be prepared by dissolving 3 ounces of soap flakes in

1 gallon of water and adding 12 ounces of derris or cube powder (containing 5 percent of rotenone). The mixture should be prepared just before use, and it should be kept well stirred at all times.

This wash is suitable for use during any season of the year except in extremely cold weather. Apply it with a brush or a cloth, spreading a thin, even coating over the entire body surface. Avoid contaminating feed, utensils, and drinking water with this preparation; do not allow pools of the mixtures to form from which the animals may drink; and do not allow the materials to drain over vegetation upon which the goats are permitted to graze.

Other suitable and safe insecticides for goats are malathion, ronnel (korlan) and pyrethrins (see section on Pesticides, Part III, for more details on these chemicals.)

SWINE

Swine producers who use sound practices of breeding, feeding, and management usually make a profit.

If you are planning to raise hogs, you should begin by finding out if a supply of feed is available. Your farm should produce abundant feed or be in a cash-grain farming section. Your farm should be accessible to markets so that you can sell the hogs you raise.

Number of Hogs to Raise

Begin hog raising on a small scale. After you develop the necessary skills, gradually increase the herd size to fit your farm.

Expanding too quickly could lead to overstocking in feed, labor, equipment, or housing, or to neglect of other farm enterprises. Be careful to avoid conflicts of your farming schedule—farrowing versus planting or harvesting. These conflicts can cause serious losses in total farm income.

Once you determine the number of hogs that best fits your particular farm plan, stick to this number unless some major change—in size of farm or in cropping—indicates a larger or smaller herd. Most successful hog raisers produce at a uniform rate and concentrate on reducing waste and increasing efficiency.

In figuring the number of hogs you can raise on the feed available, include by-products and water. Feeds that can be salvaged by hogs are skim milk, grain, field gleanings, unmarketable products from truck farms, and grain in droppings from fattening steers.

Selecting Breeding Stock

Sows

Foundation sows for the herd should have meat-type body conformation, high milk production, and good weight for age. They should be physically sound. If production-tested sows are unavailable or prices are too high, select them on individual merit.

The prospective brood sow should have a long body with a full spring of rib. The back should be uniform in width and the shoulders should be smooth. Along the topline, the back should be moderately arched and full and thick at the loin.

The sides should be long, deep and smooth; the ham should be wide and well developed, carrying down to within 2 inches of the hock. The jowl, underline, and base of the ham should be trim. The legs should be strong, of medium length, and

147

should have good feet and strong short pasterns. The sow should have 12 to 14 good teats, open and without deformity.

Select breeding females from litters of 10 or more pigs out of sows that consistently produce large litters.

Profitable Life

The profitable life of a gilt or sow differs with the type of operation and with each farm.

Do not replace all gilts after their first litter. Instead, keep the best one-third to one-half of the gilts for a second litter. having sows farrow two litters a year will give you more information for selecting young boars and gilts to be kept in the herd.

This system also permits sows to remain in the herd if they are superior to any of the gilts that would replace them. If distinctly superior, keep some of the best sows for a third or fourth litter.

When you select sows for additional litters, consider the number of pigs they produce and the weaning weight of the pigs. Also, consider the gilt's own growth and meat-type conformation.

Crossbred sows are often kept for their superior performance in prolificacy, milk production, and mothering ability.

Systematic crossbreeding programs are usually based on group standards of performance. These standards are maintained by hybrid vigor in the female line and the use of superior, production-tested males.

In order to obtain the maximum benefits from crossbreeding, sows should be replaced after producing a planned number of litters. The principal advantages of this system are lower maintenance costs for gilts and higher sale value per pound as compared to older, heavier sows.

Boars

Selecting the right boar is even more important than selecting a sow or gilt because on most farms a boar is usually bred to several sows. Use production-tested meat-type boars, especially if they are as reasonable in price as untested boars.

Ignore minor defects in a boar unless the females have similar defects. The boar's good qualities should outweigh any major weaknesses in the sows.

If you must select a boar on type and appearance alone, wait until he is at least 6 months old. At this age, defects as well as desirable traits can more readily be observed than at younger ages.

Sometimes you must choose between a boar from a herd with high performance records and a boar of superior appearance from a herd with no performance record. When you make this choice, select one on the basis of records rather than appearance.

Consider the boar's individuality and records of near relatives—dam, sisters, or brothers. The next most important qualities of a boar to consider are a moderately long body, good bone, and sound feet and legs. He should have masculine character, be smooth, not coarse, and have good muscular development in his ham and loin. His reproductive organs should be clearly visible and well developed.

Number of Boars

If the herd exceeds 15 sows and the sows are handled as a single group, use two or more boars. This will permit comparisons among the offspring of different

148

boars and provide a way to select boar replacements on a progeny-test basis.

Avoid breeding animals with ruptures of the navel, sexual abnormalities such as hermaphroditism and cryptochidism, and scrotal ruptures.

Do not use animals from litters with pigs that have defects. A single defective pig should rule out the selection of full sisters and brothers as breeders.

A boar should not be used for breeding until he is 8 months old. Keep a superior boar as long as he will fit into the breeding plan. Avoid close inbreeding such as parent-offspring or full brother-sister matings.

Crossbred Stock

Crossbred pigs have some advantages over their purebred parents. Crosses of lines or breeds usually improve prolificacy, survival, growth rate, and feed efficiency of pigs, and milk production of sows.

Two breeding plans for obtaining maximum benefits of hybrid vigor are:

• Rotational crossbreeding. It consists of using purebred sires of three or more breeds in a regular sequence or rotation. For example, females of breed A are mated to males of breed B, replacement females of AB cross are mated to breed C males and females from this mating (ABC) are mated to breed A males. This sequence is repeated as long as it gives satisfactory results.

• Crossbreeding, and rotating unrelated lines within a purebreed have similar effects. Rotating lines usually results in less vigor than a breed cross but produces greater uniformity.

The improvement obtained under either system depends on the genetic merit and the combining value of the stocks used.

Breed associations, **state** and **federal** experiment stations, and extension services sponsor programs for evaluating hog performance and quality. They also help hog breeders find superior breeding stock.

Feeds

Swine are fed chiefly cereal grains and their byproducts. To these are added protein and other supplements to provide a complete ration. This ration must contain proteins, carbohydrates, fats, minerals, and vitamins.

Corn is the staple grain used for feeding hogs. For best results, supplement corn with protein, calcium, phosphorus, and pasture or legume hay. For growing or finishing pigs, mix ground or shelled corn with a protein-mineral supplement. Grinding corn for hogs is not economical unless you plan to use it in a complete mixed diet.

Little wheat is fed to livestock. However, it is worth about 3 to 5 percent more than corn as a hog feed.

Good, sound barley, weighing 46 pounds or more per bushel, is 90 to 95 percent as good as corn. Lighter weight indicates lower feeding value. Barley should be ground or crushed. Do not feed scabbed barley.

Rye seems less palatable to hogs than other grains. Feed it ground with corn, wheat, or barley. Rye is dangerous if it contains ergot. Do not feed rye to pregnant sows; the ergot it may contain induces miscarriages.

Oats differ in feeding value—on the basis of percentage of hulls. The hulls determine weight per bushel. You can use oats as a replacement for corn—up to one-fourth of the diet. Ground oats equals the replaced corn in feeding value, pound for pound.

Oats is a better feed for growing pigs and brood sows than for market hogs. Because oats has a high fiber content, it retards excessive fat. You may want to use oats in the final stage of finishing market hogs.

Grain sorghums are nearly equal to corn as swine feed. They are slightly higher

in protein content but lower in fat. Thresh sorghum for swine. Grinding grain sorghum seldom pays unless it is handfed.

Rice is rarely fed to swine unless it is damaged, low-grade, or exceptionally cheap. It is generally worth about 85 percent as much as corn.

Grain Substitutes

If your farm is located in an area where grains are not the most plentiful feed crops or are too expensive, you can substitute other feeds in the ration.

Cull or surplus potatoes are occasionally fed to swine. Use potatoes—they should be cooked—only partially to replace the grain portion of the diet. For best results feed no more than 4 pounds of potatoes per pound of concentrates.

Yams or sweetpotatoes are fed to swine principally in the South. There, yams usually outyield corn. Their disadvantages are high labor cost and low protein, calcium, and phosphorus content. They may be fed cooked, dehydrated, or raw.

Often, yams are harvested by grazing or hogging-off. For best results supplement yams with about one-third to one-half of the usual allotment of grain, plus protein and minerals.

Molasses, when sufficiently cheap, can replace part of the grain in swine diets. Molasses and sugar are used in pelleted feeds and starter diets for baby pigs.

Root crops—mangles and turnips—are usually relished by swine. They are not economical to feed. Good legume pasture or hay is more efficient.

Combine screenings are waste products obtained from harvest operating. This might include portions of the grain harvested that is broken and an assortment of weed seeds. This can be fed as part of a ration in older pigs.

Silage is not suited for growing-finishing pigs. However, when properly supplemented with concentrates, silage is a good feed for pregnant sows. It costs less than conventional all-concentrate gestation diets.

Prosco or hog millet is grown mainly in the extreme northern section of the West North Central States. It is worth from 85 to 100 percent of the value of corn.

Many grain by products are used to feed swine either because of special nutrient content or favorable prices. Some byproduct feeds are hominy and gluten meal from corn, "oat clippings" and feeding oatmeal, wheat bran shorts and middlings, barley, rye middlings, rice bran, and rice polish.

Rice bran and broken rice are a favorite ration for family type swine raisers in Asia. Sweet potatoe cuttings are also included in this ration.

Protein Supplements

Animal Protein

Byproducts of milk, cheese, meat, and fish are valuable protein supplements to grain.

The amount of liquid skim milk or buttermilk needed to balance a corn diet differs with size and age of the pigs. Weaning pigs (56 days old) need about 4 to 5 pounds of milk product to each pound of corn.

Decrease the milk to 3 pounds when pigs weigh 50 to 75 pounds; to 2½ pounds when they weigh 100 to 125 pounds; and to 1 or 2 pounds after they weigh 150 pounds.

You can reduce the amount of liquid skim milk or buttermilk by one-third to one-half if you feed barley, wheat, or corn, on good pasture. Feed 4 to 6 pounds milk per pound of corn for 25- to 30-pound pigs; 3 pounds of milk per pound of corn for 50- to 100-pound pigs; 1½ to 2 pounds milk per pound of corn for 100- to 200-pound pigs.

If barley or wheat replaces corn or corn is fed on good pasture, reduce the amounts of milk by one-third to one-half.

Whey is worth about half as much as skim milk. If you feed whey with corn or barley, also feed a vegetable protein concentrate—linseed meal, soybean meal, or cottonseed meal.

Condensed or dried whey, skim milk, and buttermilk are good protein feeds. They are generally priced too high for economical swine feeding, except in starter diets for early weaning or creep-feeding baby pigs.

Use meat scrap and tankage as standards for evaluating other protein concentrates.

Meat or fish byproducts are most efficient in a trio-type supplement mixture. This mixture combines a legume hay or meal with protein concentrates from both animal and vegetable sources.

Vegetable Protein

Soybean oilmeal is satisfactory as the only protein supplement to grain if pigs are fed on good pasture with vitamin B_{12} and mineral supplements. The same applies to drylot feeding if a legume hay or meal is included in the diet.

Cottonseed meal alone is unsafe for unrestricted feeding to swine because of its free gossypol content. It should be fed in trio-type mixture or combined with animal byproducts.

Peanut oilmeal is a good source of protein for swine. If you feed it as the only protein source, add calcium to the ration or, you can feed peanut oilmeal with an equal amount of fishmeal, tankage, or meat scrap.

Corn and soybeans are often interplanted for grazing or hogging-off. However, raw soybeans are inferior to soybean oilmeal for all classes of swine.

Peanuts are grown in many sections of the Southern U.S., to be hogged-off. (This essentially means that swine harvests a whole or remnants of a crop in the field.) They produce soft pork but are usually an economical feed. Rate of gain may be increased by feeding a supplement such as tankage with peanuts, but this is usually not as economical as hogging-off with only salt and calcium supplements.

Garbage

Garbage feeders produce more than 2 million market hogs annually. Sterilizing or cooking garbage to prevent spread of disease is a legal requirement in almost every State since the national outbreak of vesicular exanthema in 1952.

Garbage differs widely in feeding value. The difference is due to the amount of inedible refuse in the garbage.

Carcasses of garbage-fed hogs shrink more, dress out at slightly lower weights, and are softer than grain-fed hog carcasses. However, the low cost of the feed usually makes garbage feeding profitable.

Minerals

Minerals are necessary for good swine nutrition. The minerals most needed are salt, calcium, and phosphorus. Lesser amounts of potassium, sulfur, iron, and manganese also are required. Under normal conditions zinc, cobalt, copper, magnesium, and iodine are essential in only minute or trace amounts.

Practically all feeds contain minerals. The combination of feeds that you use determines the amount of extra minerals needed in a ration. Because pasture and harvested forages have a greater percentage of minerals than seeds and their byproducts, pigs fed on pasture require less extra minerals than pigs fed in a

drylot. Animal protein concentrates are also rich sources of minerals.

Almost any mineral mixture that supplies the needs of swine and is palatable enough to be eaten freely is satisfactory. For example, a mixture of equal weights of steamed bonemeal, ground limestone (or airslacked lime), and salt is palatable. It contains the major elements needed for supplementing grain feeds. Use trace-mineralized salt that will supply requirements of the minor elements.

Supply a mineral mixture to hogs in boxes or self-feeders where it will be dry and available at all times. It may be mixed with the protein part of the diet, or incorporated at about 1.5 percent into a complete mixed diet.

Where hogs are raised in barns or on feeding platforms, mineral supplements are important. Frequently it is profitable to design mineral mixtures to fit the diets of different ages and classes of swine.

Vitamins

Most feed combinations used for swine feeding are adequate in most of the essential vitamins.

Swine fed pasture or fresh green forage, get practically all the vitamins they need except D and B_{12}. If you cannot feed fresh forage, include dehydrated alfalfa meal or high-quality legume hay in the ration.

To supply vitamin D, add small quantities of A and D feeding oil or irradiated yeast to the diet. Or, expose the pigs to sunlight. To supply vitamin B_{12}, include an animal protein concentrate or a vitamin B_{12} supplement in the diet.

Water

Hogs need a plentiful supply of water. The amount they drink depends on size, age, class of animal, and climate. A weanling pig (35 pounds) may drink about one-half gallon; a market hog (220 pounds), about 1 gallon; and a brood sow suckling a litter, about 5 gallons.

For watering troughs, allow a sow and litter (or 20 weanling pigs) at least 1 foot (on both sides) of trough space. The animals should receive all they want to drink at least two or three times a day.

Feeding

Brood Sows

To do her job efficiently, a brood sow needs an adequate diet. Overfeeding is more harmful than underfeeding. Either practice may be as harmful as a severe diet deficiency.

Pregnant sows usually are handfed a complete mixed feed. Or, you can scatter ear or shelled corn to encourage exercise and put the ground part of the ration in troughs. If you feed this way, allow a gilt about 1¾ pounds of diet daily for each 100 pounds live weight if she is in a small lot, or 2 pounds if in a large lot. A comparable sow allowance is 1¼ to 1½ pounds of complete diet per 100 pounds of body weight.

The average gilt or sow requires about ¾ ton of complete premixed diet for the gestation period (hand fed) and a lactation period (self fed) of 56 days.

In estimating feed requirements for a herd of swine, allow approximately 1 ton of feed for each litter of pigs reared to 56 days. This will provide feed for boars, creep feed for pigs, and an allowance for some delays in getting sows settled.

For self feeding during pregnancy, mix ground legume hay or other bulky feed to prevent excessive fattening of the sows. This practice reduces labor costs and produces more uniform conditions of the sows. However, more total pounds of

feed are required in this system and, for economy, you will need a cheap source of bulky feed.

Another economical gestation diet for sows includes well-eared corn silage, a protein supplement, minerals, and vitamins.

Cooking and Soaking Feeds

Cooking does not improve the feed value of grains. However, potatoes, soybeans, field beans, and velvetbeans are improved by cooking.

The protection against spread of disease more than compensates for any slight decrease in feeding value due to cooking garbage.

When it is impractical to grind whole barley or oats or when corn becomes very hard and dry, these grains may be slightly improved in feeding value by soaking.

Table 7. Methods of Feeding Pregnant Sows*

Hand Fed

Feed	Pounds
Mixed Diet (concentrate)------------------------------	6
or	
Corn silage---	12
Corn silage supplement--------------------------------	1
Yellow, shelled corn (ground)-------------------------	1

Self Fed

Mixed diet (high fiber)-------------------------------	8

*For 24 hours after farrowing give the sow water but no feed.

On the second day start her at about 2¼ to 2½ pounds of feed and increase the ration each day. She should be on full feed, about 10 to 12 pounds, when the pigs are a week to 10 days old. As soon as she is on full feed, the sow may be self fed.

If a sow becomes constipated or suffers digestive upset, she may fail to come into milk or the milk may disagree with the pigs. For mild constipation, give a warm slop of wheat bran or of the regular diet, containing a tablespoon of Epsom salt or Glauber salt.

In cases of severe constipation or complete milk failure, call a veterinarian. Proper medication may save the pigs and the sow.

If orphaned pigs have received colostrum for a day or two before the death of the sow, they are fairly easy to rear. You can feed them with a bottle and nipple or a shallow pan.

Without colostrum very rigid sanitation is needed to save the pigs. Use whole cow's milk or goat's milk as a substitute for sow's milk. Commercially prepared sow's milk substitutes, or synthetic milk, have nearly disappeared from the market but can be useful for feeding orphan pigs, if available.

The easiest way to rear orphan pigs is to put them on another sow that has extra functioning teats. This is practical only if the foster sow farrowed within a day or two of the natural dam.

Table 8. Examples of gestation and lactation diets.

Ingredient	Gestation Hand fed (complete)	Gestation Silage (supplement)	Gestation Self fed (complete)	Lactation (complete)
	Percent	Percent	Percent	Percent
Yellow shelled corn (ground)	55.00		41.25	45.00
Corn cobs (ground)			35.00	
Oats (ground)	15.00			15.00
Standard Middlings				17.50
Molasses, liquid blackstrap			5.00	
Alfalfa Meal (dehydrated 17 percent)	15.00	15.00	5.00	
Tankage or meat and bone scraps	3.60	25.00	6.00	5.00
Fishmeal	3.60			3.60
Soybean meal	3.60	52.90	6.00	3.60
Linseed Meal	2.40			7.50
Glauber's salt	.20			
Ground limestone	.40			
Bonemeal	.40	4.00	1.00	.90
Salt, trace mineralized	.50	2.00	.50	.90
Antibiotic plus vitamin B_{12}	.30			.70
Vitamin B_{12}		.50	.10	.30
Vitamin A and D supplement		.25	.05	
B-vitamin supplement		.35	.10	
Total	100.00	100.00	100.00	100.00

Table 9. Guide for preparing a premixed diet for pigs.

Age of Pigs	Approximate weight of pigs	Crude protein	Corn	Protein-mineral mixture
Weeks:	Pounds	Percent	Parts	Parts
8 to 14	30 to 90	16	75	25
14 to 20	90 to 160	14	83	17
20 to 25	160 to 225	12	92	8

Growing-Finishing Hogs

Pigs, from weaning to market, may be self fed either a free-choice diet or a complete premixed diet.

The free-choice method saves grinding and mixing costs. The disadvantages are a slightly lower rate of gain and less uniform carcass finish. For best results with this system, the grain portion and the supplement should be as near the same in palatability as possible.

Feeding a complete, premixed diet increases cost per pound of diet—the cost of grinding and mixing. However, it increases rate of gain and improves feed efficiency. This increase is not always enough to covercome the added cost.

The premixed diet permits uniform distribution of additives and usually produces more uniform carcasses than if the hogs are fed a free-choice diet.

A further advantage of this diet is that it allows changes in ingredients. You can alter levels of fiber and protein according to needs for carcass quality in market

154

hogs. The formulas in Table 9 are suitable for feeding pigs 56 days old. You can feed them these mixtures until the pigs reach market weight of approximately 225 pounds.

This protein-mineral mixture may be self fed in a separate compartment with ground, shelled, or ear corn. Or, you can make it into a complete premixed diet by combining with the proper proportion of grain.

The amount of feed needed to add 100 pounds of live weight to a hog is important for economical production of pork. This amount is influenced by age, health, inheritance of the animal, quality and combination of feeds, and environment.

Feed efficiency has been improved by the breeders' emphasis on changing from fat type to meat type as well as by advances in feeding "know-how." For instance, the complete diet just listed, when fed to good meat-type weanlings, has consistently produced 100 pounds gain up to market weight of 225 pounds for less than 350 pounds of total diet. Since these records were compiled, a number of cases have been cited of less than 300 pounds of feed producing 100 pounds of live weight gain in hogs.

Hog Pastures

Good pastures can supply a large part of the protein, calcium, and vitamins needed by swine.

With advances in swine nutrition, we are less dependent on pasture for growing-finishing hogs. However, pigs, intended for feeding out on concrete or in a drylot, will do better if they have had access to abundant green grazing during their suckling period.

Proper pasture use benefits both pasture and animals. Grazing too closely harms the plants. Undergrazing allows plants to mature too much and lowers their digestibility and palatability.

Pastures differ widely in carrying capacity, the amount depending on the crop, soil fertility, and climate. A fair-to-good pasture may carry five to fifteen 100-pound hogs per acre.

Hogs on pasture distribute manure uniformly. This saves the expense of removing and distributing manure—a considerable cost in platform feeding.

Pastures are more valuable for the breeding herd than for other classes of swine. The feed requirements of pregnant sows can be nearly filled by pasture until ideal conditions. Normally, you can count on grazing to replace one-third to two-thirds of a gestation diet.

Permanent Pastures

In most hog-growing sections, farmers plan to keep hogs mainly on permanent pastures.

Place only a limited number of hogs on permanent pasture. Allow the pasture enough growth to produce a crop of hay.

Plants used for permanent pastures are alfalfa, Ladino, red clover, alsike, white clover, bluegrass, bur clover, bermudagrass, lespendeza, carpetgrass, crabgrass and Dallis grass.

The first six are used in the northern half of the United States. Bluegrass and white clover often are grown together. Timothy often is grown with red clover. The other plants are grown in the South.

Of all the permanent pasture plants alfalfa and Ladino are preferred by hog raisers. Where these plants thrive, no other permanent pasture is necessary.

155

Temporary Pastures

You can use temporary pastures on nearly every hog farm.

Every barnyard and small lot where hogs are kept should be disked and seeded at least once a year. Disking once a year—or better twice a year—does not allow time for the permanent pasture plants to get established.

The grasses common in permanent pastures are not useful in temporary pastures where there are hogs enough to keep the pasture closely grazed.

The most common temporary pasture plants are rye, oats, wheat, rape, soybeans, and cowpeas. These plants are grown in most parts of the United States.

Seed temporary pastures heavier than a field for a grain crop. Sow rye in the fall.

In the northern areas, graze rye until it is covered by snow or made worthless by freezing. Rye may be grazed from early spring until hot weather. If the growth is rank, clip it with a mowing machine. Set the cutting bar as high as possible. In the South, rye may produce good grazing all winter.

In sections where winter oats is grown, the crop can be pastured the same way as rye. In the North, oats sown in the spring makes a good temporary pasture. The pasture period is short.

Rape is often sown with oats in the spring; Dwarf Essex is the variety of rape. You can seed rape from early spring until summer. When rye is 6 to 10 inches high, graze it heavily. It will keep growing and produce good, succulent feed.

Cowpeas and soybeans are sown in the spring. Sometimes they are planted together. Of the two, soybeans will usually make the best hog pasture. Select a variety that produces a large quantity of foliage and does well in your locality.

Turn in the hogs when the plants are 6 to 8 inches high. If the hogs eat the pasture down, take them out for a while and permit the plants to recover.

Dallis grass grows well in low, moist lands, makes a good growth in warm weather, and withstands close grazing well.

Sweetclover grows rapidly in good soil. Graze it heavily to keep the plants from becoming tough and fibrous.

Pig-Eating Sows

Killing and eating pigs is most often seen among animals that are nervous and excitable. Occasionally these sows eat one or more pigs. Some causes of pig eating are extreme heat, excessive pain in difficult or protracted labor, or loud noises.

Pig eating also occurs among sows having diet deficiencies or suffering from acute constipation due to faulty feeding or management. Although you cannot always prevent pig eating, good feeding and management should reduce it to a minimum.

Feeder Pigs

Larger farms, specialization, and labor saving systems have increased the demand for feeder pigs. Many grain producers can fit a large-scale feeding operation into their program. However, they cannot devote enough time to manage a breeding and farrowing system profitably.

Weanling pigs 6 to 10 weeks old weighing 30 to 50 pounds usually are sold as feeders. Garbage feeders and farmers who wish to graze or "hog-off" crops usually buy larger pigs, up to 120 pounds.

Most of the demand is from the Corn Belt and small grain areas. However, the Southern States have increased their swine-feeding operations and are competing for feeder pigs.

Many areas grow abundant grazing and forage crops but produce only enough grain for breeding stock on good pasture. Whenever these conditions exist and you apply approved methods of breeding, feeding, and management, producing feeder pigs should be profitable.

Managing Stock

Boars

To insure maximum usefulness of a boar:

He should have the run of a good-size lot or pasture, convenient to the breeding pen, but away from lots in which breeding sows are kept.

He should receive all the feed he will clean up twice daily during a heavy breeding season. Feed him the same diet listed for pregnant sows.

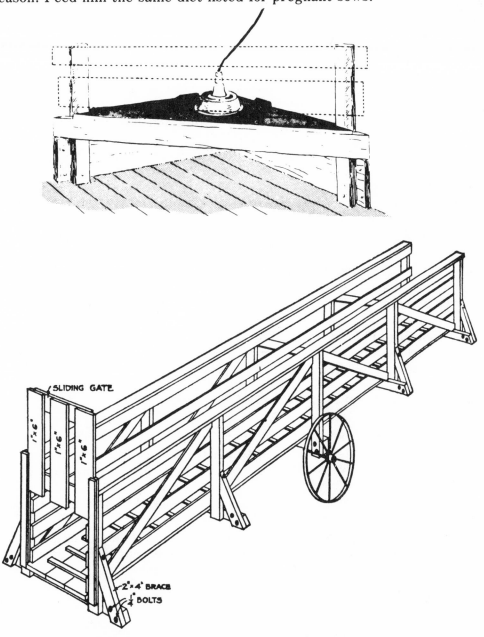

Fig. 13. Top; Corner Brooder for new born pigs. Bottom; Portable Loading Crate.

If he is used only lightly after a long or a heavy breeding season, reduce his feed to keep him in a strong, thrifty condition.

In hand-mating, allow a young boar to serve only one sow each day, except in emergencies. Limit an aged boar to this same schedule if he is used through a long breeding season. A strong, vigorous boar may serve two sows a day when necessary.

Service on each of two consecutive days will increase average number of pigs born by about one pig per litter. Have your boars use a breeding crate at least enough so that they become accustomed to it. The crate is useful for mating females and males of different size.

Group mating is practiced where group standards are emphasized rather than individual excellence. Under a group system, run two or more boars with a group of sows to settle all the sows as quickly as possible.

The advantages of group mating are maximum litter size and minimum labor. Heavy service for short periods, followed by rest, apparently is not harmful to boars.

Sows

Select only growthy, well-developed gilts for breeding. They can be safely bred at 8 months of age. Gilts bred too young may produce fewer and smaller pigs. Also, they may have more trouble at farrowing and fail to grow out well after weaning their first litters.

Under the gilt-litter system, all gilts are finished for market immediately after weaning their first litters. Immediate marketing avoids the lower price usually paid for older, heavier sows.

Under other systems, gilts are kept for a definite number of additional litters, or for as long as they produce profitable litters.

If they are fed an adequate diet, pregnant gilts have little interruption in their growth.

Sows may produce two litters a year up to 6 or 8 years of age, or even longer. Commercial producers frequently discard sows at earlier ages than 6 or 8 years. Purebred breeders usually retain the best females as long as they remain productive.

A sow usually will farrow in 112 to 115 days after she is bred. Sometimes she will farrow in 110 days or she may go a few days over 115. By keeping a careful service record you will know when to expect the pigs.

Care of Sows During Pregnancy

Breeding and pregnancy are the most critical events in profitable swine production. Sows that are too fat at breeding time have smaller litters than thrifty sows. For best results, the sow should be in good condition, neither thin nor excessively fat.

"Flushing," or increasing the ration, for 1 to 3 weeks before mating tends to increase ovulation and conception rates.

Most important during pregnancy are adequate nutrition, exercise, and protection from extreme cold or heat. Improper feeding may cause deaths among unborn pigs or poor survival of the newborn pigs.

Care of Sows and Pigs at Farrowing

About 3 days before farrowing, move the sow to scrubbed, disinfected quarters. Wash her with soap and warm water, especially her teats. Place light bedding in the farrowing pen. You can use short hay or straw, peanut hulls, or shavings.

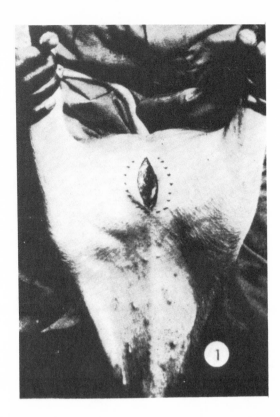
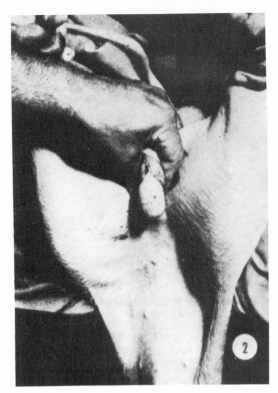
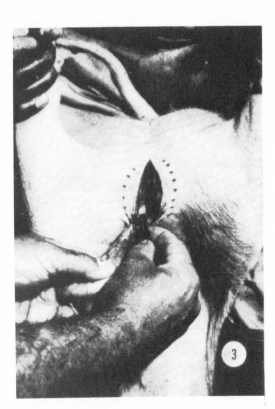
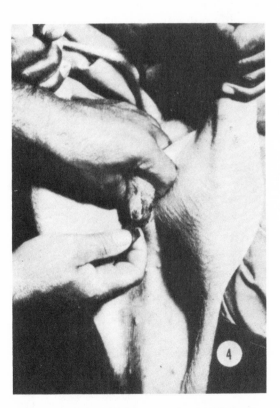

Fig. 14. Castrating A Young Pig. 1. Make the incision between the testicles as deep as a testicle is thick and twice as long as a testicle. 2. Squeeze the first testicle out through the incision. 3. Pull the testicle lightly to stretch the cord. Place your knife (or a clean, single-edge razor blade) against the cord near the edge of the incision and cut the cord. 4. Make a smaller incision inside the main incision to expose the second testicle.

159

Fig. 15. Top Left; Movable house with doors in sidewall. Top Right; Movable house with hinged wall. Bottom Left; House with removable floor panel. Bottom Right; House on skids with built-in floor.

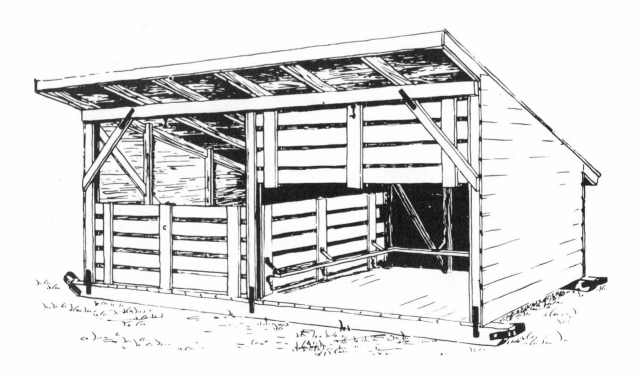

Fig. 16. A warm climate or summer hog house on skids for easy moving.

160

Reduce feed by one-third to one-half and watch for any signs of digestive upset or constipation.

Normal, healthy sows usually farrow without trouble. If possible, an attendant should be on hand to give any needed assistance. The assistance may be preventing pigs from chilling, warming them after chilling, or starting breathing in apparently lifeless pigs—by clearing the membrane covering the head and massaging or slapping the pig's sides.

After delivery, paint the navel cords with iodine. Clip the tips of the eight tusk-like needle teeth, and weigh and earmark the pigs.

The sow needs no feed for 24 hours after farrowing, but she should have water available. If at all possible, feed the sow in an enclosure separate from her pigs. This will prevent her from crippling or killing the pigs accidentally while her attention is centered on eating. It also aids in keeping the farrowing pen clean because droppings are usually voided during the feeding period.

Sows and Suckling Pigs

Some sows are not able to nurse all the pigs they bear in one litter. If the sow does not have a functioning teat for each pig, transfer pigs to a sow with a small litter. Make the change as quickly as possible.

Transferring pigs is rarely possible after more than 3 or 4 days, because teats that are not sucked dry up. Also the odors of the pigs must be masked until they are accepted by the foster dam. To do this put a little oil or some harmless ointment on both the sow's own and adopted pigs.

Unless newborn pigs have almost immediate access to the soil, you must plan a way to prevent anemia. Several procedures for preventing anemia are:

Provide clean soil or sod

Spray or paint copperas (ferrous sulfate) solution on the sow's udder

Dose with iron tablets

Use intramuscular injections of iron-dextran compounds.

Increase the sow's ration gradually until she is on full feed—when pigs are a week old. Feed the pig a starter diet in a "creep." Litters from poor-milking sows are greatly benefited by creep feedings; litters from the better milking sows do not eat enough to increase feed costs appreciably.

Pen the sow and litter separately for at least 1 week, preferably for 2 weeks.

Do not pen more than four sows and litters together under central farrowing house conditions. All the pigs should be within 1 week of the same age.

Limit the sows and pigs on one pasture to six sows with litters. These litters should be within 2 weeks of the same age.

Procedures that may cause stress in young pigs are castration, vaccination, weaning, and worming. Schedule these so that one stress effect wears off before the pig is subjected to another.

Unless male pigs are to be considered later for breeding, castrate them during the first 4 weeks. Pigs weaned at 4 weeks of age or less should be castrated at least 1 week before or after weaning. The operation should not follow cholera vaccination by less than 3 weeks.

Weaning

Most pigs are weaned at 5 to 8 weeks of age, under a 2-litter-per-year system. Reduce or cut off the sow's feed for 2 or 3 days before weaning to reduce milk flow and prevent udder trouble. Then remove the sow from the pigs, leaving the pigs in familiar quarters.

If a sow's udder appears too full, return her to the pigs for suckling; then,

remove her immediately. A second return rarely is necessary, except with very heavy milkers.

A sow normally will come in heat 3 to 7 days after the pigs are weaned. She may be bred again at this time.

Recordkeeping

Every pig should be marked at farrowing time. The most satisfactory method is to notch the ears. Eartags of different kinds are used, but they tear out easily and the identity of the pig is lost.

Even if hogs are raised for market only, earmarking the pigs will help you select animals for the breeding herd. Reliable selection can be made only if the dam of the pig is known and her performance record is examined.

Small, sharp, side-cutting pliers do a good job of earnotching. For permanent marks, notch deeply enough to include a part of the cartilage of the ear. Notch the ears soon after the litter is farrowed, when wounds heal quickly.

Record every breeding date. If you know the farrowing dates, you will be ready to feed and care for the sow.

Sanitation

Results from the best methods of feeding and breeding will be lessened by faulty sanitation.

Keep farrowing houses and sleeping quarters clean. Change bedding frequently; do not let it become wet and foul.

The floors of the sleeping quarters become dusty. Dust is irritating to the lungs and may carry eggs of parasites. To reduce dust irritation clean the floors at least every 2 or 3 weeks; disinfect floors with a 3-percent solution of cresol. To make this, add 1 pint of cresol to 4 gallons of water.

Apply lime to pens and feeding places that are not plowed. The lime will aid in drying damp places and in disinfection. At least twice a year, disk all barnyards and lots or temporary pastures on which hogs are kept. If you plant pasture crops in these lots, the disking will be profitable in two ways.

Cooling Equipment

Hogs suffer greatly from heat and must have shade. Keep farrowing and individual hoghouses closed in hot weather to prevent hogs from lying in them. Hogs will seek shade even if they suffocate in it. Trees provide good shade if there are enough of them in a clump. Or, you can make a satisfactory shading structure with a framework about 4 feet high, made of posts or poles. Cover the top with hay, straw, or weeds to a depth of at least 2 feet. When dust accumulates under this shelter, wet the covering. The water will drip through to settle the dust and cool the air in the shelter. You can make permanent shelters from pipe, lumber, and conventional roofing materials.

Farrowing Quarters and Equipment

Farrowing quarters are variations of three basic patterns.

The conventional "square" pen should be at least 6 by 8 feet for a gilt and 8 by 8 feet for a sow.

The farrowing crate or stall should be 20 by 72 inches for a gilt; 24 by 84 inches for a sow. Provide an enclosed area, 18 inches wide on each side of the crate for the pigs.

An ideal temperature for the farrowing house is 55° to 65°F., if the house is

adequately ventilated. Because a newborn pig chills easily, you should provide some heat in the protected resting area for at least 5 days.

The amount of heat needed differs. It may be supplied by infrared-heat lamps or electric hovers in cold climates. Use a 100- to 125-watt light bulb mounted in a metal reflector in warm climates. Because any type of heating device can cause fire, you should install heaters carefully. Keep the lamp from close contact with straw.

Sometimes it is difficult to make the farrowing house temperature suit both sows and newborn pigs. Extreme heat and humidity may have worse effects on farrowing than extreme cold. The nervous, restless behavior of sows suffering from heat usually causes pig deaths from mashing.

Occasionally, a sow may be lost from heat prostration. In the warmer sections of this country avoid farrowing in midsummer unless you provide some method of cooling the sows.

Farrowing house plans suitable for a particular locality may be obtained through your State extension service, county agricultural agents, or farm adviser. (See Part VIII for Swine House Plans)

If the sows have been running on pasture, move them to clean, new pasture and allow them to farrow there. Wash the sows before you move them if they are encrusted with mud and filth. This method is suitable for fall farrowing in practically all States. It is also suitable for spring farrowing in the South.

Wallows and Sprinklers

A hog wallow made of concrete and located in a convenient shady place is a benefit in a hoglot. A mud wallow made by the hogs rooting a hole in the lot or pasture is a nuisance. It should be filled in.

It is impossible to keep a mud wallow sanitary. Hogs may drink the water that has become stagnant and foul.

The concrete wallow should hold 4 to 6 inches of water. Clean it frequently and refill with fresh water. To control lice, spray enough crude oil to form a thin layer on the water. Apply the spray about every 10 days.

If you feed hogs on concrete and a pressure water system is available, use fog-type sprinkler nozzles, such as those used in fuel oil burners, to cool the hogs.

Health

Among the important health problems of hogs are cholera, erysipelas, brucellosis, tuberculosis, necrotic enteritis, atrophic rhinitis, swine influenza, and parasitic infestations.

Ask your veterinarian about the preferred times, methods, and number of vaccinations and other disease control measures needed to protect swine in your area. (See Part V, Veterinary Section for more on swine diseases.)

Diseases

If you suspect that one of your animals is sick, ask your veterinarian about the proper treatment.

Because some livestock and poultry have diseases that can be transmitted to hogs, the danger of permitting hogs to eat carcasses outweighs the feeding value. Carcasses should be burned or buried.

Parasites

Parasites affect hogs of all ages and may cause death—particularly among small

pigs—reduce vitality, and prevent best and most rapid development.

The most damaging internal parasites are large roundworms, kidney worms, thorn-headed worms, lungworms, and intestinal threadworms.

The principal external parasites are sarcoptic mange mites and suckling lice. Most of these species are found in practically all hograising areas.

Internal Parasites

Most swine parasites can be controlled by sanitation including:
Clean, disinfected farrowing pens;
Sows washed clean before farrowing;
A "clean" trip to clean pastures for sows and their litters;
Clean pastures for the pigs until they are at least 4 months old.
Internal parasites can also be controlled by feeding pigs exclusively on milk, skimmed milk, or whey for periods of 3 successive days at intervals of 2 weeks, or by feeding one of these daily instead of one grain feeding.

Pigs should be treated to control large roundworms at weaning and again about 2 months later. Use dry sodium fluoride—technical grade, tinted—at a concentration of 1 percent by weight, in *dry* ground feed for 1 day.

Pigs should be slightly underfed the day before treatment. On the day of treatment, give them about two-thirds as much medicated feed as regular feed.

Ordinarily, no other treatments are necessary or advisable. The treatments should not be given to pregnant or lactating sows, or to any animals showing symptoms of gastroenteritis.

External Parasites

For treatment of mange mites and eradication of lice, several insecticides are safe and effective—malathion, Ronnel (Korlan), pyrethrins and Rotenone. Follow directions on containers.

POULTRY

Probably no phase of a bird's life is more frequently neglected than the period from the time the bird leaves the brooder house until it reaches maturity. Yet this is an extremely important period. If stunted during the growing period, the bird never amounts to much. This is equally true for pullets, cockerels, capons and turkeys. Therefore when you learn to handle growing stock, the first important step in poultry husbandry is mastered.

To take this step, have adequate buildings, equipment, proper range, a balanced ration and above all, good chicks.

The Range, Shelters and Equipment

The Range—Provide a clean range—one where no birds have run for at least a year, preferably two or three years. This is so necessary that when you cannot provide clean range, engage in a different project. One acre will support 300 growing chickens or 150 turkeys. However it is better to plan on one acre for each 100 birds, since birds must be moved at least three times during the growing season.

If an alfalfa or green sod range can be used, the growing cost may be cut about 20%. Also birds reared on a green range are healthier and grow more rapidly. When running water (either piped or in a stream) is available the labor of handling birds is reduced and the birds grow faster.

164

The Range Shelter—When birds are fully feathered over their backs, it is time to move them to range shelters when temperatures are warm. If they can be roosted in a range shelter, they grow better than in a brooder house. Besides, a range shelter is easier to ventilate and costs less to maintain.

A shelter need not be fancy or expensive. It is merely roosts with a roof, wire sides and wire floor. Space roosts about 12 inches apart. Have the comb of the roof about five feet and the eaves about 2½ feet from the ground. The size of the shelter depends upon the size of the flock. Pullets and capons will need 8 to 10 inches linear roost room. Turkeys will need 9 to 12 inches. Thus a 7 ft. x 8 ft. shelter will accommodate 100 pullets or 50 turkeys.

Range Shade—If the birds have shade, they grow faster, feather better and do not sunburn. However don't let your birds hang around a shelterbelt or patches of underbrush where birds have run year after year. Sooner or later sickness occurs unless the ground is cleaned up. If no natural shade is available, make a shade or plant corn or sunflowers in rows to provide shade.

Range Equipment—Make range feeders and waterers movable; covered to provide shade and protection from weather. (See Self Help Engineering section, Part VIII for Poultry Equipment.)

Feeding Growing Stock

Feeding Systems—growing birds do not need as rich a diet as they did when younger. However they need a ration which will supply body building and energy materials. In addition they must have plenty of clean, cool water. To provide feed requirements any one of several systems may be used:

1. Commercial or home mixed growing mash before them in hoppers at all times plus morning and evening whole grain feedings.
   a. Give the amount of grain that will be cleaned up in an hour.
   b. If fed on the ground, choose a clean spot each time.
2. Growing mash (commercial or home mixed) plus whole grains fed in separate hoppers. Keep both feeds before the birds at all times. This is called "cafeteria style."
3. Milk plus whole grains plus green feed. To meet the bird's needs, 3 gallons of skim milk or buttermilk must be consumed daily per 100 birds. Keep the grain before them at all times in hoppers. With this system it is very necessary that the range be green. If not, feed additional greens daily.

Growing Mash Formulas—There are many good formulas for mixing growing mashes. The following has been proven satisfactory:

Table 10. A Growing Mash Ration

Ground wheat	30 pounds
Ground oats	20 pounds
Ground corn (yellow)	15 pounds
Ground barley	10 pounds
(1) Meat scrap (50% protein)	10 pounds
Dry Skimmed milk	5 pounds
Alfalfa leaf meal	5 pounds
Bone meal	2 pounds
Oyster shell (ground)	2 pounds
Salt	1 pound
(2) Cod liver oil	1 pint
Manganese Sulphate	4/10 ounce
	Total 100 pounds

165

1) When meat scrap and dry skim milk cannot be purchased and liquid skim or buttermilk is not available, substitute 2 pounds of dried whey plus 5 pounds of cottonseed meal and 8 pounds of soy bean meal.

2) When a guaranteed cod liver or other fish oil of known Vitamin D content is not available, substitute 2.4 ounces of Vitamin D supplement having 400 A.O.A.C. chick units.

Proportions of Feed-Stuffs—It is just as important to have your birds eat the right proportions of their feeds as it is to have these feeds balanced. For example, if the birds fill up on grain and eat no growing mash, they get fat and grow slowly. On the other hand, let a pullet eat only mash, she will comb up and lay before she gains body maturity. Table 11 gives an idea of the proportions of mash and grain which birds should eat at various ages.

Table 11. Proportions of Mash to Grain Consumption

Age in Weeks	% Mash	% Grain
6	95	5
8	90	10
10	80	20
12	70	30
14	60	40
16	50	50
18	40	60
20	30	70
22 to maturity	25	75

Growth to Feed Consumption—Another important feeding factor is the relation of rate of growth to amount of feed eaten. To get this, record the average weight of the flock and of feeds eaten. You are not expected to weigh each bird weekly to ascertain rate of gain. To do this would be foolish and time consuming. But weigh a sample of birds each week. At the beginning of the growing season mark five average birds in some way so that they can be easily spotted. Don't pick five extra large birds or runts.

Some poultrymen mark birds by daubing paint across their shoulders. This method requires repainting whenever birds grow new feathers. If leg banded, watch the legs. A growing chick may soon outgrow its band. This will cause sore legs, even crippled birds. Put the same five birds into a crate and weigh each week. Divide their total weight by 5, giving a fairly accurate average weight for the entire flock. Catching at night while roosting is a simple way to handle the problem.

Though the feed formulas and proportions given are not ideal for all environments, the figures will serve as a guide. In the Temperate Zone with its long growing days, birds usually eat more and make faster gains.

Young Stock Diseases

Since a special chapter is devoted to diseases, only mention of the troubles affecting growing stock will be given here. Growing chicks are apt to have coccidiosis, colds, fowl paralysis, perosis, vitamin deficiencies and troubles caused by an infestation of worms, mites or other parasites. Also growing turkeys are subject to blackhead.

As with all diseases, spot a sick bird at once, take it away from the flock and correct the cause of the disease.

166

Range Management

There is more to handling growing stock than giving them shelter and feed. A good poultryman watches his birds all the time. He heads off dangers and anticipates the birds needs.

First Nights in a Range Shelter—If birds have come from a warm brooder house, shield them from drafts and cold winds. They must be kept from crowding and taught to use their new roosts.

Storms—Until birds learn to run to shelter, see that they are driven in before a storm. Be sure the door has not blown shut. Keeping birds out in a storm may cause heavy losses as they will "corner up" and smother.

After a storm, check the range. Fill up or drain puddles. Stagnant water causes sickness.

At all times watch for any dead chicks or gophers on the range. Nothing sickens birds quicker than eating decaying flesh.

Enemies on Range—One or two species of hawks sometimes prey upon poultry on the range. Several poles may be set up with strings or wire stretched between the poles. String bits of shiny metal on the strings, for example, old lids from fruit jars. The metal catching the sunlight scares the hawks away. At night lock birds securely in the range shelter. If small animals like minks or weasels bother, a tight, inch-mesh wire under the roosts keeps them out. When young turkeys roost on exposed perches, it is well to keep a light on a pole near the roosts. If coyotes are a menace, keep birds in their shelters until after daylight. A tight fence about open roosts helps.

Dried Out or Dirty Range—You are advised to change range at least 3 times during the growing season. Yet no management detail requires your judgment and common sense as much as the decision of when to move birds. If the birds eat the green feed down to the roots, a vitamin A deficiency may show up. Then look out for colds, swollen eyes and slow growth. During a dry season when the range dries up, move birds oftener than when the range stays green.

Hot Nights—One hot night may ruin the flock. If hot nights occur, see that ventilation is adjusted to meet the condition.

Feeding—The real test of a poultryman is how he manages the feeding problem what kind of feed is needed, the proportions, and the amounts, have already been discussed. Yet under Range Management something more should be said.

The good poultryman watches the feeders. Are birds wasting feed? Are birds choosy, selecting some ingredients and leaving others? Did last night's rain wet the feed causing the mash to sour? Does the wind sometimes blow the mash away? Do the birds go on the roosts at night with full crops? A good poultryman checks all of these things each day so he can correct faults at once.

Uneven Development—Even though you feed a balanced ration and provide plenty of feeder space, all birds do not develop uniformly. If a farmer has a small number of birds, little can be done about this. But with a greater number, divide into early maturing, medium and slow maturing birds. Dividing sizes, gives a more uniform bunch of birds at the end of the project. Give the birds which grow too fast, more grain and less mash than suggested. Give the slow birds more mash and less grain than called for in the schedule. For medium birds, follow the schedule.

CAPONS AND CAPONIZING

A capon is an unsexed male bird of the dual purpose or heavy breeds. Plymouth Rocks, New Hampshires, Rhode Island Reds, Wyandottes and Orpingtons make excellent capons.

Because capons produce meat having better flavor and quality than unaltered males do, capons bring a better price and are therefore profitable to raise.

When to Caponize—The earlier the operation is performed the less the birds suffer from shock or set back. Therefore operate as soon as sex can be distinguished. With dual purpose birds this can be done by the time the birds are from 8 to 10 weeks old or when they weigh from 1 to 1½ pounds.

The Instruments—There are many sets of instruments. No matter which kind, the set must have a knife to make the incision; a spreader to hold open the cut; a hook to tear the membrane covering the intestines; a blunt instrument to press back the intestines out of the operator's way and an extractor to remove the testicle. An extractor made like a forceps does a more complete job than one shaped like a spoon.

BABY CHICKS

The care and management of baby chicks is an exacting task. Do not attempt to raise them until you are thoroughly familiar with the job of growing young stock. Further you should not tackle the raising of chicks until you can have complete charge of them.

To raise chicks successfully you must have an adequate brooder house; a good brooder stove or the equivalent; adequate brooder house equipment; a complete and adequate ration and good chicks.

The Brooder House

The essentials of a good brooder house are:
Enough floor space—Allow 1 square foot per chick. At least 1 square foot is

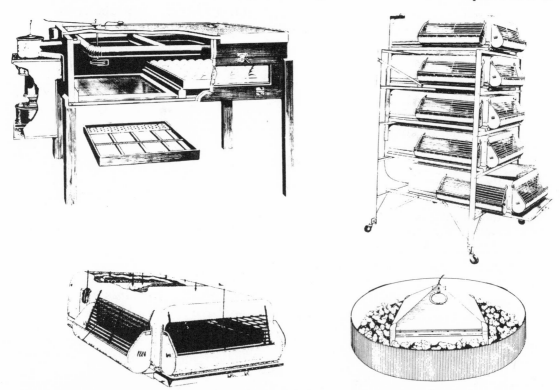

Fig. 17 Top Left; An oil/hot water incubator (the same type incubator is available in electricity). Top Right; A tier of battery brooders. Bottom Left; A single battery brooder. Bottom Right; A hover brooder with protective fence using electricity.

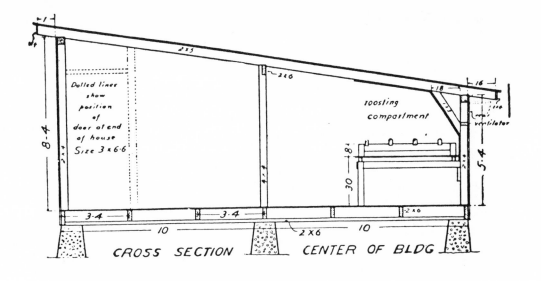

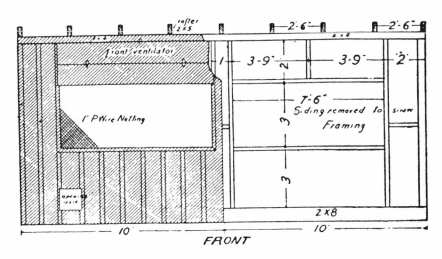

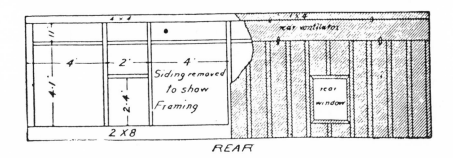

Fig. 18. A poultry house for 100 hens.

needed for every 2 chicks from one to eight weeks. Then double the floor space. Since chicks still need heat, it is better to start with 1 square foot per chick.

A well ventilated room—Although chicks need uniform heat, the room must be ventilated in order to keep the floor dry and the chicks healthy. Thoroughly study the ventilators in any brooder house plans.

The house needs a floor—Never put chicks on a dirt floor, especially if chicks have been raised on it before. A portable brooder house needs a wooden floor.

The Brooder Hen and Hover

When brooding chicks, remember that when a mother hen hovers them, she sits over them. Thus, if their backs are warm, they are warm. Therefore a good brooder stove with hover, supplies the heat above the chicks. The kind of fuel is immaterial so long as the source of heat is steady. Run the brooder heater several days before the chicks arrive. If you use an old heater, check all working parts.

The type of hover is also unimportant so long as each chick has 7 square inches hover space. Since the space should be doubled at 8 weeks, it is best to start with a generous hover.

A home made brooder may be built. Even the fireless brooder works in the brooder room if it has a steady temperature of 75° to 80°.

Fire box—The fire box may be made from an old oil barrel, heating stove, or it may be a brick or concrete fire box. The main thing is to have the fire box fitted with a tight door so that the fuel burns slowly. Place the fire box at least 18" below the surface of the ground with about a foot dug at either side of it. Fill the entire space, around and over the fire box, with rocks or bricks and sand. Start the fire at least 4 or 5 days before the chicks or poults arrive in order to have the sand and rocks thoroughly heated. Once hot, the temperature at the edge of the hover will remain constant. The temperature will not drop even after the firing of the stove has been discontinued for 36 hours.

Be sure the fire box is placed back from the sill of the house to avoid any fire risk.

Have an additional door to give additional protection. The door prevents draughts and too rapid burning of fuel. When burning wood a grate is not needed, but with coal, a grate is necessary.

The Pipe—The pipe should extend 4 or 5 feet under the floor from the fire box, in order to have all the intense heat taken from the smoke and so remove all danger of fire.

Floor—Make the floor of concrete if possible, though wooden floors have been used by cutting out the floor a few feet above the fire box and filling the space with sand and gravel.

The Hover—The hover may be made of any material, preferably metal. The main thing is to have the hover about 10" from the floor and allow 7 square inches per chick and twice that amount of space per poult.

More common types of poultry brooders utilize electricity as the main heat source. The hover type provides a canopy cover with a thermostat to control temperature (see Fig. 17). An overhead heating lamp can also be used for brooding, with a cardboard or wood enclosure to retain heat and keep out drafts. (See Self Help Engineering, (Part VIII for detailed plans on poultry equipment).

THE HOME CHICKEN FLOCK

The home chicken flock usually is kept for egg production. It should provide fresh eggs during most of the year.

Before you decide to start a laying flock, you should find out about the zoning ordinances in your area; if you live in a large city or a suburb, they may forbid poultry keeping.

No particular type of poultry house is best. Local conditions determine the house that will give good results. The poultry department of your State college of agriculture can recommend the type most suitable for your area. Prefabricated houses are available; one of these may be a good investment.

A square or rectangular house usually is more satisfactory than houses of other shapes. A small house can be about 6 feet high in front and 5 feet high at the back. Pole-type houses are usually 5 to 7 feet high at the sides and 10 feet high at the center.

Ordinarily, for a small house, a shedroof house is the most economical to build. Most shedroofs have a pitch of one to three or less. Pole-type houses have a gable roof and cost less for medium to large houses. The roof should have a pitch of one to three, or more.

The deeper the house, the less danger that drafts will reach birds roosting at the rear. A depth of at least 10 feet is desirable in a small house for both winter and summer comfort. Construction costs per square foot decrease as buildings are widened, because less foundation and wall are involved for each square foot of enclosed space. The labor required for the care of the hens is less in wider buildings. Larger houses should be about 30 feet wide and may be any length.

The number of windows and openings and the amount of ventilation needed depend on the climate. You should insulate the roof, at least, to make the house more comfortable in both summer and winter.

Frames covered with glass substitutes can be used to close part or all of the openings during winter. The glass substitutes, if kept clean, admit ultraviolet rays of the sun.

The size and breed of the flock determines the size of the house. Allow 3 square feet per bird for Leghorns or Leghorn-type strain crosses and 4 square feet per bird for medium-weight breeds—Plymouth Rocks, Rhode Island Reds, or New Hampshires.

The henhouse floor may be concrete, boards, or dirt. Concrete makes the most satisfactory floor because it is sanitary and durable; board floors are also satisfactory. Houses that have concrete or board floors can be cleaned more easily than those that have dirt floors. If you plan a dirt floor for your henhouse, make sure that the foundation is ratproof.

If you use boards for flooring, install them at least 12 inches off the ground. This will prevent dampness and rotting. Floors built this high off the ground also discourage rats from living under the henhouse.

Cover the floor with several inches of absorbent litter—wood shavings, sawdust, straw, or a commercial litter.

A system of built-up litter can be used. Put litter in the house early in the fall; add to it and stir it frequently until the droppings become well mixed. When litter is 6 to 8 inches deep and is dry, it needs no attention other than an occasional stirring. Parts of the litter that get damp and dirty should be replaced. Remove all litter at the end of the laying year.

Laying hens may be kept indoors the year round. Hens confined to the house will lay well and stay healthy if they have comfortable, well-ventilated houses and are fed adequate rations.

STARTING THE FLOCK

You can start your flock with hatching eggs, day-old chicks, started chicks, or partly grown, well-developed pullets.

Usually it is best to buy partly grown or well-developed pullets. The time and trouble in incubating and brooding chicks is not worthwhile when small numbers of pullets are raised, unless it is a hobby.

Eight to 15 birds should provide the average family with a liberal supply of eggs for most of the year.

Some breeds suitable for a home flock kept for egg production are:
New Hampshires
Plymouth Rocks
Rhode Island Reds
White Leghorns

EQUIPMENT

Most of the equipment for your henhouse can be made in the home workshop or purchased at low cost. The things you must provide for your flock are roosts, nests, a small coop, a feed hopper, a water container, and lights. You will also need a brooder if you start the flock with chicks. The sale of day-old chicks from hatcheries has largely done away with small incubators for home flocks. If started pullets are purchased, there will be no need for brooding equipment.

Preserving eggs

You can preserve your surplus eggs by refrigeration or freezing. When properly prepared for storage, fresh eggs may be kept for 6 to 9 months.

Refrigeration

Eggs laid during March, April, and May usually keep better than eggs laid later in the year.

Only fresh eggs with sound, strong shells should be preserved in the shell. Any that are soiled, cracked, or even slightly checked should not be stored.

Wash the shells. Then, coat them with clean mineral oil. You can apply the oil by dipping the eggs.

For dipping, warm the oil to thin it; have the oil no hotter than your hand can stand.

Eggs keep best if they are oiled within 24 hours after they are laid. Put several eggs in a wire basket, dip the basket, then allow the excess oil to drain off. Pack the oiled eggs in clean baskets, cases, or cartons and store them in a refrigerator or a cool cellar.

Properly oiled eggs have thick whites when broken after storage. The thick white is a sign that the oiling process was correct and storage conditions were ideal. Eggs poorly covered with oil or oiled too late will have watery whites. Oiled eggs are sometimes difficult to peel when hard boiled. To minimize this problem, hardcook oiled eggs in water that maintains a rolling boil.

Freezing

To freeze whole-egg mixtures, break the eggs and thoroughly mix the yolk and white.

172

Use an electric mixer at low speed to avoid incorporating any more air than necessary. No further treatment is needed. Pour the whole egg mixture into convenient-size containers and freeze.

For frozen, separated whites and yolks, separate the eggs in the usual way. Be careful to avoid getting any yolk into the whites; their whipping ability will be lost if yolk is mixed in. Mix the whites to a smooth consistency but avoid any foaming.

Freeze in a suitable container. The frozen, separated yolks will gel unless salt or sugar is added when they are mixed. Add 1 teaspoon of salt to each cup of yolks or 2 tablespoons of sugar, corn syrup or honey. Remember to allow for the added ingredients when using frozen yolks in recipes.

Culling the Laying Flock

Start the laying year with healthy, vigorous pullets. Remove poor layers as the year progresses. The appearance of the comb and wattles and the condition of the pubic bones, abdomen, and vent are good indicators of laying condition.

In a good layer, the comb and wattles will be full and bright red, the pubic bones thin and wide apart, the abdomen soft and deep, and the vent large and moist.

PART V — VETERINARY MEDICINE

IMMUNOLOGICAL PRODUCTS: What They Are and How They Work

"Immunity" means, in general terms, a resistance to infectious disease. Textbooks on the subject mention several types or classes of immunity, two of which are especially important from the standpoint of disease control in domestic animals and poultry. An understanding of these two types of immunity is essential if one is to obtain maximum benefits from the use of biological products.

The injection of a Bacterin, Vaccine or Toxoid into an animal stimulates the animal's tissue cells to produce substances called antibodies which serve to protect the animal against infection by the particular organisms represented in the product. Since the cells of the treated animal are active in producing the antibodies, we speak of this as an *Active Immunity*. Active immunity develops gradually, requiring from one to four weeks to reach its maximum. This type of immunity lasts a relatively long time, although there is considerable variation, depending on the age and species of the animal, nature of the disease, quality of product used and other factors. For example, pigs actively immunized with Hog-Cholera Virus and Anti-Hog-Cholera Serum will, under ordinary conditions, remain resistant to Hog Cholera for life. On the other hand, dogs vaccinated with Rabies Vaccine gradually lose their immunity after about twelve months, which make it necessary to revaccinate at least once each year.

The antibodies, which are present in the blood serum of an immunized animal, may be transferred to other animals by injections of this serum. Animals so treated acquire an immunity by virtue of the antibodies injected. This type of immunity is called *Passive Immunity* since the tissue cells of the treated animal are not involved in the production of the antibodies. Passive immunity is of short duration, lasting, on the average, about three to four weeks. Its effect, however,

174

is immediate, and for this reason immune serums or antiserums are of great value in the treatment of affected animals and also in providing immediate protection to animals that have been or are likely to be exposed to disease soon.

There are many factors which affect the degree and duration of active immunity. It is generally recognized that very young animals do not immunize as readily as older animals. Nutritional deficiencies and other debilitating conditions may possibly interfere with the development of immunity, or even cause a decrease in the resistance of an animal that has been successfully immunized some time previously. In any large number of animals, one may occasionally encounter the rare individual which, for some unknown reason, is unable to develop an immunity, even when vaccinated with products that are highly effective in the vast majority of cases. Immunity, therefore, is a relative thing, dependent on many variable factors, including the individual.

Bacterins

Bacterins are suspensions of bacteria which have been killed by heat or chemical means, thereby rendering them incapable of producing disease. The bacteria are first isolated from the blood or tissues of animals sick or dead of the disease. Their identity is established by exacting biological tests, and suitable culture media inoculated and incubated at blood temperature.

The culture medium is prepared with tissue juices and other ingredients to stimulate the body conditions, and serves as the food for bacterial development. The bacteria, by this means, can be grown in large numbers, pure and free of all contamination.

After maximum growth has been reached, the cultures are removed from the incubator and a preservative added. The preservative acts also as the killing agent. Each culture is tested for sterility to determine definitely that all the organisms have been killed. Each batch of bacterin is subjected to microscopic examinations and animal inoculation tests to determine purity and safety of the product.

VACCINES

Vaccines constitute a group of biological products which, like bacterins, are employed for the purpose of producing an active immunity. They differ in many respects from bacterins and their composition is determined largely by the methods employed in growing the bacteria or viruses which comprise the active or immunizing agent in the product.

Bacterial Vaccines are suspensions of living bacteria which have been attenuated or weakened to such a degree that they are no longer capable of producing disease when injected into the animal body. Brucella Abortus Vaccine is a typical example of a bacterial vaccine.

Virus Vaccines are suspensions of ground tissues in which the virus has grown. Viruses will not grow and multiply in artificial culture media and consequently must be grown in or on the tissues of living animals. These tissues are collected at the proper time, ground, and processed in various ways to make the finished product. Certain vaccines, as for example Fowl Pox Vaccine, contain live virus since it is essential in this instance that the virus be alive in order to produce immunity. In Rabies and Encephalomyelitis Vaccines, however, the virus is killed by chemical agents. These viruses are capable of producing an immunity even though they are killed and, further, they could not be used safely if alive.

Hog-Cholera Virus, strictly speaking, is not a vaccine, and its virulence has not been interfered with. Its action is controlled in the body of the hog by the injection of Immune Serum which prevents the development of Hog Cholera. It is the virus which stimulates the development of an active, lasting immunity.

IMMUNE SERUMS

Practically all Immune Serums are prepared from animals which have previously been immunized by injecting into their bodies large and repeated doses of Bacterins. When sufficient immunity has been developed by this treatment, the animals are injected with large and repeated doses of living bacteria, the disease-producing powers of which have not been impaired in any way.

The blood of the animals is repeatedly tested, and when found to contain sufficient amounts of antibodies, the blood is collected, clarified, pasteurized, and preserved by the addition of a suitable preserving agent.

Immune Serums contain the antibodies specific for the disease germs used in immunizing the animal, and when injected into well animals in sufficient dosage, provide an immediate immunity against the specific disease.

The Immune Serum, when injected into an animal's body, does not stimulate that animal's body cells to produce antibodies. Therefore, the immunity conferred is transitory, lasting for relatively short periods of time.

Immune Serums are used to treat sick animals and to protect animals that have been or are likely to be exposed to infection. When injected into such animals in sufficient dosage, the antibodies immediately protect the tissues from further bacterial invasion.

The dosage generally recommended has been arrived at largely through experience. It has been found that large doses, in severe cases repeated in 4 to 8 hours (less severe cases, 12 to 24 hours), are much more effective than small doses repeated at more frequent intervals. Judgment as to the dosage to be employed in any given case would depend on the severity of the symptoms manifested, and the size of the animal.

CARE OF IMMUNOLOGICAL PRODUCTS

Bacterins, Vaccines, and Immune Serums are all adversely affected by exposure to heat and light. For this reason, they should always be stored under refrigeration, preferably at 35 to 45°F., but should not be frozen. All biological products are marketed in sealed pasteboard boxes in order to protect the product from light. Live Viruses and Bacterial Vaccines are much more sensitive to the effects of heat than are Bacterins and Immune Serums; therefore, particular care should be taken to keep such products cold until ready for use.

SANITATION

This term, while familiar to everyone, has been more or less misunderstood, abused and misused until the public generally has lost sight of its real meaning, value, and importance.

Sanitation means to render wholesome or healthful, and requires the use of methods which have proved to be effective in the prevention of disease and the promotion of health.

The term, cleanliness, means the removal of all filth and dirt, freedom from whatever is foul and offensive (rubbish, animal body discharges, etc.).

Therefore, the first essential of sanitation is cleanliness. Second, disinfection. Sanitation should be maintained at all times.

Disinfection means destroying disease-producing bacteria in and about the premises, and making conditions unfavorable for their development. Disinfection is accomplished by the use of dips, disinfectants, etc.

The effectiveness of dips and disinfectants is dependent upon cleanliness. Before disinfecting, it is necessary first to clean thoroughly and remove all dirt, rubbish, etc., in order to be sure that the disinfecting agent will come in direct

contact with and destroy any disease bacteria which may be present.

Thorough cleaning and disinfection do not, in themselves, constitute sanitation. It is of equal importance to clean and disinfect the premises at periodic intervals to maintain sanitation.

Sanitation plays a most important part in the prevention of diseases by reducing the number of disease bacteria on the premises with which animals will come in contact.

It is especially important that strict sanitary measures be employed on premises where infectious contagious diseases are present. Sanitation plays an important part in preventing the spread of any infectious disease. It should be remembered that the number of disease bacteria taken within an animal's body determines whether or not the animal will contract the disease and, if so, whether or not the disease will be mild or severe.

Through cleanliness and disinfection, the number of disease bacteria is greatly decreased, and healthy animals are less apt to take within their bodies a sufficient number of the bacteria to produce disease.

DISINFECTING AGENTS

Effective disinfection depends on four things: First, the phenol coefficient of the disinfectant. Second, the dilution at which the disinfectant is used. Third, proper cleaning before application. And, fourth, thoroughness of application.

The phenol coefficient indicates the killing strength of a disinfectant as compared to phenol (carbolic acid).

Disinfectants are diluted with water for use, and the extent of dilution will depend largely on the phenol coefficient. As a general rule, disinfectants should be diluted not more than 20 times the phenol coefficient. For example, a disinfectant with phenol coefficient 5 may be diluted 100 times (20 x 5); that is, one part disinfectant to 99 parts water. In many instances stronger solutions are preferred. Obviously a disinfectant of high phenol coefficient will go farther than one of low coefficient. It is seldom economical to use disinfectants of less than coefficient 5.

Cleaning before disinfection is essential if the disinfectant is to do an effective job. Excessive amounts of dirt, filth, and organic matter interfere with the action of disinfectants.

Thorough application means applying the disinfectant to all contaminated surfaces and objects, with special attention to corners, cracks, crevices, and other points that might easily be overlooked.

The use of coal tar disinfectants, such as Dip, for general farm disinfection and many other purposes is well known. In certain operations, such as dairying, coal tar disinfectants are unsuitable because of their pronounced coal tar odor.

Pine Disinfectant is an aromatic disinfectant and deodorant concentrate with a refreshing pine odor. The pine oil is emulsified in such a manner that it retains its several valuable properties and mixes readily with water. Pine Disinfectant is especially recommended for farm, office, household, and kennel use.

Odorless Disinfectant and Poultry Disinfectant, containing quaternary ammonium compounds, are some of the developments in the sanitation field. These products have a high phenol coefficient, are odorless, tasteless, non-toxic, non-irritating, and non-corrosive. They are especially suited to all dairy and poultry sanitation needs. In suitable concentrations, they are effective deodorants as well as disinfectants. Poultry Disinfectant, in proper strength, will kill the virus of Newcastle disease in contaminated brooder houses, batteries, and other equipment, and in addition, may be used as a sanitizing agent in the drinking water.

Table 1. APPROXIMATE MEASURES

½ ounce (fluid) . . . . 4 teaspoonfuls (tsp.)
½ ounce (fluid) . . . . 1 tablespoonful
4 ounces (fluid) . . . . 1 teacupful
8 ounces (fluid) . . . . 1 glassful
1 c.c. . . . . 16 drops
4 c.c. . . . . 1 teaspoonful
15 c.c. . . . . 1 tablespoonful

USE AND CARE OF SYRINGES

All syringes and needles should be thoroughly cleaned and sterilized by boiling for at least 15 minutes just before using. Syringes and needles that have been cleaned thoroughly may be sterilized by immersing in a suitable disinfectant solution for 30 minutes.

To adjust syringe, push plunger all the way in and turn palm rest or handle to the right. If too tight, turn to the left. Place dosage nut or set screw on plunger stem in accordance with dose to be administered.

METHOD OF FILLING SYRINGE

Shake bottle well before drawing the contents of the bottle into the syringe. Force a needle through the diaphragm of the rubber stopper. Injection of a little air into the bottle between withdrawals will prevent the formation of a partial vacuum. Draw the product into the syringe direct from the bottle.

Attach another sterile needle to the syringe to inject the product.

Biological products should be used the same day the stopper is punctured. When vaccinating, protect this class of products from direct sunlight and intense heat to avoid impairment of immunizing properties.

After using syringes, they should be taken apart, thoroughly cleaned and dried, and placed in a dark cool place until again needed.

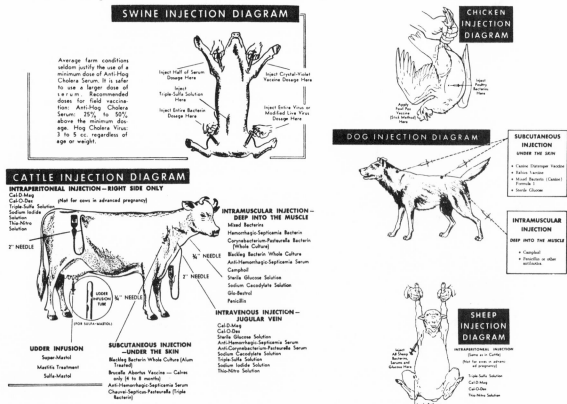

Fig. 1 Instructions For Making Various Types of Injections in Domestic Animals

178

SITE OF INJECTION

The best place to inject most bacterins, vaccines, etc., in horses and cattle is in the side of the neck, midway between the head and shoulders; sheep and swine, under the foreleg (armpit). See Fig. 1.

Needles after each injection should be rinsed in a disinfectant solution but care should be exercised to insure that the disinfectant solution is expelled from the lumen of the needle before use.

INSTRUCTIONS FOR MAKING VARIOUS TYPES OF INJECTIONS IN DOMESTIC ANIMALS

Before making an injection, read the bottle label carefully to determine indications, cautions, proper dosage, frequency of administration, and recommended method of administration. Then consult these directions for detailed instructions on how to make the type of injection recommended on the bottle label.

INTRAVENOUS: Injection directly into the veins. This method is generally used when rapid and effective action is needed to save life.

DIRECTIONS FOR MAKING AN INTRAVENOUS INJECTION IN CATTLE

Equipment Needed:

1. Choke rope—a rope or cord about 5 feet long, with a loop in one end, to be used as a tourniquet.

2. Gravity flow intravenous set. (See Fig. 5).

3. Hypodermic needles, 16 gauge, 1½ to 2 inches long and very sharp. Use new needles. Dull needles will not work. Extra needles should be available in case the one being used becomes clogged.

FIGURE 2

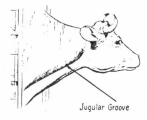

Jugular Groove

FIGURE 3

4. Scissors or clippers.

5. 70% rubbing alcohol compound or other equally effective antiseptic for disinfecting the skin. Blue Lotion is ideal for this purpose.

6. The medication to be given.

Preparation of Equipment:

Thoroughly clean the needles and intravenous set and disinfect them by boiling in water for twenty minutes.

Warm the bottle of medication to approximately body temperature and keep warm until used.

Preparation of the Animal for Injection:

1. Approximate location of vein. The jugular vein runs in the jugular groove on each side of the neck from the angle of the jaw to just above the brisket and slightly above and to the side of the windpipe. (See Fig. 3 and 4.)

179

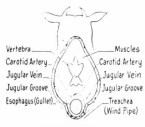

Vertebra — Muscles
Carotid Artery — Carotid Artery
Jugular Vein — Jugular Vein
Jugular Groove — Jugular Groove
Esophagus (Gullet) — Treachea (Wind Pipe)

FIGURE 4

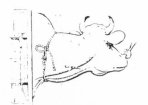

FIGURE 5

2. Restraint—a stanchion or chute is ideal for restraining the animal. With a halter, rope, or cattle leader (nose tongs), pull the animal's head around the side of the stanchion, cattle chute or post in such a manner to form a bow in the neck (See Fig. 5) then snub the head securely to prevent movement. By forming the bow in the neck, the outside curvature of the bow tends to expose the jugular vein and make it easily accessible. Caution. Avoid a tight rope or halter around the throat or upper neck which might impede blood flow. Animals that are down present no problem so far as restraint is concerned.

3. Clip hair in area where injection is to be made (over the vein in the upper third of the neck). Clean and disinfect the skin with alcohol or other suitable antiseptic.

Entering the Vein and Making the Injection.
1. Raise the vein; this is accomplished by tying the choke rope *tight* around the neck, close to the shoulder. The rope should be tied in such a way that it will not come loose and so that it can be untied quickly by pulling the loose end (See Fig. 5). In thick-necked animals, a block of wood placed in the jugular groove between the rope and the hide will help considerably in applying the desired pressure at the right point. The vein is a soft flexible tube through which blood flows back to the heart. Under ordinary conditions it cannot be seen or felt with the fingers. When the flow of blood is blocked at the base of the neck by the choke rope, the vein becomes enlarged and rigid because of the back pressure. If the choke rope is sufficiently tight, the vein stands out and can be easily seen and felt in thin-necked animals. As a further check in identifying the vein, tap it with the fingers in front of the choke rope. Pulsations that can be seen or felt with the fingers in front of the point being tapped will confirm the fact that the vein is properly distended. It is impossible to put the needle into the vein unless it is distended. Experienced operators are able to raise the vein simply by hand pressure, but the use of a choke rope is more certain.
2. Inserting the needle. This involves three distinct steps. *First*, insert the needle through the hide. *Second*, insert the needle into the vein. This may require two or three attempts before the vein is entered. The vein has a tendency to roll away from the point of the needle, especially if the needle is not sharp. The vein can be steadied with the thumb and finger of one hand. With the other hand, the needle point is placed directly over the vein, slanting it so that its direction is along the length of the vein, either toward the head or toward the heart. Properly positioned this way, a quick thrust of the needle will be followed by a spurt of blood through the needle, which indicates that the vein has been entered. *Third*, once in the vein, the needle should be inserted along the length of the vein all the way to the hub, exercising caution to see that the needle does not penetrate the opposite side of the vein. Continuous steady flow of blood through the needle indicates that the needle is still in the vein. If blood does not flow continuously, the needle is out of the vein (or clogged) and another attempt must be made. If difficulty is encountered, it may be advisable to use the vein on the other side of the neck.

180

3. While the needle is being placed in proper position in the vein, an assistant should get the medication ready so that the injection can be started without delay after the vein has been entered. Remove the rubber stopper from the bottle of intravenous solution, connect the intravenous tube to the neck of the bottle, invert the bottle and allow some of the solution to run through the tube to eliminate all air bubbles.

4. Making the injection. With needle in proper position as indicated by continuous flow of blood, release the choke rope by a quick pull on the free end. This is essential—the medication cannot flow into the vein while the vein is blocked. Immediately connect the intravenous tube to the needle, and raise the bottle. The solution will flow in by gravity (See Fig. 6.). The rate of flow can be controlled by pinching the tube between the thumb and forefinger or by raising and lowering the bottle. Bubbles entering the bottle through the air tube or valve indicate the rate at which the medication is flowing. If the flow should stop, this means the needle has slipped out of the vein (or is clogged) and the operation will have to be repeated. Watch for any swelling under the skin near the needle, which would indicate that the medication is not going into the vein. Should this occur, it is best to try the vein on the opposite side of the neck. Sudden movement of the animal, especially twisting of the neck or raising or lowering the head, may sometimes cause the needle to slip out of the vein. To prevent this, tape the needle hub to the skin of the neck to hold the needle in position. Whenever there is any doubt as to the position of the needle, this should be checked in the following manner: Pinch off the intravenous tube to stop flow, disconnect the tube from the needle and re-apply pressure to the vein. Free flow of blood through the needle indicates that it is in proper position and the injection can then be continued.

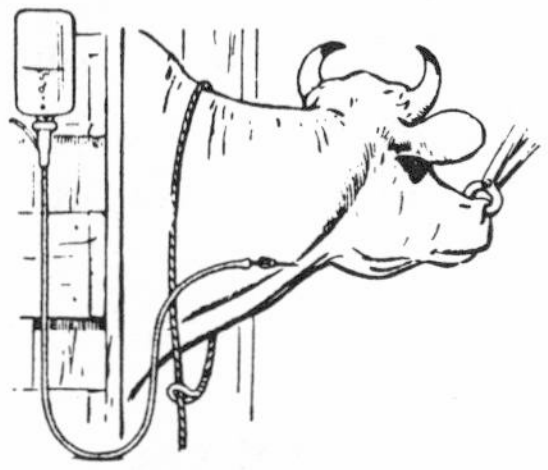

FIGURE 6.

5. Removing the needle. When injection is complete, remove needle with a straight pull. Then apply pressure over area of injection momentarily to control any bleeding through needle puncture, using cotton soaked in alcohol or other suitable antiseptic.

Precautions:

1. Inexperienced persons will find the intraperitoneal method simpler than the intravenous method and, except in cases of extreme emergencies, intraperitoneal injection is the method of preference, provided this method is recommended on the label of the product being used.

2. To reduce the likelihood of shock, intravenous solutions should be warmed to approximately body temperature before injection.

3. Rapid injection may occasionally produce shock. Administer slowly. Rate of injection may be controlled by raising or lowering the bottle or pinching the tube. The animal should be observed at all times during the injection in order not to give the solution too fast. This may be determined by watching the respiration of the animal and feeling or listening to the heart beat. If the heart beat and respiration increase markedly, the rate of injection should be immediately stopped by pinching the tube until the animal recovers approximately to its previous respiration or heart beat rate, when the injection can be resumed at a slower rate.

181

4. If symptoms of shock are seen or the animal shows any signs of distress, administration can be interrupted by pinching the intravenous tube. If symptoms persist, the injection should be terminated entirely.

INTRAPERITONEAL: Injection is made through the abdominal wall and directly into the abdominal cavity. This method is used when the large quantity of solution is to be given, rapid absorption is desired, and the vein cannot be used.

DIRECTIONS FOR MAKING AN INTRAPERITONEAL INJECTION IN CATTLE

Equipment Needed:
1. Gravity flow intravenous set.
2. Hypodermic needles, 14 or 16 gauge, 1½ or 2 inches long and very sharp. Extra needles should be available in case the one being used becomes clogged.
3. Scissors or clippers.
4. 70% Rubbing Alcohol Compound or other equally effective antiseptic for disinfecting the skin. Blue Lotion is ideal for this purpose.
5. Medication to be given.

Preparation of Equipment:
Thoroughly clean the needles and intravenous set and disinfect them by boiling in water for twenty minutes. Warm the bottle of medication to approximately body temperature and keep warm until used.

Locating the Injection Area:
An intraperitoneal injection is made through the belly wall on the animal's *right* side (never on the left) at a point about three inches below the edge of the loin muscles and midway between the point of the hip and the last rib. This is the center of a triangular depression called the "hollow of the flank," illustrated in Figure 7.

Preparation of the Animal for Injection:
The injection can be made most easily if the animal is restrained in a standing position preferably in a stanchion or cattle chute. Clip the hair from the area where the needle is to be inserted. Then swab the area vigorously with alcohol or other equally effective antiseptic to clean and disinfect the skin.

FIGURE 7

Inserting the Needle and Making the Injection:
At the center of the triangular depression, hold the needle perpendicular to the skin, thus pointing it approximately toward the center of the body. Then, with a quick thrust, insert the needle through the belly wall all the way to the hub. This will put the end of the needle into the peritoneal cavity. (In thick skinned animals where penetration is difficult, attach to the needle a sterile veterinary syringe with which the operator can obtain a better grip and make a more forceful thrust.)

When the needle is being placed in proper position, an assistant should get the medication ready by removing the rubber stopper from the bottle and attaching the intravenous tube to the neck of the bottle. Then invert the bottle and allow a small quantity of the solution to run through the tube to eliminate all air bubbles.

182

Connect the intravenous tube to the hub of the needle and elevate the bottle. If the needle is in proper position the solution will flow rapidly as indicated by a steady stream of bubbles entering the bottle through the air tube or valve. If the solution does not flow readily, disconnect the intravenous tube, withdraw the needle a short distance, and reinsert at the proper angle. If this fails to correct the trouble, the needle is probably clogged with a plug of tissue in which case a new needle should be used.

Removal of the Needle:
After the proper dosage has been administered, pinch off the tube to prevent further flow, disconnect the tube, and quickly withdraw the needle. Then swab the site of the needle puncture with alcohol or other equally effective antiseptics.

DIRECTIONS FOR MAKING AN INTRAPERITONEAL INJECTION IN SHEEP

First read the directions for making this injection in cattle. The principles involved are identical. Sheep can be easily restrained by an assistant who straddles the animal just in front of the shoulders. For sheep, use a 16-gauge needle, 1½ inches long.

Since the dosage for sheep is relatively small, an ordinary veterinary syringe of 25-cc or 50-cc capacity is generally preferred instead of an intravenous set. Sterilize needles and syringes by boiling in water for 20 minutes. Disinfect the bottle stopper before puncturing. Use a separate needle for filling the syringe.

Make injection on the animal's *right* side as described under cattle. The triangular depression is not always apparent to the eye in heavily wooled animals, but after clipping the area the depression can be easily seen or felt with the hand. Be sure to disinfect the skin, as described under cattle, before making the injection.

DIRECTIONS FOR MAKING AN INTRAPERITONEAL INJECTION IN SWINE

Equipment Needed:
1. Gravity flow intravenous set (for large hogs when dosage to be given is large) or a 25-cc or 50cc veterinary syringe (for pigs when dosage to be given is small).
2. Hypodermic needles, 16-gauge, at least 3 inches long for heavy hogs, 1 inch long for pigs.
3. Scissors or clippers
4. 70% rubbing alcohol compound or other equally effective antiseptic for disinfecting the skin. Blue Lotion is ideal for this purpose.
5. The medication to be given.

Preparation of Equipment:
Thoroughly clean the needles and intravenous set or syringes and disinfect them by boiling in water for twenty minutes. Warm the bottle of medication to approximately body temperature and keep warm until used. If the injection is to be made with a syringe, swab the stopper with disinfectant before puncturing it with the needle. Use a separate needle for filling the syringe.

Procedure for Heavy Hogs

Area of Injection:
The place to make the injection is on the animal's right side at a point about 2½ inches below the loin muscles and midway between the last rib and the point of the hip. (See Fig. 8.)

183

FIGURE 8.

Preparation of Animal:

If necessary, restrain the animal by putting a noose in the mouth behind the tusks and pulling it tight around the upper jaw. Tie the free end of the rope to a post. Clip the hair from the area where the needle is to be inserted. Then swab the area vigorously with alcohol or other equally effective antiseptic to clean and disinfect the skin.

Inserting the Needle and Making the Injection:

At the point of injection described above, hold the needle perpendicular to the skin, thus directing it approximately toward the center of the body. Then with a quick thrust, insert the needle through the belly wall all the way to the hub. This will put the end of the needle into the peritoneal cavity.

While the needle is being placed in proper position, an assistant should get the medication ready by removing the rubber stopper from the bottle and attaching the intravenous tube to the neck of the bottle. Then invert the bottle and allow a small quantity of the solution to run through the tube to eliminate all air bubbles.

Connect the intravenous tube to the hub of the needle and elevate the bottle. If the needle is in proper position the solution will flow rapidly as indicated by a steady stream of bubbles entering the bottle through the air tube or valve. If the solution does not flow readily, disconnect the intravenous tube, withdraw the needle a short distance, and reinsert at the proper angle. If this fails to correct the trouble, the needle is probably clogged with a plug of tissue, in which case a new needle should be used.

Removal of the Needle:

After the proper dosage has been administered, pinch off the tube to prevent further flow, disconnect the tube, and quickly withdraw the needle. Then swab the site of the needle puncture with alcohol or other equally effective antiseptic.

Procedure for Pigs
(Suitable for any swine not too heavy to be handled)

Area of Injection:

The injection is made thru the belly wall at a point half way between the fold of the flank and the midling. (See Fig. 9) In most pigs, this point lies between the rear nipple and the next nipple in front. The injection can be made either to the left or to the right of the midline.

FIGURE 9

184

Preparation of Animal:

The animal must be restrained by one of two methods: (1) An assistant holds the pig up by the hind legs, squeezing pig's body between assistant's knees to prevent movement. (2) The pig is placed on its back in a V-shaped trough and held down with the hind legs extended. In case the pigs are fairly large, two assistants may be required, one to hold the hind legs, and the other the fore legs. The trough should slope at an angle of 30 degrees or more with the pig's head at the low end of the trough. This sloping position practically eliminates the possibility of puncturing the intestine. Clip the hair from the area of injection and swab the skin with alcohol or other effective antiseptic to clean and disinfect the skin.

Inserting the Needle and Making the Injection:

After filling the syringe (use a separate needle) with the required dosage, attach a sterile needle, 16-gauge, 1 inch in length. At the point of injection described above, place the needle point against the skin, pointing it toward the center of the body. Quickly thrust the needle through the belly wall all the way up to the hub. Inject the full dosage and withdraw the needle. Swab the needle puncture with alcohol or more equally effective antiseptic and release the animal. If more than one syringeful is required, disconnect the syringe leaving the needle in place in the pig's belly. Refill the syringe, connect to the needle and make the second injection.

INTRAMUSCULAR: Injection is through the skin and subcutaneous tissue, directly into the muscle. Absorption is very rapid in this case.

DIRECTIONS FOR MAKING AN INTRAMUSCULAR INJECTION IN DOMESTIC ANIMALS
(Cattle, sheep, swine; horses and dogs)

Equipment Needed:
1. A 25 or 50cc veterinary syringe.
2. Hypodermic needle, 16 gauge, ¾ to 1 inch in length.
3. Scissors or clippers.
4. 70% rubbing alcohol compound or other equally effective antiseptic for disinfecting the skin and bottle stopper. Blue Lotion is ideal for this purpose.
5. The medication to be given.

Preparation of Equipment:
Clean and disinfect the needles and syringe by boiling in water for 20 minutes.

Areas of Injection:
An intramuscular injection is made directly into the muscle tissue or meat. Heavily muscled portions of the body such as the neck, shoulder and hindquarter should be utilized. Not more than 25-cc should be injected in any one spot in large animals—cattle, horses, and heavy hogs. In small animals—sheep, pigs, and dogs—not more than 10 to 15 cc should be injected in one spot. Where the dosage to be given is large, as much as 500 cc can be injected into cattle by distributing the dosage in 25-cc amounts into the heavy muscles of the neck, shoulder, and hindquarter on both sides.

Preparation of Animal:
Restrain the animal by the best means available. A stanchion or chute is ideal for large animals. Clip the hair from the area in which the injection is to be given and swab the clipped areas vigorously with alcohol or other equally effective antiseptic.

Inserting the Needle and Making the Injection:

Fill the syringe with the medication to be given, using a separate needle for filling. Disinfect the rubber stopper before inserting the needle into the bottle.

Insert a previously disinfected needle deeply into the muscle tissue with a quick thrust. Observe the hub of the needle for a moment. If blood begins to flow out of the needle, it is probably in a blood vessel and the needle should be withdrawn and re-inserted in a different direction. Attach the syringe to the needle and inject the medication slowly.

After the medication has been injected, remove the needle still attached to the syringe and massage the area with cotton soaked in alcohol so as to spread the medication through the muscle tissue. The above procedure is repeated in each injection area until the full recommended dose of medication has been given.

SUBCUTANEOUS: Injection into the tissue beneath the skin.

DIRECTIONS FOR MAKING A SUBCUTANEOUS INJECTION IN DOMESTIC ANIMALS
(Cattle, sheep, swine, horses and dogs)

First, read directions for making an intramuscular injection. The equipment needed, its preparation, and preparation of the animal are the same as for an intramuscular injection.

A subcutaneous injection is an injection made beneath the skin, i.e., between the skin and the muscle tissue. The recommended areas of injection are places where the skin is loose, particularly on the sides of the neck and behind the shoulder. In pigs and sheep the axillary space is frequently used for subcutaneous injection. The axillary space lies between the foreleg and the chest wall, and corresponds to the armpit in man.

To make the injection, pinch up a fold of skin between the thumb and fingers (not necessary if axillary space is used). Insert the needle under the fold in a direction approximately parallel to the surface of the body. When the needle is inserted in this manner, the medication will be delivered underneath the skin between the skin and the muscles. Observe the same precautions regarding clipping and disinfecting the skin as outlined under intramuscular injections.

ORAL: By the mouth—drugs are usually given by the mouth and are absorbed in the stomach and intestines. Absorption is more rapid when drugs are given in solution into an empty stomach; slower when administered in powder, pill or ball form, and on a full stomach.

OTHER METHODS OF ADMINISTERING DRUGS

INHALATION: (Inhale). Volatile drugs are used mainly for their local action on the respiratory tract.

RECTAL: By the rectum. This method is used when oral administration is inadvisable or impossible, because of paralysis of the throat, etc. Absorption here is slower.

TOPICAL: Local application to external surfaces of the body: Absorption by this method is extremely slow and the effects of the drug are limited to the treated area.

TABLE 2. BODY TEMPERATURE
Average Rectal Temperature

Horse	100.2
Ass	98.5
Cow	101.5
Sheep	102.3
Goat	103.8
Pig	101.7-103.3
Dog	101.0-102.0
Cat	101.7
Fowl	106.9-109.0
Duck	107.8-110.5

CATTLE DISEASES

Disease: Acetonema
Cause: Metabolic disturbance occuring as a complication of milk fever or as a result of poor winter feeding.
Symptom: Reduced milk flow, constipation and rapid loss of weight.
Treatment: Subcutaneous injection of 250 to 500 cc of Sterile Glucose Solution repeated in 24 hours if needed.
Prevention: Provide molasses, high-quality hay and/or good pasture grasses.

Disease: Actinomycosis (Lump Jaw) and Actinobacillosis (Wooden Tongue)
Cause: Fungus organisms.
Symptom: Tumor-like swellings or enlargements of tissues about the head and throat. Swellings contain yellowish-white pus.
Treatment: Intravenous injection of 500 c.c. of Sodium Iodide per 1,000 pounds animal weight.
Prevention: Mix one pound organic Iodide compound with 50 pounds of salt and feed free choice.

Disease: Anaplasmosis
Cause: Protozoan blood parasite.
Symptom: Anemia as shown by loss of appetite, loss of flesh, and yellowish discoloration of visible mucous membranes.
Treatment: Intramuscular injection of Sodium Cacodylate Solution; 5 cc for each 100 pounds body weight. In cases of exhaustion also give 100 cc of Sterile Glucose Solution.
Prevention: Control flies and other insects by spraying.

Disease: Anthrax
Cause: Bacterium passed in contaminated feed or water.
Symptom: Spasm, staggering, and death within a few hours. Rapid decomposition occurs after death and blood fails to clot.
Diagnosis: Laboratory blood analysis.
Treatment: 100 to 250 cc of Anti-Anthrax serum should be given daily until animal's body temperature returns to normal. Supplement large doses of Penicillin every 4 hours.
Prevention: Vaccination every 2½ to 3 months if anthrax is known to the area. Burn and bury all dead animals.

Disease: Brucellosis
Cause: Infectious disease which acts on the genital tract. Spreads by breeding of infected animals.
Symptom: Abortion.
Diagnosis: Blood Test.
Treatment: None.
Prevention: Calfhood vaccination with Brucella Abortus Vaccine, 5 cc per animal, sterilizing all syringes and needles between each vaccination.

Disease: Calf Diphtheria
Cause: Actinomyces necrophorus infection.
Symptom: Infected larynx—high temperature, distressed breathing, and death due to strangulation. Infected mouth—emaciation and salivation.
Treatment: Intraperitoneally administer 25 cc per 100 pounds of Triple-Sulpha solution. Segregate sick animals.
Prevention: Clean and disinfect all water and feed containers; generally clean the animal area.

Disease: Calf Scours (White Scours)
Cause: Colon bacillus present in the digestive tract.
Symptom: Grey or white fluid diarrhea which has an offensive odor.
Treatment: One Calf Scour Bolus for each 50 pounds of body weight. If serious, inject 50 to 100 cc of Antibacterial Serum (Bovine) also give injections of Vitamins A-D-E in oil solution.
Prevention: Sanitation.

Disease: Foot Rot
Cause: Injury to feet with subsequent infection.
Sympton: Slight lameness to complete rotting of the hoof.
Treatment: Triple-Sulfa solution given intravenously or intraperitoneally.
Prevention: Mix one pound organic Iodide compound with 50 pounds salt and feed free choice.

Disease: Hemorrhagic Septicemia (Shipping Fever)
Cause: Lowered resistance making the animal subject to Pasteurella organisms.
Symptom: Cough, difficult breathing, temperature, staggering, and death. Dead animals have blood spots on the heart, lungs and intestinal membranes.
Treatment; Isolation and 100 to 500 cc dose of Anti-Hemorrhagic-Septicemia Serum, repeated in 24 hours as needed.
Prevention: Calfhood vaccination (Whole Culture) using a 5 cc dose.

Disease: Cowpox
Cause: Filterable virus picked up through the skin of susceptible animals.
Symptom: Inflamed areas on upper teats and inner surface of thighs. Bumps and blisters may be present.
Treatment: The disease will run its course but Sulfa lotion aids healing of Cowpox sores.
Prevention: Isolate sick animals.

External Parasites of Cattle

Parasites: Horn flies, lice, gnats, mosquitoes and cattle grubs.
Treatment: Malathion, Ronnel (Korlan), Pyrethrins and Rotenone. Treatment may be given by spraying or dipping. Methods of application should follow the recommendation for the product used.
Parasite: Screw Worms
Cause: Screw worm fly lays eggs which hatch into small larvae or worms that burrow into raw tissue.
Symptom: Raw open wound with worms inside.
Treatment: Use a liquid screw worm killer containing Benzol and Chloroform.

Cattle Bloat

Cause: Accumulation of excessive gas in the paunch created by changes in feed, overeating or mechanical problems.
Treatment: Two ounces of Equi-Dine mixed with a pint of Mineral Oil given as a drench. For acute cases puncture the paunch by cutting a hole in the upper left flank midway between the last rib and the point of the hip.

Cattle Indigestion

Cause: Spoiled or damaged feeds and other indigestible substances.
Treatment: Empty the digestive tract by giving 2 ounces of Purgative every 6 hours for 3 doses or until relief occurs.

Internal Parasites of Cattle

Parasites: Stomach worms, nodular worms, hook worms, lung worms, and liver flukes.
Treatment: Pasture rotation and Phenothiazine used in a drench or feed. Use one ounce per 100 pounds body weight up to a maximum of six ounces.

Other Cattle Diseases

Disease: Leptospirosis
Cause: Germ called leptospira.
Spread: Through urine of infected animals.
Symptom: Sudden abortion, anemia, yellowish color, and blood-tinged milk.
Treatment: None effective.
Prevention: Sanitation and vaccination with Leptospira Pomona Bacterin. Vaccinate calves at 3 to 6 months of age and each year thereafter.

Disease: Malignant Edema
Cause: Clostridium septicum organism.
Symptom: Similar to Blackleg with a higher fever.
Treatment: Massive doses of penicillin.
Prevention: 5 cc dose of Triple Bacterin.

Disease: Mastitis
Cause: Streptococcus.
Symptom: Sudden decrease of milk and lumpy, stringy or bloody milk.
Treatment: Use Sulfanilamide-in-oil as an intramammary infusion. Milk frequently until cured and apply hot epsom salt water packs as needed.
Prevention: Sanitation and control of flies.

Disease: Metritis
Cause: Bacterial infection in the uterus.
Symptom: Vaginal discharge, straining and loss of weight.
Treatment: Sulfanilamide uterine boluses. Use 3 to 6 boluses and repeat in 24 hours if needed.
Prevention: Sanitation at calving. Assist, as needed, the removal of the afterbirth.

Disease: Milk Fever
Cause: Unknown.
Symptom: Nervousness, spasm and then collapse. Neck assumes S-like curve.
Treatment: Cal-O-Dex or Cal-D-Mag. Administer 250 to 500 cc intravenously and repeat in 12 to 24 hours if needed.
Prevention: Provide adequate mineral supplements especially during pregnancy.

Disease: Pink Eye
Cause: Streptococci and Staphylococci with mineral and vitamin deficiencies as a predisposing factor.
Symptom: Closed eyes, reddened eyelids, and white scum over the eyeballs.
Treatment: Pink-Eye powder; a mixture of Sulfanilamide, Boric Acid, Acriflavin, and Sulfathiazole sodium.
Prevention: Unknown.

Disease: Pneumonia
Cause: Infectious disease of the lungs brought on by chilling, crowding and malnutrition.

189

Sympton: Rapid breathing, high fever and loss of appetite. Lesions are found in the lungs of dead animals.
Treatment: 240-grain boluses of Sulfathiazole every 8 hours as needed. Give daily injections of 1 to 3 cc of Vitamin A-D-E.
Prevention: Avoid exposure to cold, crowding and malnutrition.

Disease: Red Water Disease
Cause: Bacillary Hemoglobinuria which is found in swampy and poorly-drained areas.
Symptom: Dark urine, high temperature and sudden death. Dead animals show signs of hemorrhaging on the membranes lining the chest and abdomen.
Treatment: None.
Prevention: Vaccinate all animals in infected territories with Red Water Vaccine. (Clostridium-Hemolyticum Bacterin)

Prussic Acid Poisoning

Cause: Hydrocyanic acid animals obtain by eating the second growth of canes and sorghums.
Symptom: Muscular trembles, staggering, and sudden death.
Treatment: 30 to 60 cc of Thio-Nitro Solution, intravenous.
Prevention: Keep animals away from second growths of cane or sorghums.

Warts

Cause: Filterable virus.
Symptom: Wart growth on any part of the body.
Treatment: Culling, sanitation, and use of Wart Vaccine (Bovine origin)
Prevention: Sanitation and culling of warty animals.

Wheat Poisoning and Grass Tetany

Cause: Fast growing young wheat or grass.
Symptom: Incoordination, loss of appetite and staggering. Convulsions, with periods of relaxation, occur before the animal dies.
Treatment: 500 cc of calcium gluconate by slow intravenous injection.
Prevention: Control grazing of young wheat or grasses.

Penicillin Intramuscular Dosage for Cattle
(Milk unpotable until a week after last dose)

General Rule: Allow 1 cc to each 100 pounds body weight. Use 16 gauge 1½ inch needle. Give daily for infections until 2 days after symptoms disappear.

SWINE DISEASES

Disease: Anemia
Cause: Lack of magnesium, manganese, cobalt and zinc. Deficiencies often result from pigs being farrowed on concrete or wooden floors which prevents their access to the soil.
Symptom: Sluggishness and difficult breathing.
Treatment: Intramuscular injection of 2 cc of Swi-Ron (Sterile Iron solution)
Prevention: Give pigs access to soil or inject 2 cc of Swi-Ron per pig at 2-4 days of age.

Disease: Brucellosis
Cause: Brucella suis. (Genital Disease)
Symptom: Abortion and lameness.
Diagnosis: Blood Test
Treatment: None
Prevention: Cull infected animals

Disease: Swine Erysipelas
Cause: Germ, Erysipelothrix rhusiopathiae.
Symptom: Red discolorations on skin, difficult breathing, high temperature, and swollen joints.
Treatment: Anti-Swine-Erysipelas Serum, 5 cc for pigs up to 50 pounds and proportionate increases up to 20 cc for over 100 pounds.
Prevention: Vaccinate all swine every 6 months with Erysipelas Bacterin, 5 cc up to 100 pounds and 10 cc over 100 pounds. Sows and gilts should be vaccinated 4 to 6 weeks before the farrowing period.

Disease: Hemorrhagic Septicemia
(See Cattle Section)

Disease: Swine Flu
Cause: Filterable virus affecting the respiratory tract.
Symptom: Coughing, temperature, and difficult breathing. Dead animals have a heavy mucus in the Bronchi.
Treatment: Provide warm, dry quarters and inject 2 to 5 cc of Vitamins A-D-E injectable oil solution.
Prevention: Provide warm, dry quarters during cold and rainy seasons.

Disease: Hog Cholera
Cause: Filterable virus.
Symptom: Wobbly gait, red and watery eyes, difficult breathing and diarrhea. Dead animals have bright red spots on kidneys, bladder, lungs, and lymph glands.
Treatment: None effective.
Prevention: Vaccinate each animal with 5 cc of crystal Violet Hog Cholera vaccine. Pigs should be 6 weeks old before vaccination. Always place vaccine under the skin of the foreleg. (Anti-Hog-Cholera serum may be used to provide quick immunity lasting only about 3 weeks, however, there is a danger that serum may interfere with later development of good immunity.)

Disease: Enteritis
Cause: Food upset or dietary deficiency.
Symptom: Loose bowel movements often black or bloody.
Treatment: Feed animal protein to provide B vitamins, Niacin, Riboflavin, and Calcium Pantothenate. Practice sanitation by providing clean food and water.

Disease: Infectious Enteritis
Cause: Vibro - Necrotic - Necro - Bacterial and Generalized Septicemia are all causative organisms.
Symptom: Bloody diarrhea, watery diarrhea, or other diarrhea.
Treatment: Sodium Arsanilate added to drinking water, feed some whole oats or bulky feed, put Sulfaquinoxaline in drinking water, and use antibiotics plus penicillin.
Prevention: Sanitation and proper diets.

Disease: Leptospirosis
Cause: Leptospira pomona.

191

Symptom: Abortion and litters with some dead or stunted animals.
Treatment: None effective.
Prevention: Vaccinate with Leptospira Pomona Bacterin and cull all diseased animals.

Symptom Table TABLE 3. Symptoms

ARE THEY AFFECTED WITH HOG CHOLERA, SWINE ERYSIPELAS, OR INFECTIOUS GASTROENTERITIS?

SYMPTOM TABLE

ARE THEY AFFECTED WITH HOG CHOLERA, SWINE ERYSIPELAS, OR INFECTIOUS GASTROENTERITIS?

Examine These Organs:	Acute Hog Cholera	Acute Swine Erysipelas	Acute Infectious Gastroenteritis
SKIN	Red Spots or Hemorrhages do not disappear on pressure	Scarlet areas-- disappear on pressure; "diamond skin"	Normal or extensive purple discoloration of abdomen just before death
EYES	Eyelids gummy	Normal or clear watery discharge	Normal
LIMBS	Knuckle at pastern joints	Hot, painful and frequently swollen	Normal
EPIGLOTTIS	Small petechial hemorrhages	Normal	Irregular size hemorrhages may be present
LYMPH GLANDS	Bright red, enlarged, and congested at borders	Little change in color but enlarged	Enlarged, congested, purplish-black in color
LUNGS	Real dark hemorrhages that do not run together are present	Normal; may be scattered areas of congestion	Usually scattered areas of congestion
STOMACH	Membranes usually normal.	Contains some food; membranes frequently show patchy areas of congestion and heavy sticky mucus on surface.	Contains foul-smelling ingesta. Usually acute, diffuse inflammation.
SPLEEN	Normal or slight enlargement or discoloration along edges; dark.	Frequently normal; may show slight enlargement with reddish-purple discoloration.	Enlarged, friable, dark red or purplish-black in color.
LIVER	Normal or may be congested.	Usually normal.	Frequently enlarged and congested.
SMALL INTESTINES	Normal or slight congestion.	Frequently congested.	Usually congested; may show petechial hemorrhages on mucous membrane.
LARGE INTESTINES	Generally shows moderate congestion, especially in region of ileocecal valve.	Usually normal.	Usually diffuse congestion of mucous membrane over large area.
KIDNEY	Pin-point petechial hemorrhages.	Usually some inflammation present.	Soft and congested. Petechial hemorrhages, large and irregular in size.
BLADDER	Petechial hemorrhages or congestion of mucous membrane.	Usually normal or slight congestion.	Numerous hemorrhages, irregular in size; extensive diffuse congestion.

192

External Parasites of Swine

Parasite: Mange (Mite)
Treatment: Malathion, 0.5% spray.

Parasite: Hog Louse
Treatment : A-D-A Lice powder and spraying or dipping with Malathion compound.

Internal Parasites of Swine

Parasite: Ascarids (Roundworms)
Treatment: Keno caps which contain Oil of Chenopodium. For pigs 40 to 80 pounds give one cap, over 80 pounds give 2 caps. Pen animals 18 to 24 hours; withhold feed and water for 3 hours after treatment.

Parasite: Thorn-headed Worms
Treatment: None
Prevention: Ring noses of pigs to prevent rooting.

Parasite: Nodular Worms
Treatment: Phenothiazine (Drench grade) with Bentonite. 5 grams for 25 pound pigs up to 30 grams for 200 pounds and over.

Penicillin Intramuscular Dosage for Swine

General Rule: Allow ½ cc up to 10 pounds; 1 cc up to 50 pounds, and 2 to 3 cc for hogs between 100 to 200 pounds. Use 16 or 18 gauge one inch needle. Give daily for infections until 2 days after symptoms disappear.

Vitamin Deficiency Symptoms

General Rule: All young are born with low reserves of Vitamins A, D, and E. Weakness, unthriftiness and emaciation are immediate symptoms.
Vitamin A— is obtained from green feeds and sun-cured roughage. Swine deficient in A vitamin show slow growth, lameness and will often have diarrhea.
Vitamin D—is provided in sunshine. Deficient animals have enlarged joints, abnormal walking, and humped back.
Vitamin E—acts as an anti-oxident. It stabilizes vitamin A and increases its utilization by the animal.

SHEEP DISEASES

Disease: Enterotoxemia
Cause: Organism, Clostridium perfringens Type D. (Affects Lambs)
Symptom: Walking in circles, leaning, throwing head back, convulsions and coma. Dead animals show hemorrhages of the heart.
Treatment: None effective. Antitoxin may be helpful at early stages.
Prevention: 5 cc injection of Type D Bacterin under the skin; Lambs should be at least 2 months old. Wait 4 weeks after vaccination before slaughtering. Reduce the quantity of feed if the disease is suspected.

Disease: Pink Eye
Cause: Contagious disease associated with vitamin A deficiency.
Symptom: Eyes water, swell and become inflamed.
Treatment: Isolation, dark quarters, green feed, and pink eye prescription.
Prevention: Green feed.

Disease: Lambing Paralysis
Cause: Toxemia resulting from lack of exercise.
Symptom: Slowness, leaning, paralysis of hindquarters and death within 6 or 7 days of onset. Dead animals have lesions on liver.
Treatment: Daily injections of 40 to 50 cc of Sterile Glucose Solution.
Prevention; Exercise and good feeding for pregnant animals.

Disease: Soremouth
Cause: Contagious Ecthyma
Symptom: Tiny blisters on lips which grow and become filled with pus. These eventually scab and dry if no complications develop.
Treatment: None
Prevention: Vaccination with Ovine-Ecthyma.

Disease: Stiff Lambs
Cause: Unknown (possibly Metabolic)
Symptom: Lambs show stiffness, muscular tremors and inability to rise.
Treatment: 10cc of Wheat Germ oil with 2 ounces milk—daily until improvement is noted.

External Parasites of Sheep

Parasite: Sheep Scab (Mange)
Cause: Mange mites.
Symptom: Unthrifty animals that rub and scratch.
Treatment: Malathion mixed the same as for Hog Mange.
Prevention: Quarantine and examine new animals for 10 days.

Parasite: Goat Lice
Treatment: 1 part malathion to 10 parts water.

Parasite: Sheep Ticks
Cause: Wingless Fly
Symptom: Off feed and restless.
Treatment: Malathion or Ronnel (Korlan)

Parasite: Sheep Nasal Fly
Cause: Larvae of Sheep Botfly.
Symptom: Sheep run with nose to ground during fly season.
Treatment: None.
Prevention: Smear Pine Tar on the nose.

Parasite: Foot Rot (Fungus)
Symptom: Redness and swelling of the skin above the hoof. Lameness.
Treatment: Trim feet removing loose hoof and bathe in Copper Sulfate dissolved in water—if solution is strong one or two minutes is enough. Apply a suitable antiseptic.
Prevention: Keep infected animals away from clean flocks. Sheep should be on dry ground.

Internal Parasites of Sheep

Parasites: Same as Cattle
Symptom: Anemic reaction. Sheep become weak and stunted; often have swollen stomach or jaws.
Treatment: Phenothiazine drench, boluses or feed mix. Lead Arsenate may be needed for tapeworms.

Penicillin Intramuscular Dosage for Sheep

General Rule: Lambs up to 10 pounds, ¼ to ½ cc; 10 to 20 pounds, ½ to ¾ cc; 20 to 60 pounds, ¾ to 1 cc; for 100 pounds use 1 to 2 cc. Use 18 gauge on inch needle. Give daily for infections until 2 days after symptoms disappear.

HORSE DISEASES

Disease: Colic
Cause: Improper feeds.
Symptom: Restlessness and kicking at the stomach.
Treatment: Equi-Dine
Prevention: Controlled feeding methods.

Disease: Sleeping Sickness
Cause: Filterable virus affecting the brain and spinal cord.
Symptom: Animals are first excited and then depressed. Facial paralysis and spasms of the lips precede muscular tremors, coma, and finally death.
Treatment: 250 cc of Anti-Encephalomyelitis Serum.
Prevention: Two interadermic infections of Encephalomyelitis Vaccine.

Disease: Fistula and Poll Evil
Cause: Bruising of tissues; back of the head for Poll Evil and on the withers for Fistula. Bacterial factors may create complications.
Symptom: Swelling on poll or withers which enlarges as it fills with flocculent pus.
Treatment: Cut the abscess at the lowest part to establish drainage. Irrigate daily with an odorless disinfectant (1 oz. to 1 gallon of water). Feed a mineral ration mixed with a tonic powder containing arsenic. (1 teaspoonful of tonic to a quart of oats or bran to be added to regular ration)
Prevention: Careful handling.

Disease: Influenza
Cause: Infectious and contagious filterable virus brought on by fatigue and exposure.
Symptom: Chills, coughing and mucous discharge from the nose. Complications may occur in the form of diarrhea, pneumonia and sore joints.
Treatment: None specific. Give injections of camphoil and sterile glucose solution.
Prevention: Sanitation and quarantine. Provide warm, dry quarters.

Disease: Navel Ill
Cause: Variety of organisms.
Symptom: Colts appear weak, breathe hard, have swollen joints and die within a few days.
Treatment: 100 to 150 cc of Normal Serum (Equine Origin) given daily as needed.
Prevention: Sanitation and painting of colt's navel with iodine.

Disease: Distemper
Cause: Pyogenic Streptococcus which invades tissues around the head and throat.
Symptom: Fever, discharge from the nose and swelling under the jaw with abscesses appearing in 1 to 2 weeks.
Treatment: Fresh water, rest, puncture abscesses when soft, and give Triple-Sulfa Boluses or solution.
Prevention: Segregate new or sick animals.

Disease: Tetanus
Cause: Clostridium tetani which enters tissue through wounds.
Symptom: Stiffness, anxiousness and extreme nervousness. Stiffness of the jaw muscles to the point that eating is impossible.
Treatment: 40,000 to 100,000 units of Tetanus Antitoxin for the first day. 1,500 unit doses 2 to 3 times daily after the initial dose until the animal responds. Paint wound with iodine.
Prevention: If an animal is wounded give 1,500 units of Tetanus Antitoxin.

External Parasites of Horses and Mules

Parasites: Flies, lice and ticks.
Control: Malathion, 0.5% spray.

Internal Parasites of Horses and Mules

Parasites: Bot larvae, ascarids and strongyles are most common.
Control: For ascarids (round worms) use one 6 gram Equine Worm Capsule. Phenothiazine is effective in removing strongyles. Bot larvae are difficult to control.

Penicillin Intramuscular Dosage for Horses and Mules

General Rule: Horses and foals up to 500 pounds use 5 cc; 500 to 1000 pounds use 5 to 10cc; 1000 to 2000 pounds use 10 to 20cc. Inject in the rump and use 16 gauge needle 1½ to 2 inches long. Give daily for infections until 2 days after symptoms disappear.

DOG DISEASES

Disease: Distemper
Cause: Filterable virus for first stage and bacteria for second stage.
Symptom: Fever, loss of appetite, diarrhea, vomiting, coughing and yelping.
Treatment: Difficult, attempt care and nursing.
Prevention: Canine Distemper Vaccine for healthy animals

Disease: Ear Canker
Cause: Species of mite.
Symptom: Pawing and rubbing of ears and shaking of head.
Treatment: Remove scales and wax with cotton swab, then pour a small quantity of ear canker emulsion into the canal. After rubbing the ear wipe off excess. Repeat in 30 days.
Prevention None.

Disease: Rabies
Cause: Virus disease transmitted by the bite of a rabid animal.
Symptom: Animals are irritable, attack objects in their path, paralysis develops in hind quarters and death follows.
Treatment: None.
Prevention: Annual vaccination of all dogs with rabies vaccine.

Disease: Running Fits
Cause: Unknown condition affecting the nervous system of dogs.
Symptom: Animal barks, runs wildly and champs at the jaw.
Treatment: Good diet and dark quiet quarters.
Prevention: Unknown.

Disease: Eye Irritations
Cause: Foreign matter, injuries, colds and fever.
Symptom: Check the eyes for unusual conditions.
Treatment: Remove the cause and apply an eye wash containing Zinc Sulfate and Butyn Sulfate.

External Parasites

Parasites: Fleas, lice and ticks.
Control: Flea bomb or powder. Washing and removal by hand will help if nothing else.

Parasite: Mite (Mange)
Control: Mange remedy Rotenone preparation. Disinfection of quarters and a good diet are helpful.

Nutritional Disorders

Problem: Poor condition
Control: Provide minerals, vitamins and high quality proteins.

Internal Parasites

Parasites: Roundworms, hookworms, and tapeworms
Control: Tetrachlorethylene for roundworms and hookworms. Use Arecoline Hydrobromide for tapeworms.
Prevention: Sanitation and disinfection.

POULTRY DISEASES

Management and Hygiene: Establish sanitation procedures. Adequate housing should be provided with provision for keeping chicks warm. Housing should be dry with adequate space and ventilation. Feed and water should be clean. Where disease is a problem disinfectant should be added to the drinking water. A good general disinfectant is 20% Quaternary Ammonium compound.

Nutritional Diseases:
Disease: Roup (Avitaminosis A)
Cause: Deficiency of Vitamin A.
Symptom: Cessation of growth, weakness, rough feathers and a staggery gait. Adult birds accumulate a cheesy material in the eyes. Dead birds show white pustules in the lining of the gullet.
Treatment and Prevention: Vitamin A foods such as fish liver oils and green feed.

Disease: Rickets
Cause: Vitamin D deficiency.
Symptom: Soft bones, deformities, beak is soft and birds lay soft shelled eggs.
Treatment and Prevention: Sunshine and a balanced diet.

Disease: Slipped Tendon
Cause: Lack of Manganese or a deficiency of Choline.
Symptom: Flattening of hock joints causing the tendons to slip to one side and turn the foot in or out.
Treatment: None.
Prevention: Mineral supplement or tablets.

Bacterial Diseases:
Disease: Bluecomb
Cause: Gastro-intestinal disease.
Symptom: Affects turkeys causing darkening of skin on the head and neck. A greenish or yellowish diarrhea is usually seen.
Treatment: 1 gram per gallon of water of Streptomycin Sulfate Powder.

Disease: Limberneck
Cause: Toxin from Clostridium Botulinus. Usually develops from decomposing material upon which maggots are found.
Symptom: Toxin produces paralysis.
Treatment and Prevention: Sanitation and a clean range. Give one pound of Epsom salts dissolved in water for each 100 adult birds.

Disease: Erysipelas (Turkeys)
Cause: Bacterial disease.
Symptom: Swollen combs and hemorrhaging in the muscles.
Treatment: Feed tetracycline antibiotic for 7 days. Inject 40,000 to 60,000 units of procaine penicillin in aqueous suspension.
Prevention: Vaccination after 8 weeks of age.

Disease: Fowl Cholera
Cause: Pasteurella avisepticus.
Symptom: Dying birds which may or may not show swollen wattles or diarrhea before death. Dead birds show hemorrhaging on the band of fat around the heart.
Treatment: 1½ ounces of Sulfaquin-oxaline solution for each gallon of drinking water for 3 days.
Prevention: Burn dead birds and isolate sick birds. Vaccinate susceptible birds with Avisepticus-Gallinarum Bacterin.

Chronic Respiratory
Cause: Bacteria or Virus (air-borne)
Symptom: Sneezing, coughing and hacking. Feed consumption drops and egg production falls off.
Treatment: Dissolve Streptomycin sulfate powder in drinking water.
Prevention: None

Disease: Fowl Typhoid
Cause: Acute septicemic disease.
Symptom: Yellowish or greenish diarrhea, thirst and general emaciation.
Treatment and Prevention: Disinfection, isolation of sick birds and vaccination with Avisepticus-Gallinarum Bacterin.

Disease: Infectious Coryza (Chickens)
Cause: Cold bacterium.
Symptom: Nasal discharge to coughing and sneezing. Egg production is reduced.
Treatment: Streptomycin Sulfate powder in drinking water and a source of vitamin A.
Prevention: Green feeds and good ventilation of poultry houses.

Disease: Paratyphoid
Cause: Salmonella organisms.
Symptom: Not positive; resembles other diseases. Dead birds have enlarged livers.
Treatment and Prevention: Vaccination of healthy birds with Gallinarum-Typhimurium Bacterin.

Disease: Pullorum
Cause: Bacterial infection of the ovaries.
Symptom: New chicks appear sleepy and weak. Whitish diarrhea and gasping for breath precedes death.
Treatment: None.
Prevention: Blood testing, disinfection, fumigation and burning of dead chicks.

Disease: Tuberculosis
Cause: Contagious disease.
Symptom: Emaciation, anemia, lameness and paralysis.
Treatment and Prevention None.

Disease: Aspergillosis
Cause: Infectious disease of the respiratory system.
Symptom: Rapid breathing and eventual emaciation. Dead birds show small nodules in lungs.
Treatment: None.
Prevention: Avoid moldy feed and wet or damp surroundings.

Disease: Mycosis of the Crop
Cause: Fungus infection of the crop.
Symptom: Birds are listless, droopy and fail to gain weight.
Treatment: At intermittent periods of 3 to 4 days add one level teaspoonful of copper sulfate to each 2 gallons of drinking water.
Prevention Avoid wet feed or litter.

Disease: Fowl Pox
Cause: Filterable virus often transmitted by mosquitoes.
Symptom: Wart-like growths on the comb and wattles.
Treatment: Paint cankers with iodine.
Prevention: Vaccinate with Fowl-Pox vaccine.

Disease: Infectious Bronchitis
Cause: Filterable Virus
Symptom: Gasping followed by depression and weakness.
Treatment: None.
Prevention: Bronchitis vaccine mixed in drinking water.

Disease: Laryngotracheitis (Chickens)
Cause: Filterable virus.
Symptom: Wheezing, gurgling and rattling in the throat. Death is from suffocation; birds show a dense cheesy material in the windpipe.

Treatment: None.
Prevention: Sanitation and quarantine. Laryngotracheitis vaccine may be used, but the virulent virus is a possible hazard to the user.

Disease: Leucosis (Chickens)
Cause: Filterable virus.
Symptom: Paralysis, grey eyes, and large livers with lymphoid tumors. (Birds usually have only one of the above symptoms.)
Treatment: None.
Prevention: Feed adequate rations, control internal and external parasites.

Disease: Newcastle
Cause: Filterable virus.
Symptom: Gasping followed by various nervous disorders.
Treatment: None.
Prevention: Newcastle disease vaccine (For intranasal, intraocular, or drinking water use)

Disease: Blackhead (Turkeys)
Cause: Protozoan.
Symptom: Poults are weak, sleepy, and droopy. Inflamed liver and ceca.
Control: Use Blackhead formula soluble in water for 1 to 2 weeks.
Prevention: Continuous use of Blackhead Formula. Control cecal worms.

Disease: Coccidiosis
Cause: Eimeria tenella protozoan parasite.
Symptom: Bloody droppings, dull and droopy birds which may soon die from hemorrhaging.
Control and Prevention: Sulfaquinoxaline solution in drinking water.

Disease: Trichomoniasis (Turkeys)
Cause: Protozoan.
Symptom: Ruffled feathers and foul-smelling saliva.
Treatment: One teaspoonful of copper sulfate in 2 gallons of drinking water for four days; skip three days and repeat if needed.
Prevention: Avoid poorly drained or infected areas.
Cannibalism: Habit acquired by confined birds.
Control: Salt in drinking water, ample space and green feed.

Internal Parasites:
Parasites: Roundworm, tapeworm and cecal worm are most significant.
Control: Phenothiazine, Piperazine hydrochloride and Nicotine.

External Parasites:
Parasites: Lice, mites, and blue bugs.
Control: Malathion or powders containing Rotenone, Sulfur, and petroleum oil.

External Symptoms of Birds			Probable Cause
Eyes and Nostrils	Mucus		Infectious Coryza (Colds)
	Cheesy Material		Avitaminosis A
	Blindness		Bacterial Roup
			Leucosis
Breathing	Gasping		Laryngotracheitis
			Heat Prostration
			Pneumonia
Comb	Dark Red		Fowl Cholera
			Blackhead
			Intestinal Parasites
	Pale		Tuberculosis
			Fowl Typhoid
			Fowl Leucosis
	Scabs		Fowl Pox
Feathers	Ruffled		Intestinal Parasites
			Lice
			Coccidiosis
Wings	Drooped		Severe Parasitism
			Pullorum Disease
			Coccidiosis
			Blackhead
Loss of Flesh			Tuberculosis
			Intestinal Parasites
			Fowl Leucosis
Legs	Paralysis or Weakness		Avitaminosis A or D
			Coccidiosis
			Fowl Leucosis
			Botulism
Neck	Limber		Cholera (Late Stages)
			Botulism
Diarrhea	Yellowish-Brown		Cholera
			Blackhead
	Green		Fowl Typhoid
			Fowl Leucosis
	Bloody		Coccidiosis
	Whitish		Pullorum Disease
			Intestinal Parasites

PART VI FISH RAISING

CONSTRUCTION OF PONDS

Farm fish ponds, under proper management, can contribute materially to a nation's food supply. This is particularly true in southern areas where most pond-fishes attain within one year sufficient size for table use. Farmers who own a pond site will find that with a little labor and non-critical materials they can build a small fish pond which will produce enough fish to supplement their meat supply and furnish minerals and vitamins required in the diet to maintain health. A farm fish pond one acre in size, properly fertilized and managed, can supply up to 200 or more pounds of fish a year. Production will be reduced in northern regions in proportion to the shortening of the growing season and lower water temperatures.

Pond or Water Area

The selection of the pond site is important. Primary considerations are: an adequate but not excessive water supply, a pond bottom which will hold water, a location where the dam can be constructed economically, and satisfactory and sufficient materials nearby with which to build the embankment. Secondary considerations are: reasonably fertile soil for the pond bottom, erosion control on the watershed area, gently sloping ground particularly for the pool area, and freedom from heavy overflow or flash floods. Low areas too wet to farm often make ideal pond sites for wildlife and fish.

The source of water for the pond should receive first consideration. In order to reduce the cost of construction and of fertilization after the pond is full, it is best to consider only small streams or springs or direct runoff from pastures and woodlands. It is necessary to have a constant overflow from the pond but there must be sufficient water to fill the pond and to maintain it at a rather stable level. If it is impossible to find a site where water is flowing during the summer months, then the pond should have sufficient depth to provide adequate space for the fish when evaporation lowers the amount of water-surface. A ratio of approximately 10 to 15 acres of watershed to one surface acre of pool water should be established for pasture land when the water source is only direct rainfall runoff, with a slightly larger ratio for woodland and a smaller one for lands under cultivation. These ratios will, of course, vary with the rainfall and the slope of the land, so they should be determined for each pond.

After the general location has been chosen with respect to the water supply, the next step is to select the actual site for the pond and dam. Areas where gravel beds exist or where limestone outcrops are present should be avoided as the ground may not hold water. Water draining into the pond from adjacent lands should be free of silt. If it is not possible to locate the pond where there is a wide fringe of grass or woodlands bordering the edges, it would be desirable to create such a strip so that the silt will be deposited before it reaches the pond.

The cost of construction will increase as the height of the embankment or depth of the water increases. An embankment 10 feet high will require approximately three and one-half times as much dirt as one 5 feet high. Hence, it is well to limit the depth of water to some reasonable figure unless abundant funds are available for construction. Expense must be considered also when large streams are blocked, as additional spillway capacity and freeboard on the embankment will be required as insurance against failure of the dam during floods. The minimum depth at the drain structure should be from 6 to 8 feet. If a heavy demand is made

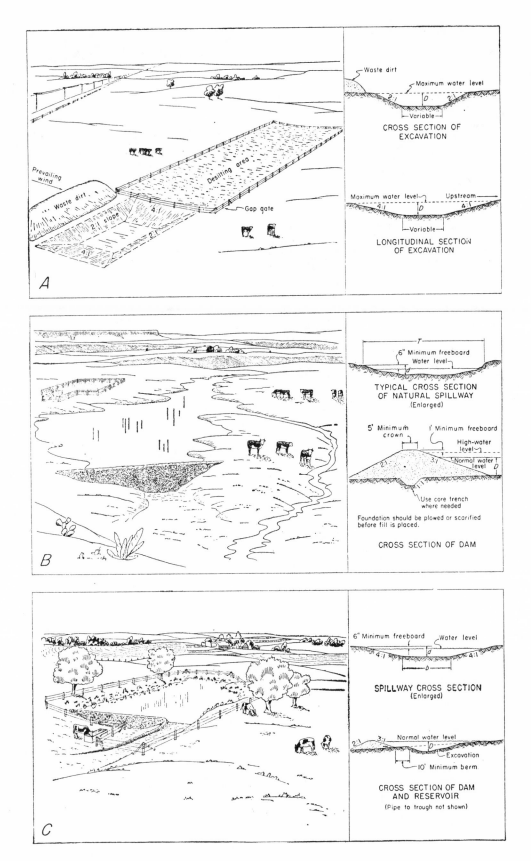

Fig. 1. —*A,* Specifications commonly used for small rectangular dugouts. Note the desilting area used with the dugout. Desilting is desirable in areas where considerable silt is carried in the run-off. *B,* A stock pond common in the West. Wherever possible, a natural spillway should be utilized. *C,* A stock pond common in the East. Note the wide entrance to the vegetated spillway.

Fig. 2. A sheepsfoot roller insures good compaction of soils used to build the dam of an embankment pond.

TABLE 1.—*Size and approximate capacity of rectangular dugouts with 2 : 1 side slopes and 4 : 1 end slopes*

Top dimensions (feet)	Depth D (feet)	Capacity			
		Cubic yards	Acre-feet	Gallons	Million gallons
50×75	6	452.0	0.28	91,292	0.09
	7	472.6	.29	95,444	.10
	8	483.7	.30	97,703	.10
	9	488.0	.30	98,563	.10
60×100	7	892.6	.55	180;273	.18
	8	937.1	.58	189,264	.19
	9	968.0	.60	195,510	.20
	10	987.7	.61	199,482	.20
65×105	8	1,110.4	.69	224,273	.22
	9	1,153.0	.71	232,875	.23
	10	1,182.1	.73	238,755	.24
	11	1,200.1	.74	242,383	.24
75×125	8	1,676.3	1.04	338,567	.34
	10	1,830.3	1.13	369,671	.37
	12	1,916.0	1.19	386,981	.39
	14	1,952.6	1.21	394,364	.39
90×155	8	2,747.4	1.70	554,896	.55
	10	3,080.3	1.91	622,138	.62
	12	3,309.3	2.05	668,398	.67
	14	3,453.6	2.14	697,542	.70
	16	3,532.3	2.19	713,430	.71
105×185	8	4,085.1	2.53	825,092	.83
	10	4,663.7	2.89	941,937	.94
	12	5,102.7	3.16	1,030,603	1.03
	14	5,421.4	3.36	1,094,973	1.09
	16	5,639.0	3.50	1,138,929	1.14

on the pond for stock watering, then, it may be necessary to have deeper water, to carry both the fish and stock over protracted dry periods.

The pond area itself should be cleared of all trees, brush, shrubs, and debris. Leaf mold and other organic mulch act as a fertilizer and should be retained. It is not considered necessary to remove stumps but the yearly maintenance will often be decreased if they are removed from those portions of the pool where the water will be less than 3 feet deep at full pool. In locations where sprouts from stumps thrive, it is particularly desirable to remove the stumps from the shallow portions as they would soon choke up that part of the pond and both the fishing and appearance would be harmed.

Water less than 18 inches in depth has little value in the fish pond. By eliminating shallows it is possible to reduce the mosquito problem, increase the forage area for the fish, and it is easier to control aquatic vegetation. These portions should be excavated and the soil deposited uniformly along the shore line, care being taken to spread it so that the normal surface drainage into the pond is not blocked. It may be desirable, also, to use some of the top-soil thus obtained in surfacing the slopes of the embankment.

Water Control Structures

In order to manage the pond properly it is necessary to provide some means for completely draining the pool. This can be done by building a drain structure, with additional attachments for controlling the elevation of the surface of the pond at the lowest point in the base of the embankment. Such a structure is useful in draining the pond when repairs are necessary, and for providing facilities for piping water to stock-watering tanks. When the source of water for the pond is constant, with no danger of flash floods, this structure can be made to serve as the overflow. The discharge opening should be large enough to permit the normal water flow to pass over it at a depth of less than 2 inches. Otherwise the pond will become depopulated by loss of fish through the discharge pipe. If excessive runoff occurs, it would be advisable to provide auxiliary spillways cut about 1 foot above the desired pond level around the end of the dam sloping no more than 3 inches per 100 feet, in earth, or as steep as desired, in rock. Sand is too erodible. The size of the outlet pipe should be determined by someone familiar with the requirements, but it should not be less than 6 inches.

Dam or Earth Embankment

The dam or earth embankment is used to stop the flow of surface water and for the creation of the pond. Careful selection of the site for the pond should include consideration of the location of the dam.

It is preferable to build it in a narrow part of the valley so that its length and height will be kept at a minimum without affecting the surface area or depth of the pond water. Primary consideration should, of course, be given to the pond site but some balance should be found between the pond acreage and the amount of embankment needed to create the pool. The larger the fill, the more expensive will be the pond.

The base of the fill should be on good soil, preferably clay, with care taken to avoid gravel beds or peaty formations. The foundation for the fill should be relatively impervious to water just as should the pond bottom.

The shape of the embankment will vary with the type of soil to be used but generally the slope will be about three feet in width for every foot in height. Sandy or similarly pervious soil should have a flatter slope, perhaps five feet in width to one in height. The top width should not be less than six feet and it can be wider to suit the needs of the owner. Often such fills are used as roadways, in which case the top should be at least eight feet wide. The top of the dam should

205

be not less than 3 feet above the desired elevation for the pool water (free board). In places where there is excessive flash runoff or high winds which cause large waves, additional freeboard may be advisable.

There should be a good bond between the embankment and the natural ground so that no seepage places exist. To insure this, it is necessary to remove all stumps, roots over two inches in diameter, vegetable matter, trash, logs, peat, etc., from the base before any fill material is moved into place. If the foundation material is found to be pervious after the removal of these materials, it is advisable to excavate a trench along the center line of the dam down to impervious soil or rock and to backfill with clay. Should rock outcrops exist, it may be necessary to pour a concrete cutoff wall into the rock and extending a few feet into the fill. After the entire base is cleaned, it should be plowed or otherwise scarified before placing the earthy fill so there will be no unbroken division between the ground and the fill.

The method of placing the fill material will vary with the type of equipment used. If a dragline or similar machine is used, the fill can be built with little compaction, but adequate allowance should be made for settling. An average allowance would be one additional foot in height for every 5 feet of final dam height; i.e., if the final dam is to be 10 feet high, it should be built to 12 feet. All dirt should be placed as nearly as possible to its final position so rehandling will not be necessary. The slopes, too, should be built in the designed ratio, which, if 3:1, would mean a rise of 1 foot for each 3 feet of horizontal measurement. As an example, if the dam is to have a final height of 10 feet, it would be necessary to start the slope out 30 feet in order to reach the designed height at the right place if it is planned to have a 6 foot top width, the outside point for the dirt would fall 33 feet from the center line of the dam.

The Soil Conservation Service (SCS) in the U. S. has provided a cost sharing plan whereas a qualified land owner approved by the SCS has to pay only a portion of farm pond construction costs.

Aside from raising fish, ponds can become invaluable for watering livestock and irrigation of gardens and orchards. In some countries of the world—where all the annual rainfall falls in a several month period—farm type ponds might provide the necessary water to carry over livestock raisers when drought conditions persist. A soil type must be available so that the pond bottom can be sealed and no leakage occurs. A clay type soil is used for this in the U.S. Without this kind of soil to seal the pond, artificial means have to be used such as plastic or bentonite.

In hot, dry climates, construction of ponds should be tailored according to conditions in that area. Ponds may need more depth or perhaps larger in surface area because of fast evaporation.

The main equipment needed for construction of smaller ponds is a medium sized dozer, a "sheepsfoot" or device to pack the earth and pipe to lay a water pipe outlet so that water can be removed by gravity force. (See Fig. 2)

A farm pond constructed in the U.S. (1974 costs) with a 13 ft. dam and holding 2.5 acre feet of water could be built for between $1,000-1,500. In certain areas of the world, this size pond might provide all the water needed for a small village's livestock and vegetable gardens.

One should be cautioned against attempting to construct ponds where the soil is extremely sandy or of porous nature. Ponds that do not leak cannot be constructed under these conditions.

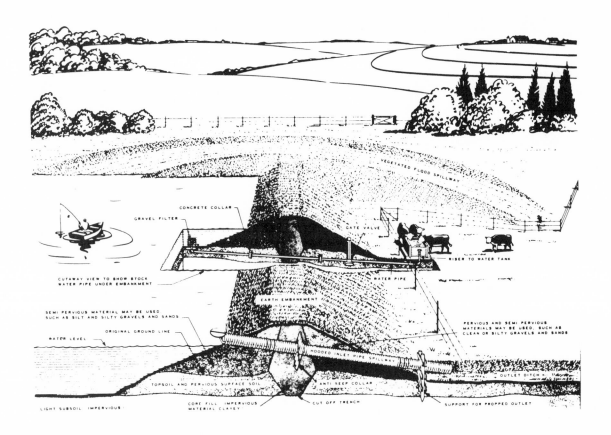

Fig. 3. Diagram of an embankment multi-purpose pond.

TROUT

Geographical Range

Ponds above 5,000 feet in the West are usually cold enough for trout. In the fog belt of the Pacific coast, in the northern tier of states, in the Appalachians, and in New England, trout thrive in ponds at lower elevations. Ponds at any elevation or in any latitude, fed by cold springs or cold wells, may be suitable.

Water Temperature

Trout can live in water between 33° and 75° F. but they make their most rapid growth in water of 50° to 65° F. Not only do trout make their fastest growth within this temperature range but they are less susceptible to parasites and diseases. It is not likely that you will be able to keep the water temperature in your pond within this range all year unless you have a source of constant-temperature water from a spring or well.

If the water in your pond is too warm for trout, you may want to stock bass, bluegills, catfish, or other warm-water fish.

Summer

In summer, the surface water of a pond is coldest just before sunrise. If the water temperature at this time is not more than 70° F., 6 inches below the surface, it is not likely to rise more than 5 to 10 degrees during the day. Trout die if the water temperature reaches 86° F. Trout may survive a few hours' exposure to high surface temperatures each day but they usually seek cooler, deeper waters.

207

Fig. 4. The gray part of the map represents areas where trout farming is most likely to be successful in the U.S. White areas approximates catfish growing areas of the country.

You can lower the water temperature and raise the oxygen level by increasing the inflow of fresh, cool water and releasing the warm water through a surface outlet gate.

Summer growth of trout is slower in the cold water of mountain ponds than in the warmer water (50 to 65 F.) at the lower elevations. Since the coldest water is at the pond bottom during summer months, the outflow from mountain ponds should be through a bottom-water outlet. This results in more favorable trout growth.

Winter

In areas where ponds are covered with ice during winter, the water temperature will be 33 F. just below the ice and about 29 F. on the bottom. Water is most dense and therefore heaviest at 39° F. Water warmer or colder becomes less dense and tends to layer above water of 39° F. Little, if any, fish growth takes place at these low temperatures. The only way you can raise the water temperature enough to benefit trout is to add a supply of water warmer than 50° F.

Stocking the Pond

To manage your trout pond best, you will need to know something about the kinds of trout you can stock and how suitable they are for your pond.

Kinds of trout

The rainbow trout is the most common choice for stocking ponds. It thrives under a wide range of conditions and grows fast. Rainbows are more widely available from hatcheries than are other kinds of trout.

208

RAINBOW

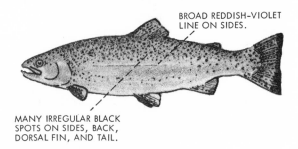

BROAD REDDISH-VIOLET LINE ON SIDES.

MANY IRREGULAR BLACK SPOTS ON SIDES, BACK, DORSAL FIN, AND TAIL.

CUTTHROAT

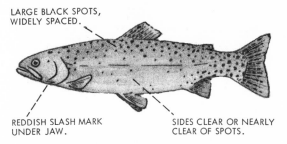

LARGE BLACK SPOTS, WIDELY SPACED.

REDDISH SLASH MARK UNDER JAW.

SIDES CLEAR OR NEARLY CLEAR OF SPOTS.

BROOK

REDDISH AND YELLOWISH SPOTS ON SIDES.

WAVY LINES ON BACK, DORSAL FIN, AND TAIL.

BELLY REDDISH-ORANGE IN FALL.

WHITE BORDERS ON FINS.

BROWN

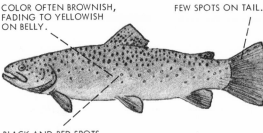

COLOR OFTEN BROWNISH, FADING TO YELLOWISH ON BELLY.

FEW SPOTS ON TAIL.

BLACK AND RED SPOTS SURROUNDED BY LIGHTER HALO.

Fig. 5. Each kind of trout has special markings that identify it.

The brook trout is favored in parts of the East although rainbows do as well and are widely available. Brook trout are a little easier to catch than rainbows and sometimes spawn in springs or trickles that are not suitable to the rainbow. Brook trout are available from some hatcheries in the West and from most hatcheries in the East.

In some sections of the country, both rainbow and brook trout are stocked in the same pond for variety. Whether you stock them singly or together is a matter of choice.

The cutthroat trout has been little used in ponds and is not widely available from hatcheries.

The brown trout is longer lived and grows larger in many ponds but it is more cannibalistic and harder to catch than are other kinds of trout. Brown trout are not recommended for stocking ponds.

Don't stock other kinds of fish with trout—they compete with the trout for oxygen and food. If your pond has 50 pounds of other kinds of fish, it will likely have 50 pounds less of trout.

If there are other fish in the pond, drain it or use chemicals to kill all fish before stocking with trout.

Number to stock

The number of trout a pond will support depends on its surface area (not volume), water quality, and size of the fish. The carrying capacity of a pond is limited and is measured in pounds of fish rather than in numbers. Therefore, for any given level of management, a pond will support more little fish than big fish.

Ponds of average fertility usually produce enough natural food to support about 100 pounds of trout per surface acre. On the basis of production records in the West, spring stocking a 1-acre pond with 500 2- to 4-inch fingerlings will give you

7- or 8-inch (4 ounces) trout the first year. Stocking at half that rate in the fall should give you 10-inch (8 ounces) trout.

In the East, the standard fall stocking rate is 600 3- to 4-inch fingerlings per acre. This stocking rate has resulted in 8-ounce trout the first year.

In general, 2- to 4-inch fingerlings are more likely to survive to pan size than are 1- to 2-inch ones.

Whether your management goal is more small fish or fewer large ones, fingerlings stocked in the fall benefit from favorable growing conditions early the following spring. As a result, they reach pan size sooner.

If winterkill or unavailability of fingerlings in the fall is a problem, you may be limited to spring stocking.

Restocking

A pond stocked in fall will contain many small but usable trout the first year. If you fish these small fish lightly, you should catch some trout weighing 1¾ to 2 pounds during the second year.

Waiting another year or two for a 2-pound trout to grow larger is not worthwhile. Trout grow slowly after they reach this size, and their death rate is high. Also, they seldom spawn in ponds. For these reasons, it is best to fish your pond hard and restock it with 4- to 5-inch fingerlings every year or two.

Some pond owners prefer to drain their pond or use chemicals to kill all the fish at the end of the second season. This prevents the few remaining large trout from eating any of the newly stocked fingerlings. Cannibalism is not considered a major problem, however, if the pond is fished hard and the population reduced so that there is plenty of food.

Where to get trout

In most cooler parts of the United States, you can buy trout for stocking from private fish hatcheries or from trout farmers. With air transportation and other modern shipping methods, trout can be sent quickly and safely to almost any location. Hatchery personnel will make shipping arrangements or tell you how to transport your fish.

The more trout you order from a private hatchery, the lower the price will be per thousand. You may be able to pool your order with other pond owners in your area to get a lower price.

Your state fish and game agency or the local Soil Conservation Service office can give you a list of hatcheries that sell trout for stocking.

How to stock

Avoid stocking trout in water above 65° F.

Because trout are sensitive to sudden changes in temperature, oxygen, carbon dioxide, and alkalinity or acidity, you should never dump the fish directly into your pond from a shipping container.

Pond water should be added slowly to the water in the shipping container until it is within 6° F. of the temperature of the pond water. An easy way to do this is to pour out about half of the water from the container. Then place the container in the pond and pour pond water slowly into it. When it is full, pour out about half the mixture and repeat the process twice more. This should take only 15 or 20 minutes.

If the trout show signs of distress such as turning on their sides, delay further mixing until they act normally. After mixing is completed, pour the fingerlings gently into the pond.

You can increase the carrying capacity of your trout pond and get steadier trout growth by supplementing natural foods with commercially prepared ones. This means that you can produce 1,000 to 2,000 pounds of trout per acre annually, which is 10 to 20 times more pounds of trout, by supplemental feeding.

In theory, you could stock as many fish as you want if you give them enough food. In practice, this doesn't work. Crowded fish are easy prey to diseases and parasites.

If you stock a 1-acre pond with 2,000 2- to 4-inch fingerlings and provide enough supplemental feed to grow 1,000 pounds of trout, you will get ½-pound trout at the end of the first year. It takes about 1 pound of feed to produce a ½-pound trout under favorable growing conditions.

Young trout may need to be fed several times a day for fast growth. But don't overfeed. Feed only what the fish will clean up promptly. If any food remains 15 minutes after feeding, it probably will not be eaten. Decomposing food uses oxygen and may cause loss of fish.

If the water in your pond is above 65° F., it is not safe to do supplemental feeding.

Dry, pelleted trout feeds, available from commercial trout feed dealers, are easy to use. Dealers furnish a detailed feeding schedule based on fish size and water temperature.

Harvesting the Fish Crop

With good management and no supplemental feeding, your pond should reach its carrying capacity in pounds of fish within a year after stocking. During the second year, trout make little growth unless the pond is fished regularly. Remember, each fish you take out allows the remaining ones to gain weight faster.

To get the greatest return in numbers of pan-size trout and in pounds of fish, start fishing as soon as the trout are 6 to 8 inches long. This will be about 6 to 10 months after you stock your pond with fingerlings.

Early in the second year, your trout should be 12 to 14 inches long and weigh about 1 pound. From then on, increase in length will be slower but the fish will weigh more.

Only a small percentage of the trout you stock will live more than 2 years. At the end of 3 years, just a few large trout will remain and their total weight will be far below the carrying capacity of your pond.

CATFISH

In the warm water areas of the U.S., the most important fish species raised in ponds is catfish which includes channel, blue and white catfish. Other fish found suitable for warm water ponds are bass and blue gills. There is a certain amount of prejudice against raising carp. In some parts of America, carp and other bottom feeding fish are referred to as "trash fish".

Water Temperature

Catfish grow rapidly in 70° F. or more water. Growth is slow between 60° and 70° F. Little growth occurs when water is colder than 60° F.

In the southern U.S. deep water is not necessary for catfish farming. Ponds constructed on flat lands should be about 2½ feet deep at the shallow end and sloped to 4 or 6 feet at the outlet. Ponds depending on rain runoffs must be deep

enough to carry catfish through a drought. Farther north, a depth of 8 feet or more may be necessary to prevent winterkill.

Stocking

For a small operation, a farmer usually buys fish for stocking. The number to stock per acre depends on the size desired at the end of the growing season. Medium size (4-6 inches) fingerlings stocked at 1,500 per surface acre usually average slightly more than 1 pound in a 210 day growing season. The same medium size fingerlings stocked at 2,000 per surface acre average slightly less than a pound. Large fingerlings (10 inches long or weighing ⅓ pound) if stocked at 1,200 per surface acre average about 2 pounds at the end of the growing season.

The following stocking rates are practical:

1. In impoundments such as farm ponds that depend on runoff water and if no lift pumps are available, 750 to 1,000 fish per surface acre.
2. In ponds having a dependable water supply:
    a. If fish are 4 to 6 inches long, 1,500 to 2,000 per surface acre;
    b. If fish are 10 inches long or weigh ⅓ pound, 1,200 fish per surface acre;
    c. If fish are 2 years old and weigh ½ to 1 pound each, 700 to 800 per surface acre.

Proper stocking can be done only by being able to determine the number of fish placed in the pond. It is impractical to actually count them, but you can determine the desired number on the basis of weight. This can be done in two ways: (1) Count the number of fish in a known weight. Example: If there are 100 fish in 1 pound and you want to stock 2,000 fish, weigh out 20 pounds of fish. (2) Measure the length of the fish and use Table 2. Example: Fish 3 inches long weigh 10 pounds per 1,000 fish. If you want to stock 2,000 fish, weigh out 20 pounds of fish.

TABLE 2.—*Average length and weight of channel catfish*

Length (inches)	Weight per thousand fish	Weight of individual fish
	Pounds	*Ounces*
1	1.3	—
2	3.5	—
3	10	—
4	20	—
6	60	—
8	112	—
10	328	5.25
12	509	8.2
14	850	13.6
16	1,290	21

Feeds and Feeding

Good catfish feed should contain 28 to 32 percent protein, no less than 5 percent fat, and 10 to 15 percent fiber. A minimum of 8 percent of the ration should be from fish meal. The rest of the ingredients may vary according to availability.

Feeds are sold as finely ground mash and as floating or sinking pellets. Floating

212

pellets cost more but enable you to observe whether the fish are feeding. If you see no feeding activity, take steps immediately to find the cause. Channel catfish must be trained to eat floating feeds. This may take a week or more. Blue catfish readily take floating feeds.

A 1/8-inch pellet is usually used for fingerlings and a 3/8-inch pellet for fish weighing ½ pound or more. Some farmers use a 5/8-inch pellet for all sizes of fish with good results. Ground mash is used primarily for feeding fry.

Check hardness of the pellets regularly. When a pellet is dropped in water, 90 percent should remain together after 10 minutes.

Feeding Fish in Production Ponds

Production ponds will average about 7 acres of surface area.

A general guide to the daily amount to feed (on basis of estimated weight of fish) according to water temperature follows:

Water temperature 6 inches below surface	Percent of Weight Amount equivalent to:
Below 45° F., feed only every 4 or 5 days	0.5 percent
45° to 60° F.	1 percent
60° to 70° F.	2 percent
Above 70° F.	3 percent

Table 3. *Monthly Feeding Schedule*

[Pounds of feed per day 6 days per week, based on 3-percent-per-day program for fingerlings that average 4 inches in length at time of stocking]

Month	Amount for 300 fish (acreage not considered)	Amount based on stocking rate of 1,500 per acre
	Pounds	*Pounds*
March	0.2	0.5
April	0.5	3.0
May	1.0	7.5
June	1.5	12.0
July	2.0	15.0
August	2.5	20.0
September	3.5	25.0
October	3.5	[2]30.0
November	2.0	20.0

[1] For December, January, and February feeding rates are reduced.
[2] Do not exceed 30 pounds per day unless water is flowing through the pond.

Feed should be scattered in 3 to 4 feet of water. Feed at the same time and place each day, either early in the morning or late in the afternoon. Fish are usually fed 6 days a week.

Check the response of the fish daily by throwing out small amounts of feed. If they fail to feed vigorously, something is wrong; stop feeding until you find the trouble.

If sinking pellets are used, feed consumption can be checked by placing a 4- by 4-foot tray on the pond bottom in the feeding area before feeding. Lift the tray slowly an hour after feeding. If all the feed has not been eaten in an hour, reduce the amount fed.

Never feed more than 30 pounds per acre a day unless water is flowing through the pond. Excessive feeding usually results in an oxygen shortage.

Winter Feeding

Catfish held over winter must be fed to prevent weight loss. They are also more resistant to disease and parasites if fed. When the water temperature is between 45° and 60° F., feed at the rate of 1 percent of the estimated total weight of the fish in the pond 6 days a week. When the water temperature is below 45° F., feed one-half of 1 percent of the weight of the fish every 4 or 5 days.

CARP

Carp raising is quite prevalent in Asia and other parts of the world. Fingerlings are available in many of these countries. Carp raising may become more important in the U.S. with the development of meat/bone separators that can separate edible meat from the bone and scales of fish.

For carp one always uses trios for parent fish—one female and two males. The female should be at least four years old, because the ova or hard roe ripens at four years. The milt or soft roe of the male ripens in the third year. There should be anything from two hundred thousand to seven hundred thousand eggs from a female, depending on conditions of temperature, weather, water, food. At established carp farms they figure on an average of at least half a million eggs per spawner.

There are several varieties of the common carp. *Cyprinus Carpio* is the name of this species. It will breed anywhere, regardless of climate and latitude. The variety, most favoured by carp farmers and the trade, is the fish called the King Carp, which has been bred for a great many years from selected parents. Environment and different feeding has made it deep-bodied or fat bellied or with longer body than the ordinary carp.

Other varieties which the carp farmer should find worth cultivating are the Mirror Carp and the Leather Carp. The Mirror Carp is a very handsome and showy fish; most suitable for a fair-sized garden pond. It is also good fish for the food markets. The aim of the carp farmer lies, mainly, toward the food market. To this end the better fish are those with the length only twice their breadth. Both Mirror and Leather Carp are European varieties.

The carp family, so far as pond culture is concerned, in addition to those mentioned, are the Crucian; the Grass; the Black; the Silver; the Bighead; and the Mud. The last five Chinese. The Crucian should be avoided. It is a nuisance, too bony for food markets and a terrific breeder. The Bighead and the Mud carp would also be useless in the U.S.

The Spawning Period

The Carp parent fish are in cool ponds while the spawning pond is getting

214

warm. When the temperature of the latter has reached, either naturally or by artificial means, from sixty degrees to seventy-five degrees—the higher the better— the parent fish are removed from the cool pond to the warm one. This should be during the last week in May or the first week in June. Spawning will take place almost immediately. Fecudation takes place outside the fish's body. Sexual organs of the female are represented by two rolls of ova, which join each other between the vent and the spine, and when ripe, occupy the largest part of the fish's abdominal cavity. As the male fish chase the female she dashes towards the bunches of twigs and leaves in the pond—or other flora which may be growing there—and swimming slowly over these she releases a stream of ova, a few seconds later another stream. In fact, there are a score or more ejections within an hour. This may continue for the whole morning and sometimes go on into the afternoon. The male fish follow the spawning and, hovering over the spot, impregnate the eggs with their milt. This has a milky appearance and curdles like milk, but is composed of microscopic spermatozoa. So quick is the follow up of the males that the eggs are impregnated as they reach the water. As may be expected very many eggs fall in the water impregnated and are lost in the mud or eaten by the parents or some pond intruder. With the impregnation of the egg the development of the embryo begins.

It is generally agreed that 10 per cent of a usual spawn can be expected to hatch into fry. A spawn of half a million eggs should, therefore, result in fifty thousand fry. The eggs include in their content a yolk which serves a double purpose. One part assists in the development of the embryo and the other remains in the yolk sac which attaches itself to the belly of the embryo and supplies it with food for the first few days. It is interesting to observe how quickly the body grows. You first recognize the head and the spine. The eyes are particularly prominent. Then the heart and the blood vessels begin to act. In six to ten days, earlier if the water is very warm, the shell is broken and the fry emerges. It is transparent, extremely delicate, and has to remain quietly existing on the remains of the yolk in the sac for another day or two. By the time this is exhausted the fry has grown much larger and much stronger. It has, moreover, got the suction and digestive organs working and is now able to move in the water and feed itself. This is a very important moment in the life of fry. There must be ample food in the pond and this food can only be microscopic fauna.

Removal of Parent Fish

Regarding the parent fish; they must be removed from the spawning pond after the spawning, otherwise they may feast upon the ova. After netting the female, she should be examined to see whether there is still ova in the abdomen. If so, this should be gently pressed out as in artificial propagation.

The young fish on removal into the fry pond should continue to be fed on the microscopic fauna for a day or two. Then gradually, as the days lengthen, minute organisms should be introduced into the pond and by July these organisms can be big enough to be seen with the naked eyes.

Carp Not Vegetarian

Many misstatements have been made in the past by mistaken scientists about the carp's habits. The carp, except the Grass, is carnivorous. But he does not chew or masticate meat, nor vegetable matter, because he cannot. The carp's mouth is loose. He sucks in food. His snout has a pump-like suction arrangement. His masticating organs are insufficient for chewing anything before swallowing it. The carp is a bottom feeder, much like the tench. On the upper lip are two to four barbels which serve as feelers searching on the bottom. But he is not a scavenger.

215

He dislikes and avoids any decayed or decaying matter.

If food in a pond is plentiful the fry will grow rapidly. On finishing the yolk sac they should be about half an inch long. A week or a fortnight later, on being transferred to a fry pond, they would be an inch or more. In a month's time the size should be two to three inches. This is the time to start sorting. Keep the smaller ones in their original fry pond and send the larger ones to other fry ponds. Until they reach the three-inch size the fry need careful handling. They are still extremely delicate, and netting and sorting into sizes disturbs them, and rough handling would kill them. The expectation, under normal conditions, is a loss of 25 per cent of fry from each hatch. But with care, fair weather and avoidance of haste, the loss may be reduced to a minimum. The rate of growth of the fry can be regulated by increasing or decreasing their number in a definite area of fertile ponds. A fertile pond is one that possesses large and continuous growth of plankton—the food of the fry. Records show that, after sorting, the larger fry, transferred to a separate pond, reached ten inches in length and one and a quarter pounds in weight during the following six months.

The Grass Carp

The habits of the Grass Carp are interesting because of its herbivorous nature. Even though it will take any kind of food that comes its way at random it prefers green grass and vegetables to any food of animal origin. All kinds of freshly-cut land grasses, weeds—if not too tough—leaves of some trees and all kinds of fresh vegetables are placed in a twenty-foot square frame in the pond. The frame is to prevent the grass, etc., from floating all over the pond. The Grass Carp, after the experience of a day or two, will come to this frame punctually for the food. During severe weather when green stuff may be difficult to procure foods like rice-bran and bean-meal are given. When well fed the growth of this fish is remarkable. Fry, at the end of the year in which they were hatched, commonly attain a length of six to ten inches and a weight of one and a half pounds. If this size fish continues to grow it attains a length of two feet and four to five pounds weight in the second year. It is not unusual for a Grass Carp of four years of age to weigh more than ten pounds. Weights of twenty and thirty pounds are quite common, and sometimes there is a fifty-pound Grass Carp in the market.

The Black Carp is a snail feeder and must be plentifully supplied with snails. It is a small feeder on other foods, but with a generous diet of snails it grows very fast, in a pond, attaining ten pounds weight in three years.

The Silver Carp is a plankton feeder. Due to the fine structure of its gill takers it can feed on big particles as well as small ones suspended in the water. The silver carp reaches maturity early and weighing from three to four pounds in the third year bears ripe ova or sperm.

These three species can be stripped and artificially propagated. They are, particularly the Grass Carp, widely distributed from Siberia to south China and should stand up to climatic conditions at almost any latitude or altitude. The fry of these species thrive on plankton. Duckweed, however, is considered the best food for fry of the Grass Carp. Unfortunately, duckweed grows rapidly in a well-fertilized pond, so much so that the fry cannot eat it quickly enough to stay its progress. This is an undesirable contingency, and as the weed becomes thick it must be cut and removed to give the nursery pond better light and ventilation.

Carp Are Lazy, Not Scavengers

The carp is a lazy, luxury-loving fish. A placid pond with the right kind of shade-giving plants and, above all, plenty of food, makes for full enjoyment of its life. The carp has no work to do except suck in food. It would never do the housework in the pond. The accusation that the carp is a scavenger may be due to

the cleanliness of carp ponds. This work is undoubtedly done by the snails, who are scavengers. Carp are fond of snails but, as already shown, can only eat them in the state of infancy when the shells of the snails are just forming and are soft. As the snail gets its hard shell the carp has, perforce, to ignore it. The consequence is that the pond is thus amply supplied with 'cleaners'.

Again, the statement that carp eats vegetable matter is, no doubt, due to the fact that the fish can be seen nibbling away among the pond flora. But it is really nibbling at the host of tiny crustaceans and other minute organisms who make their home on the leaves and stems of the plants. The Grass Carp, however, is primarily a vegetarian.

The manuring of ponds with animal excreta, poultry droppings and night soil may sound disgusting to the uninitiated, but the fish do not feed on this manure except sometimes at first out of ignorance and curiosity. They avoid the small piles made, at intervals of days, here and there in the ponds. The piles disappear very quickly, due to water action, and in their place appear swarms of infusoria and plankton, especially minute crustaceans.

A carp farm does not require a hatchery house. The culture of carp and goldfish is very similar, any informational source which gives all necessary details for the cult of the goldfish should be followed by the carp farmer. Instead of leaving the impregnated ova in the spawning ponds they can be hatched, like goldfish ova, in special aquaria or wooden tanks. In the case of a smallish establishment with only a few ponds, such hatching is advisable. From the aquaria the fry will, in due course, be removed to the fry pond.

Secret of Growth

The secret of growth lies in the operative word 'plenty'. The fish, more particularly after they are removed from the nursery pond to the rearing and growing ponds, must have plenty of water, plenty of food and plenty of water-plants. The smaller ponds are the better; they must have plenty of earth on the bottom and plenty of manure. There lies the secret of fertility.

Manures should be, preferably, of animal or other organic substances. Vegetable compost also might be useful. All manures, before being put into a pond, should be thoroughly rotted. To get them into such suitable condition the manures brought to pondside should be delimed. Each forkful, as the heaps are being made, should be dusted with lime; then a good sprinkling of lime on the top. Finally, cover the heap with earth, well patted down. While waiting the week or two for the proper rotting one can use a guano manure. The Peruvian guano is practically impossible to procure, but a guano made from poultry manure is being produced in poultry raising areas. It is rich in nitrogen and comes in pulverized form. Before putting this in a pond it should be soaked for twenty-four hours in a container. The amounts to be used in the pond are twenty pounds (dry) per one hundred gallons of water. Over-fertility in a pond is not good for the fish, so care must be taken not to use too much manure at a time.

Firm Pond Bottom Necessary

A pond becomes fertile after manuring in where organisms are created and immediately find homes in the mud bottom or on the plant life. It is here that the carp feeds—on the bottom and among the plant life. As carp feed by sucking in their food they naturally get some earth and vegetable matter with the insects, worms or general crustaceans. This matter is not much benefit to the fish, but it is not harmful until the pond bottom becomes too slimy. With loose slime the carp sucks up more of it than of food, and is not only indigestible to the fish but harmful to the small fauna living in the bottom. A firm, not loose, pond bottom is desirable and necessary. That is why each season carp ponds are emptied and

217

allowed to go dry for a period. The slime can then be scraped out and a firm bottom re-established. When empty the bottom of the pond should be ridged throughout for a time. The furrows and ridges dry quicker than if the bottom is left flat.

For some hundreds of years carp farms have existed in Europe. German scientists, some years ago, made researches into the food for carp in Europe. For ten years they examined carp stomachs from many localities under the microscope. They found that the best natural food of the carp is the small water fauna which has no hard or tough shell. With the gullet tooth of the carp the soft shell is broken and the contents swallowed without any addition of inorganic or vegetable matter. Worms and spiders are not in favour for the carp's diet, although they will be present in the pond. Water fleas and mites and all soft-shelled crustaceans are the carp's principal choice. It needs many good mouthfuls of these minute creatures, but the water fleas must help considerably, for a famous naturalist has stated that the young of a single water flea in two months is three thousand millions. In a lifetime of a single female it is estimated her progeny would reach the enormous number of four and a half billions and weigh eight tons. These daphnia varieties often form a mass in the water and the carp sucks in the lot at one go. Most gnats and caddis fly are also favourite food for carp.

In ponds which do not become properly fertilized they can be colonized by removing some of the natural food from an over-fertile pond and introducing it into the under-fertilized ones.

HOME ENERGY SAVING TIPS

Insulating Your Home

Most homes, built in the days when energy was plentiful and cheap, don't have enough ventilation. Insulation can, however, be added to any house even if some already exists.

Insulation Efficiency

Insulation efficiency is measured by its "R-Value", not its thickness (See Table 1). The R-Value stands for resistance to winter heat loss or summer heat gain and this is much more accurate than thickness. One brand of insulation might be slightly thicker or thinner than another, but if they're marked with the same R-Value, they'll resist heat flow equally well.

Attic Insulation

Insulating the attic will give you the single largest savings in your fuel bill. Adequate insulation in the attic floor generally will save up to 20 per cent on your fuel bill. The National Bureau of Standards has announced that even in a region of relatively mild climates, an investment in six inches of attic floor insulation will be returned by fuel savings within a year.

Walls and Floors

Once you have enough insulation in your attic, insulate behind your walls and under your floors if the basement or crawl space is unheated. You can place insulation under your floor using chicken wire to hold it up. Walls can be insulated with bats or blankets as you renovate or "blown-in" if your walls are already finished.

Fig. 1. Heat Transfer Comparisons

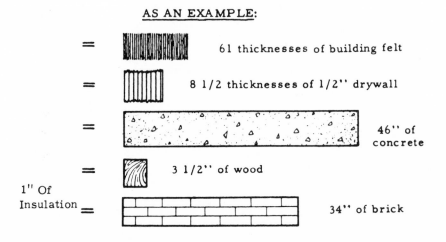

AS AN EXAMPLE:

= 61 thicknesses of building felt

= 8 1/2 thicknesses of 1/2'' drywall

= 46'' of concrete

= 3 1/2'' of wood

1'' Of Insulation = 34'' of brick

Fig. 2. Heating Zone Map

220

Heating Zone	Recommended for	
	Ceiling	Floor
0,1	R-26	R-11
2	R-26	R-13
3	R-30	R-19
4	R-33	R-22
5	R-38	R-22

R-Values	Batts or Blankets		Loose Fill (Poured In)		
	glass fiber	rock wool	glass fiber	rock wool	cellulosic fiber
R-11	3½"-4"	3"	5"	4"	3
R-13	4"	4½"	6"	4½"	3½"
R-19	6"-6½"	5¼"	8"-9"	6"-7"	5"
R-22	6½"	6"	10"	7"-8"	6"
R-26	8"	8½"	12"	9"	7"-7½"
R-30	9½"-10½"	9"	13"-14"	10"-11"	8"
R-33	11"	10"	15"	11"-12"	9"
R-38	12"-13"	10½"	17"-18"	13"-14"	10"-11"

Table 1. Top: Recommendations of R-Values for floors and ceilings (corresponds with zones in Fig. 1).

Bottom: Types of insulation and thickness needed for various R-Values.

221

Fig. 3. Batts — glass fiber, rock wool

Where they're used to insulate:

unfinished attic floor

unfinished attic rafters

underside of floors

— best suited for standard joist or rafter spacing of 16" or 24", and space between joists relatively free of obstructions

— cut in sections 15" or 23" wide, 1" to 7" thick, 4' to 8' long

— with or without a vapor barrier backing — if you need one and can't get it, buy polyethylene except that to be used to insulate the underside of floors

— easy to handle because of relatively small size

— use will result in more waste from trimming sections than use of blankets

— fire resistant, moisture resistant

Fig. 4. Foamed in Place — ureaformaldehyde-based

Where it's used to insulate:

finished frame walls

— moisture resistant, fire resistant

— may have higher insulating value than blown-in materials

— more expensive than blown-in materials

— quality of application to date has been very inconsistent — choose a qualified contractor who will guarantee his work

Fig. 5. Blankets — glass fiber, rock wool

Where they're used to insulate:

unfinished attic floor

unfinished attic rafters

underside of floors

— best suited for standard joist or rafter spacing of 16" or 24", and space between joists relatively free of obstructions

— cut in sections 15" or 23" wide, 1" to 7" thick in rolls

— with or without a vapor barrier backing

— a little more difficult to handle than batts because of size

— fire resistant, moisture resistant

Fig. 6. Rigid Board — extruded polystyrene bead board (expanded polystyrene) urethane board, glass fiber

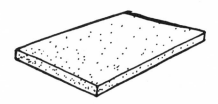

Where it's used to insulate:

basement wall

— extruded polystyrene and urethane are their own vapor barriers, bead board and glass fiber are not

— high insulating value for relatively small thicknesses, particularly urethane

— comes in 24" or 48" widths

— variety of thicknesses from 3/4" to 4"

NOTE: Polystyrene and urethane rigid board insulation is best installed by a contractor. They must be covered with 1/2" gypsum wallboard to assure fire safety.

Fig. 7. Loose Fill (poured in) — glass fiber, rock wool, cellulosic fiber, vermiculite, perlite

Where it's used to insulate:

unfinished attic floor

— vapor barrier bought and applied separately

— best suited for non-standard or irregular joist spacing or when space between joists has many obstructions

— glass fiber and rock wool are fire resistant and moisture resistant

— cellulosic fiber chemically treated to be fire resistant and moisture resistant; treatment not yet proven to be heat resistant, may break down in a hot attic; check to be sure that bags indicate material meets Federal Specifications. If they do, they'll be clearly labelled

— cellulosic fiber has about 30% more insulation value than rock wool for the same installed thickness (this can be important in walls or under attic floors)

— vermiculite is significantly more expensive but can be poured into smaller areas

— vermiculite and perlite have about the same insulating value

— all are easy to install

Fig. 8. Loose Fill (blown-in) — glass fiber, rock wool, cellulosic fiber

Where it's used to insulate:

unfinished attic floor

finished attic floor

finished frame walls

underside of floors

— vapor barrier bought separately

— same physical properties as poured-in loose fill

— because it consists of smaller tufts, cellulosic fiber gets into small nooks and corners more consistently than rock wool or glass fiber when blown into closed spaces such as walls or joist spaces

— when any of these materials are blown into a closed space enough must be blown in to fill the whole space

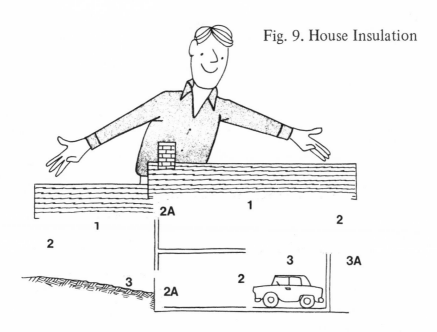

Fig. 9. House Insulation

The diagram in Fig. 9 shows where insulation goes in a house. The numbers on it are keyed to the list below:

1. Ceilings with cold spaces above.

2. Exterior walls. The short walls of a split-level house (2A) should not be neglected. Walls between living space and unheated garages or storage rooms should be insulated, too. Walls that are enclosed on both sides can be insulated only by an insulation contractor.

3. Floors above cold spaces — vented crawl spaces, garages, open porches, and any portion of a floor in a room that is cantilevered beyond the wall below (3A).

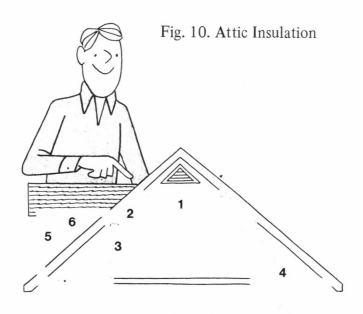

Fig. 10. Attic Insulation

Insulate attic living space as indicated in the diagram above:

1. Between "collar beams."

2. Between sloping rafters. Be sure to leave an air space for ventilation between the insulation and the roof deck (select insulation thickness accordingly)

3. Between the studs of "knee walls."

4. Between the joists of the floor outside the living space.

5. Dormer walls

6. Dormer ceilings

CONTRACTOR INSTALLATION

— Make sure to choose a reputable contractor.

— To locate a contractor, ask your utility company, consult friends, look in yellow pages

— Obtain cost estimates from at least three different contractors. Make sure you describe the job identically to each.

— Check a contractor's reliability with your local Better Business Bureau listed in the phone book.

— Ask a contractor for references including previous customers. Check them out.

— If your state requires licensing, find out if the contractor is licensed. If the state requires bonding, make certain the contractor is bonded.

— Check with your local building-code authorities for guidance in purchasing an insulating material.

— Talk with a contractor in terms of R Values. If a contractor won't deal with you in R Value language, don't deal with him.

— Bags of insulation should be marked with R Values and figures indicating the area the contents will cover to achieve the desired R Value.

— After selecting a contractor, have a specific contract drawn up for the job; sign it only when you are fully satisfied that it details everything you want done.

— Any warranty for the insulation should be in writing and part of the contract.

Fig. 11. Caulking Windows. Drawing a good bead of caulk will take a little practice. First attempts may be a bit messy. Make sure the bead overlaps both sides for a tight seal.

Fig. 12. Weather-stripping Windows. In weatherstripping windows, rolled vinyl or foam rubber with adhesive backing can be used.

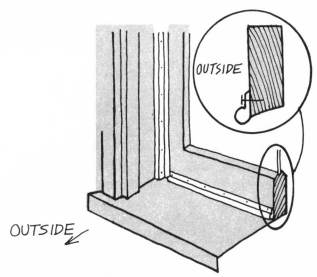

Fig. 13. Weather-stripping Doors. You can weatherstrip your doors even if you're not an experienced handyman. There are several types of weatherstripping for doors, each with its own level of effectiveness, durability and degree of installation difficulty. Select among the options given the one you feel is best for you. *The installations are the same for the two sides and top of a door,* with a different, more durable one for the threshold.

227

Fig. 14. Filling Cracks. Fill extra wide cracks like those at the sills (where the house meets the foundation) with oakum, glass fiber insulation strips, etc.

Fig. 15. Build Storm Windows. Storm window suppliers will build single pane storm windows to your measurements that you then install yourself. Another method is to make your own with do-it-yourself materials available at most hardware stores.

Fig. 16. Fireplace Air Vent

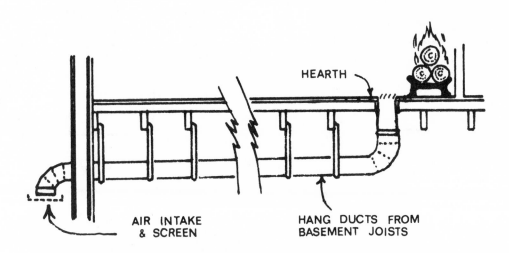

Put a vent under your floor to feed air to the fireplace. This will reduce the amount of air which is drawn across the room from cracks around windows and doors.

The easiest way to connect a vent to the outside is to use a series of rectangular metal ducts. You can get these ducts at a plumbing supply store. Different sizes are available, but try to buy ducts which are at least 3 inches deep by 10 inches wide. You will need enough to stretch under your floor from just in front of the fireplace to the *nearest* opening in the basement.

Fig. 17. Air Heating Grate

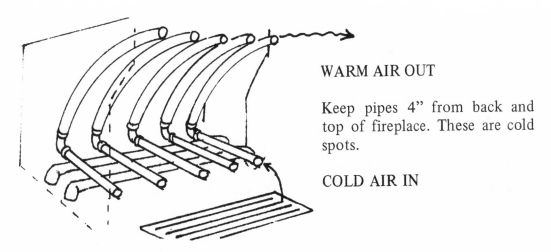

WARM AIR OUT

Keep pipes 4" from back and top of fireplace. These are cold spots.

COLD AIR IN

This air heater works by sucking cold air from the floor. The air is heated by the fire, and then flows out into the room.

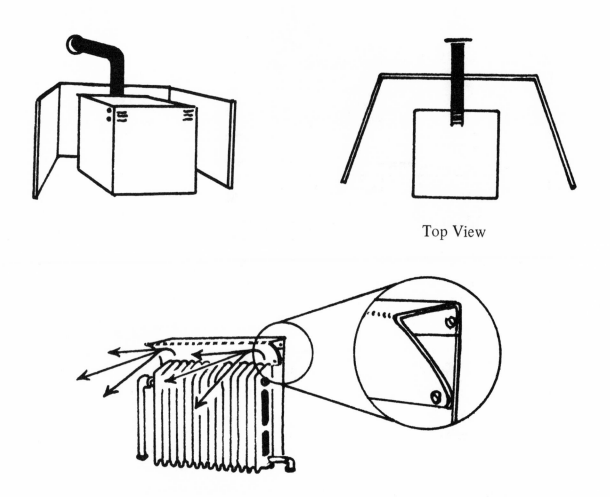

Top View

Fig. 18. Top: Wood or oil stove with aluminum reflector between stove and wall.
Bottom: Radiator with curved reflector on top that is also between heater and wall.

TIRE CHAIN

Fig. 19. Cleaning A Capped Chimney. You can clean a chimney using a chain. Attach a rope and lower it down the chimney a few feet. Then pull it up and down. Once this area is clean, drop it a few more feet and clean again. Do this until you get the whole chimney clean.

230

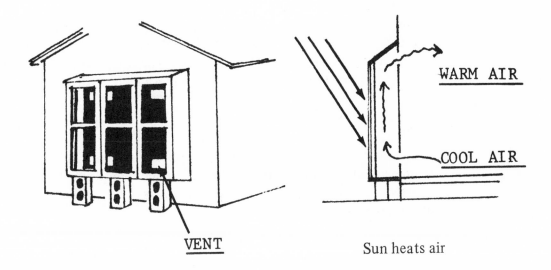

VENT

Sun heats air

WARM AIR

COOL AIR

Fig. 20. A solar wall heater made from old storm windows. The windows are placed in a box made with 1" x 6" lumber. Vents are 4" x 14" in size. Principle is to allow cold air from lower vents to enter the heater from room. After sun heats the cool air, it rises and re-enters room through upper vents. The heater wall is painted black. Vents can be closed at night or when the sun is not shining.

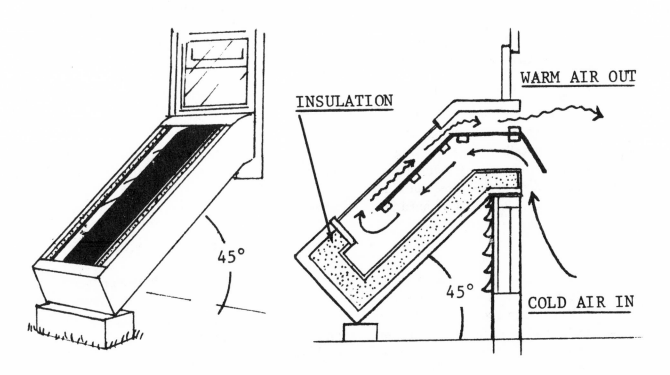

45°

INSULATION

WARM AIR OUT

45°

COLD AIR IN

Fig. 21. This solar window heater uses the same principle as above wall heater. 1" x 10" lumber is used for side and 3/8" exterior plywood for bottom. The heater is covered with glass. The 3" of insulation on bottom and sides keeps the sun's heat from escaping through sides and top.

SOAP

Soap has been used as a cleansing agent for more than 2,000 years. It is a good detergent when used in soft or softened water. It cleans well because it can be dissolved in warm or hot water to form suds which penetrate quickly and deeply into the fibers of a fabric; it emulsifies grease; and holds the dirt in suspension until it can be rinsed away. Making soap at home is a thrifty practice for any family. It's a way to use fat from butchering and cooking which is often wasted.

Ingredients for Soap

Only three ingredients are needed to make soap—cold water, lye, and fat. Six pounds of fat and one can of lye can be made into nine pounds of soap. Fat from butchering can be used to make an excellent quality soap. Used fat can be clarified to make clean fat suitable for soapmaking.

Lye

When you buy lye notice the sodium hydroxide content. Since there are many different brands on the market read the label and be sure the sodium hydroxide content is 94 to 98 per cent. It is usually sold in cans containing about 13 ounces.

NOTE: ANTIDOTE FOR LYE — LYE IS POISON — IT BURNS

For protection when making soap, keep a small bowl of vinegar near, so if you spatter lye on your hands you can dip them immediately into the vinegar to neutralize it. If burns are serious, call a doctor immediately. Drench burned spot as soon as possible with water and bathe with vinegar. If lye has been swallowed, give juice of lemon, orange, rhubarb or grapefruit, or if you don't have these use vinegar. Give as much as the person will take.

Fats

You can use any animal or vegetable fat but not mineral oil.

Mutton tallow has a very high melting point and is hardest of all animal fats. It will make a hard, dry soap unless additional water is added or it is mixed with soft fats as lard, goose grease or chicken fat.

Beef tallow is next in hardness and should be mixed with softer fat or have additional water added.

Poultry fat used alone makes a soft spongy bar, so should be used with harder fats.

Any of these fats can be mixed and will make good soap. Soap made from oils or soft fats requires less water and needs to dry longer than soap made from tallow.

Store fat in a cool dry place while collecting enough for soap-making. However, it's best to make fat into soap promptly and let the soap age rather than to let the fat get old and rancid. Soap improves with age, but fat does not.

To Render Fat

1. Grind fat using the coarse blade or cut into small pieces.
2. Put into a large kettle on top of range or in roaster in the oven. Add a quart of water for each 10 pounds of fat.

3. Use moderate temperature and stir occasionally.

4. When cracklings begin to brown and settle, strain and squeeze all of the fat from the cracklings. Cracklings themselves don't make soap.

To Clarify Drippings and Remove Salt

1. Put drippings into kettle with equal amount of water.

2. Bring to a boil, remove from heat and stir. (Caution: fat boils over easily)

3. For each gallon of hot liquid pour 1 quart of cold water over the surface of the fat. (Caution: if fat spatters cool a little) Stir slightly.

4. Cool and skim fat from the surface.

To Remove Rancidity

1. Boil sour or rancid fat in a mixture of 5 parts of water to one part of vinegar.

2. Cool and skim fat from the surface.

3. Remelt the fat and for each gallon of hot liquid add one quart of cold water. Stir slightly.

4. Cool and skim fat from the surface.

Other Ingredients

If perfume is desired use oil of citronella, oil of sassafras, oil of lavender or oil of lemon.

Uncolored soap is usually most satisfactory. However, when making toilet soap if a slight yellow color or marbled effect is desired, use liquid butter coloring. Other colors are not easily available.

Pumice stone powder for mechanics' soap.

Oil of tar for tar soap.

Castor oil to prevent abrasive from settling.

Borax to quicken sudsing action.

Coconut oil to produce a fine sudsing soap.

Equipment Needed

Utensils should be iron, enamel, crockery or glass. You will need:

Large round bottom bowl or utensil (6 quarts)

Small bowl or utensil (2 quarts)

Standard tablespoon, cup and pint measures

Slotted wooden spoon

Dairy thermometer

Household scales

Flat wooden box soaked in water and lined with wet cotton cloth.

Making Soap: The "Saponification" Process

Making soap is a chemical process. When lye and fat are brought together under the right conditions, they react to make entirely different products. Fat plus lye produces soap and glycerine. This process is called saponification. It may

take several weeks for complete saponification to take place. When it is saponified, the product never separates into fat and lye again. In homemade soap, glycerine is left in. Commercially it is separated and sold as glycerine.

If proportions used are correct and saponification complete, the soap formed will be neutral. If any free lye is present, the soap "bites" when touched with the tongue.

Precautions

1. Don't use aluminum utensils for making soap.
2. For excellent soap use *exact* weights, measures and temperatures.
3. Always add the lye slowly to the water.
4. Always add the lye solution slowly to the melted fat.
5. Rapid addition of lye to fat or jerky, uneven stirring may cause separation.
6. Pour mixture into the mold carefully.
7. Don't allow new soap to freeze.

Correct Temperatures Are Important

Table 2. Temperatures for Lye Solution and Melted Fat.

Type of Fat	Temperature of Melted Fat	Temperature of Lye Solution
Tallow	120° F – 130° F	90° F – 95° F
Lard and tallow (half and half)	100° F – 110° F	80° F – 85° F
Sweet lard or other soft fats	80° F – 85° F	70° F – 75° F
Soft rancid fat	97° F – 100° F	75° F – 80° F

Recipes for Cold Process

Soap with Soft Fat

Soap from Tallow

5 cups cold soft water
1 can lye (13 oz.)
6 pounds soft fat (lard or mixed fats.)
2 tablespoons of borax may be added
1 to 2 tablespoons of perfume if desired.

7 cups cold soft water
1 can lye (13 oz.)
6 pounds of mutton or beef tallow
2 tablespoons of borax may be added
1 to 2 tablespoons of perfume if desired.

Note: Use lower range temperatures in warm weather.

Method

1. Put correct amount of cold water into a 2 quart utensil (earthenware or heatproof glass). Add slowly one can of lye and stir until dissolved. Cool solution to temperature given in chart.

2. Put melted fat into a six quart utensil (earthenware or glass). Add the lye solution in a slow steady stream. Stir slowly until the mixture is thick and creamy.

234

3. If desired add any or all of the following: borax, perfume and color.

4. For *bar* soap pour carefully into a soaked wooden box lined with a wet cloth. When well set remove and cut into convenient sized cakes. Pile so air circulates around each cake.

5. For granular form leave in container and stir occasionally over a period of several hours, until it becomes dry and crumbly. You can also grind bar soap through a food chopper for granular form. If you prefer flakes, cut bar soap with a slaw cutter. Granular soap or flakes can be stored in a pasteboard box or any other convenient container.

Curing Soap

Best results are obtained if homemade soap is cured at room temperature. It can be used at the end of a month, but since aging improves it a longer period is better.

Other Soaps

Toilet Soap: Made like other soap, only the fat used is from butchering instead of drippings. It gives a whiter, better quality soap.

Floating soap: Made by folding the air into any soap when it begins to have a creamy consistency. Test for floating by dropping a few drops on cold water. Except for the convenience of soap staying on top of the water, floating soap is no better than other soaps.

Tar soap: As any plain lard or tallow soap becomes creamy, add eight ounces of oil of tar. Work in well by stirring to prevent small lumps from forming. Tar soap is used frequently for shampoo.

Shaving soap: To one-half recipe of soap add 3 ounces of coconut oil. Or use all lard for the fat.

Mechanic's hand Soap: (Makes 11 pounds)

3 pounds homemade soap
6 cups water (7 cups if the soap is very dry)
1 tablespoon borax
3 ounces light mineral oil
5 pounds of pumice stone powder

Method: Dissolve 3 pounds of homemade soap in 6 cups of water. Add borax and mineral oil. When cooled to a creamy consistency work in the pumice stone. Pour into wide mouth jars or cans which are then tightly covered and use as a paste, or pour into a mold and when hard cut into cakes.

If You Have "Bad Luck". . . .

If soap separates, it can be reclaimed. Cut or shave soap into an enamel or iron kettle. Use rubber gloves or cut soap without touching. Be sure to use any lye that has separated out and about ⅔ pint of water for each pound of soap. Stir slowly and evenly and bring gradually to the boiling point. Watch carefully for it will boil over easily. Boil until the mixture drops from the spoon in sheets. Pour into molds and cover as before.

Good Soap Should. . . .

Be neutral, no lye or fat present
Be attractive
Have a clean, wholesome odor
Curl when shaved (if fresh)

CANDLES

Candles are run in molds. For this purpose melt together one quarter of a pound of white wax, one quarter of an ounce of camphor, two ounces of alum, and ten ounces of suet or mutton tallow. Soak the wicks in limewater and saltpetre, and when dry, fix them in the molds and pour in the melted tallow. Let them remain one night to cool; then warm them a little to loosen them. Draw them out, and when hard, put them in a box in a dry, cool place.

To make dipped candles, cut the wicks of the right length, double them over rods, and twist them. They should first be dipped in limewater or vinegar and dried. Melt the tallow in a large kettle, filling it to the top with hot water when the tallow is melted. Put in wax and powdered alum to harden them. Keep the tallow hot over a portable furnace, and fill up the kettle with hot water as fast as the tallow is used up. Lay two long strips of narrow board, on which to hang the rods; and set flat pans under on the floor to catch the grease. Take several rods at once, and wet the wicks in the tallow; when cool, straighten and smooth them. Then dip them as fast as they cool until they become of the proper size. Plunge them obliquely, not perpendicularly; and when the bottoms are too large, hold them in the hot grease till a part melts off. Let them remain one night to cool; then cut off the bottoms and keep them in a cool, dry place. Cheap lights are made by dipping rushes in tallow.

CERAMICS

Ceramics, a term applied to all useful or ornamental clay objects that are baked. Ceramics includes both pottery and porcelain. Any clay object fashioned from earth and hardened by baking, either in the sun or by firing, is considered pottery. Porcelain is one particular kind of pottery. Translucent, vitreous, and basically white, true porcelain is formed from specific types of clay, rock, and quartz or quartz substitutes.

The making of pottery is an ancient art, antedating, in most cultures, the knowledge of metals or even of textiles. Porcelain, however, is a much later development, first appearing in China as late as A.D. 600, and in Europe, in the eighteenth century.

Techniques

Material

Clay is the basic material in the making of ceramics. When it is first dug from the earth, the clay is mixed with sand, small stones, decayed vegetable matter, and other foreign material, all of which has to be removed before the clay can be used. This is accomplished today, as it was in ancient times, by mixing water with

the clay and letting the mixture stand in a large basin. The impurities fall to the bottom, and the upper layer of clay and water is pumped or bailed into an adjoining basin. The process is then repeated sometimes several times, each succeeding settling purifying the clay still further until the desired quality is achieved.

The damp clay is stored indoors until needed. Storage of the clay for several months actually improves its working qualities. It allows the clay to take a "set" so that although remaining malleable, the clay will hold its shape while it is being molded. The fresh clay is often mixed with old clay from a previous mixed batch; this increases bacterial action and also seems to improve the quality of the material.

A piece molded in clay undergoes a certain amount of shrinkage, both while it is drying and during the firing process. To insure uniform drying and to minimize shrinkage, coarsely ground bits of fired terra cotta, usually broken pottery known as "grog," are added to the clay. The grog also increases the stiffness of the clay, thus reducing its tendency to slump while being modeled.

Forming the Pot

Freehand Technique. The earliest technique for making pottery, invented about 5,000 B.C., at the beginning of the Neolithic period, was the freehand forming of a vessel from a lump of clay. This was accomplished by pushing and pinching the clay until the desired shape was achieved. Examples of this early work have been found in Jordan, Iran, and Iraq. This technique is still used today by some potters.

Coil Technique

A later development was the coil technique, whereby the pot was built up from a number of strands of clay. A thick strand was coiled around a flat, hand-formed clay base and then pinched and smoothed to form a good joint. Additional strands were added until the pot reached the desired height and shape. To assist in the building and smoothing operation, a rounded stone was sometimes held inside the wall of the pot while the outside surface was beaten with a paddle. This technique produced very fine pottery with walls of uniform thickness. The coiled pottery method has been compared to the technique of basket weaving in which baskets are woven with long ropes of fiber, and it may be that the coiled pottery technique derived from basket making.

A refinement of the coil technique involvedforming the pot on a small piece of rush matting or a curved potsherd (a fragment of a broken pot). The mat or potsherd acted as a base during the building of the pot and as a convenient pivot so that the vessel could be readily rotated between the hands of the potter. This manual rotation gave the potter an opportunity to continually smooth the pot and adjust its symmetry as he built it. Some primitive groups, such as the American Indians, never progressed beyond this technique, and all of their pottery was produced by this method. The coil method continued to be employed in the construction of very large storage jars even after the invention of the potter's wheel.

The Potter's Wheel.

The invention of the potter's wheel occurred near the end of the fourth millennium B.C. Its use was not immediately widespread, some areas having adopted it far ahead of others. One of the first areas to use the wheel was Sumer, in ancient Babylonia, about 3250 B.C. In Egypt it was used as early as the latter part of the Second Dynasty, abut 2800 B.C., and in Troy, wheel-made pottery was found at the Troy IIb level, about 2500 B.C.

The ancient potter's wheel was a heavy, sturdily built disk of wood or terra cotta. On the underside of the disk was a socket which fitted over a low fixed pivot. The entire wheel was balanced to run true without wobble or vibration. It was customary practice in Greece to have a boy, presumably an apprentice, turn the wheel by hand, adjusting the speed at the command of the potter. The large size and weight of the wheel provided ample momentum once the wheel was put in motion. Having an assistant for the labor of wheel-turning allowed the potter to use both hands in forming the vase and to devote his entire attention to it. The kick-wheel, or foot-operated wheel, apparently was not used until Roman times. In the seventeenth century the wheel was spun by means of a cord working over a pulley, and in the nineteenth century a steam-driven wheel was introduced.

The process of making a pot on a wheel starts with wedging the clay to remove air bubbles, to make it homogeneous, and to get it to the proper working consistency. A ball of clay is then centered on the rotating wheel and firmly held in cupped hands until it runs true without wobbling. Pressure of the thumb in the center of the ball of clay forms a thick-walled ring which is slowly pulled upward between the thumb and fingers, creating a cylinder. The cylinder can then be opened into a bowl shape, drawn up as a long tube, flattened into a plate, or closed to form a sphere, at the pleasure of the potter. This concludes the "throwing" operation, and the vase is set aside to harden. The following day, when the clay has dried leather-hard, the pot is centered upside down on the wheel. As the wheel rotates, metal, bone, or wooden tools are used to "turn," or refine, the shape by shaving off unwanted clay. The modeling of the pot is now finished and the pot is ready for decorating and firing. (The foot or other sections of the pot may be thrown and turned separately and then joined to the body of the pot with clay slip—liquid clay used by the potter as a cement.)

Casting

Casting is a technique used in making a series of identical pieces of pottery. First, a plaster mold is made from the piece to be reproduced. A liquid clay slip, called a casting slip, is then poured into the mold. It is allowed to remain there until the plaster absorbs the moisture of the clay slip near the surface of the mold, causing this layer to solidify. This takes about an hour. The mold is then inverted, and the remaining slip is poured out. After the thin-walled clay casting has hardened slightly, the mold is carefully opened and the casting removed. The hollow clay casting is retouched and finished by hand and subsequently fired.

In ancient times, the soft, pliable clay was pressed into the mold by hand. It was not poured, as it is in casting. The manufacturing procedure began with the forming of the original model. The patrix, or master model, was made from clay by a sculptor, keeping in mind the ultimate use of the vase and the intermediate manufacturing steps. In most of these so-called plastic vases, the mold-made

section was joined to a part, usually the mouth, formed on the potter's wheel. Therefore, the patrix was made for only the molded section.

Firing

The technique of treating dried clay with heat to change it from a soft, fragile substance to a hard, vitreous material was discovered by man about 5000 B.C. The discovery was undoubtedly accidental, possibly as a result of building a campfire over a deposit of clay. When the fire burned itself out it was undoubtedly noticed that the clay underneath had become extremely hard. The inventive first potter must have repeated the phenomenon by shaping something from the soft clay and placing it in the fire. When this piece emerged from the firing intact and in a hard, permanent form, an industry was born.

Primitive methods

The early potters did not use a kiln; they arranged their dried clay vessels in a small pile and then covered them with whatever fuel was available, such as wood, charcoal, twigs, straw, or dried dung. Primitive groups in Africa and in both North and South America have continued this particular practice to the present day. Since the temperature is not uniform in a mound of pots and some of them do not reach the proper temperature for the vetrification of the clay, this type of firing produces uneven results and causes the loss of a substantial number of pots by breakage. When the unvitrified pots are filled with water they dissolve and revert back to soft clay. the color of this pottery is also rather unpredictable, as some areas of the fire are oxidizing in character and others are reducing. Therefore, some of the pottery is a brownish-red in color and some is grayish or black.

The Kiln

A kiln is a specially built chamber for firing pottery which allows the potter more control over the process than does an open fire. Usually the area for burning the fuel is separate from the area in which the pots are placed. Openings are provided for tending the fire, for the placement and removal of the ware, for observation of the firing, and for control of the flow of air through the kiln.

Procedure

Most pottery is fired twice. The first firing, done after the pot is formed, hardens the clay, producing what is known as "biscuit"; the second firing, done after the pot is glazed, fixes the glaze.

In the first stage of firing, the moisture in the clay is slowly removed. The firing is done slowly, to avoid cracking the ware. When the temperature reaches 112°F. the clay is completely dehydrated. The clay is now red throughout and is brittle, porous, and absorbent. In the second firing, after glazing, the temperature reaches 1112°-1652°F. If the air is freely admitted to the kiln during this process, the clay is thus oxidized and all carbonaceous matter is removed. If the air is excluded from the kiln, the clay will be black and is said to be "reduced."

Decoration

There are three basic types of decoration: underglaze, inglaze, and overglaze. Glazes are smooth, glassy coatings made of mixtures of minerals such as lead, flint, borax, feldspar, or lime.

Underglaze

As the term implies, underglaze decorations are applied before the ware is covered with a transparent glaze. Colors are produced by the use of colored oxides of elements such as colbalt, nickel, chrome, manganese, and iron. The coloring oxides are mixed with materials which will fuse during subsequent heat treatment, thus adhering to the ware. Decoration is applied by hand painting, application of decalcommania, silk-screening, or spraying through other types of stencils. One method of decoration, called sgraffito, entails painting the entire piece with a clay slip of a different color than the original and then scratching the desired design through the coating. Underglaze decoration is extremely durable, being protected from wear and chemical attack by the covering glaze.

Inglaze

Inglazed decoration is merely the application of a solid-colored glaze to a piece. This method is very widely used. It is quite difficult to produce sharp images of any design within the glaze itself, because of the melting process and the diffusion which take place upon firing the glaze. However, a number of pleasing effects are produced by application of different colored glazes which flow together partially during the heat treatment.

Overglaze

In overglazing both colored-oxide media and materials which actually form deposits of a metal are applied over the glaze. Since overglazes are fired at relatively low temperatures (1300°-1600°F), a great many coloring materials which would not be stable at the higher temperatures needed for the firing of underglazes can be used. Thus, overglaze decorations allow the use of the greatest palette of colors in ceramic work. Metalic decorations consist of either a metal salt or very finely divided metal particles suspended in a medium which produces a consistency suitable for painting or silk-screening onto the ware. During firing, the medium volatilizes, leaving the metal behind. If the coating is sufficiently thin the metal does not appear metallic but rather produces a mother-of-pearl type of luster. The color of this luster can be varied by the use of different metals. If the decorating medium is compounded to leave a somewhat thicker coating, the result will be a shiny metallic coating; gold, silver, and platinum are the metals normally used for this. The media containing powdered metal particles are usually applied quite thickly by silk-screening and thus produce the most durable metallic decoration. These materials are dull rather than shiny after firing and must be burnished.

CHARCOAL

Charcoal is the black, porous, brittle material consisting mainly of carbon that remains after burning vegetable and animal matter with limited access of air. The term is popularly applied to the material thus obtained from wood; this was earlier known as coal simply, until mineral coal came into use. When the production of charcoal as such for domestic cooking and heating and for

metallurgical purposes originally began is unknown, but the smelting of metals from their ores was practiced before 4,000 B.C. and charcoal was the only known fuel capable of producing the high temperatures necessary.

Wood consists essentially of carbon, hydrogen and oxygen, but the latter two elements are present in the same proportions as in water. During the combustion of wood only the carbon contributes towards the heat released, and a proportion of this becomes used in evaporating the moisture in the wood, of which even seasoned timber contains 15-20%. If wood is first converted into charcoal this burns with intense heat, without any visible flame and has about twice the heating power of the same weight of wood. These properties and the high chemical activity of charcoal compared with most other forms of carbon (diamond as the other extreme) are responsible for its economic importance.

History in Europe

Throughout the middle ages the increasing demands for fuel for metal-smelting and glass-making led to the concentration of these industries in the European forest lands, some of which became relatively densely populated. Much of the deforestation of Europe during this period can be attributed to charcoal-burning. In spite of legal restrictions the process continued: In England, the Sussex Weald and the Midland forests were cut; yet towards the end of the 16th century Archbishop Grindal could complain of the smoke caused by charcoal-burners at Croydon, so that timber must still have been available there. By the beginning of the 20th century 95% of the forests which once covered Great Britain had been felled and in parts of western Europe the proportion was nearly as high. The evolution during the 18th century of metallurgical processes using coke prevented complete denudation of the European forests. Charcoal is now little used for iron-smelting except in remote ore-fields without local coal supplies (e.g., Zapla, in Argentina), but metallurgical operations requiring a carbonaceous material of low ash content, especially sulphur and phosphorus, still consume large quantities.

Preparation

Wood charcoal was formerly produced by slow partial combustion of wood in circular stacks (Ger. Meiler, hence 'meiler charcoal') with a central chimney. When this process is used the stacks contain about 200 cu. yd. of material and two to three weeks are required for its completion; with skilled attention the yield approaches 26% by weight of the wood or 60% by bulk. To avoid the loss of many valuable by-products into the atmosphere, carbonizaiton is now carried out in kilns or retorts fitted with condensers. The former are of either beehive or rectangular shape, externally fired and may contain 250-400 cu. yd. of wood. The temperature is raised in stages first to about 275° C, when an exotheric reaction occurs, then to 400 or 500° C; the process normally takes up to three weeks but can be shortened by the use of forced draught. The main liquid product is Stockholm tar or creosote, a valuable preservative for timber.

Better yields of both charcoal and distillates are obtained with retorts; the process was introduced into England in 1783 when an improved quality of charcoal was required for making gunpowder. For this purpose light woods such as alder or willow are best. During the second world war small portable kilns were designed for use in Britain and elsewhere. Sporting cartridge powder often contains red charcoal or charbon roux, prepared by subjecting wood to superheated steam at two atmospheres pressure in iron cylinders.

241

Recently, especially in the United States, low temperatures (200° rising to 340°C) have been employed for the distillation of wood; this and the selection of woods to give the maximum volume of liquid reduce the quantity and quality of charcoal, which becomes a by-product, but a variety of spirits and oils in addition to creosote are obtained. Formerly horizontal iron retorts were used but in modern America practice the process is continuous, wood being fed in at the top of the retort and charcoal withdrawn at the base. A swiss process, also continuous, utilizes furnace gases for direct heating of the wood. In Scandinavia horizontal tube ovens and large vertical iron retorts containing 500 cu. yd. of wood are employed.(cu. yds. x .765 = cu. meters)

The residue of charcoal from distillation is usually 20-35% by weight; in addition 10-40 gallons of turpentine, up to 120 gallons of resin oil and creosote, and smaller amounts of acetic acid, wood spirit (methyl alcohol) and various oils are obtained per cord (c=4,000 lb.) of wood. Inflammable gas and pitch are also produced.

A 'charcoal' or char can be prepared by carbonizing peat and various commercial processes for its manufacture have been operated but none has proved an economic success in the long run.

Properties

Wood charcoal retains the original shape and cell structure of the wood from which it is made, rings when struck and has a bright fracture; it is tasteless and odorless. Its apparent density ranges from 0.1 gm/ml if made from soft wood to 0.5 if made from hard wood. Its calorific value varies from 12,000 to 14,000 B.Th.U./lb. Excluding the associated mineral matter the composition of a typical 'meiler charcoal' prepared at 500°C corresponds approximately to the formula $C_{16}H_6O$; the proportion of carbon increases with higher carbonization temperatures. In the literature the 'carbon' content of a charcoal is frequently referred to as the residue after re-carbonizing to a high temperature; this ignores the carbon present in volatile matter driven off and the appreciable hydrogen and oxygen content of the residue. The non-combustible portion, usually amounting in a commercial charcoal to 1-5% by weight on the dry basis, consists of adventitious matter and the mineral residues from plant cells, the latter being mainly phosphates, carbonates, silicates, chlorides and sulphates of the elements Na, K, Mg, Ca, Fe, and Mn. Owing to its capacity for absorbing gases and vapours, charcoal normally contains up to 9% of moisture.

One of the principal uses of wood charcoal today is for the manufacture of carbon disulphide. Beech or birch wood yields the best charcoal for this purpose and its reactivity is highest when the carbonization temperature does not exceed about 500°C. In countries with ample timber resources but dependent on imported petroleum supplies (e.g. France and Australia) charcoal has been used as a fuel for mobile gas generators. The low density of the fuel and size of the generator have, however, tended to restrict this application.

When wood charcoal, especially that made from coconut shell, is kept at red heat for many hours, with only limited access of air, its capacity for absorption of gases is greatly enhanced; it is then said to be active.

TANNING

The directions for tanning need not be memorized, but they must be studied carefully until thoroughly understood before the work is begun. All supplies and equipment should be on hand and all plans should be carefully made before the work is started. It may be necessary to modify the directions, especially those dealing with equipment or tanning conditions. Success in modifying them depends

largely upon the individual.

Tanning operations are done best at a uniformly moderate temperature. A cellar, which is naturally fairly warm in winter and cool in summer, is a suitable place. A supply of fresh water near at hand and a drain are convenient.

All the operations can be done in tight, clean wooden barrels, preferable oak, having a capacity of from 40 to 60 gallons. When not in use the barrels should be kept clean and full of water. Half barrels and wooden or fiber buckets are useful for many purposes. Iron containers should never be used. Tools useful in tanning are shown in Figure 22.

Tanning Hides and Skins for Leather

The kind of leather which can be made from a hide or skin depends largely upon the weight and size of the hide or skin. In the tanning trade distinctions in hides and skins are based mainly upon the size and age of the animal and upon the class of leather. Hides from large and adult animals are suitable for sole, harness, belting, or heavy leathers. Skins from small animals, such as sheep, goats, calves, and deer, are made into light and fancy leathers. While there are other commercially important sources of hides and skins, the most important ones are the usual domesticated farm and range animals. As a general rule, the thickness of the finished leather will be about the same as that of the untanned hide. This should be a guide in selecting skins for different kinds of leather. The first essential for a satisfactory yield of good leather is a sound, clean hide or skin. Skinning should be done properly, without cutting or scoring the hide, and at the same time all of the fat and flesh should be removed; for, if left on, they increase the tendency of the hide to rot or spoil.

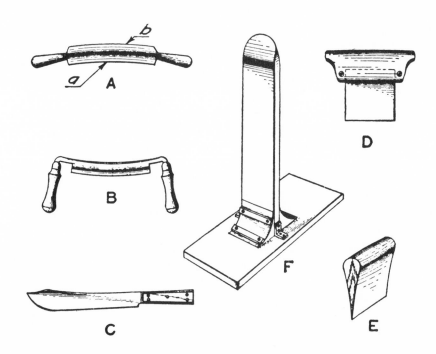

Fig. 22. Tools For Tanning

(A) Tanner's fleshing knife, having a blade 15 to 17 inches long: (a) Dull edge for scraping off the hair after liming; (b) very sharp edge for shaving off the flesh.

(B) Eight-inch blade drawing knife, which may be used instead of A, especially if both handles are bent straight. The back edge may be used for unhairing and the cutting edge for shaving off the flesh.

(C) Twelve-inch-blade butcher knife, which may be used instead of A or B when the point has been driven into a wooden handle or wrapped with leather.

(D) Metal slicker—a dull steel blade about 5 inches square, 1/32 to 1/16 inch thick, mounted in a wooden handle.

(E) Wooden slicker, made of hardwood, about 6 inches square, 1½ inches thick at head, shaved down in the shape of a wedge to a thin edge.

(F) Stake for breaking up and softening skins and leather. A board about 3 feet long, 6 inches wide, and 1 inch thick is braced in upright position to a heavy base or to the floor. The top of the board is rounded and thinned in the shape of a wedge to an edge about 1/8 inch thick.

Preparation of the hide or skin for tanning may be begun as soon as it has been taken off the animal, drained, and cooled from the body heat. Overnight will be long enough. If tanning is not to be started at once or if there are more hides than can be handled at one time, the hides may be thoroughly salted, using about 1 pound of clean salt for each pound of hide. They may be kept for from 3 to 5 months. The hides must never be allowed to freeze or heat during storage or tanning. Some tanners state that salting before tanning is helpful. It can do no harm to salt a hide for a few days before it is prepared for tanning.

The directions here given have been prepared for a single heavy cow, steer, or bull hide weighing from 40 to 70 pounds or for an equivalent weight in smaller skins, such as calf or kip skins. The heavy hides are best suited for sole, harness, or belting leather. Lighter hides weighing from 20 to 40 pounds should be used for lace leather.

Preliminary Operations

Before it is tanned a hide or skin must be put through the following preliminary operations, which are the same for all the leather-making processes given in this section. As soon as the skin has been put through these processes, start the tanning, following the directions given for the particular kind of leather desired.

Soaking and Cleaning

If the hide has been salted, shake it vigorously to remove most of the salt. Spread it out, hair side down, and trim off the tail, head, all ragged edges, and shanks (See Fig. 22A)

Place the hide, hair side up, lengthwise, over a smooth log or board, and with a sharp knife split it from neck to tail, straight down the backbone line, into two half hides, or "sides." It will be more convenient in the later handling, especially when the hide is large, to then split each side lengthwise through the "break," just above the flanks, into two strips, making the strip with the backbone edge about twice as wide as the belly strip. Thus a whole hide will give two sides or four strips. Small skins need not be split. In these directions "side" means side, strip, or skin, as the case may be.

Fill a 50-gallon barrel with clean, cool water. Place the sides, flesh side out, over short sticks and hang them in the barrel of water. The sticks must be short enough to fit crosswise in the barrel and should have a cord or small rope, a foot or so long, attached to each end. The cords or ropes are fastened to nails on the outside of the barrel after adjusting them so the sides are completely covered by water. Let the sides soak for 2 or 3 hours. Stir them about frequently to soften, loosen, and wash out the blood, dirt, manure, and salt. (See Fig. 22B)

After they have soaked for about 3 hours take out the sides, one at a time, and place them, hair side up, over a "beam." A ready-made beam can be bought. A fairly satisfactory one may be made from a very smooth slab, log, or thick planed board, from 1 to 2 feet wide and 6 to 8 feet long. The slab or log is inclined, with

one end resting on the ground and the other extending over the box or trestle so as to be about waist high. With the side lying hair side up over the beam scrub off all dirt and manure, using if necessary a stiff brush. Wash off with several bucketfuls of clean water. (See Fig. 22B)

Turn the side over, flesh side up, and scrape or cut off any remaining flesh. Work over the entire flesh side with the back edge of a drawing or butcher knife held firmly against the hide, pushing away from the body. Wash off with one or two bucketfuls of clean water. This working over should always be done.

Refill the soak barrel with clean, cool water and hang the sides in it as before. Pull them up and stir them about frequently until they are soft and flexible. Usually a green or fresh hide needs to be soaked for not more than from 12 to 24 hours and a green salted hide for not more than from 24 to 48 hours.

When the sides are properly softened—that is, when they are about like a fresh hide or skin—throw them over the beam and thoroughly scrape off all remaining flesh and fat.

The side must be soft, pliable, and clean all over before being put into the lime, which is the next step.

Liming

Wash out the soak barrel, put in from 9 to 11 pounds of hydrated lime (use lime from a fresh bag, not old, air-slaked lime) and 4 or 5 gallons of water. Stir with a paddle until the lime is thoroughly mixed with the water, then nearly fill the barrel with clean, cool water and again stir thoroughly. Again place the sides, hair side out, over the short sticks and hang them in the barrel so that they are completely covered by the limewater. See that the sides have as few folds or wrinkles as possible, and also be sure that no air is trapped under them. Keep the barrel covered with boards or bags. Pull up the sides and stir the limewater three or four times each day until the hair will come off easily. This takes from 6 to 10 days in summer and possibly as many as 16 days in winter.

When thoroughly limed, the hair can be rubbed off readily with the hand. Early in the liming process it will be possible to pull out the hair, but the hide must be left in the limewater until the hair comes off by rubbing over with the hand. For harness and belting leathers leave the hide in the limewater for from 3 to 5 days after this condition has been reached.

Unhairing

After the side has been limed, throw it hair side up, over the beam and with the back edge of a drawing or butcher knife held nearly flat against the side push off the hair from all parts. If the side is sufficiently limed, a curdy or cheesy layer of skin rubs off with the hair. If this layer does not rub off, the side must be returned to the limewater. Now thoroughly work over the grain or hair side with a dull-edged tool to "scud" or work out as much lime, grease, and dirt as possible.

Fleshing

Turn the side over and scud it again, being sure to remove all fleshing matter. Shave down to the hide itself, but be careful not to cut into it. Remove the flesh by scraping and by using a very sharp knife, with a motion like that of shaving the face.

Now proceed as directed under Bark-Tanned Sole and Harness Leather, Chrome-Tanned Leather, or Alum-Tanned Lace Leather, depending upon the kind of leather desired.

245

The lime, limewater, sludge, and fleshings from the liming process may be used as fertilizer, particularly for acid soils. The hair, as it is scraped from the hide, may be collected separately and after being rinsed several times may be used for plastering. If desired, it can be thoroughly washed with many changes of water until absolutely clean and after being dried out in a warm place used for padding, upholstering, insulation of pipes, etc.

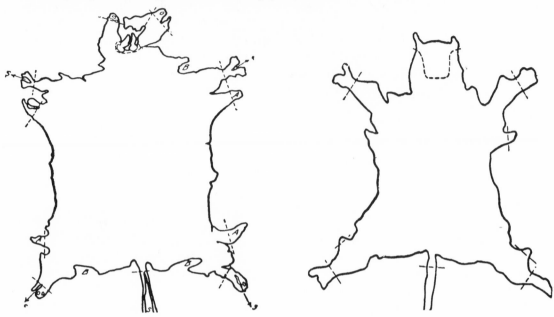

Fig. 22A. Left; A hide of poor pattern and trim. Right; A Calfskin of good pattern and trim. The dotted lines indicate amount cut off before tanning.

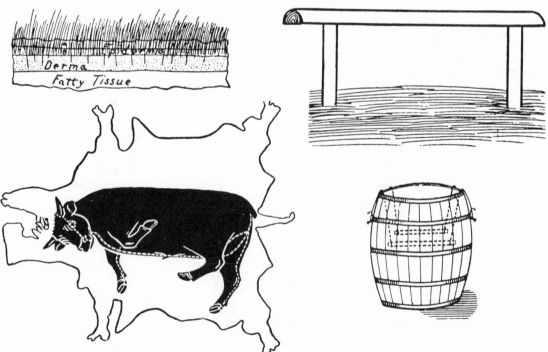

Fig. 22B. Top left; Section of skin or hide magnified. Top right; Hide beam, not adjustable, good for large hides. Bottom left; Proper ripping cuts for a correct pattern. Bottom right; Arrangement for hanging hides in place in a barrel.

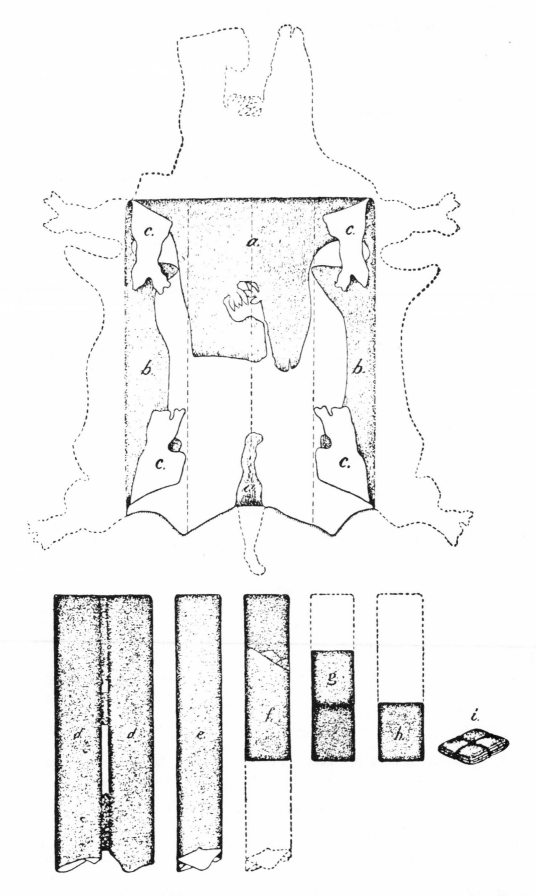

Fig. 22C. Folding and bundling hides. **a.** the first step and **i.** the hide bundled and tied.

Bark-Tanned Sole and Harness Leather

Deliming

After the sides have been put through the unhairing and fleshing operations, rinse them with clean water. Wash the sides in cool, clean water for from 6 to 8 hours, changing the water frequently.

Buy 5 ounces of U.S.P. (United States Pharmnacopoeia) lactic acid (or 16 ounces of tannery 22 percent lactic acid). Nearly fill a clean 40-to 50-gallon barrel with clean, cool water, stir in the lactic acid, and mix the water and acid thoroughly with a paddle. Hang the sides in the barrel and leave them there for 24 hours, pulling them up and stirring them frequently.

Take out the sides, work over or scud them thoroughly, as directed under Unhairing, and hang them in a barrel of cold water. Change the water several times, and finally leave them in the water overnight.

If lactic acid cannot be obtained, use a gallon of vinegar instead.

Tanning

The sides are now ready for the actual tanning. From 15 to 20 days before this stage will be reached, weigh out from 30 to 40 pounds of good quality, finely ground oak or hemlock bark and pour onto it about 20 gallons of boiling water.

Finely ground bark, with no particles larger than a grain of corn, will give the best results. Simply chopping the bark into coarse pieces will not do. Do not let the tan liquor come into contact with iron vessels. Use the purest water available. Rain water is best.

Let this bark infusion stand in a covered vessel until ready for use. Stir it occasionally. When ready to start tanning, strain off the bark liquor through a clean, coarse sack into the tanning barrel. Fill the barrel about three-quarters full with water, rinsing the bark with this water so as to get out as much tannin as possible. Add 2 quarts of vinegar. Stir well. Place the sides, from the deliming, over sticks, and hang them in this bark liquor with as few folds and wrinkles as possible. Move the sides about and change their position often in order to get an even color.

Just as soon as the sides have been hung in the bark liquor, again soak from 30 to 40 pounds of ground bark in about 20 gallons of hot water. Let this second bark liquor stand until the sides have become evenly colored, or for from 10 to 15 days. Take out of the tanning barrel 5 gallons of liquor and pour in about one-quarter of the second bark liquor. Also add about 2 quarts more of vinegar and stir it in well. Five days later take out a second 5 gallons of tanning liquor from the barrel and add another fourth of the tan liquor only (no vinegar). Do this every 5 days until the second bark liquor is used up.

The progress of the tanning varies somewhat with conditions and can best be followed by inspecting a small sliver slit from the edge of the hide. About 35 days after the actual tanning has been started a fresh cut should show two dark or brown narrow streaks about as wide as heavy pencil line coming in from each surface of the hide.

At this stage weigh out about 40 pounds of fine bark and just moisten it with hot water. Do not add more water than the bark will soak up. Pull the sides out of the bark liquor and dump in the moistened bark, keeping in the barrel as much of the old tan liquor as possible. Mix thoroughly and while mixing hang the sides back in the barrel. Actually bury them in the bark. All parts of the sides must be kept well down in the bark mixture. Leave the sides in this bark for about 6 weeks and move them about once in a while.

At the end of 6 weeks pull the sides out. A cutting should show that the tanning

has spread nearer to the center. Pour out about half the liquor. Stir the bark in the barrel, hang the sides back, and fill the barrel with fresh, finely ground bark. Leave the sides in for about 2 months, shaking the barrel from time to time and adding bark and water as needed to keep the sides completely covered.

At the end of this time the hide should be evenly colored all the way through without any white or raw streak in the center of a cut edge. If it is not struck through, it must be left longer in the wet bark, and more bark may be needed.

For harness, strap, and belting leather the sides may be taken out of the bark liquor at this stage, but for sole leather they must be left for 2 months longer. When fully tanned through, the sides are ready for oiling and finishing.

Oiling and Finishing

Harness and Belting Leather

Take the sides from the tan liquor, rinse them off with water, and scour the grain or hair side thoroughly with plenty of warm water and a stiff brush. Then go over the sides with a "slicker", pressing the slicker firmly against the leather while pushing it away from the body and work out as much water as possible. "Slick" out on the grain or hair side in all directions. For harness, belting, and the like this scouring and slicking must be done thoroughly. (See Fig. 22 for tools).

A slicker can be made from a piece of copper or brass about one-fourth inch thick, 6 inches long, and 4 inches wide. One long edge of the slicker is mounted in a wooden handle and the other long edge is finished smooth and well rounded. A piece of hardwood, about 6 inches square, 1½ inches thick at the head, and shaved down wedge-shape to a thin edge will also serve as a slicker.

While the sides are still damp, but not very wet, go over the grain or hair side with a liberal coating of neat's-foot or cod oil. Hang up the sides and let them dry out slowly. When dry, take them down and dampen well by dipping in water or by rolling them up in set sacking or burlap.

When uniformly damp and limber, evenly brush or mop over the grain or hair side a thick coating of warm dubbin. The dubbin is made by melting together about equal parts of cod oil and tallow or neat's-foot oil and tallow. This dubbin when cool must be soft and pasty, but not liquid.

Hang up the sides again and leave until thoroughly dry. When dry, scrape off the excess tallow by working over with the slicker. If more grease in the leather is desired, dampen again and apply another coating of the dubbin, giving a light application to the flesh side also. When again dry, remove the tallow and thoroughly work over all parts of the leather with the slicker. Rubbing over with sawdust will help to take up any surface oiliness.

If it is desired to blacken the leather, this must be done before greasing. A black dye solution can be made by dissolving one-half ounce of water-soluble nigrosine in 1¼ pints of water, with the addition, if handy, of several drops of ammonia. Evenly mop or brush this solution over the dampened but ungreased leather and then grease as directed in the preceding paragraph.

Sole Leather

Take the sides from the tan liquor and rinse them thoroughly with clean water. Slick out on the grain or hair side as described for harness leather. Hang them up until they are only damp and then apply a good coating of neat's-foot oil or cod oil to the grain or hair side. Again hang them up until they are thoroughly dry.

When repairing shoes with this leather it is advisable, after cutting out the piece for soling, to dampen and hammer it down well, and then, after putting it on the shoe, to make it waterproof and more serviceable by setting the shoe in a shallow pan of melted grease or oil and letting it stand for about 15 minutes. The

grease or oil must be not hotter than the hand can bear. Rubber heels should not be put in oil or grease. The soles of shoes with rubber heels may be waterproofed in the same way, using a piepan for the oil or grease and placing the heels outside the pan. Any good oil or grease will do. The following formulas have been found satisfactory:

Table 3. Waterproofing Leather

	Ounces
Formula 1:	
Neutral wool grease	8
Dark petrolatum	4
Paraffin wax	4
Formula 2:	
Petrolatum	16
Beeswax	2
Formula 3:	
Petrolatum	8
Paraffin wax	4
Wool grease	4
Crude turpentine gum (gum thus)	2
Formula 4:	
Tallow	12
Cod oil	4

Chrome-Tanned Leather

For many purposes chrome-tanned leather is considered to be as good as the more generally known bark or vegetable-tanned leather. The chrome process, which takes only a few weeks as against as many months for the bark-tanning process, derives its name from the use of chemicals containing chromium. It is a chemical process requiring great care. It is felt, however, that by following exactly the directions here given, never disregarding details which may seem unimportant, a serviceable leather can be produced in a comparatively short time. The saving in time seems sufficient to justify a trial of this process.

Deliming

After the sides have been put through the unhairing and fleshing operations rinse them off with clear water.

If sole, belting, or harness leather is to be tanned, soak and wash the sides in cool water for about 6 hours before putting them into the lactic acid. Change the water four or five times.

If strap, upper, or thin leather is to be tanned, put the limed white sides into a wooden or fiber tub of clean, lukewarm (about 90°F.) water and let them stay there for from 4 to 8 hours before putting them into the lactic acid. Stir the sides about occasionally. Be sure that the water is not too hot. It never should be so hot that it is uncomfortably warm to the hand.

For each large hide or skin buy 5 ounces of U.S.P. lactic acid (or 16 ounces of tannery 22 percent lactic acid). Nearly fill a clean 40- to 50-gallon barrel with clean, cool water, and stir in the lactic acid, mixing thoroughly with a paddle.

Hang the sides in the barrel, and leave them there for 24 hours, plunging them up and down occasionally.

For light skins, weighing less than 15 pounds, use only 2 ounces of U.S.P. lactic acid in about 20 gallons of water.

If lactic acid cannot be obtained, use 1 pint of vinegar for every ounce of lactic acid. An effort should be made to get the lactic acid, however, for vinegar will not be as satisfactory, especially for the medium and smaller skins.

After deliming, work over both sides of the side as directed under Unhairing.

For sole, belting, and harness leathers, hang the sides in a barrel of cool water overnight. Then proceed as directed under Tanning.

For thin, softer leathers from small skins, do not soak the sides in water overnight. Simply rinse them off with water and proceed as directed under Tanning.

Tanning

The tanning solution should be made up at least 2 days before it is to be used—that is, not later than when the sides are taken from the limewater for the last time.

Remember that this is a chemical process and that all materials must be of good quality and accurately weighed and the specified quantities of water carefully measured.

The following chemicals are required: Chrome alum (chromium potassium sulfate crystals); soda crystals (crystallized sodium carbonate); and common salt (sodium chloride). Insist upon pure chemicals of the United States Pharmacopoeia quality. Get them from the nearest drugstore or find out from it the address of a chemical manufacturing concern which can supply them.

For each hide or skin weighing more than 30 pounds use the following quantities for the stock chrome solution:

Dissolve 3½ pounds of soda crystals (crystallized sodium carbonate) and 6 pounds of common salt (sodium chloride) in 3 gallons of warm, clean water in a wooden or fiber bucket. The soda crystals must be clear or glasslike. Do not use the white crusted lumps.

At the same time dissolve in a large tub or half barrel 12 pounds of chrome alum (chromium potassium sulfate crystals) in 9 gallons of cool, clean water. This will take some time to dissolve and will need frequent stirring. Here again it is important to use only the very dark, hard, glossy, purple or plum-colored crystals of chrome alum, not the lighter, crumbly, dull-lavender ones.

When the chemicals are dissolved, which can be told by feeling around in the tubs with a paddle, pour the soda-salt solution slowly in a thin stream into the chrome-alum solution, stirring constantly.

Take at least 10 minutes to pour in the soda solution. This should give one solution of about 12 gallons, which is the stock chrome solution. Keep this solution well covered in a wooden or fiber bucket, tub, or half barrel.

To start tanning, pour one-third (4 gallons) of the stock chrome solution into a clean 50-gallon barrel and add about 30 gallons of clean, cool water; that is, fill the barrel about two-thirds full. Thoroughly mix the solution in the barrel and hang in it the sides from the deliming. Work the sides about and stir the solution frequently, especially during the first 2 or 3 days. This helps to give the sides an even color. It should be done every hour or so throughout the first day. Keep the sides as smooth as possible.

After 3 days, temporarily remove the sides from the barrel. Add one-half of the remaining stock chrome solution, thoroughly mixing it with that in the barrel, and again hang in the sides. Move the sides about and stir frequently as before.

251

After the sides have been in this solution for 3 or 4 days, cut off a small piece of the thickest part of the side, usually in the neck, and examine the freshly cut edge of the piece. If the cut edge seems to be evenly colored greenish or bluish all the way through, the tanning is about finished. Boil the small piece in water for a few minutes. If it curls up and becomes hard or rubbery, the tanning is not completed and the sides must be left in the tanning solution for a few days longer, or until a small piece when boiled in water is changed little if at all.

The foregoing quantities and directions have been given for a medium or large hide. For smaller hides and skins the quantities of chemicals and water can be reduced. For each hide or skin weighing less than 30 pounds, or for two or three small skins together weighing not more than 30 pounds, the quantities of chemicals may be cut in half, giving the following solutions:

For the soda-salt solution, dissolve 1¾ pounds of soda crystals (crystallized sodium carbonate) and 3 pounds of common salt (sodium chloride) in 1½ gallons of clean water.

For the chrome-alum solution, dissolve 6 pounds of chrome alum (chromium potassium sulfate crystals) in 4½ gallons of cool, clean water.

When the chemicals are dissolved pour the soda-salt solution slowly into the chrome-alum solution as already described. This will give one solution of about 6 gallons which is the stock chrome solution. For the lighter skins tan with this solution, exactly as directed for medium and large hides, adding one-third, that is, 2 gallons, of this stock chrome solution each time, and begin to tan in about 15 gallons instead of 30 gallons of water. Follow the directions already given as to stirring, number of days, and testing to determine when tanning is completed. Very small, thin skins probably will not take as long to tan as will the large hides. The boiling-water test is very reliable for showing when the hide is tanned.

Washing and Neutralizing

When the sides are tanned, take them out of the tanning solution and put them in a barrel of clean water. The barrel in which the tanning was done can be used after it has been thoroughly washed.

When emptying the tanning barrel be sure carefully to dispose of the tanning solution. Although not poisonous to the touch, it probably would be fatal to farm animals should they drink it, and it is harmful to soil.

Wash the sides in about four changes of water. For medium and large hides, dissolve 2 pounds of borax in about 40 gallons of clean water and soak the sides in this solution overnight. For hides and skins weighing less than 25 pounds, use 1 pound of borax in about 20 gallons of water. Move the sides about in the borax solution as often as feasible. After soaking overnight in the borax solution, remove the sides and wash them for an entire day, changing the water five or six times. Take the sides out, let the water drain off, and proceed as directed under Dyeing Black, or, if it is not desired to blacken the leather, proceed as directed under Oiling and Finishing.

Dyeing Black

Water-Soluble Nigrosine: One of the simplest and best means of dyeing leather black is to use nigrosine. Make up the dye solution in the proportion of one-half ounce of water-soluble nigrosine dissolved in 1¼ pints of water. Be sure to get water-soluble nigrosine. Evenly mop or brush this solution over the damp leather after draining as already directed and then proceed as directed under Oiling and Finishing.

Iron Liquor and Sumac: If water-soluble nigrosine cannot be obtained, a fairly good black may be secured with iron liquor and sumac. To make the iron liquor,

mix clean iron filings or turnings with one-half gallon of good vinegar and let the mixture stand for several days. See that there are always some undissolved filings or turnings in the vinegar. For a medium or large hide put from 10 to 15 pounds of dried crumbled sumac leaves in a barrel containing from 35 to 40 gallons of warm water. Stir well and when cool hang in it the wet, chrome-tanned sides. If you cannot get sumac leaves, use 20 or 30 pounds of finely chopped oak or hemlock bark but pour hot water on the bark and let stand a couple of days before use. Leave the sides in this solution for about 2 days, pulling them up and mixing the solution frequently. Take out the sides, rinse off all bits of sumac, and evenly mop or brush over with the iron liquor. Rinse off the excess of iron liquor and put the sides back in the sumac overnight. If not black enough the next morning, mop over again with iron liquor, rinse, return to the sumac solution for a day. Take the sides out of the sumac, rinse well, and scrub thoroughly with warm water. Finally wash the sides for a few hours in several changes of water.

While both of these formulas of dyeing have been given, it is recommended that water-soluble nigrosine be used whenever possible, as the iron liquor and sumac formula is somewhat troublesome and may produce a cracky grain. After blackening, proceed as directed under Oiling and Finishing.

Oiling and Finishing

Thin Leather: Let the wet tanned leather from the dyeing, or, if not dyed, from the neutralizing, dry out slowly. While it is still very damp go over the grain or hair side with a liberal coating of neat's-foot or cod oil. While still damp, tack the sides out on a wall or tie them in frames, being sure to pull them out tight and smooth, and leave them until dry. When dry take down and dampen well by dipping in warm water or by rolling them up in wet sacking or burlap. When uniformly damp and limber go over the sides with a "slicker", pressing out slicker firmly against the leather, while pushing it away from the body. Slick out on the grain or hair side in all directions.

After slicking it may be necessary to "stake" the leather. This is done by pulling the damp leather vigorously back and forth over the edge of a small smooth board about 3 feet long, 6 inches wide, and 1 inch thick, fastened upright and braced to the floor or ground. The top end of the board must be shaved down to a wedge shape, with the edge not more than one-eighth inch thick and the corners well-rounded. Pull the sides, flesh side down, backward and forward over this edge, exactly as a cloth is worked back and forth in polishing shoes.

Let the sides dry out thoroughly again. If not sufficiently soft and pliable, dampen them with water, apply more oil, and slick and stake as before. The more time given to slicking and staking, the smoother and more pliable the leather will be.

Thick Leather: Thick leather from the larger hides is oiled and finished in a slightly different manner. For harness and strap leather, let the tanned sides, dyed if desired, dry down. While they are still quite damp slick over the grain or hair side thoroughly and apply a liberal coating of neat's-foot or cod oil. Tack on a wall or tie in a frame, stretching the leather out tight and smooth, and leave until dry. Take the sides down, dampen them with warm water until limber and pliable, and apply to the grain side a thick coating of warm dubbin. The dubbin is made by melting together about equal parts of cod oil and tallow or neat's-foot oil and tallow. When cool it must be soft and pasty but not liquid. If too nearly liquid, add more tallow. Hang up the sides again and leave them until thoroughly dried. When dry, scrape off the excess tallow by working over with the slicker. If more grease in the leather is desired, dampen again and apply another coating of the dubbin. When again dry, slick off the tallow and thoroughly work over all parts of the leather with the slicker. Rubbing over with sawdust helps to take up surface oiliness.

253

Chrome-tanned leather is stretchy, so that in cutting the leather for use in harness, straps, reins, and similar articles it is best to first take out most of the stretch.

Chrome leather for shoe soles must be heavily greased, or, in other words, waterproofed, unless it is to be worn in extremely dry regions. Waterproofing may be done after repairing the shoes by setting them in a shallow pan of oil or grease so that just the soles are covered by the grease. The soles should be dry before they are set in the melted grease. Melted paraffin wax will do, although it makes the soles stiff.

Alum-Tanned Lace Leather

Deliming

After the sides have been put through the unhairing and fleshing operations, rinse them off with cool, clean water for from 6 to 8 hours, changing the water frequently.

Buy 5 ounces of U.S.P. lactic acid (or 16 ounces of tannery 22 percent lactic acid). Nearly fill a clean 40- to 50-gallon barrel with clean, cool water and stir in the lactic acid, mixing thoroughly with a paddle. Hang the sides in the barrel and leave them there for 24 hours, pulling them up and stirring them about frequently. Take out the sides, work over or scud thoroughly, as directed under Unhairing, and hang them in a barrel of cool water. Change the water several times, and finally leave them in the water overnight. If lactic acid cannot be obtained, use a gallon of vinegar instead.

Tanning

While the sides are being delimed, thoroughly wash out the barrel in which the hide was limed. Put in it 15 gallons of clean water and 12 pounds of ammonia alum or potash alum and stir frequently until it is completely dissolved.

Dissolve 3 pounds of washing soda (crystallized sodium carbonate) and 6 pounds of salt in 5 gallons of cold, clean water in a wooden bucket. The soda crystals must be clear and glasslike. Do not use white crusted lumps.

Pour the soda solution into the alum solution in the barrel very, very slowly, stirring the solution in the barrel constantly. Take at least 10 minutes to pour in the soda solution in a small stream. If the soda is poured in rapidly the solution will become milky and will not tan. The solution should be cool, and enough water to nearly fill the barrel should be added.

Hang each well-washed side from the deliming in the alum-soda solution. Pull up the sides and stir the solution six or eight times each day. Do not put the bare hands in the liquor if they are cut or cracked or have sores on them.

After 6 to 7 days remove the sides from the alum-soda solution and rinse well for about a quarter of an hour in clean, cold water.

Oiling and Finishing

Let the sides drain and dry out slowly. While still very damp go over the grain or hair side with a liberal coating of neat's-foot or cod oil. After the oil has gone in and the sides have dried a little more but are still slightly damp, begin to work them over a "stake." The time to start staking is important. The sides must not be too damp; neither must they be too dry. When light spots or light streaks appear on folding it is time to begin staking. Alum-tanned leather must be thoroughly and frequently staked.

254

Staking is done by pulling the damp leather vigorously back and forth over the edge of a small, smooth board. The sides must be staked thoroughly all over in order to make them pliable and soft, and the staking must be continued at intervals until the leather is dry.

When dry, evenly dampen the sides by dipping them in water or by leaving them overnight covered with wet burlap or sacks. Apply to the hair side a thick coating of warm dubbin. The dubbin is made by melting together about equal parts of neat's-foot oil and tallow or cod oil and tallow. When cool, the dubbin must be soft and pasty but not liquid. If too nearly liquid, add more tallow. Leave the greased sides, preferably in a warm place, until dry. Scrape off the excess tallow and again stake the sides. If the leather is too hard and stiff, dampen it evenly with water before staking.

After staking, go over the sides with a slicker, pressing the slicker firmly against the leather, while pushing it away from the body. Slick out on the grain, or hair side, in all directions.

Alum-tanned leather almost invariably dries out the first time hard and stiff. It must be dampened again and restaked while drying. In some cases this must be done repeatedly, and another application of dubbin may be necessary. By repeated dampening, staking, and slicking the leather can be made as soft and pliable as desired.

Tanning Fur Skins

Much of the value of a fur skin depends upon the manner in which it is handled in the raw state. After the animal has been caught, every effort should be made to follow the best practices in skinning and curing, in order to obtain a skin of the greatest possible value. Certain trade customs also must be followed to secure the top price.

Requests for directions for tanning fur skins are constantly received by the U. S. Department of Agriculture. There is, however, less need for such information than there is for information on farm or home tanning of hides and skins into leather. Fur skins as a protection are a necessity for those living in cold climates, but comparatively few are used for this purpose. Most of the fur skins are made into articles which are more or less of a luxury and, as such, are valued largely on the basis of their appearance and finish, which an inexperienced worker can seldom make sufficiently pleasing. Furthermore, raw fur skins are valuable, and, if well cared for, usually find a ready market. Nevertheless, the spread between the prices paid for raw furs and those demanded for finished fur articles is enormous. No doubt, this spread in many instances inspires the attempts at home manufacture.

An inexperienced person should not try to tan valuable fur skins or large hides, such as cattle, horse, or bear, for making into coats, robes, or rugs. The risk of damage or of an unsatisfactory product, as measured by the usual standards of finish and appearance, is too great. The difficulties in properly handling large hides make the chances of success remote, except by those having suitable equipment and experience. Moreover, tanning the skin is only one step in the production of the finished article. After being tanned, all skins must be tailored, many must be dyed, and small ones must be matched, blended, and sewed together. All these operations require experience and practice to secure the attractive appearance desired by wearers of furs. Some of the operations, such as those of bleaching and dyeing, are so highly specialized that their undertaking should not even be considered by an amateur. From the standpoint of serviceability and usefulness, inexperienced persons might meet with a fair degree of success in tanning and tailoring fur skins, but few can ever hope to

255

make a fur piece or garment which will compare favorably in appearance with the shop or factory product. The tanning and dressing of fur skins, then, are best left to those who are experienced and equipped to carry out the tedious operations required.

To satisfy the demand upon the USDA for information on the home tanning for fur skins and to provide those who insist upon carrying on such work with correct information and with detailed methods which offer the best chances for success, the following directions are given. These directions are meant primarily for small fur skins no larger than that of the fox and for skins of low market value.

No formulas for tanning are foolproof, and success can be attained only by close observation, plenty of work, and the exercise of care and patience. All skins are not treated just alike. In fact, each skin has its own peculiarities, which only experience can show how to treat. Some skins are tough and fairly thick and will stand mistreatment; others are very thin and tender and are easily ruined. Some are fat and greasy and require thorough working out of the grease; others do not. An inexperienced person should experiment with the least valuable skins. If a number of skins of the same kind are to be tanned, one or two of the poorest should be tried first.

Soaking and Fleshing

The first step is to get the skin thoroughly softened, cleaned, and free from flesh and grease.

Split the tail the entire length on the underside. If the skin is "cased," split it nearly down the middle of the belly. Soak it in several changes of clear, cool water. When the skin begins to soften, lay it on a beam or smooth pole and begin working over the flesh side to break up the adhering tissue and fat. All dried skins have a shiny, tight layer of tissue. This tissue must be broken up and entirely removed, which is best done by repeated alternate working and soaking. A good tool for scratching the tissue is a metal edge of any kind, such as a drawing knife or an ordinary knife with dull saw teeth or notches filed in it. Working over with these dull teeth scratches or breaks up the tissue so that it can be scraped off after further soaking.

At the same time the grease and oil are worked out of the skin. This operation is of the utmost importance. It is utterly useless to start tanning until all the tissue and grease have been removed and the skin is uniformly soft and pliable, without any hard spots.

The time of soaking depends upon the condition of the skin. Some skins require only about 2 hours, while others need a much longer time. Very hard skins often must be thoroughly dampened, rolled up, fur side out, and put away in a cool place overnight to soften. While a skin must be soaked until soft, it should not stay wet longer than necessary, as the hair may start to slip.

In fleshing and scraping, care also must be taken not to injure the true skin or expose the hair roots, especially on thin skins.

When the soaking is well advanced and the skin is getting in good shape, work it in lukewarm water containing an ounce of soda or borax to the gallon. Soap also may be added. This treatment promotes softening, cleans the skin, and cuts the grease.

Work again over the beam and finally rinse thoroughly in lukewarm water. Squeeze out most of the water, but do not wring the skin. Without further drying, work the skin in gasoline, using several changes if very much dirt and grease are present. Squeeze and hang up the skin for a few minutes.

The skin should now be ready for tanning. When painting or pasting of the tan liquor on the flesh side only is included in the directions for tanning, it is best to

dry out the hair or fur side first by working in sawdust. In this way any heating of the fur side while the skin is tacked out is avoided, as are also matting and stiffening of the fur. If while drying out the fur, the flesh side becomes too dry, it must be evenly dampened with a wet cloth before applying the tan liquor.

Combination Tannage

A combination tannage is a combination of mineral and vegetable tanning. It has an advantage over the salt-acid or salt-alum processes in giving a soft and flexible skin, as well as a more lasting tannage.

One of the most popular and successful formulas for a combination tannage is given by M. C. Lamb. A pasty mixture of alum, salt, gambier, and flour, with or without glycerin or olive oil, is made as follows: Dissolve 1 pound of aluminum sulfate and 1 pound of salt together in a small quantity of water. Dissolve 3 ounces of gambier or Terra Japonica in a little boiling water. (Instead of gambier, 3 or 4 ounces of finely powdered sumac leaves may be used.) Mix the two solutions and make up to 2 gallons with water. As this solution is used, mix it with enough flour to make a moderately thin paste. If the skin has a hard texture and lacks natural grease, thoroughly mix a little olive oil or glycerin with the paste.

Soak, soften, and clean the skin as previously described and tack it out flat and smooth, flesh side up. Apply from two to three coatings of the paste, depending upon the thickness of the skin. Only thick skins require three coatings. Each coating should be about one-eighth inch thick and should be applied at intervals of a day. Between applications the skin should be kept covered with sacking or paper. Scrape off most of the old coating before putting on a new one. After the last coating has been applied, spread out the skin uncovered or hang it up to dry slowly.

When practically dry, wash off the flour paste, rinse for several minutes in water containing an ounce of borax to the gallon, then in water alone. Squeeze out most of the water. Put the skin over a beam and slick it out well on the flesh side with the back of a knife or edge of a wooden slicker, thus working out most of the water. Again tack the skin out smoothly, flesh side up, and apply a thin coating of any animal fat, fresh butter, being particularly good, or a nondrying oil, such as neat's-foot, castor, or olive oil. Glycerin or a soap may be used instead of the grease or oil. If the skin originally was very greasy, it may not be necessary to apply any oil.

When nearly dry, but still slightly damp, begin to work the skin in all directions, stretching it from corner to corner and working the flesh side over a stake or a wooden edge, as given in Fig. 22.

The time to begin working is important and is best judged from experience. The skin must not be too wet; neither must it be too dry. The appearance of a few light spots or a light streak on folding is a good indication of the time to start working the skin.

Work the skin in all directions back and forth, as if shining shoes with a cloth. The skin may also be worked this way through smooth metal rings. Much of the success in getting a soft skin lies in this repeated working, which must be done while the skin is drying out, not after it is dry. If the skin is soft enough when dry, it must be evenly dampened and worked again while drying. This may be repeated several times if necessary.

After softening and drying out it is well to give the skin a hasty bath in gasoline. If the skin is greasy, this must be done. This also helps to deodorize some skins, such as those of the skunk.

Finally, to clean and brighten the tanned skin, tumble or work it repeatedly in

dry, warm sawdust, preferably hardwood sawdust, or bran or cornmeal. Clean these out of the fur by gentle shaking, beating, combing, and brushing.

The flesh side may be smoothed if necessary by working over a sandpaper block. This also helps to soften the skin further. If desired, the thicker sections of the skin may be made thinner and more flexible by shaving off some of the skin or hide.

Salt-Alum Tannage

The salt-alum process, an old method for furskin tanning, is widely used. It is considered slightly better than the salt-acid tannage, being a little more permanent and, when properly carried out, giving skins which have a little more stretch and flexibility. It often happens, however, that alum-tanned skins come out stiff and hard and must be worked repeatedly and sometimes retanned.

A salt-alum tanning solution may be made up using the following proportions: 1 pound of ammonia alum or potash alum dissolved in 1 gallon of water; 4 ounces of washing soda (crystallized sodium carbonate) and 8 ounces of salt, dissolved together in one-half gallon of water. When dissolved, pour the soda-salt solution very slowly into the alum solution while stirring vigorously.

A skin, cleaned and softened as previously described, may be tanned by immersion in this solution for from 2 to 5 days, depending upon its thickness. Because of the action of alum on some furs it may be best, as a general rule, to apply the tanning liquor as a paste to the flesh side only.

Mix the tan liquor as used with sufficient flour to make a thick paste. Add the flour in small quantities with a little water and mix thoroughly to avoid lumps. Tack the skin out smoothly, flesh side up. Apply a coating of the paste about one-eighth inch thick and cover the skin. The next day scrape off most of the paste and give another coating. Apply altogether, at intervals of a day, from two to three coatings, depending upon the thickness of the skin. Only thick skins should need as many as three treatments. Leave the last coating on for 3 or 4 days. Finally scrape off and rinse clean in water, putting in about an ounce of borax to a gallon of water. Rinse at last in water only.

Work over a beam to remove most of the water. Stretch the skin out flat and sponge over the flesh side with a thin soap paste. After this has gone in, apply a thin coating of oil. Leave the skin stretched out to dry, and while it is still damp, work and stake, wetting and working repeatedly if necessary. Finally, clean in gasoline and sawdust and finish as described above.

Salt-Acid Tannage

One of the oldest processes of tanning requires various mixtures of common salt and sulfuric acid. Tanning, or, more correctly speaking, tawing, by this means is open to the objection that sulfuric acid must be used very cautiously, and must be completely neutralized to prevent later damage to the skin. Skins tanned with salt and acid also show a tendency to become damp and clammy in wet weather and, if repeatedly subjected to wetting, lose their tanned effect.

A salt-acid tanning solution may be made up in the following proportions: For each gallon of water use 1 pound of common salt and one-half ounce of concentrated sulfuric acid. Dissolve the salt and carefully pour in the acid while stirring. This tan liquor must be made and used in jars or wooden vessels, never in metal containers of any kind. (When pouring in the acid, do not inhale any more of the fumes given off than is necessary, and also be careful not to get any of the strong acid on the skin or clothing.) As soon as the acid-salt solution has cooled, it is ready for use.

Put the cleaned, softened skin in the solution so that it is entirely covered and leave it for from 1 to 3 days, depending upon its thickness. During this time stir the skin about frequently. If desired, the solution may be painted on instead. In this case, tack out the skin smoothly, flesh side up, paint over with the solution, and cover the skin with well-dampened sacking or cloth. At the end of 6 hours, paint over it again. With thicker skins, give one or two more applications of the solution about 6 hours apart, keeping the skin covered between applications. After the last application, hang up the skin or spread it, flesh side up, without cover, and let it dry.

After tanning, either by immersion or by painting, rinse the skin in clear water and squeeze out most of the water, but do not wring it. Then work the skin for about 10 minutes in a solution made up in the proportion of an ounce of borax in a gallon of water, and finally rinse well in clear water and squeeze.

Work over the skin with a slicker to remove most of the water, tack it out flat, flesh side up, and apply a thin coating of grease or oil. Leave the skin stretched to dry, and while it is still damp work and stake it.

Finally clean in gasoline and sawdust, and finish by shaking, beating, sandpapering, brushing, and combing.

HAND-LOOM WEAVING

A Simple Loom—In all hand weaving the loom is the structure forming a frame upon which the materials are woven. It would be quite possible to carry out simple weaving without a frame by attaching one end of a set of threads to a hook in a wall, holding the other ends, and working other threads across these. Therefore the loom or frame is merely a simple device to hold one set of threads firmly in position while working through them with another thread or threads. There are many types of looms, and it should be made quite clear that it is not essential for the beginner to commence with a simple, small loom and work through all the types of looms mentioned; the beginner can commence with quite a large loom, such as the four-shaft "Kentish Loom," if it can be afforded. The purpose of describing the simple looms is to demonstrate by illustration and explanation the simple technique of weaving. However, it is suggested that construction of the loom illustrated in Fig. 23 and using it to practice the early stages of the work will assist the learner-weaver in appreciating the simplicity of the craft.

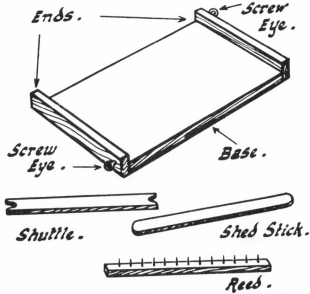

Fig. 23 A Simple Practice Loom

The loom illustrated consists of a piece of wood, which is narrower than it is long, with two smaller pieces of wood fixed at each end. At the top left corner a small screw-eye is fitted and another screwed into the wood at the bottom right corner. To set up this simple loom, the end of a piece of long string should be firmly tied to the small screw-eye at the top-left corner, and the string wound round the wood frame in the manner illustrated in Fig. 24. The string should be wound tightly and the tension should be even; twelve winds of string are all that are necessary for initial practice. The loose end of the string should be firmly tied to the small screw-eye at the bottom of the frame after winding. It should be obvious that only a very simple form of weaving can be done on the loom illustrated.

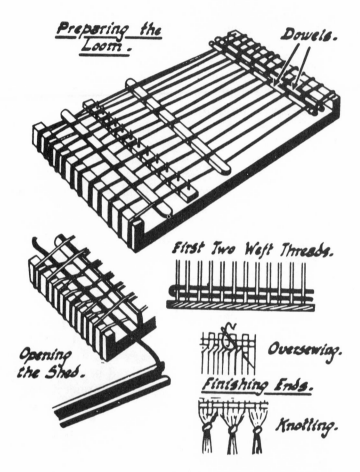

Fig. 24. Setting up the Practice Loom

The Warp: This term is common to all forms of weaving and it is used to describe the fixed strings or threads described above, which are the foundation of the fabric. Various means are used with the different types of loom for holding the warp firmly and keeping the strands separate. In the simple loom described, this can be done by fitting two dowel rods across the frame over and under alternate threads of the warp. The rods are illustrated in Fig. 24. and it will be seen that the tension can be easily increased by drawing the two rods closer together. The rods should be attached to the back end of the frame, as shown in the illustration. Thus the warp is set up on the frame of this loom. Variations of setting up the warp will be explained in detail when describing other types of looms.

The Weft: This is another term common to all forms of weaving, which is used to describe the long thread woven through the warp (fixed threads). For the

260

purpose of practice on this simple loom the weft material can be cotton rug yarn. The material woven by passing the weft thread through the warp is known as the "web."

So now we have the three main items of weaving. The loom [the simple framework] on which the warp threads are set up, and the weft [the thread woven into the warp to form the web.] Before commencing weaving it is necessary to have three more pieces of equipment. These are a shed stick, a shuttle, and a reed.

The Shed Stick: This is shown in the illustration (Fig. 23,) and it is used to separate the warp threads. It is a narrow piece of thin wood with rounded ends, which is passed through the warp under and over alternate threads. Two shed sticks are used in this form of weaving, and it will be seen from the illustration that they are passed through the warp threads in alternate order. When weaving is being done, one of the shed sticks is turned on edge to separate the warp threads for passage of the weft.

The Shuttle: This is another basic item of equipment used in all forms of weaving. There are many different types of shuttles used with different looms, but for the purpose of explaining the fundamentals of weaving the shuttle described and illustrated (Fig. 23) is a narrow thin piece of wood with a U-shaped notch cut at each end. Like the other equipment described, the shuttle can quite easily be made at home.

The Reed: Also known as the "comb" is shown in the illustration (Fig. 23) in the form of a flat piece of wood with nails hammered into it, and for the purpose of this explanation, thirteen nails are shown and spaced to separate the warp threads. (The spaces between are known as "Dents"). This piece of equipment is not attached to the loom illustrated, and it may be different in shape and form for use with some of the other looms described later in this book. The reed is used to beat up the "pick": (The pick is the term used to describe the weft threads as they are passed through the warp) to make a firm web (the woven material).

Weaving on the simple loom: After setting up the warp on the simple loom, the rods should be fastened in place, and one of the shed sticks inserted through the warp threads over and under in alternate order. The weft material of course yarn should be wound round the shuttle between the U-shaped notches, with the end of the material free, and the reed should be put in place behind the first shed stick as illustrated in Fig. 24. Darn the shuttle through the warp threads from right to left, under and over alternate threads, a short distance from the front of the loom, leaving two or three inches of yarn hanging over on the right of the weft. With the right hand hold the yarn where it meets the first warp thread on the right, and darn the shuttle back through the warp threads—this time from left to right—under and over alternate threads in opposite order to those first worked. Hold the left edge weft and warp and pull the yarn straight, but not too tight. Bring the reed forward, with the nails between the warp threads, and press it firmly against the darned pick, and your two rows of yarn should look like those in the illustration (Fig. 24). The odd end of the yarn is afterwards darned in the web.

To continue, turn the reed down and bring the shed stick forward to a distance of four or five inches from the pick, and turn it on its side (this is also shown in the illustration—Fig. 24). The shed stick separates the warp threads and the space thus formed in front of the pick (the weft threads already woven) permits easy passage of the loaded shuttle. This space is known in weaving as the "shed," and the term is common to all forms of weaving done on any kind of loom. Before passing the shuttle through the shed, insert the second stick, flat on its side, through the warp behind the reed, and ensure that it is worked under and over alternate threads to those separated by the first shed stick. Pass the shuttle through the shed from right to left to the third warp strand of yarn; pull the yarn

firm, remove the first shed stick, and turn the reed up to bring it forward to beat up the pick.

Continue in the same way, repeating the sequence of actions. After beating up the pick, turn down the reed and bring the shed stick forward, turning it on edge to open the shed; place the other shed stick in position through the warp (always in alternate order to the first one for this simple weave), and pass the shuttle back through the shed alternately from left to right. As the web progresses it may be observed that it is drawn in and is not so wide as the warp threads. This loss of width is due to the compression of the warp in weaving, and this can be largely avoided by adjusting the tension of the weft strands before they are beaten down. The edges should be watched as the work progresses, and the tension on the weft should be even throughout the work. This is not always easy for the beginner to do, but if it is carefully watched in the early stages, and the reason for the looseness fully understood, it should be a simple matter to overcome the fault with practice. It may be found that the tension on part of a weft thread is greater than that of the rest, causing the weft to curve. The tension, of course, should always be even throughout the work and tightness or looseness of the weft adjusted immediately when observed.The pressure on the reed should also be even throughout the work, and after a little practice on this very simple loom, the beginner will soon find how to regulate the tension of the warp threads, and beat up the pick evenly to form the web with firm straight edges.

Continue weaving the practice piece on the simple loom, as described above, to within four or five inches of the end of the loom. The web formed by passing alternate weft threads through alternate warp threads is described as plain weaving or "tabby" weave. There are many variations which will be explained later in the book. The ends of woven fabric may be finished in several different ways, and these are best done on the loom rather than cutting the warp threads and finishing the ends off the loom. The ends may be oversewn with strong yarns as illustrated in Fig. 24, and the stitches should be sewn through each of the weft and warp threads, and fastened off firmly, or the ends of the warp threads may be knotted to form a fringe—this is also illustrated in Fig. 24—when securing the ends of the web, the woven material should be removed from the loom, by cutting through the warp threads.

It may be found in working on larger looms that there may be some slight variations of the usages and methods described; for instance, shed sticks are used slightly differently in larger looms—the object at this stage is to clarify the preliminary instructions.

The information given above has been written in very simple style to give the beginner a working knowledge of the elementary principles of hand-loom weaving, and includes most of the technical terms used in weaving. But it should not be assumed that the simple loom described is only suitable for practice—it can be used to weave some very good, small articles.

To modify the practice loom, screw four cup hooks into the ends of the frame at the top, as shown in illustration Fig. 25. Position the cup hooks so that the closed sides of them face inside the loom. Cut two pieces of dowel rod to rest in the cup hooks which may be bent a little to prevent the rods falling out. Drill a small hole through both ends of each rod and insert a short piece of strong wire through the holes at each side of the frame at both ends; hammer a small nail into position, as shown in the illustration.

All the other items used with the simple practice loom will be required for use with this loom—the cross rods (dowel rods), the reed, shed-sticks, and the shuttle. For practice, the worker can again use string for the warp, which for this loom is attached to the two roller rods. To set up the loom, place the two dowel rods in the cup hooks and tie a piece of string to the ends of the dowel rods, as shown in the illustration Fig. 25, to keep them in place while setting up. The warp

threads should be about six inches longer than double the length of the piece of material which is to be woven. The string should be doubled and looped over the warp rod at the back of the frame, as shown in the illustration Fig. 25. Pass the end of the string through the loop, which should be closed very tightly to prevent the warp slipping round the dowel in a later stage of the work. Fasten the required number of warp threads to the warp dowel, then fasten the ends of the warp strings to the dowel rod at the front of the loom, and fasten them very tightly. It will obviously be necessary to have the strands all exactly the same length to maintain even tension of the warp.

After fastening the ends of the warp strands to the rod at the front of the loom, wind the back roller rod round clock-wise, as shown in the illustration, to tighten the warp, and finish with the pieces of wire at the end of the back dowel lodged against the small nails in the side of the loom. Before inserting the cross rods and tying them to the frame, ensure that the tension on each warp string is even; if any are loose it will affect the firm texture of the weaving. Work the cross rods through the warp, as previously described, and fasten them to the frame.

Insert one of the shed-sticks over and under alternate warp strands if a plain tabby weave is to be worked, or under and over two strands at a time if a twill weave is to be done. As explained above, weave in the same way by passing the shuttle backwards and forwards through the shed, beating up each pick as it is formed, and when several inches of the web have been completed release the tension on the warp rod at the back of the frame and tighten up and twist the warp rod at the front of the frame. Lock the dowel rods in position, and before commencing the next stage of the work make any adjustments to the cross rods necessary to take up any slackness of the warp. This simple modification of the practice loom demonstrates how the length of the material can be increased beyond that of the length of the loom.

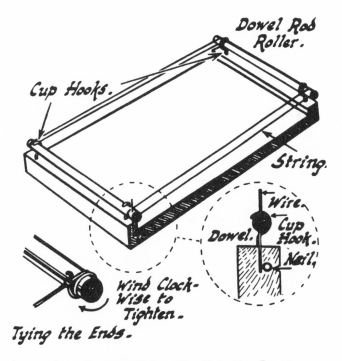

Fig. 25. Modifying the Practice Loom

Looms of more advanced design than the simple practice loom—with the roller modification—previously described, takes the learner beyond the beginner stage into the realm of Table Looms. The structure of table looms may vary according to the ideas of individual manufacturers, but in principle their actions are similar.

263

The table loom illustrated in Fig. 26 is a step forward from the practice loom pictured in previous illustrations, but it has several points of similarity; it will be remembered that the "loom" is the frame upon which the weaving is done. In our first loom the warp was set up by winding string round the wood frame—in the table loom (Fig. 26) it will be seen that the warp is stretched between two rollers similarly positioned and controlled to the dowel-rod rollers of our first loom, that is, one roller at each end of the loom, which is wound tight, or freed, by adjusting control pins or pieces of wire held in place by nails or pegs in the side of the frame. Our simple board, with a piece of wood attached at each end, has developed into a box-like frame with rounded slots cut in the sides to hold the rollers in position (instead of the cup-hooks), and the wire peg, or nail inserted in the side of the frame can be placed in more than one position to adjust the tension of the warp when rolling off the web. The shed-sticks used with our last model and the reed have been combined in the form of a heddle-reed, which is included in the illustration (Fig. 26). The heddle-reed separates the warp threads to form the shed through which the shuttle is passed (this is only suitable for tabby weave). The cross-rods remain, but in this loom they are narrow flat pieces of wood (also known as 'shed-sticks') and as before they are positioned at the end of the frame.

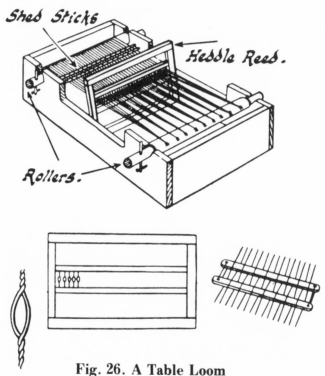

Fig. 26. A Table Loom

A table loom such as the one illustrated, could quite easily be made at home, but if this is done care should be taken to form the joints of the frame carefully so that it is rigid and the ends square with the sides. A broom-handle could be pressed into service for the rollers, and the cross-rods could be made from builder's laths; a strip of canvas should be firmly tacked to each roller to help to secure the ends of the warp. Two dowel rods should be attached to the canvas of each roller, as illustrated. A home-made loom of this type would be quite suitable for practicing weaving, but if the craft is to be made the subject of a commercial venture the hand-weaver should purchase a craftsman-made loom. Some very attractive and useful articles can be woven on this table loom—in which the length is not controlled by the length of the framework, because of the rollers; but, of course, the width of the web is slightly less than the width of the loom. The heddle-reed can also be made at home. It consists of a light wooden frame which

264

should be strong and rigid, upon which is strung fine wire twisted as shown in Fig. 26, to form a row of holes. Additional heddle-reeds can be made for use with this loom for weaving some of the more intricate patterns. In setting up the loom, some of the warp threads are passed through the holes in the heddles. It will be observed that the loose pieces of equipment prominent in the practice loom are incorporated in the table loom. The only loose part is the shuttle.

The shuttle can be the same shape as the one previously described and illustrated, but it should be long enough to pass through the shed, or roller shuttle may be used with this type of loom. The roller, or hand shuttle, is illustrated in Fig. 27. The advantage of this type of shuttle is that it can be thrown through the open shed, making the work very much easier and quicker. The best roller shuttles are made of hardwood with a very smooth finish. Sizes vary, but usually they are six to eight inches long; these shuttles are shaped like a boat, and carry a bobbin in a hollow center. The bobbin freely rotates on its spindle and the thread is passed through a hole in the side of the shuttle; the bobbin is held in the body of the shuttle by means of a spring which in some hand shuttles can be regulated to adjust the tension of the weft. Shuttles used in weaving fine yarns may not be fitted with rollers at the bottom, the smoothness and shape of them being relied on to pass freely over the delicate threads; but shuttles used in weaving coarser yarns may be fitted with rollers to assist them in gliding over the lower warp strands when the shed is open. In action the hand shuttle is held with the point inserted in the open shed and is flicked to glide along the threads to be caught in the other hand. There is quite a knack in manipulating this type of shuttle, and after practice the worker will find that not only can the action of weaving be speeded up, but the quality of the web can be improved by controlling the weft at an even tension best suited to the yarn used. It may be considered that the use of a hand or roller shuttle is not necessary with such a narrow loom as the one described, but it will be found as the weaver progresses beyond the learner stage, that the quality of weaving with this type of shuttle is much superior to the method previously described. The roller shuttle will again be referred to in later instructions.

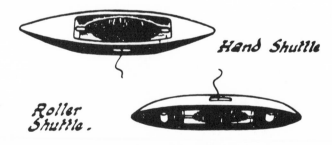

Fig. 27 Shuttles

Warping: With our simple practice loom the warp was set up by winding string round the body of the loom. To set up the table loom a different method of setting up is adopted, and this is known as "warping". Only a very simple method of preparing the warp is described. Before warping it will be necessary to estimate the warp, and the amount of yarn required, for the warp of a particular object will vary according to the type of yarn being used—wool, linen, cotton and silk, and synthetic yarns of different weights and qualities will obviously vary in thickness, and to estimate the number of threads of the warp it will be necessary to determine the number of strands of whatever yarn is used to the inch. For the purpose of clarifying this explanation, the weaving of a simple scarf is described as being the first practice piece made on the table loom.

265

The width of the scarf is to be 9 inches, and the length 40 inches (not including the length of the fringe); it is to be made with 2-ply wool and one color only used for the warp.

As previously explained, the spacings between the warp threads may vary according to individual requirements, but for our scarf of 2-ply wool we will count 12 threads to the inch across the warp. Therefore, if the scarf is to be 9 inches wide and there are 12 threads to the inch, the number of threads required for the warp will be 9 x 12, which equals 108 threads; and extra thread should be added each side for the selvedge, and these two additional threads bring the total up to 110 in the warp. To determine the length of the warp the amount of loom wastage and shrinkage should be added to the length of the scarf (although described as wastage, not all is waste as some will be taken up by the knotted fringe at each end of the scarf). Loom wastage may vary according to the construction of the loom, and shrinkage also may vary according to the yarn material being used. The length of shrinkage and wastage for this scarf is estimated at 11 inches. Therefore, if the scarf is to be 40 inches long and the wastage is estimated at 11 inches, the total length of the warp will be 40 + 11, which is 51 inches. A simple warping board, used for preparing the warp, is illustrated in Fig. 28. It is a flat piece of wood with holes drilled in it; the dimensions of the board and the distance between the holes are shown in the illustration (Fig. 28). Pegs are fitted into the holes, and although they should fit tightly for winding the warp, they should be removable in order to adjust them for winding warps of different lengths. By adjusting the number and groupings of the pegs, warps of almost any length for the table loom described, can be prepared. The importance of sturdiness in the warping board cannot be overstressed. The pegs should be substantial in make and they should firmly fit into their holes—the strain of numerous threads wound round the pegs can be considerable.

To prepare the warping board for a 51 inch warp (the length of the scarf plus an allowance for wastage), set the pegs in the board as illustrated in Fig. 28. Only half the board is used, and only seven pegs are set in holes in the positions shown in the illustration. To clarify these instructions the pegs have been numbered from 1 to 7. The peg-holes in this board are three inches apart, and if those used in Fig. 28 are counted it will be noted that there are 17 three-inch spaces between peg No. 1 and peg No. 7. Thus the length of the warp is regulated at 51 inches. (It will be obvious that by changing the positions of the pegs in the holes longer or shorter warps can be prepared on the board.)

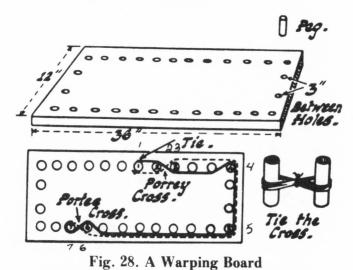

Fig. 28. A Warping Board

266

After positioning the pegs and setting them firmly in their holes to take the strain of the threads of yarn, the end of the yarn should be tied to peg No. 1. When firmly tied it should be taken along to peg No. 2 which passes, and should cross outside this peg to the inside of peg No. 3. Continuing round the board to the right the yarn should be brought round the outside of peg No. 4 then along the end of the board round the outside of peg No. 5. From peg No. 5 the yarn should be taken round the inside of peg No. 6, then round the outside of peg No. 7. This completes the winding of the first warp thread.

To wind the second warp thread on the numbered pegs, keep the tension on the yarn and bring it round peg No. 7. From peg No. 7 pass the yarn round the **outside** of peg No. 6 (this is in opposite order to the first wind). Continue round the outside of pegs No. 4 and 5 at the corners, **outside** peg No. 3, over the first thread and **inside** peg No. 2 to peg No. 1 which the yarn is wound round to commence the third warp thread. Continue winding the yarn round the numbered pegs in the same order until 51 threads are wound on. Keep the tension on the yarn even all through the winding process; this is very important, and if care is taken at this stage to keep the tension even much trouble will be saved when the warp is on the loom. To secure the warp, tie the yarn at the end of the 51st wind firmly to peg No. 7.

Before removing the warp from the board the crosses should be tied. These crosses are identified in the illustration (Fig. 28) by their names; the crossed threads between pegs 2 and 3 form the "Porrey" cross, and the crossed threads between pegs 6 and 7 form the "Portee" cross. To tie the crosses, pass a piece of cord through the threads at each side of the crosses (as illustrated in Fig. 28) and tie the cord. Of the two crosses, the porrey is the most important. After tying the crosses, the warp can be removed from the warping board. There is a certain way to remove the warp from the board to prevent the warp threads becoming tangled. To remove the warp, ease it off the pegs (if it is very tight remove the corner pegs— Nos. 4 and 5); hold the warp with the left hand at the portee cross (as shown in the illustration— Fig. 29) and place the right hand through the looped threads at the top of the warp; when doing this be careful not to disturb the threads more than can be avoided. Turn the right hand down to grasp the warp under the portee cross and draw the threads through the first loop, thus forming a second loop. Repeat his process by again placing the right hand through the second loop, grasping the warp threads and pulling them through the second loop to form a third loop and continue to the end of the warp. This is known as "Chaining" and is similar to the simple crochet stitch of that name.

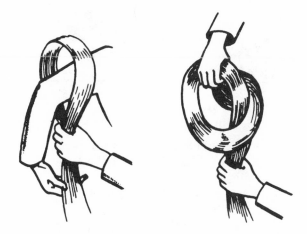

Fig. 29. Chaining The Warp

It is suggested that the beginner should practice several warps until the process is thoroughly understood before preparing the warp for the scarf—the practice warps can be prepared with string, and not only should practice be carried out in preparing the warp on the warping board, but also in chaining the warp, and releasing the chain. When the end of the warp at the last chain is pulled it should slide freely from the loop above it. It may be found—before experience is gained in practice—that although the worker was careful in forming the chain not to disturb the threads in the warp they may be inadvertently twisted and the chain is locked. If this happens, the threads should not be tugged to release them; tugging will only tighten the lock in the chain, and the only way to release it is to pass the other end of the chain through the first loop, unchaining the warp and forming the chain afresh. Time spent in practice at this stage is never wasted.

Setting up the Loom: After preparing a sound warp for the scarf it is ready for "beaming". Beaming is the term used to describe the process of fitting the warp to the loom. There are several ways of doing this which may vary considerably according to the type and manufacturer of the loom, and for the table loom mentioned in this chapter a simplified form of beaming is described.

First pass the two shed-sticks through the end of the warp—one each side of the porrey cross—as illustrated in Fig. 30. Spread the warp between the shed-sticks thread by thread in order, to a width of 11 inches (the width of the scarf), and tie the ends of the shed-sticks to the front roller, which should then be placed in the slots at the front of the frame. Next clamp the heddle-reed to the frame (illustrated in Fig. 30).

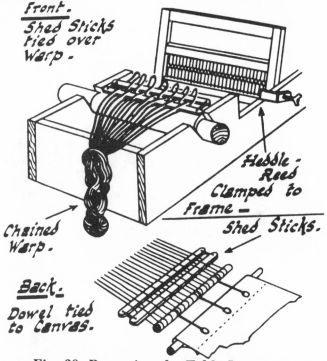

Fig. 30. **Preparing the Table Loom**

The next part of the work is best done by two persons; one at the back of the loom and the other at the front. The person at the back of the loom should have a crochet hook to pass through the holes in the heddle-reed for the person at the front of the loom to hook the looped threads on. After each looped thread is hooked on the crochet hook it should be drawn back through the holes in the heddle-reed and passed over one of the dowel rods from the back roller of the loom. The hooking and looping should commence in the center of the spread warp, working a central looped thread of the warp through a central hole in the heddle-reed, and after passing the looped thread through the hole in the

268

heddle-reed (this is known as a "dent") and passing the loop over the dowel rod, the remaining threads should be passed through alternate dents in a definite order. After securing the first thread, take the thread next to it and pass that one through the next dent but one from the first one and loop it over the dowel rod.

The third thread treated should be the next thread on the other side of the first thread, and the work of threading should proceed in the same order—that is from the center working alternately from side to side. It is of the greatest importance to take care with this part of the work not to get the threads tangled and crossed.

After passing all the threads of the warp through alternate dents in the heddle-reed and looping them over the dowel rod, the rod should be secured to the canvas of the back roller and firmly tied, as illustrated in Fig. 30. The next thing to do is to unchain the warp, and holding it at the end, ensure that all the threads are firmly fastened to the beam at the back of the loom and that the tension is even throughout the warp.

Still holding the warp taut, commence turning the roller back in its groove. As the canvas is taken up, strips of stout brown paper slightly wider than the warp should be inserted between the roller and the warp. Keep the tension on the warp and when about 10 inches of the warp is left in front of the clamped heddle-reed lock the back roller. Release the shed-sticks from the front roller and insert them through the warp behind the heddle-reed under and over to form a cross in the warp between them, as illustrated in Fig. 30. After doing this, cut through the loops of the warp threads at the front of the loom, and wind the back roller to draw the cut threads through the dents in the heddle-reed, until they hang from the back roller, as shown in Fig. 31. At this stage the warp is now ready for entering, which simply means that the threads must once again be passed through the dents of the heddle-reed in their proper order and this time back to front.

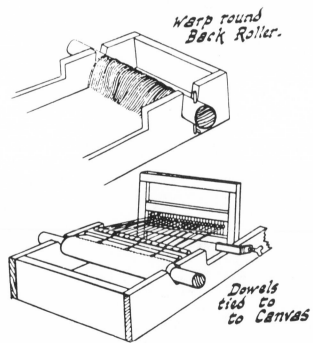

Fig. 31. Entering the Warp

It is advisable for two persons to do the entering or threading, and the person at the front of the loom should have a crochet hook. Commence again at the center of the warp; the person at the front of the loom should put the crochet hook through the center dent of the heddle-reed, and the person working at the back of the loom should bend the end of the center thread and fasten it over the hook,

269

which is then drawn through the dent. The second thread of the pair should be passed through the space between the dents; this threading and spacing should be carefully done not to cross any of the threads. Work from both sides of the center of the wrap in alternate order and when 12 threads have been passed through the heddle-reed, secure them to the dowel removed from the canvas of the front roller. The threads should be tied to the dowel in the manner illustrated in Fig. 31, and the work of entering should be continued, tying each group of 12 threads until the last threads at the sides of the warp are reached—after tying eight groups of 12 strands each to the dowel rod; the last tie each side should consist of six threads each, thus making a total of 110 warp threads in all, including the two extra each side allowed for the selvedge.

When tying has been completed the heddle-reed may be released from the clamps and moved to the back of the loom, and the dowel rod should be firmly tied to the rodded canvas (see Fig. 31). Make any adjustments necessary to the ties to evenly tension the warp, unlock the back roller, and wind the front roller round (with the canvas rolled over the top) to prepare the loom behind the heddle-reed, as in Fig. 31. The loom is now ready to receive the weft. By raising and lowering the heddle-reed it will be found that the shed is opened for passage of the shuttle. Lowering the heddle-reed presses down the alternate strands threaded through the dents below the threads between the dents, and raising it reverses the action, so that if the heddle-reed is alternately lowered and raised the shed is opened, in the correct order passage of the weft, to form tabby weave. The scarf is woven in the same way as on the simple practice loom previously described, by working the shuttle across the shed, rolling the web back as it is completed, and knotting a fringe at the ends. The only difference is that between each pick the heddle-reed is brought back on the warp to beat up the pick. Color schemes and patterns can be worked out on squared paper as is also the method of winding the bobbin of the roller shuttle, if it is used at this stage.

DYEING

Dyeing Wool: Wool is obtainable in three different conditions: these are "in grease" wool, "washed" wool and "scoured" wool. "In grease" wool is so called because it is supplied in its original state of impurity and has not been washed to remove the grease. "Washed" wool, as its name implies, has been washed to render it clean, and has had some of the grease removed. "Scoured" wool is wool that has been made perfectly clean with all grease and impurities removed.

Before commencing to dye wool, it is important to make certain that your wool is free from grease, and if "in grease" wool or "washed" wool is to be dyed, it should first be washed to free it from all traces of grease. The wool is washed in water to which ammonia and soft soap are added in the following proportions, which are given for a ten-gallon bath: to ten gallons of water add 6 oz. of ammonia and 3 oz. of soft soap.

After mixing, heat the water to a temperature of not more than 140° Fahrenheit. Care should be taken in washing wool not to felt it; the water should not be too hot, and while washing it the wool should be squeezed as little as possible. When the wool has been thoroughly washed and is free from grease, dyeing and mordanting should be proceeded with. There are several methods of dyeing wool according to the nature of the dye; these are given as under:

(1) Some dyes do not require mordanting and the wool can be heated direct in the dye.

(2) The wool can be heated with the mordant and dyed in the same bath.

(3) The wool is separately mordanted, then dyed and after dyeing is mordanted again. This method ensures that the dyes will be extremely fast.

(4) With this method the wool is heated first with the dye and when it has

270

Table 4. Simple Dyeing Chart for Wool

Colour	Quantity of wool	Dyestuff	Mordant	Time and Method	Time of year	Remarks
Brown	3 lbs.	Walnuts	None	Boil shells and cool. Enter wool. Heat for 1 hour at 140° F.	When nuts are ripe	
Yellow	3 lbs.	6 lbs. fresh birch leaves	3/4 lb. Alum	Boil leaves for 1 hour. Enter wool. Heat 140° for 1½ hours	Summer	
Lemon	3 lbs.	Mignonette	3/4 lb. Alum	Boil for 3 hours. Enter wool. Heat for 1 hour at 140°	Summer	Use whole plant. Gives very fast colour
Yellowy Green	3 lbs.	Nettles	3/4 lb. Alum	Boil nettles for 1 hour. Enter wool. Heat for 1½ hours at 140°	During May	
Crimson	3 lbs.	4½ oz. Cochineal 3 dessert-common salt	3/4 lb. Alum 4½ oz. cream of tartar	Bring to 140°. Simmer for 1 hour. Enter wool. Keep at temperature of 140° for 2 hours	All the year round	Many shades can be obtained by varying the quantities
Rust	3 lbs.	18 oz. Madder	As above	Bring to 140°. Simmer for 20 mins. Enter wool. Continue to simmer for 1 hour	All the year round	
Grey Blue	3 lbs.	3 lbs. crushed sloe berries	None	Boil berries for 1 hour. Enter wool and heat for 1 hour at 140° F.	Autumn	Place berries in a muslin bag to boil

absorbed color the mordant is added to the bath to fix the color.

Mordanting should be carried out as follows, there being some slight difference in the method of using two mordants:

Alum: Fill your bath with sufficient water to cover the wool, then, before placing the wool in the bath, add alum in the proportion of ¼ lb. of alum to every 1 lb. of wool being dyed. When the alum has dissolved in the water, the wool should be put in. Heat the bath and bring the water to a temperature of 140°F., stirring occasionally, and after one hour at this temperature take out the wool and wrap it in a cloth while it is still damp. After wrapping the wool it should be left for two or three days, and before dyeing should be lightly washed to rid it of superfluous mordant.

Chrome: To mix a chrome mordant, fill a bath with sufficient water to cover the amount of wool to be treated, and add the water before placing the wool in the bath 3 oz. of chrome to 1 lb. of wool. Allow the chrome to dissolve in the water, place the wool in the bath, bring the water to a temperature of 140°F. and maintain it at this point for three-quarters of an hour.

A dyeing chart for wool, which gives full information about colors, quantities to be dyed, description of the dyestuff, mordants, and the time for dyeing is given in Table 4.

It is important in all stages of preparation of mordant and dyeing wool not to allow the temperature of the bath to exceed 140°F. or the material may be thickened and damaged.

Dyeing Silk: The dyeing of silk, providing information of colors, quantities, dyestuffs, etc. is given in Table 5.

Silk is obtainable for hand weaving in two kinds, one of which is waste silk (which is generally known as Spun silk), the other variety is raw silk. Raw silk is coated with a gummy substance which has to be removed before it can be dyed. To clean raw silk place it in a canvas bag, which should be tied at the mouth, and heat it in a strong solution of soap for several hours until all the gummed coating is removed.

Silks for hand-loom weaving can be dyed in the same way as wool, but lower temperatures are used in the dyeing of silk than used in dyeing wool. In some

Table. 5. Simple Dyeing Chart for Silk

Colour	Quantity of silk	Dyestuff	Mordant	Time and Method	Time of year	Remarks
Orange	1 lb.	½ lb. Madder 2 oz. Flavin 1 oz. Tin	Alum Acetate	Enter Tin in a cold bath. Mix Flavin and Madder to paste. Add to bath and bring to boil. Enter silk and heat 10 mins. at 140° F. Wash in soap.	All the year round	
Black	1 lb.	6 oz. Logwood 3/4 oz. Flavin 1 oz. Iron	Alum Acetate	Mix all dyestuffs together in bath. Enter silk and heat ½ hour. Wash thoroughly.	All the year round	Put dyestuffs in muslin bag to boil.
Grey	1 lb.	A quantity of Bracken tips	1 oz. Iron 2 oz. Cream Tartar	Boil quantity of young Bracken tips for ½ hour. Strain. Enter silk and heat for ½ hour	When Bracken tips available	
Red	1 lb.	5 oz. Cochineal 1 oz. Tin	1 oz. Tannic Acid	Dissolve 1 oz. Tannic acid in hot water. Enter silk and leave for 24 hours. Rinse well. In clean bath put 4 oz. cochineal. Enter silk and heat till blue colour develops. Lift silk. Add 1 oz. cochineal and 1 oz. tin. Re-enter silk. Heat well. Wash in soap.	All the year round	While silk is in tannic acid bath stir from time to time.
Brown	1 lb.	Quantity of lichen according to shade required	Alum Acetate	Put into dye bath. Quantity of lichen. Add 1 tsp. acetic acid. Enter silk. Heat for 1 to 3 hours at 140° F.	When lichen obtainable	Vary the quantity of lichen to obtain different shades of brown.

cases soaking in a cold solution of the mordant is sufficient preparation of the silk. For treating bright colored silks an Alum mordant should be used; if it is necessary to brighten the colors, tin mordant should be used. When black dyes are to be used an Iron mordant is required.

To prepare Alum mordant for silk, dissolve 3 lbs. of Alum and 3 oz. of chalk in a gallon of water. Add 2 lbs. of white acetate of lead. Stir the mixture occasionally and allow it to remain for about thirty-six hours. After the final stirring let the mixture stand for twelve hours and decant the clear liquor. To the residue, add two gallons of water and leave it twelve hours. Decant it and add the clear liquor to the first decanted. Stir and bottle the mixture.

Colour	Quantity of Cotton	Dyestuff	Mordant	Time and Method	Time of year	Remarks
Red	1 lb.	12 ozs. Madder	Boil out in soda, wash and dry. Steep overnight in a hot bath of 1½ oz. tannic acid. Dry, then steep in cold solution of ¼ lb. alum and ½ oz. chalk dry. Add 2 ozs. more alum and steep as before. Wash and dry.	Add Madder to cold bath. Enter cotton and bring to boil in 1 hour. Rinse and re-dye as above. Rinse in warm bath with 2 ozs. soap. Wash and dry.	Any time of year	All cotton should be mercerised before dyeing. See text.
Yellow	1 lb.	1½ oz. Flavin	Steep overnight in hot bath with 1½ oz. tannic acid. Wring dry. Work in bath containing ¼ lb. alum., ½ oz chalk (dry). Pass through weak chloride of lime. Dry. Return to alum bath and repeat process. Wash well.	Add Flavin to cold bath. Bring to boil and dye slowly.	Any time of year	4 ozs. Galls may be used in place of Tannic Acid.

Table 6. Simple Dyeing chart for Cotton

Colour	Quantity of cotton	Dyestuff	Mordant	Time and Method	Time of year	Remarks
Brown	2 lbs.	12 ozs. Fustic	Put 2 ozs. cutch and 1 oz. chrome in separate baths	Enter cotton in cutch bath. Boil for 20 mins. Wring. Boil 10 mins. in chrome bath. Add 6 ozs. of fustic to cutch bath. Enter cotton. Repeat process till shade required is obtained.	Any time of year	Colour may be darkened by adding 1 dracum of copper sulphate.
Black	2 lbs.	12 ozs. Logwood 2½ ozs. Madder 6 ozs. Fustic	Wash cotton, steep overnight in hot bath containing 2 ozs. tannic acid. Wring out and work in 1¼ oz. soda bath at temperature of 50° to 60° C. Wring and work in cold bath containing 1¼ oz. copper as for ½ hour. Return to soda bath for ¾ hour.	Mix dyestuffs in cold bath. Enter cotton and bring to boiling point. Boil for ½ hour. Pass through warm solution of 1 oz. chrome. Wash and work through warm bath containing soap.	Any time of year	To obtain Greys. Dye with 1 to 5 per cent. of logwood after mordanting in iron.

Then using the mixture, add two parts of it to one of water and work the silk into the solution. Leave it in the mixture for two hours, then take it out and allow to dry. After drying, wash it well in clean water before dyeing.

Dyeing Cotton: Cotton is difficult to dye unless it has first been mercerized. Cotton is always best dyed with chemical dyes, and it should be boiled in Alum mordant, then boiled in dye. Before commencing mordanting and dyeing cotton, it should be boiled for several hours to completely rid it of all impurities.

Dark colored cottons should be boiled in plain water. For boiling light colored cottons carbonate of soda should be added to the extent of 5 per cent (by weight) of the quantity of water used, or caustic soda may be used, in which case the quantity should be only 2 per cent.

Brown cotton—when dyeing use a chrome mordant; boil the cotton first in the dye, then boil it in the chrome solution for a short time. For treating pale and light colored cotton, use a tannic acid mordant, adding 10 per cent of tannic acid by volume to the water.

In the last-named case, the bath may be hot or cold, but if hot, the temperature should not exceed 140° Fahrenheit. Work the cotton in the mordanting solution, then leave it to soak for twelve hours. After soaking, wring it out and wash it.

A dyeing chart for cotton, showing colors, dyestuffs, quantities, mordants, time, etc. is in Table 6 (Linen is dyed in the same way as cotton).

Plants for Dye Colors: Plants for making red dyes are: Birch, Common Sorrel, White Madder, Potentil and Gromwell.

Plants for making blue dyes are: Elder, Privet, Sloe, Woad, and Yellow Iris.

Plants for making yellow dyes are: Ash, Barberry, Birch leaves, Gorse, Bog Myrtle, Bramble, Broom, Crab-apple, Marsh Marigold, Nettle, Pear and Plum.

Plants for brown dyes are: Hop, Onion, Larch, Oak, Walnut, and Dulse Seaweed.

Plants for purple dyes are: Dandelion, Deadly Nightshade, Dock and Meadowsweet, and it must be recognized that many of the plants included in these lists are poisonous. They must be handled carefully and should be safely stored to prevent any damage or danger of accidents.

In addition to the plants listed above, dyes may be made from lichen. Many

ordinary lichens make extremely good fast dyes of shades of brown, and they are largely used in the Highlands of Western Ireland. For dyeing materials brown, no mordant is needed with lichen dyes and the colors are the fastest known in the vegetable group. The lichens are collected in the summer, in July and August, and after drying in the sun are put into a bath containing sufficient water to cover them, and the water is then boiled.

After the lichen dye bath is cool, cotton may be immersed in the liquid and then boiled until the shade of brown required is obtained.

The information given above is sufficient to enable the home weaver to dye materials. There are, of course, other dyes and mordants, but those described are the ones chiefly used. It is, of course, obvious that yarns should be dyed before they are woven into textiles.

Finishing Treatments of Textiles: After weaving textiles on hand looms, some treatment may be necessary to finish them, and there is some difference of treatment for various kinds of yarns. Soft water is best for treatment of the finished fabrics, and in the case of wool, if the water is hard, ammonia should be added.

Before woven textiles are washed they should be carefully examined in a good light for faults, and, if possible, any found should be rectified before the material is finished.

To wash tweed, which is woven wool yarns, place the tweed into warm soapy water, which should not be too hot. Leave the tweed to soak for about twelve hours, then repeat the process, following by rinsing in clear water. All the grease is removed when the tweed squeaks in the fingers. After washing, rinse the tweed thoroughly in warm water and wring it by twisting.

After wringing the tweed before it is nearly dry, roll it round a smooth stick, which should afterwards be withdrawn from the roll. Leave the lengths of tweed rolled for several hours and then press lightly with a warm iron. This treatment is for yarns which have been oiled to make the process of weaving easier.

Unoiled wool should be washed in warm water, adding a little soap only, and should be wrung out but not twisted too hard, then hung until nearly dry before rolling over a smooth piece of wood, later ironing with a moderate iron.

To finish linen, place it in a bath of hot water and add soap if the linen is dirty. After soaking, put the linen through the mangle, then hang to dry before rolling it. After the linen has been rolled for several hours it should be ironed on the wrong side of the material with a hot iron.

Woven silk should be soaked in warm water only, then squeezed to remove as much water as possible, and after hanging until nearly dry, it should be ironed on the wrong side of the material with a moderately heated iron.

To finish cotton, soak it in clear warm water and only add soap if the cotton is dirty. After soaking squeeze out as much water as possible, hang the cotton to dry and when nearly dry, iron it on the wrong side with a fairly hot iron.

Rayon should be finished in clear warm water and soap should not be added unless the work is dirty. When wringing out rayon handle it very carefully, hang the material until it is nearly dry and iron with a warm iron. A hot iron should not be used on rayon.

SUN DRYING YOUR FRUITS AND VEGETABLES

Drying the surplus food in the season of plenty can mean more good health foods for the family in seasons when these foods are not available fresh. It can add variety to the diet and make cooking easier because there are more foods from

274

which to plan meals. Drying is not difficult and it requires very little equipment. For the equipment you can use things you already have or can make the necessary pieces easily at home. Drying need cost nothing.

What is Drying

Drying foods does two things. 1) It removes the water and 2) It checks the chemical change that takes place naturally in food, as for example, fruit when it ripens.

What Foods Can You Dry

Many different foods are being dried today in various parts of the world. Some foods, which in one country may seem unsuitable for drying, are being dried in others. The tomato is an example of this. In the United States it has been less commonly dried than some other vegetables. In some Middle East countries it has been dried frequently. Here are some of the foods most commonly dried. They have been divided into two groups; those which are easier and those harder to dry.

Fruits
Easier: Apples, Apricots, Cherries, Cocoanut, Dates, Figs, Buava, Nectarines, Peaches, Pears, Plums, Prunes.
Harder: Avocado, Blackberries, Banana, Bread Fruit, Dewberries, Loganberries, Mamey, Grapes.

Vegetables
Easier: Beans, Mature (Kidney, Lima, Mongo, Pinta, Pole, Red, Black, Soy), Beans, Dried in green state, (Lentils, Soy), Chili (Peppers), Herbs (Parsley, Celery tops, etc.), Peas, mature (Sugar pea, Cow pea, Chick pea, Pigeon pea), Sweet Corn, Sweet Potatoes, Cassava Root, Onion, Soup Mixture.
Harder: Asparagus, Beets, Broccoli, Carrots, Celery, Greens, (Kintsay, Talinum, Kangkong, Collards, Mustards, Turnip Tops, Sweet Potato Leaves), Green Snap Beans, Green Peas, Okra, Peppers, Pimentos, Pumpkin, Squash, Tomatoes.

Cleanliness Every Step of the Way

Cleanliness is of the greatest importance. It is necessary to follow clean practices every step of the way. What causes food to become dirty? Dust and dirt which fall on the food may contain harmful bacteria. Flies or other insects also carry bacteria on their feet. Some of these bacteria may cause it to spoil more easily. Here are some rules for keeping the food clean as you pick it, prepare it, dry it and store it.
1. Wash hands before handling food.
2. Pick or collect food into clean containers.
3. Wash food carefully in clean water.
4. Cover food drying on trays with clean cloths to keep dust, dirt, flies, and other insects out of it.
5. Wash these covering cloths frequently in clean water.
6. Place trays of food while drying away from dust, insects, and flies.
7. Never lay drying food directly on sand, or ground.
8. Store in tight containers from which dirt and insects can be excluded.
9. Scrub trays or mats after using.

Check the air

If you are thinking of drying be sure you have conditions which will bring you success. You need to have these three for the best results.

1. DRYNESS OF AIR—Unless the air is reasonably dry the moisture cannot be removed from the food. If it rains all the time it will be hard to dry food.

2. WARM OR HOT AIR—Hot days when the sun is shining brightly are best for drying food. Then the food can be dried quickly, which is desirable.

3. CIRCULATION OF AIR—There needs to be free circulation of air around the drying food. Make sure that air can reach the foods from all sides, around and underneath, as well as the top of the food.

How to Dry Fruits—Equipment Needed

Equipment can be very simple for drying fruit. In order to work rapidly after the fruit is picked it will help to get the equipment ready ahead of time. Be sure it is clean. You will need—

1. Sharp knife—to pare and cut fruits. (A stainless steel knife prevents discoloration)

2. Wooden board—to make cutting easier

3. Pan, kettle or pot—in which to wash fruit

4. Equipment for sulphuring—Large box to cover trays, Small container for sulphur, Sulphur, Small piece of paper, Matches

5. Plenty of clean water.

6. Trays or mats on which to spread fruit to dry. Trays should be thoroughly scrubbed and dried.

7. Pieces of clean, loosely woven cloth—One for each tray or mat. Each piece should be 2 inches (5 centimeters) longer and 2 inches (5 centimeters) wider than tray.

Steps in Drying Fruits—How, Why, When

1. Gather fruit
   a. **Select Good Quality Food**
   The finished food can be no better than the fruit with which you start. Select fresh, ripe, firm and sound fruit. Gather it as early in the morning as possible. When fruit is right for eating it is right for drying.
   b. **Handle Carefully**
   Fruits bruise easily. Handle with care.

2. Wash fruit
   Place fruit in pan. Pour clean water over fruit. Wash carefully. Lift fruit from water. Empty water from pan and repeat if necessary.

3. Peel or pit fruit—As needed

4. Cut fruit—As needed. Slice into thin pieces. Thick slices dry slowly.

5. Sulphur fruit—Most fruit is improved by sulphuring. Read chart, later in text, to see which fruits should be sulphured. See directions for how to sulphur, also later in text.
   Why sulphured fruit has better color and flavor—Fruit requires less soaking before cooking. Sulphuring helps to—retain vitamins, prevent souring, prevent insect attacks.

6. Spread fruit on clean dry trays or mats—Spread evenly. One layer in thickness.

7. Cover with loosely woven clean cloth, mosquito netting, or wire screen. To keep insects and dust from getting on the food. Fasten cloth so it will not blow off.

8. Place trays of fruit in sun to dry.
   a. In direct sunlight. This may mean placing the tray flat or it may require raising one edge of the tray.
   b. Where air can circulate freely over and under food. This may require putting tray on blocks or stones.
   c. Away from dust and dirt.
   d. Off the ground.
   e. Away from animals and people.
   f. Protect from storms and dew.
   g. Take in when danger of rain.

9. Turn food. Two or three times each day to speed drying.

10. Continue drying. For several days until $2/3$ dry.

11. Test for dryness. Squeeze a handful. If there is no moisture left on the hand and the fruit springs apart when hand is opened, the fruit is properly dried. Berries should rattle on trays.

12. Condition fruit. Gives fruit opportunity to complete drying process and prevents growth of mold.
    Take fruit from trays and put in large container. Cover container with cloth or wire screen to prevent insect and dirt from getting in. Stir fruit 2 or 3 times daily. Leave 8 to 10 days.

13. Put dried food in containers for storage. Containers in which food is stored need to—
    a. Be moisture proof.
    b. Keep insects out.
    c. Keep dirt from food.

    Some good containers are—
    a. Stone jars.
    b. Jars or pots made of clay or metal.
    c. Dry gourds.
    d. Paper bags.
    e. Cloth bags
    f. Glass jars.
    G. Tin boxes with tight fitting tops.
    Small containers are better than large because the food is less likely to become contaminated by mold or insects.

14. Seal containers of food. For containers with loosely fitting lids—Place lid on container, dip strip of cloth (about 1" wide) ($2\frac{1}{2}$ centimeters) in melted paraffin or beeswax. Wrap, while warm, around container at joining of lid. Be sure all space between container and lid is covered by strip of cloth.

15. If the food has been put in bags, place the small bags in a large container. Large container may be a jar, crock, or pot. Seal large container when filled with small packages.

16. Store. In a clean, dry, dark and cool place. It is well to check food often to see that it remains dry.

How to Sulphur Fruit: Materials and Equipment Needed

1. **Trays or rack** on which the fruit is spread for drying must not be made of metal.

2. **Platform**—stones, bricks or blocks of wood to build a platform 6-8 inches (15-20 centimeters) high on which the trays can be stacked.

3. **Sulphuring Box**—wood or cardboard box to cover trays for sulphuring, needs:

   to be deep enough to cover the stacked trays, plus the platform. It must be wide enough to cover not only the trays but also a small pan of sulphur which will be placed at the side of the stack of trays.

4. **Pan, tin can or pottery bowl** in which to burn sulphur. It should be shallow and clean.

5. **Paper**—square piece in which sulphur is wrapped. Minimum size—large enough to wrap around a walnut.

6. **Sulphur**—Allow one level teaspoon of sulphur to each pound (450 grams) of prepared fruit. Don't use too much sulphur.

7. **Matches**

8. **Tray dividers**—pieces of wood, or bamboo, which are as long as the width of trays and 1½ inches (about 4 centimeters) wide. Allow two pieces for each tray —stones may be substituted for the pieces of wood. Allow four stones per tray.

Getting Ready

1. Cut opening about 1 inch by 6 inches (3 by 15 centimeters) at bottom of box for ventilation.

2. Build platform of bricks, blocks or stones on which trays can be stacked.

3. Place sulphur on small piece of paper, roll loosely and twist ends so that end of paper may be lighted.

Sulphur Fruit Out of Doors: Steps in Doing the Job

1. Place fruit on trays. The fruit should be only one layer deep.

2. Stack the trays one on top of the other with a space of 1½ inches (about 4 centimeters) between them. Use strips of wood, piece of bamboo or stones to separate the trays. Fumes of sulphur must be able to circulate freely around the fruit.

3. Place twist of paper containing sulphur in small metal or crockery container.

4. Set the sulphur container by side of the stack of trays and set fire to the twist of paper containing sulphur.

278

Table 7. Condensed Directions for Preparing and Sun Drying Some Fruits and Vegetables

ITEM	Selection and Preparation	Treatment before Drying Method	Time in minutes	Tests for Dryness
FRUITS:				
Apples	Peel and core. Cut into slices or rings about 1/8 inch thick.	Sulfur	60	leathery; glove-like; section cut in half, no moist area in center
Pears	Peel, cut in half lengthwise, and core Section or cut into slices about 1/8 inch thick	Sulfur	(60, sliced) (120 quartered)	Springy feel
Large stone fruits	Peel and slice peaches. Cut in half and pit apricots, nectarines, and large plums and prunes. Fruits dry more rapidly if cut in quarters or sliced.	Sulfur	(60, sliced) (120, quartered)	pliable; leathery; a handful of prunes properly dried will fall apart after squeezing.
Berries (except strawberries)	Pick over; remove defective, wash.	Steam	½ to 1	hard; no visible moisture when crushed.
Cherries	Pick over, remove defective, wash, pit.	No further treatment		leathery but sticky
Figs	If figs are small or have partly dried on the tree, they may be dried whole without blanching. Otherwise, cut in half	Steam	20	leathery; flesh pliable; slightly sticky.
Grapes	Only seedless varieties should be dried Pick over, remove defective.	No further treatment		Pliable; leathery
VEGETABLES:				
Asparagus	Cut tender green tips only	Steam	4 - 5	Brittle, greenish black
Beans-green snap	Remove defective pods. Wash and remove strings from string varieties. Split pods lengthwise, to hasten drying.	Steam	15 - 20	Brittle
Beets	Select small, tender beets of good color and flavor, free from woodiness. wash; trim the tops but leave the crowns; steam for 30-45 mins. until cooked through. Cool; trim off the roots and crowns; peel, Cut slices about 1/8" thick.	No further treatment		tough; leathery
Broccoli	Trim and cut as for serving. Wash. Quarter stalks lengthwise	Steam	8 - 10	Brittle
Cabbage	Remove outer leaves, quarter, and core Cut into shreads about 1/8" thick	Steam	5 - 6 wilt	tough to brittle
Green chili or Peppers	Use full grown pod, bright green Peel and slit pod; remove seeds and dry	No treatment		Crisp, brittle medium green
Red chili or peppers	Use mature pod, dark red. String and hang in sun.	No treatment		Shrunken pod, flexible, dark red
Carrots, turnips rutabagas	Select crisp, tender, free from woodiness. Wash. Trim off roots and tops. Peel thin. Cut into slices or strips about 1/8" thick	Steam	8 - 10	tough; leathery
Corn, cut	Select tender sweet corn. Husk. Steam 10-15 min., or until milk is set. Cut from cob	No further treatment		dry; brittle
Leaves for seasoning; celery; parsley	Wash	No treatment		brittle
Onions, garlic	Remove outer discolored layers. Slice	No treatment		brittle; light colored
Peas	Select young, tender peas of a sweet variety. Shell	steam immediately	10	hard; wrinkled; shatter when hit with a hammer
Potatoes	Peel, cut into shoestring strips 3/16" in cross section, or cut into slices about 1/8" thick.	Rinse in cold water steam	4 - 6	Brittle
Spinach and other greens	Select young, tender leaves. Wash. See that leaves are not wadded when placed on trays. Cut large leaves crosswise into several pieces to facilitate drying	Steam	4, or until thoroughly wilted	Brittle
Squash	Wash, peel, and slice in strips 1/4" thick.	Steam	6	tough to brittle
Squash(Hubbard) Pumpkin, yellow	Cut into strips about 1" wide. Peel off the rind. Scrape off the fiber and seeds. Cut peeled strips crosswise into pieces about 1/8" thick.	Steam	Until tender	tough to brittle
Sweet potatoes	Wash, peel, trim and cut into 1/4" slices (alternate method-steam before peeling).	Steam	Until tender	tough to brittle
Tomatoes for stewing	Select tomatoes of good color. Steam or dip in boiling water to loosen skins. Chill in cold water. peel, Cut into sections, not over 3/4" wide. Cut small pear or plum tomatoes in half.	No further treatment or may sulfur	10 - 20	leathery

---

5. Quickly cover stock of trays and sulphur dish with box. It should cover trays completely. Close opening in box as soon as sulphur is burned to prevent loss of fumes.

6. For length of time fruit should be sulphured see Table 7.

7. Remove cover and place trays to dry.

HOW TO DRY VEGETABLES: Equipment Needed

Collect equipment before gathering vegetables.
1. Knife (for most vegetables).
2. Wooden board for cutting.
3. Pans or pots in which to wash vegetables.
4. Plenty of clean water for thorough washing.
5. Pot or kettle in which to steam vegetables.
6. Lid which fits the pot or kettle in which vegetables are steamed.
7. Equipment for steaming. A rack and basket or a cloth bag and stick.
8. Rack, trays or mats on which the vegetables can be spread to dry.
9. One piece of loosely woven, clean cloth for **each** tray or mat above. These should be slightly larger than the tray or mat on which they are to be used.

Steps in Drying Vegetables.

Steps	How, Why, When
1. Gather vegetables.	Select good quality, firm sound vegetables. Avoid overripe vegetables. Harvest early in the morning or late in the day. Avoid delay between harvesting and processing.
2. Wash vegetables.	Use plenty of clean water. Place vegetables in pan. Pour clean water over vegetables. Wash thoroughly. Scrub if necessary. Lift from water. Empty water from pan. Repeat if necessary.
3. Prepare vegetables.	Follow directions for each vegetable. This may be: Shelling Hulling Peeling Slicing Work rapidly.

4. Steam most vegetables.	Steaming helps to: a. Retain vitamins. b. Retain minerals. c. Give better color and flavor. d. Reduces time needed for soaking before cooking.
5. Spread vegetables on clean dry trays or mats.	One layer in thickness Spread evenly.
6. Cover with loosely woven clean cloth, mosquito netting or wire screen.	To keep insects and dust off food. Fasten cloth down so it will not blow off.
7. Place trays in sun to dry.	a. In direct sunlight. b. Where air can circulate freely. c. Away from dust and dirt. d. Off ground. e. Away from animals and people. f. Protect from storms and dew.
8. Turn food.	Two or three times each day to speed drying.
9. Continue drying.	For several days until 2/3 dry.
10. Test for dryness.	Squeeze handful.
11. Condition vegetables.	In large containers for 8 to 10 days.
12. Put in containers for storage.	Several small containers are better than large ones.
13. Seal containers.	To exclude air. To keep out insects.
14. If food is in bags, place the small bags in a large container.	Seal large container.
15. Store.	In clean, dry, dark, cool place.

HOW TO STEAM VEGETABLES

To steam vegetables they must be suspended in live steam above rapidly boiling water in such a way that the steam reaches all the pieces of the vegetables quickly without the vegetables resting in the water. This means the vegetables must be held loosely and not be allowed to pack. Small amounts of the vegetable pieces need to be steamed at one time to insure the steam reaching all the vegetables and to avoid overcooking some while others remain raw.

Two methods of steaming have been used successfully in different countries. Each method with equipment used is described in the following:

Equipment Needed—Method I

1. A deep container with tight fitting cover. A pot or kettle used for preparing soups, main dish or stew for the family would be fine for this. If it does not have a cover which fits tightly, something should be improvised to serve as a cover and hold the steam inside the kettle. A board could be laid over the opening. The board needs to be large enough to cover the opening completely and hold in the steam. Placing a weight on top will help with this.

2. Rack which can be put in the bottom of this container and used to hold the vegetables up out of the boiling water. It will need to be 1½ to 2 inches (3½-5 centimeters) high and be so constructed that it permits the water to boil freely around or through it. A wooden rack made of slats is often used for this. An equally satisfactory rack can be made of bamboo, or woven of reeds.

3. Container to hold vegetables while being steamed. This must:
(a) Fit inside the steaming pot;
(b) Hold the vegetables loosely,
(c) Be open enough in construction that the steam can reach all parts of the vegetables.
This container can be a colander, wire basket, or reed basket. Improvised baskets can be made of wire fencing, wire screening, weaving materials such as grasses, reeds, or vines. If none of these are available, a second pot could be set on the rack inside the larger pot.

Steps in Steaming Vegetables

Steps	How, Why, When
1. Put rack in bottom of deep container.	As a support for the steaming basket.
2. Put 1 inch (2½ centimeters) of water in deep container and bring to boil.	Put lid on container to hasten boiling.
3. Put layer of prepared vegetables in basket.	Make layer of vegetables thin – not more than 2½ inches (7 centimeters) deep.
4. Place basket on rack in bottom of deep container.	Vegetables should not touch water.
5. Place lid on container.	Lid needs to fit tightly to keep steam in container. Place weight on lid if necessary.

| 6. | Count time as soon as kettle fills with steam. | Minimum time indicated on chart has been found best, except when vegetables are older, have been gathered longer, or were grown under very dry conditions. These vegetables may need longer steaming. |
| 7. | Test to see if vegetables are completely steamed. | Each piece of vegetable must be heated through and wilted. Remove a piece from center of steamer and press it. It should feel tender but not completely cooked. |

Equipment Needed—Method II

1. Deep container with tight fitting lid.
2. Piece of loosely woven, clean cloth in which vegetables can be tied loosely and hung in the container. The size of this will depend on the size of the steaming kettle used. It is important not to crowd the vegetables or the steam will be unable to reach all of them.
3. A piece of wood, stick or bamboo which can be wedged across the kettle near its opening, to which the bag of vegetables can be hung.

Steps in Steaming Vegetables

Steps   *How, Why, When*

1.	Place piece of wood, stick or bamboo in top of deep container	Just far enough below rim edge of container to permit lid to be placed tightly on container.
2.	Put 1 inch ($2\frac{1}{2}$ centimeters) of water in container and bring to boil.	Put lid on container to hasten boiling.
3.	Place vegetables in piece of loosely woven clean cloth.	Vegetables must be very loose in bag.
4.	Tie cloth to form a bag.	Bring opposite corners of cloth together and tie. Repeat with remaining two corners. This knot should be tied far enough from the corners to: (a) Leave ends long enough to tie over stick in top of container. (b) Keep the bottom of the bag from touching the water when the bag is tied on the stick.

5. Tie bag to stick securely.	So that bag of vegetables does not touch water.
6. Place lid on container.	Lid needs to fit tightly to keep steam in container.
7. Count time as soon as container fills with steam.	Minimum time on chart has been found best, except when vegetables are older, have been gathered longer, or were grown under very dry conditions. These vegetables may need longer steaming.
8. Test to see if vegetables are completely steamed.	Remove a piece from center of vegetables and press it. It should be heated through and wilted. It should feel tender but not completely cooked.

Drying Trays

Size

Here are some guides and suggestions to help you select or make your own trays.

1. Since you will need to move the trays after they are loaded they should be no larger than you can handle easily.

2. Under most circumstances a few larger trays will be easier to care for and spread food on than many small trays.

3. Where are you going to place trays so that the sun can reach the food? How large is this space? Will a few large trays rest better here or several smaller trays?

4. What do you already have on hand which can be used for drying trays? It may be better to improvise with something you have in the home now than go to the expense or spend the time to make new ones.

5. Trays of uniform size are easier to stack when you must bring them in at night or out of the rain. It also may make it easier to store them in seasons when you are not using them.

6. A size of trays which has been found to be convenient is 14 by 24 inches. (35 x 60 centimeters)

Shape

Any shape—round, square, rectangular—is satisfactory. Trays of uniform shape can be easily and quickly stacked.

Bottom of Tray

The bottom of the tray needs to have openings to allow passage of air. Air needs to reach all sides of the food for rapid drying. For trays made of wood, allow spaces between slats. If trays are made of reeds or grasses, use an open work weaving pattern. Do not make the bottom of the tray solid.

Side on Trays

Trays with sides on them are better than those without sides because they:
1. Keep foods from sliding off when you move the trays.
2. Make stacking easier.
3. Keep trays from resting on food when you stack them.
4. Provide an edge to which cloth may be fastened.

Materials for Trays

Trays can be made of many materials. Here are a few:
a. Scrap lumber of wooden boxes are sources of wood to use in building trays.
b. Bamboo, or similar wood.
c. Small limbs of tree for frame and vines like honeysuckle woven in between to form drying surface.
d. Frame of wood with thongs of leather woven in to form the rack.
e. Screen wire attached to bottom of wooden frame.
f. Grass or straw matting woven or cut in suitable sizes.

Some Good Places to Dry Fruits and Vegetables

1. On the roof of the house.
2. On an improvised table by the house.
3. On an elevated platform built a few feet above the ground level. Below are suggestions.
   (a) Wooden or bamboo rack.
   (b) Mound of adobe bricks or stones.

Oven Drying Fruits and Vegetables

Apples to turnips
Most food successfully dried in the sun or in a home drier can be dried in an oven.

Home drying doesn't suit lettuce, melons, cucumbers, radishes. Asparagus can be dried, but is not so good as most dried vegetables.
Understand at the start
1. Oven drying is small-scale drying. An oven can take four to eight pounds — preferably six — of a prepared fruit or vegetable at one drying load. It takes most of a day for the load to dry.
2. Oven drying is a *watchman's* job. Never go off and leave food drying in an oven. Gas pressure may change. If trays should catch fire, turn off the heat and close the oven door.
If you buy trays
You can buy trays or make them. Be very sure ready-made trays are right size for your oven. If bought trays have wire surface, cover with cotton netting so food won't stick, and so shredded or tiny pieces won't slip through. Metal trays cannot be used in sulfuring.

Tray making
Materials: soft lumber, nails or corrugated fasteners, coarse curtain netting, string, carpet tacks or thumbtacks.
Work Job: Measure the oven's inside length and width. Make each tray frame with outside dimensions 1½ inches smaller than the oven's inside length and width. This amount of space is needed for air to circulate.

Tack strings diagonally between corners of each frame. Stretch the strings tight and twist where they cross. Stretch a single layer of netting on top of the strings, tightly across the frame, turn in a hem, and tack down on the underside of the frame.

Care of Trays: These trays can be cleaned without taking apart. Just wash the netting with a brush and warm soapy water. Rinse, then dry trays in oven or sun.

Blocks for Tray Stacking: Cut blocks 1¼ by 1¼ by 3 inches. Cut as many as you need. See section on Loading and Stacking.

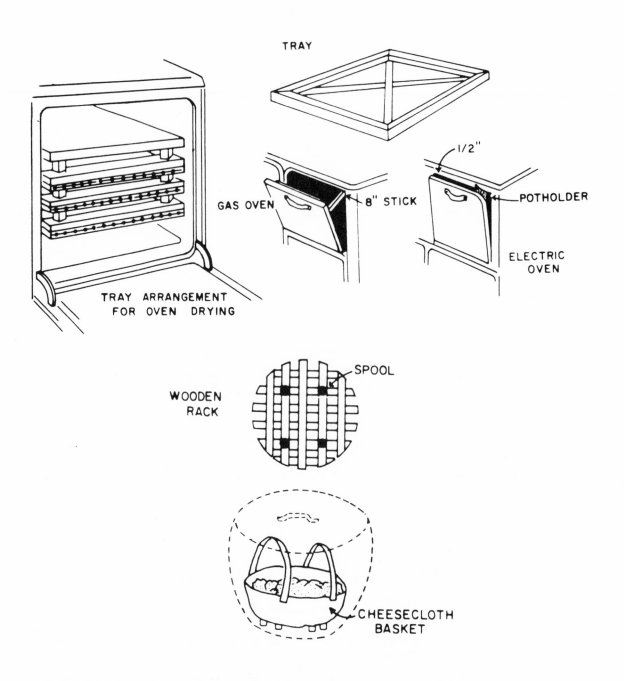

Fig. 32. Top; Equipment for oven drying. Bottom; Equipment for steaming.

286

Thermometer needed

Without a thermometer it is almost impossible to control temperature in oven drying.

Any deep-fat, candy, dairy, or oven thermometer will do, provided it registers below 150° and up to 250° or higher.

Loading and stacking

Spread food evenly, one or two pounds to each tray. The lighter load dries faster. If a gas-oven floor has corners cut out, don't spread food on tray corners — it will scorch.

If you dry different foods at one time, don't include onions, celery, kale, or other foods with strong flavor or odor.

Stack two loaded trays together, using a wood block at each corner, so air can circulate between trays. Place on stack or stack on each oven rack; or, if there is only one rack, use extra blocks and stack three or four layers together.

Number trays "1" to "4" and mark front and back to help keep track of tray positions.

Steam

To steam fruits, use a preserving kettle or any good-sized cooking vessel.

A steamer can be made: Use a kettle with tight-fitting lid and colander, strainer, deep-fat frying basket, or cheesecloth basket resting on a rack of wire or wood. An easy-to-make rack with spool legs is pictured.

To make a cheesecloth basket: Cut a cheesecloth circle about ten inches larger in diameter than your kettle. Run through a small hem a wire not likely to rust. Make the wire rim the right size to go into the kettle easily. Use wire or cord for handles. Then you can lift the handles with a fork.

Drying temperatures for fruits and vegetables

1. Spread in single layers on trays.
2. Usual drying temperature is 150°F. Onions or cabbage require temperature not above 135°F. Open oven door if temperature cannot otherwise be controlled.

Not too hot

Put the thermometer on the top tray. Temperature should stay about 150° F. Prop an electric oven door open by tucking a folded hot pad holder on top corner to make about a half-inch crack. Prop a gas oven door open eight inches at top. The right opening helps control heat and lets out moist air.

If you can't keep the heat down to 150°F., prop the door a little wider; or in a gas range, reduce the flame by turning oven-valve handle toward "off" position. As you turn it, watch lest the flame go out.

Oven-drying arithmetic

The tabulation below gives some idea of the yield of dried food that can be obtained from a peck of a fruit or vegetable, as bought or picked. Weights per peck given below are approximate:

Apples	12 lb. yield 1¼ lb. (3 pt.)
Beans, lima	7 lb. yield 1¼ lb. (2 pt.)
Beans, snap	6 lb. yield ½ lb. (2½ pt., 1-inch pieces)
beets	15 lb. yield 1½ lb. (3-5 pt.)
broccoli	12 lb. yield 1¼-1½ lb. (12-15 pt.)
Carrots	15 lb. yield 1¼ lb. (2-4 pt.)
Corn	18 lb. yield 1¼ lb. (2-4 pt.)

Greens	3 lb. yield ¼ lb. (5½ pt.)
Onions	12 lb. yield 1½ lb. (11½ pt., sliced; 4½ pt. shredded)
Peaches	12 lb. yield 1-1½ lb. (2-3 pt.)
Pears	14 lb. yield 1½ pt. (3 pt., quarters)
Peas	8 lb. yield ¼ lb. (1 pt.)
Pumpkin	11 lb. yield ¼ lb. (5 pt.)
Squash	10 lb. yield ¼ lb. (5 pt.)
Tomatoes	14 lb. yield ½ lb. (2½-3Pt.)

How to Prepare Dried Food For Use

Restoring [Soaking]

Most fruits and vegetables should be covered with cold water and soaked to restore the moisture removed by drying. Usually soaking ½ hour to 2 hours will give an acceptable product, although longer soaking, 2 to 6 hours, may result in increased tenderness.

The food should be kept covered while soaking. The amount of water used for soaking should be as near to that which the food can take up as possible. It is better to add water during the soaking process than to start out with more than is needed.

Cooking

Cook the food in the same water in which it has been soaked because there are some minerals dissolved in the water.

Boil vegetables until tender. Add water for cooking if all the water used in soaking has been absorbed.

Cook greens, cabbage, tomatoes, soup mixtures and powdered vegetables without soaking. Drop them into enough water to cover and cook until tender.

Dried tomatoes, okra, pepper, string beans and corn added to a meat stew or soup make an excellent dish when fresh vegetables are not available in the family garden.

Flavoring

Vegetables on drying lose much of their fresh flavor. Therefore, the addition of such flavoring as basil, garlic, onion or other herbs will be desirable.

Fruits

Usually ¼ cup of sugar per cup of dried fruit is sufficient for dried apples, pears, or peaches. Less sugar is needed for dried than for fresh fruit because in the drying process the starch in the fruit is changed to sugar. When sugar is used it should be added at the end of the cooking period so as not to interfere with the absorption of water by the fruit. Adding a few grains of salt helps to bring out the natural sweetness of the fruit. Lemon, orange, or grapefruit juice added to the dried fruit just before serving will give a fresh fruit flavor and add vitamin C to the dish.

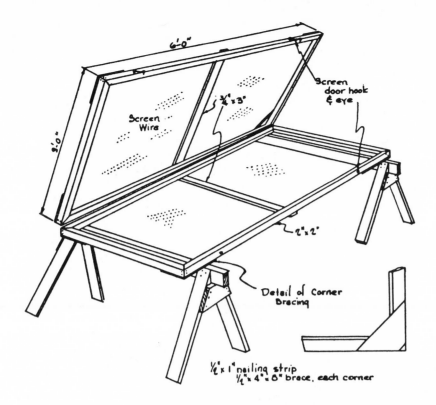

Fig. 33. Combination Sun and Stove Drier for Fruits and Vegetables. Economical drying is obtained by removing trays and placing in sun during favorable weather. Sun drying requires use of cheesecloth or screen wire to keep out insects.

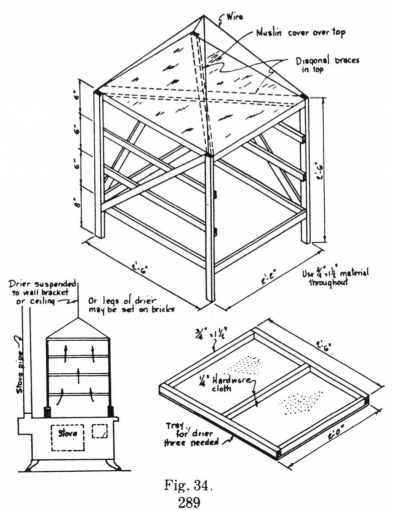

Fig. 34.

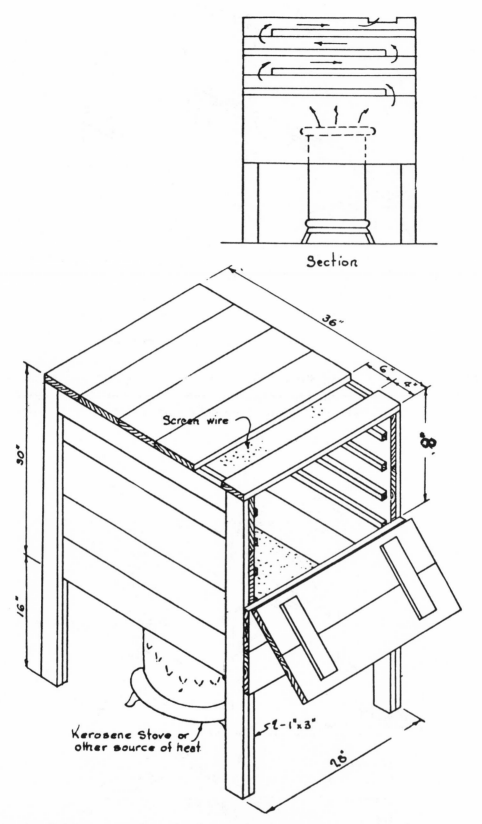

Section

Screen wire

36"

6"
4"

8"

30"

16"

Kerosene Stove or
other source of heat

2-1"x3"

20"

Fig. 35. Cabinet type drier for fruits and vegetables.

This drier is also designed for use with artificial and sun drying. The trays are built to the exact size and specification as for the combination stove and sun drier. The cabinet is 6 inches deeper to allow for staggering the trays from top to bottom to permit better air flow.

290

Bill of Materials for Fruit and Vegetable Driers

Fig. 33. Sun Drier:
4 pcs. 2" x 2" x 6'0"—sides of top and bottom
4 pcs. 2" x 2" x 3'0"—ends of top and bottom
2 pcs. ¾" x 2" x 3'0"—cross braces
8 pcs. ½" x 4" x 0'8"—corner braces
12 feet 36" galv. screen wire—top and bottom; 2-3" butt hinges: 36 lin. feet ½" x 1" nailing strip material; tacks and nails; 2 screen door hooks and eye.

Fig. 34. Combination Sun and Stove Drier
18 ¾" x 1½" x 2'6" legs and side pieces and side of trays
4 ¾" x 1½" x 2'½" bottom and top braces
1 ¾" x 1½" x 14' 0" diagonal braces (cut as needed)
9 ¾" x 1½" ends and braces for trays
30 lin. feet ¼" x 1" stripping for bottom of trays
3 ¼" mesh hardware cloth 2'0" x 2'6" trays
2 lb. 6d finishing nails; 1 lb. 3d common nails; staples

Fig. 35.. Cabinet Type Drier
Approximately 40 sq. ft. of 5/8" plywood
30 lin. feet 1" x 3"—legs and frame work
24 lin. feet 1" x 1"—tray runners
44 lin. feet 1" x 1½"—material for trays
10 feet 24" x ¼" mesh hardware cloth—trays
36" x 36" screening—tacks, nails, etc.

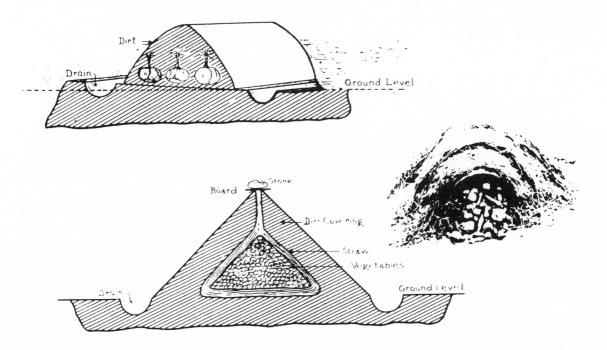

Fig. 36. Top; Cabbages are placed head down in a pit for storage. Bottom; Cone shaped pit shows storage of vegetables. Middle; Straw and soil-covered barrels are adequate for keeping small quantities of vegetables or fruits.

291

TABLE 9.   DRYING TABLE FOR FRUITS AND VEGETABLES

FOOD	PREPARATION FOR DRYING	DRYNESS TEST
Fruits		
Apples	Pare, core, and cut in ¼″ slices or rings. Sulfur outdoors 30 minutes, or dip in solution. Spread not more than ½″ deep on trays—overlap rings.	Pliable, springy feel, creamy white.
Apricots	Same as peaches.	Pliable and leathery.
Berries	No pretreatment. Leave whole, except cut strawberries in half.	No visible moisture when crushed.
Cherries	Remove stems and pits. If juicy, drain about 1 hour.	Leathery but sticky.
Grapes	Leave whole, remove stems. Dip in boiling water to crack skins.	Pliable, dark brown.
Peaches	Peel if desired. Cut in halves, remove pits. Sulfur outdoors—peeled 30 minutes, unpeeled 2 to 3 hours; or dip in solution; or precook. Dry pit side up.	Pliable and leathery.
Pears	Pare and remove core and woody tissue. Cut into ¼″ slices or rings, or into quarters or eighths. Sulfur outdoors 2 to 4 hours, according to size of pieces; or dip in solution; or precook.	Leathery, springy feel.
Prunes	Cut in halves and remove pits or leave whole. Halves: No pretreatment. Whole: To soften and crack skins and to help fruit dry better, hold in steam or boiling water for 2 minutes, or dip in boiling lye bath (3 tablespoons lye to 1 gallon water) for one-half minute.	Pliable and leathery.
Vegetables		
Beans— green, lima	Shell. Steam 15 to 20 minutes, or until tender but firm.	Shatter when hit with a hammer.
Beans, snap	Trim and slice lengthwise or cut in 1-inch pieces. Steam about 20 minutes or until tender but firm. Spread about one-half inch deep on trays.	Brittle, dark green to brownish.
Beets	Trim off all but 1 inch of tops and roots. Steam whole from 30 to 60 minutes depending on size, or until cooked through. Cool and peel. Cut in ¼″ cubes, or slice ⅛″ thick. Spread not more than ¼″ deep on trays.	Brittle, dark red.
Carrots and Parsnips	Scrape or peel. Steam whole about 20 minutes, or until tender but firm. Slice crosswise ⅛″ thick or dice in ¼″ cubes or shred before steaming. Spread not more than ½″ deep on trays.	Very brittle, deep orange.
Corn	Select tender, mature sweet corn. Husk. Steam on the cob 10 to 15 minutes. Cut from cob. No further treatment necessary.	Dry, brittle.
Mushrooms	Peel the larger mushrooms. Dry whole or sliced, depending on size. No precooking necessary. If stems are tender, slice for drying; if tough, discard. Spread not more than ½″ deep on trays.	Leathery to brittle.
Onions	Select mature onions. Remove outer, discolored layers. Slice about ¼″ thick. No further treatment necessary.	Brittle, light colored.
Peas, green	Steam shelled peas 15 minutes, until tender but firm. Stir frequently during the first few hours of drying.	Shatter when hit with a hammer.
Peppers and Pimentos	Cut in ½″ strips or rings. Remove seeds. Steam 10 minutes. Spread rings 2 layers deep—strips not more than 1½″ deep.	Pliable.
Pumpkin and Squash	Quarter, remove seeds and pith, cut in 1″ strips, and peel. Slice strips crosswise, ¼″ thick. Steam 8 to 13 minutes, until slightly soft but not sticky.	Leathery.
Parsley and other Herbs	No precooking is necessary. Hang bunches of whole plant in dry warm place to dry. When dry, crush leaves and remove stems. Store in tightly closed container.	Brittle.

TABLE 10. *Freezing points, recommended storage conditions, and length of storage period of vegetables and fruits.*

Commodity	Freezing point	Storage conditions			Length of storage period
	°F.	Place to store	Temperature	Humidity	
			°F.		
Vegetables:					
Dry beans and peas		Any cool, dry place	32° to 40°	Dry	As long as desired.
Late cabbage	30.4	Pit, trench, or outdoor cellar	Near 32° as possible	Moderately moist.	Through late fall and winter.
Cauliflower	30.3	Storage cellar	do	do	6 to 8 weeks.
Late celery	31.6	Pit or trench; roots in soil in storage cellar.	do	do	Through late fall and winter.
Endive	31.9	Roots in soil in storage cellar	do	do	2 to 3 months.
Onions	30.6	Any cool, dry place	do	Dry	Through fall and winter.
Parsnips	30.4	Where they grew, or in storage cellar.	do	Moist	Do.
Peppers	30.7	Unheated basement or **room**	45° to 50°	Moderately moist.	2 to 3 weeks.
Potatoes	30.9	Pit or in storage cellar	35° to 40°	do	Through fall and winter.
Pumpkins and squashes	30.5	Home cellar or basement	55°	Moderately dry.	Do.
Root crops (miscellaneous).		Pit or in storage cellar	Near 32° as possible	Moist	Do.
Sweetpotatoes	29.7	Home cellar or basement	55° to 60°	Moderately dry.	Do.
Tomatoes (mature green).	31.0	do	55° to 70°	do	4 to 6 weeks.
Fruits:					
Apples	29.0	Fruit storage cellar	Near 32° as possible	Moderately moist.	Through fall and winter.
Grapefruit	29.8	do	do	do	4 to 6 weeks.
Grapes	28.1	do	do	do	1 to 2 months.
Oranges	30.5	do	do	do	4 to 6 weeks.
Pears	29.2	do	do	do	See text.

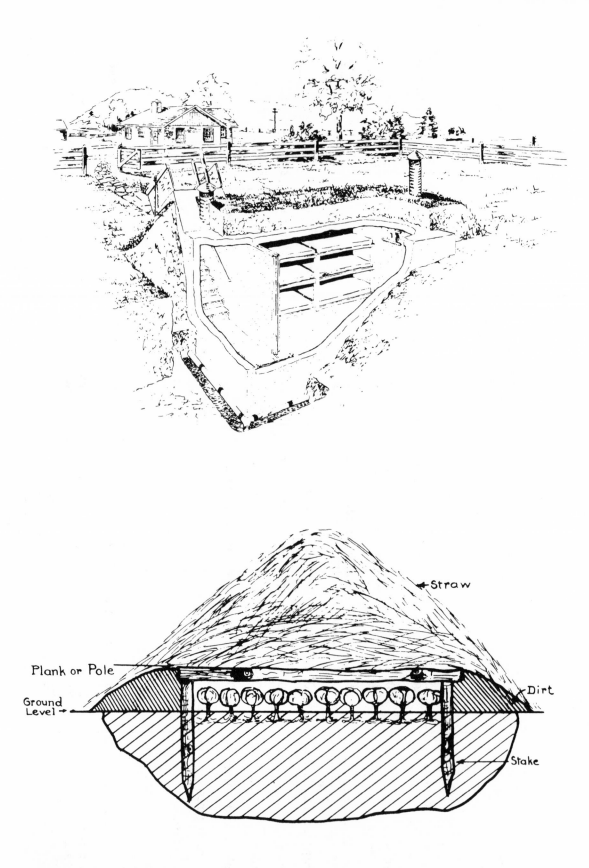

Fig. 37. Top; Underground cellar that can also serve as a fallout shelter. Bottom; Cabbages are stored by placing them upright in a trench framed with stakes and covered by straw.

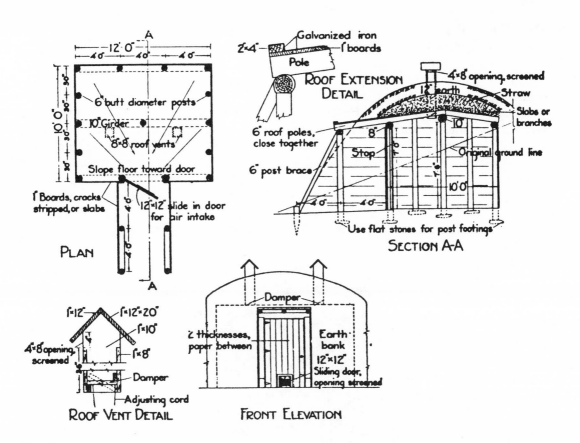

Fig. 38. A 10' x 12' pole and board fruit storage cellar.

295

MEAT PREPARATION
Stunning, Killing and Hide Removal

Cattle

Kill the beef animal as humanely as possible and in a way that will insure thorough drainage of blood. Fasten the animal's head securely in a position that will enable you to stun it with one sharp blow with a mechanical stunner or by shooting. The proper place to strike is at the intersection of two imaginary lines extending from the right horn or edge of poll to the left eye and from the left horn or edge of poll to the right eye (Fig. 39). A sharp blow at this point will immobilize the animal for several minutes. Stunning an animal is preferable to shooting it. After shooting, complete and efficient bleeding is not probable, and the results are bloody cuts, hastened spoilage, and unsightly roasts and steaks.

Fig. 39. Intersection of two lines locates point to stun animal.

As soon as the animal is down, draw a chain securely around the animal's hind legs and hoist it from the ground. The head of the animal should clear the floor by 18 to 24 inches. Grasp the left foreleg of the animal with your left hand and bend the leg back slightly. With the sharp skinning knife in your right hand, make an incision through the hide a little to the right of the middle of the dewlap. Extend the incision from the crease in front of the forelegs to the jawbone in the head.

The next step is to turn the knife over (sharp edge up) and, while holding the knife at a slightly upward angle, insert the point into the prepared incision and push it upward toward the point of the breastbone (Fig. 40). When you reach the breastbone, follow downward with the point of the knife until the blade just slips under the breastbone (Fig. 41) and between the first ribs. Cut straight to the backbone on either side of the gullet, then turn the knife over and downward. This will sever the carotid arteries as they fork just under the point of the

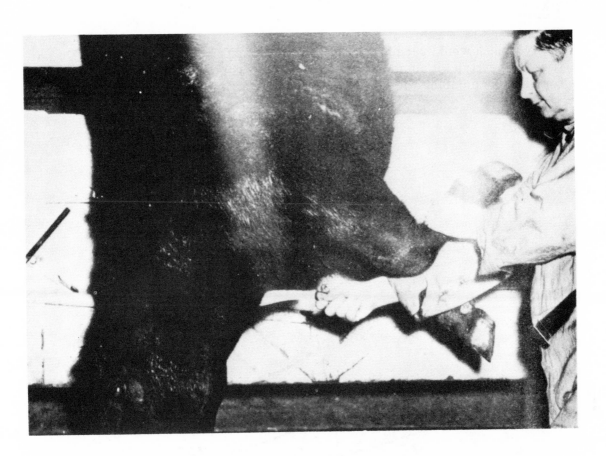

Fig. 40. Opening skin under neck.

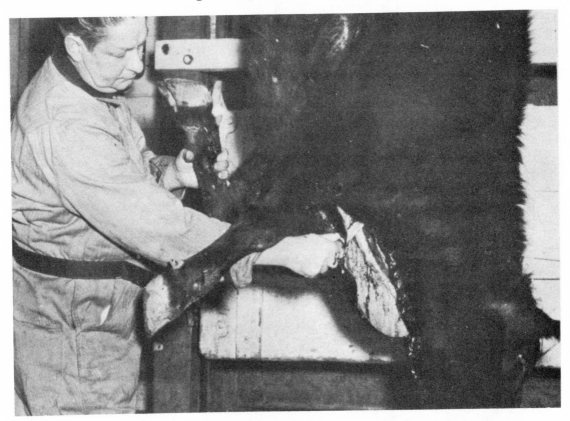

Fig. 41. Inserting knife below breastbone.

297

breastbone. Take care not to stick too deeply and too far back into the chest cavity, which would permit the blood to accumulate in the chest cavity. Do not stick the heart; let it pump out the blood as long as possible. Make bleeding more complete by pumping the forelegs up and down a few times.

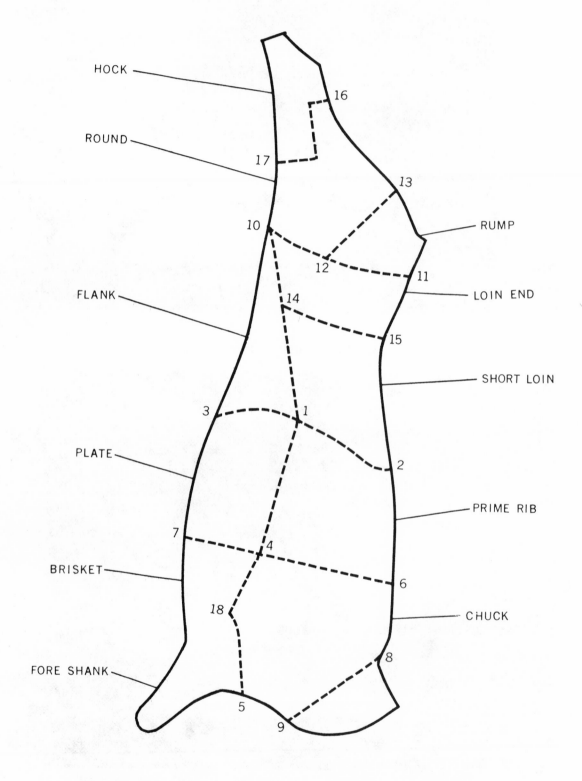

Fig. 42. Side of beef with primary cuts outlined and named.

Hogs

Stun the hog by striking it one sharp blow with a sledge hammer or heavy instrument in the middle of the forehead. The animal can be shot in the same area.

Bleed by severing carotid artery with a 6-7 inch knife (see Fig. 43). Bristles are removed by scalding in 150°F. water and scraped. Entrails are removed after bristles have been removed.

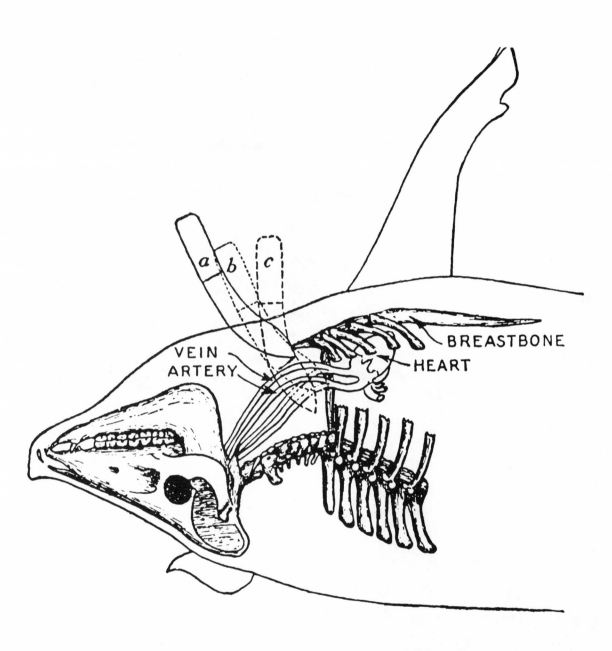

Fig. 43. The three positions of the knife in sticking a hog: a. The knife inserted in the fat; b. The knife above the artery; C. After downward thrust has been made and the artery severed.

Fig. 44. Scalding the hog. Keeping it in motion lessens the danger of setting the hair and works the water into the wrinkles of the skin.

Fig. 45. Left Illustration; Hog hoisting arrangement. Right; Scalding. To make scalding easy, you need plenty of hot water at the right temperature. Here are several suggestions. A galvanized tank, set so a fire can be built under it, is an ideal arrangement. Beside it build a heavy solid table for scraping. Or, there's nothing much better than a big, old bathtub for scalding. Fire can be built under it. It's heavy and lasts indefinitely. It makes it easy to slide the hog in and out. Many farmers use a tight barrel, leaned at a 45° angle, at one end of a scraping table. Water can be heated in a large kettle or old wash boiler and emptied into the barrel. A little lye or wood ashes added to the water makes scraping easier. The water should be heated to around 150°.

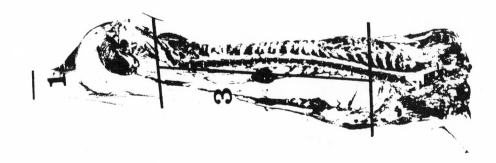

Fig. 46. Hog Carcass. Cut or slice the ham (1), loin (2), and shoulder (4) into roasts, steaks, or chops. Trim the thin bacon strip (3) for curing, or cut into boiling pieces. Trim all meat closely, using lean for sausage and fat for lard.

Sheep

   A sharp blow on top of the poll will stun sheep that do not have horns. A blow with a heavy hammer is sometimes necessary for horned sheep. Place stunned sheep on a table or platform. Grasp jaw with the left hand, insert the knife behind the jaw, blade-edge outward, and draw the knife out through the pelt across the throat area. This will cut the main artery and allow bleeding. Fleece is removed by skinning.

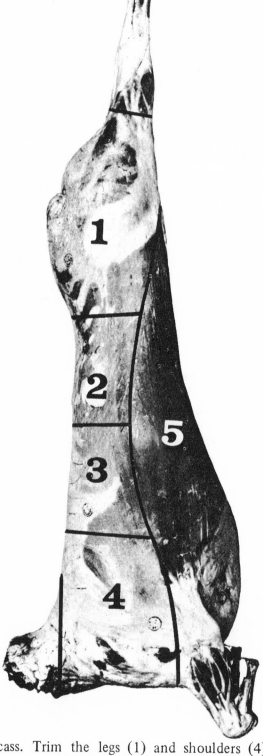

Fig. 47. Lamb Carcass. Trim the legs (1) and shoulders (4) into uniform sized roasts; cut rib (3) and loin (2) into chops; bone breast (5) shanks and neck for stew or ground lamb.

Approximate yields of trimmed beef cuts from animal having a live weight of 750 pounds and a carcass weight of 420 pounds

Trimmed cuts	Yield	Live weight	Carcass weight
	Pounds	*Percent*	*Percent*
Steaks and oven roasts	172	23	40
Pot roasts	83	11	20
Stew and ground meat	83	11	20
Total	338	45	80

Approximate yields of trimmed beef cuts from dressed forequarters weighing 218 pounds

Trimmed cuts	Yield	Weight of forequarters
	Pounds	*Percent*
Steaks and oven roasts	55	25
Pot roasts	70	32
Stew and ground meat	59	37
Total	184	84

Approximate yields of trimmed beef cuts from dressed hindquarters weighing 202 pounds

Trimmed cuts	Yield	Weight of hindquarters
	Pounds	*Percent*
Steaks and oven roasts	117	58
Stew, ground meat, and pot roasts	37	18
Total	154	76

Approximate trimmed pork cuts from a hog having a live weight of 225 pounds and a carcass weight of 176 pounds

Trimmed cuts	Yield	Live weight	Carcass weight
	Pounds	*Percent*	*Percent*
Fresh hams, shoulders, bacon, jowls	90	40	50
Loins, ribs, sausage	34	15	20
Total	124	55	70
Lard, rendered	12	15	27

Yields of trimmed lamb cuts from a lamb having a live weight of 85 pounds and a carcass weight of 41 pounds

Trimmed cuts	Yield	Live weight	Carcass weight
	Pounds	*Percent*	*Percent*
Legs, chops, shoulders	31	37	75
Breast and stew	7	8	15
Total	38	45	90

Table 11. Meat Yields from Livestock Carcasses. All trimmed meat cut yields are figured after surplus fat and bone have been removed from carcasses.

Table 12:

The recommended storage periods for home-frozen meats and fish held at 0° F. are given below. For best quality, use the shorter storage time.

Product	Storage period (months)	Product	Storage period (months)
Beef:		Pork, cured:	
Ground meat	2 to 3	Bacon	Less than 1
Roasts	8 to 12	Ham	1 to 2
Steaks	8 to 12	Pork, fresh:	
Stew meat	2 to 3	Chops	3 to 4
Fish	6 to 9	Roasts	4 to 8
Lamb:		Sausage	1 to 2
Chops	3 to 4	Veal:	
Ground meat	2 to 3	Cutlets, chops	3 to 4
Roasts	8 to 12	Ground meat	2 to 3
Stew meat	2 to 3	Roasts	4 to 8
		Organ meats	3 to 4

[1] Frozen cured meat loses quality quickly and should be used as soon as possible.

Part VIII
SELF-HELP ENGINEERING

HAND GRINDER

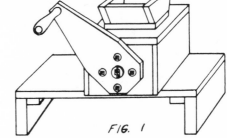

FIG. 1

Tools and Materials

Tools
Hammer
Hand cross cut saw
Auger brace and 1/4, 1/2 and 7/8
   inch auger bits.
Round file
Coping saw or key hole saw
Breast drill and 1/8" twist drill
One flat file
One three corner file
1/2" x 13" die and die handle
5/16" die
Wood chisel
Half round wood file
Tin shears
Screw driver

Materials
12 feet of 1" x 6" seasoned sheathing lumber
2 feet 1" x 10" sheathing lumber
2 feet 2" x 8" framing lumber
3 feet 2" x 4" framing lumber
1 piece 1/2" x 14" cold rolled steel
12 - 1 1/2" x 8" flat head wood
   screws
3 - 1/2" steel washers
4 - 1" x 4" carriage bolts
1 - 1/2" wing nut
1 - 3/8" x 5" carriage bolt
2 cast iron burrs.

Details

Through the following discussion 1" lumber refers to the standard board thickness for surfaced sheathing lumber in the United States. It actually measures only about three quarters of an inch in thickness. All dimensions are in inches. Lumber used should be flat and well seasoned. The numbers in the next section refer to part numbers shown in Figure 2 and subsequent detailed part sketches.

1. Grinder Body: make of 1" x 6" pine or hard wood lumber. Circular hole can be cut with coping saw or jig saw but for a better and quicker way to cut see Notes 1 and 2, Figures 3 and 4.

2. Rotor: See Note 2. Take care to bore the ½" holes thru each part where required accurately and at right angles to the surface of the part. If when placed on the assembly post, it does not lie flat to the assembly post surface marked "A" in Figure 3 or against an adjacent part because the hole is not bored straight, remove it from the assembly post and use a round file in the hole carefully until it will lie flat. Use a few spots of glue between parts. Be careful in nailing so nails will not interfere with boring the ¼" holes later. Keep the nails within 1" of the center post. 1½" finishing nails are about right.

It is a help in getting the metal band snugly on the rotor drum to form the 3/8" lip on one end first, then bend the band around some round object that is about 3" in diameter. Next put it on the rotor drum with the one lip engaged in the slot. Use strong twine or flexible wire to pull band snugly around drum and mark position of the second lip. Remove from rotor, form the second lip and cut off excess. The band may need to be formed a little with the fingers. It should now fit snugly.

305

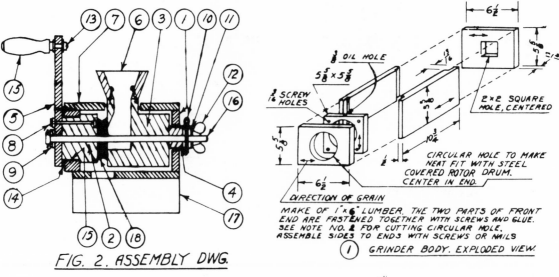

FIG. 2. ASSEMBLY DWG.

① GRINDER BODY. EXPLODED VIEW.

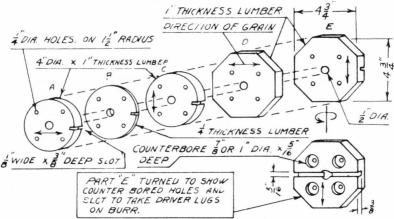

② EXPLODED VIEW OF ROTOR

3. Stationary Burr Holder: In boring ½" holes and assembling follow the instructions given under (2). Assemble the parts using a few spots of glue and nails. 1½" finishing nails are about right.

4. Follow instructions under (2) Rotor for assembling parts of the thrust block.

5. The ¼" holes can best be located by placing the rotor and crank all on the assemply post. With bolts in place thru rotor, mark location for holes on crank by tapping with a hammer. Oil hole in the crank is bored to reach the ½" hole. This will supply oil to the steel shaft.

6. Attach hopper to top of stationary burr holder with screws. See Figure 2.

7. Cover

8. Four ¼" x 4½" carriage bolts with nuts and 8 washers.

9. Two steel washers for ½" diameter bolts.

10. Two 1/8" diameter x 2" cotter key. If a larger diameter cotter key is used, drill the hole to suit. The hole should not in any case be more than 5/32".

11. Three steel washers for ½" bolt.

12. One ½" winged nut.

13. One 5/16" diameter carriage bolt threaded 1½". File square shank under head to roundness. Length 4½".

14. Clearance Block—The purpose of the clearance block is to keep the crank

306

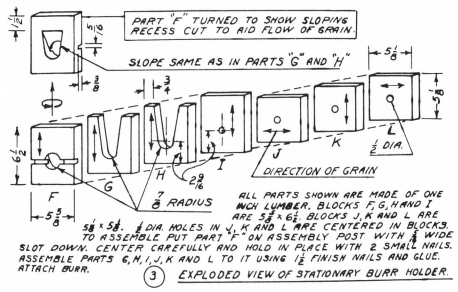

PART "F" TURNED TO SHOW SLOPING RECESS CUT TO AID FLOW OF GRAIN.

SLOPE SAME AS IN PARTS "G" AND "H"

DIRECTION OF GRAIN

$\frac{7}{8}$ RADIUS

ALL PARTS SHOWN ARE MADE OF ONE INCH LUMBER. BLOCKS F, G, H AND I ARE $5\frac{5}{8}$ × $6\frac{1}{2}$. BLOCKS J, K AND L ARE $5\frac{1}{8}$ × $5\frac{1}{8}$. $\frac{1}{2}$ DIA. HOLES IN J, K AND L ARE CENTERED IN BLOCKS. TO ASSEMBLE PUT PART "F" ON ASSEMBLY POST WITH $\frac{3}{4}$ WIDE SLOT DOWN. CENTER CAREFULLY AND HOLD IN PLACE WITH 2 SMALL NAILS. ASSEMBLE PARTS G, H, I, J, K AND L TO IT USING $1\frac{1}{2}$ FINISH NAILS AND GLUE. ATTACH BURR.

③ EXPLODED VIEW OF STATIONARY BURR HOLDER.

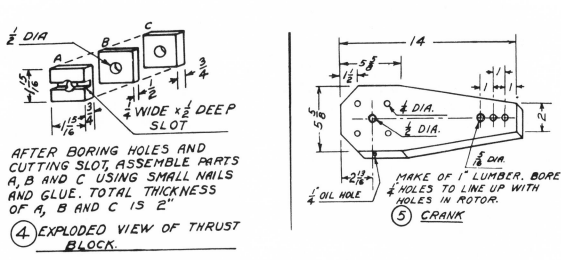

AFTER BORING HOLES AND CUTTING SLOT, ASSEMBLE PARTS A, B AND C USING SMALL NAILS AND GLUE. TOTAL THICKNESS OF A, B AND C IS 2"

④ EXPLODED VIEW OF THRUST BLOCK.

MAKE OF 1" LUMBER. BORE $\frac{1}{4}$ HOLES TO LINE UP WITH HOLES IN ROTOR.

⑤ CRANK

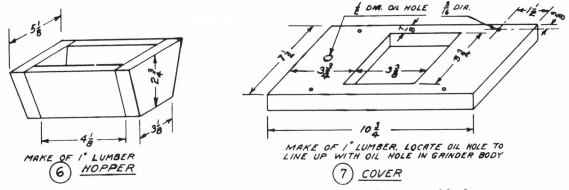

MAKE OF 1" LUMBER
⑥ HOPPER

MAKE OF 1" LUMBER. LOCATE OIL HOLE TO LINE UP WITH OIL HOLE IN GRINDER BODY

⑦ COVER

from rubbing the front of the grinder. Locate the clearance blocks at even quarters around circular opening in front of grinder body.

15. Rotor Drum Band—In making this part and attaching it to rotor read the discussion under Rotor (2).

16. Steel Shaft—Threading is U.S. standard, $\frac{1}{2}$" x 13 threads per inch.

17. Grinder Stand.

18. Two cast iron burrs. See materials.

Final Assembling

After all parts are completed the next step is to fully assemble the mill. The rotor with burr attached is placed in its position in the circular opening. Attach the crank. Next put the stationary burr holder in position and insert the steel shaft thru both parts. Put the thrust block in place, insert the cotter key, put on the thrust block in place, insert the cotter key, put on steel washer and run up the winged nut. In making the final adjustment it may be necessary to add one or more steel washers between thrust block and burr holder or to shorten the thrust block. When the winged nut is tight, there should be little play between the cotter key and the bottom of the slot in thrust block.

Before putting on the cover turn the rotor and observe the burrs carefully. They should remain flat to each other when rotor is turned. If there is an opening which travels around as the rotor turns, a shim is needed under the burr on the rotor. Mark the place and note thickness of shim required. If the opening remains stationary a shim is needed under the burr on the burr holder. Remove the necessary part and add a shim. Of course, both burrs may need shims. A little glue under the shims makes a permanent job.

Notes:

The purpose of the following is to facilitate and speed up the job of making the mills. It is assumed the mills will be made in a carpenter shop as a business. The notes along with Figures 3 and 4 describe two devices that will be found very useful in shops making these mills.

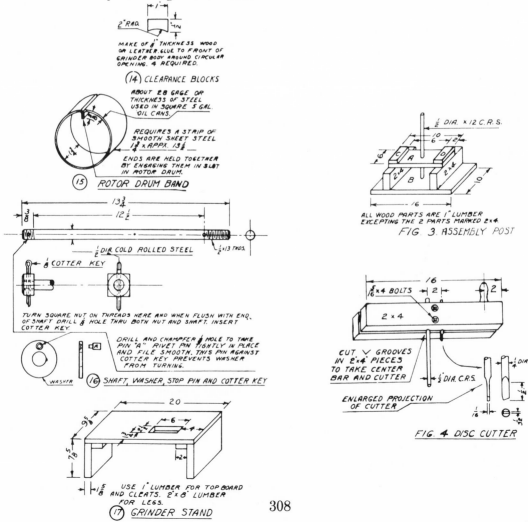

308

Note 1: See Figure 3. Use of the assembly post is described under (2) and (3). In constructing the assembly post, care should be taken to make it very solid and strong and the steel post must be square with the surface marked "A" in Figure 3. A good way is to build the entire wood part of the device "C" and "D" before boring the holes for the steel post. When ready to bore these holes, bore thru "A" first, then push the bar thru to "B" and testing carefully with a square move top of bar until it tests square both ways then strike the bar on its top end to mark position of the auger hole in "B". Last, put on "C" and "D".

Note 2: See Figure 4. The purpose of this device is to cut the curcular discs out of the end boards of the grinder body. Test each on the assembly post to be sure the holes are square thru these members. Use a round file if the member does not lay flat on 'A' of the assembly post. Place the pieces one at a time on the rod of the disc cutter. Remove the steel rod from the assembly post and pass the steel rod of the disc cutter thru both holes of the assembly device. The assembly device with disc cutter in place should now be held in a bench vise or fastened to a wall so the shaft is horizontal and at a convenient height for turning. Turn the crank and exert a gentle pressure to bring the cutter into play.

The steel cutter should be of tool steel. A six inch length of drill rod is excellent. If this is not available, a screw driver with approximately a ¼" diameter shank can be shaped up with a file to do the job. In operating the disc cutter cut only half way thru the member then reverse and complete from other side.

For greater strength the cutter can be made more than 1/16" in thickness. This will make the discs that compose the rotor drum fit too loosely even after the steel band is on but the difficulty is easily corrected by giving the drum several turns of heavy wrapping paper before the steel band is applied. The paper should be glued to the drum.

SEED CLEANING SIEVES

Abstract

The set of sieves described here will clean your crop seeds effectively, which is an important step for improved crop production.

Tools and Materials

12—boards: 2½ x 5 x 46 cm. (1" x 2" x 18")
12—wood strips:1 x 2½ x 43½ cm.(¼" x 1" x 17")
1—46 cm (18 in.) square of ¼" galvanized screen.
1—same but 3/16" screen
1—same but 1/8" screen
Hammer, saw, nails.

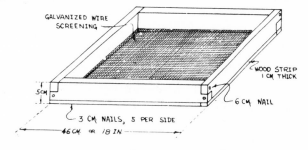

Details

Fig. 5—Seed Cleaning Sieve

The exact size of these sieves is not important, but 1/8" , 3/16" and 1/4" mesh make convenient sizes for cleaning wheat, barley, corn and seeds of similar size. Grading consists of removing the small, weak seeds which will produce small weak plants or will not grow at all. Less seed can be planted per acre, if it is properly cleaned and graded, and still produce a good crop.

BUCKET SPRAYER

This simple sprayer works on the same principle as the inertia pump, and it is designed so that local shops can make it. Two people operate it; one sprays while the other pumps.

Tools and materials

Galvanized iron 30 cm x 30 cm
    plus 10 cm x 20 cm
Barrel metal 10 cm x 20 cm
1/4" hose (high pressure) 4 m.
1/4" pipe (truck brake line may
    be used) 50 cm
Wood for handle 2 cm x 15 cm
    x 30 cm.
3/4" galvanized iron pipe (thin-
    wall) 120 cm long
4 mm wire-20 cm
Truck inner tube material 10 cm
    x 20 cm
1 mm galvanized wire 30 cm
4 - 3/16" bolts 1 cm long
2 - 3/16" bolts 3 1/2 cm long

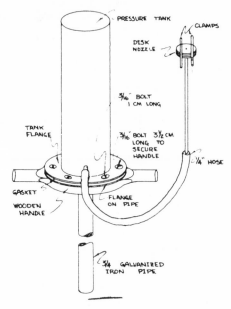

Fig. 6

Details

The bucket sprayer described here has been designed primarily to meet the need for a sprayer which can be built in an area where production facilities are limited. This sprayer can be made by the local artisans. It is intended only for water solutions of insecticides or fungicides.

The sprayer pump is of the inertia type which consists of a ¾" iron pipe with the top plugged and a simple valve located 8 cm. from the top. The valve is a piece of truck inner tube rubber wrapped around the pipe and held in place by wire. One corner of the rubber is over a hole in the pipe. Some careful adjustment is necessary when placing the rubber to make sure it works properly and does not leak.

The pressure tank encloses the valve assembly and, as the liquid is pumped into the tank, builds up pressure sufficient to operate the simple disk type spray nozzle. The tank is built so that it can be removed in order to service the valve.

The length of the hose can be determined by the maker of the sprayer but should be about 4 meters to allow the man doing the spraying to cover quite a large area before having to move the bucket. Also, the length of the small pipe and the angle of the spray nozzle will be determined by the kind of crops being sprayed.

At times it will be necessary to "prime" the sprayer pump. This is caused by two things. Either the valve rubber is too tight and the air cannot be forced through the valve, or the rubber is stuck to the pipe. To prime the pump turn it up-side-down and fill the pipe with water. Holding the thumb over the pipe, turn

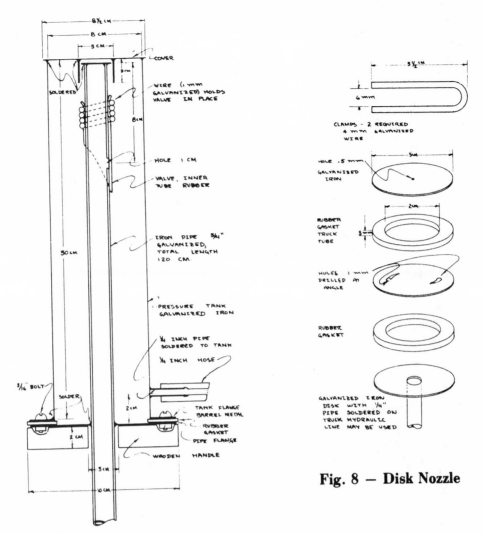

Fig. 8 — Disk Nozzle

Fig. 7 — Pump Cross Section

the pump over and lower it into the bucket of liquid and start pumping in the usual manner. If priming does not start the pump it will then be necessary to remove the pressure tank to inspect and repair the valve.

Only very clean water should be used to make the mixture for spraying and it should be strained through a cloth after mixing to remove any particles which might cause the nozzle to plug. If a very fine brass screen is available, it should be put in the nozzle to keep the dirt from plugging the holes.

GRAIN CLEANER

Abstract

This device removes round seeds from wheat. Sieved grain poured slowly down the chute collects at the base of the inclined platform while round seeds, rolling faster, fall over the far side.

Tools and Material

```
1 - 70 x 70 cm. galvanized       1 - 2 x 8 x 30 cm.
    iron                             wood
1 - 24 x 140 cm. galvanized      1 - 2 x 8 x 34 cm.
    iron                             wood
4 - 2 x 4 x 68 cm. wood          Hammer, saw, nails.
1 - 2 x 4 x 25 cm. wood
1 - 2 x 8 x 80 cm.
    wood
```

311

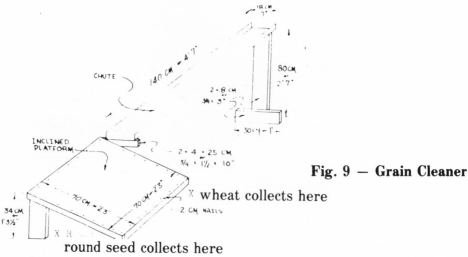

Fig. 9 — Grain Cleaner

wheat collects here

round seed collects here

DRAG GRADER

Tools and Materials

```
3" x 12" lumber
  2 pieces 8' long
  1 piece  5' long
  2 pieces 1' long
3" x 6" lumber
  1 piece 4 1/2' long
4 metal edges 1/4" to 1/2"
  thick, 4" wide, 8' long.
17 lag screws 7" long,
  5/8" diameter.
2 eye bolts, 3" diameter
  eye large washers
12 feet heavy chain
32 woodscrews, 3" flat-
  head steel.
```

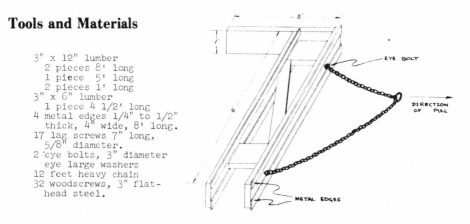

Fig. 10. Drag Grader

Details

The angle between the 5' and 8' beams should be made 30° if ditch cleaning is anticipated. The unit can be scaled down for use with one animal. The metal edge overhangs the surfaces of the 8' beam by one inch. Each is screwed on with eight large woodscrews or carriage bolts.

The position of the scraper is adjusted by changing the hitching point on the chain. The metal edges are attached to both top and bottom so the drag can be turned over to reverse the direction in which material is cast.

LIVESTOCK EQUIPMENT

Chicken Brooder

This brooder is sufficient size for 200 chicks, and is hinged for easy access to corral and brooder. Dimensions are shown in meters.

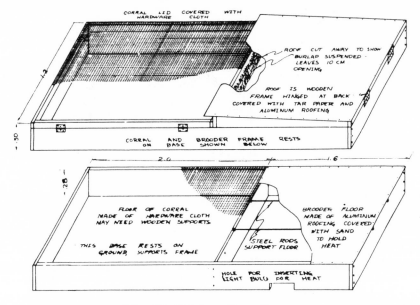

Fig. 11 Chicken Brooder

TOOLS AND MATERIALS

Hardware cloth 1.2 x 2 m., 2 pieces this size needed.
Aluminum roofing - 1.2 m. x 1.6 m., 1.2 m. x 1.7 m.
Wood, approximately 30 cm x 2 cm x 20 m..
Steel rod 1 cm diameter x 3.2 m.
4 hinges about 8 cm long
Woodscrews for hinges
2 buckets clean dry sand
Nails, tacks, staples
Small tools

Details

This chick brooder is heated by a regular electric light bulb, placed under the brooder floor. Sand placed on the floor of the brooder holds and distributes the heat, and helps keep the area clean and dry. Depending on the temperature rise required, the wattage of the light bulb will have to be chosen by experimentation. The metal floor and roof prevent predators such as rats from entering the brooder. If electric power is not available, an excavation can be made for a lantern. Be sure the lantern has adequate ventilation.

Evaluation

This type of brooder has been used successfully in Ecuador and other places by the indigenous people to raise broilers for a cash crop.

313

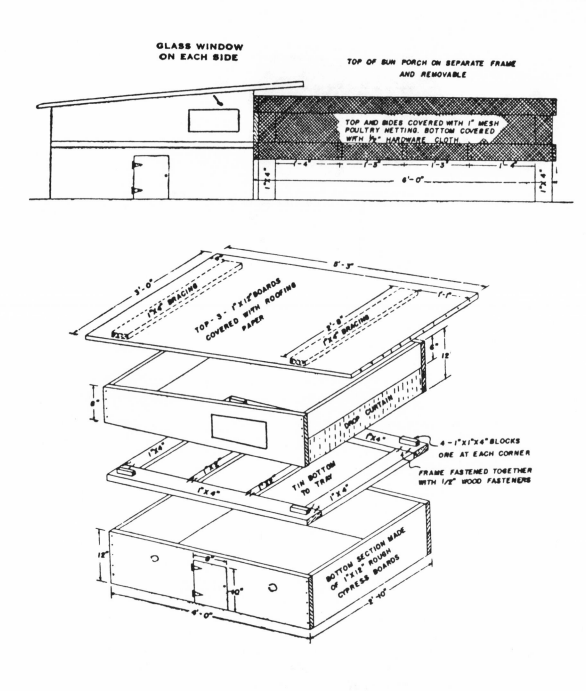

Fig. 12. Homemade lamp brooder for 75 to 100 chicks.

The brooder is heated with an ordinary low type kitchen lamp. (The type of lamp is usually fastened on the wall.) In placing the lamp, care should be taken so as to allow about 1 inch space between the top of the lamp chimney and the floor of the top section. during extreme cold spells it will probably be necessary to use two lamps in heating the brooder. The bottom of the brooder is covered with tin. The tin that is nailed to the frame should come next to the lamp.

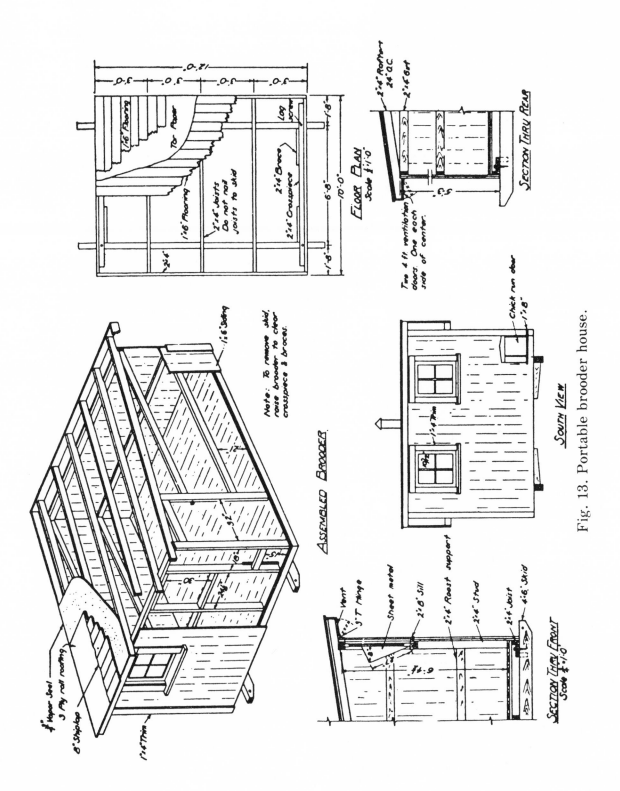

Fig. 13. Portable brooder house.

315

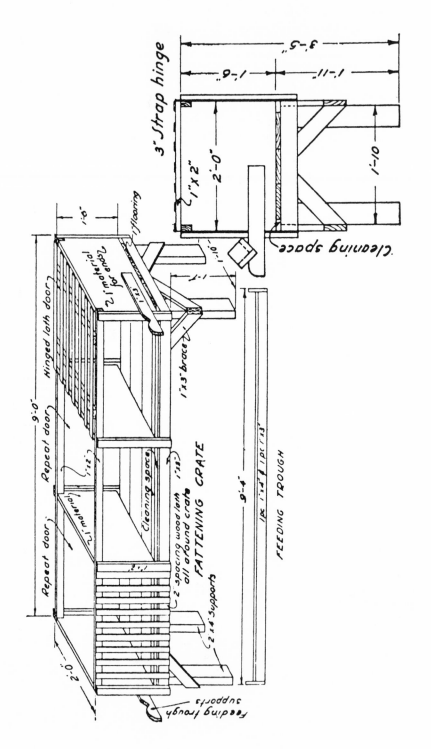

Fig. 14. Top: Fattening crate. Bottom: End view fattening crate. This coop may be constructed as a single compartment battery or multiple batteries.

316

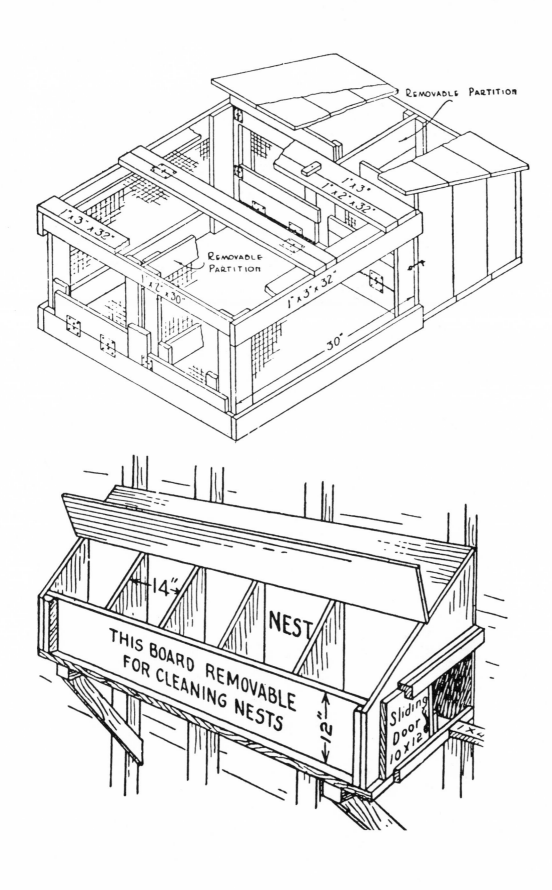

Fig. 15. Top: A portable, inexpensive coop for hen hatching. Bottom: A battery of simple practical nests.

317

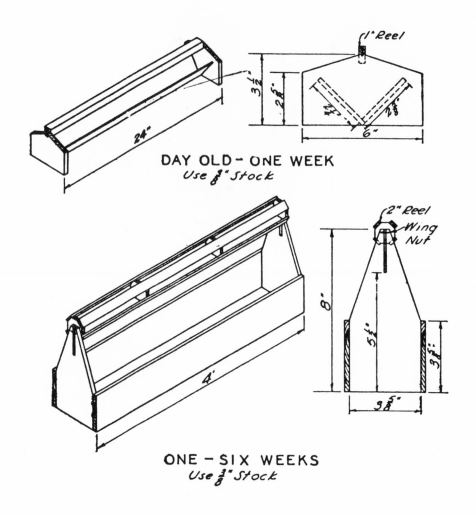

DAY OLD - ONE WEEK
Use ⅜" Stock

ONE - SIX WEEKS
Use ⅜" Stock

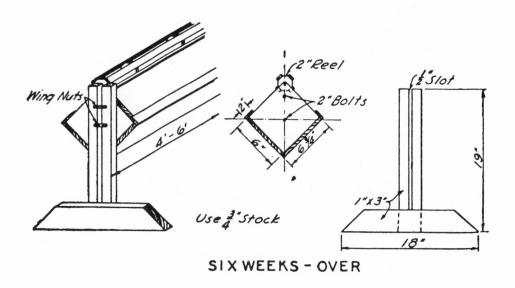

SIX WEEKS - OVER

Fig. 16. Feed hopper equipment for chicks.

318

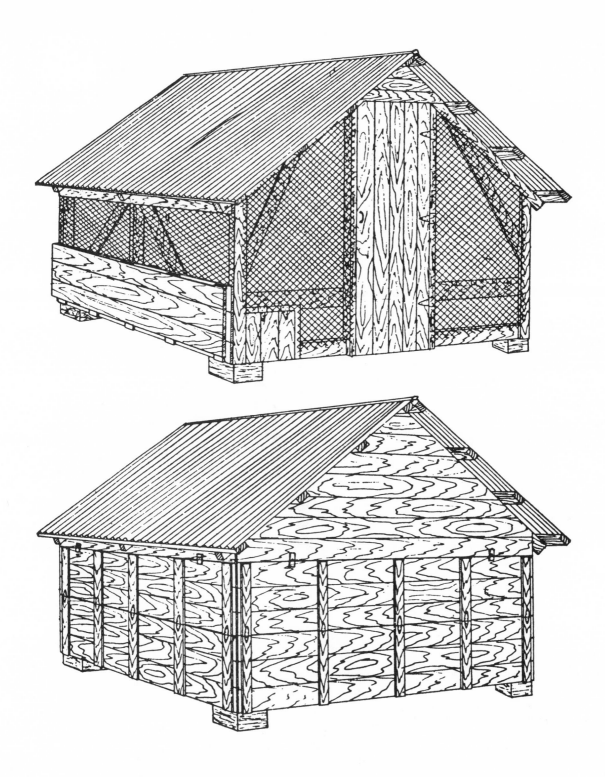

Fig. 17. A convertible poultry shelter house.

The shelter house illustrated above is so planned that it can be used with open sides and ends for hot weather, or it can be enclosed as is shown, for early pullets. And, by further enclosing the front end, it can be pressed into service as a brooder house. The lower illustration shows one end and two sides closed for early season use on the range. If the house is used for brooding, the front end could also be enclosed.

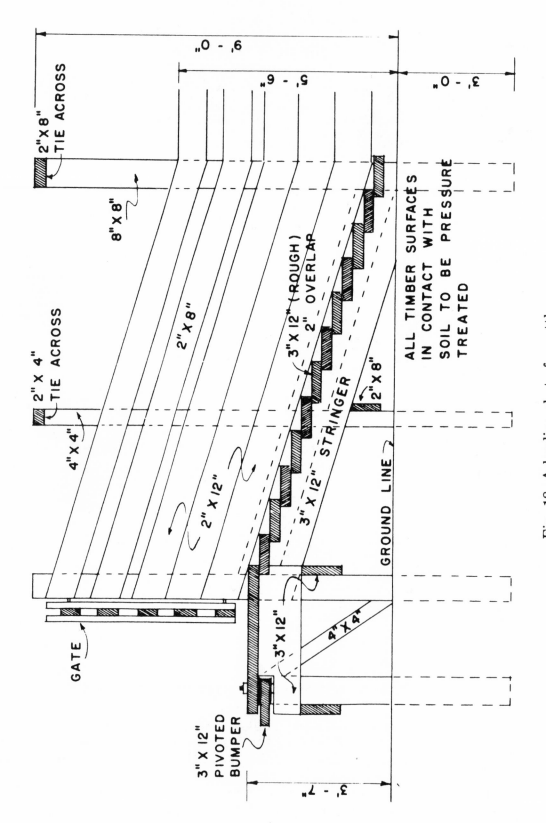

2" x 8"
TIE ACROSS

9' - 0"

5' - 6"

3' - 0"

8" x 8"

2" x 8"

3" x 12" (ROUGH)
2" OVERLAP

ALL TIMBER SURFACES
IN CONTACT WITH
SOIL TO BE PRESSURE
TREATED

2" x 4"
TIE ACROSS

4" x 4"

2" x 12"

3" x 12" STRINGER

2" x 8"

GROUND LINE

GATE

3" x 12"

4" x 4"

3" x 12"
PIVOTED
BUMPER

3' - 7"

Fig. 18. A loading chute for cattle.

320

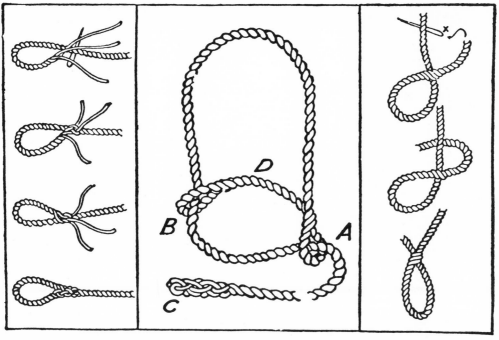

Steps in making eye splice B	Completed halter. A, eye splice; B, loop splice; C, crown knot; D, nose piece	Steps in making loop splice A

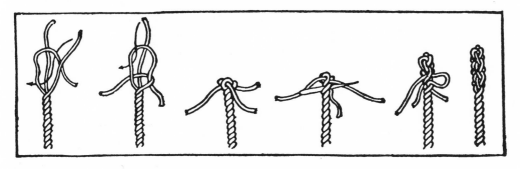

Steps in making crown knot, C

Fig. 19. A completed rope halter, and steps showing method of making.

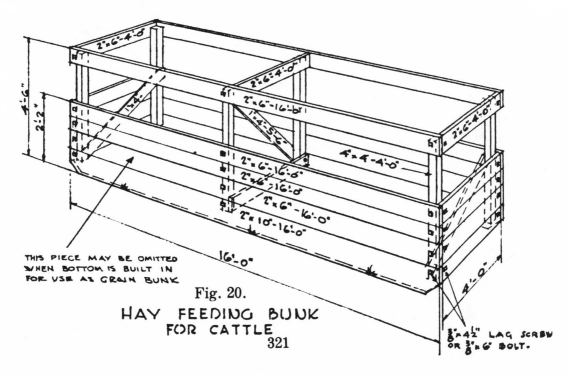

THIS PIECE MAY BE OMITTED WHEN BOTTOM IS BUILT IN FOR USE AS GRAIN BUNK

Fig. 20.
HAY FEEDING BUNK
FOR CATTLE

321

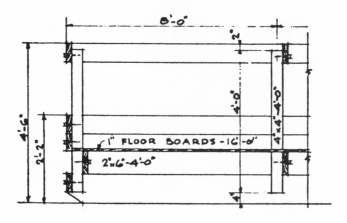

GRAIN & SILAGE FEEDING BUNK.
FOR CATTLE

CONSTRUCTION OF GRAIN & SILAGE FEEDING BUNK
SAME AS HAY FEEDING BUNK WITH FLOOR ADDED.

(con'd.) Fig. 20. Hay, grain and silage feeding bunk.

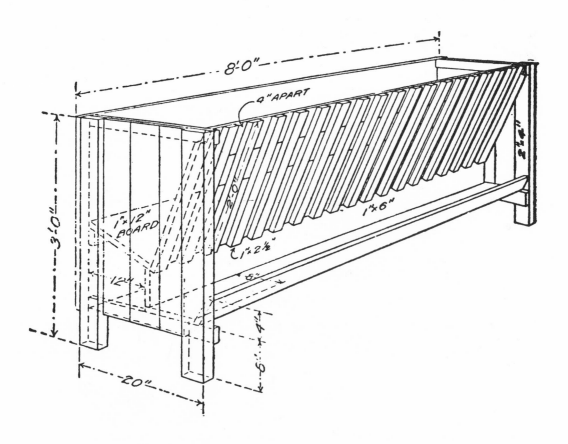

Fig. 21. A stationary or wall hay and grain rack for goats.

322

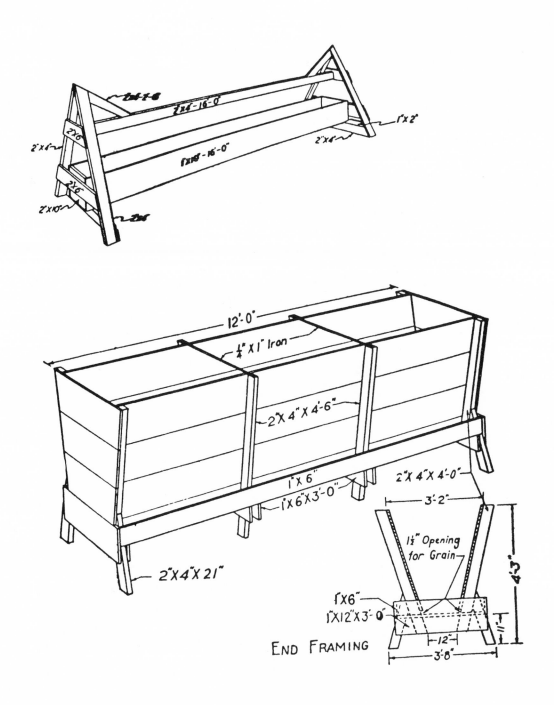

Fig. 22. Top: A simple grain feeder for goats. Bottom: A self feeder for grain.

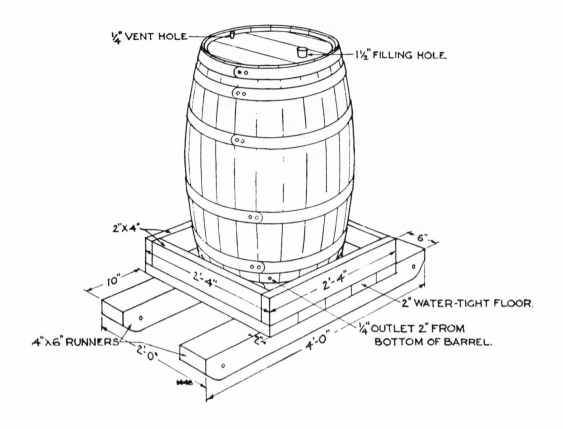

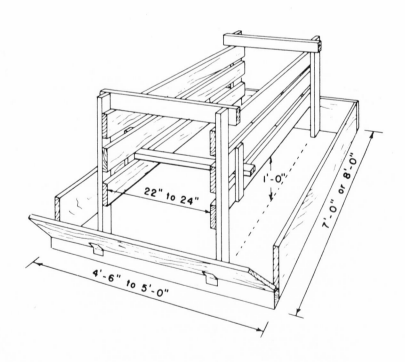

Fig. 23. Top: A waterer for swine (metal or wood barrel). Bottom: A swine
farrowing stall.

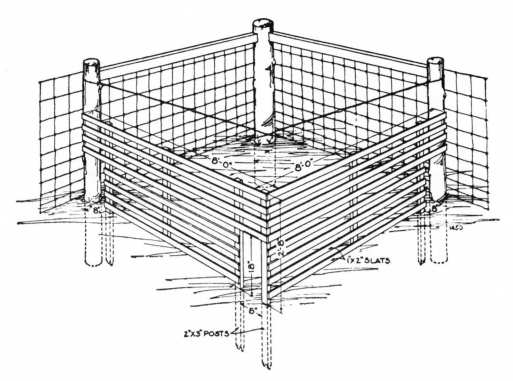

Fig. 24. Creep feeder for young pigs.

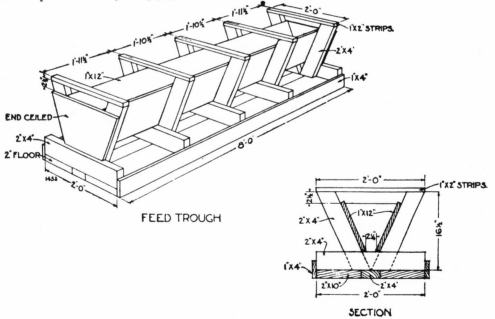

FEED TROUGH

SECTION

Fig. 25. Flat bottomed feed trough.

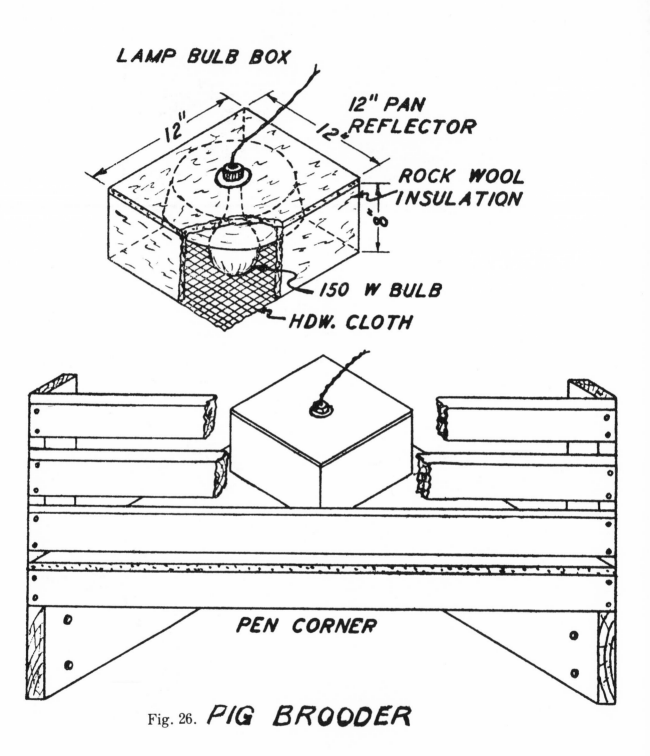

LAMP BULB BOX

12" PAN REFLECTOR

12"

12"

ROCK WOOL INSULATION

8"

150 W BULB

HDW. CLOTH

PEN CORNER

Fig. 26. *PIG BROODER*

Fig. 27. *LAMB BROODER*

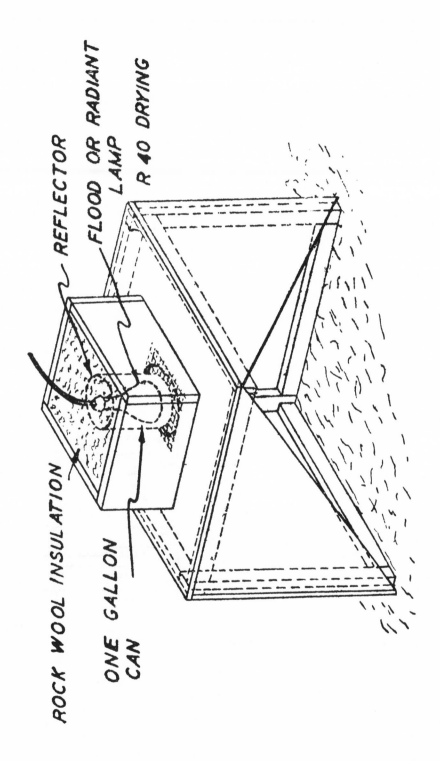

REFLECTOR

FLOOD OR RADIANT LAMP

R 40 DRYING

ROCK WOOL INSULATION

ONE GALLON CAN

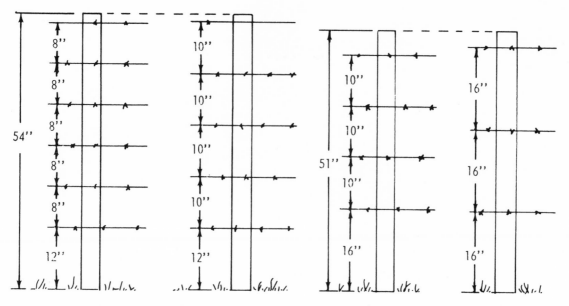

Common spacings of wires in barbed wire fences.

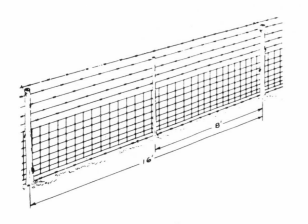

Fence for protecting sheep from dogs and coyotes.

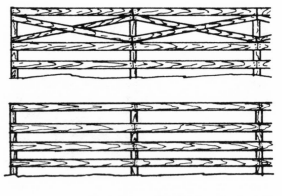

Common designs of board fences.

Fig. 28

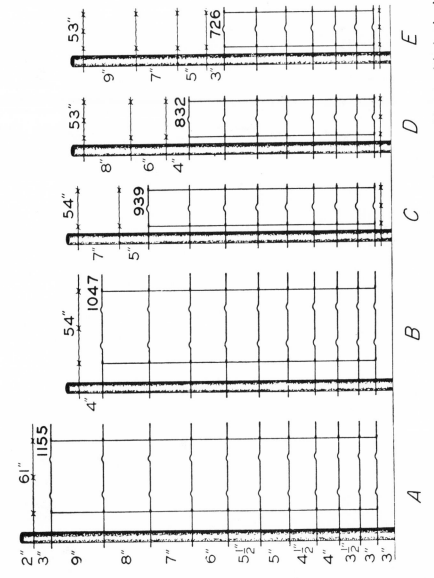

Fig. 29 —Standard styles or designs of woven wire fencing combined with barbed wire. Stay (vertical) wires are spaced 12 inches in fences A and B and 6 inches in C, D, and E.

329

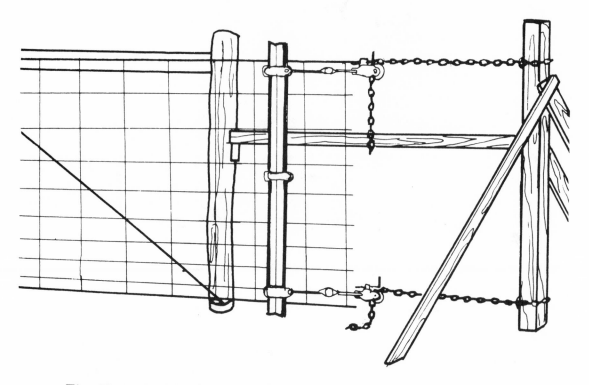

Fig. 30. Fence stretcher in position. Note braced "dummy" post at right.

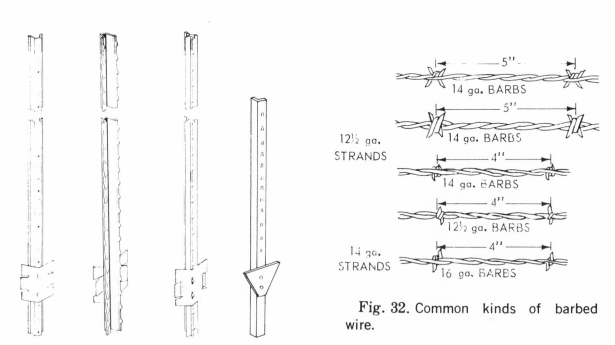

Fig. 31. Common kinds of steel posts.

Fig. 32. Common kinds of barbed wire.

330

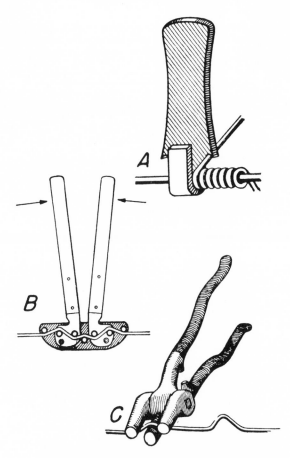

Fig. 33 Fencing tools: **A,** Splicing tool; **B,** double-crimp tool; and **C,** single-crimp tool.

The following figures show the average labor requirements for various fencing operations on fairly level ground:

Amount of work 2 men can accomplish in 10-hour day:

A. Number of wood line posts set 3 feet deep _____ 50 to 60
B. Number of steel line posts driven 2½ feet deep _____ 300 to 500
C. Number of rods of 47-inch woven-wire fence (type 1047) with 1 barbed wire, stretched and attached to:
    Wood posts _____ 90 to 100
    Steel posts _____ 80 to 90
D. Number of rods of 26-inch woven-wire fence (type 726) with 4 barbed wires, stretched and attached to:
    Wood posts _____ 75 to 80
    Steel posts _____ 60 to 75
E. Number of rods of 5-line, barbed-wire fence stretched and attached to:
    Wood posts _____ 60
    Steel posts _____ 50 to 60
F. Number of rods of old fence with wood posts torn down _____ 100

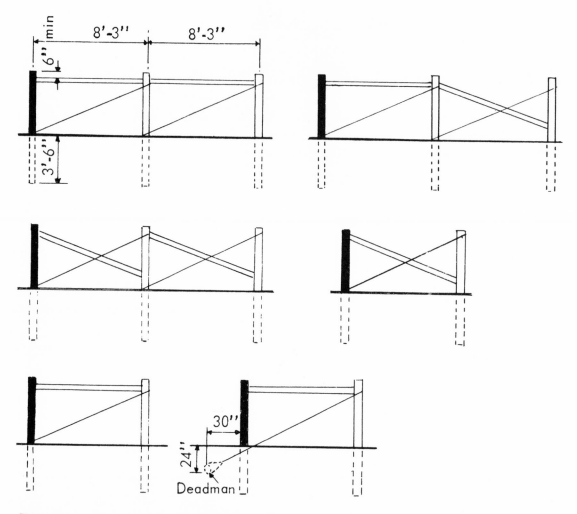

Fig. 34. —Wood corner· or end-post assemblies. Corner or end posts are shaded.

Minimum sizes recommended for the components of the assemblies are:

Single spans:
    Corner post _____ 6-inch diameter
    Brace post _____ 5-inch diameter
    Brace _____ 4-inch diameter
    Tie _____ 2 double strands
                   of No. 9-gage
                   wire.

Double spans:
    Corner post _____ 5-inch diameter
    Each brace post ___ 4-inch diameter
    Each brace _____ 4-inch diameter
    Each tie _____ 2 double strands
                   of No. 9-gage
                   wire.

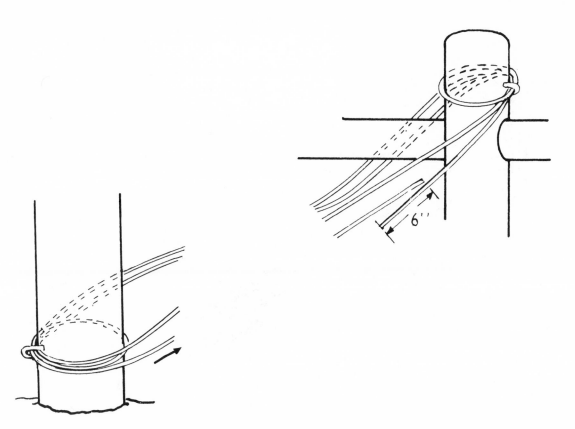

Fig. 35 Fastening of wire brace or tie in wood corner- or end-post assembly.

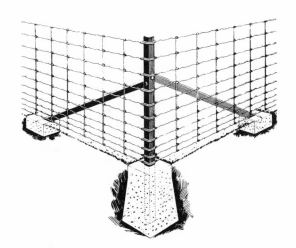

Fig. 36 Steel corner- or end-post assembly.

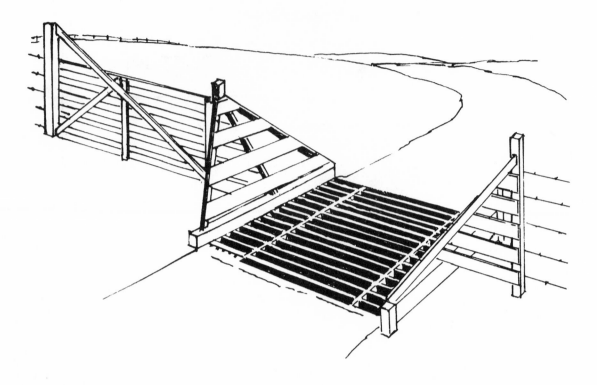

Cattle guards allow vehicles to pass through the fence line,
but restrain livestock.

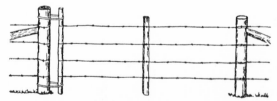

A cheap gate can be made of
3 or 4 strands of wire fastened to a
wood or steel bar and held by loops of
wire at the gatepost.

Fig. 37

Fig. 38. Common kinds of farm gates. **Top left:** Strong, lightweight aluminum gates are available in many designs and sizes. **Top right:** A support wire from the gatepost to the swinging end of the gate reduces the strain on the hinges and prevents sagging. **Bottom:** Planks nailed to the gateposts and fenceposts protect the wire fence when livestock pass through the gate.

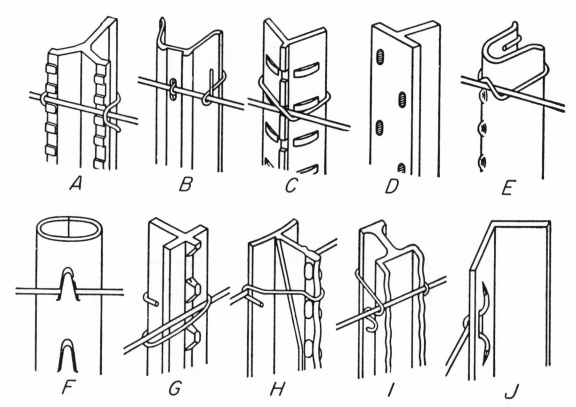

Steel farm fence posts, showing typical shapes, wire binders, and surface treatment. Shapes or forms: Angles, *C* and *J*; Y-form, *A*; tees, *D*, *G*, *H*, and *I*; channel or U-bar, *B* and *E*; circular, *F*. Binders: Twisted wire, *C*; staples, *D* and *J*; slip on *G* and *I*; clip and twist, *A*, *B*, *E*, and *H*; lipped, *F*. Surfaces: Studded, *C* and *G*; embossed, *A*, *C*, and *E*; channelled, *A*, *B*, and *I*; perforated or punched, *B*, *D*, and *J*.

A common method of fastening tie wires in bracing assemblies is to loop the wire around brace or corner posts and secure the loop with a short piece of wire in the manner illustrated (left, front view; right, back view). Tie wires are sometimes wrapped completely around the post.

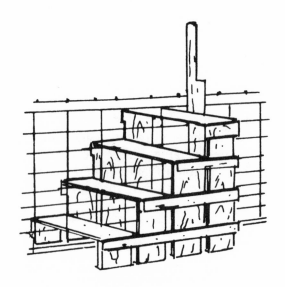

A stile should be used where a fence must be climbed over frequently.

Fig. 39.

TABLE 1 —*Weight of commonly used staples required for various spacing of posts*

Post spacing in feet	Posts per 80 rods	Weight of staples required for 80 rods of fence			
		1 inch	1⅛ inches	1¼ inches	1½ inches
	Number	*Pounds*	*Pounds*	*Pounds*	*Pounds*
8	165	11. 5	12. 5	15. 0	16. 8
10	132	9. 2	10. 0	11. 1	13. 4
12	110	7. 6	8. 3	9. 2	11. 2
16½	80	5. 6	6. 1	6. 7	8. 1

TABLE 2 —*Number of line posts required at various spacings for 100 rods of fencing* [1]

Post spacing (feet)	Number of posts	Post spacing (feet)	Number of posts
8	205	20	83
10	165	25	66
12	138	30	55
14	118	40	42
16½	100	50	33

[1] Corner and gate posts are additional.

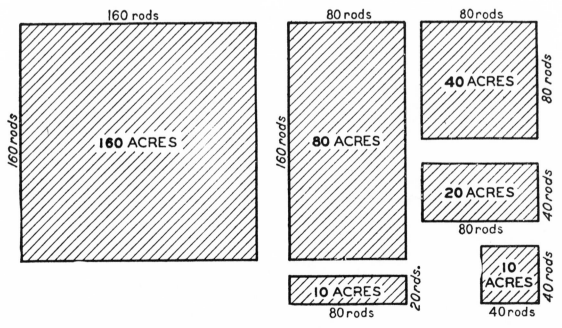

Fig. 40 The length of fencing required per acre varies with the size and shape of the fenced area.

NOTE: 1 rod = 16½ feet — Barbed wire normally is sold in rods.

337

Fig. 41

HOME GREEN HOUSE

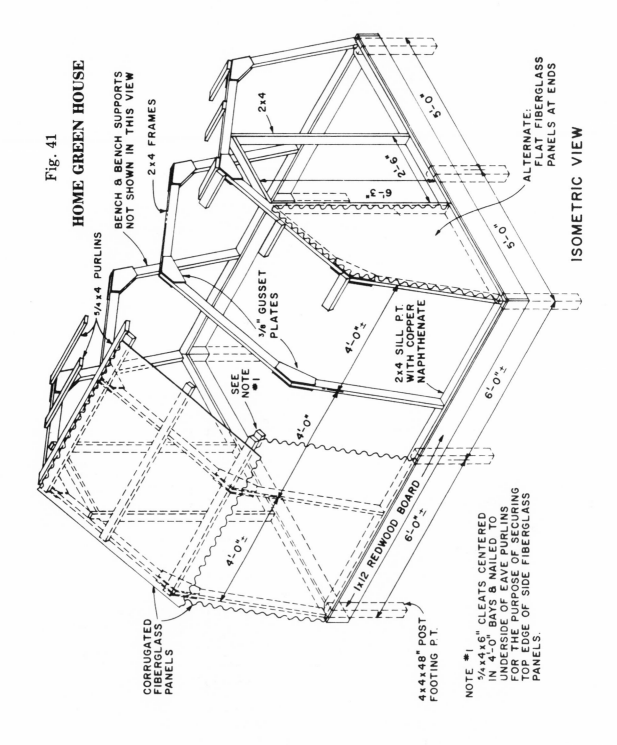

5/4 x 4 PURLINS

BENCH & BENCH SUPPORTS
NOT SHOWN IN THIS VIEW

2x4 FRAMES

2x4

5'-0"

2'-6"

6'-3"

ALTERNATE:
FLAT FIBERGLASS
PANELS AT ENDS

5'-0"

ISOMETRIC VIEW

3/8" GUSSET
PLATES

4'-0"±

2x4 SILL P.T.
WITH COPPER
NAPHTHENATE

6'-0"±

SEE
NOTE
#1

4'-0"

1x12 REDWOOD BOARD

6'-0"±

4'-0"±

CORRUGATED
FIBERGLASS
PANELS

4x4x48" POST
FOOTING P.T.

NOTE #1
5/4x4x6" CLEATS CENTERED
IN 4'-0" BAYS & NAILED TO
UNDERSIDE OF EAVE PURLINS
FOR THE PURPOSE OF SECURING
TOP EDGE OF SIDE FIBERGLASS
PANELS.

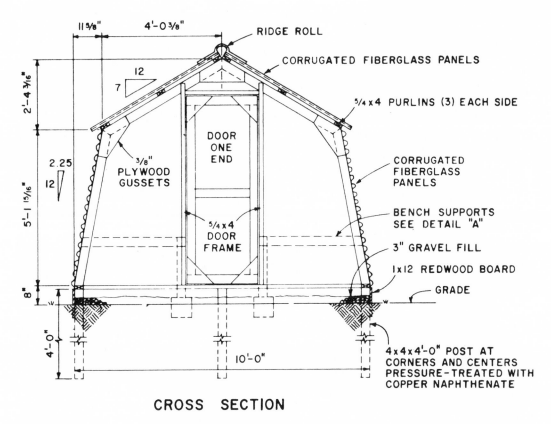

RIDGE ROLL

CORRUGATED FIBERGLASS PANELS

12
7

2.25
12

⁵/₄ x 4 PURLINS (3) EACH SIDE

DOOR
ONE
END

³/₈"
PLYWOOD
GUSSETS

CORRUGATED
FIBERGLASS
PANELS

⁵/₄ x 4
DOOR
FRAME

BENCH SUPPORTS
SEE DETAIL "A"

3" GRAVEL FILL

1x12 REDWOOD BOARD

GRADE

4x4x4'-0" POST AT
CORNERS AND CENTERS
PRESSURE-TREATED WITH
COPPER NAPHTHENATE

11 ⁵/₈"   4'-0 ³/₈"

2'-4 ³/₁₆"

5'-1 ¹⁵/₁₆"

8"

4'-0"

10'-0"

CROSS   SECTION

Fig. 42.

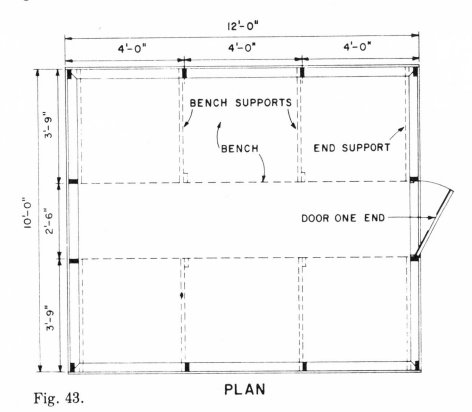

12'-0"

4'-0"   4'-0"   4'-0"

3'-9"

10'-0"

2'-6"

3'-9"

BENCH SUPPORTS

BENCH   END SUPPORT

DOOR ONE END

PLAN

Fig. 43.

339

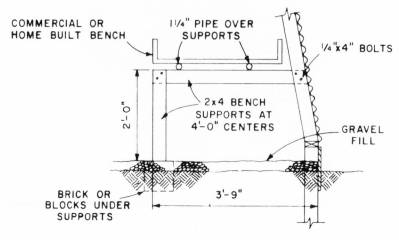

COMMERCIAL OR HOME BUILT BENCH

1¼" PIPE OVER SUPPORTS

¼"x4" BOLTS

2'-0"

2x4 BENCH SUPPORTS AT 4'-0" CENTERS

GRAVEL FILL

BRICK OR BLOCKS UNDER SUPPORTS

3'-9"

Fig. 44.

DETAIL "A"

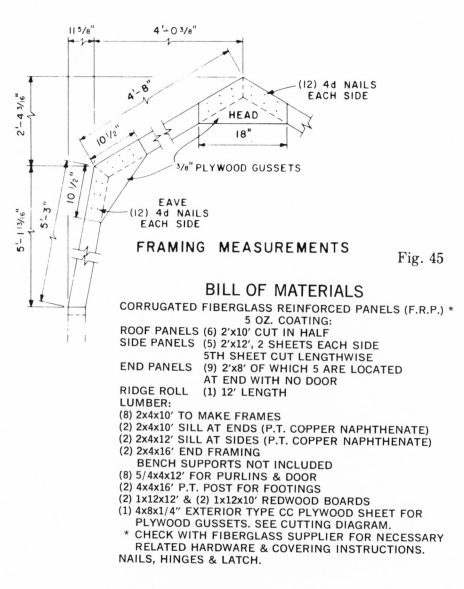

11 5/8"

4'-0 3/8"

4'-8"

(12) 4d NAILS EACH SIDE

2'-4 3/16"

10 1/2"

HEAD

18"

3/8" PLYWOOD GUSSETS

10 1/2"

5'-3"

5'-1 13/16"

EAVE
(12) 4d NAILS EACH SIDE

FRAMING MEASUREMENTS

Fig. 45

BILL OF MATERIALS

CORRUGATED FIBERGLASS REINFORCED PANELS (F.R.P.) *
5 OZ. COATING:
ROOF PANELS (6) 2'x10' CUT IN HALF
SIDE PANELS (5) 2'x12', 2 SHEETS EACH SIDE
5TH SHEET CUT LENGTHWISE
END PANELS (9) 2'x8' OF WHICH 5 ARE LOCATED
AT END WITH NO DOOR
RIDGE ROLL (1) 12' LENGTH
LUMBER:
(8) 2x4x10' TO MAKE FRAMES
(2) 2x4x10' SILL AT ENDS (P.T. COPPER NAPHTHENATE)
(2) 2x4x12' SILL AT SIDES (P.T. COPPER NAPHTHENATE)
(2) 2x4x16' END FRAMING
BENCH SUPPORTS NOT INCLUDED
(8) 5/4x4x12' FOR PURLINS & DOOR
(2) 4x4x16' P.T. POST FOR FOOTINGS
(2) 1x12x12' & (2) 1x12x10' REDWOOD BOARDS
(1) 4x8x1/4" EXTERIOR TYPE CC PLYWOOD SHEET FOR
PLYWOOD GUSSETS. SEE CUTTING DIAGRAM.
* CHECK WITH FIBERGLASS SUPPLIER FOR NECESSARY
RELATED HARDWARE & COVERING INSTRUCTIONS.
NAILS, HINGES & LATCH.

340

COLD FRAME

FOR AVERAGE HOME GARDEN

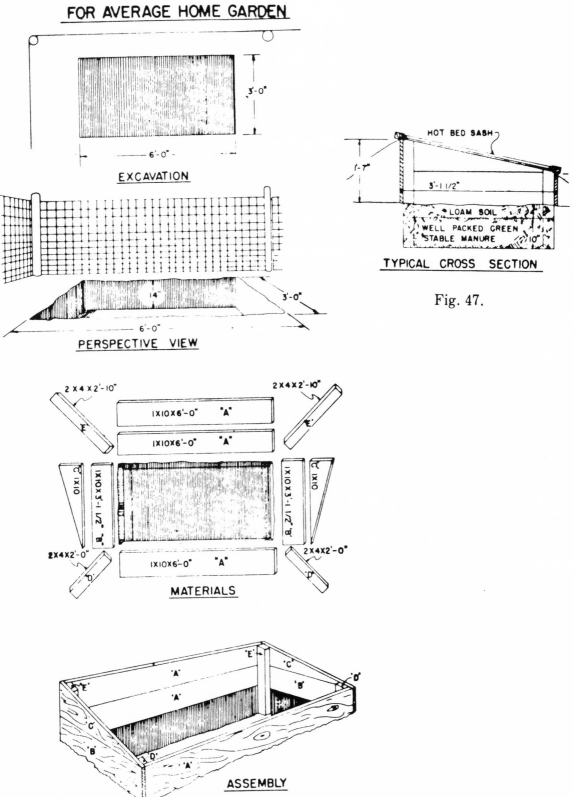

EXCAVATION

3'-0"

6'-0"

PERSPECTIVE VIEW

14"

3'-0"

6'-0"

HOT BED SASH

1'-7"

3'-1 1/2"

LOAM SOIL

WELL PACKED GREEN

STABLE MANURE

10"

TYPICAL CROSS SECTION

Fig. 47.

MATERIALS

2 X 4 X 2'-10"

2 X 4 X 2'-10"

1X10X6'-0"   "A"

1X10X6'-0"   "A"

1X10   1X10X3'-1 1/2"   "B"   1X10X3'-1 1/2"   "B"   1X10

2X4X2'-0"   1X10X6'-0"   "A"   2X4X2'-0"

ASSEMBLY

Fig. 46. Cold Frame for starting vegetable plants in the early spring — large enough for average home garden. 4-6 mil plastic can be used to cover frame.

341

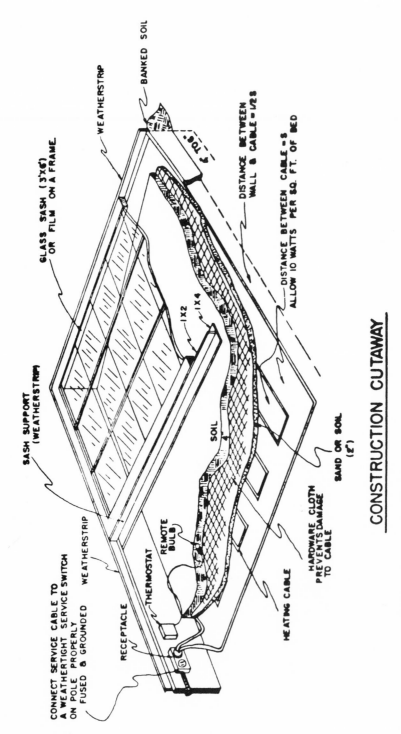

BANKED SOIL

WEATHERSTRIP

GLASS SASH (3'X6')
OR FILM ON A FRAME

DISTANCE BETWEEN
WALL & CABLE = 1/28

DISTANCE BETWEEN CABLE = 8
ALLOW IO WATTS PER SQ. FT. OF BED

SASH SUPPORT
(WEATHERSTRIP)

1X2

1X4

SOIL

CONNECT SERVICE CABLE TO
A WEATHERTIGHT SERVICE SWITCH
ON POLE PROPERLY
FUSED & GROUNDED   WEATHERSTRIP

SAND OR SOIL
(2')

RECEPTACLE

THERMOSTAT

REMOTE
BULB

HARDWARE CLOTH
PREVENTS DAMAGE
TO CABLE

HEATING CABLE

CONSTRUCTION CUTAWAY

Fig. 48. Electrically heated hot bed for starting vegetable plants in early spring.

342

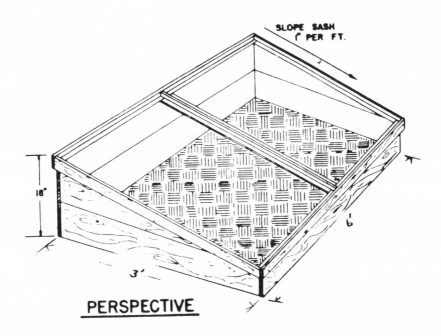

PERSPECTIVE

COVERING

GLASS SASH IS THE BEST TYPE OF COVERING FOR HOTBEDS, BUT IT IS ALSO THE MOST EXPENSIVE. OTHER MATERIAL, SUCH AS PLASTIC-COATED FABRIC, OR TREATED MUSLIN, PROVIDES A SATISFACTORY COVERING.

HEATING CABLE

BOTH LEAD-COVERED AND PLASTIC-COVERED CABLE GIVE SATISFACTORY RESULTS. WHEN USED PROPERLY, IN SOUTHERN AREAS 10 WATTS PER SQ. FOOT HAVE PROVED ADEQUATE. YOUR POWER SUPPLIER OR QUALIFIED DEALER CAN ASSIST YOU IN SELECTING HEATING CABLE.

LAY THE CABLE ON THE SOIL AT THE BOTTOM OF THE BED, OR, IF THE BED WAS EXCAVATED, LAY IT ON THE SAND THAT WAS SPREAD ON THE CINDERS OR GRAVEL.

THE SPACING BETWEEN LOOPS OR SECTIONS OF THE CABLE IS IMPORTANT. THE FORMULA FOR THIS IS AS FOLLOWS—

$$\text{SPACING (IN INCHES)} = \frac{12 \times \text{WATTS PER FOOT OF CABLE}}{\text{WATTAGE REQUIRED PER SQ. FT OF BED}}$$

THE SPACING BETWEEN THE OUTSIDE CABLE AND THE WALL IS HALF THE SPACING BETWEEN CABLE.

MAKE ALL CONNECTIONS TO THE HEATING CABLE WATERTIGHT TO EXCLUDE MOISTURE. THE WIRING SHOULD CONFORM TO THE NATIONAL ELECTRICAL CODE AND TO THE REQUIREMENTS OF THE LOCAL POWER SUPPLIER. IT SHOULD BE INSTALLED BY A REPRESENTATIVE OF THE POWER SUPPLIER OR BY A QUALIFIED ELECTRICIAN.

CONNECT A THERMOSTAT WITH AN OPERATING RANGE OF 30° TO 120°F (5° F. DIFFERENTIAL) IN THE ELECTRIC CIRCUIT TO CONTROL THE TEMPERATURE IN THE BED. THE THERMOSTAT MUST HAVE SUFFICIENT CURRENT-CARRYING CAPACITY TO HANDLE THE BED OR SECTION OF BED THAT IT CONTROLS. DO NOT PLACE THE THERMOSTAT OR BULB DIRECTLY ABOVE A HEATING CABLE OR ALLOW IT TO COME IN CONTACT WITH A CABLE.

Fig. 48B. Perspective, covering and heating cable for hot bed in Fig. 48.

343

TABLE 3. **Bedding Information For Growing Plants in Electric Hotbeds**

Kind of Plant	Hotbed Temperature	Seed Needed per 18 sq. ft.	Plants per 18 sq. ft.	Width Rows (feet)	Spacing Drill (feet)	Plants per Acre	Time from Seeding to Transplanting
Sweet Potatoes	80° - 85°	1½ bu.	3,500	3½	1	12,500	3-4 weeks
Cabbage	70°	¾ oz.	3,750	3	1½	10,000	4-6 weeks
Egg Plant	70°	1½ oz.	3,000-4,000	4	3	3,630	6-8 weeks
Pepper	70° - 75°	3 oz.	2,000-3,000	4 3½	2½ 3	4,356 4,150	7-8 weeks
Tomato	70° - 75°	1¼ oz.	2,500-3,500	4	2½	4,356	5-7 weeks
Onion	70°	2 oz.	6,000	2½	4 inches	40,000	5-7 weeks
Celery	65° - 68°	½ oz.	5,000	2	6 inches	43,560	8-10 weeks
Lettuce	60° - 65°	½ oz.	4,000	2	1	24,000	3-4 weeks

In the Hot Bed   **Transplanted to Field**

Fig. 49. Arrangement of cable and thermostat in an electric hotbed.

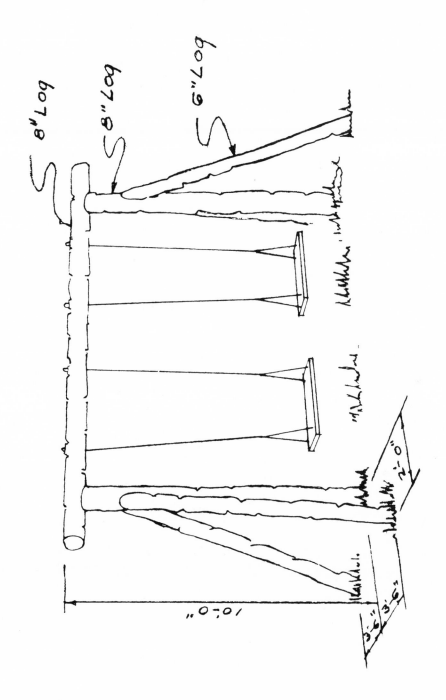

Fig. 50.

SWINGS

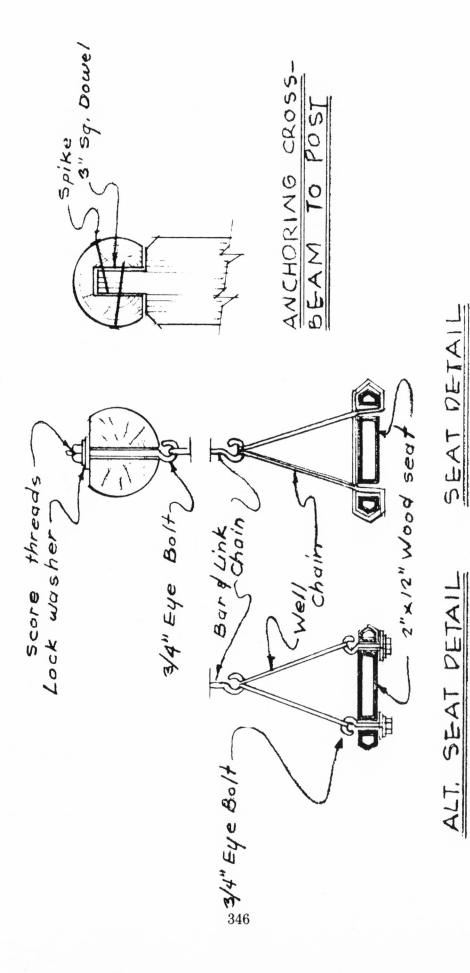

Spike 3" sq. Dowel

ANCHORING CROSS-
BEAM TO POST

Score threads
Lock washer

3/4" Eye Bolt

Bar & Link
Chain

Well
Chain

2"×12" Wood seat

3/4" Eye Bolt

ALT. SEAT DETAIL

SEAT DETAIL

Fig. 51.

346

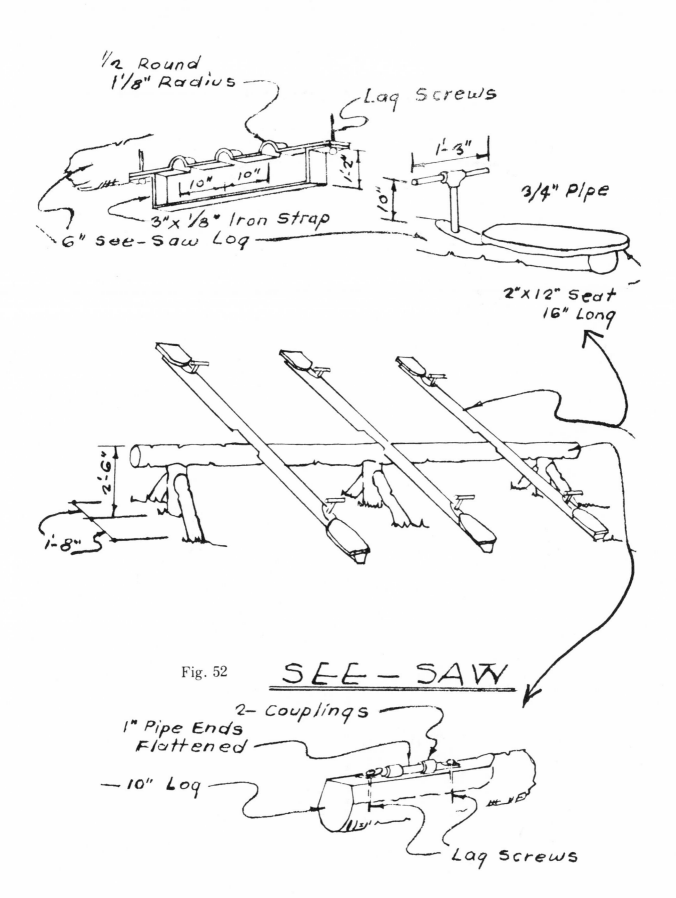

½ Round
1⅛" Radius

Lag Screws

3" × ⅛" Iron Strap

6" See-Saw Log

1'-3"

10"

3/4" Pipe

2"×12" Seat
16" Long

10"
10"

2'-6"

1'-8"

Fig. 52   SEE – SAW

2 – Couplings

1" Pipe Ends
Flattened

10" Log

Lag Screws

347

KITCHEN CABINET

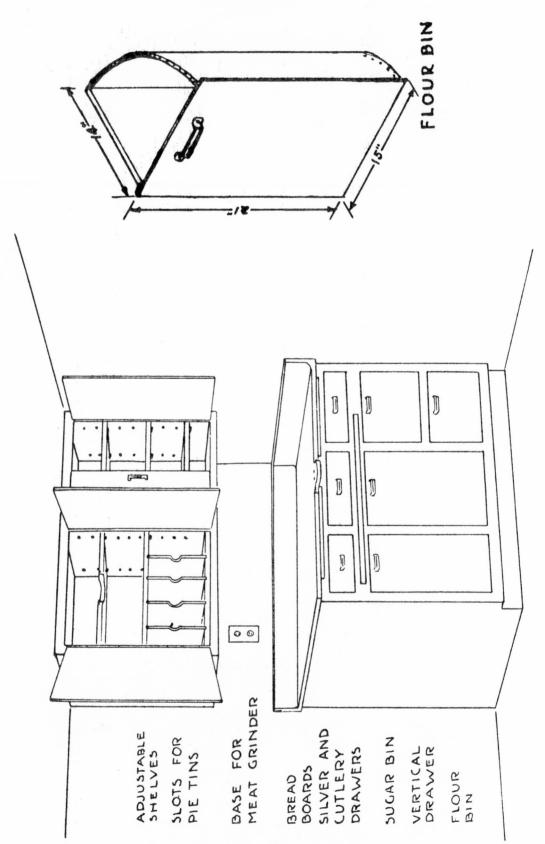

Fig. 53.

FLOUR BIN

ADJUSTABLE SHELVES

SLOTS FOR PIE TINS

BASE FOR MEAT GRINDER

BREAD BOARDS

SILVER AND CUTLERY DRAWERS

SUGAR BIN

VERTICAL DRAWER

FLOUR BIN

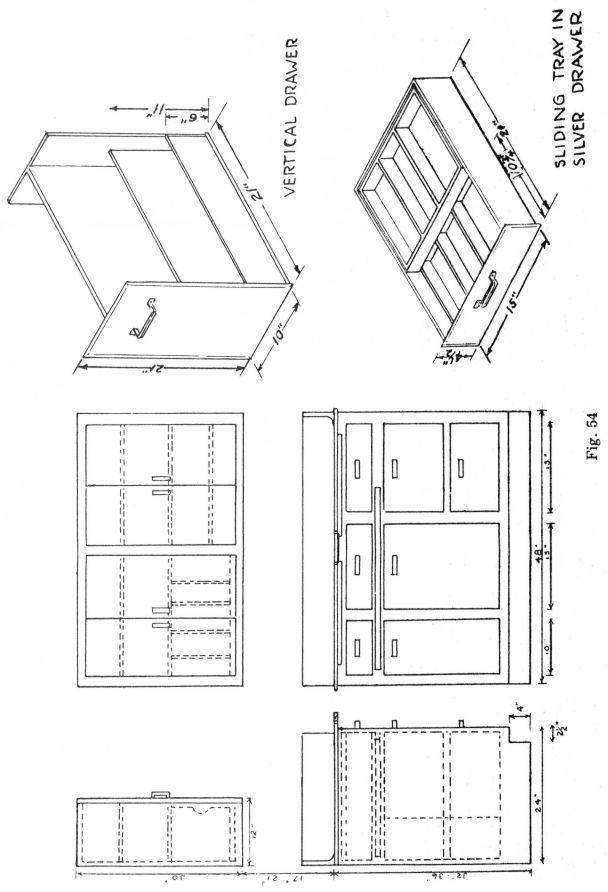

VERTICAL DRAWER

SLIDING TRAY IN SILVER DRAWER

Fig. 54

349

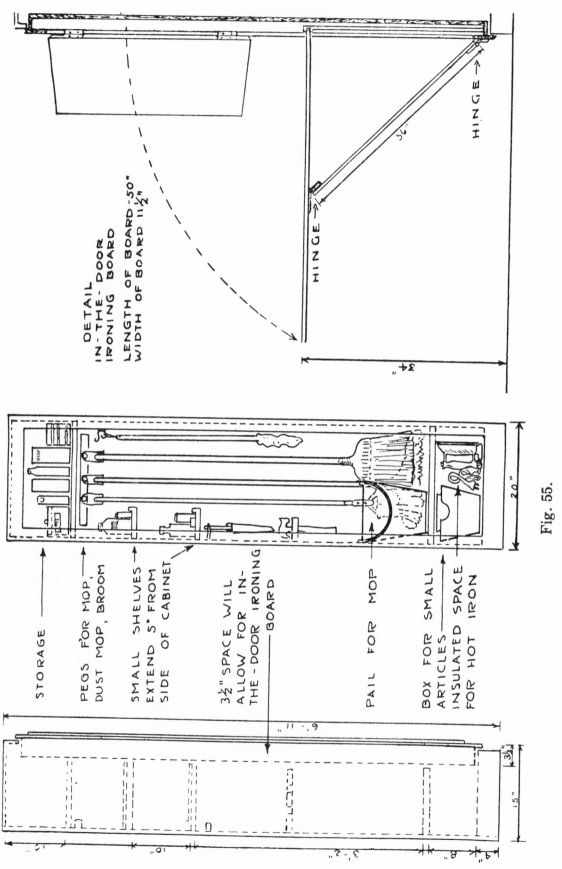

DETAIL
IN-THE-DOOR
IRONING BOARD
LENGTH OF BOARD-50"
WIDTH OF BOARD 11½"

HINGE

HINGE

HINGE

34"

STORAGE

PEGS FOR MOP,
DUST MOP, BROOM

SMALL SHELVES
EXTEND 5" FROM
SIDE OF CABINET

3½" SPACE WILL
ALLOW FOR IN-
THE-DOOR IRONING
BOARD

PAIL FOR MOP

BOX FOR SMALL
ARTICLES
INSULATED SPACE
FOR HOT IRON

20"

Fig. 55.

6'-11"

3½"

15"

5"

10"

3'-2"

8"

4"

350

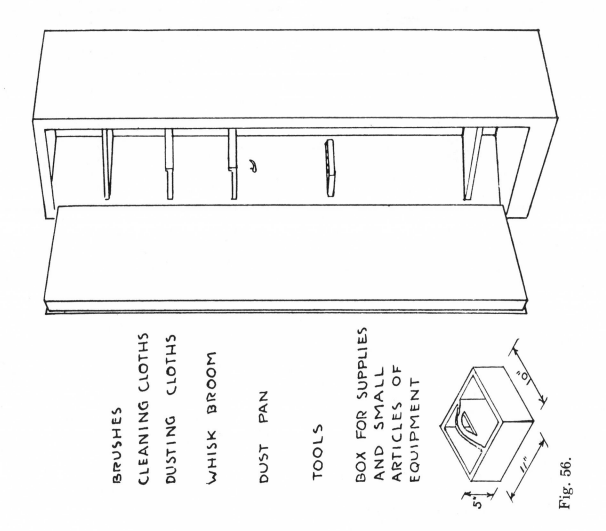

BRUSHES

CLEANING CLOTHS

DUSTING CLOTHS

WHISK BROOM

DUST PAN

TOOLS

BOX FOR SUPPLIES
AND SMALL
ARTICLES OF
EQUIPMENT

5" 11" 10"

Fig. 56.

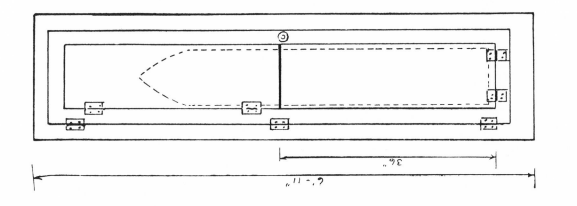

36"

5'-11"

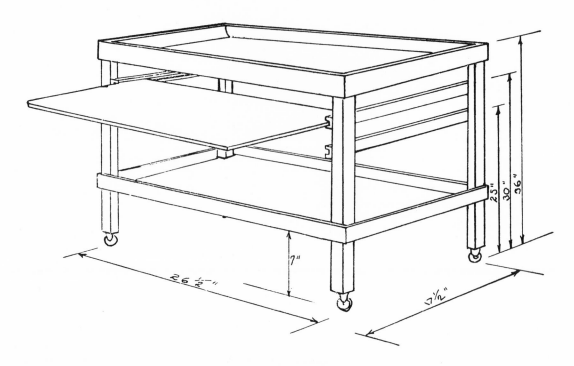

Fig. 56b. Work Table

BOILER FOR POTABLE WATER

Abstract Boiler for Potable Water

To provide safe storage and preparation
of drinking water in areas where pure
water is not available and boiling
is practical.

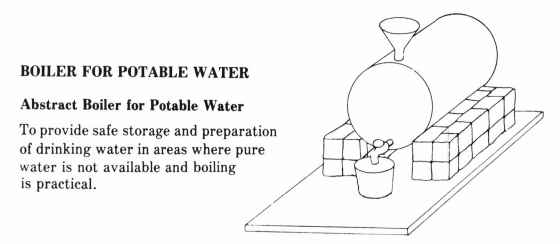

Fig. 57. Boiler For Potable Water

Tools and Materials

1 — 55 Gallon drum
1 — ¾" Pipe Nibble 2" long. Quantity of bricks for two layers of bricks to support drum.
1 — bag of cement plus sand for mortar and base of fireplace.
1 — large funnel and filter medium for filling.
1 — Metal plate to control draft in front of firebox.
1 — ¾" valve, preferably all metal such as a gate valve to withstand heat.

Details

This drum for boiling of drinking water is intended for use in your residence to provide a convenient method for preparation and storage of sterile water. The fireplace is simple, oriented so that the prevailing wind or draft goes from front to back of the drum between the bricks. A chimney can be provided but is not necessary.

Evaluation

The unit has been tested in workcamps in Mexico and elsewhere. A 55 gallon drum would normally last a 20 person camp group for an entire week, and certainly would provide adequate safe water supply for two or three individuals for a much longer time. Water must boil at least 15 minutes with steam escaping around the completely loosened filler plug. Be sure that the water in the pipe nipple and valve reach boiling temperatures by purging about two liters of water out through the valve while the drum is at a full boil.

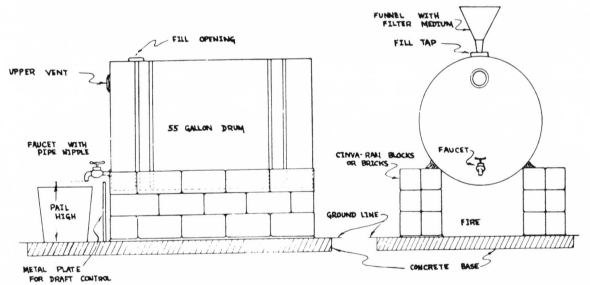

Fig. 58. Front & Side View of Potable Water Boiler

Thus, depending on your water, different amounts of chlorine are needed for adequate protection. Measuring the amount of free chlorine after the 30 minute holding period is the best way to control the process. A simple chemical test using a special organic indicator (orthotolidine) can be used. When this is not available, the chart (Table 4) can be used as a rough guide.

Table 4. Treatment of Water

Water Condition	Initial Chlorine Dose in Parts Per Million(ppm)	
	No hard-to-kill organisms suspected.	Hard-to-kill organisms present or suspected.
Very Clear, few minerals.	5 ppm	Get expert advice; in an emergency boil and cool water first, then use 5 ppm to help prevent recontamination. If boiling is impossible, use 10 ppm.
A coin in the bottom of an 8 oz. glass of the water looks hazy.	10 ppm	Get expert advice; in an emergency boil and cool first. If boiling is impossible use 15 ppm.

In the chart, parts per million or "ppm" means the ratio of:

$$\frac{\textbf{Weight of active material [chlorine]}}{\textbf{Weight of water}}$$

In water supply terminology, ppm means exactly the same thing as milligrams per liter or "mg/L".

The second chart, Table 5, gives the amount of chemical to add to 1000 gallons of water to get a solution of 1 ppm. Multiply the amount of chemical shown in Table 5 by the number of ppm recommended in Table 4 to get the amount of chemical you should add to 1000 gallons of water. Usually it is convenient to make up a solution of 500 ppm strength which can then be further diluted to give the chlorine concentration needed. The 500 ppm solution must be stored in a sealed container in a cool dark place, and should be used as quickly as possible since it does lose strength. Modern chlorination plants use bottled chlorine gas, but this can only be used with expensive machinery by trained experts.

CHLORINATION FOR POLLUTED WATER

Abstract-Chlorination Polluted Water

Chlorination, when properly applied, is a simple way to insure and protect the purity of water. These guidelines include tables to give a rough indication of the amounts of chlorine bearing chemicals needed.

Tools and Materials

Chlorine in some form
Container to mix chlorine

Details

The surest way to treat water for drinking is to boil it—see "Boiler for Potable Water." However, under controlled conditions chlorination is a safe method, and often more convenient and practical than boiling. Water properly treated has residual free chlorine which resists recontamination. The chlorine in water is not harmful, since water with a harmful amount of chlorine in it is extremely distasteful. Proper treatment of water with chlorine requires some knowledge of the process and its effects.

When chlorine is added to water, it attacks and combines with any suspended organic matter as well as some minerals such as iron. There is always a certain amount of dead organic matter in water, and almost always live bacteria, virus, and perhaps other types of life. Enough chlorine must be added to oxidize all of

the organic matter, dead or alive, and to leave some excess uncombined or "free" chlorine.

Some organisms are more resistant to chlorine than others. Two particularly resistant varieties are amoebic cysts (which cause amoebic dysentary) and the cercariae of schistosomes (which cause schistosomiasis). These, among others, require much higher levels of residual free chlorine and longer contact periods than usual to be safe. Often special techniques are used to combat these and other specific diseases. It always takes time for chlorine to work. Be sure that water is thoroughly mixed with an adequate dose of the dissolved chemical, and that it *stands for at least 30 minutes before consumption.*

Since both combined and uncombined chlorine has an unpalatable taste, it is best (and safest) to choose the clearest water available. A settling tank, and simple filtration can help reduce the amount of suspended matter, especially particles large enough to see. Filtration that can be depended upon to remove all of the amoebic cysts, schistosomes, and other pathogens normally requires professionals to set up and operate. *NEVER* depend on home-made filters alone to provide potable water. However, a home-made slow sand filter is an excellent way to prepare water for chlorination.

Table 5. Addition of Chemicals

Compound	% by weight of active material	Quantity to add to 100 gallons of water to get a 1 ppm solution
High Test (Calcium hypochlorite) $Ca(OCl)_2$	70%	1/5 ounce
Chlorinated lime	25%	1/2 ounce
Sodium hypochlorite NaOCl	14%	1 ounce
Sodium hypochlorite	10%	1.3 ounces
Bleach - a solution of chlorine in water	usually 5.25%	2.6 ounces

SILK SCREEN PRINTING

Abstract-Silk Screen Printing

Silk screen printing is a simple and inexpensive method for producing multiple copies of visual aids, posters, etc. A squeegee is used to force very thick paint through the parts of the silk screen exposed by the stencil to the paper placed underneath.

Tools and Materials

Fig. 59

Hinges (about 1" x 3")
Wing or regular nuts
Squeegee
Trigger support
Frame
Baseboard or smooth table top
Silk or other sheer cloth
Thumbtacks
Silk screen paint
Paper for copies

FRAME
SHOWING VARIOUS JOINT CONSTRUCTIONS
HINGE
WING NUT
ADHERE STENCIL TO UNDER SIDE OF SILK SCREEN
SILK TACKED TO FRAME
TRIGGER SUPPORT
PAPER TO BE PRINTED GOES UNDER SCREEN
REGISTRATION GUIDES - USED TO LINE UP PAPER STRAIGHT
BASEBOARD OR WOODEN TABLE TOP

355

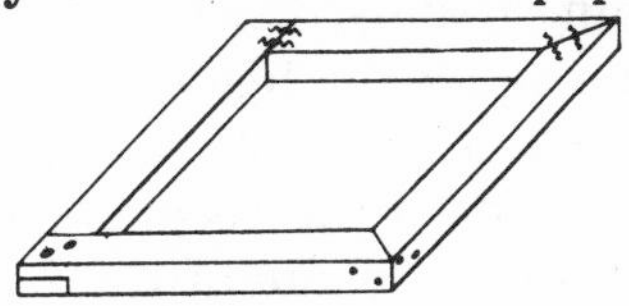

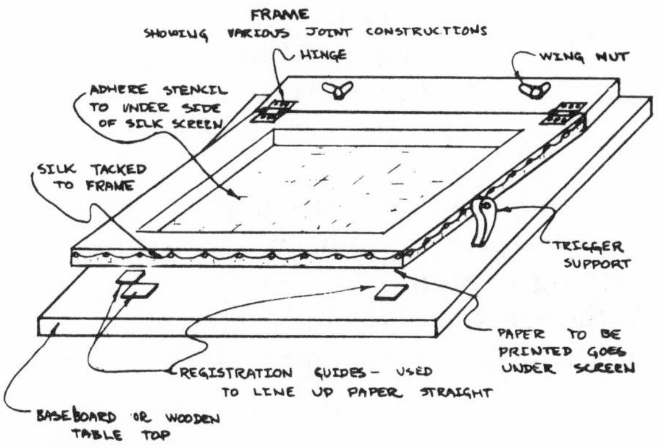

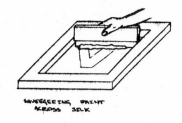

SQUEEGEEING PAINT
ACROSS SILK

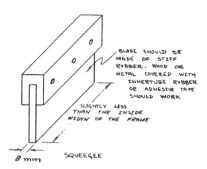

BLADE SHOULD BE
MADE OF STIFF
RUBBER. WOOD OR
METAL COVERED WITH
INNERTUBE RUBBER
OR ADHESIVE TAPE
SHOULD WORK

SLIGHTLY LESS
THAN THE INSIDE
WIDTH OF THE FRAME

8 mm   SQUEEGEE

Fig. 59 continued

Details

1. Study the drawings, then construct a frame as illustrated using approximately (1.9 x 5 cms.) (¾" x 2") plywood or other wood. The exact size of the frame is determined by the size of the largest prints to be made. Average inside frame dimensions might be (38.1 cm. x 50.8 cm.) (18" x 24"). Make sure the corners are square and that the frame lies flat against a flat baseboard or table top, which can also be made of 1.9 cm (¾") plywood.

2. Stretch the silk *very tightly* over the underside of the frame using tacks or thumb tacks every 1" or 2 cm. Tack either in the center of the underside of the frame or pull the silk over the outside bottom edges and tack around the outside. Make sure that the threads of the fabric are lined up with the frame edges. A few coats of shellac over wooden frame will make it more durable and less apt to warp.

3. Cut stencil and adhere to screen according to instructions.

4. Place the paper cardboard, etc, to be printed under the screen and stencil; draw a couple of spoonfulls of finger paint or other water-soluble paint in a line across the edge of the silk just inside one end of the frame.

(Oil soluble paints work well, but require a solvent cleanup; also, the viscosity of the paint should be like auto transmission grease, not thin enough to fall through the screen of its own accord.)

5. Pull the paint across the silk surface using an edge of the squeegee blade. This squeezes the paint through all the open areas of the paper stencil. Lift screen. Remove print and replace with next piece to be printed. Pull paint back the other way for the next print. The desired technique is to place an amount of paint on the screen which, together with the right blade pressure, will produce an acceptable print with one stroke of the squeegee.

Make certain that dried paint particles do not get in the paint as they could damage the screen.

6. If more than one color is to be printed, registration becomes an important feature and can be achieved by the following method:

(a) Print the first color *using registration guides*. Registration guides can be made of thin cardboard or several layers of tape. (Thicker guides can cause silk to break when squeegee blade presses the silk against the guides.)

(b) A piece of wax or thin translucent paper is taped on one edge to the baseboard beneath the second screen to be printed.

(c) Print a trial image of the second screen onto this paper.

(d) Raise the screen.

(e) Slide the sample of the first printing into position beneath the taped wax paper until the desired registration with the first printing is achieved.

(f) Once registered *carefully* hold the first printing sample in position, and remove the wax paper.

(g) Tape new registration guides on three sides of the first printing sample.

(h) Now proceed to print the second color. Subsequent colors are printed by returning to Step (b).

7. Several colors can be printed over one another if transparent paints are used. The size of the printed area can be restricted by using paper masks.

DRYING RACK MADE WITH
2" × 2" UPRIGHTS WITH
1" × 1" CROSS BARS ABOUT
AN INCH APART

Fig. 60

8. Pull up stencil. Clean wet paint out of silk and frame by unscrewing wing bolts, taking the frame to a convenient wash area and holding under running water.

9. Optional: A drying rack pictured here is helpful when many prints are to be dried.

BAMBOO OR REED WRITING PENS

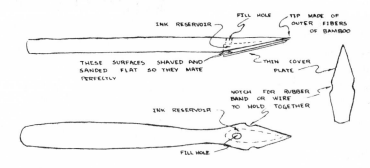

Fig. 61

EVAPORATIVE FOOD COOLER

Abstract- Evaporative Food Cooler

In warm, dry climates an evaporative food cooler will extend the period for keeping food fresh and allow saving leftovers. It also helps to keep crawling and flying insects away from food.

Tools and Materials

Saw
Hammer
Nails, tacks
Burlap or other cloth 2 m. x 2 m.
Wood for frame 3 cm x 3 cm x 13 m.
Pan 10 cm deep, 24 x 30 cm for top.
Screen, hardware cloth or galvanized
   iron 2m. x 2m. (non-rusting)
2 pair hinges
Pan larger than 30 cm x 36 cm for legs to stand in
Paint for wooden parts.

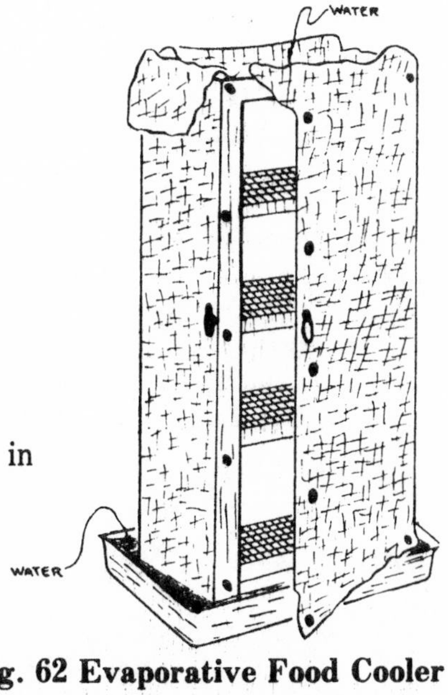

Fig. 62 Evaporative Food Cooler

357

Details

Make the wooden frame to fit the upper pan. This might be the bottom of a discarded 5 gallon oil can. Screen and bracing sticks on the inside top of the frame prevent the pan from falling into the refrigerator. Hinge the door carefully so it swings easily, and make a simple wooden or thong latch. Paint or oil all the wooden parts. Shelves and frame are covered with screening or hardware cloth and tacked in place. Cutting this screen diagonally uses a bit more material, but will strengthen the frame considerably. Make the shelves adjustable by providing several shelf supports.

Two covers of canton flannel, jute burlap (not sisal or henequin burlap) or heavy grade absorbent coarse cloth are made to fit the frame. Wash and sun one cover while using the other. Button or lace the cover to the frame, with the smooth side out. On the front, fasten the cover to the door instead of the frame. Allow a wide hem to overlap the door closing. The bottom of the cover should extend down into the lower pan. Strips 20 cm wide should be sewed to the top of the cover. These form wicks that dip over into the upper pan. Keep both the upper and lower pans filled with water.

Evaluation

If the cooler is kept in a breezy spot in the shade, and the climate is dry, it will cool food considerably. The cover keeps flying insects out, while the lower pan discourages roaches and other crawling types. To be safe, the cooler must be kept clean.

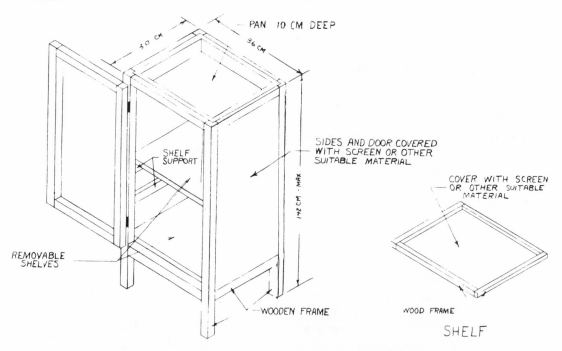

Fig. 63. Frame of Iceless Refrigerator.

CHARCOAL OVEN

Abstract-Charcoal Oven

This simple charcoal-fired oven is made from two discarded 5 gallon oil tin cans. With practice, all types of baking can be expertly done.

358

Tools and Materials

Nail for scriber and punch
Tinsnips
Heavy knife to start cuts
Hammer
Screwdriver
Pliers
Metal bar 20 cm long with square corner for bending
Two 5 gallon oil cans
Tin cans to provide shelf material
Light rod 50 cm long, 5 to 7 mm diameter
Two pairs of light hinges
12 machine bolts, nuts, lockwashers, size 8/32 or soft rivets
Bricks for base
Sand

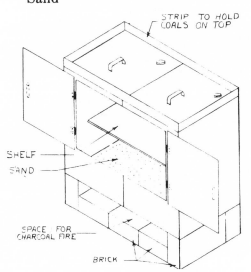

Fig. 64 Charcoal Oven

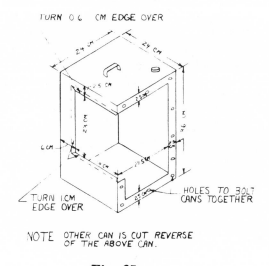

Fig. 65

Details

Cut the material from the side of the oven with care so as to preserve the material removed for making the door. Don't cut out the corner with a vertical seam; it is too hard to do, weakens the oven, and the removed material is hard to make into the doors. Fold the edges of the door and door opening back (1 cm wide) and hammer flat to remove sharp edges. The latch can be made of three thicknesses of metal scraps left over. Clean the oven thoroughly and heat at least once before baking to burn out any residual oil. The strip around the top forms a rim to contain burning coals, to make the oven hotter, or to brown the surface of baked goods.

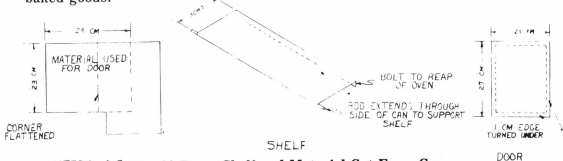

Fig. 66 Door, Shelf and Material Cut From Can

359

Evaluation

This oven is being used successfully in a number of countries. Baking and roasting are quite effectively done with this simple and inexpensive appliance. Any recipes which involve these processes may be used.

FIRELESS COOKER

Abstract-Fireless Cooker

In some places where fuel is scarce, this easy-to-build fireless cooker can be a real contribution to better cooking. It works by heat retention through insulation.

Tools and Materials

Outside container with lid—(15" to 24" in diameter)
Inside container or well— at least 6" smaller in diameter and 6" shorter than outside container
Cooking pot with lid
1½ yards cloth for cushion
50 sheets newspaper or other insulation.
Cardboard
6 cups sand
4 cups cement
½ yard oilcloth for collar (optional)

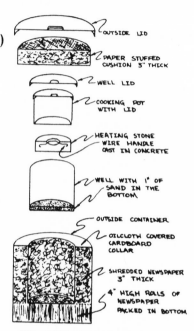

Fig. 67. Fireless Cooker

Details

The principle of the fireless cooker is to keep food cooking with the small amount of heat stored in hot stones by preventing heat loss with a thick layer of insulating material around the pot.

The outside container can be a wooden bucket, kerosene can, garbage can, packing crate or even a hole in dry ground. The inside container or well can be a pail or can with a lid. It must allow for the three inches of insulation between it and the outside container and should hold the stone and cooking pot without much vacant space.

Insulation can be made of shredded newspapers, wool, cotton, sawdust, straw, rockwool, fiberglass or other material. The insulation should be at least three inches thick on all sides, top and bottom. Be sure that it is very dry. The bottom layer of insulation must be strong enough to support the weight of the well, stone, and cooking pot. A natural stone carved to shape or a piece of concrete may be used for the heating stone. The cushion is a three-inch-thick cloth sack filled with shredded newspapers or other insulation and should fit snugly in the outside container. The cooking pot must have a right lid, and fit nicely into the well with the stone in place. Be sure it can be easily removed when full of hot food.

Directions for building —
    Wash and dry the containers and lids.
    Cut 4" wide strips of newspaper several layers thick. Roll each into a cylinder

360

with a center hole no greater in diameter than a pencil. Pack these on end into the bottom of the outside container. They will support the well, stone, and cooking pot.

Put the well in place and pack the insulation around it to within ½" of the top.

Make a cardboard collar covered with oilcloth. Though this is not necessary, it improves appearance and cleanliness.

Place about an inch of clean sand in the bottom of the well. This will prevent the hot stone from scorching the paper rolls and possibly causing a fire. The stone should never be heated enough to scorch paper.

To make a concrete heating stone, place a 2" wide cardboard band or collar on heavy paper or board to form a circle the size of the stone desired. Mix 4 cups each of cement and sand washed free of silt, then add 1½ cups of water or until a stiff mush is formed. Fill the collar, casting in a handle for lifting the hot stone. Let the stone stand for 48 hours, then remove the collar, place it in cold water and boil for 30 minutes. Cool it slowly.

Use of the Cooker:

It is important to keep the cooking pot and well carefully washed and open, in sunshine of possible, when not in use. The cooker's lid should be left partly open and the stone kept clean and dry.

It is not necessary to use much water when cooking in a fireless cooker for there is little loss by evaporation. Most foods should be brought to a boil and cooked for 4 to 5 minutes on a stove. Then, the covered cooking pot is set on the hot stone in the cooker and the lid is placed on the well. Cereal may be left in the cooker all night. Rice and cracked or whole wheat are especially good. Beans should be soaked over night, boiled for 5 minutes and then placed in the cooker for 4 to 5 hours. Dried fruit should be washed, soaked for an hour in 2 parts water to 1 part fruit, boiled for 5 minutes, then placed in the cooker for 4 hours.

Evaluation

Fireless cookers have been used and found very successful in many countries.

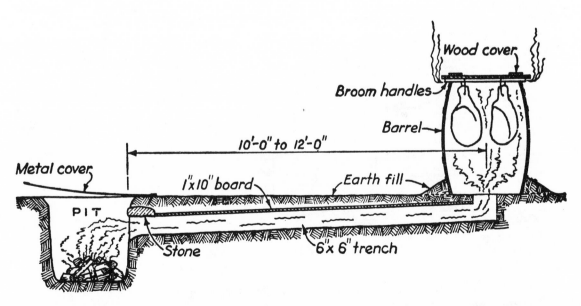

Fig. 68. Barrel for smoking meats. A small frame construction can be substituted for barrel stovepipe or tile could be used for the flue.

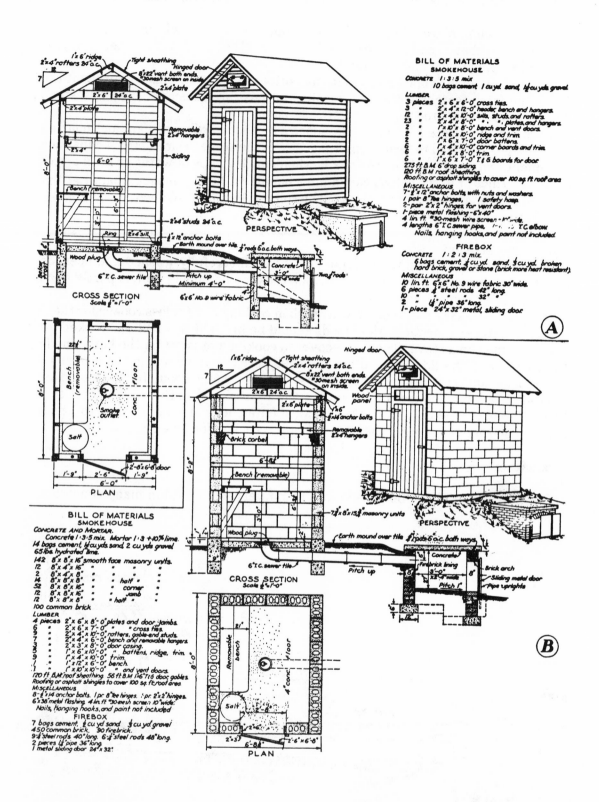

Fig. 69. Smokehouse (A) drawings and materials for frame construction. (B) Cement block construction.

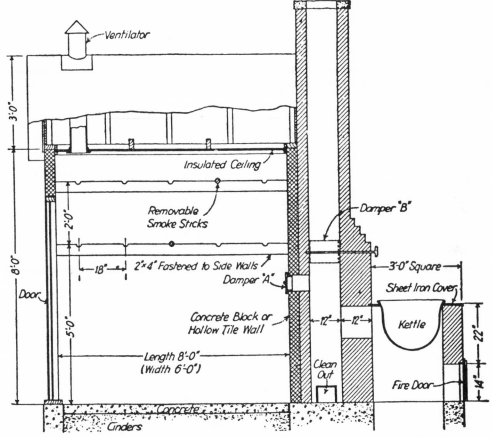

A 6'x6'x8' COMBINATION SMOKE AND STORAGE HOUSE AND COOKER

Fig. 70. Plan for a Combination Smokehouse and Cooker. There are two tiers of removable smoke poles made from 2-inch pipe, drilled and pegged every 18 inches, the metal pegs extending through either side of the pipe for hangers. The oven with a 28-inch (50 gal.) cast-iron, open fire kettle built in, is used for rendering and cooking as well as being the firebox for generating smoke. This fire-box is made of brick and can be erected at the end of any building that is to be used as a smokehouse. When the kettle is to be used for cooking purposes, close damper A and open damper B. When smoking meat, keep water in the kettle, close damper B after the fire is started and open damper A. Two inches of concrete laid over 6 to 9 inches of rock and cinders will make satisfactory floor.

SOLAR WATER HEATER

Abstract-Solar Water Heater

To provide hot water, primarily for washing clothes, in areas where fuel is scarce and sunshine is plentiful.

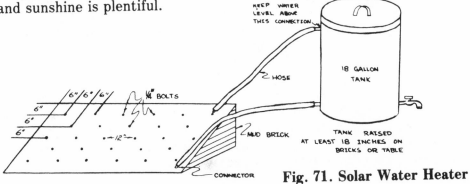

Fig. 71. Solar Water Heater

363

Tools and Materials

2 pieces galvanized sheet metal, 3' by 6' for heater.
2 pieces galvanized sheet metal pipe, 6" long by 1" in diameter for connectors.
2 pieces rubber hose, 4' long by 1" in diameter.
56 metal washers for ¼" bolts.
56 rubber washers cut from heavy truck inner tube. Inside hole diameter should
 be 1/8", outside diameter same as metal washers.
28 stove bolts, galvanized, ¼" long.
1 galvanized sheet metal tank, 18 gallon capacity with faucet, removable lid, 1"
 hose connectors near the top and bottom.
Tinsmith's tools: hammers, anvils, soldering equipment, etc.
Drill and ¼" bit.
Screw driver and wrench to fit ¼" bolts or a pair of pliers.
Quantity of mud bricks.

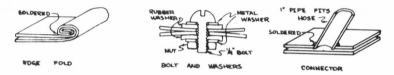

Fig. 72. Construction of Heater

Details

The heater is made by placing the two sheets of galvanized sheet metal together in the form of an envelope. The edges of the sheets are double folded and soldered to make an air tight seal. (See Fig. 72.) To prevent the sheets from being forced apart when the heater is filled with water, it is necessary to reinforce it with ¼" bolts placed at regular intervals, like buttons in a mattress. To make the bolts water-tight they must have rubber and metal washers on both sides.

Inlet and outlet connections are provided in the upper and lower right hand corners of the heater for connection to the tank. The front of the heater is painted black to absorb the sunlight rather than reflect it. A flat black paint is better than an enamel.

The tank does not have to be of any definite shape but should hold approximately 18 gallons of water. The hot water will rise to the top and, with the removable lid, it is possible to dip out the hottest water when only a small quantity is needed. When all of the water is to be used it may be drained out of the faucet. The water level must be maintained above the upper hose connection.

When the solar water heater is set up, the heater should be facing southeast to take advantage of the morning sun. The back of the heater should be raised about 18" so the sunlight will strike it as directly as possible. A simple way to raise the heater is to build up the back and sloping sides with mud bricks. Use three small boards (2" by 4") to prop up the back while putting the mud bricks in place. Then, remove the boards and seal any holes with mud to form a dead air space under the heater which will serve as insulation and increase the efficiency.

The heater is connected to the tank in such a way as to allow the water to circulate as it is heated. The upper connectors of the tank and heater are connected with one hose and the lower connectors with the other. The tank is raised approximately 18", using a small table or a brick platform, so the coolest water will be in the heater. As the water in the heater is warmed, it rises and flows out the upper hose into the top of the tank. Cool water from the bottom of the tank enters the heater at the bottom. Insulating the tank will increase the efficiency of the solar water heater by cutting down the heat losses. Any suitable local material may be used, such as straw or sawdust.

364

Evaluation

The solar water heater described here was made and tested in Kabul, Afghanistan, for the purpose of providing hot water for use in the hand operated washing machines. Three sizes were made and tested: 2½' x 4½', 3' x 6', and 3' x 8' which are the sizes of sheet metal available in Kabul. The 3' x 6' heater with an 18 gallon tank was most suitable from the standpoint of cost and water requirement. In Kabul, where there is lots of sunshine, the 18 gallons of water were heated to 140°F. between sun up and noon on a clear summer day.

HAND-OPERATED WASHING MACHINE—I

Abstract-Hand-Operated Washing Machine—I

This easily operated washing machine can be built by a semi-skilled carpenter of materials readily found in most countries. It can wash six pounds of clothes, can be shared by several families, and is easy on clothes while being effective and sanitary.

Tools and Materials

Tub Construction: Moderately firm softwood free from large heartwood growth.
2 pieces—2.5 x 45.7 x 96.5 cm.—sides 1" x 18" x 38"
2 pieces—2.5 x 30.5 x 40.6 cm.—ends 1" x 12" x 16"
2 pieces—2.5 x 15.2 x 40.6 cm.—bottom 1" x 6" x 16"
1 piece— 2.5 x 40.6 x 66.0 cm.—bottom 1" x 16" x 26"
4 pieces—2.5 x 10.2 x 76.2 cm.—legs 1" x 4" x 30"
2 pieces—2.5 x 25.4 cm. diameter—round plungers 1" x 10" diameter
2 pieces—3.8 x 12.7 cm. diameter—round plungers 1.5" x 5" diameter
2 pieces—2.5 x 20.3 x 91.4 cm.—cover (may be omitted) 1" x 8 " x 36"
6 pieces—2.5 x 7.6 x 20.3 cm.—cover (may be omitted) 1" x 3" x 8"

Operating Parts: Moderately firm hardwood
1 piece— 2.5 x 7.6 x 121.9 cm. long—lever 1" x 3" x 48"
2 pieces—2.9 cm. square 38.1 cm. long-plungers 1 1/8" square 15" long
2 pieces—2.9 x 7.6 x 61.0 cm. long—uprights 1 1/8" x 3" x 24" long
2 pieces—3.2 cm. round 45.7 cm. long—pivot and handle 1¼" round 18" long

Metal Parts
4 pieces iron or brass plate—.64 x 3.8 x 15.2 cm. long (¼" x 1½" x 6" long)—plunger connection
10 rods—3.6 or .79 cm. diameter (1.4" or 5/16" diameter) 45.7 cm. (18") long with threads and nuts on each end—iron or brass.
20 washers about 2.5 cm. (1") diameter with hole to fit rods
1 rod—.64 x 15.2 cm. (¼" x 6") with loop end for retaining pivot
6 bolts—.64 x 5.1 cm. long (¼" x 2" long)
24 screws—4.4 cm. x #10—flat head (1¾" x #10)
50—6.35 cm. (2½") nails
Strip Sheet Metal with turned edge—6.4 cm. wide, 152.4 cm. long (2½" wide, 72" long)
Small quantity of loose cotton or soft vegetable fiber for caulking seams

Minimum Tools Needed
Tape measure or ruler
Hatchet, Saw
Wood chisel 1.3 or 1.9 cm. wide (½" or ¾")

Screw Driver
Adjustable Wrench
0.64 cm. (¼") drill, gimlet or similar tool
Draw knife or plane and coping saw (would be useful but not essential)

Details

This model of washing machine should be a decided improvement to conserve clothing over methods now in use in many countries. This is especially true where clothes are beaten or scrubbed on rocks. It will also save a considerable amount of labor. If the cost of this machine is too great for one family, it could be used by several. However, too many users will probably mean severe wear or breakage and competition for times of use.

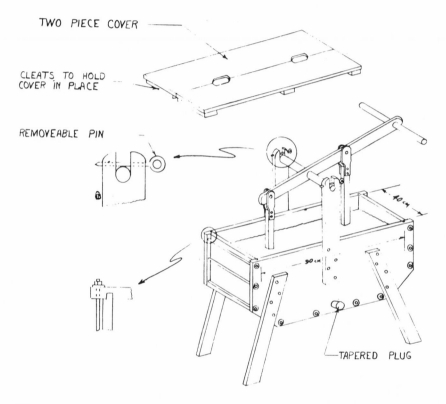

Fig. 73.

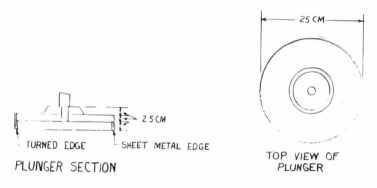

The machine reverses the principle employed in the usual commercial washers in which the clothes are swished through the water for various degrees of a circle until the water is moving and then reversed. To keep this machine simple, the clothes stay more or less stationary while the water is forced back and forth through the clothes by the piston action of the plungers. One plunger creates a

366

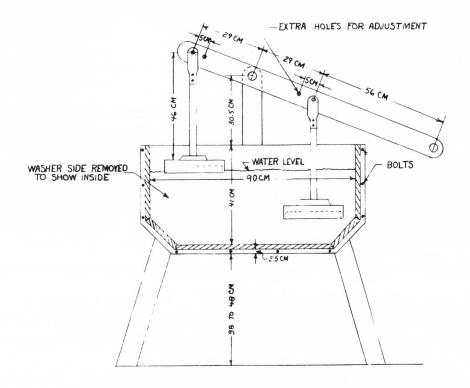

Fig. 74 Side View of Washing Machine

suction as it rises and the other plunger creates a pressure as it moves downward. Since the principle involves the churning action of the water, the slope at the corners of the machine bottom is important for best action.

The machine needs a rectangular tub for this method of operation. The rectangular box also is easy to build and does not require skilled carpentry methods. In general, any moderately strong wood that will not warp excessively will be satisfactory. The sides should be grooved for the ends and bottom of the tub as indicated and bolted with threaded rods extending through both sides with washers to permit it to be drawn tight. The through bolting is important, otherwise, leaks are inevitable.

The size indicated on drawings is considered sufficient for an average family in the U.S. The same principle may be used for a larger or smaller machine provided basic proportions are maintained. The tub should be slightly less than half as wide as it is long to get a proper surge of water. The pistons should be wide enough to move within a couple of inches of each side of the tub. The lever pivot should be high enough to permit the plungers to move up and down several inches without the edge of a lever hitting the edge of the tub. Likewise, rods on the plungers must be long enough to permit plungers to go well into the water so that clothes come completely out of the water at the highest position.

For efficient use of the above washer, several suggestions are made. Fill the washer with fifteen gallons of warm or hot water depending on what is available. Stains should be removed, soap rubbed into areas of garments which come in close contact with the body, and especially dirty clothes should be soaked before placing them in the washer. Shaved soap may be dissolved by heating it in a small quantity of water before adding it to the wash water. A six-pound load of clothes is recommended for best cleaning. Wash at a moderate speed (about fifty strokes per minute) for at least ten minutes or longer if it seems necessary. After washing and rinsing clothes, rinse the washer until clean and then replace the stopper. To prevent the wood from drying out and the washer leaking, add one to two inches of water to the washer when not in use.

367

Instructions for making washer

Mark and groove sides for end and bottom members.
Drill holes for cross bolts.
Cut off corners and trim ends of side members to length.
Level ends and bottom pieces to fit into groove in side members.
Miter bottom and end members together.
Assemble and bolt.
Cut and install legs.
Caulk seams between ends and bottom members with loose cotton or other vegetable fiber to make seams watertight. If joints to side members are carefully made, they probably will not need caulking.
Bore hole and make plug for draining tub. NOTE—This is shown on side in drawing but it is better in bottom of tub.
Make and install pivot members(upright).
Make and install plunger lever. NOTE—the cross pivot member (round) should be shouldered or notched at each pivot to prevent side movement.
Make plungers and install.

HAND WASHING MACHINE—II

Abstract-Hand Washing Machine—II

This hand washer is simple to construct and simplifies washing considerably.

Tools and Materials

Tinsnips
Pliers
Hammer
Soldering equipment
Galvanized iron sheeting: 140 cm x 70 cm for tub
   100 cm x 50 cm for lid and bottom
   36cm x 18 cm for agitator
Wooden handle—4 cm diameter, 140 cm. long

Fig. 75

Hand Washing Machine

Details

The tub, lid and agitator are made of the heaviest galvanized tin available which can be worked by a tinsmith.

To operate the washing machine the agitator is worked up and down with a quick motion but with a slight pause between strokes. The movement of the water caused by the agitator will continue for a few seconds before additional agitation is needed. On the upward stroke the agitator should come completely out of the water. The agitator should not hit the bottom of the tub on the downward stroke as this would damage both the tub and the clothes.

368

Abstract-Sewage Disposal in a Rural Home

The sewage system described in this section was similar to units used in the U.S. in the 1940's and 1950's. There have been changes in materials used and sanitary codes since that time period. The basic sewage disposal system used in rural areas today, however, is still quite similar to the earlier period.

Before installing a sewage system, always check with your county health authorities in order to comply with regulations for your area. In rural areas abroad, see what materials are available locally that can be used to develop the desired system.

CHARACTERISTICS OF SEWAGE

Household sewage ordinarily consists principally of human excrement, toilet paper, garbage, dish water, and other wash water from the various plumbing fixtures and floor drains.

Many kinds of bacteria, at times disease-producing ones, are contained in the discharges from the human body. Epidemics of typhoid fever, dysentery, diarrhea, cholera, and other water-borne diseases may result from the pollution of the water supply with sewage. Pollution is carried by water moving underground, as well as by water flowing on the surface. This is especially true in limestone regions, where underground channels and rock crevices permit water to flow for considerable distances with little filtering action. Sewage used for fertilizing or irrigating crops may contaminate vegetables. Anthrax, cholera, and parasitic worms may be present in the surface drainage from fields and barn lots. It is wise to regard all sewage as dangerous and to dispose of it promptly in a sanitary manner, so that disease germs will not pollute the water supplies or be spread by flies, animals, or an.

PROTECTION OF WATER SOURCES FROM HOUSEHOLD WASTES

Under most farm conditions a safe place for the disposal of wastes is in the upper 3-foot layer of soil, where the action of bacteria tends to render it harmless. Tile disposal fields, such as are used with septic tanks, and earth-pit privies accomplish this if the water table remains several feet below the surface and if the location is remote from water supplies.

Sewage or other wastes discharged into abandoned wells or other pits that reach to the water table or below it are almost certain to contaminate the ground water.

It is generally poor practice, and illegal in the U.S. to discharge wastes into surface streams. Streams do not necessarily purify themselves in 50 feet, 100 feet, or some other stated distance, as is commonly believed. They do tend to purify themselves over long distances through the action of sunlight, aeration, and other factors but may not be safe for domestic use for many miles below the source of pollution. Clear, sparkling water is not always safe drinking water.

SEPTIC-TANK SYSTEMS

Septic-tank systems, if installed and maintained properly, provide the most sanitary method of sewage disposal for farmhouses equipped with running water.

Ground water or rock close to the surface, lack of sufficient fall for the sewage to flow by gravity, and too small an absorption area for the effluent limit the satisfactory operation of a septic tank. When these conditions exist, special advice should be sought from a competent local sanitary authority. Adverse soil conditions can be overcome if sufficient fall and space are available.

The five essential parts (Fig. 76) of a septic-tank system are (1) the house sewer; (2) the septic tank; (3) the effluent sewer; (4) the distribution box; and (5) the disposal field. To facilitate inspection and repairs it is good practice to keep in the house a chart showing the location of the tank and other parts of the system.

A septic tank does not necessarily purify the sewage, eliminate odor, or destroy all solid matter. Its purpose is to condition the sewage or domestic waste by bacterial action, so that it can be disposed of in a more satisfactory manner.

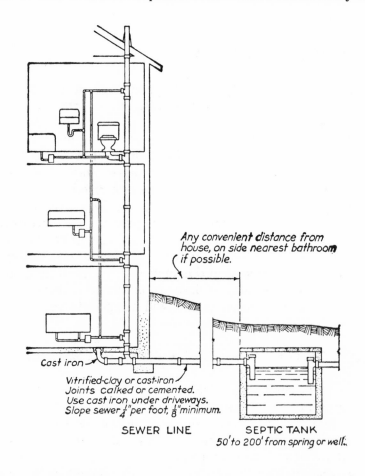

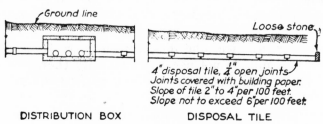

Fig. 76 A septic-tank system.

370

Operation of a Septic-Tank System

In a septic-tank system the sewage flows by gravity from the farmhouse through the sewer into the tank, where it should remain at least 24 hours. While passing through the tank the solids are acted upon by anaerobic bacteria, which work only in the dark and where there is little air. The heavy particles settle to the bottom as sludge, the lighter particles float as scum, and the remainder passes out of the tank through the effluent sewer to the disposal field. The gas released in the process escapes through a vent provided either in the T to the house sewer or the effluent sewer.

A tank that is too small may fill up with solids in a short while, because sufficient time is not allowed for breaking them down by fermentation, or the sewage may be pushed right through into the disposal field and clog it.

The effluent may contain even more disease germs than the original sewage, and though it may be as clear as spring water it is far from pure and may cause foul odors if discharged or allowed to pool on the surface of the ground.

The final disposition of the effluent into the upper layer of the soil exposes it to the action of aerobic bacteria. These bacteria, unlike those in the tank, need air and cannot work in saturated soil or live much more than 3 feet below the surface of the ground. The "living earth," or upper stratum, teems with these bacteria, which convert the dangerous sewage and disease germs into harmless matter and thus tend to purify the effluent if it remains long enough in the top layers of soil before seeping into the subsoil and thence to the ground water. Effluent discharged deep in the soil does not receive the benefit of this purifying action.

Several types of septic tanks are in common use. The one described in this section is the single-chamber type. This should meet all average needs. It would be advisable to consult the local health department as to their recommendations because frequently local conditions and larger establishments require special installations.

Selecting the Site

First install the tile disposal field where there will be the least danger of polluting water supplies, at least 100 feet from water sources if possible and always at a lower surface elevation. This is of greatest importance. Even though selecting a more distant location would result in greater initial cost, it would be a good investment as protection against diseases that might result from pollution of water sources. The site should slope away from the house and away from the source of water. Gentle unshaded slopes free of trees or shrubbery are best. Root-free locations are important because open-jointed tile cannot be "rootproofed." Porous, well-drained, gravelly, or sandy soil allows greater purification. Do not have the disposal field in vegetable gardens, under roadways, in swampy land, in muck soils, or in areas having rock substrata sloping toward the water supply. Allow sufficient area, where available, to enlarge the field later if needed.

The septic tank may be close to the house, but a more distant site would reduce the likelihood of odors if leakage occurs. The tank should also be kept 50 feet or more from any source of water supply and at a lower elevation. It should not be placed under driveways, pavements, or flower beds, as these would make it not readily accessible for periodic inspection. Care should be taken to insure that surface drainage from the area around the tank will not reach the vicinity of the water supply.

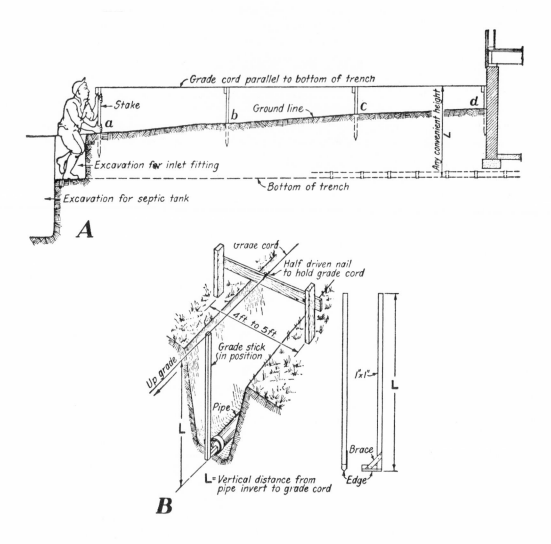

Fig. 77 — Establishing grade for sewer. A, 2- by 4-inch stakes are set each side of the trench at convenient distances *a, b,* and *d.* Then a board is nailed horizontally on the stakes at *d* at a convenient height above the bottom of the trench, that is, the bottom of the sewer leaving the house. A board is nailed likewise to the stakes at *a* the same height above the inlet to the tank that *d* is above the bottom of the trench. Similarly, boards are set at *b* and *c* by sighting from *a* to *d* so the tops of the intermediate boards will be in line. *B,* The exact grade of the sewer is obtained by measuring from the grade cord with the 1- by 1-inch stick, shown in detail. The length of the stick must equal the height of the board above sewer at *d.*

The House Sewer—Material

Vitrified salt-glazed clay well-made concrete sewer pipe, castiron soil pipe and plastic pipe are the standard materials for house sewers on farms.

Size

The tank should be large enough to retain the sewage at least 24 hours. The size should be determined by the largest number of persons that may live in the house, rather than by the number actually living there at the time the tank is built. The additional cost of a large tank over a small one is relatively little. If there is any question as to which of two sizes should be built it is wise to choose the larger. The dimensions recommended in the table in Fig. 78 are based on an average production of 50 gallons of sewage per person per day.

Unusually large quantities of sewage call for a tank of large capacity. In no case should the capacity of the tank below the flow line be less than 500 gallons. A tank length of two to three times the width should be maintained, and it is advisable to provide a depth of at least 4 feet below the flow line.

Allow about 1 foot of "freeboard," or air space, above the flow line for the accumulation of gases. This space is generally vented through the soil stack of the house.

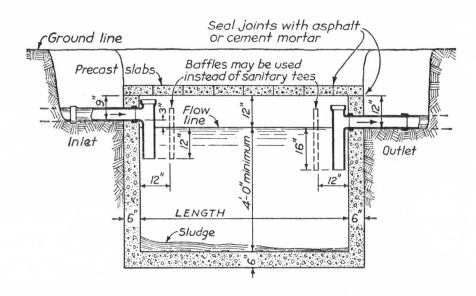

CAPACITIES, DIMENSIONS, AND CONCRETE MATERIALS FOR SEPTIC TANKS SERVING INDIVIDUAL DWELLINGS								
Maximum number of persons served	Liquid capacity of tank in gallons	Recommended inside dimensions				Materials for concrete 1 : 2½ : 4 mix		
		Width	Length	Liquid depth	Total depth	Cement sacks	Sand cubic yards	Gravel cubic yards
4 or less	500	3'-0"	6'-0"	4'-0"	5'-0"	16	1½	2½
6	600	3'-0"	7'-0"	4'-0"	5'-0"	17	1¾	2¾
8	750	3'-6"	7'-6"	4'-0"	5'-0"	19	2	3
10	900	3'-6"	8'-6"	4'-0"	5'-0"	21	2¼	3¼
12	1100	4'-0"	8'-6"	4'-6"	5'-6"	24	2¼	3½
14	1200	4'-0"	9'-0"	4'-6"	5'-6"	25	2½	3¾
16	1500	4'-6"	10'-0"	4'-6"	5'-6"	28	2¾	4¼

Fig. 78. Single-chamber septic tank. Note alternate use of baffle boards

Building A Concrete Tank

A convenient method of assuring correct location of the tank is to build a frame as shown in Fig. 79. Care is necessary to aline it with the center line of the inlet and outlet and to level it so that the distance from the bottom of the 2 by 4's on the form to the lower edge of the inlet hole in the form will permit it to be set at the grade of the house sewer. This frame is used to support the form for the tank. To avoid caving the edges, drive the stakes supporting the frame before beginning the excavation. The lumber in the frame can be used later to make part of the tank baffles.

Figure 80 shows how an inside form can be built and hung in place. The inlet and outlet tees should be carefully set and tied in place before the concrete is poured. A single length of pipe should be joined to the tee, so that the two can be set in the form as one unit. In most cases the earth walls of the excavations will serve as the outside forms unless the soil is sandy or gravelly and the excavation is deeper than 5 feet. If outside forms are used, space must also be provided for them. Forms should be constructed before the excavation is made and the tank built as soon as practical, to avoid warping of forms and caving of earth walls.

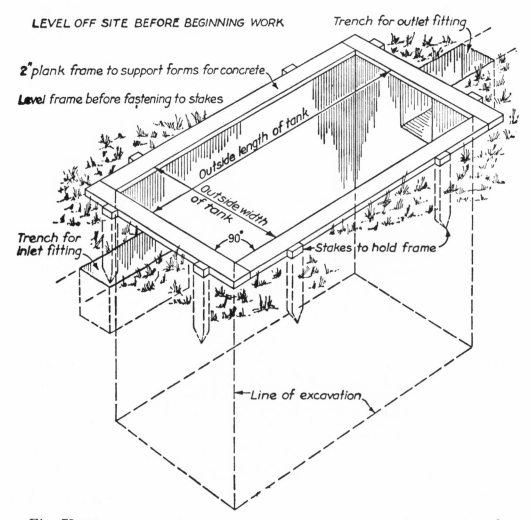

Fig. 79. **Method of outlining a septic-tank excavation on the ground surface.**

374

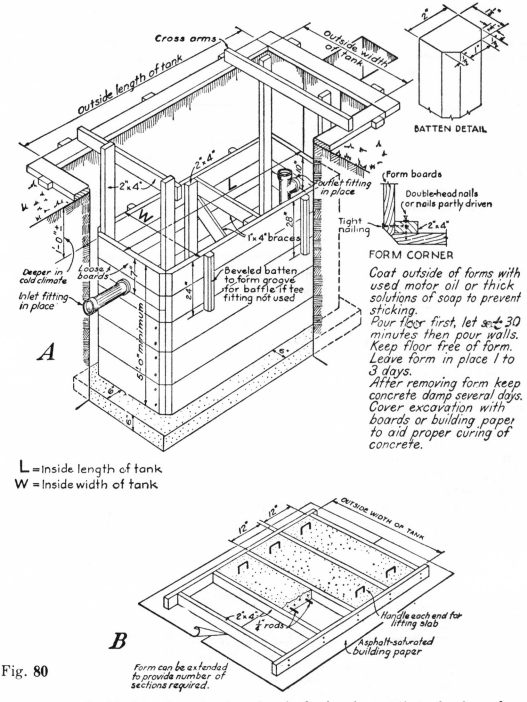

BATTEN DETAIL

Cross arms

outside length of tank

outside width of tank

2"x 4"

W

2"x 4"

Form boards

Double-head nails (or nails partly driven)

outlet fitting in place

28"

10"

Tight nailing

2"x 4"

1"x 4" braces

FORM CORNER

Deeper in cold climate

Loose boards

Beveled batten to form groove for baffle if tee fitting not used

7"

Coat outside of forms with used motor oil or thick solutions of soap to prevent sticking.
Pour floor first, let set 30 minutes then pour walls. Keep floor free of form. Leave form in place 1 to 3 days.
After removing form keep concrete damp several days. Cover excavation with boards or building paper to aid proper curing of concrete.

Inlet fitting in place

24"

1'-0"

5'-0" minimum

6"

6"

6"

6"

A

L = Inside length of tank
W = Inside width of tank

12"

12"

OUTSIDE WIDTH OF TANK

2"x 4"

¼" rods

Handle each end for lifting slab

Asphalt-saturated building paper

B

Form can be extended to provide number of sections required.

Fig. 80

Inside form hung in place for single-chamber septic tank, also a form for casting concrete-slab cover in sections.

Care and Maintenance of Septic Tanks

A septic tank when first used does not need starters to promote bacterial action, although starter bacterial action is available in many stores. A good septic tank normally requires no maintenance other than a yearly inspection and an occasional cleaning. Frequency of cleaning depends on the capacity of the tank and the quantity and composition of the sewage. Tanks of the size recommended in this section may require cleaning at intervals of 3 to 5 years.

The tank should be cleaned when 18 to 20 inches of sludge and scum has accumulated. If a drain has not been provided, sludge may be removed by bailing or by pumping with a sludge or bilge pump. It is not necessary to remove the entire liquid contents. Burial in a shallow pit or trench with at least 18 to 24 inches of earth cover at a point remote from water sources is the most practical method for disposing of these wastes.

A septic tank is intended to handle sewage only. Coffee grounds and ground garbage may be included if there is an ample supply of water for flushing and the tank is cleaned more frequently than would otherwise be done. The size of the tank should be increased at least 25 percent if these materials are included in the sewage.

Do not use matches or an open flame to inspect a septic tank, as the gasses produced by decomposing sewage may explode and cause serious injury.

Effect of Drain Solvents and Other Materials

Soap, drain solvents, and other mild cleaning or disinfecting solutions used for normal household purposes cause no trouble in the tank. Constant use in large quantities may prove harmful.

Wastes from milk rooms, strong chemicals used in sterilizing equipment or in photographic work, and the wastes from filters or water softeners not only reduce bacterial action but also cause abnormally rapid accumulations of sludge and clogging of the tile lines.

Protection Against Freezing

Septic-tank systems seldom freeze when in constant use. Warm water and the decomposition of the sewage usually maintain above-freezing temperatures. In cold regions there is trouble from freezing if various parts of the system are not covered adequately. If the system is to be out of service for a period of time or if exposure is severe, it may be advisable to mound over the poorly protected parts of the system with earth, hay, straw, brush, leaves, manure, snow, or the like.

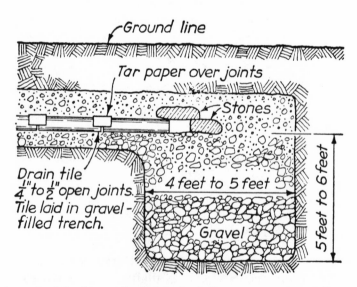

Fig. 81. Disposal of drainage from kitchen fixtures, using a line of terra cotta or plastic drain tile surrounded with gravel. One or two rock-filled pits at the end of the line increase the absorption area and are desirable where there are several fixtures or the soil is nonporous. The pits may be lined with boards or masonry laid without mortar and provided with a tight cover.

376

In sewage disposal, clogging of the disposal field is the most common trouble. This may be caused (1) by a tank too small for the volume of sewage, (2) by failure to clean the tank regularly, (3) by interior arrangement that does not provide slow flow through the tank or that allows scum or sludge to pass out with the effluent, or (4) by a disposal field that is too small or is incorrectly built.

The remedy for a clogged disposal field is to dig up and clean the tiles and re-lay them 3 or 4 feet to one side of the other of their former position. Sometimes a tile line can be cleaned by opening up the line at each end and flushing it thoroughly with a hose. With this method provision must be made to drain off and safely dispose of the water used for flushing.

Tile lines laid with improper slope allow the effluent to collect in a limited area and saturate the soil, causing odors. Bacteria cannot work in such areas, where the soil becomes sour, or "sewage-sick." These lines must be relaid on the correct slope. Odors or a water-logged soil may also indicate that the disposal field is too small.

House sewers frequently clog. This is due, in most cases, to roots and less frequently to trash, garbage, or other foreign materials discharged with the sewage. Greases in the sewer may cause trouble, especially when the slope is insufficient to give the sewage a cleansing velocity. Drain solvents will sometimes remove the obstruction, but more often it is necessary to clean the sewer by rodding. In some cases it may be necessary to dig up the line to reach the obstruction or, at least, to open the line so that it can be rodded from two directions. When it has been cleaned, a manhole could be built for use in case of future trouble. If stoppage is due to roots it may be necessary to re-lay the sewer with root-tight joints, or to move either the sewer or the vegetation so that roots cannot reach the line.

PRIVIES

A privy when safely located and properly built and maintained is satisfactory for some purposes. Privies should be built 50 to 150 feet from the farmhouse, preferably on the opposite side of the house from prevailing winds, and at least 50 feet from the well. A site downhill from the well is generally safest. In some cases, however, the ground water may flow in a direction opposite to the slope of the surface, in which case the privy should be built on the other side of the well. Direction of flow may sometimes be learned from soil surveys, well-driller's data, or other similar sources. A distance of at least 6 feet from fences or other buildings allows for proper mounding of the privy and keeps it away from roof drainage from adjacent buildings.

Good, tight construction with screened ventilators keeps insects and birds from entering, prevents rapid deterioration of the building, and provides greater comfort for the user.

The earth-pit privy is the simplest to build and the one most widely used. It is not generally recommended in localities where underground rock has crevices.

For a sanitary type of privy with reinforced concrete floor, riser, and supporting sills see Fig. 82. Because privy units are commonly used as urinals, the use of impervious materials for risers and floors facilitates cleanliness. In the colder climates, wood treated with a preservative is durable and reduces the problem of moisture condensation. Therefore, wood could be used if approved by the State Department of Health.

When it is considered impracticable to build the slab and riser of concrete, these parts may be of wood, as shown in Fig. 83. The building itself may be as

shown in either illustration. A wood structure is easy to move to a new location.

A pit with a minimum capacity of 50 cubic feet will usually serve five people over a period of 5 to 10 years. The privy should be moved when the pit is filled to within 18 or 20 inches of the top and a strong disinfectant spread in the old pit before covering it with earth.

It is important to have the earth-pit privy more than 50 feet from the well even where the water table is not near the surface. The ground water should flow from the well toward the privy, and it is important that this direction of flow be determined in advance.

Wood is most commonly employed for the main part of the building. The ground outside should be sloped as shown, to shed water away from the building, and the roof should extend beyond the walls to shed water away from the pit.

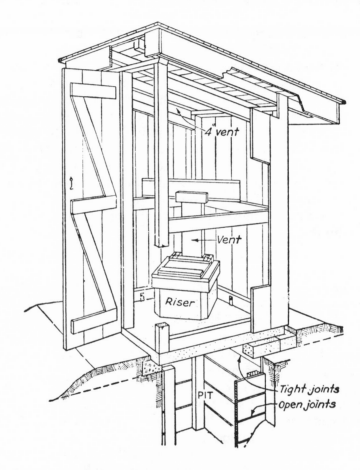

Fig. 82. Sanitary type of privy.

Care and Maintenance

All privies require periodic attention. Seats and covers should be washed weekly with soap and water or with disinfectants.

During the fly season fly and mosquito eggs will be destroyed by pouring half a pint of crude oil, crankcase oil, fuel oil, kerosene, or borax solution (1 pound powdered borax dissolved in about 10 gallons of water) over the contents of the pit about once a week.

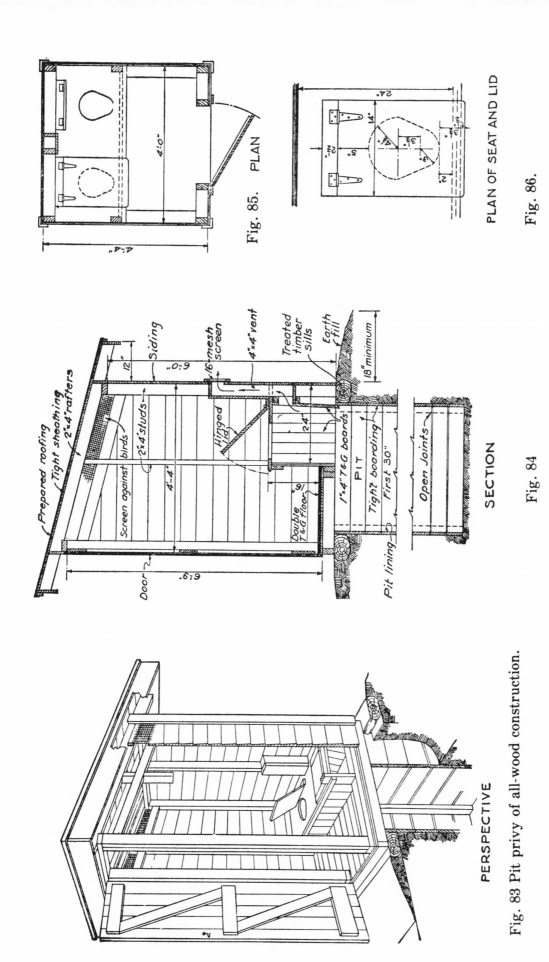

Fig. 85. PLAN

PLAN OF SEAT AND LID

Fig. 86.

SECTION Fig. 84

PERSPECTIVE

Fig. 83 Pit privy of all-wood construction.

INTRODUCTION TO CONCRETE CONSTRUCTION

Abstract-Introduction to Concrete Construction

Concrete is a strong, durable and inexpensive construction material when properly prepared. This brief summary in conjunction with later entries will give you a good introduction to concrete construction.

Tools and Materials

None — general information

Details

After concrete has set, there is no simple non-destructive test to evaluate how strong it is. Therefore, the entire responsibility for making concrete a strong material in accordance with specifications rests with the supervisor on the job and the people who prepare, measure and mix the ingredients, place them in the forms, and watch over the concrete while it hardens.

The most important factor in making strong concrete is the amount of water. Beginners are likely to have too much. See the entry on a slump cone for further details.

The proper proportion of all the materials, designed for the application, is essential. The concrete calculator will help give the proper proportions and amounts for your job.

Properly graded, clean, sharp agregate and sand is required to make good concrete. When we glue two pieces of paper together, we spread the glue evenly and in a thin layer, and press firmly to eliminate air holes. In concrete, the cement is the glue, and the sand and aggregate the material being joined.

By properly graded we mean that there are not too many of any one size grains or pebbles. Visualize this by thinking of a large pile of stone all 1½" in diameter. There would be spaces between these stones where smaller pebbles would fit. We could add to the pile just enough smaller stones to fill the largest voids. Now the voids would be smaller yet, and even smaller pebbles could fill these holes; and so forth. Carried to an extreme, the pile would become nearly solid rock, and only a very small amount of cement would be needed to stick it together. The resulting concrete would be very dense and strong.

Sharp aggregate and sand is desirable. Smooth, rounded stones and sand can make fairly good concrete, but sharp, fragmented particles work better because the cement as a glue can get a better grip on a rough stone with sharp edges.

It is extremely important to have the aggregate and sand clean. Silt, clay, bits of organic matter will ruin concrete if there is very much present. A very simple test for cleanliness makes use of a clear wide-mouth jar. Fill the jar about half full of the finer material available, the sand and small aggregate, and cover with water. Shake the mixture vigorously, and then allow it to stand for three hours. In almost every case there will be a distinct line dividing the fine sand suitable for concrete and that which is too fine. If the very fine materials amounts to more than 10% of the suitable material, then the concrete made from it will be weak.

This means that other fine material should be sought, or the available material should be washed to remove the material that is too fine. This can be done by putting the sand (and fine aggregate if necessary) in some container such as a drum. Cover the aggregate with water, stir thoroughly, and let stand for a minute, and pour off the liquid. One or two such treatments will remove most of the very fine material and organic matter.

Another point to consider in the selection of aggregate is its strength. About the only simple test is to break some of the stones with a hammer. If the effort required to break the majority of aggregate stones is greater than the effort required to break a similar sized piece of concrete, then the aggregate will make strong concrete. If the stone breaks easily, then you can expect that the concrete made of these stones will only be as strong as the stones themselves.

In very dry climates several precautions must be taken. If the sand is perfectly dry, it packs into a smaller space. If you put 20 buckets of bone dry sand in a pile, stirred in two buckets of water you could carry away about 27 buckets of damp sand. Charts do not take this extremely dry sand into account. If your sand is completely dry, add some water to it or else do your measurements by weight instead of volume. The surface of the curing concrete should be kept damp. This is because water evaporating from the surface will remove some of the water needed to make a proper cure. Cover the concrete with building paper, burlap, straw, or anything that will hold moisture and keep the direct sun and wind from the concrete surface. Keep the concrete moist by sprinkling as often as necessary; this may be as often as three times per day. After the first week of curing, it is not so necessary to keep the surface damp continuously.

Mixing the materials and getting them in place quickly, tamping and spading to a dense mixture is important. This is covered on the entry on mixing.

Reinforcing concrete will allow much greater loads to be carried. Design of reinforced concrete structures can become too complicated for a person without special training, if they are large or must carry high loads.

HAND MIXING CONCRETE

Abstract-Hand Mixing Concrete

Proper mixing of ingredients is necessary to get the highest strength concrete. Hand mixed concrete made with these tools and directions can be as strong as machine mixed concrete.

Tools and Materials

Lumber—2 pieces 6' x 1' x 2"
Galvanized sheet metal—6' x 3'
Nails

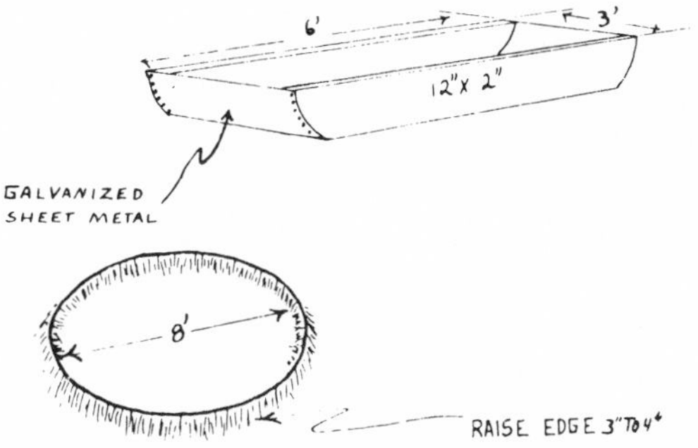

Figure 87

Saw, hammer—or concrete for making a mixing floor, (about 10 cubic feet of concrete are needed for an 8' diameter mixing floor made 2" thick with 4" high rim.)

Details

On many self-help projects the amount of concrete needed may be small or it may be difficult to obtain a mechanical mixer. Under these circumstances hand mixing of the concrete will be necessary and, if a few precautions are taken, the quality of concrete can be made equivalent to that from a mechanical mixer.

The first requirement is a watertight and clean base upon which the mixing can be done. This can be a wood and metal mixing boat (Figure 87) or a simple round floor made of concrete (Figure 87).

The ends of the wood and metal mixing boat are curved to make emptying easier. The raised edge of the concrete mixing floor serves to prevent loss of water from the concrete.

The procedure for mixing is similar to that for mechanical mixers in that the dry materials should be mixed first. As a minimum it is recommended that the pile of stone, sand, and cement be turned completely once. It should be completely turned a second time while the water is being added. Then it should be turned a third time. Anything less than this will not adequately mix all materials. When this last step is completed the mix can be placed as usual.

Correctly placing the fresh concrete in the forms or "shuttering" is important in making strong structures. The wet concrete mix should not be handled roughly either in carrying to the shuttering or putting into the shuttering. In either case it is very easy, through joggling or throwing, to separate the fine from the coarse material. We have said before that the strongest concrete comes when the various sizes of aggregate and cement are well mixed together. The concrete mix should be firmly tamped into place with a thin (¾") iron rod.

Be sure to rinse concrete from the mixing boat and tools when finished each day with the work. This will prevent rusting and caking of cement on them for smooth, shiny tools and boat surfaces make mixing surprisingly easier, and the tools will last much longer. Also try to keep wet concrete off your skin, for the material is somewhat caustic.

When the shuttering is full the hard work is done, but the process is not finished. The shuttering must be removed and the concrete protected until adequate strength is attained. The hardening action of cement begins almost immediately after the water is added, but the action may not be fully completed for several years.

Concrete reaches the strength used in the designing after 28 days and is strong enough for light loading after 7 days. In most cases the shuttering can be removed from standing structures such as bridges or walls after 4 to 5 days. In small ground supported structures such as street drains it is possible to remove the shuttering within 6 hours of completion provided this is done carefully. Special conditions, usually specified on the plans, may require leaving the shuttering in place for a much longer time.

During the early stages of hardening or curing the cement in the concrete continues to need moisture. If there is insufficient water available the cement is unable to complete its job of gluing the aggregate together. Because of this, it is recommended that new concrete be protected from drying winds and the sun, and that the surface of the new concrete be kept damp. For cement floors or open construction a covering of banana or palm leaves will be adequate, but these should be given a sprinkling of water at least once and perhaps twice each day for a period of not less than one week.

382

CONCRETE SLUMP CONE

Abstract-Concrete Slump Cone

The use of this simple device will enable you to determine if the proper amount of water has been added to the mix, which will insure maximum strength in the finished concrete.

Tools And Materials

Heavy galvanized iron

Strap iron 4 pieces 1/8" x 3" x 1"
16 iron rivets 1/8" diameter x ¼" long
Wooden dowel 24" long, 5/8" diameter

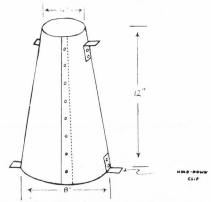

Fig. 88. Concrete slump cone

Details

In making reinforced concrete, it is important to have just enough water to make the concrete settle firmly into the shuttering (forms) and around the reinforcing when it is **thoroughly tamped.**

The easiest way is to look at the mix and at the way the workmen place the wet concrete. If the mix appears soupy and the aggregate shows up clearly in the mix, then it is too wet. At the same time it will be noticed that the workmen dump the mix into the shuttering and do very little tamping because, if they do any amount of tamping, a large amount of water will immediately appear on the surface. The workmen will soon complain if the mix is too dry.

A more accurate method of making a decision on the proper amount of water is to use the slump test. This test requires a small cone made of fairly strong metal and open at both ends. Dimensions of the cone and tamping rod are shown in the sketch. Once this simple equipment is available the slump test becomes very easy. The steps to follow are listed below.

1. Set the slump cone on a smooth clean surface and stand on the hold-down

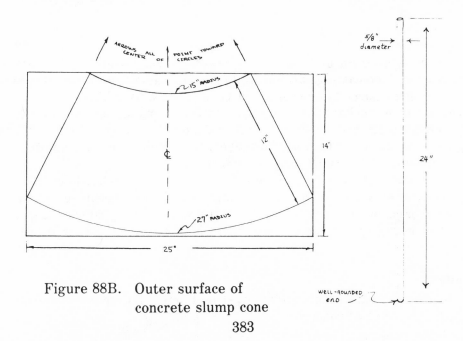

Figure 88B.   Outer surface of
concrete slump cone

383

clips at the bottom of the cone.

2. Have someone fill the cone to ¼ of its height and tamp this layer 25 times.

3. Fill the cone to ½ its height and tamp this layer 25 times. Avoid tamping the first layer again.

4. Fill the cone to ¾ its height and tamp 25 times. Avoid tamping the previous layers.

5. Complete filling of the cone and tamp this layer 25 times.

6. Step off the hold-down clips and lift the cone vertically and very carefully off the concrete.

Since this process will have taken only a few minutes the concrete will still be very soft when the cone is removed and the top will fall to some extent while the sides bulge out. This is called the slump. Obviously, if the mix is too wet the concrete will lose its shape completely and become just a soft pile. A good mix, as far as the water-cement ratio is concerned, will slump about 3" to 4" when the cone form is removed. It is well to keep in mind that dirty or muddy water can cause as much trouble as aggregate with excessive fine materials. Use clean or settled water.

Evaluation

The slump test is a standard test for evaluating wet concrete. This particular cone and rod has been recommended for village construction projects in Ghana.

QUICK SETTING CEMENT

Abstract-Quick Setting Cement

Using calcium chloride as an additive in making concrete results in a faster setting product with high initial strength.

Tools And Materials

Ingredients for regular concrete (any Portland cement), and measured amount of calcium chloride.

Details

In some applications a quick setting concrete is very useful. Situations arise when many repeated castings are desired from the same form or mold. Using an accelerator allows parts to be cast about twice as fast as without it.

However, the mixed batch must be put into the forms faster since the concrete sets up sooner. In general, the batches are small for these applications so that fast setting up is no particular trouble. Moreover, the accelerator does not impair the ultimate strength of the concrete.

The accelerator is best added by mixing one pound clean calcium chloride in each quart of water (½ kilogram for each litre) and then using this solution as part of the water used in the concrete mix. Use the solution at a ratio of 2 quarts (2 litres) for each bag of cement (94 lbs. or 43 kg.). Mix the concrete in the usual way.

Evaluation

This is the method recommended by the Portland Cement Association to accelerate the curing of concrete.

384

For the most of human history, shelter has been provided by the self-help method. Within recent years many governments and peoples have found that when included as a part of the process of economic development, aided self-help methods will contribute greatly to shelter improvement. They are particularly useful in countries where economic development is in its early stages, providing an opportunity for the people to make significant improvements with regard to housing within available resources by using the greatest resource of all, the manpower of the families themselves.

Thus, aided self-help in housing is a method to utilize the many man hours available in the form of heretofore unused leisure time—often enforced leisure because of seasonal unemployment, used in conjunction with some practical form of aid from the state, or others, enabling man to improve his shelter through his own efforts using profitably his spare time to an extent that he never could alone and unaided.

Perhaps the most important consideration is that this formula permits many governments to not wait for economic development but to proceed now within available resources and to both improve living conditions and also actually contribute to economic development.

The production of better shelter by the aided self-help housing method involves certain responsibilities both on the part of the sponsor of aid and on the part of the families or groups of families who are engaged in the effort to obtain better housing. The sponsor often assists with technical advice in design and construction. Sometimes he arranges for the provision of limited amounts of hard-to-get building materials which may greatly improve the end product. Long term building loans at low interest rates are often necessary. At times the sponsor must assist in arranging for secure land tenure through title or long term lease. Often a combination of some or all of these forms of aid make up an aided self-help housing program. In any event, the sponsor must be organized and equipped to promptly furnish such aid as is deemed necessary and advisable.

The family or group to be aided must assume the responsibility for contributing its labor to the joint effort. Frequently the family gathers together all of the local materials which will be necessary. Usually it repays the cost or a portion of the cost of the aid.

The aided self-help method of improved housing and shelter encourages private ownership of property. It provides constructive opportunity for the use of spare time. It gives the family an opportunity to improve its economic position and its social status in the community. It gives each participating family a stronger interest in the economic and political stability of the country. It adds hope for a better future for many, even though their government has comparatively few resources.

The program reported in this section is only one of those which are well under way in many places. Each program can learn from the other programs, particularly new ones. This can be done through film and documents, but by far the best way is to call in people who have experience, especially those who have shown imagination and ingenuity in initiating new programs in new places. Technical cooperation in this field is developing rapidly through agreements between individual governments (bilateral); and agreements between international organizations with individual governments (multilateral) and, also, through private contracts.

EXAMPLE OF SELF HELP HOUSING

After World War II, while most of Europe was rebuilding, Greece was still fighting against a Communist inspired revolutionary army. When the communists were defeated late in 1949, immediate reestablishment of Greece's agricultural economy was necessary. Ninety thousand war damaged houses in over 2100 farm villages had to be rebuilt. Funds, labor, materials and transportation were in short supply. At this point, Greece turned to aided self-help housing, as a technique to rebuild for most of the homeless families.

In conference with village leaders and others, the Ministry of Housing and Reconstruction developed a plan so that returning farmers could quickly rebuild their own homes with aid from the Government. The State provided technical advice and the organization to make possible the huge building program. It furnished the scarce (often imported) materials and it delivered these materials to local points of distribution. In addition, the State supplied small amounts of cash, so that the returning farmers could purchase materials which were produced locally, and could employ a limited amount of skilled labor to show them how to rebuild and to assist them in the most difficult phases. Periodic release of aid was on the basis of eligibility and the progress which the family made in reconstruction. Living areas were limited to 300 square feet per family, with provision for future expansion.

The families accepted the responsibility for organizing the reconstruction of their homes. They gathered together the local materials which were available near the site, such as stone, adobe earth and sometimes timber, and purchased locally manufactured products such as lime. They transported the hard-to-get materials supplied by the State from the nearest distribution center to their home site. Then, with the entire family working, they rebuilt their own homes with the advice and sometimes the assistance of the limited supply of skilled labor and government technicians which were available.

Fig. 89. A Stone and Cement Self-Help Home

EARTH BLOCK PRESS

Building blocks and tiles for small houses, farm buildings, walls, floors, patios, and walks can be made from a simple, portable, low-cost, hand-operated machine using common earth and cement or lime. The all-steel machine, tough and durable, is constructed for long and hard use. Oiling and ordinary care to keep it rust-free are the only maintenance requirements. In many areas earth blocks, if made by the user, cost only about 1/20 as much as conventional building blocks.

Earth blocks are used in the same way as other masonry building materials. In laying them up, apply the same mortar you would normally use. Blocks of heavier densities need no surface protection. They may be painted.

*The
Cinva-Ram
Block
Press*

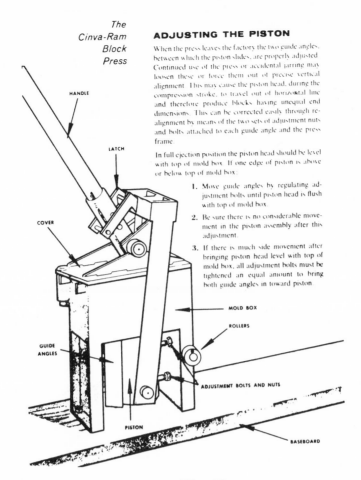

ADJUSTING THE PISTON

When the press leaves the factory the two guide angles, between which the piston slides, are properly adjusted. Continued use of the press or accidental jarring may loosen these or force them out of precise vertical alignment. This may cause the piston head, during the compression stroke, to travel out of horizontal line and therefore produce blocks having unequal end dimensions. This can be corrected easily through re-alignment by means of the two sets of adjustment nuts and bolts attached to each guide angle and the press frame.

In full ejection position the piston head should be level with top of mold box. If one edge of piston is above or below top of mold box:

1. Move guide angles by regulating adjustment bolts until piston head is flush with top of mold box.

2. Be sure there is no considerable movement in the piston assembly after this adjustment.

3. If there is much side movement after bringing piston head level with top of mold box, all adjustment bolts must be tightened an equal amount to bring both guide angles in toward piston.

Fig. 90

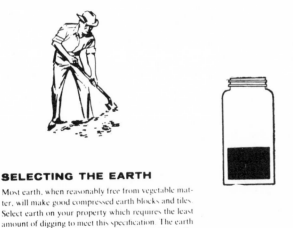

SELECTING THE EARTH

Most earth, when reasonably free from vegetable matter, will make good compressed earth blocks and tiles. Select earth on your property which requires the least amount of digging to meet this specification. The earth from foundation or basement excavations will usually be suitable.

STEPS IN
TESTING YOUR EARTH

1. Fill a straight-sided glass jar about one-third full of earth.

2. Add water to fill jar about two-thirds full.

3. Cover jar and shake vigorously until all of the earth is in suspension.

4. Allow earth to settle until you can see the various particle-size divisions. (About 30 minutes.)

Although any earth will make a suitable block, one should attempt to use earth which will make the best block. This is made from earth having particle-sizes from very fine to fairly coarse. The coarse particles should not be less than one-third, nor more than two thirds of the earth in the jar. The only earth which is not suitable is earth having only one particle-size. However, it is often possible to add sand to make fine-particle earth suitable.

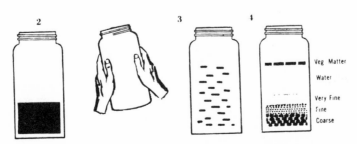

Fig. 91   Steps in Testing Earth

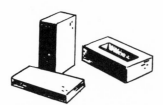

Blocks and Floor Tiles

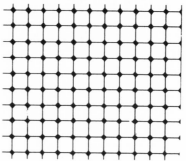

PREPARING THE EARTH

Only the simplest of implements are required to properly prepare the selected earth.

¼" mesh: actual size —

SCREENING THE EARTH

The selected earth must be screened through mesh having openings of about ¼" square.

Screening the soil

ADDING THE CEMENT

Depending upon the intended use of the blocks and the climatic conditions, excellent results can be obtained with 5 to 10 percent cement. After screening the earth, sprinkle the measured amount of cement evenly and mix thoroughly. Generally, a higher percentage of cement will result in a block having greater resistance to erosion, absorption, and abrasion.

Moistening the soil

NOTE: Lime may be substituted for Cement, but in doing so, double the quantity of Lime used and also Double the Curing Time of the Blocks or Tiles.

MOISTURE CONTENT

determining the dampness

The amount of moisture in the earth mixture is one of the *most important requirements*. A simple test to determine the correct amount of moisture in the mix is to squeeze a ball of the soil mix in your hand. If the ball can be broken in two without crumbling and without leaving any moisture on your hand, the moisture content is correct. Should the mix be too dry, sprinkle small amounts of water evenly and mix thoroughly until it is of the right consistency.

Fig. 92

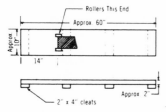

Standard 2" x 10" x 6' long
Rollers This End
Approx. 60"
Approx 10"
14"
2" x 4" cleats
Approx. 2"

MOUNTING THE PRESS

The press must be attached to a wooden baseboard for necessary stability.

OPERATING THE PRESS

In order to make good compressed earth blocks and tiles, enough earth mix must be loaded into the mold box to require a *hard pull* on the handle. Make a few test blocks and tiles to determine the quantity of your earth mix which must be loaded into the press to give you this adequate, hard pull.

There are three basic operations in making the compressed earth blocks or tiles:

1. Loading the mold box.
2. Compressing the mix.
3. Ejecting the finished product.

Detailed Movements

1. Place the handle in the rest position and open the mold box by swinging the cover horizontally until its stop is reached; then fill the mold box with the prepared earth.

2. Close the mold box, skimming off excess earth, and bring the handle to the vertical position; then release the latch.

3. Pull down the handle until it is parallel with the ground. This applies the necessary pressure to form the block. If the mold box is properly filled, this should require a *"hard pull"*.

1.

2.

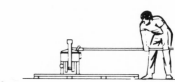

3.

Fig. 93

388

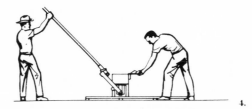

4.

4. Return the handle to the original rest position, swing cover back and open the mold box.

5. Pull down on the handle in the opposite direction until it is parallel with the ground. This ejects the block.

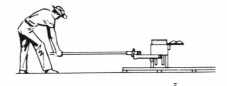

5.

6a *Removing blocks from the press:* Place hands flat at the ends of the block, being careful not to damage the corners or edges and then gently lift the block from the mold box. Place on edge at the curing site.

6b *Removing tiles from the press:* Place one flat hand on top of the tile. Keeping the tile and wooden insert together, slide both off the mold box until the other hand can be placed beneath the insert. Place both on edge at the curing site and then gently separate the insert from the tile.

NOTE: One of the greatest advantages of a compressed earth block or tile is that it can be removed immediately from the press without the use of a pallet.

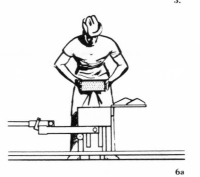

6a

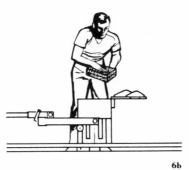

6b

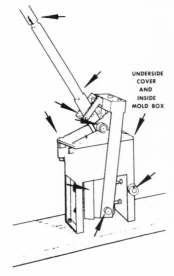

Fig. 94 Lubrication Points

LUBRICATING THE PRESS AND ACCESSORIES

Before and during operation, oil all moving and wearing parts; especially the underside of the steel cover, the inside of the mold box, the metal face of the insert, and the wooden form. FREQUENT oiling of the form and insert DURING OPERATION will prevent finished blocks and tiles from sticking when removing them from the press. A light coating of oil over the entire press after operation or during storage for long periods of time will keep it free from rust.

MAKING BLOCKS AND TILES

To make a solid block, do not use the wooden form or the insert. Remove both from the mold box. If the wooden form is attached to the piston head, it can be released by removing the two screws at the top of the wooden form.

To make a semi-hollow block, attach only the wooden form to the piston head by means of the two screws supplied.

To make a tile, place only the insert at the bottom of the mold box, *Metal face up.*

NOTE: Each Cinva-Ram comes equipped with 5 inserts to fabricate blocks for field drains, grilles, lintels, shelf-supports, conduits and pipes, as well as semi-hollow, tile, and half blocks.

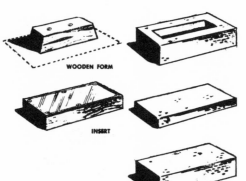

Fig. 95. Inserts For Fabricated Blocks

CURING THE BLOCKS AND TILES

The instructions for curing Cinva-Ram blocks and tiles should be followed carefully. In general, they are cured similarly to cement blocks or concrete. The moisture in Cinva-Ram blocks must be eliminated slowly, under cover and protected from sun and rain. They should not be stacked upon each other during the first three or four days after making. They should be separated, in single rows away from direct contact with the ground. For the first three or four days they must be sprinkled lightly with water twice a day. On the eighth day blocks may be laid-up in a wall where they continue to cure and gain full strength in about 30 days.

Tiles should not be laid-up until they have fully cured (about 25 days).

NOTE: If Lime is used in making the Blocks or Tiles, Remember to Double the Curing Time.

Fig. 96 Curing Blocks & Tiles

390

POLE FRAME CONSTRUCTION AND POST PRESERVATION

Layout

Once the site is decided upon, set up batter boards and string lines to represent the outline of the building as shown in Fig. 97A. Square the corners by laying out any right triangle whose sides are in the proportion of 3,4,5. This can be 3 feet on one side, 4 feet on the other, and 5 feet on the hypotenuse or long side of the triangle. Any multiple of these figures will do so long as the triangle is laid out the same way. It may be 6,8,10 as in Fig. 97A corner A. It could be 9,12,15; 12,16, 20, etc.

Most builders space their poles 12 to 15 feet apart. Measurements are made from the outside of each corner pole to the center of the next pole as indicated in Fig. 97A. Spacings are then determined from the center of each pole to the center of the next. The proposed pole locations are marked by measuring in from the outside wall a distance equal to half the diameter of the large end of the pole and driving a stake as indicated by "b" and "d" in Fig. 97A.

Holes

The depth the poles are set into the ground depends upon the wind forces and rigidity needed in the building. For most pole-frame buildings the needed depth of the pole hole is shown in Table 6. This table is limited to buildings with pole spacings of 15 feet or less:

Table 6. Depth of Pole Hole

Total pole length	Ordinary and gravelly soils
15 feet or less	4 feet
16-20 feet	4½ feet
21-25 feet	5 feet

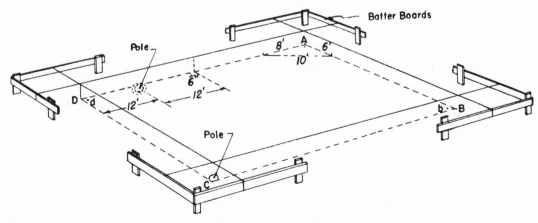

Fig. 97A. How to lay out the site for a pole frame building.

391

Fig. 97B. Framing detail for the outside row of plates.

POLES

Pressure or hot and cold bath treated poles are best and should be used for building construction. The poles are obtained directly from pole treating yards or through a local lumber dealer or construction firm. Untreated poles that come in contact with moist soil will last 5 years or less while treated poles can be expected to last 20 years or more. Although commercially treated poles are recommended, on-the-site, cold-soak treatment of most woods will give good results if done right. (See this section on cold soaking.)

Use poles that are 1 or 2 feet longer than the distance from the bottom of the pole to the roof. This allows for final trimming at the plate line. For most structures, poles with a 5- or 6-inch top diameter are suitable.

Aligning poles

Select the four straightest poles for the corners and carefully align them on the outward side with the ground line as established in Figure 97A. Put just enough dirt in the hole to hold the butt ends from shifting out of line. **Do not tamp at this time.**

Set the sidewall and endwall poles in place and line them up with the corner poles. Irregularities in sidewall poles must be taken care of as much as possible by rotating these poles so that any crookedness lies parallel to the siding. This will minimize distortion in the sidewall.

Poles are next aligned vertically on the outward side as shown in Fig. 98. Braces from near the top of the poles to stakes hold the poles in place. Locate a grade-level mark on the outward side of each pole as shown in Fig. 98. See that

these marks are at the same level. Locate them by using a farm level or a carpenter's level and a straight edge. Check these grade marks to make sure they are all at the same elevation, then make them permanent with a nail or a level saw-cut.

Framing

From the grade mark on each pole, measure up the required distance to locate the plate. Measure this height on each outside pole and drive a nail in each pole as a mark. The outside plate can then be set directly on the nails and spiked to the poles as shown in Fig. 97B. For best results, use ring or spiral shanked nails of the type shown in Fig. 100.

For stronger construction in windy and heavy snow areas, use bolts or notch the poles for the plates before nailing. To support the rafters, the inside plate is placed higher than the outside one (Fig. 97B.) Put the inside plate in place after the rafters are up. To increase the load-carrying ability of the plates, 2" x 4" x 3' blocks are often nailed under the plates and purlins as shown in Fig. 99.

Purlin plates are fastened to the poles supporting the center of the roof. These inside poles are spaced the same as the outside poles. Fig. 99 shows two methods of construction. Notice that the rafters are lapped and spiked to the poles.

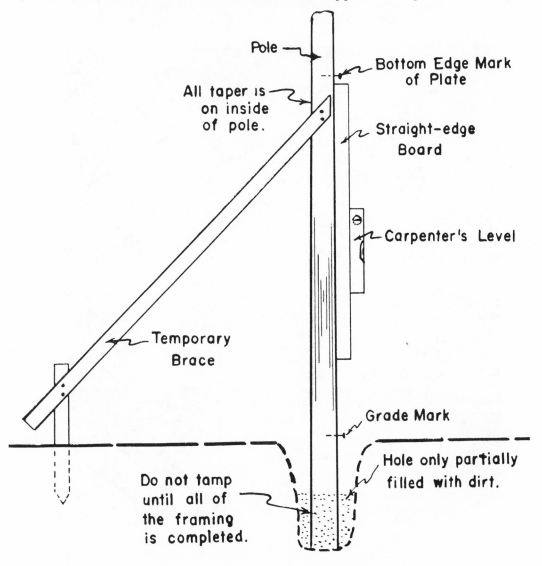

Fig. 98. A method of aligning the poles.

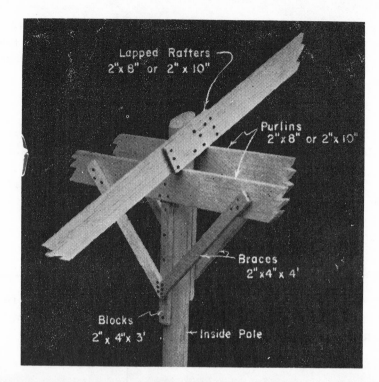

Fig. 99. Top: A method of framing for the interior poles using braces. Bottom: An alternate method of framing the interior poles. Support for the purlins is provided by notching the pole.

394

Fig. 100 shows construction at the roof peak. Rafters and girts are lapped and spiked together to save sawing and fitting. The pairs of rafters on each end of the building are cut and butted together. Rafters can be spaced from 2 feet to 6 feet apart depending on the size of the rafter material and the type of roofing to be used. When poles are spaced 12 to 15 feet apart, 2" x 10" rafters spaced 4 feet apart are satisfactory.

After the rafters are in place, the tops of the poles may be sawed off. The 2" x 4" girts are nailed on edge and spaced 2 feet apart when corrugated roofing is used. Fasten the 2" x 4" girts to the rafter with a tie block as shown in Fig. 101. If the rafters are spaced 3 feet or less apart, the 2" x 4" girts shown in Fig. 100 may be nailed flat or 1-inch solid sheathing may be used.

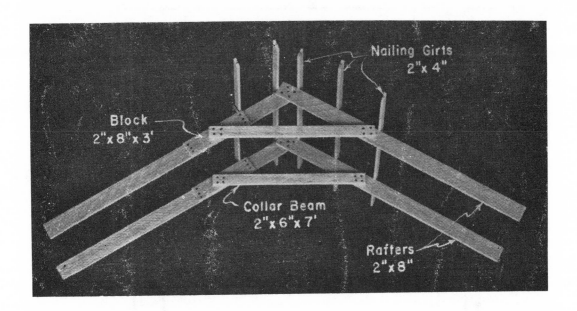

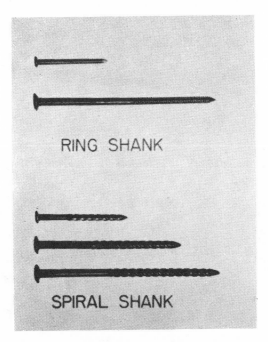

Fig. 100. Top; Ridge framing details. Bottom: Ring or spiral shanked nails of the type shown here increase the strength of pole-type buildings. This type of nail is also recommended for attaching metal roofing and siding.

395

Siding

To hold the siding, 2" x 6" girts usually are nailed on the outside of the poles as shown in Fig. 101. To stiffen the girts a 2" x 4" can be nailed along the top edge of the girt to form an L-shaped member. Vertical wood siding or corrugated metal sheet is then nailed over the girts.

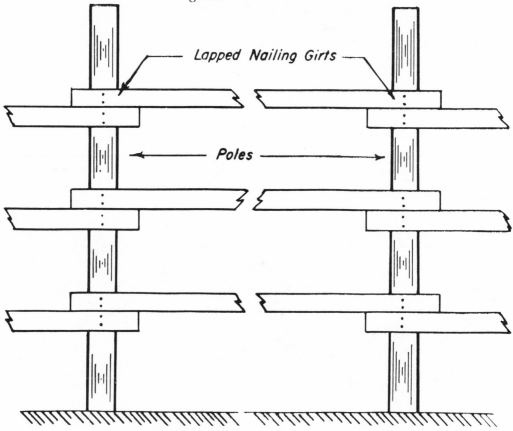

Fig. 101. Top; Side framing details showing how girts are lapped to eliminate sawing. Bottom; A tie-block has been used here to fasten the between-the-poles rafter to the plate. The same type block can also be used to tie the roof nailing girts to the rafter.

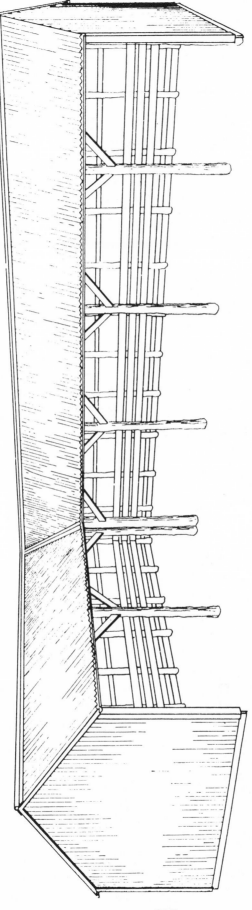

Fig. 102. This pole-frame, L-type loafing shed will provide good shelter for animals. It is flexible in regard to size and construction materials. You can easily change the design size and shape to fit your location and needs. Remember to build the front high enough to allow easy operation of the tractor manure-loader.

397

Fig. 103. A combination Pole and Frame Hay Storage Feeding Shed.

398

Cold Soaking Method of Treating Poles

Any method of fence post treatment that calls for a lot of hard, disagreeable work, extreme care in watching the details, and a lot of time for the process is not likely to be popular with farmers. The treating method known as cold soaking is not unduly burdensome either as to work involved, details of treating, or actual operating time. Its cost is in an in-between class and its benefits, so far as proved by service to day, are in the same class.

The groupings in the following tabulation, based on kinds of wood that the Forest Projects Laboratory has treated by cold soaking, give an idea of what woods to treat by this method. In interpreting these groupings it should be borne in mind that the treatment gives good results only with seasoned posts and that good or fair retentions do not offset poor penetrations. The poor distribution of the preservative indicated by such a combination would mean only uncertain results with high cost.

The results reported for the following groups apply to seasoned posts after a soaking period of 48 hours or longer.

Group 1. *Retentions fair to good, penetrations in sapwood reasonably good.*

Round softwood posts
Pine, eastern white
Pine, jack
Pine, lodgepole
Pine, ponderosa
Pine, red
Pine, southern yellow

Round hardwood posts
Oak, black (high sapwood content)
Oak, red (high sapwood content)
Oak, southern red
Oak, white

Group 2. *Retentions and penetrations poor to fair.*

Round softwood posts
Douglas-fir (coast, inter-
  mountain and mountain type)
Fir, balsam
Fir, white[1]
Larch, European
Larch, western
Redcedar, western
Spruce, black
Spruce, Norway
Tamarack
White-cedar, northern

Round hardwood posts
Ash, green
Beech, American[1]
Birch, yellow
Butternut
Catalpa
Cherry, black[1]
Elm, American
Elm, slippery
Hackberry
Hickory, mockernut[1]
Hickory, shagbark

[1] Penetrations in some cases fair to good but not consistently so.

Group 3. *Retentions good, transverse sapwood penetrations generally poor.* (Good end penetration is usually obtained but material over 2 to 3 feet in length could not be expected to show good results.)

Round hardwood posts

Aspen
Basswood
Birch, white or paper
Boxelder
Cottonwood, eastern
Maple, hard

Maple, soft
Sweetbay
Sweetgum
Tupelo, swamp (blackgum)
Willow
Yellow-poplar

The cold soaking treatment consists in submerging posts for 1 to 2 days or longer in coal-tar creosote, solutions of coal-tar creosote and domestic fuel oil, a solution of pentachlorophenol in fuel oil, or a solution of copper naphthenate in fuel oil. Solutions of 5-percent (by weight) pentachlorophenol are used. The copper naphthenate solutions should be prepared to contain a copper metal equi-

valent of at least one percent (by weight). Copper naphthenate and pentachlorophenol are usually sold in concentrated solutions. Directions for diluting the product to get treating solutions of these concentrations should come with the preservative.

Cold soaking in coal-tar creosote or in creosote-petroleum solutions may not result in satisfactory penetrations of the wood unless the creosote and the oils used with the creosote are applied during warm weather and are thin (low in viscosity). The low-viscosity oils may not perform as well in service as the heavier oils which can be used in treatments involving heating.

Cold soaking calls for a single tank without heating equipment. For woods that treat easily, 48 hours of soaking in low-viscosity and preservative oils gives good penetrations of preservative into the wood as much as you would get with a week of soaking. In most cases soaking more than a week would not be worthwhile. Cold soaking works best with round pine posts that are well seasoned. Posts of other species and split or sawed posts do not treat so well.

Pine posts having a high moisture content (over 30 percent) have been found to be poorly penetrated and to absorb insufficient amounts of preservative. Posts containing surface mold, excessive blue stain, and the beginnings of decay on the other hand absorb too much preservative. With such material the treating time can be reduced to 3 or 4 hours to cut down the absorption of preservative so long as this does not seriously reduce the depth of penetration. It is seldom worth while or economical to treat posts that are rotted.

The preservative for cold soaking may cost 35 to 50 cents a gallon or even more and an absorption of at least half a gallon per post is what you should try for. If you hire labor for treating either by the hot-and-cold-bath method or cold soaking and add the cost of preservative and are obliged to charge the cost of tanks to a fairly small group of posts, the cost of treatment may cost as much as or more than the cost of pressure-treated posts. The initial cost will be appreciably less if the owner already has a suitable tank or can buy one cheap and then does his own treating.

Posts treated by cold soaking in petroleum solutions containing pentachlorophenol have been in service only since 1942. The posts that have been in service long enough to justify any estimates of service life happen to be those consisting of species to which the treatment seems to be least adapted. Aspen, birch, and cottonwood posts in 13 installations are estimated to have an average life of 7.0 years in comparison with 4.1 years for untreated posts of the same species.

Tests have been running somewhat longer in the case of posts treated with straight coal-tar creosote by cold soaking. In 6 installations of basswood, elm, cottonwood, and red oak posts treated and installed in 1909 the average life of the posts is 23.2 years. The average life of untreated posts of these species is 7.1 years.

Cold soaking can effectively be done in a 55 gallon oil drum or similar type containers. One end is removed from the drum and then it is filled with the preservative. The posts are placed in the drum with the preservative for the proper amount of soaking time.

METHODS OF PLACER GOLD MINING

Formation of Placers

Gold found in placers originally existed in place as deposits of various forms in areas intruded by igneous rocks. In some cases it was deposited in the igneous rock itself in finely disseminated particles; in other cases it was originally in quartz veins, cutting through the igneous and other rocks and formed as a result of the igneous intrusions. Due to disintegrating processes (change of temperature, wind, rain, earth movements, and chemical action), the rock containing the gold has been reduced to such a state that it is easily broken and the gold freed. Through the action of running water, and of glaciers in some instances, the gold-bearing rock is transported away from its source. The moving water causes the heavier gold particles to work slowly toward the bottom of the stream bed. On reaching bed rock, or hard pan, the gold moves slowly down stream until it lodges in crevices, cracks, or other irregular openings in the stream bed.

Placer deposits may be moved many times, depending upon the volume of water and the velocity with which it is flowing, and this generally depends upon the rising and subsiding of that particular part of the earth's crust. There is no fixed rule as to where the gold is apt to occur in the stream bed. The velocity of the stream is not the same at all points in its cross section. Points where the bed has widened, with resultant decrease in velocity, are the most favorable. The reason for this is that the gold is given the chance to settle to the bottom, when velocity of water decreases. Placers may be found in old dry stream beds. At the

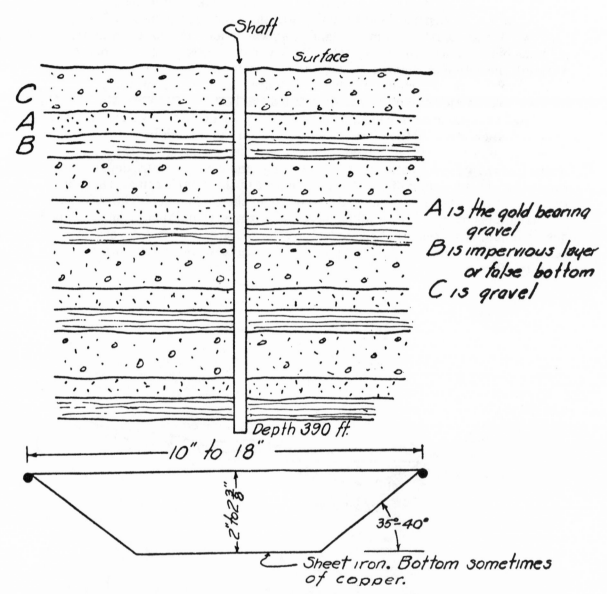

Fig. 104. Bench gravels; where well rounded particles indicate materials carried by water; gold bearing gravel layer; a gold pan.

402

time of this formation, water was, of course, present. Later disturbances may have caused the stream to change its course. Or climatic conditions may have been responsible for its drying up.

There have been very few instances where the gold in a placer deposit has been traced back to its source. The reason is that the source has been either completely eroded away, or has been deeply covered with other material, such as lava flows, sediments, etc., or the gold may have traveled great distances. It has been rather definitely proven that there are cases where placer gold was found over one hundred miles from its original source.

Position of Gold in Deposit

In general the various sized particles of gold or other placer minerals will be found in the following section of the stream when the water has flowed continuously in one direction:

1. The coarse gold will be deposited in the upper part of the stream.
2. The finer gold will be deposited in the lower portions of the stream.
3. The richest and coarsest gold will be deposited in the layers of comparative coarse gravel wash.
4. The finer gold will be deposited in the finer sandy drifts.
5. The best gold should occur in the layers of wash containing black sand and pebbles of magnetite or other heavy mineral.
6. On a favorable bottom gold will ordinarily lodge on the down side of a bar of rock running across the bed of a stream.

Associated Minerals

Black sand (magnetite, an oxide of iron) is nearly always found in placers with gold. Its presence or absence is not positive proof of the presence or absence of gold. Ilmenite (an iron titanium oxide) resembles magnetite to a large extent. It is usually present. Garnet (ruby sand) and zircon commonly occur in gold placers. In Alaska, and in at least one locality in Idaho, cinnabar (mercury sulphide) has been found in gold placers. Scheelite (calcium tungstate) and cassiterite (tin oxide) have been found in some placers. Pyrite is commonly found, and by the inexperienced prospector may be confused with gold. A very simple test quickly distinguishes between the two. Pyrite is very brittle. A slight pressure between two hard surfaces reduces it to fragments. Gold is simply flattened without breaking. Biotite mica which has altered to a bronze color is sometimes confusing. It is readily recognized from gold by the readiness with which it breaks when bent back and forth.

Descriptions of the Simpler Mining Methods and Apparatus

The size of the gold to be recovered has an important bearing on the details of the appliance to be used. Finely divided gold is much more difficult to save than the coarser variety.

The following table will give some idea of the size of gold particles and their value.

Nuggets
    Coarse gold — that which remains on a 10-mesh screen (ten openings per linear inch).
    Medium gold — that which remains on a 20-mesh and passes a 10-inch screen (about 2200 colors to 1 oz.).

403

Fine gold — that which passes a 20-mesh and remains on a 40-mesh screen (about 12,000 colors to 1 oz.).

Very fine gold — that which pases a 40-mesh screen (about 40,000 colors to 1 oz.).

Flour gold

170 colors to 1 cent (314,500 to 1 oz).

280 colors to 1 cent (436,900 to 1 oz).

500 colors to 1 cent (855,000 to 1 oz).

Of the many methods that are used for recovering gold from placer deposits there are only three that merit description in so far as the prospector is concerned. In the order of simplicity, the construction of the apparatus and operation of these three methods follow.

Panning

The ordinary sheet-iron gold pan varies from about 10 to 18 inches in diameter at the top. The depth is about three inches. The ordinary 10-inch frying pan with the handle removed is quite often used. This pan holds about five pounds. The 18-inch pan holds about 25 pounds of dirt. Figure 104 illustrates the gold pan.

The gold pan is made of stiff sheet-iron. The inner surface must be kept clean and bright, and free of grease. Some pans are made with a copper bottom. Copper amalgamates readily with mercury. By rubbing mercury on the copper bottom, fine gold is retained through amalgamation.

Operation of pan

The pan is filled about two-thirds full of dirt and placed under water. While in this position the contents are stirred or "kneaded" with both hands. This procedure is necessary to break up the lumps and to free the gold from clay-like material. As the disintegration proceeds, the large stones and pebbles are thrown out. When the material has been thoroughly broken up and the large rocks removed, the pan is taken in both hands for the panning operation. The position of the hands is slightly back of the middle of the pan. This permits the pan to be inclined down and away from the operator. The pan is now raised until it is just covered with water. It is now given a slight oscillating, circular motion, with the result that the contents are shaken from side to side. This motion keeps the lighter material in suspension and washes it out of the pan. It also enables the gold and heavy minerals (magnetite, etc.,) to work their way to the bottom of the mass. This operation is continued until only the gold and black sands are left. This material is now dried and the magnetite removed with a magnet. Other material such as stream tin, and heavy non-magnetic minerals, are separated from the gold either by amalgamating the gold or by picking out the gold, piece by piece.

About 100 pans of dirt are the most that can be panned by an experienced miner in 10 hours. Assuming that placer gravel weighs 135 pounds per cubic foot, and that the gold pan holds 15 pounds, 100 pans would be equivalent to about 11 cubic feet or 4/10 of a cubic yard. With the large pan (18 inch diameter) a good panner may handle one cubic yard.

Rockers

There are many forms and sizes of rockers. The rocker handles about three to five cubic yards of material per 10 hours, its capacity depending upon the size of the gold and the amount of clay present. Large amounts of clay slow the operation down. It is necessary that all the clay be washed free of the gold, otherwise, the

fine gold is floated away. The sketch shown as Figure 105 illustrates a convenient form of knockdown rocker.

Description of Rocker—

The inside of one side of the rocker and an end view of the rocker is shown.

A — Cleats for holding the back of the rocker.

B — Cleat for holding bottom of rocker, L.

C — Cleats for holding back of rocker.

D — Cleat for holding canvas-apron frame.

E — Cleats for holding brace at top of rocker.

F — Cleat for holding sieve box.

X — Bold holes for ½ inch iron bolts used in holding rocker together.

I — Riffles ¾ inch high by 1 inch wide.

K — Rockers

H — Handle for rocking apparatus.

L — Bottom board of rocker.

M — Spike projecting 1½ inches to prevent rocker from slipping down grade.

The bottom board, L, of the rocker should be in one piece. This is to prevent leakage of fine gold which might occur if two poorly fitted boards were used. Material of construction is preferable finished ¾ inch. The six ½ inch rods should have nuts and washers for the ends. This permits tearing the rocker down for transportation purposes.

The dimensions of the sieve box are as shown in the sketch. It should just fit loosely in the top of the rocker. The bottom is made of heavy sheet iron perforated with about ½ inch diameter holes.

The apron is a framework made of 1 inch by 1½ inch material well fitted together and covered with canvas. The canvas is not stretched tight, but allowed to sag somewhat at the bottom. This gives a slight depression in which gold is caught.

The grade or inclination of the rocker is obtained as follows:

Two heavy planks are firmly placed on the ground such a distance apart that each of the rockers will fall about in the center of a plank. The planks must have holes in them to receive the spike in the bottom of the rockers. The plank under the front or discharge end of the rocker is placed two inches lower than the rear plank. This arrangement, therefore, gives a drop of two inches in three feet. The grade is influenced directly by the following conditions:

1. Rapidity with which material can be fed to the rocker.
2. Amount of clay present.
3. Fineness of gold.

If the gravel is finely bound together with clay, the grade should not be less than two inches. If very little clay is present, and the gold is not too fine, the grade can be increased. In any event, the grade must be such that the clay is completely removed from the gold before the discharge is reached, and if the gold is very fine it should be given a chance to settle. In cases of very fine gold and considerable clay, it might be adivisable to add one more riffle.

Operation of rocker

For the operation of the rocker much more water is required for the gold pan. Where there is a shortage of water it is usually better to carry the gravel to a point near the source of water. The gravel is placed in the screen box and the rocker is shaken back and forth with a vigorous motion. At the same time, water is poured over the gravel, or a small stream of water is permitted to run over it. If water is scarce, the discharge can be caught in a small pool and rinsed. Good judgment must be exercised in the use of the water. If too rapid a flow is used, the smaller gold particles will be washed over the riffles and lost with the discharge. At the same time, sufficient water must be used to completely disintegrate the

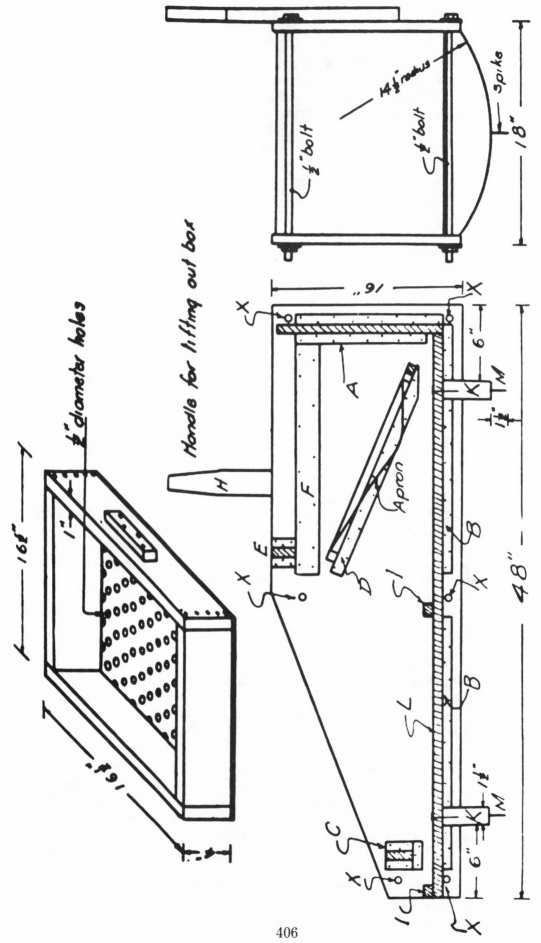

Fig. 105. Knock Down Rocker

406

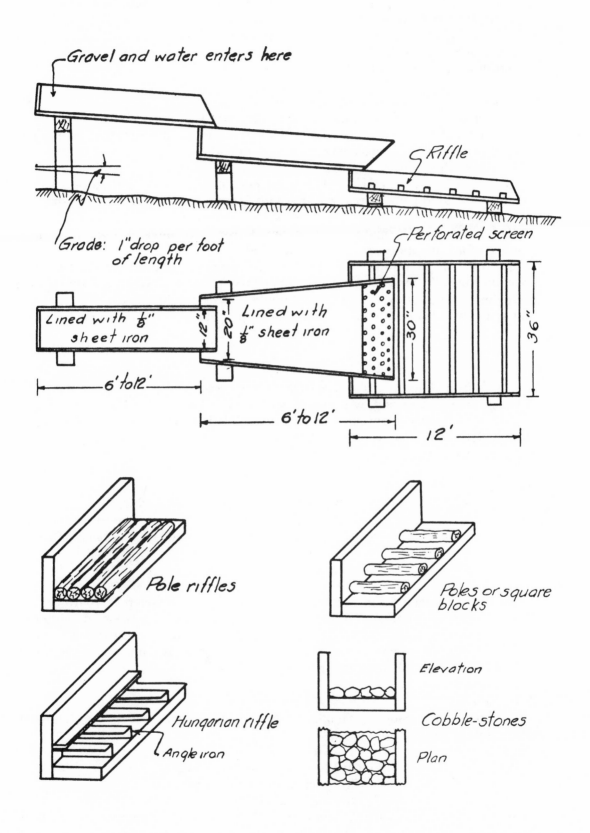

Fig. 106. Top; A Tom. Bottom; Various types of Riffles

407

gravel and remove the clay. An attempt should be made to keep a fairly steady stream flowing, rather than an intermittent, surging supply. The amount of water must be just sufficient to carry the tailings over the riffles. The motion of rocking is a quick jerk with a sudden stopping of the motion. The heavy sands must not be permitted to build up back of the riffles. If this is allowed, the gold will wash over these sands and be lost.

Clean up

The canvas or blanket forming the apron is rinsed off in a tub of water two or three times a shift. The gold and sands back of the riffles are removed as often as thought necessary. The concentrates are dried and the gold removed in the same manner described under panning.

The rocker is not very efficient. It does permit the handling of more material than does the gold pan. Mercury sometimes is placed back of the riffles to catch some of the fine gold.

When the over-size material is removed from the sieve box, it should be inspected for nuggets before being discarded.

The "tom" or "long tom" is sometimes used in place of the rocker. It is illustrated in Fig. 106. Six to twelve foot sluice boxes are used. One man shovels the gravel into the head box, others lift out boulders with pitchforks and break up the lumps of clay. Clean up is made in the same manner as for the rocker.

Sluices

In the use of sluice boxes two conditions may arise. First, where the box rests on the ground, and second, where it is necessary to elevate the sluice on trestles, necessitating also the elevating of the gravel. Only the first case will be discussed. The construction of the boxes and the manner of retaining the gold are the same in either case.

Material

The material from which the sluice is made is rough-finished lumber. There are some instances, such as dredging and large scale hydraulics, where metal boxes are used. In many cases the box will be made of lumber which has been hewn out by the prospector himself.

Dimensions

The sluice is made up in sections. These sections vary from 12 to 16 feet in length, depending upon the locality. Twelve foot sections are the most common. The width varies from one foot to five feet, but is usually between 12 and 18 inches. The depth is from eight to ten inches. The boards from which the boxes are made are about one and one-half inches thick.

Construction

The boxes are made of rough lumber. For ordinary work the following dimensions are sufficient:

Length: 12 feet
Width: 1 foot inside measurement
Depth: 8 inches inside measurement
Thickness of material: 1½ inches

One end of each box should be narrower than the other. This permits the telescoping of the boxes. As the gravel bank recedes, boxes from the discharge end are brought to the head end. Thus, it is not necessary to move the entire sluice in order to keep close to the working face.

Head Box

The box into which the gravel is shoveled is called the "head box." It is equipped with a grizzly or bars to prevent the large boulders and rocks from entering the sluice. This is also where the water enters the sluice.

Grizzly

The grizzly is made of iron bars or heavy pipe. The spacing between the bars will depend upon the size of the gravel. If only medium sized gravel with a very few large rocks is to be encountered, a perforated sheet may be used.

Riffles

The riffles can be constructed of many different things; wooden blocks, angle irons, poles, cobblestones, boulders, etc., have been used. They may run the length of the box or across it. Fig. 106 shows some of the riffles in common use. The boxes are shown with one side removed.

In Fig. 107 is shown a section of a sluice. The number of boxes making up the sluice depends upon the amount of material to be handled and the size of the gold. Fine gold requires more time to settle.

When real fine gold is present, the last sluice box may be replaced by a very wide table (about 16 feet) from 10 to 20 feet in length. A screen is placed over the end of the sluice box so that only the sands and fine gold can get onto the table. The table is divided into sections eight feet wide, and each half covered with burlap tightly stretched. The material is allowed to flow over one half for about 12 hours. Then it is changed to the other side. The burlap is removed and washed off in a tub.

In some instances, mercury may be placed back of the riffles in the boxes near the discharge end of the sluice. This helps to retain the fine gold through amalgamation. If the gold is not clean, it will not combine with mercury.

It may be necessary to elevate parts of the sluice on trestles or other devices to maintain approximately a grade of six inches drop for each twelve feet of sluice.

The riffles should not be fastened in the sluice box permanently as it is necessary to remove them for the clean up. They may be held in place by nailing the side boards of the box to the ends of the riffles. The nail should not be driven all the way in. Or they may be wedged in place.

Clean up

The frequency of the clean up depends upon the richness of the gravel being washed. It may vary from a few days to the entire season. The first few riffles should be cleaned up at least once every two weeks. In making the clean up the gravel is discontinued and a stream of water, just large enough to wash the heavy sands, mercury, and amalgam, is permitted to flow down the sluice. The riffles are taken up and the sand washed down the sluice. Occasionally, the contents are scraped up with a spoon. All cracks and crevices are thoroughly cleaned. Blankets and burlap that may have been used are washed in a tub.

Operation

In order to use a sluice, plenty of water must be available as a continuous stream is run through the system. If sufficient water is not at hand, it is useless to construct the sluice. For large scale operations, water may be brought to the gold-bearing deposit by means of a flume.

The gravel is shoveled on to the grizzly at the head box and the water run over it. The over-size is raked or shoveled off to one side. The amount of water flowing down the sluice should be just enough to wash the gravel, passing through the grizzly, over the riffles, and out the end of the sluice. For this reason, the grizzly bars should not be spaced too far apart. If so, the velocity of the water may have

to be so great as to prevent the settling of the fine gold. When the wooden riffles become so worn that they no longer hold back the heavy sands, they should be replaced. This condition exists when the riffles become rounded or are worn thin.

Fig. 107 illustrates the method of working a gravel bed where it is not necessary to elevate the material.

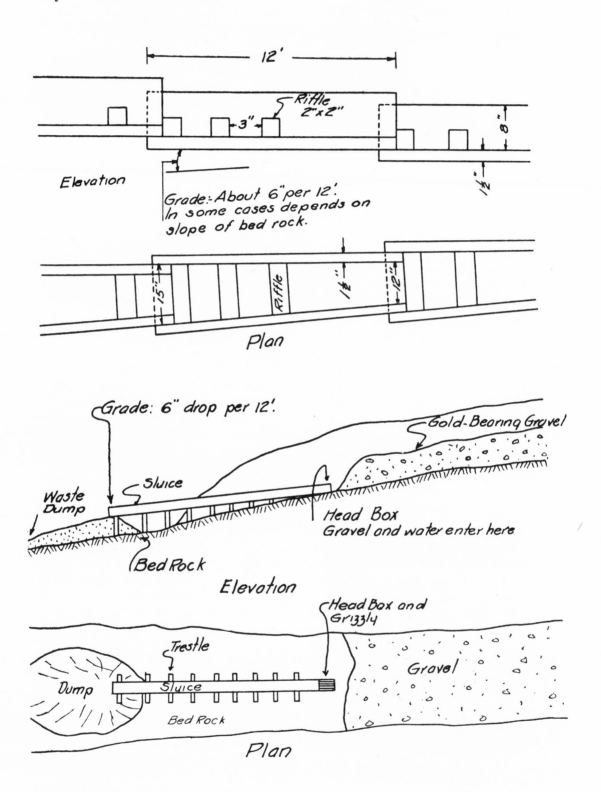

Fig. 107. Top; Section of Sluice. Bottom; Sluice lay-out.

Recovery of Fine Gold

Very fine gold is usually recovered in one of two ways or a combination of both. These methods are the use of undercurrents and gold saving tables. The essential difference between the two is that the tables are usually covered with carpet, burlap, hides, matting, or some similar material and quite often have a flatter grade than do the undercurrents proper. They are also much wider.

Descriptions of these two additions to the main sluice follow:

Undercurrents

The conditions existing in the operation of the main sluice do not permit the settling of the fine gold. This is because of the comparatively high velocity necessary to move the large quantity of gravel and sand and to prevent them from lodging and building up back of the riffles. It is essential that everything larger than the very fine gravel (about ¼ inch in size and preferably nothing larger than coarse sand) be excluded from the undercurrent. This is accomplished by inserting a grizzly or perforated iron plate near the end of the sluice and above the trough leading to the undercurrent.

The undercurrent consists of a series of shallow wooden sluices. Their width is eight to ten times the width of the main sluice. This fulfills one of the main requirements of the undercurrent, *a large decrease in volocity of the water*. The length of the undercurrent is two to four times its width. For example, a main sluice 12 inches wide would require an undercurrent of about eight feet in width and about 20 feet long. The bottom of the undercurrent is made of planks about one and one-half inches thick. The joints must be tight. The sides are about ten inches high. The bottom must be thickly covered with riffles. Material used for the riffles may be wooden strips, cobble stones, blocks, etc. They are spaced about one inch apart and are about two inches deep. The grade varies from one foot drop in 12 feet of length to one foot in nine feet. The exact grade depends on the type of riffle, size of gold, amount of water flowing, etc., and must be determined by experimenting with the conditions present. In some cases the lower riffles of the undercurrent are replaced by an amalgamating plate.

It is very necessary that the sandy material flow over the undercurrent in a thin layer. Wide experience has shown that about ten per cent of the gold recovered on undercurrents. In many instances, of course, it is much greater.

Fig. 108 shows a sketch of the undercurrent.

Gold saving tables

The construction of tables is identical with undercurrents with the exception of the material used for riffles. Burlap, carpet, blankets, hides, etc., are used. They are held in place by tacks and chicken wire and in some instances by means of wooden strips. Only the fine sands should be permitted to pass over the gold tables, and they should do so in a thin film. The clean up is made by removing the covering and washing in a tub. At the end of the season the covering should be turned and the ashes panned for gold.

If wooden blocks are used on the undercurrent they should be burned at the end of the season.

Recovery of Gold From Sands

As the gold dust is mixed with more or less sand, iron, and other materials it is necessary that it be cleaned. The larger pieces of foreign material are picked out by hand, the iron and magnetite are removed with a magnet. The finer sand can be removed by blowing it away.

If mercury has been used, the amalgam formed is softened with an excess of

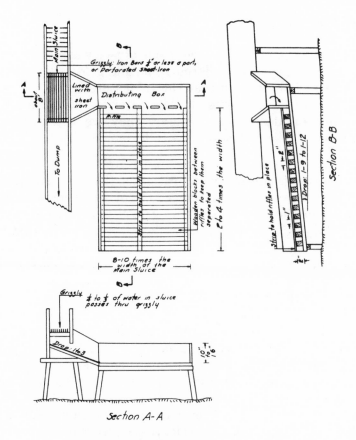

Fig. 108. Undercurrent

mercury and the mixture stirred. This procedure causes the base material to rise to the top where it can be skimmed off. The excess mercury is removed from the cleaned amalgam by squeezing through a chamois skin or strong, cotton cloth.

Cleaning heavy sands

The heavy material from the sluices, and from cleaning the gold dust and the amalgam, may contain other metals or minerals besides gold and amalgam. The most important of these are — native copper, silver, platinum, iridosmine, monazite, pyrite, marcasite, hematite, chromite, galena, cinnabar, cassiterite, wolframite, scheelite, barite and stibnite. Of the rock-forming minerals, the following may be present: Magnetite, ilmenite, rutile, garnet, zircon, tourmaline and others.

As platinum does not amalgamate with mercury, it will be left behind in the sands when the gold is amalgamated. The sands should, therefore, be carefully examined for flakes of platinum.

When the fine gold is rusty or coated with materials which prevent it from amalgamating, it may sometimes be cleaned by agitating with a solution of cyanide and lye in a clean-up barrel. This operation takes from 20 minutes to several hours, and then may not prove effective. The gold is brightened up by this procedure. The mercury may be added in the barrel.

Use of cyanide

If the cyanide is used too carelessly, solution of the gold will result. Solutions of certain strengths dissolve the gold more readily than others.

The greatest amount of gold is dissolved in a solution of potassium cyanide of 0.25 per cent strength. A safe means of using cyanide is to make up a solution of one ounce of 98 per cent potassium cyanide to one-half gallon of water, and then use four ounces, or about one-half teacup of this solution to 10 gallons of water.

412

Fig. 109. Two prospectors using a pan to look for colors (See Fig. 104)

413

Fig. 110. Gold bearing gravel shoveled on to a sluice (See Fig. 107).

Fig. 111. A mode of using a rocker to remove coarse gravels (See Fig. 105).

Fig. 112. Using a pan for finishing or to remove the gold from the finer materials after using a rocker or a sluice on the coarse gravel.

PART IX
BASIC HEALTH AND HYGIENE

HYGIENE
1. Keep Clean

Germs which cause sickness live in dirt, insects, and stale air. Bathe every day. If you swim in salt water, rub your body with sand and swim again. If you swim or shower in fresh water, use soap, but wash it all off. Wash your hands with soap and water before eating and after going to the latrine. Keep dirty hands away from body openings, wounds, and ulcers. Clean, medicate, and bandage all sores.

Brush your teeth and rinse your mouth after eating. Show your teeth to a dentist twice a year. Keep your tooth brush clean and do not use another's. Chew hard foods like corn, cane, and gristle to strengthen the teeth. Do not scratch teeth with needles, pins, sand, etc. Do not put dirty things into your mouth.

Comb your hair two or three times a day and keep your comb clean. Wash your hair in fresh water every week and keep it free from lice. One louse can lay 300 eggs which hatch in two weeks. In two more weeks the young lice lay eggs.

2. Clothing

Do not wear wet or dirty clothing. Wash dirty clothes and dry them in the sun. Put clean clothes on clean bodies. Do not use another's towel or clothing. Do not wear at night what you wore during the day. Wear few and simple clothes to allow sunlight and air to reach your body. Sunlight helps to make strong teeth and bones and kills germs.

3. Food and Water

Good food help to maintain health, cure sickness, mend broken parts, keep us warm, and give us energy. Eat meat (including fish and other seafoods), eggs, milk, or nuts each day. Also eat one or more of these foods each day: ham, taro, bread, rice, green vegetables, yellow vegetables, coconut, sugar cane, honey, fruits, unpolished rice, rich in vitamin B, prevents beriberi.

Eat only good, clean, fresh food prepared with clean hands and clean utensils. Avoid fruits that are unripe or too ripe. Vegetables are spoiled if boiled too long. Make the water boil and then put the vegetables in for a short time. Keep the water for making soup. Fresh vegetables prevent vitamin A deficiency.

Keep food in a clean safe place away from flies and rats. Keep the kitchen clean and tidy. Wash all clothes often. Wash dishes and utensils in hot water and soap as soon as a meal is finished and put them in a box away from flies.

Drink pure water, tea, or juice whenever you are thirsty. Alcohol, except in small amounts, is a poison. Do not drink or eat from the same dishes or utensils as a sick person unless you have washed and dried them well. Do not eat food that a sick person has touched.

4. Sleep

Sleep enough so that you do not feel sleepy during the day. New babies need to sleep nearly all the time and children need much more sleep than adults do. Sleep on a comfortable bed, not on the ground, away from a fire or drafts, with plenty of fresh air and under a mosquito net (where mosquitoes are prevalent).

To keep the air fresh, do not close all doors and windows and do not have too many people sleeping in one room. Isolate sick persons because the germs they breathe out can infect others. Keep children out of sick persons' rooms.

5. Care of House and Village

Keep your house clean and tidy. Sweep the dust out of your house every day with the windows open. Do not spit because spitting puts germs into the air which can cause sickness. Burn or bury all rubbish outside the home every day. Keep latrines clean and covered so that flies cannot get in. Keep animals away from houses. If possible, have a separate room for the kitchen. Have clean mats on a coral, lime, wood or other floor. Have good windows to let in plenty of fresh air and light. Have clean wide roads and paths and plenty of room between the houses for playing. Keep the grass cut short and pull out the weeds. Keep a big piece of land for playing and have some trees for shade. If you are to be healthy and strong, you must have good gardens and plenty of good water.

6. Care of your Feet

Keep your feet clean. Dry thoroughly between toes. Change socks daily. If you acquire a fungus infection, get medical aid. Do not cut a corn or callous. Get medical aid. Keep toenails clean and short. To avoid ingrown effects, cut toenails straight across; do not round them. Do not wear socks with holes, with poorly darned spots, or that fit poorly. Break in shoes before wearing them on a trip.

ADVANCED SANITATION AND HYGIENE

DEFINITIONS

1. Sanitation is the effective use of measures which will maintain healthful environmental conditions. Among these measures are the safeguarding of food and water, and the control of disease-bearing insects and rodents.

2. Hygiene is the employment, by the individual, of practices which will keep him healthy. Among these measures are proper eating, body cleanliness, and the avoidance of known sources of disease.

3. Communicable Disease is a disease, the causative agent of which may pass or be carried from one person to another, or from animal to man.

4. A Vector is a carrier, especially an animal (usually an insect), which transfers infection from one person to another, or from animal to man.

THE THREE LINKS IN THE CHAIN OF DISEASE TRANSMISSION

1. The Source may be a case, carrier, or animal. A **case** is one who is actually ill with the disease; a **carrier** is one who harbors infection without actually being ill himself; many animals can also harbor infections which will affect man.

2. The vehicle, or method of transmission, may be by direct contact with an infected case or carrier; or indirect via insects, food and water, air or fomites. Fomites are objects which have become contaminated with infective organisms, and include bed linen, clothing, utensils, etc.

3. The susceptible individual is an individual without immunity, or resistance, to an infecting organism. Immunity may be natural, i.e., acquired by having the disease, or artificial, i.e., acquired by the injection or swallowing of vaccine produced from killed or weakened organisms.

417

THE VARIOUS CATEGORIES OF DISEASE

1. Respiratory Diseases include the common cold, influenza, small pox, diphtheria, meningitis, and tuberculosis. The best protection against tuberculosis is the maintenance of good living habits, i.e., *plenty of rest and good nutrition.* Intestinal tuberculosis and tuberculosis of the skin can be acquired by drinking unpasteurized milk, or eating dairy foods made from unpasteurized milk.

2. Intestinal Diseases include typhoid fever, amoebic and bacterial dysentery, cholera, food poisoning, and various parasitic infections. These are all spread through food and water, contaminated with feces or urine from an infected case or carrier. To protect yourself, *eat nothing which has not been thoroughly cooked; drink no water which has not been disinfected or boiled.* Salad vegetables should be scalded by immersing them in boiling water for ten seconds, or by disinfecting them in chlorine disinfectant solution for 30 minutes. One package of "Disinfectant, Chlorine, Food Service" dissolved in ten gallons of water provides a good disinfectant for this purpose. Some disease organisms are resistant to chlorine. Among these are the cysts of amoebae which produce amoebic dysentery and certain liver flukes. The flukes are acquired by eating water vegetables such as watercress, water caltrod, and water chestnuts. *Avoid these, if possible.* Still other parasites can be acquired by eating the flesh of raw, smoked, or pickled fish. *Eat only fish which has been thoroughly cooked.*

WATER can be the vehicle of infection for hepatitis, typhoid fever, cholera, dysentery, and many of the parasites. Almost no water supply can be consumed in safety unless boiled or disinfected with chlorine or iodine. Water used to make ice should be treated in the same manner. *Calcium hypochlorite, two ampules per 36-gallon Lyster Bag, provides sufficient chlorine; or iodine, one tablet per canteen if the water is clear, two if the water is cloudy.* Permit the water to stand for 30 minutes before drinking. Water for bathing should also be purified to avoid the disease leptospirosis.

INSECT-BORNE DISEASES include malaria, dengue fever, encephalitis, scrub typhus, and plague. The antimalarial tablet, taken faithfully once a week, will prevent malaria. The standard U.S. Army insect repellent, mosquito nets, and impregnated clothing are other individual measures which can be taken to avoid infection with other such insect-borne diseases.

THE DEEP FUNGUS INFECTIONS can be prevented by proper utilization of your protective clothing, and by immediate first aid treatment of even the most minor injuries. The superficial infections, such as "jock itch" and athlete's foot, can be prevented by faithful cleaning and drying of armpits, groin, and feet; frequent changes of clothing, including socks; and the application of Desenex foot powder to these areas.

VENEREAL DISEASES include syphilis, gonorrhea, chancriod, and lymphogranuloma inguinale. All are transmitted through intercourse, though syphilis can also be acquired by kissing. Individual prophylaxis includes the use of a condom; and urinating and washing the genitalia after intercourse. If you suspect that you have acquired an infection, don't delay treatment. Tuberculosis and other non-venereal diseases can be acquired through intimate contact.

VENOMOUS SNAKES, LEECHES AND PREDATORY ANIMALS represent animals of minor medical importance. Anti-venom is the only satisfactory treatment for snakebite. Leech bites should be treated as any other minor wound. Animal bites from predatory animals should arouse the suspicion that the animal is rabid. If the animal escapes, so that examination of the head for rabies cannot be accomplished, treatment against rabies should be started immediately. This applies to domestic animals also.

FIRST AID

The Four Life-Saver Steps [for all injuries]

1. *Stop the Bleeding.* Apply pressure to wound with first aid dressing, clean cloth, or even the bare hand. Fold the dressing to form a wad and bandage it tightly against the wound. Do not remove it when it becomes reddened by blood, just add more dressing. Elevate wounded part if pressure does not stop bleeding, but splint suspected fractures before elevating. Pressure directly over the wound may not stop bleeding if a large artery is injured. In such cases, apply pressure between the wound and the heart by placing your hand or finger where the artery lies close to the bone. *Pressure points* for wounds on *head and scalp*: Just in front of ear; *face below eye level:* along jawbone; *neck or throat:* beside windpipe; *upper arm, armpit, or shoulder:* behind the inner third of the collarbone against the first rib; *leg and foot:* in groin against pelvic bone or on inner side of thigh; *arm and hand:* inner side of upper arm.

If pressure and elevation do not stop bleeding, or if blood is spurting from wound, as a last resort apply tourniquet between wound and heart. A tourniquet should be a flat band at least two inches wide. It can be made from a triangular bandage, handkerchief, belt, or stocking, but never rope or wire. The most convenient places to apply a tourniquet are around the upper arm and around the thigh.

Place the tourniquet close to the wound but leave unbroken skin between the tourniquet and the wound. Tighten tourniquet by inserting a stick and twisting just enough to stop bleeding. Bind stick used to tighten tourniquet to limb or prevent unwinding. A tourniquet should not be loosened by anyone except competent medical personnel. Leave tourniquet exposed if casualty has not been clearly marked to call attention to it.

2. *Insure Breathing.* Unless there are fractures, especially of the back or neck, position casualty in chin up position with head tilted back. Clear mouth and throat. If casualty is having trouble breathing, start artificial respiration immediately. *Artificial Respiration.* The mouth-to-mouth or mouth-to-nose method permits more air to enter the casualty's lungs than any other known manual method.

(1) Place casualty on back immediately. Don't waste time moving to a better place, loosening clothing, or draining water from lungs.

(2) Quickly clear mouth and throat. Remove mucus, food and other obstructions.

(3) Tilt head back as far as possible in a chin up position with the neck stretched.

(4) Lift lower jaw forward by grasping it with thumb in corner of mouth. Do not hold or depress tongue.

(5) Pinch nose shut (or seal mouth) to prevent air leakage.*

(6) Open your mouth wide and blow. Take a deep breath and blow forcefully (except for babies) into mouth or nose until you see chest rise.

(7) Listen for exhalation. Quickly remove your mouth when chest rises. Lift jaw higher if casualty makes snoring or gurgling sounds.

(8) Repeat (6) and (7) 12 (for men) to 20 (for infants) times per minute. Continue until casualty begins to breathe normally.

*For infants seal both mouth and nose with your mouth. Blow with small puffs of air from your cheeks.

3. *Prevent or Treat Shock.* Shock is a condition of great weakness of the body caused by a disturbance of the nervous system that prevents proper blood

circulation and can result in death. Any injury, either with or without bleeding, can cause shock. A person in shock may have glassy eyes, cold perspiration, rapid and weak pulse, and nausea; he may feel cold, tremble and appear nervous, may be thirsty, may become very pale, wet with sweat and pass out. Shock may not appear for some time after an injury. Treat for shock before it occurs. It is much easier to prevent than to cure. Make comfortable, loosen belt and clothing, handle gently. Position level in order that blood may flow to brain (unless there is a head or chest injury). Splint fractures before moving. Keep warm, but not hot, by wrapping with blankets, poncho, etc., placed under as well as over casualty. If unconscious, place on side or belly with head turned slightly to one side. If conscious and no belly wound, replace lost fluid by giving one teaspoonful of salt and one-half teaspoonful of baking soda in one quart of water or by giving water to which contents of a salt and soda pack have been added, or coffee, tea, cocoa, soup or plain water. No alcohol—it is not a stimulant.

4. *Protect the Wound.* Cover it with first aid dressing. Wrap tails of dressing around it to exert even pressure over entire surface and cover edges to keep out dirt. Splint fractures before moving.

Poisons Taken Internally

Get the patient to a doctor or a hospital at once. If this is impossible and you are sure that poison has been taken, give water to drink at once. This will dilute the poison in the stomach, thereby slowing its absorption. Then induce vomiting, *unless it is an acid or lye poisoning,* by giving several glasses of water containing two teaspoonfuls of baking soda, giving soapy water, lukewarm water, or milk. Tickling the back of the throat with the finger helps.

When the stomach is well washed out, give an antidote if you know what it is and have it; but don't waste time with an antidote before you wash out the stomach. You can give a heaping tablespoonful of Epsom salts after the stomach is emptied. It is good treatment for almost any poison.

For acid or lye poisoning, do not cause vomiting. For acid, first give several glasses of baking soda in water to neutralize the acid, and then give milk. For lye, give several glasses of water containing lemon juice or vinegar to neutralize the lye, and then give milk. Keep the patient warm.

Puncture Wounds

These are caused by pointed things such as wire, nails, sharp sticks, or tines and are serious because of the danger of lockjaw. Wash the wound well with soap and water and soak with Epsom salts. Get the patient to a doctor. If the patient has not been immunized against tetanus (lockjaw), he will need a dose of tetanus antitoxin. If he has been immunized against tetanus, he will need only a dose of tetanus toxoid.

Chest Wounds. The chest wound itself may not be as dangerous as the air which may enter through it into the chest cavity and collapse the lungs. Seal wound and make airtight by covering it directly with the plastic or metal foil side of the first aid dressing wrapper. Apply regular dressing over foil or plastic. Use additional bandaging material if necessary (poncho, shelter half, etc.) to create enough pressure over dressing to make wound airtight. Casualty may be most comfortable in sitting position; if not, lie on injured side. Do not place in shock position.

Belly Wounds. Cover wound and protruding intestines with dry, sterile dressings. Do *not* try to replace intestines, moisten dressing, or bind dressing over protruding intestines tightly. Give *nothing* to EAT OR DRINK. Treat for shock before it occurs (casualty on side, level).

420

Jaw Wounds. Remove broken teeth, pieces of bones and false teeth from mouth and throat. Bind dressing in place to protect wound. If jaw is broken support by additional dressing placed under jaw and tied on top of head. Do *not* cover mouth. Permit escape of vomitus and other fluids. If unconscious place on side or belly with body level and head turned slightly to one side.

Head Wounds. Suspect head wound if casualty is or has been unconscious, has blood or other fluid escaping from nose or ears, has slow pulse or headache, is vomiting, has had convulsion or is breathing very slowly. Do not give morphine and do *not* place with head lower than rest of body. If conscious evacuate on litter with head raised about 45°; if unconscious remove false teeth and other objects from mouth and place on side or belly with head turned to one side to prevent choking on blood or vomitus.

Burns. Minor burns (no blistering or charring) of small skin areas should be covered with first aid packet or other dry sterile dressing, if available. Otherwise leave uncovered. If *severe* burn (blistered or charred *or* covers large area of body) infection and shock must be prevented. Cover burned area with dry, sterile dressing. Do not touch burn with anything except sterile dressing except in case of mass casualties. Then cover with clean sheets, T-shirts, etc. Only as *last* resort leave uncovered. DO NOT: pull clothes over burned areas, try to remove pieces of cloth sticking to skin, try to clean burned area, break burn blisters, or put grease, vaseline or ointment on burn. Prevent shock by placing body level and by replacing body fluids and salts. If casualty is conscious, is not vomiting and has no belly wound give small amounts of cool or cold water to which salt or salt and soda have been added. Add contents of 1 packet of Sodium Chloride-Sodium Bicarbonate Mixture from first aid pouch to 1 canteenful (1 quart) of water, if available. If not, dissolve 4 salt tablets or ½ teaspoonful of loose salt plus 2 sodium bicarbonate tablets or ¼ teaspoonful of baking soda in 1 quart of water. Give a few sips every few minutes; increase amount until ⅓ canteen cupful is drunk every hour. If casualty vomits or acts as if he might, do not give any more of this solution. Do not warm water (warm salt water can cause vomiting).

Fractures. Signs of broken bones: tenderness over injury with pain on movement; inability to move injured part; unnatural shape; swelling and discoloration of skin. All these signs may or may not be present with fracture; if not sure, give casualty benefit of doubt and treat as a fracture. Handle with care! Prevent shock and further injury. Broken ends of bone can cut nerves, blood vessels, etc. Do not move unless necessary. If casualty must be moved *splint fracture first*—"Splint them where they lie." If there is wound apply dressing as for any other wound. If bleeding, it must be stopped. If tourniquet is necessary do not place over site of fracture. If time permits, improvise splints (sticks, blankets, poncho, etc.); if weapon is used, unload it first; pad splints well with soft material to prevent pressure and rubbing; splint should extend from above joint above fracture to below joint below fracture; bind splints securely at several points but not tight enough to interfere with blood flow (check pulse).

One of the quickest ways of splinting a broken leg is by tying it to uninjured leg (do not use narrow materials, such as wire; use padding between legs, and tie at several points above and below the break; tie feet together).

Support fracture of arm or shoulder with sling (do not try to bend injured elbow if it is straight).

Broken Neck. Extremely dangerous; bone fragments may cut spinal cord just as in case of broken back. Keep casualty's head straight and still with neck slightly arched. Caution him not to move.

Moving him may cause his death. Place rolled bath towel or roll of clothing about same bulk as bath towel under neck for support and padding (roll should be thick enough only to arch neck slightly). Raise shoulders in order to place roll

under neck—do not bend neck or head forward. *Do not twist or raise head.* Place roll so that when casualty is lying flat the back of his head touches ground. To keep head motionless after roll is in place put large padded rock or pack at each side of head. If man must be moved, get help. One person should support head and keep it straight while others lift casualty. Transport on hard litter or board. Never turn over a casualty with broken neck! If casualty is found with neck in abnormal position do not try to straighten head and neck; immobilize head in position found.

Dislocations

When a bone gets out of place at the joint, it is called a dislocation. The patient feels intense pain and usually cannot move the injured part. You can often feel the end of the bone that is out of place. The injured area swells quickly, and the patient may suffer from shock.

The first thing to do in case of a dislocation is to call a doctor. Then splint the injured part and place the patient in as comfortable a position as possible. You can lessen the pain by applying cold wet cloths to the dislocated joint.

It is best to have a doctor replace dislocations whenever possible. But you can treat less serious dislocations in emergencies. Hold a dislocated finger firmly with one hand on each side of the dislocation. Slowly pull the end of the finger in a straight line with the hand until it slips into place.

A dislocated jaw is very painful and should be replaced at once. Protect your thumbs with several layers of bandage or cloth and put them into the patient's mouth far back on the lower teeth. Your fingers should be under his chin. Press steadily down and back with the thumbs on the back teeth; pull upward with the fingers under the chin.

Never try to replace a dislocated bone if there is an open wound near the joint. Dress the wound and send a patient to a doctor.

Heat Injury. Can be prevented by common-sense management, by taking salt tablets or extra salt with food and by drinking enough water (as much as 3 gallons a day when working hard in high temperatures) to replace the salt and water lost in sweat. It is not possible to train men to get along on less than the required amount of salt and water!

Heat Cramps. Are cramps of the muscles of the legs, arms, or belly. They occur when a person has sweated a lot and has not taken extra salt to replace the salt lost in his sweat. He may also vomit and be very weak. Give him large amounts of salt water (See Heat Exhaustion, below).

Heat Exhaustion. Casualty may have headache, become dizzy, faint, weak, and pale. He is *sweating* and his skin is *moist* and *cool.* This occurs when person has sweated a lot and has not taken extra salt and water to replace the salt and water lost in his sweat. Lay casualty down in shaded or other cool area, remove outer clothing, elevate feet, give him cool salt water to drink if he is conscious. (Dissolve 2 crushed salt tablets or ¼ teaspoonful of table salt in a canteen (1 quart of cool water). He should drink 3 to 5 canteens in 12 hours.

Heatstroke. Very serious and may be fatal. Casualty *stops sweating* (this is a *warning,* and should be watched for) and skin is *dry* and *hot.* Body temperature becomes very high, casualty may have headache, becomes dizzy, may become delirious and unconscious. *Lower the body temperature as quickly as possible.* Carry to shade, remove clothing, and immerse in cold water bath containing ice, if possible. If ice is not available, use the coldest water available. Keep entire body wet by pouring water over him and cool him by continuously fanning his wet body. *Get to medical aid!* Continue cooling of casualty's body during evacuation to medical facility.

Cold Injury. Can be prevented by preventing loss of body heat.

Trench Foot is a serious condition that can require amputation of the feet. It results from a combination of cold weather and wet socks and boots. It occurs at temperatures *above freezing* (can occur at temperatures as high as 50 F!). It can be prevented. Avoid standing in water, snow or mud. Whenever possible, exercise feet and legs and move toes and ankles about in boots. Massage feet for several minutes each day, clean and dry feet thoroughly and put on dry socks at least once daily (carry an extra pair of socks and dry by carrying inside shirt); do not wear tight boots, socks or laces.

Frostbite. Is actual freezing of a part of the body (usually the face, hands and feet). There may be no pain. Frostbitten part of body becomes grayish or white and loses feeling (use a buddy system to keep watching one another's face for signs). May occur quickly in cold weather, especially if wind is blowing. *Prevent* by wearing warm, loose clothing and by keeping dry. Don't overheat and perspire in cold climates—wear fewer clothes when exercising to avoid overheating and perspiration that will freeze later on. Dry or change wet clothing at once. *Treat* by removing any clothing (boots, gloves, socks) that fits closely over site of injury: thaw frozen part rapidly by putting it in warm (not hot) water, by placing it next to a warm part of your own or someone else's body, or by exposure to warm air. *Do not* rewarm by such measures as walking, massage, exposure to open fire, cold water soaks or rubbing with snow. Wrap the casualty in blankets and give him warm drinks. After the part has thawed, wrap it loosely in dry, sterile dressings. Do not apply ointments or vaseline and do not open blisters. If feet or legs are frostbitten do not let casualty walk—evacuate on litter to a medical facility. If hand or arm is frostbitten put arm in sling.

Unconsciousness. If you can determine cause (bleeding, heatstroke, head injuries, etc.) give first aid. It is often impossible to determine cause. If casualty has merely fainted he will regain consciousness in a few minutes. Take off equipment, loosen clothing. Do not pour liquids into mouth of an unconscious person—if you do you may choke him. Remove false teeth, chewing gum or other objects which might choke him from mouth or throat. If individual is about to faint while sitting up, lower head between knees so that blood may flow to head; hold so that he does not fall and injure himself.

Foreign Body in the Eye. Do not rub eye. Tears will frequently flush out particle. If not, pull eyelid up or down, attempt to remove with moist, clean corner of handkerchief. If unsuccessful, or if the foreign body is of glass or metal, blindfold *both* eyes and evacuate to medical installation.

Foreign Body in Ear, Nose or Throat. Never probe for foreign object in ear or nose. An insect in the ear may be removed by attracting with a flashlight, or by drowning by pouring water into ear. Do not attempt to flush foreign object out of ear with water if it will swell when wet. Remove foreign object from nose by blowing. Coughing will frequently dislodge foreign object from the throat. If this fails and object can be reached try to remove it with the fingers; but be careful. Do not push it deeper down the throat!

Care of Feet. Prevention of foot trouble is best first aid for the feet! Keep clean, dry thoroughly between toes, use foot powder twice daily, and change socks daily. Do not cut a callous or corn. Keep toenails clean and short and cut straight across. If blister develops wash it and surrounding area with soap and water; sterilize a needle by heating it in a flame; open the blister by sticking it at the lower edge with needle that has been sterilized by heating in flame.

Snake Bite. Keep bitten person quiet and do not let walk or run; kill snake if possible and keep so that it can be identified and proper antivenom serum given. Make casualty as comfortable as possible (preferably in sitting position); immediately immobilize bitten limb in a position below level of heart. Improvise tourniquet (handkerchief, strip of cloth, etc.) and place it between bite and heart,

about 2 to 4 inches above site. Tighten tourniquet enough to stop flow in superficial blood vessels (the veins will stand out prominently under the skin) but not tight enough to stop the pulse. If swelling occurs release tourniquet and reapply it further up arm or leg ahead of the swelling. Send someone to summon assistance. If litter or vehicle is available transport casualty to nearest medical treatment facility at once. Should casualty stop breathing start artificial respiration at once.

Animal Bites

Bites from dogs, cats, or any other animals are dangerous. Most animals carry germs that may cause the wound to become infected. If the animal has rabies, the bitten person will get hydrophobia and die unless the Pasteur treatment is started early enough.

Wash the wound thoroughly to remove the animal's saliva. Rinse with clear water. Dry with clean gauze, apply iodine and, when the iodine has dried, dress the wound as you would any other.

Even minor scratches caused by animals should be treated by a doctor as soon as possible. He will treat the wound further and give the Pasteur treatment if necessary.

The animal that has bitten the patient should be confined securely for 14 days and observed by a veterinarian. If the animal does not develop rabies during this time, the bitten person is safe. Hydrophobia develops 2 weeks to 3 months after a person has been bitten. Generally, the doctor will consider it safe to delay starting the treatment for several days while waiting to see if the animal is diseased, except when the patient's head, face, or hands have been bitten.

If the animal is killed or dies during the 14-day period, its head should be sent to a laboratory for examination. Animals can be protected from rabies by yearly vaccinations.

Bruises

A bruise is an unopen wound. It is caused by a blow that breaks the small blood vessels under the skin. As a result, the area becomes discolored and swollen.

Cold wet cloths on the bruise, if applied at once, will keep down the swelling and ease the pain. After several hours, apply warm wet cloths.

Morphine. Use with caution only in case of severe pain. Use only if pain cannot be relieved by simple measures such as keeping casualty quiet, splinting injured arm or leg, carefully changing position. If syrette contains 30 mg. (½ grain) of morphine, give only one-half of the syrette. If it contains 16 mg. (¼ grain) give contents of whole syrette. *Do not* use morphine: within 2 hours of previous injection, when casualty is unconscious, has a head injury, a fractured neck, is breathing less than 12 times per minute, is in shock, has chest wounds, has difficulty with breathing, or has severe abdominal pain.

Dressings and Bandages

Dressings are put directly over wounds to help keep the wounds free from dirt and germs. Dressings also help to control bleeding and absorb liquid material from the wound.

Bandages are used to hold dressings in place. They may also be used to keep splints in place, to make slings, and to help stop bleeding.

Kinds of Dressings

Gauze is the best material to use for dressings. It is more absorbent and allows more air to circulate than other cotton cloth. Dressings must be clean and sterile (free from germs) or as nearly sterile as possible.

Sterile gauze squares may be purchased for the first aid kit. They are usually 3½ by 3½ inches and are sealed in individual wax paper packages. They may be used on any small wound. You can get other sizes of sterile gauze for larger wounds.

You can also buy small dressings on strips of adhesive tape. They are very good to use on small cuts and scratches, wounds of the fingers and toes, and other small wounds.

If sterile gauze dressings are not available, the next best material is freshly washed and ironed old white cotton cloth, such as sheets or pillow cases.

When you handle a dressing, do not touch the part that will be put next to the wound.

Kinds of Bandages

Bandages can be made from gauze or other cotton cloth, such as muslin. In an emergency bandages may be made from a large handkerchief or scarf, a piece of sheet, a napkin, or a towel. Sometimes adhesive tape is used instead of a bandage to hold a dressing in place.

There are several kinds of bandages. The triangle bandage is one of the best to use for first aid. It stays on well and is easy to make. The triangular bandage is made from a firm piece of cloth 36 or 40 inches square. It is folded diagonally. Or it may be cut diagonally to make two bandages.

A cravat or necktie bandage can be made from a triangular bandage or from a strip of cloth. To fold a triangular bandage as a cravat, bring the point of the cloth to the middle of the base. Make another fold in the middle of the cloth as you see in the picture. Continue to fold the cloth until the bandage is the right width.

Rolled bandages are often used by doctors, but they are difficult to use properly. It is hard to keep them from being too tight; and it is hard to keep them on without using adhesive tape.

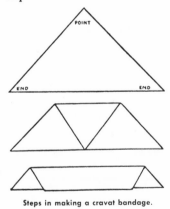

Steps in making a cravat bandage.

How to Use Bandages

A bandage should be snug but not tight. If it is too tight it may cause swelling and pain. If it is too loose it may slip. Be sure to put it on smoothly.

Do not cover the ends of the fingers or toes unless they have been injured. Never use a wet bandage because it may shrink and become too tight as it dries.

A square knot is usually used to tie bandages. Or the end of the bandage may be fastened down with adhesive tape. Learn to tie a square knot properly. Tie the knots where they are easy to reach and are comfortable.

To Tie a Square Knot. A square knot is easy to tie. It does not matter with which end you do the tying. If you are right-handed you will use one end; if left handed, the other (see page 476).

425

Step 1. Cross one end (a) over the other, turn it under and up.

Step 2. Turn the lower end (b) back in the opposite direction from which it is pointing.

Step 3. Bring the first end (a) down over the other end (b) then under it and out the loop or opening that is formed.

Step 4. Pull on both ends to tighten the knot.

To Make an Arm Sling. An arm sling is good to use for a serious injury to the arm or hand. Put one end of a triangular bandage over the shoulder on the uninjured side. Let the other end hang straight down over the chest. Have the point of the bandage behind the elbow. Bring the lower end up over the shoulder on the injured side. Tie the two ends together at the side of the neck. Fold the point of the bandage over and pin it to the sling.

To Bandage The Hand. Turn the hand palm up and lay a narrow cravat bandage across the wrist. Have one end extended about 12 inches past the thumb.

Bring the other end around the back of the hand, then between the thumb and index finger, across the palm, and up to the wrist. Encircle the wrist. Then bring the bandage across the back of the hand, between the thumb and index finger and across the palm again. Wrap both ends around the wrist and tie them in a square knot.

To Bandage an Elbow or Knee. Use a cravat bandage 8 inches wide for the elbow and wider for the knee. Put the middle of the cravat over the bent elbow. Smooth it out and bring the ends around, crossing them in the hollow of the elbow. Bring the upper end entirely around the arm above the elbow. Bring the lower end entirely around the arm below the elbow. Tie the ends on the outside of the arm just above the bend of the elbow.

The knee is bandaged the same way.

To Bandage an Arm or Leg. An injury above or below the elbow or the knee can be bandaged with a cravat. Make it 2 inches wide for a small injury, wider for a larger injury. Place it diagonally across the arm or leg over the injury. Have the longest end down. Hold the upper end firmly as you bring the lower end down around the arm or leg and back up again using a spiral motion. Tie the ends in a square knot.

The following medical information is offered for the times when a physician is not available to treat injury or illness. Treatments should be confined if possible, to those with some medical training if physicians are not available. Over-treatment may be more serious than doing nothing at all.

ADDITIONAL TREATMENT AND GENERAL INFORMATION

There are only two medical problems requiring *immediate* action: severe bleeding and stoppage of breathing. Methods of artificial respiration and control of severe bleeding are important. You must know them before you need them—when you need them it is too late to learn them.

Other medical problems do not require immediate action. IF YOU DON'T KNOW WHAT TO DO—DON'T. Take time to think. Decide what the problem is, think through your actions before you act.

If a medical problem displays only general symptoms—WAIT. It is better to wait a few hours, a day until more specific symptoms appear which lead you to proper treatment than to do the wrong thing. Keep patient under observation.

Medical problems can be divided into two general categories—INJURIES and INFECTIONS/DISEASES. Problems not included in these categories require highly specialized medical care.

Injuries. Do Only What is Absolutely Necessary.

1. Examine a person until you have determined all injuries. If you find one, don't stop, there may be other more serious injuries.

2. Examine first for severe bleeding, stoppage of breathing. Artificial respiration and control of severe bleeding must be started at once.

3. Don't hurry. If a person is breathing and is not bleeding severely, speed is not required. Hasty action will only aggravate injuries.

4. Don't aggravate injuries. Always protect injuries with bandages, padding, splints before you move a person. Move a person slowly, carefully.

5. Keep the injured person warm, comfortable and at rest to protect against shock. Give him plenty of fluids to drink if he is not unconscious.

6. Do as little as possible beyond above. Allow the body to heal itself. There is little you can do to help or speed this healing process—there is much you can do to interfere with it.

7. For day to day care—keep injuries from becoming infected. If infection develops, treat it.

Diseases/Infections. Remember—Dirt Causes Infections/Diseases.

Most infections/diseases are caused by germs. Germs do not move about under their own power, they are transmitted from place to place by dirt. It will be easier to think out disease transmission, prevention and treatment if you remember that dirt, something you are familiar with, causes disease/infections. One of the few diseases not caused by dirt is Malaria. Other medical problems not caused by germs require physician/hospital care.

Prevention of Disease/Infection.

Prevention is as important as treating medical problems after they develop. Dirt causes disease/infection; dirty clothing touching an injury will rub dirt into the injury and cause infection. Dirty clothing may rub skin raw, then rub dirt into the raw area causing infection. Dirty skin which is injured can become infected. Dirty food and water eaten can cause diarrhea/dysentery. Germs from dirt eaten can enter the body from the stomach and cause internal infections/illnesses. Flying and crawling insects can bring dirt on their feet from the garbage pail to food, water, the body and uncovered injuries. Insects can also carry infection from the sick to health persons.

During treatment of disease/infection, it is very important to:

a. keep the patient's clothing and bedding, and the patient himself clean.

b. keep flying/crawling insects from the sick.

c. provide the sick with food/water which has been cleaned by boiling/cooking well.

d. sterilize used bedding materials by boiling before using again.

e. keep used bandage materials, sick room debris away from flying/crawling insects. Such debris should be burned.

IT IS EXTREMELY IMPORTANT TO YOU WHO ARE HANDLING AND TOUCHING SICK PERSONS, THAT INFECTED MATERIALS BE SCRUPULOUSLY CLEAN. NEVER GO FROM ONE PATIENT TO ANOTHER WITHOUT WASHING YOUR HANDS THOROUGHLY.

Medical Treatment.

Since dirt is the major cause of infections/diseases—surgical soap and clean water are basic treatment medications. A wound must be cleaned before medicine

427

is applied to prevent infection. An external body infection must be cleaned of dirt and infection material before medicines are applied to treat infection.

Whenever the instructions include the use of sterile water this means to:

1. Obtain the cleanest possible water (include rain water, spring water, well water). Water containing dirt, debris should be allowed to stand until dirt has settled out.

2. Boil this clean water at least 15 minutes before use.

Clean boiled water is the best. If for some reason you cannot boil water, you can add one tablet of potassium permanganate to a quart of clean water. This can be used where sterile water is required EXCEPT IT CANNOT BE USED FOR DRINKING WATER, IN THE EYES OR EARS.

Skin Injuries

Foreign Bodies: Splinters, Glass, Thorns, etc.
1. Clean the area with surgical soap and water.
2. Wash a scalpel blade with surgical soap and water. Open the skin over the complete length of the foreign body.
3. Lift out the foreign body gently so pieces are not broken off. Make sure all pieces are out.

Open Wounds: Injuries where the skin is broken.

Small cuts, scratches, blisters:
1. Wash with surgical soap and water.
2. Apply Bacitracin-Neomycin Ointment and a bandaid or gauze pad bandage.

Large, deep wounds:
1. If the wound is bleeding, put sterile gauze pads directly over the injury and hold tightly in place so pressure will allow blood to clot and stop the bleeding. Hold this pressure at least 5 minutes before lifting the pads or removal of bandage will tear clots loose and restart bleeding.
2. After bleeding stops, wash the skin widely around wound with surgical soap and water. Do not allow soap to get into the wound.
3. Gently pour sterile water into the wound to wash out any dirt.
4. Apply Bacitracin-Neomycin in a thin layer around, but not in, the wound. Cover with a loose bandage.
5. Give one Oxytetracycline (Terramycin) tablet four times daily for four days to prevent infection.
6. Change the bandage only every third day unless the patient gets the bandage dirty or wet.
7. If pain is severe, give one Codeine Tablet three or four times daily.

Closed Wounds: The injury is under the skin, the skin is not broken.

Bruises:
1. Restrict movement of severely bruised area and allow body to heal.
2. Cold compresses may be applied.

Sprains: It may be difficult to distinguish between a sprain and a broken bone. A sprain occurs at a joint and generally firm pressure on the bones on the side opposite the area of swelling will not pain. If in doubt, treat as a broken bone.
1. Prop the sprain up and apply cold compresses to keep down the swelling. After 24 hours, hot compresses may be used to bring down the swelling.

2. The sprain may be wrapped with a tight bandage or taped firmly with adhesive tape to prevent movement of injured joint. Do not tape too tightly; check often to make certain circulation has not been cut off.

3. Limit patient's use of sprained joint—allow body time to heal.

Fractures: Broken bones should be set properly by physician/hospital. Bones not properly set may heal into a permanent deformity.

1. Splint the broken bone; apply the splint before patient is moved from site of injury. A splint must be functional; it need not be a work of art:

—a splint must be long enough so it can be fastened above and below the break and surrounding area of swelling.

—it must be fastened securely to support the broken bone in a natural position and to prevent the movement of the broken bone ends.

—it must be well padded where it touches the skin so it will not rub the area raw.

Poison Ivy Type Injuries: Itching, burning, red skin; watery blisters may form. Appears only on skin not covered by clothing; skin areas that can rub against poison plants.

1. Wash with surgical soap and water two or three times daily.

2. Dibucaine (Nupercaine) Ointment may be applied to reduce itching, pain.

Burns: Seriousness of burns is judged by the severity of the burn and the size of the body involved.

Minor Burns: small area of the body burned.

1. When the skin is not broken, put a pad bandage over the area for protection against further injury.

2. Do not rupture blisters—they are the fluid protective pad of the body.

3. When skin is broken, treat as a small cut.

Deep Burns: Small area of the body burned. Treat as a deep wound.

Deep Burns: large areas of the body burned.

This is a serious medical problem which, even with the best medical care, may be fatal. These injuries require physician/hospital care as soon as possible. Do nothing except cover the injured person with a clean sheet, and give as much fluid as you can force the patient to drink. Two Codeine tablets may be given every four hours for pain.

Sunburn:

1. Protect the burn against further injury; keep clothing off burned areas, keep the person out of the sun.

2. Dibucaine (Nupercaine) Ointment may be applied to relieve pain.

3. If pain is severe, one Codeine tablet may be given three or four times daily.

4. Severe sunburn with blistering over large areas of the body can be as serious as deep burns; should have physician/hospital care if possible.

Infected Injuries:

Small cuts, scratches, blisters: Treat as similar uninfected injuries. With blisters, if the blister fluid becomes cloudy or redness develops around the blister it must be opened and drained. Puncture the blister at THE OUTER EDGE with a scalpel blade. Do not remove the skin from the blister unless pus begins to ooze from the blister later, then remove the skin.

Infected deep cuts, wounds: Treat as similar uninfected injuries except change the bandage and wash out the wound with sterile water *every day.*

Boils:
1. Apply hot compresses to boil four or five times daily for 15 minutes. Continue hot compresses even after boil breaks and drains.
2. Apply Bacitracin-Neomycin Ointment to boil and cover with a bandage.
3. After boil breaks, wash out boil with sterile water, dry gently and put Bacitracin-Neomycin around, but not into the boil. Cover with a bandage.
4. If boil does not rupture but spreads under the skin, give one Oxytetracycline (Terramycin) tablet four times daily.

Skin Infections:
Skin areas which are red, painful, usually hot to touch, with oozing of pus and scab formation.
1. Wash with surgical soap and water twice daily.
2. After each washing, cover the affected area with gauze pads soaked in Potassium Permanganate treated water. Keep these pads wet and in place for at least 15 minutes.
3. Apply Bacitracin-Neomycin Ointment and cover with a bandage.
4. If area affected is large, or if infection spreads under the skin, give one Oxytetracycline (Terramycin) tablet four times daily.

Skin Fungus Infections:
Red, painful areas with cracked, peeling skin and watery blisters oozing a watery fluid.
1. Wash with surgical soap and water twice daily.
2. After each washing, cover the affected area with gauze pads soaked in Potassium Permanganate treated water. Keep these pads wet and in place for at least 15 minutes. For Athlete's Foot, soak the feet in a basin of Potassium Permanganate treated water. Dry areas thoroughly. Allow the area to air dry for five minutes.
3. Apply Undecylenic Acid Ointment (Desenex) to affected areas twice daily after washing except feet. Apply ointment to feet only at night.

Skin Rashes:

Rashes accompanied by internal disease symptoms: (Chills and fever, general muscular aching and ill-feeling, nausea, diarrhea). These rashes are external symptoms of an internal condition.
1. Give two Oxytetracycline (Terramycin) tablets four times the first day, then one tablet four times daily after that.
2. Give one Aspirin tablet four times daily for aches, fever, headache.
3. Give one Meclizine (Bonine) tablet four times daily for nausea.

Rashes not accompanied by internal disease symptoms:
1. Wash with surgical soap and water two to three times daily.
2. After washing, apply wet compresses of potassium permanganate treated water to affected areas.
3. If body lice are present (and causing the rash), rub Undecylenic Acid (Desenex) Ointment in the affected areas instead of using potassium permanganate wet compresses. The patient's clothing should be boiled to kill lice so patient is not reinfected by his clothing.

Eye

Foreign Bodies:
1. If the foreign body can be seen, remove it with the corner tip of a sterile gauze pad.

430

2. Wash out the eye with sterile water. Potassium Permanganate treated water cannot be used.

3. Put Butyn and Metaphen Eye Ointment in the eye to ease pain and protect against infection. Keep the eye COVERED with two gauze pads adhesive taped in place as long as Butyn and Metaphen Ointment is used in the eye.

Burns, Minor Injuries. Treat as for Foreign Bodies in the Eye.

Infections. Accompanied by redness, swelling of the lids, with/without pus.
1. Wash out the eye with sterile water three times daily.
2. Put Oxytetracycline (Terramycin) Ointment in the eye after each washing.
3. If infection is severe or affects both eyes, give one Oxytetracycline (Terramycin) tablet four times daily.

Sty: Similar to skin boil.
1. Apply hot compresses to eye four or five times daily for 15 minutes. Continue hot compresses even after sty breaks and drains.
2. Put Oxytetracycline (Terramycin Ointment) in the eye after each heat application.
3. If the sty does not break, or spreads under the skin, give one Oxytetracycline (Terramycin) tablet four times daily.

Ear

Earache:

1. Put Antipyrine and Benzocaine (Auralgan) Ear Drops in the ear twice daily. Put a large plug of cotton in the outer ear to keep liquid in ear.
2. If earache is accompanied by a sore throat, in addition to the drops give one Chlorpheniramine (Chlor-Trimeton) tablet four times daily.
3. If there are signs of pus drainage, or if the earache is accompanied by fever, pain in the head in front or behind the ear lobe, give one Oxytetracycline (Terramycin) tablet four times daily.

Injuries: almost always to the outer ear and lobe. Treat as skin injuries.

Nose

Common Cold. Cannot be cured, but symptoms can be relieved. Antibiotics do no good and should be saved for more serious illnesses requiring them.
1. Give one aspirin tablet four times daily for fever and headache.
2. Give one Chlorpheniramine (Chlor-Trimeton) tablet four times daily as antihistamine.
3. Gargling with warm salt water will help relieve throat soareness, cough.

Nosebleed. Even though there SEEMS to be a lot of blood lost, this is not serious.
1. Bend the head forward on the chest of the sitting patient. Apply pressure on the nostrils just below the nose bone with fingers to squeeze nose shut.
2. Ice or cold compresses placed on the nose and at back of neck may help.

Fracture. Correct as soon as possible after fracture occurs.
1. If the nose is not noticeably deformed and the patient can breathe through both sides of nose, tape firmly with adhesive tape across bridge of nose. Put gauze pads over this tape and fasten with adhesive tape to protect nose against further injury.

2. If the nose is noticeably deformed, the patient cannot breathe through one/both sides of the nose, gently mold the nose with your fingers until it appears normal and patient can breathe through both sides. Then tape firmly with adhesive tape across the bridge of the nose and a padding bandage for protection.

Teeth

Toothache. Can only be permanently relieved by dental care. For temporary care soak a small pledget of cotton in Eugenol and place in the top of the hurting tooth. This can be repeated if pain returns later.

Bleeding Socket. After tooth loss.
1. Dry out the socket with a sterile gauze pad.
2. Place a dry sterile gauze pad into the socket and have the patient bite down on the pad to apply pressure to bleeding socket. Leave pad in place for several hours. During this time patient should not eat or drink.

Tongue

Injuries. Unless the tongue is so badly lacerated that it requires stitching, injuries to tongue will heal by themselves. The patient should take only liquid or soft food for 24 to 48 hours to prevent further injury to tongue.

Trench Mouth. Highly contagious. Bleeding from inflamed, swollen gums without signs of injury.
1. Dry gums with a sterile gauze pad.
2. Put Oxytetracycline (Terramycin) Eye Ointment on finger tip and smear on gums, both inside and outside teeth, three times daily.

Throat

Sore Throat. Associated with cold symptoms—treat as common cold.

Infected Throat. Difficulty in swallowing, painful swellings at angle of jaws under skin, throat behind mouth appears inflamed and swollen with/without yellowish spots resembling pimples or dirty white pus patches. Usually accompanied by fever, chills, ill-feeling.
1. Give two Oxytetracycline (Terramycin) tablets four times the first day then one tablet four times daily after that.
2. Give one aspirin tablet four times daily for headache and fever.
3. Keep the patient in bed; give only liquid or soft foods.

Stomach

Do not confuse location of stomach (just below breastbone in triangle made by downward curving of lower ribs) with the intestinal area (around navel) and the bowel area (triangular area bounded by the two groin lines and a line drawn across the belly between the tops of the hip bones.)

Indigestion (Heartburn). One Belladonna-Phenobarbital tablet four times daily. Usually one or two tablets will clear up the problem.

Nausea/Vomiting, Motion Sickness.
1. Give one Meclizine (Bonine) tablet four times daily.
2. Patient should take a liquid or semi-solid starchy diet without spices or seasoning.

432

3. Give the patient as much liquids as he will take.

Lung, Chest

Flu. Symptoms of a bad cold with mild fever, soreness of the chest.
1. Patient should stay in bed, eat liquid or light foods and take large quantities of fluids.
2. Give one aspirin four to six times daily for muscle ache, headache, fever.

Pneumonia. Symptoms similar to Flu but with sharp chest pains, difficulty in breathing and high fever. If in doubt whether patient has flu or pneumonia, treat as pneumonia.
1. Patient should stay in bed, eat liquid or light foods and take large quantities of fluids.
2. Give one aspirin four to six times daily for muscle ache, headache, fever.
3. Give two Oxytetracycline (Terramycin) tablets four times the first day, then one tablet four times daily after that.

Intestines, Bowels

Diarrheas/Dysentery. May be accompanied by chills and fever, nausea, bowel cramps and pain. Regardless of cause, treat:
1. Give two Oxytetracycline (Terramycin) tablets four times the first day then one tablet four times daily after that.
2. Insist the patient take large quantities of fluids. If the diarrhea is severe and lasts for several days, make up a salt solution of one teaspoonful salt to a pint of water, and have the patient sip as much of this as often as he can. This is better than plain water in diarrheas of long duration.
3. Give one Meclizine (Bonine) tablet four to six times daily for nausea.
4. One Codeine tablet every four hours may be given for severe bowel cramps and to help control diarrhea.
NOTE: Diarrhea will dimish but may not stop until treatment with Oxytetracycline (Terramycin) tablets is discontinued. Do not stop Oxytetracycline treatment until 48-72 hours after all other symptoms have disappeared.

Amoebic Dysentery. If diarrhea treated above returns in a milder form with/without periodic acute attacks of short duration, give two Iodochlorhydroxyquin (Entero-Vioform) tablets three times daily for ten days.

Appendicitis. General ill-feeling, fever, characterized by nausea particularly on trying to eat, pain in lower right abdominal area with belly muscles becoming rigid and hard, which prevents patient from standing up straight. If you suspect appendicitis treat:
1. Give two Oxytetracycline (Terramycin) tablets four times daily.
2. Put ice or cold compresses over painful lower right belly area.
3. The patient should remain in bed and should take nothing by mouth but medications and small quantities of water.
This treatment may prevent rupture of the appendix, clear up symptoms temporarily but the patient should have physician/hospital care as soon as possible.

Urinary Tract

Infections. Painful, frequent urination, may be accompanied by chills and fever, pain in the lower back.
1. Give two Oxytetracycline (Terramycin) tablets four times daily for five days.
2. Patient should take large quantities of water.

Gonorrhea. Painful, frequent urination accompanied by a thick, yellowish pus discharge from the penis. Treat as urinary infection above.

Ulcer on Penis: Treat as Urinary Tract infection above but continue the Oxytetracycline tablets for 10 days.

Lymphogranuloma. Large, painful, round swelling in one or both groins. Skin over swelling may be inflamed or discolored and hot to touch. An infection of long duration may break through the skin and become a large ugly ulcer.

Treat as Urinary Tract infection above but continue Oxytetracycline tablets for ten days.

Malaria

Symptoms are varied, but high fever and shaking chills occuring every second to third day are almost always present. Attacks of shaking chills terminate rapidly with a rapid temperature fall to normal. Patient usually falls into a deep sleep, awakes and feels well until next attack.

Prevention: Give one Chloroquine Phosphate (Aralen) 0.5 Gm. tablet weekly on the same day each week.

Treatment: On the first day give four Chloroquine Phosphate (Aralen) 0.5 Gm. tablets the first dose. Six hours later give a second dose of two more Chloroquine Phosphate 0.5 Gm. tablets. On the second day and the third day, give one dose of two Chloroquine Phosphate (Aralen) 0.5 Gm. tablets. If symptoms recur, re-treat as above.

NOTE: 1. Chloroquine is very poisonous when overdoses are given. GIVE ONLY AS INSTRUCTED ABOVE to prevent poisoning patient.

2. Two strength sizes of Chloroquine Phosphate tablets are in common use. Be sure you know which strength—the 0.5 Gm. or the 0.25 Gm. tablet—you are using. If you have the 0.25 Gm. tablets, double the quantities of tablets in the instructions above.

Snake Bite

The snake bite kit includes all required materials and instructions for proper use of these kits.

Serious Wounds/Injuries

Extremely serious wounds which require immediate hospital care. What you do while getting the patient to the hospital.

Penetrating Chest Wounds. Chest wounds which do not penetrate into the chest cavity can be treated as skin injuries. Chest wounds which penetrate into the chest cavity are characterizing by sucking, bubbling passage of air into and out of the hole each time the patient breathes.

1. Do not attempt to clean the wound.

2. Smear Bacitracin-Neomycin Ointment on the skin around the hole.

Apply more Ointment to sterile gauze pads. Place the pads over the wound so as to form an air-tight covering. Completely cover these pads with adhesive tape.

3. Place the patient in a semi-sitting position and lean him on the SIDE OF HIS CHEST WHICH IS INJURED. This lung is not working so lean him on this side and allow the remaining lung freedom of motion.

4. Do not give anything for pain.

434

Abdominal Wounds Which Expose the Intestines

1. Place the patient in a semi-sitting position.
2. If the intestines have spilled out of the belly, DO NOT ATTEMPT TO PLACE THEM BACK INSIDE.
3. Place sterile gauze over the wound and any intestines which have spilled out. Keep this gauze moist with sterile water. Potassium Permanganate treated water *cannot be used* for this.
4. Do nothing else but get the patient hospital care.

Patient Response to Treatment

Response to treatment is divided into three general phases: (If injuries are not infected phase I and II are not seen).

I. Initial Treatment. Treating an infection/disease is a fight. During this phase consider that the germs fight back. There may be no noticeable improvement, in fact the symptoms may become slightly more severe. Do not take this as a sign of treatment failure. Once a medical treatment has been started, it should not be considered a failure or changed for at least 48 to 72 hours.

II. Healing Phase. During this phase the germs are killed, the patient shows considerable improvement. Treatment should be continued until the patient has been symptom-free for at least 48 hours. It is better to treat a little longer than necessary, than to stop too soon and have the illness recur.

III. Recuperation Phase. During this phase the germs have been killed, but the body injury caused by these germs must heal. The patient may be symptom-free, but does not feel strong, completely well.

Alternate Treatment Medications

Oxytetracycline (Terramycin) tablets, a wide-spectrum antibiotic is used for many of the illness/diseases in the preceding instructions. If an illness/disease does not respond to Oxytetracycline, change to:

1. Potassium Phenoxymethyl Penicillin (Pen-Vee) tablets, two tablets four times daily for all medical problems except:
2. Diarrheas/dysenteries and Urinary Tract Infections. For these medical problems change to Sulfamethoxypyridazine (Kynex) tablets, two tablets the first day, then one tablet *daily* after that.

MIDWIFERY

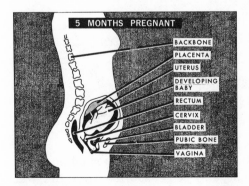

The uterus has grown large and is easily felt through abdomen. The abdomen protrudes. The baby is growing, and looks like a baby, though it would be too small to live if born now. The placenta, through which the baby gets nourishment, is shown attached to the uterine wall.

435

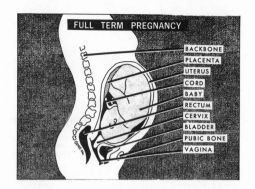

At full term, or after 40 weeks of pregnancy, the baby is ready to be born. The cervix through which baby must leave the uterus is shown clearly here, still closed. The contractions of the muscles of the uterus will open the cervix, and force the baby down through the vagina, or birth canal to the outside.

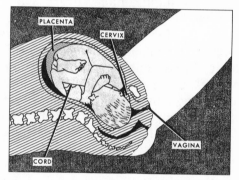

At the end of the first stage of labor the cervix is completely open and the baby's head is beginning to come down through the vagina. Contractions begin in the lower back and later are felt in the lower abdomen. At the time shown here, contractions are probably coming every 2 minutes, lasting 40-60 seconds and are very strong.

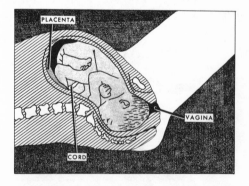

The first stage of labor usually lasts several hours and is hard work. The mother needs to relax, rest, and be reassured. Give her water and fruit juices. In this picture the second stage of labor is well along. It is shorter than the first stage and the mother will now be pushing down with each contraction, helping to force the baby into the world.

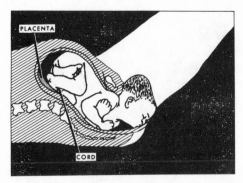

The head of the baby has been partially born. This shows the usual position with the face down and the back of the head up. The bag of water in which the baby is enclosed throughout pregnancy may have broken at the beginning of labor, before or during the first stage. It may break now, or have to be torn with the fingers.

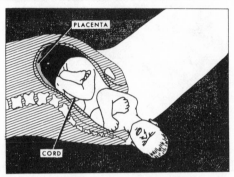

Here you see the baby's head turned to the right which is the usual position. The shoulders are about to be born. The head turns so that the baby's body can fit into the birth canal and come through more easily. After the birth of the baby there will be further uterine contractions and the placenta will be separated from the uterine wall and expelled.

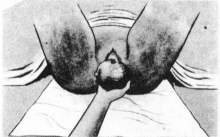

The attendant supports the emerging head of the baby with the hand. *Wash hands thoroughly first.* The head turns by itself to allow the rest of the body to fit into the birth canal. The attendant does not turn the head and never *pulls* or pushes on the head or the body. *Do not try to hurry the delivery.*

Baby is now almost completely delivered. Attendant's hands are supporting body, not pulling or hurrying the delivery. Legs will soon appear and delivery will be complete. Time of delivery is noted now. Right hand of attendant supports baby's head and back, and keeps it out of fluid and other material on floor.

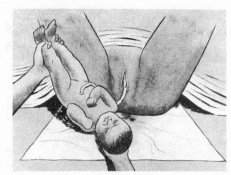

Keep right hand under the baby's head and shoulders for support. Use left hand to grasp ankles of baby as shown. Baby is slippery. Grasp ankles with a towel, if available. Elevate body enough to aid drainage of mucus from chest and throat. Baby should start crying now. His color will be a reddish purple.

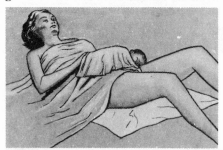

Put baby on mother's abdomen facing you, head slightly lowered to right. Wrap him to keep him warm. He should be crying and becoming healthy pink color now. Mother may hold him in place. Do not place him too far back on abdomen. Do not pull on cord.

Use fingers to "milk" baby's throat; stroke from base of throat to chin. Clear the air passages so the baby can breathe well. If the baby is not breathing well by now, use mouth-to-mouth breathing. Be gentle. Do not blow too hard. Breathe gently into baby's mouth every 5 seconds. Stop as soon as baby is breathing.

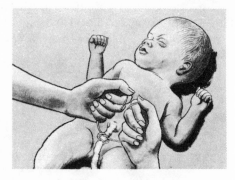

Tie a square knot in the cord about 4 inches from baby. Use strong cotton tape or cloth. Do not use ordinary string. Tie second knot 2 to 4 inches from first and cut between. Wait to tie cord until tape and scissors have been boiled or cleansed. This will usually be after placenta has been expelled and mother's uterus is firm. Then baby can be moved and cared for.

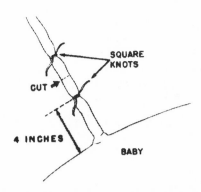

Cut between the square knots. Tie a square knot by bringing right tape over left tape for first loop, and left tape over right for second loop. Tighten each loop firmly as tied. Use scissors or a razor blade to cut cord. Placenta will usually be expelled 20 to 30 minutes after baby is delivered. After placenta is out, keep uterus firm by gentle massage. Massage only if it is not firm.

Remember
1. Childbirth is normal
2. Let nature take her course
3. Wait for Baby —
   Do not hurry birth
   Do not interfere
   Do not hurry to cut cord
4. Cleanliness of hands and surroundings are important
5. Reassure mother
6. Make sure baby is warm and breathing well

After care of mother
1. Check uterus regularly after first hour
2. Allow food and fluids as desired
3. Encourage rest. May be up and around for a short period after 8 hours.

After care of baby
1. Keep baby warm and breathing well
2. Do not wash white material off baby. It protects skin.
3. Do nothing to eyes, ears, nose or mouth
4. Put to breast every 3-4 hours after first 12 hours
5. Keep people away
6. Handle as gently and as little as possible.

19th CENTURY CURES, REMEDIES AND HELPFUL HINTS

The information in this part was published during the last quarter of the 19th century. It recognizes at least in some circles the use of chemicals in the food chain as being detrimental to good health. Accurately — and without medical evidence at the time — some of these authors predicted that smoking cigarettes can cause cancer. And for those who think that the campaign against contaminated foods is a recent thing, they will be surprised at the information provided in this part.

Some of the cures, remedies etc., may be considered outdated by today's standards. There is also the comical side in its passages. There are, however, many helpful hints that pertain as much to this century as the last.

The photos in this part show how America looked—in rural areas—before the turn of the last century and shortly thereafter. This is about the time that the cures, remedies and hints found in this section were put into print.

To prevent Jars From Cracking

To prevent the cracking of glass fruit-jars or jelly glasses when pouring boiling fruit or felly into them, stand the jar on a steel or silver knife blade, or place a silver spoon in the jar while filling. No other precaution is necessary except to avoid drafts of air when filling.

Washing Fluids [Soap]

To make good washing fluid, take one pound each of potash lye, washing soda, and borax, and mix together in an enameled pan containing four quarts of boiling water. When cold, add to this mixture one pint of ammonia, and pour into glass jars or an earthen jug. About half a cupful of this fluid will be enough for a common-sized washing.

A very good fluid may also be made of equal parts of sal soda and concentrated lye. Dissolve separately one pound of each in two quarts of water. Mix and bottle as above. As soon as thoroughly dissolved and mixed it is ready for use. About half a teacupful of this fluid will be sufficient for a boiler full of clothes. Put into the water before it is hot, and stir well before putting the clothes in. Add about half this amount to each additional boiler full of clothes.

Grease Spots

1. If the grease spot is from sewing maching oil, wash with soap in cold water. Hot water is liable to make the stain permanent.

2. If the stain is an old one, rub with lard, and let stand for a few hours before washing with the cold water and soap; or tepid rain-water with baking-soda may be used.

3. A common grease spot, if fixed by long standing may be removed with naphtha, ether, or chloroform. But be careful, as they are highly explosive.

440

The birth of a town . . . at its beginning in northern Idaho in 1891 called Vollmer (later name was changed to Troy, its present day name).

To Remove Old Varnish Before Redressing

To sandpaper varnished furniture is a tedious task. A much quicker and more satisfactory way of removing varnish and paint is to scrub the surface with a strong solution of sal soda. To each pint of water add enough common washing soda to equal the bulk of a hen's egg; heat it, and apply while warm. If the varnished surface be moistened with this, and let stand a few moments, it can be cleaned off easily with a scrubbing brush.

All foreign material will thus be removed from the wood, and it will be just as it was turned out from the mill. Rinse off with clear water. When dry, it may be revarnished, stained, or painted. One advantage of this method is that it leaves the edges clear cut, instead of uneven and blunt as does the sandpaper.

Traps

Even with precautions, flies will get inside, and some other means must be taken to keep the house free from them.

There are numerous little fly-traps which are more or less familiar to every one. Here is a good old-fashioned one;—

Take a glass of water, and put over it a slice of bread; cover the under side of the bread with molasses, and make a small hole in the center; in a short time the flies will all go through the hole and not come back again.

It is claimed that castor beans, planted near the doors and windows, will keep away flies and mosquitoes. The remedy is inexpensive and very decorative, and it will do no harm to try it.

Two or three sheets of tanglefoot fly-paper will pick them up in a few hours.

Did you ever wonder why there are no flies around soda fountains, where one would expect them by the millions? It is because there is essence of sassafras scattered about to keep them away. A few drops of the oil will drive them out of the house.

Pennyroyal and Quassia Chips

If mosquitoes are troublesome in the sleeping-room, uncork a bottle of the oil of pennyroyal, and they will leave in haste; or, put in each window a saucer containing water and a pinch of quassia chips. Renew about twice a week. This remedy is clean, non-poisonous, and economical, and is a sure preventive.

Rats and Mice

Take equal quantities of corn-meal, or rye-meal, and unslacked, finely powdered lime. Mix well without wetting, and place on pieces of boards. Put water in a flat dish near by. They will eat the mixture readily, and soon become thirsty, drink the water, which slacks the lime, and the gas destroys them quickly.

Mix equal parts of brown sugar, corn-meal, and plaster of Paris, and place this compound where they can eat it. After moistening by eating, the plaster sets or hardens in the stomach and kills the rat.

Catch one rat alive, cover it with oil of phosphorous and set free. Being luminous in the dark, it will frighten away all its companions. This has been tried with great success.

Ants

Mix equal quantities of powdered sugar and powdered borax and strew on shelves and floors. The ants will eat so much of the sweet mixture that the borax will kill them.

442

The town of Troy growing in 1909.

Roaches

These troublesome insects have a peculiar aversion to borax. One-half pound, powdered, and sprinkled about their haunts, will drive them out of the house. Cayenne pepper sprinkled about will also drive them away.

Suggestions To The Tormented On Fleas

All the remedies known cannot enable a "tenderfoot" entirely to escape the annoyance of these little pests when he lands in a country infested by them. Some people remain "tenderfeet" all their lives. To people who are seriously poisoned by their bites they are a constant terror, particularly at night.

1. Wear close-meshed underclothing and stockings. The underclothing should lap and button up closely, particularly around the neck. Roll the stockings up over the bottoms of the drawers. If the mesh is fine enough so that the fleas cannot get through, and if the garments fit tightly about the neck and wrists, there is but little danger of trouble by day.

2. Bedding should be kept up from the floor. If allowed to hang near enough to the floor so fleas can jump onto it, or if allowed to drag on the floor in the morning before the bed is made, the fleas will get into the bed, if there are any about.

3. Do not sit or lie on the bed with your clothes on, or throw wraps or clothing onto the bed at any time.

4. Finish running about before putting on your nightclothes. Fleas will always jump for anything white, and you are most likely to pick them up on your bare feet or nightclothes if the slightest opportunity is offered.

5. Before getting into bed, sit down on the edge of it and brush your feet.

6. If you find a flea is in bed with you, do not toss and roll, or try to fight him or catch him in the dark; do not throw back the bedclothes. Shake yourself thoroughly under the covers, then slip out quickly without turning back the sheet. Place a light where it will shine into the bed when you partially lift the covers. Straighten out the top sheet so there are no wrinkles for hiding-places, then, with the sheet pulled to a fairly good tension, lift it gently and watch for him. He is almost certain to be on the upper sheet; that is why so many persons hunt for a flea several times in one night without finding him. Roll the covers back little by little until you find him, then wet your forefinger and thumb, put your finger over him quickly, pick him up and drop him into a vessel of water. Do not try to kill him over the bed; if you do, the chances are about equal that he will get away and give you a harder chase next time. A hunt of this kind should be pursued as systematically and scientifically as a bear hunt, or the hunter will miss his game.

Pennyroyal, oil of lavender, bronco flea-driver, and many other remedies are used with some success in keeping away fleas, but none of them can be made to take the place of cleanliness and carefulness.

Where fleas are very troublesome, it is well to keep alcohol or some other simple antidote on hand to rub on the bites to relieve the smarting of the poison.

The Wholesome Part of Doughnuts

The health journals and the doctors all agree that the best and most wholesome part of the New England country doughnut is the hole. The larger the hole, they say, the better the doughnut.

Catarrhal difficulties, kidney disease, headache, and heart troubles are the result of immoderate eating.

Cane sugar is the least digestible of all foods. It is not digested in the stomach, but in the small intestine. There is only one fluid that will digest cane sugar.

Mrs. Oldtimes — These new notions about sterilizing mild and boiling water to

444

drink are all nonsense. They make a heap of work all for nothing. I had eleven babies and I ought to know something about it.

Young Mother — And did your children all grow up to maturity?

Mrs. Oldtimes — Two of them did.

The Physical Endurance of Vegetarians

The following interesting facts on the subject of vegetarianism are given by Gautier, an eminent French authority on dietetics . . .

"According to J. Sinclair, the Hindu messengers who carry despatches for long distances eat only rice, while covering each day, in running from one village to another, a distance of at least twenty leagues (sixty miles), and do this not for a single day only but for every day consecutively, week after week.

"The Russian peasants, who live upon vegetables, black bread, milk, and leeks, work from sixteen to eighteen hours a day, and their strength often exceeds that of American sailors.

"The Norwegian peasants scarcely know the taste of animal food. They cover on a continuous run, however, in accompanying the carriages of tourists, a distance of three of four leagues without stopping.

"The modern Egyptian laborers and sailors, a class who, from time immemorial, have lived almost exclusively upon melons, onions, beans, lentils, dates, and corn, are remarkable for their muscular strength.

"The miners of South America, very temperate laborers, who never eat meat, carry on their shoulders burdens of two hundred pounds, with which the climb, twelve times a day, vertical ladders sixty to eighty meters high (one hundred ninety-six to two hundred sixty-two feet).

"The Turkish soldier is surpassing frugal. He drinks only water or lemonade, and lives upon a diet of rice anf figs, scarcely ever touching flesh. It is well known that the vigor of the Turk is remarkable, and his courage indisputalbe. The porters of Salonica and Constantinople, who live upon the same diet, are proverbially strong; hence the saying, "Strong as a Turk."

"Addressing himself to his friend, Firmus, who abandoned the Pythagorean doctoring to become an eater of flesh, the philosopher Porphyry wrote as follows:

"It is not among the eaters of simple vegetable foods, but among the eaters of flesh, that one meets assassins, tyrants, and robbers."

In the religious communities where the use of meat is forbidden, appendicitis is unknown.

It is a well-established fact that a leg of mutton caused a revolution in the affairs of Europe. Just before the Battle of Leipsic, Napoleon the Great insisted on dining on boiled mutton, although his physician warned him that it would disagree with him. The Emperor's brain resented the liberty taken with its colleague, the stomach; the monarch's equilibrium was overturned, the battle lost, and a new page opened in history.

Helpful Hints

In making paste, or thickening for gravy, add a pinch of salt to the flour and water, and it will mix much more smoothly and easily. Use a fork instead of a spoon for blending.

To make certain when a cake is done, put your ear down and listen; if it has ceased sounding, it is done. This is easier than trying with a straw.

Try a good, strong can opener for cutting open a Hubbard squash, and you will never use any other instrument. A very little cornstarch mingled with salt will prevent it from packing and will not interfere with its flavor.

Drop a little lump of sugar among the turnips while cooking; it will improve them very much.

Acid fruits should not be eaten with starchy foods, as the acid prevents digestion of the starch.

It is not possible to give definite rules that every one can follow in a matter of combining foods. What agrees perfectly with one is poison to another.

Nature of Condiments [Seasonings]

Condiments are defined as articles which add nothing to the nutritive value of food; they simply make it taste better. But this is wholly a matter of habit. The Englishman would object to having his food seasoned with asafetida because he is not used to it, while the Frenchman considers it a delicate flavoring.

All condiments are poisons, and when used in any considerable quantity, clog the liver and irritate all the digestive organs.

Applied to the skin, they will blister. The mucus membrane of the stomach is inflammed by their use, and after they are taken into the blood, they circulate to the tissues and do much mischief.

It is the duty of the liver to eliminate these substances from the blood, and, in consequence, it suffers more than any other organ of the body.

Condiments are used most in hot countries, and, consequently, diseases of the liver are almost universal.

People who use condiments to excess claim that their food will not digest if eaten without them. To some extent this is true. Their stomachs have become so benumbed that unless they are goaded by these irritants, they will not secrete sufficient gastric juice to perform the work of digestion.

A stomach in this condition must be allowed time to rest before it will be able to relish simple food.

Incentives to Strong Drink

Highly seasoned food leads to intemperance in drinking as well as in eating. The irritated, inflamed condition of the alimentary canal caused by the hot food, creates a craving for something stronger.

All stimulants must be continually increased in quantity, or they soon lose their effect. The same is true of the person who habitually takes some drug; to maintain the effect, the dose must be continually increased. The poisons in the drug and in the condiments have such a stimulating effect upon the system that there is a constant clamoring for something stronger.

Tea and Coffee

Probably tea and coffee are most universally used as drinks, but the millions that use them daily scarcely give a thought to the poisons they contain. Both will produce intoxication. Theine is the active property of tea, and caffeine of coffee, the two poisons being identical. It is for the effect of these poisons on the system that people drink them.

It has been found by experiment that twenty grains of theine is a poisonous dose. Tea contains from three to six per cent of theine. A teaspoonful of tea weighs a dram. There are sixty grains in a dram; hence there are three and five-tenths grains of theine in a teaspoonful of tea. A dram of tea, at least, is used for a cup. Two cups of tea would contain seven drains of theine, which would be enough to kill any small animal the size of a cat or rabbit. Six cups of tea would contain enough poison to make a person insensible. A smaller amount will excite the nerves, cause sleeplessness, and incite a spirit of gossip.

It is said that a cup of strong tea contains more poison than an equal quantity of

446

beer is more harmful. Few persons would drink as many cups of strong tea as they would of beer. By this we do not recommend beer, but we condemn the tea.

Tannin, another property of tea and coffee interfere with digestion by its action upon the gastric juice (one of the most important of the digest fluids), hindering its secretion and rendering it almost lifeless. Tea has even been known to cause delirium tremens.

There is imported into the United States annually more than one billion pounds of tea, or five hundred thousand tons (prior to 1900). Figuring only three per cent of poison to the pound, it would still reach the enormous figure of fifteen thousand tons, enough to exterminate the whole human race.

Tea and Coffee Cause of Rheumatism

Dr. J. C. Walton, in a very sensible article on the prophylaxis and treatment of uric acid conditions, published in the Charlote Medical Journal or April, 1904, mentions a case of rheumatism in which, notwithstanding rigid diet and thorough-going treatment, no improvement was noticed until after the patient gave up his coffee, when the disease promptly subsided. The doctor states that he has observed a number of similar cases. This is quite in accord with Aige's theory that theine or caffeine produces the same pernicious effect in the body that uric acid does. The doctor has observed excellent results from the use of hot air and other sweating procedures, followed by a gradual cold bath.

The loving mother who places rich and highly seasoned food upon her table for her husband and children is surely paving the way for tobacco and strong drinks. A perverted taste and apetite created by wrong methods of cooking and eating are accountable for much of the misery and sorrow abroad in the world today.

Effect of Alcohol Upon The Nervous System

The brain and spinal cord of a drinking man are in a constant state of congestion. The walls of the arteries and blood-vessels become weakened, and a rupture of a blood-vessel, or apoplexy, is liable to occur at any time. The brain-cells shrivel and become hard, and their power to act is partially destroyed. After a night of drinking, the head is dizzy and sore, and the hands shaky. All the finer sensibilities of the man are blunted.

Alcohol paralyzes the nerves that control the flow of blood to the different organs, and often congestion and inflammation are the result. For this reason the drunkard's face has an unnatural flush, and the vital organs of the body become diseased.

There is no temperance drink more palatable and refreshing than unfermented grape juice.

Unfermented Grape Juice

Choose ripe Concord or other suitable grapes, and remove the stems and any imperfect fruit that may be found. Then place in a wooden bowl, and mash well with a potato masher. Put a small quantity at a time into a jelly bag, and press out all the juice, or pass through a fruit press; then strain the liquid through flannel. Pour the liquid into bottles until they are nearly full. Then cork tightly, and stand in an upright position in a wash-boiler, the bottom of which has been covered with slats. Wrap each bottle in a cloth. Pour in cold water to within an inch of the corks, and stand the boiler over the fire. Let heat slowly, and note the time at which the water begins to boil. Let boil for twenty minutes, remove from fire, and allow the liquid to become cold in the water. Store in a cool place, laying the bottles on their sides.

447

If you find your soup is too salty, add a few slices of raw potato and cook a few minutes. The potato will absorb the salt.

Avoid the unpleasant odor from boiling vegetables by placing a piece of charcoal in the pot.

Improve the flavor of applesause by adding a pinch of salt.

If when serving tomatoes raw, you do not wish them to have the slightest taste of cooked tomatoes, as they will when they are immersed in hot water, rub the surface of the tomato all over with the flat edge of a sharp knife, being careful not to break the skin, and it will peel nearly as easily as when hot water is poured over it.

Drinking at Meal-Time

Much water or liquid of any kind taken with the meals diminishes the secretions of the salivary glands and encourages little mastication. Drinking to wash down the food quickly is one of the evils accompanying hasty eating. Eat slowly, allowing the saliva to mingle with and moisten the food, and there will be less desire for drinking.

Proper Food Combinations

Two important principles should be observed in combining foods:

First, the combination should be such as to bring to the body the proper food elements in the right proportion.

Second, the foods should be so combined that there will be harmony in the digestive process. Food which is digested in the stomach should not be mixed with food that requires long intestinal digestion. Combine foods that will digest together in about the same length of time. Albuminous substances, with the exception of casein, are digested chiefly in the stomach. Starchy foods are digested in the mouth and intestines.

The stomach may be trained to digest meat, milk or bread; but it is utterly impossible for it to digest all food substances at the same time. This is just as impossible as it is for a man to be working as a blacksmith and training for a soldier at the same time. If we mix too many kinds of foods together, we are certainly making trouble. All breads or cereals digest well together. All fruits and nuts digest well together; but meat is a bad thing in combination with most other foods. An exclusive diet of meat is far easier on digestion than a mixed diet. That is why multitudes of poeple who have suffered from indigestion, when put on an exclusive meat diet, feel better. An exclusve mild diet often agrees with an invalid. Some people put on an exclusive bread diet would feel better, because the stomach can digest each one of these different articles by itself, but not the combination.

Milk and apples digest in about the same time, and are a good combination. The fact that fruits are acid is no reason why they should not be eaten with milk. The acid simply curdles the milk but does not sour it. It simply separates the whey from the casein. Instead of making it more difficult of digestion, it facilitates its digestion. Taking acid with milk prevents large, hard curds from being formed in the stomach.

The albluminous element of peas, beans, and milk is casein, which is digested chiefly in the intestines, thus making them an excellent combination.

Vegetables and acid fruits are one of the worst food combinations.

Grains and milk, grains and fruits, grains and meats or eggs, and grains and vegetables are considered to be good combinations. Grains, sweet fruits, and milk, and meat and vegetables are fair combinations. Fruits and vegetables, milk and vegetables, and milk and meat are bad combinations.

How the food was produced. . . a grain harvest crew and cook shack. The cow was brought along to provide fresh milk.

The harvest crew at work threshing grain with a stationary thresher.

449

Tobacco

Tobacco is one of the greatest curses of modern times. It is less than three hundred years since its introduction into the civilized world, yet in that short space of time it has conquered every nationality and blighted and ruined the lives of millions of people.

Every pound of tobacco contains three hundred eighty grains of poison; chiefest among these is nicotine, one of the most deadly poisons known to chemists. It is found in tobacco in proportions varying from two to eight percent. Scientists tell us that there is poison enough in one pound of the noxious weed to kill three hundred men if administered in a manner to receive its full effect. One-tenth of a grain is sufficient to kill an animal the size of a dog.

Smoking injures the throat, weakens the vocal cords, and frequently causes cancer of the lip and throat.

Items of Interest on Tobacco

As to cigarette smoking among boys, there is just this much to say: The boy who smokes, whether it be the cigarette or any other form, between the ages of fourteen and eighteen, may bid adieu to all hopes of scholarship. He can do next to nothing in the high school grades.

Railroads

"Cigarette smokers are unsafe. I would just as soon get railroad men out of the insane asylum as to employ cigarette smokers." — Chairman Harriman, of the Board of Directors, Union Pacific and Southern Pacific Railroads.

Some years since a great railroad corporation in the West, having occasion to change the gauge of its road throughout a distance of some five hundred miles, employed a force of three thousand workmen upon the job, who worked from very early in the morning until late at night. Alcoholic drinks were strictly prohibited, but a thin gruel made of oatmeal and water was kept on hand and freely partaken of by the men to quench their thirst. The results were admirable; not a single workman gave out under the severe strain, and not one lost a day from sickness. Thus, this large body of men was kept well and in perfect health and spirits, and the work was done in considerably less time than counted on for its completion.

Exercise

My pallid friend, is your pulse beating low?
Does the red wine of life too sluggishly flow?
Set it spinning through every tingling vein
By outdoor work, till you feel once again
Like giving a cheery schoolboy shout;
    Get out!

Are you morbid, and, like the owl in the tree,
Do you gloomily hoot at what you can't see?
Perhaps now, instead of being so wise,
You are only looking through jaundiced eyes;
Perhaps you are bilious, or getting too stout;
    Get out!

A wire tie pull binder that tied grain into bundles that were carried into the stationary threshers.

Out in an air where fresh breeze blow
Away all the cobwebs that sometimes grow
In the brains of those who turn from the light
To all gloomy thoughts instead of the bright.
Contend with such foes and put them to rout;
   Get out!

Activity is a manifestation of life; and a more abundant life is the reward of activity. Stagnation is the immediate forerunner of death. When a tree ceases to grow, it dies; still water soon becomes stagnant; running water is the purest, for its activity affords a means for purification. The Dead Sea is a stagnant sink, and is called the Sea of Death, for it has no outlet, and therefore, no activity. Fish cannot live in its waters, for it has become a reservoir of poisons, which have been accumulating and multiplying for centuries.

This law of life holds good in the operation of every organ of the body. Muscles little used, become weak; teeth not used, soon decay; eyes little used, lose their power; and so with all the other organs of the body. They fulfill their respective functions with a strength in direct proportion to their proper exercise.

The chief reason for weakness and disease is that through inactivity the blood becomes sluggish, and fails to fulfill its functions, which are, chiefly, to carry off the waste, effete matter from the organs and muscles and bones of the body, and then rebuild with new and better strength that which is broken down. It is impossible for the blood to do this work unless the lungs are supplied with fresh, pure air, and the body with good food; then the habits of life must be such that the blood will be sent vigorously upon its life-giving mission to every extremity of the body.

The value of regular intelligent exercise cannot be overestimated. It is the law of life in every living thing.

Suggestion To Women

A woman cannot work at dressmaking, tailoring, or any other sedentary employment, ten hours a day, year in and year out, without enfeebling her constitution, impairing her eye-sight, and bringing on a complication of complaints; but she can sweep, cook, wash, and do the duties of a well-ordered house, with modern arrangements, and grow healthier every year. The times in New England when all women did housework a part of every day were the times when all women were healthy.— Harriet Beecher Stowe

The Daily Bath

A bath should be taken every morning unless there is some unusual physical condition to prevent it. The best time for this bath, and fortunately the time most convenient for nearly every one, is in the morning, before dressing. It is not necessary that this bath should be elaborate, nor consume more than five minutes time. A gentleman who has been greatly benefited by these morning baths, in giving a friend directions how to take them, said that his bath was made up of one part water, four parts rough towel-rubbing, and five parts friction with the bare hand. Almost everyone can take a bath like this and be benefited by it. Persons who might receive serious injury from cold plunge baths can almost invariably take this bath with benefit.

If the weather is cold, it is not necessary to remove all of the clothing at once. Drop the nightclothes down to the waist; wet the hands and briskly splash the face, arms, and body. The water should not be very cold, if tepid water can be readily obtained. In most cases, however, if only a little be used, cold water will

Over 60 horses plowing, harrowing and seeding in one large farm.

453

not be unpleasant or cause a chill, if the rubbing is brisk. This splash may be finished in a minute; then rub vigorously and thoroughly dry with a rough turkish towel. A smooth cotton or linen towel is about as good for drying the skin as super-calendered paper is for a blotter.

This will finish one-half the bath, according to the above directions. Now comes the hand friction. Beginning with the wrist, rub the arms, neck, and body lightly and rapidly, until every inch of the surface is aglow. Then put on a woolen shirt or some other short, warm garment, if the temperature of the room is too cold for comfort. Carefully avoid any reaction or chill. Bathe the rest of the body as described above. Although this early bathing may seem a little unpleasant at first, in a few days it will seem a luxury. The exercise is invigorating, the skin is stimulated, and all the organs of the body are toned up for the days work; and the glow of warmth thus created will remove the temptatiion to overheat the house by fires to warm up a sluggish system.

A Good Bath Powder

A delightful bath powder, and one that will relieve excessive perspiration, is made by the following recipe: Powdered starch, eight ounces; powdered orris-root, two ounces; camphor, one dram. Reduce to a powder, and put in small cheese-cloth bags.

Cosmetics

The most perfect complexion is given by health. No effort is generally made to improve such a complexion; but when age, sickness, or sorrow have taken away the bloom, many people are so unwise, or, perhaps, so ignorant of the results, that they resort to the use of cosmetics or face-creams, and lotions. Many of these cosmetics which are manufactured, advertised, and sold so extensively, contain the most powerful poisons. Unscrupulous manufacturers take advantage of the pride and vanity of thousands of foolish people, who care more for looks than for health, and develop a thriving business by the sale of these poisons.

Instead of improving the complexion, these lotions are an injury. By their continued use the skin becomes rough, and loses its fresh, natural tint.

Instead of cosmetics, use plenty of soft water and pure toilet soap.

Cucumber Lotion

The cucumber lotion is excellent for whitening the skin, also for its astringent properties. Put the juice of a cucumber into a pint bottle, add two drams of eau de Cologne and six ounces of rose-water, shake well, and add drop by drop two drams tincture of benzoin. Shake thoroughly. This preparation is delightful, and will give tone to the skin.

Cleansing the Skin

Many otherwise good skins are kept in poor condition by using hard water; this is not necessary, as a solution of borax will soften the water. Fill a bottle with warm water, add a teaspoonful of borax at a time until the water absorbs all it can in solution. Keep the bottle on the toilet table and add to the wash water.

Select unscented soap that has little alkali and no coloring in it. Such soap will not harm the most delicate skin.

Soap does not agree with fine, dry skins, the alkali in the soap taking away the natural oil. In such cases take a little almond meal in the hand and use the same as soap.

Pure almond-oil will not hurt the most delicate skin.

Food for the work horses. . . A hay stacking crew using all horse power.

One dram of tincture of benzoin to four ounces of rose water is the proportion for making a delightful, milky preparation for the skin. The benzoin should be added a few drops at a time to avoid curdling. If more benzoin is added than the above given proportion, curdling is liable to result.

Equal parts of bay rum and glycerin is an excellent lotion for the face after shaving.

Cold Cream

An excellent cold cream is quickly and easily made by the following recipe:

Two and one-half ounces of spermaceti, two and one-half ounces of sweet almond-oil, one-fourth ounces white wax. Melt together and after removing from the fire, add one and one-half ounces of rose-water. Beat until it creams.

Drying The Hair

Dry the hair by rubbing with warm towels, followed by a good dry massage with the fingertips, till the whole head is aglow. By this procedure, the requisites of beauty and health — cleanliness and vigorous circulation — have been fulfilled. Whenever possible, the hair should be dried in the sun. A sun bath brings out its glinting lights as nothing else can. The polish of the hair, if we may call it so, is more essential to its beauty than either its texture or color.

When sunshine is not available, fanning is a good substitute for drying the hair. If the air is warm, the process will be much shorter. The lock should be shaken from time to time during the drying. It is well in the case of long hair to braid it very loosely before washing, as then it will not be so likely to tangle. Instead of the water bath, a sun bath alone will make the hair fresh and sweet, and, together with brushing, does much to keep it in order. After shampoo, especially if the hair is naturally dry, it is a good plan to have rubbed into the scalp — for it is very difficult to do it properly one's self — a little bland oil, such as almond oil, oil of benne, or a little vaseline. But whatever you use must be sweet and not rancid. Any one of these oils will help to nourish the hair and offest any possible unhappy result of the shampoo.

A Good Habit

Many housekeepers see bits of poetry and prose which they would like to memorize, but where is the time in which to learn them? For years I have learned bits of this sort, and anything else I wish to commit, by fastening them on my mirror. At night when preparing for bed, and at times when I comb my hair or dress during the day, my eyes, lighting upon the lines, communicate them to my brain, and I have learned them almost unconsciously.

False Standards

One standard has been erected for men and another for women. This is not right. We should require as much from our boys as from our girls — as much from men as from women. As a woman has as much right to require a high standard of morals from the man with whom she associates, the man has to require the same from her. This should be remembered in all home teaching and practice.

Improper Jokes and Stories

A very common practice among men, and we fear to a shameful degree among women, is the habit of telling vile stories, and indulging in lewd jokes. It is a pity that all such human vultures could not be shot with the good weapon once used by

A team of 39 horses pulling a grain harvesting combine.

457

General U. S. Grant. At a cabinet meeting on one occasion when the business lagged, a certain member proposed to a story which he considered proper, as "there were no women present". "But please bear in mind," said the General, "that there are gentlemen present."

Sunshine

Nature's greatest agent for disinfecting and deodorizing is the bright sunshine. It is free to all, and needs no bottles or jugs to preserve it, nor "poison" lables to warn against carelessness in using it.

Dry Earth

This is one of the best absorbents and deodorants if finely powdered and very dry. It should be gathered up from dusty roads, or dried in an oven, and preserved in boxes or barrels for use in wet weather or in the winter. Use freely; it is of great service.

Charcoal

Powdered charcoal, mixed with clear water is also a good disinfectant and deodorant.

Insomnia

Never resort to drugs as a remedy for sleeplessness. Use some of the simple, common-sense remedies that are always at hand.

1. A neutral bath just before retiring is soothing to the nerves. It equalizes the circulation, warms the hands and feet, induces sleep.

2. A cool hand bath, taken with very little friction, is good if there is not time or opportunity for a neutral bath.

3. Be sure that the last meal is properly digested before retiring. Appease any feeling of hunger by a cup of hot water, hot lemonade, a bit of easily digested fruit, or even a glass of milk sipped slowly.

4. If the head is hot and weary from some mental strain, bind a cold compress around it, and place a bag of hot water to the feet. Then lie down quietly in a favorite position and encourage sleep. If it does not come in due time, try deep breathing. Let each inhalation be slow and steady, filling the lungs to their utmost capacity. This exercise will draw the blood from the head, and give relief to the tired nerves. Sometimes a slight physical exercise, such as regular movement of the toes and fingers will induce sleep.

To Remove Rust From Steel

Cover the steel with olive oil; after twenty-four hours rub it with powdered unslacked lime until the rust disappears.

To Strengthen Glassware

All glassware that one wishes to keep from cracking must be put into a dish with slightly salted cold water. Let it come to a boil slowly, then boil well, and again, cool slowly. The slower the process, especially that of cooling, the more effective will be the results.

To Treat New Ironware

To prepare new iron kettles for use and prevent rust, fill them with potato peelings and boil for an hour, then with hot water and rub with a little lard.

To Keep Glue Liquid

Dissolve the glue in whiskey instead of water. Pour it into a bottle and cork it tight. This will keep for years.   458

A way or rest station for stage coaches.

Cement For Cracks In Stoves

A good cement may be made of wood ashes and salt, in equal parts. Make a paste with cold water and fill the cracks when the stove is cool. It soon hardens.

How To Crystallize Grasses

Take one and one-half pounds of rock alum, pour on three pints of boiling water; when quite cool put into a wide-mouthed vessel. Hang in the grasses, a few at a time. Do not let them get too heavy, or the stems will not support them. Again heat the alum and add more grasses. By adding a little coloring it will give variety.

The Varied Uses Of Lemon

Every toilet table should be liberally supplied with lemons. Their uses are so varied and so valuable that no one can overlook them. Among them is the fact that a teaspoonful of lemon juice in a cupful of black coffee will drive away the headache. But if, on rising, the juice of one-half of the lemon be squeezed into a cupful of very hot water and drunk with no sugar there will be no headache to drive away. A slice of lemon rubbed on the temples and back of the neck will also cure the headache. A solution of lemon juice should always be at hand. A little rubbed on the skin at night will whiten and soften its texture. A paste made of magnesia and lemon juice will bleach the face and hands when applied to them. A fine manicure acid is made from a teaspoonful of lemon juice in a cupful of warm water (soft). It will whiten discolored and stained finger nails. Lemon juice in water will loosen the tartar that accumulates on the teeth. It makes the breath sweet. A slice of lemon rubbed over tan shoes which are then wiped off with a soft cloth will remove black stains from their surface.

Beef Tea

Take one pound of lean beef, cut it fine, put it in a bottle corked tightly, and put the bottle into a kettle of warm water; the water should be allowed to boil for a considerable time; the bottle should then be removed and the contents poured out. The tea may be salted a little and a teaspoonful given each time. Another way of preparing it is as follows: Take a thick steak, broil slightly on a gridiron until the juices have started, and then squeeze thoroughly with a lemon squeezer. The juice thus extracted will be highly nutritious.

Barley Coffee

Roast barley until well browned and boil a tablespoon of it in a pint of water for five minutes; strain and add a little sugar, if desired. A nourishing drink toward the close of fever and during convalescence.

Beef Jelly
(Excellent for Convalescents.)

Make some beef tea with a very little salt. Place one-eighth of an ounce of gelatine in a saucepan with a little cold water and soak. When sufficiently swollen place on the fire and boil until dissolved. Take the beef tea extract when nearly cold, add the gelatine, stir well, and turn into molds.

A pioneer farm family in front of their battered wood home.

Beef Tea

Take two pounds of lean rump of beef, remove every particle of fat, cut into small pieces and place in a tightly corked bottle. Place the bottle in a deep saucepan of cold water, reaching two-thirds of the way to the top of the bottle, place over a slow fire, and keep it boiling slowly for fifteen minutes, take out the bottle, pour out the liquor, and use as required.

Hiccough Cure

Small pieces of ice applied suddenly, so as to surprise the patient, will stop persistent hiccoughing. Also hot drinks of weak coffee and milk taken frequently has the desired effect.

For swollen and bleeding gums rinse the mouth with a wine-glassful of warm water in which is placed about seven drops of myrrh. This will harden the gums and keep them from working off the teeth, which always gives them a bad appearance.

Choking

To prevent choking, break an egg into a cup and give it to the person choking to swallow. The white of the egg seems to catch around the obstacle and remove it. If one egg does not answer the purpose try another. The white is all that is necessary.

Cure For External Cancer

Apply as poultice bruised stramonium leaves. Stramonium affects some persons as the poison ivy does. In this case the antidote is strong salt water freely applied.

Internal Cancer Cure

Take the dried blossoms of the common red clover, put them in hot water, let them steep over night and this will be a clover tea. Take a tablespoonful of this tea five or six times daily. Cases of virulent cancer have been cured by this simple remedy.

To Cool The Blood

Take eight ounces of sasparilla, three ounces of root licorice, six ounces of wild cherry bark, one-half ounce of mandrake, one ounce of gentian, one-half teaspoonful each of cinnamon and red pepper. Boil in three gallons of rain water till reduced to one-half. Sweeten a very little. This is a fine drink for cooling the blood. Abstain from sweets while using it.

Blood Purifier

Clover tea is a fine blood purifier, drank freely, removing pimples and whitening the skin. It is also a sleep-inducing draught. Its efficiency in early stages of cancer is unquestioned.

To Remove Proud Flesh

Pulverize loaf sugar very fine and apply it to the part affected. This is an easy remedy and is said to remove it entirely without pain.

A single horse pulling a huge load of logs on a sled. The wood from these logs eventually ended up in homes across America.

To Cure Dry Piles

The dry piles can readily be cured by a bruised onion, roasted in ashes.

Inward Piles

A small pitch pill taken after fasting a day will usually kill the bleeding piles. Or, take twice a day of the thin skin of walnuts as much as will lie on a 25 cent piece.

Quinsey [Sore Throat]

Roast four large onions. Peel them quickly and slightly pound. Add to them a little sweet oil. Place them while hot in a thin muslin bag that will reach from ear to ear, first thoroughly rubbing the throat and in this way getting up a good circulation of blood. Apply as warm as possible to the throat. Change when the strength of the onions appears to be exhausted. Flannel must be worn round the neck after the onion is removed.

Nightmare

This is a complaint which comes when the sleep is disturbed. It is the dreaming of something horrible and the person feels that it is something from which he cannot escape but is the victim. He attempts to scream for help but usually his effort is in vain. Nervous and over-worked people are especially subject to it. It is due to poor circulation. It is not only unpleasant but dangerous. The best remedy is to bathe each morning in cold water on arising, eat plain foods, little or no meat, tea or coffee, and breathe deeply for fifteen minutes each night before retiring.

Cough Syrup — Fine

One ounce each of hoarhound and licorice, two ounces of gum arabic, one pint of molasses and one teacupful of vinegar. Boil the hoarhound in one quart of water; dissolve the licorice and gum arabic in a little water first. Strain the hoarhound before adding the other ingredients. Do not put in the vinegar until it is nearly done.

Excellent Cream For The Complexion

A cream that is perfectly harmless, so harmless, indeed, that mothers need not hesitate to rub in on infants faces, has the juice of strawberries as a principal ingredient. The formula is:

One-half ounce of white wax, one-half ounce of spermaceti, two and one-half ounces of oil of sweet almonds, three-fourths of an ounce of strawberry juice, three drops of tincture of benzoin, two drops of oil of rose.

Be sure that your druggist gives you only one-half ounce of the wax and of the spermaceti. More than this will make the emollient hard and crumbly. The correct amount will give you a cream of perfect consistency. Take large, fresh strawberries, wash and drain thoroughly, macerate and strain through muslin. Shave the wax and spermaceti and put in a porcelain kettle over a slow fire. When they have melted add the almond oil. Heat slightly, remove from the fire and pour in the strawberry juice. Fluff up quickly with an egg beater. When the mixture begins to cream add the benzoin and the perfume. Put into little jars and keep in a cool place. Apply at any time. Excellent for tan, sunburn, or rough skin.

Wrinkles

If you have lost any teeth they will account for the lines, otherwise you should not have wrinkles before sixty. There is no other treatment that will take the place of massage for obliterating wrinkles.

Rules For The Reduction Of Flesh

Avoid all starchy and sweetened food, all cereal, vegetables containing sugar or starch, such as peas, beans, corn, potatoes, etc. Have your bread toasted; sprinkle it with salt instead of butter. Milk, I regret to say, if it be pure and good, is fattening. Hot water is an excellent substitute for other liquids. Add a little of the juice of limes or lemons to it if you choose. Limit your sleeping hours to seven at the outside. No naps. You must take exercise.

If you cannot walk at least five miles a day and do not wheel, go to one of the institutions where mechanical massage is given. Several correspondents report excellent results from this method of getting the vigorous exercise they require. The system is thoroughly wholesome. In reducing flesh the one fact to recollect is that fat is carbon—oxygen destroys or burns out carbon. You must consume the carbon by the oxygen you take through your lungs. The more exercise the more oxygen and consequent destruction of fat by the one healthful method of curing obesity. The more starch and sugar you eat the more carbon you burn away.

To Make The Hair Grow

The following remedy is excellent, as everyone who has tried it can testify. Have it put up at the drugstore. Seventy five grains of beta napthol, seventy five grains of hydrarg ammon, two ounces of lanoline and ungt. aqua Rosal in equal parts. Mix and apply to scalp after each shampoo.

To Remove Warts

These unsightly excrescences can be effectually removed by steeping or soaking a small piece of beef all night in vinegar. Cut what will cover the wart and tie it on. Strips of sticking plaster will fasten it on. Take the meat off in the daytime and put it on at night. In two weeks the wart will die and fall off.

Where the goods were bought. . . a grocery store in any small town in America about 1910-1915.

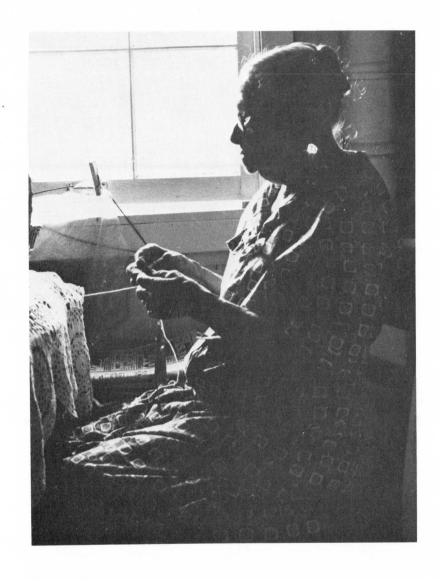

A pioneer born in 1873 during the presidency of General Ulysses S. Grant. The grandmother of the author, crocheting in this photo, lived to be 101 years of age.

Part X
MATH, KNOTS AND TIME

MEASUREMENTS AND CONVERSIONS

Apothecaries' Fluid Measure
(Used in compounding medicines)

```
.00369 l = 60 minims     = 1 fluid dram
.0296 l = 8 fluid drams  = 1 fluid ounce
       16 fluid ounces   = 1 pint
        8 pints          = 1 gallon
```

Dry Measure
(Used in measuring dry articles)

```
        .0164 l = 1 cubic inch
1.1 l = 2 pints (pt.) = 1 quart (qt.)
8.81 l = 8 quarts     = 1 peck (pk.) U.S.
35.24 l = 4 pecks     = 1 bushel (bu.) U.S.
Note: U.S. bushel = 2150.42 cu. in. = 35.24 l
      British bu. = 2218.2 cu. in.  = 36.35 l
      British pk. = 9.09 l
```

Cubic Measure
(Used in measuring things which have three dimensions, length, breadth, and thickness)

```
1728 cubic inches (cu. in.) = 1 cubic foot
765 l = 27 cubic feet (cu. ft.) = 1 cubic yard
       24-3/4 cubic feet = 1 perch
           1 cubic foot = 7.5 gal. approx.
```

Liquid Measure
(Used in measuring liquids)

```
1 gill   = .1183 l
4 gills  = 1 pint (pt.)
2 pints  = 1 quart (qt.) = .9463 l
4 quarts = 1 gallon (gal.) = 3.785 l
Note: U.S. gal. contains 231 cu. in.
      Usually a barrel contains 31 gals.
      and a hogshead 63 gals. Barrel
      & hogshead sizes vary. One gal.
      imperial (277 cu. in.) = 4.543 l
```

Long or Linear Measure
(Used in measuring lengths and distances)

```
 1 inch (in.) = 2.53977 cm.
12 inches (in.) = 1 foot (ft.) = 30.48 cm.
 3 feet        = 1 yard (yd.)
5-1/2 yds. or
16-1/2 feet    = 1 rod (rd.) or pole (p.)
40 rods        = 1 furlong (fur.)
 8 furlongs    = 1 mile (m.) = 1.6 km.
320 rods or
5280 feet      = 1 mile = 1609.35 m.
 3 miles       = 1 league
```

Mariners' Measure

```
  6 feet      = 1 fathom
100 fathoms   = 1 cable length or
                  cable
 10 cable-lengths = 1 mile
5280 feet     = 1 statute mile
6085 feet     = 1 nautical or
                  geographical mile
```

Measure of Angles or Arcs

```
 60 seconds (")  = 1 minute (')
 60 minutes      = 1 degree (°)
 90 degrees      = 1 right angle or
                     quadrant (L)
360 degrees      = 1 circle
```

Square Measure
(Used in measuring the area of surfaces)

```
    .0006452 m2 = 1 square inch (sq. in.)
   144 square inches = 1 square foot (sq. ft.)
.836 m2 = 9 square ft. = 1 square yard (sq. yd.)
30-1/4 square yards or
272-1/4 square feet    = 1 square rod (sq. rd.)
4047 m2 = 160 sq. rods = 1 acre (A.)
        640 acres      = 1 square mile (sq. mi.)
Note: A perch (P.) is a square rod
      A rood (R.) = 40 sq. rd.
```

Wood Measure
(Used in measuring wood and other merchandise)

```
16 cubic feet                    = 1 cord foot
 8 cord feet or 128 cubic feet   = 1 cord (cd.)
Note: A cord of wood, as generally piled, is
      8 ft. long, 4 ft. wide, and 4 ft. high.
```

METRIC SYSTEM EQUIVALENTS

Measures of Length

Metric Denomination and Value			Equivalent in Common Use
Myriameter		10,000 m	6.214 miles
Kilometer	(km)	1,000 m	0.62137 mile (3,280 feet, 10 inches)
Hectometer		100 m	328 feet, 1 inch
Decameter		10 m	393.7 inches
Meter	(m)	1 m	39.37 inches
Decimeter	(dm)	1/10 m	3.937 inches
Centimeter	(cm)	1/100 m	0.3937 inch
Millimeter	(mm)	1/1000 m	0.03937 inch

Metric Denomination and Value		Cubic	Equivalent in Common Use
Name	Liter	Measure	Dry Measure
Kiloliter (stere)	1,000	1 m³	1.308 cu. yds.
Hectoliter (hℓ)	100	1/10 m³	2 bush., 3.35 pecks
Decaliter (daℓ)	10	10 dm³	9.08 qts.
Liter (ℓ)	1	1 dm³	0.908 qt.
Deciliter (dℓ)	1/10	1/10 dm³	6.1022 cu. in.
Centiliter (cℓ)	1/100	10 cm³	0.6102 cu. in.
Milliliter (mℓ)	1/1000	1 cm³	0.061 cu. in.

Metric Denomination and Value		Cubic	Equivalent in Common Use
Name	Liter	Measure	Liquid Measure
Kiloliter (stere)	1,000	1 m³	264.17 gals.
Hectoliter	100	1/10 m³	26.42 gals.
Decaliter	10	10 dm³	2.64 gals.
Liter	1	1 dm³	1.0567 qts.
Deciliter	1/10	1/10 dm³	0.845 gill.
Centiliter	1/100	10 cm³	0.338 fl. oz.
Milliliter	1/1000	1 cm³	0.27 fl. dr.

Measures of Surface

Metric Denomination and Value		Equivalent in Common Use
Hectare (ha)	10,000 m²	2.471 acres
Are (a)	100 m²	119.6 square yards
Centare	1 m²	1550 square inches

TABLE OF CONVERSION FACTORS

To change	To	Multiply by
Inches	Centimeters	2.54
Feet	Meters	.305
Miles	Kilometers	1.609
Meters	Inches	39.37
Kilometers	Miles	.621
Square inches	Square centimeters	6.452
Square yards	Square meters	.836
Square centimeters	Square inches	.155
Square meters	Square yards	1.196
Cubic inches	Cubic centimeters	16.387
Cubic yards	Cubic meters	.765
Cubic centimeters	Cubic inches	.061

Weights

Metric Denomination and Value		Water at Maximum Density	Equivalent in Common Use
Name	Gram		Avoirdupois Weight
Millier (tonneau)(t)	1,000,000	1 m³	2,204.6 pounds
Quintal (q)	100,000	1 hℓ	220.46 pounds
Myriagram	10,000	10 ℓ	22.046 pounds
Kilogram (kg)	1,000	1 ℓ	2.204 pounds
Hectogram	100	1 dℓ	3.527 ounces
Decagram	10	10 cm³	0.353 ounces
Gram (g)	1	1 cm³	15.432 grains
Decigram (dg)	1/10	1/10 cm³	1.543 grains
Centigram (cg)	1/100	10 mm³	0.154 grain
Milligram (mg)	1/1000	1 mm³	0.015 grain

Apothecaries Weight
(Used in compounding medicines)

20 grains (gr.) = 1 scruple
3 scruples = 1 dram
8 drams = 1 ounce
12 ounces = 1 pound

Note: The pound, ounce and grain have the same weight as those of Troy Weight.

Troy Weight
(Used in weighing gold, silver and precious stones)

24 grains (gr.) = 1 pennyweight (pwt.)
20 pennyweights = 1 ounce (oz.)
12 ounces = 1 pound (lb.)

Note: 1 lb. Troy = 5,760 grains. In weighing diamonds, 1 carat = 3.168 Troy grains, and is divided into quarters which are called carat grains.

Avoirdupois Weight
(For all articles except drugs, gold, silver, and gem-stones)

27 11/32 grains = 1 dram (dr.)
16 drams = 1 ounce (oz.)
16 ounces = 1 pound (lb.) = 0.45257 kg
25 pounds = 1 quarter (qr.)
4 quarters)
100 pounds)
20 hundredweight or) = 1 hundredweight (cwt.)
2,000 pounds) = 1 ton (T.)

Note: 1 lb. Avoirdupois = 7,000 grs. The ton and hundredweight above given (often called *short ton* and the *short hundredweight*) are those in common use in the United States. The ton of 2,240 lbs., and the hundredweight of 112 lbs. (often called the *long ton* and the *long hundredweight*) are used at U.S. Custom Houses and in wholesale transactions in coal and iron, and are in general use in Great Britain.

Temperature

Degrees Centigrade = 5/9 x (Degrees Fahrenheit -32)
Degrees Fahrenheit = 1.8 x (Degrees Centigrade +32)

U. S. GOVERNMENT LAND MEASURE

A township—36 sections, each a mile square.

A section—640 acres.

A quarter section—half a mile square—160 acres.

An eighth section—half a mile long, north and south, and a quarter of a mile wide—80 acres.

A sixteenth section—a quarter of a mile square—40 acres.

The sections are all numbered 1 to 36, commencing at the northeast corner.

The sections are divided into quarters, which are named by the cardinal points. The quarters are divided in the same way. The description of a forty-acre lot would read: The south half of the west half of the southwest quarter of section 1 in township 24, north of range 7 west, or, as the case might be, and sometimes will fall short and sometimes overrun the number of acres it is supposed to contain.

LAND MEASURE RULE

To find the number of acres in a body of land, multiply the length by the width (in rods) and divide this product by 160. When the opposite sides of the area are unequal but parallel, add them and take half of the sum for the mean length or width.

EXAMPLE: How many sq. rods, also acres, in a field 80 rods long and 62½ rods wide?

80×62½=5000 sq. rods; 5000÷160=31¼ acres. Ans.

470

ACREAGE PER MILE OF VARIOUS WIDTHS

Width	Acres	Width	Acres
1 foot	0.121	15 feet	1.815
5 feet	0.605	16 feet	1.936
8 feet	0.968	18 feet	2.178
10 feet	1.21	20 feet	2.42
12 feet	1.452	24 feet	2.904
14 feet	1.694	25 feet	3.025

One Side of a Square Tract of Land Containing

1	Acre, is 208.7 ft.	=	43560 sq. ft.		
1½	" " 255.6 "	=	65340 " "		
2	" " 295.2 "	=	87120 " "		
2½	" " 330 "	=	108900 " "		
3	" " 361.5 "	=	130680 " "		
5	" " 466.7 "	=	217800 " "		
10	" " 660 "	=	435600 " "		
1/10	Acre, is 66 ft.	=	4356 sq. ft.		
1/8	" " 73.8 "	=	5445 " "		
1/6	" " 85.2 "	=	7260 " "		
1/4	" " 104.4 "	=	10890 " "		
1/3	" " 120.5 "	=	14520 " "		
1/2	" " 147.6 "	=	21780 " "		
3/4	" " 180.8 "	=	32670 " "		

DRAINS REQUIRED FOR ACRE OF LAND

The following Table shows the number of tiles, of the different lengths made, which are required for an acre, and will be useful to those who may desire to purchase just enough for a particular piece of ground:

DISTANCE APART	12-in. Tiles	13-in. Tiles	14-in. Tiles	15-in. Tiles
Drains 12 ft. apart require	3,630	3,351	3,111	2,934
" 15 " "	2,904	2,681	2,489	2,323
" 18 " "	2,420	2,234	2,074	1,936
" 21 " "	2,074	1,914	1,777	1,659
" 24 " "	1,815	1,675	1,556	1,452
" 27 " "	1,613	1,480	1,383	1,291
" 30 " "	1,452	1,340	1,245	1,162
" 33 " "	1,320	1,218	1,131	1,056
" 36 " "	1,210	1,117	1,037	968

In reference to tile-pipe drain, it must be remembered that the ditch may be much narrower than when stones are used, thus making a considerable saving in the expense of digging. The upper part of the earth is taken out with a common spade, and the lower part with one made quite narrow for the purpose, being only about 4 in. wide at the point.

Distance Traveled in Plowing 1 Acre

FURROW WIDTH INCHES	DISTANCE MILES	FURROW WIDTH INCHES	DISTANCE MILES
10	9 9/10	14	7
11	9	15	6 1/2
12	8 1/4	16	6 1/6
13	7 1/2		

DUTY OF FARM MACHINES

Probably the simplest and easiest method of determining the duty of a tractor or horse-drawn implement in acres covered *per 10-hour* day is to multiply the effective width of cut in feet by the rate of travel in mile per hour.

Width cut in feet X Miles per hour = acres per day.

EXAMPLE: 1 ft. cut X 2 m.p.h. = 2 acres per day. The average speed of mules is 2 m.p.h. The average speed for tractors: plowing, 3 m.p.h.; harrowing, 4 m.p.h.; cultivating 2-4 m.p.h.; mowing, 3-4 m.p.h.; and combining, 3-4 m.p.h.

QUANTITY OF SILAGE REQUIRED AND MOST ECONOMICAL DIAMETER OF SILO FOR DAIRY HERD

Number of dairy cows in herd	Feed for 180 days			Feed for 240 days		
	Estimated tonnage of silage consumed	Size of silo		Estimated tonnage of silage consumed	Size of silo	
		Diameter	Height		Diameter	Height
	Tons	Feet	Feet	Tons	Feet	Feet
13	47	10	26	63	10	34
15	54	10	30	72	12	28
20	72	12	28	96	12	35
25	90	12	33	123	14	34
30	108	14	30	144	14	39
35	126	14	34	168	16	35
40	144	14	39	192	16	39
45	162	16	34	216	16	43
50	180	16	37	240	18	39
60	216	16	44	288	18	46
70	252	18	41	336	20	44

Figures based on 40 lb. silage per day per cow.

CAPACITIES OF ROUND SILOS IN TONS

Depth of Silage*	10-ft. Diameter	12-ft. Diameter	14-ft. Diameter	16-ft. Diameter	18-ft. Diameter	20-ft. Diameter
FEET	TONS	TONS	TONS	TONS	TONS	TONS
10	13.7	19.8	27.0	35.2	44.5	55.0
11	15.3	22.0	29.9	39.0	49.3	61.0
12	16.8	24.2	32.9	42.9	54.3	67.1
13	18.3	26.4	35.9	46.9	59.3	73.3
14	19.9	28.7	39.0	50.9	64.4	79.6
15	21.4	30.9	42.0	54.9	69.3	-85.7
16	23.1	33.2	45.2	59.0	74.6	92.2
17	24.6	35.5	48.3	63.0	79.7	98.5
18	26.2	37.8	51.4	67.1	84.8	104.8
19	27.8	40.1	54.6	71.2	90.0	111.3
20	29.5	42.4	57.8	75.4	95.3	117.8
21	31.0	44.7	60.8	79.4	100.3	124.0
22	32.7	47.0	64.0	83.6	105.6	130.5
23	34.3	49.4	67.3	87.8	110.5	137.2
24	35.9	51.1	70.4	91.9	116.1	143.6
25	37.6	54.2	73.7	96.2	121.6	150.3
26	39.2	56.5	76.9	100.3	126.8	156.8
27	40.9	58.9	80.2	104.7	132.4	163.6
28	42.6	61.3	83.4	108.8	137.6	170.1
29	44.3	63.7	86.9	113.4	143.3	177.1
30	45.9	66.1	90.1	117.6	148.6	183.7
31	47.6	68.5	93.4	121.1	154.1	180.9
32	49.3	70.9	96.7	126.2	159.5	196.2
33	51.0	73.4	100.0	130.5	165.0	202.4
34	52.7	75.8	103.3	134.8	170.5	208.0
35	54.4	78.2	106.6	139.1	175.9	214.9
36	56.1	80.7	110.0	143.5	181.4	221.2
37	57.8	83.1	113.3	147.8	186.9	227.4
38	59.5	85.8	116.6	152.1	192.4	233.7
39	61.2	88.0	119.9	156.4	197.8	239.9
40	62.8	90.4	123.2	160.7	203.3	246.2
41	64.5	92.8	126.5	165.0	208.8	252.4
42	66.2	95.2	129.8	169.3	214.2	258.6
43	67.9	97.7	133.1	173.6	219.7	264.9
44	69.6	100.1	136.4	177.9	225.2	271.2
45	71.3	102.7	139.7	182.2	230.6	277.4

*Depth measured after silage has settled 30 days or more.

Approximate number of animals required to remove 2 in. of silage per day*, from silos of various diameters and at different rates of feeding.

Diameter feet	Pounds of silage to be removed daily	Number of animals that may be fed with daily allowance of:			
		40 lb.	30 lb.	20 lb.	15 lb.
10	525	13	18	26	35
12	755	19	25	38	50
14	1,030	26	34	52	69
16	1,340	34	45	67	90
18	1,700	42	57	85	113
20	2,100	53	70	105	140

*This is for winter feeding; 3 in. should be removed in summer.

DETERMINING HAY TONNAGE

To find the number of tons of hay in a given stack, simply divide the number of cubic feet in the stack, as calculated, using the system outlined

CUBIC FEET PER TON OF SETTLED HAY

Type of Hay	Cu. Ft.	Type of Hay	Cu. Ft.
Alfalfa	470	Straw (baled)	200
Baled Hay (closely stacked)	175	Straw (loose)	800
Chopped Hay	210	Timothy	625
Clover	500	Wild Hay	450

MEASURING CORN

Owing to the many varied conditions affecting the size and quality of kernel and cob, it is difficult to give a universal measurement rule. The following simple rules, however, are recognized in most sections of the country.

● Figuring Bushels of Ear Corn in Crib: Determine the number of cubic feet in the crib and multiply by 4½, then divide by 10; this rule applies for average corn. If the cobs are well filled and the corn is sound and dry and well settled in the crib, do as above, but divide by 9 instead of 10. If the cobs aren't well filled or the corn is damp and of inferior quality, divide by 11.

● Figuring Bushels of Shelled Corn in Bin: Determine the number of cubic feet of shelled corn in the bin and divide by 2, if the corn is heavy grain on small cob. For medium cob, medium grain, do the same, only divide by 2¼ instead of 2. For medium cob, light grain, divide by 2¾.

MEASURING HAY IN STACKS
Round Stacks

The volume in cubic feet of round stacks is best figured by using this formula:

$$\text{Volume} = [(.04 \times O) \text{ minus } (.012 \times C)] \times C \times C$$

In this formula, O equals the **over**, or distance in feet from the ground on one side up and over the peak down to the ground on the other side; it is advisable to take two measurements of O from different spots and then average them. C equals the **circumference**, or distance in feet around the stack at the ground.

Example: If O measures 40 ft. and C measures 60 ft., the volume in cu. ft. is figured this way.

$$\text{Volume} = [(.04 \times 40) \text{ minus } (.012 \times 60)] \times 60 \times 60$$
$$\text{"} = [1.6 \text{ minus } .72] \times 60 \times 60$$
$$\text{"} = .88 \times 60 \times 60$$
$$\text{"} = 3,168 \text{ cu. ft.}$$

Oblong or Rectangular Stacks

The volume of an oblong or rectangular stack equals its length times the area of its cross section. The **length**, of course, can be easily measured, but an accurate formula is needed to figure the area of the cross section from the two other measurements obtainable, namely the over and the width. The over, O in the formulas below, is the distance from the ground on one side up and over the peak down to the ground on the other side. The **width**, W in the formulas below, is the width of the stack at the ground. The **length**, L in the formulas below, is the average length of the stack at the ground.

The three major styles of stacks, with the formulas for each one, are as follows:

For low, round-topped stacks.
$$\text{Volume} = [(.52 \times O) \text{ minus } (.44 \times W)] \times W \times L$$

For high, round-topped stacks.
$$\text{Volume} = [(.52 \times O) \text{ minus } (.46 \times W)] \times W \times L$$

For square, flat-topped stacks.
$$\text{Volume} = [(.56 \times O) \text{ minus } (.55 \times W)] \times W \times L$$

Example: Determine cu. ft. in a square, flat-topped stack if L measures 50 ft., W measures 35 ft., and O measures 70 ft. Using these numbers in the proper formula, we have:

$$\text{Volume} = [(.56 \times 70) \text{ minus } (.55 \times 35)] \times 35 \times 50$$
$$\text{"} = [39.20 \text{ minus } 19.25] \times 35 \times 50$$
$$\text{"} = 19.95 \times 35 \times 50$$
$$\text{"} = 34,912.5 \text{ cu. ft.}$$

HANDY ROPE INFORMATION

The safe working strength of various diameters of new manila and sisal rope, approximate weight, and the corresponding sizes of block.

Diameter of rope (inches)	Safe working stress		Approximate length per pound	Size of block
	Manila	Sisal		
	Pounds	Pounds	Feet	Inches
¼	100	70	51.0	2
⅜	200	140	24.5	3
½	400	280	13.6	4
⅝	800	560	7.5	5
¾	980	686	6.2	6
⅞	1,400	980	4.5	7
1	1,640	1,148	3.7	9
1¼	2,500	1,750	2.4	12
1½	3,500	2,450	1.7	15

WATER REQUIREMENTS OF ANIMALS

HORSE—7 to 10 gallons daily, average about 8½ gallons
COW—6 to 10 gallons daily, average about 8½ gallons
HOG—2 to 3 gallons daily, average about 2½ gallons
SHEEP—1 to 2 gallons daily, average about 1½ gallons
100 Chickens need 40 pounds of water a day—5½ gallons

RULES FOR MEASUREMENT

To find diameter of a circle multiply circumference by .31831.

To find circumference of a circle multiply diameter by 3.1416.

To find area of a circle multiply square of diameter by .7854.

To find surface of a ball, or sphere, multiply square of diameter by 3.1416.

To find volume of a ball, or sphere, multiply cube of diameter by .5236.

To find area of a triangle multiply the perpendicular height times the base and divide by two.

To find the area of trapezoid multiply half sum of parallel sides times perpendicular height.

To find area of ellipse multiply long diameter times short diameter times .7854.

To find area of parallelogram multiply base times perpendicular height.

RECTANGULAR BODIES are reduced to cubic feet or inches by multiplying the length, width, and height together. Thus a bin 8 ft. long, 5 ft. wide, and 4 ft. high contains $8 \times 5 \times 4 = 160$ cubic feet.

CYLINDRICAL BODIES are reduced to cylindrical feet or inches by multiplying the square of the diameter by the depth; and they are reduced to cubic feet by multiplying the cylindrical feet by .7854. Thus a tank, diameter 5 ft., depth 4 ft., contains $5^2 \times 4 = 100$ cylindrical feet; and $100 \times .7854 = 78\frac{1}{2}$ cubic feet.

THE HEIGHT of tall objects like trees and buildings may be measured by using this simple system. Set up a stick in the ground and measure its shadow. Measure the length of the shadow of the tree, or other object. The height of the tree equals the length of the tree's shadow times the height of the stick divided by the length of the stick's shadow.

Tables Convenient for Taking Inside Dimensions

A box 25 x 24 x 14.7 inches will hold a barrel of 31½ gallons.

A box 15 x 14 x 11 inches will hold 10 gallons.

A box 8¼ x 7 x 4 inches will hold a gallon.

A box 4 x 4 x 3.6 inches will hold a quart.

A box 24 x 28 x 16 inches will hold five bushels.

A box 16 x 12 x 11.2 inches will hold a bushel.

A box 12 x 11.2 x 8 inches will hold a half-bushel.

A box 7 x 6.4 x 12 inches will hold a peck.

A box 8.4 x 8 x 4 inches will hold a peck, or four dry quarts.

A box 6 x 5.6 x 4 inches deep will hold a half-gallon.

A can 7 inches in diameter by 6 inches deep will hold a gallon.

USEFUL INFORMATION

Double diameter of pipe increases its capacity **4 times.**

Double riveting is 16-20% stronger than single.

To find the pressure in lbs. per sq. in. at the base of a column of water (a vertical water pipe, for instance), multiply the column height in ft. by **434.**

A bunch of laths (unit size 4 ft. long by 1½ in. wide) will cover about 3 sq. yds. 70 sq. yds. of surface requires about 100 laths and 11 lbs. of lath nails.

100 sq. ft. of roof area, 4 in. to the weather, requires about 1000 standard shingles and 5 lbs. of nails.

5 courses of brick will lay 1 ft. in height on a chimney.

To determine the field speed of a tractor, walk beside it for 20 sec., counting the number of 3-ft. steps you take during that period. Then point off one place to get speed in m.p.h.

To figure value of items sold by the ton, you can multiply the number of lbs. by the price per ton, point off 3 places and divide by two.

A standard single roll of wallpaper is 22 in. wide and 252 in. (21 ft.) long.

Steam rising from water at its boiling point (212° F.) has a pressure of 14.7 lbs. per sq. in. (same as atmospheric normal).

Each nominal horsepower of a boiler requires 30-35 lbs. of water.

A wagon bed 3 ft. wide and 10 ft. long will hold 2 bushels for every inch in depth.

GRANARIES — WAGON-BEDS
To Find Contents, in Bushels

RULE: Determine the number of cubic feet and multiply by .8 (exact .8036).

EXAMPLES: Find the contents of a granary 14 ft. long, 7½ ft. wide, and 6 ft. high. 14 x 7½ x 6 = 630 cu. ft.; 630 x .8 = 504 bu. Contents of wagon-bed 10 ft. x 3 ft. x 1½ ft. = 45 cu. ft.; 45 x .8 = 36 bu.

BARRELS — CASKS
To Find Contents, in Gallons

RULE: Multiply the square of the mean diameter by the depth and that resulting product by .0034 to find the gallon capacity.

EXAMPLES: Find the capacity of a barrel whose mean diameter is 20 in. with a depth of 32 in. 20^2 x 32 = 12,800; 12,800 x .0034 = 43½ gals. Find the capacity of a cask whose mean diameter is 12½ in. with a 20 in. depth. $12\frac{1}{2}^2$ x 20 x .0034 = 10⅝ gals.

RECTANGULAR TANKS
To Find Contents, in Gallons

RULE: To determine number of gallons multiply cubic volume in feet by 7½ (exact 7.48); for contents in barrels multiply by .2375.

EXAMPLE: Find the capacity of an oblong tank 10 ft. long, 3 ft. wide, and 1⅔ ft. deep. 10 x 3 x 1⅔ = 50 cu. ft.; 50 x 7½ = 375 gals.; 50 x .2375 = 11⅞ bbls.

ROUND CISTERNS AND TANKS
To Find Contents, in Gallons

Depth in Feet	Diameter in Feet								
	4	5	6	7	8	9	10	11	12
4	376	588	846	1,152	1,504	1,904	2,350	2,844	3,384
5	470	735	1,058	1,439	1,880	2,380	2,938	3,555	4,230
6	564	881	1,269	1,727	2,256	2,855	3,525	4,265	5,076
7	658	1,028	1,481	2,015	2,632	3,331	4,113	4,976	5,922
8	752	1,175	1,692	2,303	3,008	3,807	4,700	5,687	6,768
9	846	1,322	1,904	2,591	3,384	4,283	5,288	6,398	7,614
10	940	1,469	2,115	2,879	3,760	4,759	5,875	7,109	8,460
11	1,034	1,616	2,327	3,167	4,123	5,235	6,463	7,820	9,306
12	1,128	1,763	2,537	3,455	4,512	5,711	7,050	8,531	10,152

NOTE: The U. S. Standard gallon contains 231 cu. in. while the English Imperial gallon contains 277.274 cu. in. To change U. S. gals. to English gals. multiply the number of U. S. gals. by 5/6. 100 U. S. gals. (100 x 5/6) = 83 1/3 Eng. gals. To change English gals. to U. S. gals. multiply the English gals. by 1 1/5. 100 Eng. gals. (100 x 1 1/5) = 120 U. S. gals.

WEIGHTS AND VOLUMES OF WATER

One cubic inch of water weighs .03617 pounds. One cubic foot weighs 62.5 pounds.

One cubic foot equals 7.48052 gallons. One pint (liquid) weighs 1.044375 pounds. One gallon weighs 8.345 pounds. One gallon equals 231 cubic inches. One liquid quart equals 57.75 cubic inches.

MISCELLANEOUS EQUIVALENTS

A pint's a lb. (approximately of: water, wheat, butter, sugar, or blackberries.

196 lbs. of flour make 1 bbl.

200 lbs. beef or pork make 1 bbl.

165 lbs. potatoes make 1 bbl.

135 lbs. apples make 1 bbl.

280 lbs. salt make 1 bbl.

1 bbl. fish weighs 200 lbs.

1 gal. water weighs about 8⅓ lbs.

1 gal. milk weighs about 8.6 lbs.

1 gal. cream weighs about 8.4 lbs.

46½ qts. of milk weigh 100 lbs.

1 cu. ft. water weighs 62½ lbs., contains 7½ gals.

1 gal. kerosene weighs about 6½ lbs.

1 bbl. cement contains 3.8 cu. ft.

1 bbl. oil contains 42 gals.

1 bbl. dry commodities contains 7,065 cu. in. or 105 dry qts.

1 standard bale cotton weighs 480 lbs.

1 keg of nails weighs 100 lbs.

1 keg of powder weighs 25 lbs.

1 stone or lead of iron weighs 14 lbs.

1 pig of lead or iron weighs 21½ stones.

1 cu. ft. Anthracite broken coal averages about 54 lbs.

1 cu. ft. Bituminous broken coal averages about 49 lbs.

1 ton of loose Anthracite occupies 40-43 cu. ft.

1 ton of loose Bituminous occupies 40-48 cu. ft.

1 horsepower (hp.) is equivalent to raising 33,000 lbs. 1 ft. per minute.

⅓ in. equals one size in measuring shoes.

4 in. equal 1 hand in measuring horses.

9 in. equal 1 span.

6 ft. equal 1 fathom.

6,080 ft. equal 1 nautical mile.

1 board ft. equals 144 cu. in.

1 cylindrical ft. contains 5⅞ gals.

1 cu. ft. equals .8 bushel.

12 dozen (doz.) equal 1 gross (gr.).

INTEREST TABLE

This will be found convenient in the absence of extended interest tables. To find the interest on a given sum, for a given period, at a given rate:

At 3% multiply the principal by the number of days and divide by	120
At 4% as above, and divide by	90
At 5% as above, and divide by	72
At 6% as above, and divide by	60
At 7% as above, and divide by	52
At 8% as above, and divide by	45
At 9% as above, and divide by	40
At 10% as above, and divide by	36
At 12% as above, and divide by	30

SIZES AND WEIGHTS OF WIRE USED IN FARM FENCING

Gauge No.	Diameter	Surface Area Per Pound	Weight Per 100 Feet	Length Per Pound	Weight Per— Mile	Weight Per— Rod
	Inches	Sq. Feet	Pounds	Feet	Pounds	Pounds
9	0.1483	0.66	5.87	17.05	309.7	0.97
10	.1350	.73	4.86	20.57	256.7	.80
11	.1205	.82	3.87	25.82	204.5	.64
12	.1055	.93	2.97	33.69	156.7	.49
12½	.0990	.98	2.64	37.82	139.4	.43
13	.0915	1.08	2.23	44.78	117.9	.37
14	.0800	1.23	1.70	58.58	90.1	.28
14½	.0760	1.29	1.54	64.93	81.3	.25
19	.0410	28.7	.44	223.00	23.7	.07
20	.0348	33.8	.32	309.60	17.0	.05

APPROXIMATE AMOUNT OF BARBED WIRE REQUIRED FOR FENCES

2 strand, 12½ gauge hog wire with 2 point, 14 gauge barbs, 3 inches between barbs

	1 line	2 lines	3 lines
1 rod in length	1 lb.	2 lbs.	3 lbs.
100 rods	100 lbs.	200 lbs.	300 lbs.
100 feet	6¹⁄₁₆ lbs.	12½ lbs.	18³⁄₁₆ lbs
1 square acre	50⅔ lbs.	101½ lbs.	152 lbs.
1 square mile	1,280 lbs.	2,564 lbs.	3,840 lbs.
1 side of square mile	320 lbs.	640 lbs.	960 lbs.

GENERAL WOOD CHARACTERISTICS

1. Degree of Workability with Hand Tools; **2.** Tendency to Warp; **3.** Tendency to Shrink or Swell; **4.** Relative Hardness; **5.** Comparative Weight.

Wood	1	2	3	4	5
Black Ash	L	I	H	H	I
White Ash	L	I	I	H	H
Basswood	H	I	H	L	L
Beech	L	H	H	H	H
Yellow Birch	L	I	H	H	H
Eastern Red Cedar	I	L	L	H	H
Western Red Cedar	H	L	L	L	L
Northern White Cedar	H	L	L	L	L
Southern White Cedar	H	L	L	L	L
Cherry	L	L	I	H	I
Chestnut	I	L	I	I	I
Cottonwood	I	H	H	L	I
Southern Cypress	I	I	I	I	I
Rock Elm	L	I	H	H	H
Soft Elm	L	H	H	H	H
Balsam Fir	I	I	I	L	L
Douglas Fir	L	I	I	I	I
White Fir	I	I	I	L	L
Red Gum	I	H	H	I	I
Eastern Hemlock	I	I	I	I	I
Western Hemlock	I	I	I	I	I
Pecan Hickory	L	I	H	H	H
True Hickory	L	I	H	H	H
Western Larch	L	I	I	H	H
Black Locust	L	I	I	H	H
Honey Locust	L	I	I	h	H
Mahogany	I	L	I	H	H
Hard Maple	L	I	H	H	H
Soft Maple	L	I	I	H	H
Red Oak	L	I	H	H	H
White Oak	L	I	H	H	H
Ponderosa Pine	H	L	I	L	I
Arkansas Soft Pine	H	L	L	L	L
Sugar Pine	H	L	L	L	L
Northern White Pine	H	L	L	L	L
Western White Pine	H	L	I	L	I
Southern Yellow Pine	L	I	I	H	H
Yellow Poplar	H	L	I	L	I
Redwood	I	L	L	I	I
Eastern Spruce	I	L	I	L	I
Englemann Spruce	I	L	I	L	L
Sitka Spruce	I	L	I	L	I
Sycamore	L	H	H	H	H
Tupelo	L	H	I	H	H
Walnut	I	L	I	H	H

H—High I—Intermediate L—Low

BOARD MEASURE

Size		Length in Feet						
Nom.	Actual	8	10	12	14	16	18	20
		Board Feet						
1x 2	25/32x 1⅝	1⅓	1⅔	2	2⅓	2⅔	3	3⅓
1x 3	25/32x 2⅝	2	2½	3	3½	4	4½	5
1x 4	25/32x 3⅝	2⅔	3⅓	4	4⅔	5⅓	6	6⅔
1x 6	25/32x 5⅝	4	5	6	7	8	9	10
1x 8	25/32x 7½	5⅓	6⅔	8	9⅓	10⅔	12	13⅓
1x10	25/32x 9½	6⅔	8⅓	10	11⅔	13⅓	15	16⅔
1x12	25/32x11½	8	10	12	14	16	18	20
1x14	25/32x13½	9⅓	11⅔	14	16⅓	18⅔	21	23⅓
1x16	25/32x15½	10⅔	13⅓	16	18⅔	21⅓	24	26⅔
2x 2	1⅝x 1⅝	2⅔	3⅓	4	4⅔	5⅓	6	6⅔
2x 3	1⅝x 2⅝	4	5	6	7	8	9	10
2x 4	1⅝x 3⅝	5⅓	6⅔	8	9⅓	10⅔	12	13⅓
2x 6	1⅝x 5⅝	8	10	12	14	16	18	20
2x 8	1⅝x 7½	10⅔	13⅓	16	18⅔	21⅓	24	26⅔
2x10	1⅝x 9½	13⅓	16⅔	20	23⅓	26⅔	30	33⅓
2x12	1⅝x11½	16	20	24	28	32	36	40
2x14	1⅝x13½	18⅔	23⅓	28	32⅔	37⅓	42	46⅔
2x16	1⅝x15½	21⅓	26⅔	32	37⅓	42⅔	48	53⅓
3x 3	2⅝x 2⅝	6	7½	9	10½	12	13½	15
3x 4	2⅝x 3⅝	8	10	12	14	16	18	20
3x 6	2⅝x 5⅝	12	15	18	21	24	27	30
3x 8	2⅝x 7½	16	20	24	28	32	36	40
3x10	2⅝x 9½	20	25	30	35	40	45	50
3x12	2⅝x11½	24	30	36	42	48	54	60
3x14	2⅝x13½	28	35	42	49	56	63	70
3x16	2⅝x15½	32	40	48	56	64	72	80
4x 4	3⅝x 3⅝	10⅔	13⅓	16	18⅔	21⅓	24	26⅔
4x 6	3⅝x 5⅝	16	20	24	28	32	36	40
4x 8	3⅝x 7½	21⅓	26⅔	32	37⅓	42⅔	48	53⅓
4x10	3⅝x 9½	26⅔	33⅓	40	46⅔	53⅓	60	66⅔
4x12	3⅝x11½	32	40	48	56	64	72	80
4x14	3⅝x13½	37⅓	46⅔	56	65⅓	74⅔	84	93⅓
4x16	3⅝x15½	42⅔	53⅓	64	74⅔	85⅓	96	106⅔
6x 6	5½x 5½	24	30	36	42	48	54	60
6x 8	5½x 7½	32	40	48	56	64	72	80
6x10	5½x 9½	40	50	60	70	80	90	100
6x12	5½x11½	48	60	72	84	96	108	120
6x14	5½x13½	56	70	84	98	112	126	140
6x16	5½x15½	64	80	96	112	128	144	160
8x 8	7½x 7½	42⅔	53⅓	64	74⅔	85⅓	96	106⅔
8x10	7½x 9½	53⅓	66⅔	80	93⅓	106⅔	120	133⅓
8x12	7½x11½	64	80	96	112	128	144	160
8x14	7½x13½	74⅔	93⅓	112	130⅔	149⅓	168	186⅔
8x16	7½x15½	85⅓	106⅔	128	149⅓	170⅔	192	213⅓
10x10	9½x 9½	66⅔	83⅓	100	116⅔	133⅓	150	166⅔
10x12	9½x11½	80	100	120	140	160	180	200
10x14	9½x13½	93⅓	116⅔	140	163⅓	186⅔	210	233⅓
10x16	9½x15½	106⅔	133⅓	160	186⅔	213⅓	240	266⅔

TO FIND NUMBER OF BOARD FEET IN A LOG

Subtract 4 inches from the diameter and square the remainder. The result will be the number of board feet in a 16-foot log. Add ⅛ for 18-foot logs, ¼ for 20-foot logs. Subtract ⅛ for 14-foot logs, ¼ for 12-foot logs.

TO FIGURE CORD WOOD

A cord of wood is 4 ft. wide, 4 ft. high, and 8 ft. long; it thus contains (4x4x8) 128 cu. ft. To figure cordage, determine cu. ft. of wood in pile, or on wagon, and divide by 128.

Example: How many cords in a load 8 ft. x 2⅔ ft. x 12 ft.? 8 x 2⅔ x 12=256; 256÷128=2 cords.

COMMON NAILS REFERENCE TABLE

Size*	Length	Gauge No.	Diameter Head	Approx. No. to Pound
2d	1"	15	11/64"	845
3d	1¼"	14	13/64"	540
4d	1½"	12½	¼"	290
5d	1¾"	12½	¼"	250
6d	2"	11½	17/64"	165
7d	2¼"	11½	17/64"	150
8d	2½"	10¼	9/32"	100
9d	2¾"	10¼	9/32"	90
10d	3"	9	5/16"	65
12d	3¼"	9	5/16"	60
16d	3½"	8	11/32"	45
20d	4"	6	13/32"	30
30d	4½"	5	7/16"	20
40d	5"	4	15/32"	17
50d	5½"	3	½"	13
60d	6"	2	17/32"	10

APPROXIMATE QUANTITIES OF MATERIALS REQUIRED FOR MAKING ONE CUBIC YARD OF CONCRETE

Cement	Sand	Gravel or Stone	Cement	Sand (damp and loose)	Gravel (loose)
	Proportions of Concrete or Mortar			Quantities of Materials	
			Sacks	(Cu. Yds.)	(Cu. Yd.)
1	1.5		15.5	0.86	
1	2.0		12.8	.95	
1	2.5		11.0	1.02	
1	3.0		9.6	1.07	
1	1.5	3	7.6	.42	0.85
1	2.0	2	8.2	.60	.60
1	2.0	3	7.0	.52	.78
1	2.0	4	6.0	.44	.89
1	2.5	3.5	5.9	.55	.77
1	2.5	4	5.6	.52	.83
1	2.5	5	5.0	.46	.92
1	3.0	5	4.6	.51	.85
1	3.0	6	4.2	.47	.94

Quantities may vary 10% depending on aggregate used.

PIPE DIMENSIONS

Nom. Inside Dia.	Actual Outside Dia.	Actual Inside Dia.	Nom. Inside Dia.	Actual Outside Dia.	Actual Inside Dia.
⅛	0.405	0.270	3	3.5	3.067
¼	0.540	0.364	3½	4	3.548
⅜	0.675	0.494	4	4.5	4.026
½	0.840	0.623	4½	5	4.508
¾	1.05	0.824	5	5.563	5.045
1	1.315	1.048	6	6.625	6.065
1¼	1.66	1.38	7	7.625	7.023
1½	1.9	1.61	8	8.625	7.982
2	2.375	2.067	9	9.625	8.937
2½	2.875	2.468	10	10.75	10.019

NOTE: Dimensions above are in inches, and are for standard steel and wrought-iron pipe.

Capacity of 100 feet of pipe—based on actual internal diameter:

¾ "	2.8 Gals.	2 "	17.4 Gals.
1 "	4.5 Gals.	2½"	24.8 Gals.
1¼"	7.8 Gals.	3 "	38.3 Gals.
1½"	10.6 Gals.		

CAPACITY OF ELECTRICAL WIRE, Rubber Covered

(Choose Fuse Sizes Accordingly)

Wire Size	8 B.S.	10 B.S.	12 B.S.	14 B.S.
In Cable or Conduit	48 amps	35 amps	26 amps	15 amps
In Knob-and-Tube Work	50 amps	35 amps	30 amps	20 amps

HOUSEHOLD MEASURES
(with approximate equivalents)

1 teaspoon (tsp.)	= 4 cc.	= 1 fl. dr.
1 dessertspoon	= 8 cc.	= 2 fl. dr.
1 tablespoon (tbsp.)	= 15 cc.	= ½ fl. oz.
1 wineglass	= 60 cc.	= 2 fl. oz.
1 teacup	= 120 cc.	= 4 fl. oz.
1 tumbler	= 240 cc.	= 8 fl. oz.

TABLE OF WEIGHTS AND MEASURES

Fruit or Vegetable	Measure	Weight	Quart Jars
Red Raspberries	24 pt. crate	16 lbs. net	8
Strawberries	16 qt. crate	22 lbs. net	8
Cherries	16 qt. crate	22 lbs. net	12
Peaches	1 bushel	48 to 50 lbs.	25
String Beans	1 peck	6 lbs.	6-8 pints
Carrots	1 bushel	50 lbs.	40 pints
Corn	1 bushel	70 lbs.	16 pints
Tomatoes	1 peck	14 lbs.	7-9 pints

NUMBER OF SHRUBS OR PLANTS FOR AN ACRE

Distance Apart	No. of Plants	Distance Apart	No. of Plants	Distance Apart	No. of Plants
3 x3 inches	696,690	4 x 4 feet	2,722	13 x13 feet	257
4 x4 "	392,040	4½x 4½ "	2,151	14 x14 "	222
6 x6 "	174,240	5 x 1 "	8,712	15 x15 "	193
9 x9 "	77,440	5 x 2 "	4,356	16 x16 "	170
1 x1 foot	43,560	5 x 3 "	2,904	16½x16½ "	160
1½x1½ feet	19,360	5 x 4 "	2,178	17 x17 "	150
2 x1 "	21,780	5 x 5 "	1,742	18 x18 "	134
2 x2 "	10,890	5½x 5½ "	1,417	19 x19 "	120
2½x2½ "	6,960	6 x 6 "	1,210	20 x20 "	108
3 x1 "	14,620	6½x 6½ "	1,031	25 x25 "	69
3 x2 "	7,260	7 x 7 "	881	30 x30 "	48
3 x3 "	4,840	8 x 8 "	680	33 x33 "	40
3½x3½ "	3,555	9 x 9 "	537	40 x40 "	27
4 x1 "	10,890	10 x10 "	435	50 x50 "	17
4 x2 "	5,445	11 x11 "	360	60 x60 "	12
4 x3 "	3,630	12 x12 "	302	66 x66 "	10

ROPE ON THE FARM

Safe working strength of new fiber rope, by size of rope and kind of fiber

[Actual breaking strengths are at least 5 times the figures given]

Rope diameter	Working strength					
	Natural fiber		Synthetic fiber			
	Manila	Sisal	Nylon	Dacron	Polyethylene	Saran
Inches	*Pounds*	*Pounds*	*Pounds*	*Pounds*	*Pounds*	*Pounds*
3/8	200	150	400	390	300	150
1/2	440	350	780	745	600	300
5/8	880	700	1,710	1,355	1,100	620
3/4	1,080	865	2,000	1,870	1,600	800
7/8	1,540	1,230	2,700	2,520	2,120	1,140
1	1,800	1,440	3,600	3,220	2,800	1,600

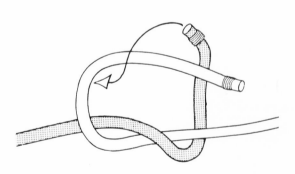

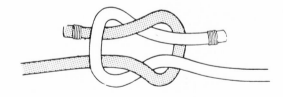

The square knot

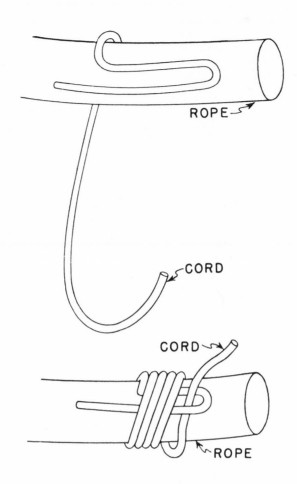

Whipping a rope

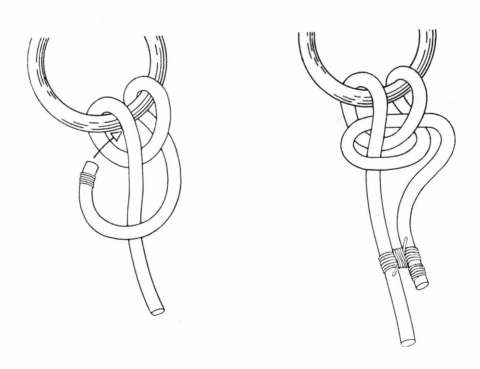

The anchor bend

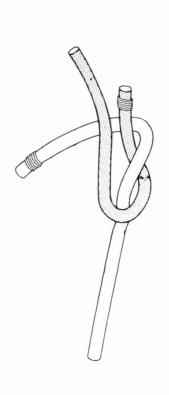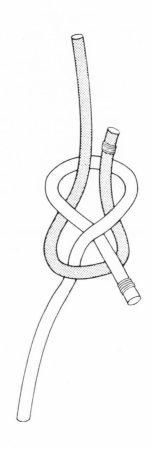

The sheet bend

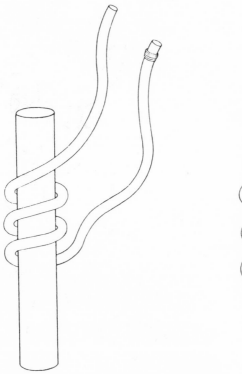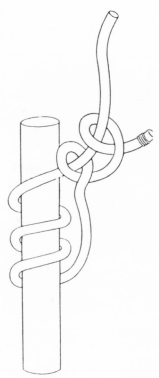

The pipe hitch

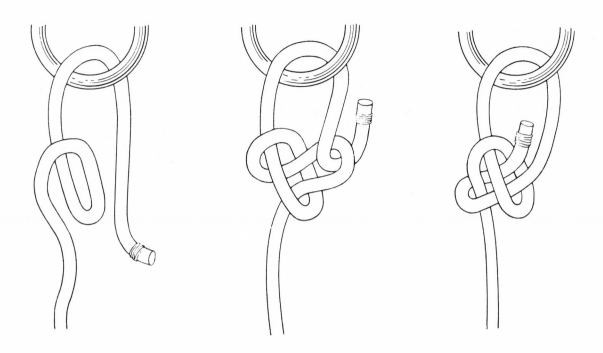

The bowline

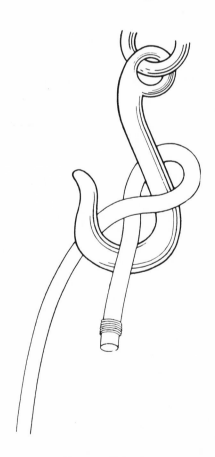

The Blackwall hitch

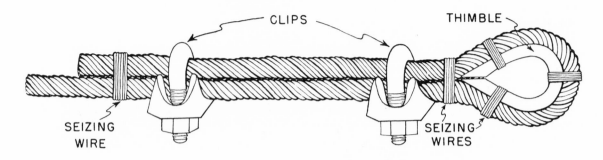

Use of clips, seizing wire, and a thimble to make an eye loop on wire rope.

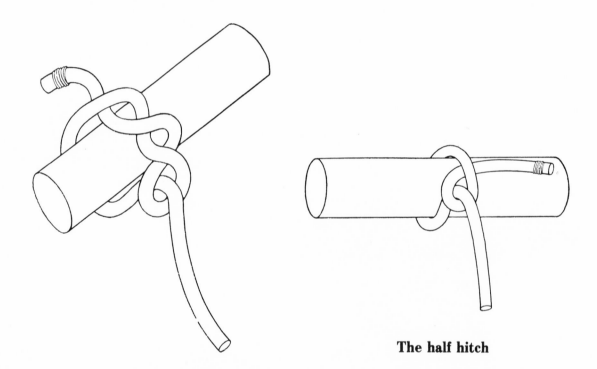

The timber hitch

The half hitch

480

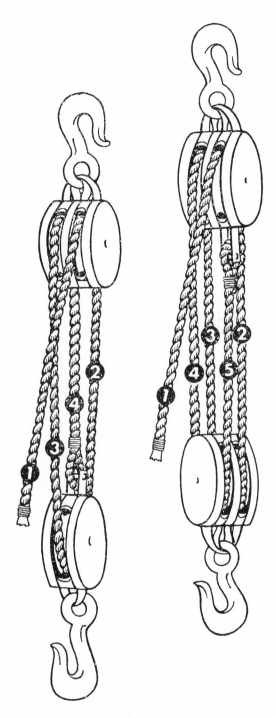

Block and tackle. *A*, Single-and-double block and tackle; *B*, double-and-double block and tackle. In these examples, the mechanical advantage is equal to one less than the number of ropes between the blocks.

CALENDERS – 1776 TO 2000

INDEX

1776	9	1801	5	1826	1	1851	4	1876	14	1901	3	1926	6	1951	2	1976	12
1777	4	1802	6	1827	2	1852	12	1877	2	1902	4	1927	7	1952	10	1977	7
1778	5	1803	7	1828	10	1853	7	1878	3	1903	5	1928	8	1953	5	1978	1
1779	6	1804	8	1829	5	1854	1	1879	4	1904	13	1929	3	1954	6	1979	2
1780	14	1805	3	1830	6	1855	2	1880	12	1905	1	1930	4	1955	7	1980	10
1781	2	1806	4	1831	7	1856	10	1881	7	1906	2	1931	5	1956	8	1981	5
1782	3	1807	5	1832	8	1857	5	1882	1	1907	3	1932	13	1957	3	1982	6
1783	4	1808	13	1833	3	1858	6	1883	2	1908	11	1933	1	1958	4	1983	7
1784	12	1809	1	1834	4	1859	7	1884	10	1909	6	1934	2	1959	5	1984	8
1785	7	1810	2	1835	5	1860	8	1885	5	1910	7	1935	3	1960	13	1985	3
1786	1	1811	3	1836	13	1861	3	1886	6	1911	1	1936	11	1961	1	1986	4
1787	2	1812	11	1837	1	1862	4	1887	7	1912	9	1937	6	1962	2	1987	5
1788	10	1813	6	1838	2	1863	5	1888	8	1913	4	1938	7	1963	3	1988	13
1789	5	1814	7	1839	3	1864	13	1889	3	1914	5	1939	1	1964	11	1989	1
1790	6	1815	1	1840	11	1865	1	1890	4	1915	6	1940	9	1965	6	1990	2
1791	7	1816	9	1841	6	1866	2	1891	5	1916	14	1941	4	1966	7	1991	3
1792	8	1817	4	1842	7	1867	3	1892	13	1917	2	1942	5	1967	1	1992	11
1793	3	1818	5	1843	1	1868	11	1893	1	1918	3	1943	6	1968	9	1993	6
1794	4	1819	6	1844	9	1869	6	1894	2	1919	4	1944	14	1969	4	1994	7
1795	5	1820	14	1845	4	1870	7	1895	3	1920	12	1945	2	1970	5	1995	1
1796	13	1821	2	1846	5	1871	1	1896	11	1921	7	1946	3	1971	6	1996	9
1797	1	1822	3	1847	6	1872	9	1897	6	1922	1	1947	4	1972	14	1997	4
1798	2	1823	4	1848	14	1873	4	1898	7	1923	2	1948	12	1973	2	1998	5
1799	3	1824	12	1849	2	1874	5	1899	1	1924	10	1949	7	1974	3	1999	6
1800	4	1825	7	1850	3	1875	6	1900	2	1925	5	1950	1	1975	4	2000	14

DIRECTIONS FOR USE

Look for the year you want in the index at left. The number opposite each year is the number of the calendar to use for that year.

1

JANUARY

S	M	T	W	T	F	S
1	2	3	4	5	6	7
8	9	10	11	12	13	14
15	16	17	18	19	20	21
22	23	24	25	26	27	28
29	30	31				

MAY

S	M	T	W	T	F	S
	1	2	3	4	5	6
7	8	9	10	11	12	13
14	15	16	17	18	19	20
21	22	23	24	25	26	27
28	29	30	31			

SEPTEMBER

S	M	T	W	T	F	S
					1	2
3	4	5	6	7	8	9
10	11	12	13	14	15	16
17	18	19	20	21	22	23
24	25	26	27	28	29	30

FEBRUARY

S	M	T	W	T	F	S
			1	2	3	4
5	6	7	8	9	10	11
12	13	14	15	16	17	18
19	20	21	22	23	24	25
26	27	28				

JUNE

S	M	T	W	T	F	S
				1	2	3
4	5	6	7	8	9	10
11	12	13	14	15	16	17
18	19	20	21	22	23	24
25	26	27	28	29	30	

OCTOBER

S	M	T	W	T	F	S
1	2	3	4	5	6	7
8	9	10	11	12	13	14
15	16	17	18	19	20	21
22	23	24	25	26	27	28
29	30	31				

MARCH

S	M	T	W	T	F	S
			1	2	3	4
5	6	7	8	9	10	11
12	13	14	15	16	17	18
19	20	21	22	23	24	25
26	27	28	29	30	31	

JULY

S	M	T	W	T	F	S
						1
2	3	4	5	6	7	8
9	10	11	12	13	14	15
16	17	18	19	20	21	22
23	24	25	26	27	28	29
30	31					

NOVEMBER

S	M	T	W	T	F	S
			1	2	3	4
5	6	7	8	9	10	11
12	13	14	15	16	17	18
19	20	21	22	23	24	25
26	27	28	29	30		

APRIL

S	M	T	W	T	F	S
						1
2	3	4	5	6	7	8
9	10	11	12	13	14	15
16	17	18	19	20	21	22
23	24	25	26	27	28	29
30						

AUGUST

S	M	T	W	T	F	S
		1	2	3	4	5
6	7	8	9	10	11	12
13	14	15	16	17	18	19
20	21	22	23	24	25	26
27	28	29	30	31		

DECEMBER

S	M	T	W	T	F	S
					1	2
3	4	5	6	7	8	9
10	11	12	13	14	15	16
17	18	19	20	21	22	23
24	25	26	27	28	29	30
31						

2

JANUARY

S	M	T	W	T	F	S
	1	2	3	4	5	6
7	8	9	10	11	12	13
14	15	16	17	18	19	20
21	22	23	24	25	26	27
28	29	30	31			

MAY

S	M	T	W	T	F	S
		1	2	3	4	5
6	7	8	9	10	11	12
13	14	15	16	17	18	19
20	21	22	23	24	25	26
27	28	29	30	31		

SEPTEMBER

S	M	T	W	T	F	S
						1
2	3	4	5	6	7	8
9	10	11	12	13	14	15
16	17	18	19	20	21	22
23	24	25	26	27	28	29
30						

FEBRUARY

S	M	T	W	T	F	S
				1	2	3
4	5	6	7	8	9	10
11	12	13	14	15	16	17
18	19	20	21	22	23	24
25	26	27	28			

JUNE

S	M	T	W	T	F	S
					1	2
3	4	5	6	7	8	9
10	11	12	13	14	15	16
17	18	19	20	21	22	23
24	25	26	27	28	29	30

OCTOBER

S	M	T	W	T	F	S
	1	2	3	4	5	6
7	8	9	10	11	12	13
14	15	16	17	18	19	20
21	22	23	24	25	26	27
28	29	30	31			

MARCH

S	M	T	W	T	F	S
				1	2	3
4	5	6	7	8	9	10
11	12	13	14	15	16	17
18	19	20	21	22	23	24
25	26	27	28	29	30	31

JULY

S	M	T	W	T	F	S
1	2	3	4	5	6	7
8	9	10	11	12	13	14
15	16	17	18	19	20	21
22	23	24	25	26	27	28
29	30	31				

NOVEMBER

S	M	T	W	T	F	S
				1	2	3
4	5	6	7	8	9	10
11	12	13	14	15	16	17
18	19	20	21	22	23	24
25	26	27	28	29	30	

APRIL

S	M	T	W	T	F	S
1	2	3	4	5	6	7
8	9	10	11	12	13	14
15	16	17	18	19	20	21
22	23	24	25	26	27	28
29	30					

AUGUST

S	M	T	W	T	F	S
			1	2	3	4
5	6	7	8	9	10	11
12	13	14	15	16	17	18
19	20	21	22	23	24	25
26	27	28	29	30	31	

DECEMBER

S	M	T	W	T	F	S
						1
2	3	4	5	6	7	8
9	10	11	12	13	14	15
16	17	18	19	20	21	22
23	24	25	26	27	28	29
30	31					

3

JANUARY

S	M	T	W	T	F	S
		1	2	3	4	5
6	7	8	9	10	11	12
13	14	15	16	17	18	19
20	21	22	23	24	25	26
27	28	29	30	31		

MAY

S	M	T	W	T	F	S
			1	2	3	4
5	6	7	8	9	10	11
12	13	14	15	16	17	18
19	20	21	22	23	24	25
26	27	28	29	30	31	

SEPTEMBER

S	M	T	W	T	F	S
1	2	3	4	5	6	7
8	9	10	11	12	13	14
15	16	17	18	19	20	21
22	23	24	25	26	27	28
29	30					

FEBRUARY

S	M	T	W	T	F	S
					1	2
3	4	5	6	7	8	9
10	11	12	13	14	15	16
17	18	19	20	21	22	23
24	25	26	27	28		

JUNE

S	M	T	W	T	F	S
						1
2	3	4	5	6	7	8
9	10	11	12	13	14	15
16	17	18	19	20	21	22
23	24	25	26	27	28	29
30						

OCTOBER

S	M	T	W	T	F	S
		1	2	3	4	5
6	7	8	9	10	11	12
13	14	15	16	17	18	19
20	21	22	23	24	25	26
27	28	29	30	31		

MARCH

S	M	T	W	T	F	S
					1	2
3	4	5	6	7	8	9
10	11	12	13	14	15	16
17	18	19	20	21	22	23
24	25	26	27	28	29	30
31						

JULY

S	M	T	W	T	F	S
	1	2	3	4	5	6
7	8	9	10	11	12	13
14	15	16	17	18	19	20
21	22	23	24	25	26	27
28	29	30	31			

NOVEMBER

S	M	T	W	T	F	S
					1	2
3	4	5	6	7	8	9
10	11	12	13	14	15	16
17	18	19	20	21	22	23
24	25	26	27	28	29	30

APRIL

S	M	T	W	T	F	S
	1	2	3	4	5	6
7	8	9	10	11	12	13
14	15	16	17	18	19	20
21	22	23	24	25	26	27
28	29	30				

AUGUST

S	M	T	W	T	F	S
				1	2	3
4	5	6	7	8	9	10
11	12	13	14	15	16	17
18	19	20	21	22	23	24
25	26	27	28	29	30	31

DECEMBER

S	M	T	W	T	F	S
1	2	3	4	5	6	7
8	9	10	11	12	13	14
15	16	17	18	19	20	21
22	23	24	25	26	27	28
29	30	31				

4

JANUARY

S	M	T	W	T	F	S
			1	2	3	4
5	6	7	8	9	10	11
12	13	14	15	16	17	18
19	20	21	22	23	24	25
26	27	28	29	30	31	

MAY

S	M	T	W	T	F	S
				1	2	3
4	5	6	7	8	9	10
11	12	13	14	15	16	17
18	19	20	21	22	23	24
25	26	27	28	29	30	31

SEPTEMBER

S	M	T	W	T	F	S
	1	2	3	4	5	6
7	8	9	10	11	12	13
14	15	16	17	18	19	20
21	22	23	24	25	26	27
28	29	30				

FEBRUARY

S	M	T	W	T	F	S
						1
2	3	4	5	6	7	8
9	10	11	12	13	14	15
16	17	18	19	20	21	22
23	24	25	26	27	28	

JUNE

S	M	T	W	T	F	S
1	2	3	4	5	6	7
8	9	10	11	12	13	14
15	16	17	18	19	20	21
22	23	24	25	26	27	28
29	30					

OCTOBER

S	M	T	W	T	F	S
			1	2	3	4
5	6	7	8	9	10	11
12	13	14	15	16	17	18
19	20	21	22	23	24	25
26	27	28	29	30	31	

MARCH

S	M	T	W	T	F	S
						1
2	3	4	5	6	7	8
9	10	11	12	13	14	15
16	17	18	19	20	21	22
23	24	25	26	27	28	29
30	31					

JULY

S	M	T	W	T	F	S
		1	2	3	4	5
6	7	8	9	10	11	12
13	14	15	16	17	18	19
20	21	22	23	24	25	26
27	28	29	30	31		

NOVEMBER

S	M	T	W	T	F	S
						1
2	3	4	5	6	7	8
9	10	11	12	13	14	15
16	17	18	19	20	21	22
23	24	25	26	27	28	29
30						

APRIL

S	M	T	W	T	F	S
		1	2	3	4	5
6	7	8	9	10	11	12
13	14	15	16	17	18	19
20	21	22	23	24	25	26
27	28	29	30			

AUGUST

S	M	T	W	T	F	S
					1	2
3	4	5	6	7	8	9
10	11	12	13	14	15	16
17	18	19	20	21	22	23
24	25	26	27	28	29	30
31						

DECEMBER

S	M	T	W	T	F	S
	1	2	3	4	5	6
7	8	9	10	11	12	13
14	15	16	17	18	19	20
21	22	23	24	25	26	27
28	29	30	31			

5

JANUARY

S	M	T	W	T	F	S
				1	2	3
4	5	6	7	8	9	10
11	12	13	14	15	16	17
18	19	20	21	22	23	24
25	26	27	28	29	30	31

MAY

S	M	T	W	T	F	S
					1	2
3	4	5	6	7	8	9
10	11	12	13	14	15	16
17	18	19	20	21	22	23
24	25	26	27	28	29	30
31						

SEPTEMBER

S	M	T	W	T	F	S
		1	2	3	4	5
6	7	8	9	10	11	12
13	14	15	16	17	18	19
20	21	22	23	24	25	26
27	28	29	30			

FEBRUARY

S	M	T	W	T	F	S
1	2	3	4	5	6	7
8	9	10	11	12	13	14
15	16	17	18	19	20	21
22	23	24	25	26	27	28

JUNE

S	M	T	W	T	F	S
	1	2	3	4	5	6
7	8	9	10	11	12	13
14	15	16	17	18	19	20
21	22	23	24	25	26	27
28	29	30				

OCTOBER

S	M	T	W	T	F	S
				1	2	3
4	5	6	7	8	9	10
11	12	13	14	15	16	17
18	19	20	21	22	23	24
25	26	27	28	29	30	31

MARCH

S	M	T	W	T	F	S
1	2	3	4	5	6	7
8	9	10	11	12	13	14
15	16	17	18	19	20	21
22	23	24	25	26	27	28
29	30	31				

JULY

S	M	T	W	T	F	S
			1	2	3	4
5	6	7	8	9	10	11
12	13	14	15	16	17	18
19	20	21	22	23	24	25
26	27	28	29	30	31	

NOVEMBER

S	M	T	W	T	F	S
1	2	3	4	5	6	7
8	9	10	11	12	13	14
15	16	17	18	19	20	21
22	23	24	25	26	27	28
29	30					

APRIL

S	M	T	W	T	F	S
			1	2	3	4
5	6	7	8	9	10	11
12	13	14	15	16	17	18
19	20	21	22	23	24	25
26	27	28	29	30		

AUGUST

S	M	T	W	T	F	S
						1
2	3	4	5	6	7	8
9	10	11	12	13	14	15
16	17	18	19	20	21	22
23	24	25	26	27	28	29
30	31					

DECEMBER

S	M	T	W	T	F	S
		1	2	3	4	5
6	7	8	9	10	11	12
13	14	15	16	17	18	19
20	21	22	23	24	25	26
27	28	29	30	31		

6

JANUARY

S	M	T	W	T	F	S
					1	2
3	4	5	6	7	8	9
10	11	12	13	14	15	16
17	18	19	20	21	22	23
24	25	26	27	28	29	30
31						

MAY

S	M	T	W	T	F	S
						1
2	3	4	5	6	7	8
9	10	11	12	13	14	15
16	17	18	19	20	21	22
23	24	25	26	27	28	29
30	31					

SEPTEMBER

S	M	T	W	T	F	S
			1	2	3	4
5	6	7	8	9	10	11
12	13	14	15	16	17	18
19	20	21	22	23	24	25
26	27	28	29	30		

FEBRUARY

S	M	T	W	T	F	S
	1	2	3	4	5	6
7	8	9	10	11	12	13
14	15	16	17	18	19	20
21	22	23	24	25	26	27
28						

JUNE

S	M	T	W	T	F	S
		1	2	3	4	5
6	7	8	9	10	11	12
13	14	15	16	17	18	19
20	21	22	23	24	25	26
27	28	29	30			

OCTOBER

S	M	T	W	T	F	S
					1	2
3	4	5	6	7	8	9
10	11	12	13	14	15	16
17	18	19	20	21	22	23
24	25	26	27	28	29	30
31						

MARCH

S	M	T	W	T	F	S
	1	2	3	4	5	6
7	8	9	10	11	12	13
14	15	16	17	18	19	20
21	22	23	24	25	26	27
28	29	30	31			

JULY

S	M	T	W	T	F	S
				1	2	3
4	5	6	7	8	9	10
11	12	13	14	15	16	17
18	19	20	21	22	23	24
25	26	27	28	29	30	31

NOVEMBER

S	M	T	W	T	F	S
	1	2	3	4	5	6
7	8	9	10	11	12	13
14	15	16	17	18	19	20
21	22	23	24	25	26	27
28	29	30				

APRIL

S	M	T	W	T	F	S
				1	2	3
4	5	6	7	8	9	10
11	12	13	14	15	16	17
18	19	20	21	22	23	24
25	26	27	28	29	30	

AUGUST

S	M	T	W	T	F	S
1	2	3	4	5	6	7
8	9	10	11	12	13	14
15	16	17	18	19	20	21
22	23	24	25	26	27	28
29	30	31				

DECEMBER

S	M	T	W	T	F	S
			1	2	3	4
5	6	7	8	9	10	11
12	13	14	15	16	17	18
19	20	21	22	23	24	25
26	27	28	29	30	31	

483

INDEX